THE RAPE OF SOCIALISM

'It is your duty to know and to be haunted by your knowledge.'

Arthur Koestler

'The only thing necessary for the triumph of evil is for good men to do nothing.'

Edmund Burke

'None are more hopelessly enslaved than those who falsely believe they are free.'

Goethe

'It is not the King and the generals who make history, but the masses of the people.'

Nelson Mandela

THE RAPE OF SOCIALISM

How Labour Lost the Millennium

by

DONOVAN PEDELTY

Prometheus Press
Powys, Wales

Prometheus Press
Tir Celyn
Aberedw
Builth Wells Powys LD2 3SQ

Published by Prometheus Press 1997

A catalogue record for this book is available from the British
Library

ISBN 0 9529993 1 5

Printed and bound in Great Britain by T. J. International Ltd,
Padstow, Cornwall

CONTENTS

CONTENTS

LOOKING BACKWARD

In September 1987 a young man who had lived since his birth, in 1857, in Boston, Massachusetts, awoke from a state of suspended animation to find his native city changed beyond all recognition, had it not been that, raising his eyes towards the horizon, he could discern, to the west, the familiar blue ribbon of the sinuous River Charles winding away to the sunset and, to the east, Boston harbour, stretching before him within its headlands, not one of its green islets missing. In the course of the next seven days, however, young Julian West was to discover that, if the fabric of the city was so greatly changed, the society it sustained was utterly transformed. And it is on this transformation of the social ethos that his own account concentrates.

He comes to see that the common assumptions of his social class that had kept the toiling masses in or on the verge of destitution throughout the nineteenth century were not only false but were themselves the primary causes of the most pernicious ills of society. The two principal beliefs underpinning the dominant ideology at the time of his birth and upbringing had concerned human nature and the 'laws' of economics. What the latter were conceived to be is explained in the opening pages of the account, in which the author outlines his own privileged position in society, conferred on him by an inheritance that had come down to him from his great-grandfather and that, despite having already supported three generations in idleness, had, strangely, not diminished, but actually grown in size - a mystery revealed as being due to an 'unnatural and preposterous arrangement' of giving what was called 'interest on investments' and which amounted to 'a species of tax in perpetuity upon the product of those engaged in industry which a person possessing or inheriting money was able to levy.'

He then turns to the condition of the common people and refers to the great 'labor troubles' of those days, which had particularly exercised him because a strike of building workers, some of whom were engaged in putting up a new house for him, had caused a delay in his intended marriage. 'The working classes had quite suddenly and very generally become infected with a profound discontent with their condition, and an idea that it could be greatly bettered if they only knew how to go about it.' The trouble was that, however understandable they might be, their aspirations were in fact 'chimerical' since 'it was in the very nature of things impossible that the new hopes of the workingmen could be satisfied, simply because the world had not the wherewithal to satisfy them. It was only because the masses worked very hard and lived on short commons that the race did not starve outright, and no considerable improvement in their condition was possible while the world, as a whole, remained so poor. *It was not the capitalists whom the laboringmen were contending with...but the iron-bound environment of humanity, and it was merely a question of the thickness of their skulls when they would discover the fact and make up their minds to endure what they could not cure.*' [my emphasis]

In addition to this apparently perpetual social condition of mass deprivation, the young Julian West and his contemporaries had accepted, as though they were natural disasters, the five- to ten-year devastations of severe trade depression. Unable to prevent or control these calamities, 'it only remained to endure them as necessary evils, and when they had passed over, to build up again the shattered structure of industry, as dwellers in an earthquake country keep on rebuilding their cities on the same site.'

Most of West's account of those troubled times, and of the almost unbelievable contrast they present when compared with the modern age he has so miraculously survived to enjoy, take the form of conversations with his new-found friend Dr Leete, in whose home he is now living. 'In our day,' he tells his host, 'the market rate determined the price of labor of all sorts, as well as of goods. The employer paid as little as he could, and the worker got as much. It was not a pretty system ethically, I admit; but...there seemed to be no other practicable way of doing it.'

'It would have been a pity if humanity could never have devised a better plan,' replies Dr Leete, 'for yours was simply the application to the mutual relations of men of the devil's maxim, "Your necessity is my opportunity." The reward of any service depended not upon its difficulty, danger, or hardship, for throughout the world it seems that the most perilous, severe, and repulsive labor was done by the worst paid classes...' And he goes on to astonish his young friend by telling him that nowadays all people get the same share of the social product for their services to the community.

To West's objections that 'some men do twice the work of others' and that while some are clever, others are indifferent workers, Dr Leete replies: 'We require of each that he shall make the same effort; that is, we demand of him the best service it is in his power to give.' He points out that 'desert is a moral question' and that the amount of the effort alone is pertinent to the question of desert. All men who do their best, do the same. A man's endowments, however godlike, merely fix the measure of his duty. The man of great endowments who does not do all he might, though he may do more than a man of small endowments who does his best, is deemed a less deserving worker than the latter, and dies a debtor to his fellows.'

And he draws West's attention to a number of other advantages of the modern way of dealing with rewards for services rendered. No longer need a worker demean himself by haggling for his price in the marketplace, as he was formerly obliged to do, whatever his calling. No longer is every member of society 'in a position of galling personal dependence upon others as to the very means of life, the poor upon the rich, or employed upon employer, women upon men, children upon parents...' No longer are natural aptitudes wasted by force of circumstance and talents perverted by mercenary considerations. No longer do bribery and corruption flourish, while venal crimes in general, 'which the machinery of law, courts, and police could barely prevent from choking your civilization outright,' have effectively been abolished. This means the virtual eradication of crime as a whole, since 'in your day fully nineteen twentieths of the crime...resulted from the inequality in the possessions of individuals: want tempted the poor, lust of greater gains, or the desire to preserve former gains, tempted the well-to-do.'

He said that such great social changes had combined to produce a transformation in people's attitudes to one another; they were no longer supercilious or patronising, servile or malevolent, but reflected mutual esteem. For, Dr Leete declares, 'It is the worst thing about any system which divides men, or allows them to be divided, into classes and castes, that it weakens the sense of a common humanity. Unequal distribution of wealth, and, still more effectually, unequal opportunities of education and culture, divided society in your day into classes which, in many respects, regarded each other as distinct races.'

On another occasion he remarks to West: 'If I were to give you, in one sentence, a key to what may seem the mysteries of our civilization as compared with that of your age, I should say that it is the fact that the solidarity of the race and the brotherhood of man, which to you were but fine phrases, are, to our thinking and feeling, ties as real and vital as physical fraternity.' Such perceptions, he has already made clear, have made war a thing of the past, for 'in heaven's name, who are the public enemies? Are they France, England, Germany, or hunger, cold and nakedness?'

And they are perceptions rooted in a clear understanding of the realities of social life. 'Who is capable of self-support?' he demands, when West starts to talk of charity. 'There is no such thing in a civilized society as self-support... As men grow more civilized, and the subdivision of occupations and services is carried out, a complex mutual dependence becomes the universal rule. Every man, however solitary may seem his occupation, is a member of a vast industrial partnership, as large as the nation, as large as humanity. The necessity of mutual dependence should imply the duty and guarantee of mutual support; and that it did not in your day, constituted the essential cruelty and unreason of your system.'

Accompanying this growth in understanding of social realities and their implications was a new perception of human nature. This is most fully and explicitly expressed in the author's report of a sermon he has heard. The preacher, a Mr Barton, stresses the cruel necessity that people of former times were driven by to fight for survival. 'For the sake of those dependent on him, a man might not choose, but must plunge into the foul fight - cheat, overreach, supplant, defraud, buy below worth and sell above...grind his laborers, sweat his debtors, cozen his creditors. Though a man sought it carefully with tears, it was hard to find a way in which he could earn a living and provide for his family except by pressing in before some weaker rival and taking the food from his mouth.'

Mr Barton attributes this savage situation to a most extraordinary assumption made by most people in those unhappy times. 'It was the sincere belief of even the best of men at that epoch that the only stable elements in human nature, on which a social system could be safely founded, were its worst propensities. They had been taught and believed that greed and self-seeking were all that held mankind together, and that all human associations would fall to pieces if anything were done to blunt the edge of these motives or curb their operation. In a word, they believed - even those who longed to believe otherwise - the exact reverse of what seems to us to be self-evident; they believed, that is, that the anti-social qualities of men, and not their social qualities, were what furnished the cohesive force of society. It seemed reasonable

4

to them that men lived together solely for the purpose of overreaching and oppressing one another, and of being overreached and oppressed, and that while a society that gave full scope to these propensities could stand, there would be little chance for one based on the idea of co-operation for the benefit of all.'

Looking on the 'inhuman spectacle' of that society, ministers of religion 'bitterly bemoaned *the depravity of human nature*; as if angelic nature would not have been debauched in such a devil's school!' [my emphasis] So we should not think of 'the stupendous change' that has taken place since those tragic times as some kind of miracle. 'It is not necessary to suppose a moral new birth of humanity, or a wholesale destruction of the wicked, and survival of the good, to account for the fact before us. It finds its simple and obvious explanation in the reaction of a changed environment upon human nature...Ceasing to be predatory in their habits,' the people of our age have become 'co-workers, and found in fraternity, at once, the science of wealth and of happiness.'

Mr Barton is right, of course, to curb whatever childish tendencies we may still have to jump to supernatural conclusions when amazed; and Julian West's account of the stark contrast between his times and ours provides ample explanation for the transformation of human conduct. Nevertheless, the differences are of such magnitude that it requires a prodigious feat of the imagination to think ourselves back into those distressful days. Mr West's vivid account of his strange experience and its profound effects on him helps us to take that great leap in time and to realise how nearly we have come to the millennium of which men have dreamt throughout the ages.

Wye Valley
Mid-Wales
Autumn 1987

UTOPIA AND REALITY

Mr Barton shared with his audience his reflections on the extraordinary fact that they had amongst them 'a living representative of the epoch of our great- grandparents' - a fact which, he suggested, could only 'leave us more than ever amazed at the stupendous change which one brief century has made in the material and moral conditions of humanity.' But whatever may be thought about the material changes that have occurred during the past hundred years - and in certain respects they have unquestionably been very great - such a remark could only have been made in 1987 (and could only be made now) with satirical intent. In fact, like Dr Leete and his family, and like Julian West himself, Mr Barton is of course a fictitious character, and the book he comes from was first published in 1888. Its author's intentions were not satirical at all; they were to portray 'a social order at once so simple and logical that it seems but the triumph of common sense.' It was, in short, a utopia, a dream of better times, written not as mere fantasy or escapism, but in the firm conviction that such times could be brought about.

Utopias are of course quite out of fashion. But Edward Bellamy's *Looking Backward: 2000-1887* was not only a great success in its own time and place (it sold more than 300,000 copies in America within two years of its first appearance and spawned a movement known - confusingly to our ears, living as we do in an age which has witnessed the rebirth of fierce, not to say ferocious, nationalistic feuds in several part of the world, including that old powder-keg the Balkans, at the same time as frontiers are fast becoming essentially irrelevant - as Nationalism, to promote its ideas on the 'nationalisation' of the production and distribution of wealth), but it was translated into many foreign languages and was given a new lease of life at the end of the Second World War, when, as Bellamy's son Paul wrote in 1945 in the introduction to a new edition, 'The yeast of social change is working in every country of the globe' and 'every statesman is drawing up blueprints, if not of Utopia, at least of something different and better than the economic order we have.'

If this quite restrained statement be accepted - and it would be difficult to deny that the upheaval of war waged on every inhabited continent, following as it did the great trade depression of the thirties and the unrelenting repression and exploitation of colonial peoples by European powers, as well of course as the ravages of the dictatorships, produced an all but universal clamour for a better life - we owe it to ourselves to stop our ears to the jeers and sneers of those who haven't the imagination to envisage a better world, and to ask in all seriousness why so little has changed in the common lot of mankind in the hundred years since Bellamy dreamt and wrote. For even if we turn our backs on the three-quarters of the human race who live in the 'underdeveloped world' (to use one euphemism) and further restrict our consideration to the 'free world' (to use a bigger one), we cannot justly claim that the condition of mankind has in most respects fundamentally improved. If we took as our yardstick Franklin D. Roosevelt's 'Four Freedoms' - freedom of speech and expression, freedom of worship, freedom from fear, and freedom from want - we might maintain with some plausibility that in the more genuine 'parliamentary democracies' the first two were substantially guaranteed (although even in the freest bits of the 'free world', anybody who has made a habit of exercising the first of these hard-won constitutional rights will know that to do so can cost one dearly in one's working life, leave one open to financial ruin from libel action, and in some circumstances bring one directly into conflict with the forces of the State); but we would have to admit that the other two were far from assured.

In the closing pages of Bellamy's utopia, his hero dreams that he has been dreaming and has woken up in nineteenth-century Boston. Before going in his dream out into the streets of the city and looking again (but with his perceptions awakened by having seen a nobler future) at the nightmare spectacle of 'the festering mass of human wretchedness' about him, and then suffering the scorn of his own social circle when he pleads the cause of the dispossessed, he glances at a summary of world events in his morning newspaper which reads as follows:

'FOREIGN AFFAIRS. - The impending war between France and Germany. The French Chambers asked for new military credits to meet Germany's increase of her army. - Great suffering among the unemployed in London. They demand work. Monster demonstration to be made. The authorities uneasy. - Great strikes in Belgium. The government preparing to repress outbreaks. Shocking facts in regard to the employment of girls in Belgian coal mines. - Wholesale evictions in Ireland.

'HOME AFFAIRS.- The epidemic of fraud unchecked. Embezzlement of half a million in New York. - Misappropriation of a trust fund by executors. Orphans left penniless. - Clever system of thefts by a bank teller; $50,000 gone. - The coal barons decide to advance the price of coal and reduce production. - Speculators engineering a great wheat corner at Chicago. - A clique forcing up the price of coffee. - Enormous land grabs of Western syndicates. - Revelations of shocking corruption among Chicago officials. Systematic bribery. - The trial of the Boodle aldermen to go on at New York. - Large failures of business houses. Fears of a business crisis. - A large grist of burglaries and larcenies. - A woman murdered in cold blood for her money at New Haven. A householder shot by a burglar in this city last night. - A man shoots himself in Worcester because he could not get work. A large family left destitute. - An aged couple in New Jersey commit suicide rather than go to the workhouse. - Pitiable destitution among the women wage-workers in the great cities. - Startling growth of illiteracy in Massachusetts. - More insane asylums wanted. - Decoration Day addresses. Professor Brown's oration on the moral grandeur of nineteenth century civilisation.'

The remarkable fact is that the picture of the world reflected in this 1887 news summary, far from seeming a historical curiosity, remains chillingly close to experienced reality a century later. Making due allowance for the big geopolitical changes that have made military conflict between the Western-style powers improbable, for major reforms concerning the rights of women and children in the advanced 'democracies' and for the general provision in such countries of safety- nets that has made utter destitution largely a thing of the past, most of the items in Julian West's paper have their shocking parallels today.

On the eve of what was to prove a third successive general election victory for the Tory Party led by Margaret Thatcher, Britain's second biggest circulation daily paper, *The Daily Mirror*, published a special edition dedicated to the millions living in or on the margins of poverty. Its photographs of inner city poverty and squalor recalled irresistibly those social campaigning issues of *Picture Post* that had once so shocked the conscience of the nation. 'Britain is divided, the *Mirror* editorial roundly declared, between those who have and those who will never have. Between those who hope and those who have no hope.' It is 'the Britain of her creation,' the indictment of the Tory leader read, and 'She doesn't care. Do you?' Too many of those who used their vote either did not know what they were doing or didn't care, so that with only 43 per cent of the total poll in their pockets, Maggie Thatcher's New Model Tories were given a third term in office. Five years later, in defiance of the opinion polls, they won yet again - even if, as some argued, their victory was largely due to the assumption of gullible voters that having a new leader, decent little John Major, made them to all intents and purposes a new party.

The years in between those two British general elections brought two sequences of events of epic, mould-breaking dimensions: in southern Africa the dismantling of the laager of apartheid, in eastern Europe and the Russian empire the collapse of 'Soviet Communism'. The capitalist 'democracies' of the Western alliance had won the Cold War which had cost their citizens and many others so dearly. Surely that famous victory meant, for 'the free world' at any rate, that 'the market' would at last be able to deliver that milk and honey? Of the 'moral grandeur' of civilisation in America, Britain, and the world at large as the twentieth century draws to a close, we may judge from the following facts and comments (all of which appeared in the columns of one of the world's great liberal newspapers, *The Guardian*, which Julian West might have known as *The Manchester Guardian*), mainly from 1996, which the United Nations had designated the International Year for the Eradication of Poverty:

> THE TRIUMPH OF GLOBAL CAPITALISM - 'If you choose a day and make a total of the movement of money that has taken place that day, and you then calculate the sum of all the transfer of merchandise that has taken place, you will find it represents only one thousandth part of monetary movement. This is terrifying.' (French political economist Alain Minc, talking to Peter Lennon, *Guardian* 31st January 1994) - Transnational corporations account for one third of global output. TNC sales, at $4,000 billion worth, exceed the market value of total international trade. (UN Conference on Trade and Development, World Investment Report, 1994) - The top ten British supermarkets have an annual turnover equal to the income of the world's poorest 35 countries. (Alex Bellos, *Guardian* 28th October 1996) - The wealth of the world's 358 billionaires is greater than the combined annual incomes of countries with nearly half the world's people. In 1961 the richest 20 per cent of the world's population were 30 times better off than the poorest 20 per cent; in 1996 they were 61 times better off. The share of global income received by the poorest 20 per cent fell from 2.3 per cent to 1.4 per cent. (UN Human Development Report 1996) - In the financial year 1995/96 the World Bank lent a record $19 billion to help countries develop their economies. Through the payment of interest and other debts, it recouped $1.7 billion more from Third World countries than it lent. (Annual Report of the World Bank, 1996) - 'Although I have made a fortune in the financial markets, I now fear that the untrammelled intensification of laissez-faire capitalism and the spread of market values into all areas of life is endangering our open and democratic

society. The main enemy of the open society, I believe, is no longer the communist but the capitalist threat.' (George Soros, *Guardian* 18th January 1997).

CAPITALIST DEMOCRACY LIBERATES LATIN AMERICA - 'The US and capitalism have won, and in few areas of the world is that victory so clear- cut, sweet, and spectacular as in Latin America. Democracy, free market economies, and pro-American outpourings of sentiment and policy dot the landscape...' Such euphoria seems distant now...By 1990, 240 million people in Latin America were believed to be living below the poverty line. (Martin Woollacott comments on Jorge Castañeda's reflections on the dividend from the end of the Cold War, *Guardian* 1st February 1995) - Some 86 million Latin Americans survive on less than a dollar a day, and if income distribution is left to market forces, everything indicates that their number can only increase. There are 35 dollar billionaires in Latin America according to Forbes [magazine], of whom 15 are Mexicans. A country in which, according to United Nations figures, half the population cannot afford an adequate calorie intake ranks fifth in the world by number of billionaires, behind the United States, Germany, Japan and Hong Kong...Between 1960 and 1990 the share of Brazil's national income received by the poorest 50 per cent fell from 17.7 per cent to 10.4 per cent of the total. (Phil Gunson, *Guardian* 15th July 1996).

PROPAGANDA BY DEED - Peru is a country where half the 24 million population live in poverty and four million of these cannot satisfy basic food and health requirements. Next week's news magazines will prove the point: a dramatic piece of guerrilla action does wonders for the world media's social consciousness. (*Guardian* leader of 21st December 1996 on the seizing of the Japanese embassy in Lima

11

by Tupac Amaru revolutionaries) - 1; This is that
brief moment when the hundreds of millions of poor
and illiterate people, through sheer force of numbers,
have an equal voice to the privileged few who
generally dominate public life. 2: On a lane leading to
an Allahabad slum, local people have put up
barricades of wood and rubbish and a sign, 'Political
leaders prohibited. Give us water, and then come and
ask us for our vote.' (Suzanne Goldenberg reporting
on the 1996 general election campaign in the world's
largest parliamentary democracy, *Guardian* 30th
March 1996 and 27th April 1996).

THE PEACE DIVIDEND - Annual military spending
around the world amounted to $778 billion. (*UN
Human Development Report 1996*) - With a slump in
the arms trade from the 1988 peak of $61 billion
during the Gulf War down to $15.4 billion in 1995,
Russian arms sales to the developing world for the
first time overtook US sales. At $6 billion Russian
sales equalled 40 per cent of the total, followed by
the US at $3.8 billion, France at $2.4 billion, Italy at
$800 million, and Britain at $500 million.
(Congressional Research Service, Washington DC,
20th August 1996) - Contrary to an assurance by
Prime Minister John Major, British-made armoured
vehicles supplied in the 1960s were used to repress
the democratic movement in Indonesia, the Ministry
of Defence has admitted. (*Guardian* 19th October
1996).

BUYING HEALTH - One sixth of the world's
population, 800 million or so people, have no access
to health care. It costs at least £8 a person a year to
provide basic health care. Sixteen countries spend
less than this, as do Bangladesh, Nepal, India,
Vietnam, and Pakistan. Britain spends £723 a head a
year. The worst decline in health services in fifty
years means that simple, preventable diseases will be
killing more children by the end of the century.

Immunisation costs 40p per head of population, more than half the entire national health budget for countries like Mozambique and Uganda. Most African countries spend considerably or hugely more on 'defence' than on health. Zaire spends per capita 26.5p on health and £6.50 on defence, Liberia 46.5p to £11.10, Tanzania 46.5p to £70...Aid as a proportion of the income of donor countries is at its lowest level for twenty years, with Britain's contribution standing at about 0.26 per cent of GNP, scarcely more than a third of the way to the target of 0.7 per cent. (Save the Children report, April 1996).

OUR SHELTER FROM THE STORMY BLAST - 'Send these, the homeless, tempest-tossed, to me.' (One of the lines of verse by Emma Lazarus inscribed on the Statue of Liberty) - On any given night there are about 700,000 homeless people sleeping out in America. Here in New Orleans and in more than forty cities across the United States the homeless are facing a determined push of new laws aimed at banishing them from the streets. 'The general public is fed up. We have certain standards we must uphold. People should be able to use public spaces. When other people come in and build cardboard tents and so on, the area becomes inaccessible for everyone else,' said New Orleans city council president Peggy Wilson, author of the [eviction] proposal. (Sue Anne Pressley, *The Washington Post* 2nd January 1996) - President Clinton deprived America's poor of a 61-year-old safety net yesterday when he signed into law a radical overhaul of the United States welfare system. The law removes the guarantee of federal cash for the poor for the first time since the New Deal. It was condemned by trade unions, women's groups, ethnic minorities and immigrant organisations as a betrayal of the Democratic Party's heritage and a shameless attempt to outflank his Republican rival, Bob Dole. Mr Clinton said he hoped his action would help reduce 'the terrible, almost physical isolation' of the

poor from the rest of American society. (Joseph
Freedland, reporting from Washington DC, *Guardian*
3rd August 1996).

SUFFER LITTLE CHILDREN - Intolerable forms of
child labour are so grave an abuse of human rights
that the world must come to regard them in the way it
does slavery, as unjustifiable under any circumstance.
(From a UNICEF report published on its fiftieth
birthday, 12th December 1996) - In very poor
countries every family member has to work if they
are to survive. (Oxfam comment) - Britain prevented
the final communiqué at the Lille G7 jobs summit
from including a call for the World Trade
Organisation to investigate whether some developing
countries win markets by using slave or child labour.
(Larry Elliott, *Guardian* 3rd April 1996) - Reebok
yesterday called on its arch rival Nike, the market
leader in trainers, to join it in a bid to end child labour
and improve working conditions at their Asian factories.
Christian Aid says only £1.20 from the price of a £50
pair typically goes to workers who made the shoes and
Chinese workers would have to work nine hours a day,
six days a week for fifteen centuries to earn the
£929,113 paid to Nike boss Phil Knight last year.
(Roger Cowe, *Guardian* 28th September 1996) - One in
three children in Britain is growing up in a family
without anybody in a full-time job. (*Households Below
Average Income*, Stationery Office, 14th November
1996) - According to Barnardo's one in four children in
Britain, around three million, is growing up in poverty.
'The shocking reality is that many of the problems
Thomas Barnardo faced in the East End of the 1860s are
still facts of life in London today. Homeless children
carving out a meagre existence on London's streets,
begging for their supper in the West End, sleeping
rough in parks and subways, they're easy victims for the
pimps who prey on their vulnerability.' (Roger
Singleton, director of Barnardo's, in conversation with
Margaret Hughes, *Guardian* 30th September 1995).

GIVE US THIS DAY... - At an aggregate level, the world still has enough to eat. But individual people do not eat around an aggregate table. Many dine in comfort. Others continue to get by. And a large minority, 800 million, struggle for food in overcrowded slums, on impoverished soils, often amidst an abundance which they cannot afford...The World Development Movement points out that even in the US an estimated 30 million people suffer from malnutrition. (*Guardian* leader of 12th November 1996 on the forthcoming World Food Summit in Rome) - The World Food Summit opens here today to a chorus of protest from charities who argue it will merely serve to endorse a set of free-market principles favouring the richer countries...Save the Children denounced the summit as a 'forum for legitimising a new international code of practice which basically subordinates basic rights to the market philosophy.' (John Hooper, *Guardian* 13th November 1996).

THE POOR ARE ALWAYS WITH US - Nearly one household in six in Britain is living below the poverty line [half average income], putting the country on a par with the poorest states in the European Union. (European Commission report, 6th November 1996) - Between 1979 and 1993 the number of people living below the poverty line in Britain rose from 5 million to 14.1 million. The fall of 400,000 during the next two years marks the first time the gap between rich and poor stopped widening since *1976*. [my emphasis] Average real income after allowing for housing costs rose by 40 per cent from its 1979 level, but while the richest tenth of the population enjoyed a 65 per cent rise, the poorest tenth suffered a 13 per cent fall. (*Households Below Average Income*, 1996) The US system of state provision is driven and defined by politics rather than principles...the American poor are the least likely [to vote], and children cannot vote at all. Accordingly, 21 per cent

15

of US children live in poverty, double the rate of any other industrialised country, Unicef reported last year. (Martin Walker, *Guardian* 27th January 1996).

THE RESERVE WORKFORCE - Worldwide unemployment has reached one billion, representing crisis levels not experienced since the depths of the 1930s depression...almost one in three of the global labour force is now out of work or underemployed...At least 34 million people in the world's richest nations which belong to the Organisation for Economic Co-operation and Development are jobless. Unemployment rose to an average 11.3 per cent in European countries last year, compared with 2 per cent in the 1960s. (International Labour Organisation report, 26th November 1996) - The number of people out of work in Britain is twice the level suggested by official unemployment figures: 4.2 million men and women who want paid work are currently out of a job, compared to the Government's figure of 2.16 million. (The Employment Policy Institute, 16th July 1996) - 'For nearly 200 years, the heart of the social contract and the measure of individual human worth have centred on the value of each person's labour. Every nation will have to grapple with the question of what to do with the millions of people whose labour is needed less, or not at all.' (Jeremy Rifkin, *Los Angeles Times* 17th October 1995).

THE PARTNERSHIP OF CAPITAL AND LABOUR - In 1995/96 the ten most highly remunerated of Britain's bosses all earned more than £1 million, the equivalent of £19,230 every week, almost exactly what the average full-time male worker earns in a year. Top executives gave themselves pay rises last year of nearly 19 per cent, roughly five times both inflation and the average increase in earnings. (Lisa Buckingham and Sarah Whitebloom, *Guardian* 1st June 1996) - Directors of the UK's 250 largest quoted companies received a median increase of 8.6 per cent in total earnings...in the most recent financial year...well over twice the 3.75 increase in average earnings over the same period...Top earners received an *increase* last year worth twice as much as the entire pay of an average worker. (*Guardian* leader 28th December 1996) - A group of power industry executives scooped £26.9 million in pay-offs and compensation payments as a result of last year's takeovers and mergers in the electricity industry. One executive, former Norweb chairman Ken Harvey, received a total package of nearly £3 million including a last-minute pay rise of £377,000, enough to pay the power bill of an average family for 1,350 years...The huge payouts will infuriate unions in an industry which has seen 50,000 jobs axed in the six years since privatisation. They are braced for further job cuts following the takeovers. (Chris Cowe, *Guardian* 15th November 1996) - Estimates of people who cannot afford to heat their homes, people in 'fuel poverty', run to about 6.6 to 8 million. Winter deaths, associated with cold temperatures and poorly-insulated homes, exceed summer deaths by around 30,000 annually. This is a particularly British problem not seen in a range of other countries with much more severe winter weather. (Dr Hugh Crombie, Research Manager, Royal Society of Health, in a letter to *The Guardian*, 19th April 1996) - Chief executives in top American corporations earn 120 times more than the average worker, compared with 35 times more in the 1970s. Among men about 70 per cent of all earnings growth has been captured by the top one per cent of earners. (Robert Frank of Cornell University to the American Association for the Advancement of Science, reported by Tim Radford, *Guardian* 10th February 1996).

OUR SENIOR CITIZENS - Britain's top directors are being given company pension contributions worth on average half their salaries, more than five times the

value of pension payments for most employees...
More than forty companies gave their executives
contributions running into six figures in their latest
financial year, nearly 60 per cent up on the previous
12-month period. (Labour Research report, 2nd
January 1997) - Some 5 million people out of the 8
million people, half the working population,
employed by smaller British companies are facing an
impoverished old age because of a huge shortfall in
the pension provision. (Association of Consulting
Actuaries report, 17th September 1996) - Of Britain's
10 million or so pensioners, 3.8 million 'only survive
through means-tested benefits and another 600,000
who should be claiming, either through pride or
ignorance, do not. Where the basic pension
represented 21 per cent of average earnings in 1979,
it has now shrunk to 14 per cent today because of the
1980 decision by ministers to break its link to the
earnings index. On current trends it will shrink to 9
per cent by 2020. (*Guardian* leader, 13th September
1996).

In its 1987 election campaign special edition *The Daily
Mirror* numbered the have-nots for whom it was pleading at 18
million - near to a third of the nation. In the lifetime of Edward
Bellamy and his English contemporary George Gissing, whose
fiction is a sustained threnody on the plight of the disinherited,
these 'submerged classes' constituted a clear majority in all the
wealthiest nations. To that extent George Orwell was right in
saying in his 1948 essay on Gissing that his novels were one
reason 'for thinking that the present age is a good deal better
than the last one' and that 'we have improved perceptibly on
that black- coated, money-ruled world of only sixty years ago.'
But despite 'the shadow of the atomic bomb', he was writing at
a time of hope replenished, a new dawn after a long dark night.
Had he foreseen how degraded and fettered life would still be
for millions of his fellow countrymen forty years on, we may be
sure that his comments on Britain's social progress would have
been a deal more abrasive. In the concluding passage of the
grimmest of Gissing's novels, published in 1889, he reflects on

the blighted hopes of his two principal characters that 'at least their lives would remain a protest against those brute forces of society which fill with wreck the abysses of the nether world.' A century later such language may sound melodramatic; but to our shame we still have that 'nether world' and those insensately consigned to it. How is this possible, when at any rate since Orwell was writing those encouraging words, Britain has had the benefit of having one of the strongest 'democratic socialist' movements in the world? The purpose of this book is to answer that question.

PART ONE

MAKING AND MARRING A NATURAL PARTY OF GOVERNMENT

'I remember very well, in a discourse one day with the King, when I happened to say there were several thousand books among us written upon the *Art of Government*, it gave him (directly contrary to my intention) a very mean opinion of our understandings. He professed to despise all *mystery*, *refinement*, and *intrigue*, either in a prince or in a minister. He could not tell what I meant by *Secrets of State*, where an enemy or some rival nation were not in the case. He confined the knowledge of governing within very *narrow bounds*; to common sense and reason, to justice and lenity, to the speedy determination of civil and criminal cases; with some other obvious topics which are not worth considering. And, he gave it for his opinion, that whoever could make two ears of corn, or two blades of grass to grow upon a spot of ground where only one grew before, would deserve better of mankind, and do more essential service to his country, than the whole race of politicians put together.'

**Jonathan Swift, *Gulliver's Travels*
(A Voyage to Brobdingnag)**

CHAPTER 1

The hijacking of the Tory Party

'The Tories have ceased to be gentlemen without
becoming democrats.'

William Rees-Mogg (1963)

'Melmotte was the Conservative candidate for
Westminster. It is needless to say that his committee
was made up of peers, bankers, and publicans, with all
that absence of class prejudice for which the party
has become famous since the ballot was introduced
among us.'

Anthony Trollope, *The Way We Live Now* **(1875)**

If the Labour Party is, as is often said, a 'broad church', embracing
very diverse points of view on the kind of polity at which it should
aim ('a house divided', as its enemies gleefully proclaim), then the
Conservative Party is close to being an inexplicable enigma, since
it succeeds in uniting for political action social groups, economic
interests, and ideological persuasions that are almost totally
disparate. Tory zealots hail this as their party's greatest glory. Its
more thoughtful supporters might secretly subscribe to the view of
opponents that in its ability to mean 'all things to all men' (of any
sex, of course) the party is a masterpiece of Machiavellian
statesmanship. At all events, the Thatcherite Revolution has
dangerously exposed the deep fissures in the Conservative Party.

It is a little too early to predict the demise of the Conservative
Party, but should its latter-day history come to be seen in this way,
the supreme irony which will have to be recorded is that its *first
cause* is to be found in the machinations of its demi-gods, the inner
circle of grandees who had controlled the party throughout most of
its life. When Harold Macmillan announced his resignation of the
leadership to the party conference at Blackpool in the autumn of
1963 (a resignation determined not by illness, as was given out,
but by a loss of will, of that spirit which had made him revel in the
mocking nickname 'Supermac') a train of events was set in motion
that was to lead to a wholly unforeseen revolution in the

Conservatives' collective concept of the *final cause*, the kind of polity for which they should strive. At that time the Party picked its leader by what Bernard Levin, in *The Pendulum Years*, has described as 'a mysterious and undefinable process' and Iain Macleod characterised as a 'magic circle of Old Etonians'. There was at the time a handful of credible claimants to the succession. The one who emerged from the dubious straw-poll procedures of Cabinet, MPs, peers, and executive committee members of the National Union of Conservative and Constitutional Associations (the Party's approximation to a national organisation of members) as the most credible consensus candidate was, for a party striving for a modern image, quite *in*credible, as he himself was later to admit.

Amongst the credible claimants, foremost by right of experience and distinction in office, of standing with the nation, and ironically, of the kindredness of his concept of modern Conservatism to Macmillan's own 'middle way' stance, was Rab Butler. His selection as leader to succeed the man chosen in preference to him on Anthony Eden's resignation following the Suez debacle, might have ensured both the continuance of progressive paternalism in a democratic packaging *and* (for a while at least) of a preponderant influence in the party for its grandees. In his memoirs, Macmillan records his surprise that Lord Home had come out of the consultation proceedings as the favourite, but the suspicion remains that the mantle fell on him because Supermac was, as Macleod believed, 'determined that Butler, although incomparably the best qualified of the contenders, should not succeed him,' and so cast his 'blockvote' against him.

Inevitably, Home's consequential elevation to the pinnacle of power prompted a repeat performance of the protest and derision that had erupted in 1960. Then Macmillan had promoted him to one of the highest and most politically important offices in the realm, the post of Foreign Secretary, contrary, as it was claimed, to what had become the accepted constitutional practice of only filling such posts from the elected chamber. Now the newly-elected Labour leader, Harold Wilson, made much of the fact that his opponent was a hereditary peer, 'the fourteenth earl' and mocked him as an 'elegant anachronism'. Home retorted with spirit that he supposed that when you came to think of it Mr Wilson was 'the fourteenth Mr Wilson' and asked, ironically, 'Are we to say that all men are equal except peers?' Nevertheless, to reach the summit he was obliged to cast aside the ermine and reappear centre stage in commoner's guise as Sir Alec Douglas-Home.

In an unseemly scramble for top-billing, one of his rivals, Lord Hailsham, had actually announced at the Blackpool Conference that he was on the point of divesting himself of his peer's robes so that he might run - or 'streak' perhaps - in the race for the premiership. Like Home, he proved adept at the quick-change act, gliding from 'Lord Hailsham' to 'Quintin Hogg' (an unavailing enticement as it turned out) and back again, with consummate artistry, thus allowing him eventually to sit, like his father before him, on the Woolsack. History's bigger joke, however, was that these noble scions were enabled to compete for the top job through the determination of another politician (who, notwithstanding his personal ambitions, undoubtedly had better credentials for taking on the role of true commoner) to renounce his succession to the peerage, in order to retain his seat in the Commons. Disqualified from sitting when his father, the first Viscount Stansgate, died, Anthony Wedgwood Benn appealed to his Bristol constituents in the ensuing by-election and was voted in again, but his election was declared invalid and his Tory opponent returned for Bristol South-West. The disquiet caused, however, by this frustration of the will of the electorate, led to the Peerage Act, passed with perfect timing for the climax of the Tory leadership pantomime (while Benn regained his seat unopposed when his former adversary honoured his pledge to resign if the law were changed).

Whether or not the antics attendant on choosing a new leader played any part in the Tories being pipped at the post in the general election of October 1964, it cannot have done them any good that their old leader was so clearly disinclined to allow 'the winds of change' to blow away the cobwebs of his own party's rituals. 'The way in which Home had been chosen did the Conservatives no good,' one historian (T.O. Lloyd) comments. 'Wilson had been elected leader of the Labour Party in a straightforward way that everybody could understand; Home had been presented as Prime Minister after consultations that were never intended to be understood by the public. Being elected gives a leader legitimacy in the modern world; emerging as the result of consultations is not a process that commands general respect.' Another historian (C.J. Bartlett) tartly observes: 'Significantly the Conservatives never used this system to choose a leader again.'

Their removal from office (even though it was by such a small margin that the new government had the smallest ever overall majority won in a British general election - four seats precisely) made it clear to all but the most incorrigible traditionalists amongst them that they must do something to tart up their image; above all, that they must show that no future Tory government would be open to the gibe that the fate of nation and empire (or what was left of it) was settled on the grouse-moors of England or Scotland. Especially so as they were now confronted by a party led by a dynamic economist who spoke with evident conviction of reshaping the country in the 'white heat of the technological revolution.' Home was to say later, in explaining his relinquishment of the leadership: 'One of the reasons why I resigned was just that I'd been on the scene a long time, and I thought that the Tory Party needed somebody else who would have a slightly more modern outlook, perhaps, or be *thought* to have a more modern outlook.'

After an inquiry had been set up by Home, it had been agreed that in future the Tories would follow the practice of the other principal political parties in leaving it to their parliamentary party to choose the leader. And so it was that Edward Heath, victor of a three-way contest with Reginald Maudling and Enoch Powell, became the first leader of the Conservative Party to be elected instead of 'emerging' from the steaming cauldron of the 'magic circle'.

The change in the procedure of appointing the leader naturally helped to give Heath the appearance of having 'a more modern outlook'; but his elevation did in fact mark a major - and almost certainly irreversible - change in the nature of the Tory Party leadership. The landed gentry had given way to the class that had long formed the party's backbone of loyal ensigns; public school *noblesse oblige* had retired in favour of grammar school commonsensical assumptions of the civic rights and responsibilities of 'the responsible classes'. And in keeping with this, Ted Heath authentically represented a newer managerial breed of Tory to match the 'new model socialist' elite, fired not by millennial dreams of social justice and a true commonwealth, but by Vorticist visions of social order and scientific revolution. 'Butskellism' had paved the way; but now was the real apotheosis of post-war consensual politics, for each of the leading protagonists, despite their strenuous efforts at differentiation, equally embodied the spirit of the age.

What inevitably ensued - teasing steps to left or right notwithstanding - was a decade of manoeuvring to occupy the middle ground, not simply because it was generally accepted that the party which succeeded in doing so would govern (though a strongly pragmatic approach to politics was one of the things the top contenders had in common), but because of the genuine similarity of outlook between these modern men of affairs. Each was so essentially 'moderate' that to talk of one as of the Left and the other as of the Right obscures rather than illuminates the reality. If one were to remove the shadow cast by opposing rhetoric and consider the substance only, one might well muddle up in one's mind the measures taken by Heath's administration and those taken by the Wilson and Callaghan governments. And the truth was that their underlying political philosophies of a 'mixed economy' supervised by government as and when it considered it necessary in the interests of national prosperity, abetted by such adjustments from time to time in the provision of incentives and disincentives as were felt to promote this, accompanied by paternalistic concern for the provision of 'decent' standards of welfare (or as some would say, of indigence) for the less successful members of society - these politicial philosophies, or concepts of wise 'governance' (to use one of Wilson's favourite words) were difficult to distinguish except in detail and emphasis.

To prepare to demolish, brick by brick, the consensus they so hated but which seemed at the time so solidly built, the Thatcherite faction (as we may now call them) in the Tory Party had first to oust their own leader. And it suited their purpose to charge Heath with reneging on his election promises, with caving in to opposition forces and making a series of U-turns. 'The free-market philosophy on which he was elected in 1970,' says Patrick Cosgrave in *Thatcher: The First Term*, 'was not all that dissimilar to the one on which she was elected in 1979. But Heath changed - indeed reversed - his policies in 1972, because he had become convinced that they did not work.' It is, of course, a matter of historical record that he came into office with a strategy of removing shackles on business enterprise, but as for his 'free-market philosophy', it is of a markedly different species from that of Thatcherism. As he himself put it in 1966: 'It is the job of Government to help industry overcome problems and to help modern capitalism to work...our task is to remove the obstructions...to enterprise and competition in our business world.' However disinclined they might be to put it quite like that, that is the position of every modern social democrat and of the great majority of leading Labour politicians. And there is no more reason to think that, speaking honestly, they would need to qualify Heath's words to make their own political creed clear than would Heath himself. In short, such a statement is itself an expression of the consensus which the Thatcherites were bent on destroying, since for them it was 'the hidden hand' of 'spontaneous market forces', not the helping hand of government, that makes the magic of capitalism.

Put simply, while impatient of custom and practice that impeded efficiency, it is clear that Heath always was a paternalist Conservative, not a 'free-for-aller'. He is also a reasonable man who, despite strong and durable convictions which some feel distinguish him from that master pragmatist Harold Wilson, has shown himself capable of learning from his mistakes and changing his mind, a virtue to which Cosgrave's caustic comments on Heath's changes of policy pay unintended tribute. Considering his obviously fundamental belief in the democratic virtue of compromise, it is highly ironic (and not a little tragic - and not only in a personal sense either) that a leader in effect accused of funk by enemies within his own party, should at the same time have gone down in history for practising what Alan Sked and Chris Cook call in the chapter on his government in their *Post-War Britain*, 'The Politics of Confrontation'.

However much the 'hidden hand' Tories might grind their teeth at Heath's unnatural practices in propping up 'lame ducks' and so forth, they could hardly deny that in such matters he was in large measure a victim of circumstances beyond his control. In interfering with the natural *dis*order of the market in respect of prices and incomes, on the other hand, Heath chose to confront the unions, appealed to the country in the 'Who Governs Britain?' election of February 1974 when they would not knuckle under, and lost power for his party by a whisker. (The Tories actually secured the highest number of votes, nearly a quarter of a million more than Labour, but five fewer seats, with the Liberal and nationalist parties holding the balance but declining to use it to sustain the Tories in power.) Needless to say, it was not the confrontation with the unions as such to which the Tory troops objected, only to the fact that, in a situation far less favourable to State power than that enjoyed by Margaret Thatcher in her relentless campaigns to bring the unions to heel, Heath lost.

Clearly ripe for a bit of the Brutus treatment, Heath engineered his own downfall in more specific way. Beaten on points in a return bout in October with Wilson (who gambled on securing an overall majority and got it, by just three seats), Heath clung to his dignity. He agreed under heavy pressure to the setting up of a committee under Lord Home to consider changes to the Party's leadership election procedures (at that time they contained no formal provision for removing a leader who was not prepared to fall on his own sword after defeat in battle) and accepted the committee's recommendations, with the greatest reluctance, after sitting on them for over a month.

The reluctance was understandable. Under the procedures then implemented, a formal challenge for the party leadership could be made once a year. No party with democratic pretensions could take exception to this; but one particular provision for entering the contest was another matter and led to its being called a 'coward's charter'. This allowed for the entry of previously undeclared candidates in the event of no one gaining a lead of at least 15 per cent over the nearest challenger in the previous ballot. Which is precisely what happened in the scramble for the succession to Heath. Though not obliged to withdraw on being beaten in the first ballot (by 130 votes to 119, with Hugh Fraser picking up 11 as a stalking-horse and 12 MPs abstaining) by the woman he had appointed his Secretary of State for Education, Heath rightly took it as a vote of no confidence. At this stage, with Fraser and Heath himself dropping out, four more former cabinet ministers, William Whitelaw, Sir Geoffrey Howe, James Prior, and John Peyton, each of them with greater experience and - or so it was thought - carrying more weight in the party than Margaret Thatcher, entered the contest. In the second ballot they were routed. Thatcher won an overall majority with 146 votes out of the 271 cast, Willie Whitelaw (whose awesome fate was to be nominated by Mrs Thatcher as 'my Willie') collected 76, Howe and Prior 19 each, and Peyton trailed with 11. The first woman to become leader of a major British political party had won the position because, as Geoffrey Rippon put it: 'She had the courage to declare herself in time. I think people respected that.'

That at least is undeniably half the story. The other half, however, is of greater importance in considering the fate of the Conservative Party and the consequences for the country. Those in the know are agreed that Thatcher's commanding lead (only nine votes short of an absolute majority) in the first ballot did not reflect a general infatuation with Maggie but rather a general jilting of Ted. It appears that a decisive proportion of the parliamentary party voted tactically to try to ensure a second ballot. Cosgrave claims to have identified at least sixteen backbenchers who were determined to get rid of Heath, but 'did not want a Thatcher victory either: they wanted her to damage Edward Heath sufficiently to allow the entry of further candidates the second time around.' But in employing what Phillip Whitehead, in *The Writing on the Wall*, calls this 'ingenious way of smoking out an unpopular leader' which was provided by the new election procedures, they failed to reckon with the disinformation stratagems of Thatcher's master-agent, Airey Neave (who had been, as Whitehead puts it, 'left to rust by Heath'), or to calculate the possible consequences of the kind of runaway lead the lady took in the first ballot. The amateur plotters, along with whichever of the heavyweights who hung around outside the ropes had calculated all along to be in the ring for the final round, had hoist themselves with their own petard.

Beyond the frisson it gave them at having, to the amazement of everyone, outpaced the parvenu parties by becoming the first party to pick a woman to lead them into battle, it is doubtful if more than a handful or two of the more thoughtful Tory legionaries had much conception of what they had done. In tribute to her intuitive mastery of political timing we now need to remind ourselves that, while forceful and effective enough on the floor of the House, Margaret Thatcher had been admirably discreet in the airing of her fundamental views of society. Only her intimates had much idea what she really stood for. As I have already made clear, while Heath's election as leader marked a significant sociological shift in the nature of the Tory Party, it did *not* mean a major change in the ideology that sustained it. Now the brigadiers of the Old Guard had lost more than a skirmish for the leadership: without yet realising it, they had lost the commanding heights where the strategic decisions were taken and the war aims declared. As a discreetly anonymous dissident was to put it, the party had been 'hijacked'.

The Tory Party had been such an effective instrument for the subliminal control by the Elders of affairs of state in a representative democracy precisely because it was *not* a democratic machine. Until the wisest and most astute of the party's twentieth-century statesmen drew attention to the artifice, by allowing his personal prejudice to cloud his judgement, it worked like a dream. The very obscurity of the grandees' deliberations - including their arrogation of the right to choose the party's leader - somehow seemed (as with the election of Popes) to legitimise them. In the not-so-long run, however, the constitutional metamorphosis from 'magic circle' ministrations to the elevation of leaders with a clear mandate from the parliamentary party, was to let the populist genie out of the Tory bottle. After which, we did not have to wait long to witness the forging of an unholy alliance between popular prejudice and militant capitalist individualism.

CHAPTER 2

New model Tories

'Mrs Thatcher undoubtedly inserted into Conservative
policy an ideological, if not religious, fervour and
a dogmatic tone that had previously been lacking...
Thatcherism largely consisted of nineteenth-century
individualism dressed up in twentieth-century
clothes. As with the Manchester Liberalism of the
last century, economic dogma was at its core.'

Ian Gilmour, *Dancing with Dogma*

When our discreet dissident spoke of the hijacking of the Tory Party,
he was saying a lot more than 'this woman outsmarted us in seizing
the reins'. Maggie's coup it was. But she and her henchmen had
not broken the rules of the game. The real point was much more
fundamental. It denoted a radical change in destination for the
Conservative omnibus, since what the more immediate changes in
style and stress were ultimately to add up to was a change in
ideology.

While the changes in style and stress that occurred between
Mrs Thatcher's startling triumph in the party leadership contest
and her first victory at the polls were obvious enough, they did not
in themselves constitute a break with the past. Tory rhetoric,
especially since the great social upheaval of the French Revolution,
has always played heavily on the themes of freedom and individual
rights being under threat from absolutist or collectivist power
embodied in the State or in political creeds dependent on capturing
the State as a weapon or instrument to further their aims. The
preservation of the citizen's rights and liberties by maintaining the
'proper constitutional balance' between the three estates of the
realm - sovereign, peers, and the people's representatives in
the Commons - has always been represented as the party's
paramount concern. Until the Russian Revolution its bogeymen
were generally dubbed Jacobins; since then they have more
commonly been called Reds.

As a rule Tory ideologues do not speak plainly (and advisedly
so); but they *see* very clearly: that the capture of the citadel of State

power by those intent (or purportedly intent) on the redistribution of wealth threatens the very core of the Tories' *real* concern, which is with 'property rights'. Against egalitarian charges of defending privilege and perpetuating social injustice, they have only the 'freedom' card to play; but for two centuries, from the days of Burke and the Younger Pitt till our own times, they have used it again and again triumphantly to trump the 'equality' card of their collectivist opponents. (Even though, in the representative democracies, the collectivists have won a trick or two, as, notably, Labour did in 1945 when Churchill, unscrupulously conflating black-shirted National Socialism with State Socialism of whatever hue, flung down his impending- 'Gestapo-State' challenge but failed to frighten the voters into the arms of the Conservatives.) So in using, with great seductive force, the 'our ancient liberties' rhetoric in the 1979 campaign, Margaret Thatcher was in the mainstream of Conservative tradition.

At the time it was not so easy to see that a radical break with the past had already been made, especially since, although the leading lady was for most of the action centre stage, the old praetorian guard of Willie Whitelaw, Jim Prior, Peter Walker, Francis Pym, Ian Gilmour, and the like, still surrounded her, providing a reassuring connection with family traditions, while, from the wings, the speeches of the ousted autocrat seemed not so very different in substance, however dissimilar they might be in tone. And after the victory, Mrs Thatcher's first appointments to office appeared to promise a considerable measure of continuity, not to presage violent change. We might go even further than this and aver that if fate or the electorate had deprived her of a second term, we would hardly now talk of 'the Thatcherite Revolution'.

Furthermore, in her campaign speeches Mrs Thatcher brought out equally strongly the Tories' traditional claim to being England's truly national party, the party best able to hold the country together and to lead it in pursuing generally recognised common purposes. They concede the special concern of the Liberals for individual liberties and of Labour for social welfare; but their party alone, they aver, by appropriately qualifying enthusiasm for these ideals with equal concern for national prosperity and stability and sufficient skill in maintaining them, assures concord at home and concerted action abroad. Civil strife and national disunity, according to this view, are primarily the consequence of sectional interests pressing

31

their claims too imperiously or too impatiently: where change in the balance of advantage between social groups or classes is desirable, it should be brought about gradually and with the general consent of those affected. Thus, in her adoption speech on the opening day of the official general election campaign in 1979, Mrs Thatcher declared: 'I seek confrontation with no one...Our Conservative message is not one of strife but of reconciliation. The things we have in common as a nation far outnumber those that divide us. We want not to uproot or destroy, but to rebuild.' More memorably (but some might think more hubristically), on taking possession of the keys of No.10 she quoted the celebrated prayer of St. Francis of Assisi: 'Where there is discord, may we bring harmony. Where there is error, may we bring truth. Where there is doubt, may we bring faith. Where there is despair, may we bring hope.'

The Tories' 1979 manifesto, and their whole campaign, did of course lay great stress on what they saw as the need to restore incentives (especially in the form of tax cuts) for the creation of wealth; but, needless to say, the emphasis was not put primarily on the vulgar right to make money (which could be the one kind of equality in which modern Conservatives of every degree of humidity really believe) but on what this would do for national prosperity. 'The State takes too much of the nation's income. Its share must be steadily reduced. When it spends and borrows too much, taxes, interest rates, prices and unemployment rise, so that in the long run there is less wealth with which to improve *our standard of living* and our social services,' the manifesto argued. (My emphasis: as with the word *national*, *our* does not reveal reality but obscures it. There is, of course, no common standard of living but a multitude of almost infinitely diverse standards of living.) The tasks were: 'to restore the health of our economic and social life...'; to ensure that 'genuine new jobs are created in an expanding economy'; and, most cosily of all, 'to support family life' and raise standards of education, while 'concentrating welfare services on the effective support of the old, the sick, the disabled and those who are in real need.' Far from heralding the end of caring, the objective presented was to construct a better, more effective as well as less bossy, Welfare State. No one could say this was not wholly in accord with Disraeli's declaration that 'another great object of the Tory Party, and one not inferior to the maintenance of the Empire, or the upholding of our institutions, is the elevation of the condition of the people.'

Yet the portents *were* there, in the spring of '79 (not to mention earlier indicators in speeches by Margaret Thatcher and her henchmen). They pointed to a change in the nature of the Tory beast as big as those signposted by Peel's Tamworth Manifesto and the 'two nations' admonishments of Disraeli - and notwithstanding the populist character of Thatcherism, in one fundamental sense, to a change in the opposite direction!

'A change in style, stress, and ideology,' I called it. But there is a sense peculiar to conservative political philosophies in which it is not really possible to distinguish between these three terms. Their adherents commonly disclaim having any ideology at all, and normally employ words like 'doctrine' and 'dogma' only as sticks with which to goad and beat their opponents. Conservatives have a weakness for emotive abstractions like 'loyalty' and 'patriotism' and for what one might call institutional abstractions like 'Crown' and 'constitution' but distrust purer ideological abstractions. For example, although they have been obliged by historical 'progress' to let 'democracy', 'freedom' and even 'equality' out on probation, they display an almost invincible disinclination to defining them.

'It is easier to identify a Conservative than it is to define Conservatism,' writes Philip Buck in the introduction to his anthology *How Conservatives Think*. 'Indeed, this might be pressed further: it is easier for a Conservative to identify a fellow-Conservative than it is for either of them to define what each, or both, believe to be Conservatism, as a political theory or a system of ideas. The problem of definition is as great, or greater, if an attempt is made to trace the history of Conservative thought.' Similarly, R.J. White describes Conservatism as 'less a political doctrine than a habit of mind, a mode of feeling, a way of living'; while Lord Coleraine says it is 'an attitude of mind, not a corpus of doctrine or a carefully worked out system of political theory.'

All of which helps to explain the difficulties the Conservatives tend to have with the intelligentsia. Conservative thinking is religious rather than philosophical in the Western sense, if only because their basic premises (or perhaps one should say, even if it arguably puts the cart before the horse, basic purposes) force them into the philosophically absurd position of having to make virtues of inconsistency and illogicality. Well the truth is that, in the *expression* (if not in the thinking) of Conservative political philosophy, they *are* virtues (political virtues, that is), precisely because they do not illuminate but obscure the realities they purport to represent.

Nevertheless, Tory ideology is real enough, and like any other ideology with some claim to sense, it prides itself on addressing itself to the harsh realities of life. In essence, these concern Tory perceptions of 'human nature' and 'economic laws' and the interaction of these two intractables. The former, as they see it, is more or less immutable and determines the economic relationships between one human being and another unless those 'natural' relationships are distorted by the intervention of 'artificial' (i.e. devised or imposed) practices or institutions. Inasmuch as they are so distorted by meddlers, the inescapable consequence is waste and inefficiency, i.e. bad economics, since (according to this view) economics is just as much subject to 'laws' as is physics.

In one *extreme* view, this means that society is of its nature essentially atomistic; which is to say that it does not really exist. In Margaret Thatcher's words: 'There is no such thing as society; only individuals and families.' The paradox is, of course, that every political party or grouping, of whatever persuasion, must in some measure strive to refute the assumption of atomism; and in fact the bonds of nationhood which are so strongly felt (or so they tell us) and so insistently invoked by Conservatives are utterly incompatible with such a divisive view of human relationships.

The Tory manifesto which heralded the country's resounding rebuff to a divided, dispirited, and above all directionless Labour Movement declared: 'We want to work with the grain of human nature, helping people to restore that self-reliance and self-confidence which are the basis of personal responsibility and national success,' going on to argue, in a passage quoted above, that in taking too much of the nation's income, the State reduces the nation's wealth, and therefore its standard of living. As I have already observed, such arguments marked no break with Tory tradition. However, in retrospect at least (and precisely because of the pains taken to emphasise the continuity of the new Tory administration with its predecessors) it is easy to see a momentous shift in stress, barely a year after the election, in the words of the man who was to become the key figure - second only to Herself - in implementing the Thatcherite Revolution.

In a lecture given to the Bow Group in August 1980, Nigel Lawson (at that time a junior minister in the Treasury) concluded:

> 'All that is new is that the new Conservatism has embarked on the task - it is not an easy one: nothing worthwhile in politics is; but at least it runs with rather than against the grain of human nature - of re-educating the people in some old truths. They are no less true for being old.'

The lecture was published by the Centre for Policy Studies under the title *The New Conservatism*, and the very fact that it was given to a Tory ginger group especially characterised by its concern for 'the condition of the people' made it a clear declaration of intent to capture the party for the new thinking - thinking which is rooted not in Tory tradition but in classical economics and the Manchester school of liberalism.

Patrick Cosgrave says of Thatcherism that its combination of market-place liberalism in domestic policy and nationalism in foreign (including foreign economic) policy 'has been unknown in British politics since the middle of the nineteenth century.' But while conceding that Mrs Thatcher's Tory critics are right in saying that 'she has by her words and actions sought to establish a strand of Conservatism as the whole tradition,' he stresses that 'at least it *is* a strand, and an important one.'

So lenient a judgement comes close to a Humpty Dumpty effrontery with regard to terminology. None of the British political parties represented in Parliament subscribes, as a party, to anything approaching a clearly defined ideology. Some of them, indeed, glory in this haziness, while the leader of one party is embarrassed that he cannot pronounce his party totally free of such foreign infections. For practical, psychological, and historical reasons the Conservative Party is in most respects even more of a pantechnicon than its rivals. This does not mean, however, that anything goes, that it is a mere transitory alliance of shifting sectional interests. Such expediency could never have brought it such enduring success. Equally, however, it can never be itself by leaning too far in one particular direction. If ever it does so, its innate centrifugal forces threaten to fragment it.

Nigel Lawson was perfectly right to reject, in his Bow Group lecture, the notion 'that Conservatism is nothing more than a technique of government.' (Though it is that and, in a sense, centrally so.) But to do so in the context of repudiating consensus politics in the name of conviction politics was to pose a false antithesis. Strong (and even contradictory) convictions can accommodate themselves to the politics of conservatism; blind obsessions cannot.

The whole point about British Conservatism is its fine sense of balance - between the estates of the realm, between social classes, between self-interest and communal concerns, between privilege and duty, and so on and so forth. It is precisely its generally skilful balancing of interests and concerns that has enabled the Conservative Party to pose so successfully for a hundred and fifty years as a (even as *the*) truly national party. There is even a sense in which it can rightfully claim to have been, during the historical period of 'representative democracy', the natural party of government.

If we dig beneath those great accretions of sentiment regarding King, Country, Church, and suchlike (which are admittedly of real concern to true Conservatives) for the keystones of the old Conservatism, we will find that they are PROPERTY & PATERNALISM. Enough of the latter, at least, to preserve the former! In their boundless enthusiasm for the shining splendours of capitalism, the cohorts of Thatcherism have upset the 'natural' balance of traditional Conservatism by knocking out the keystone of 'paternalism' and replacing it with 'economic liberty', the better to accumulate 'property' - which, needless to say, *does* remain safe in their hands! In practical terms this boils down to one all-embracing slogan, namely, PROPERTY: The Right to Procure, Deploy, and Dispose of it as one pleases; or, in the universal question-begging phrase: the right to do what one likes with one's own.

Just so long as 'the New Conservatism' appears to be delivering general prosperity, it may continue to be widely popular; and since it has been instrumental in dispersing the mists concealing the realities of the old Conservatism (while at the same time laying down some of its own), it is doubtful if the old kind of Conservative equilibrium can ever be restored. That is no reason for not recognising that, despite having some important constituents in common, the old and the new Conservatisms are quite distinct creeds. And, since, despite the triumphant ascendancy of the Thatcherites, the battle for the soul of the Tory Party is not by any means over and may still result in a major realignment of political forces, it is of some practical importance to understand the issues dividing the new from the old and the drys from the wets.

CHAPTER 3

The Tory heritage

'Every history of the creation, and every traditionary
account, whether from the lettered or unlettered
world, however they may vary in their opinion or
belief of certain particulars, all agree in establishing
onepoint, *the unity of man*; by which I mean, that all
men are of *one degree*, and consequently that all men
are born equal, and with equal natural right, in the
same manner as if posterity had been continued by
creation instead of *generation*...'

Tom Paine, *The Rights of Man* (1791-92)

That Thatcherism is just a strand or two ripped out of the whole
complex tapestry of Conservatism can be easily seen by a brief
survey of the salient ideas of the twenty-five Conservative
thinkers, spanning nearly three hundred years of British politics,
represented in Philip Buck's anthology.

Buck starts in Restoration times with George Savile, the
first Marquis of Halifax (1633-1695), of whose influence on
bringing about what came to be called by its beneficiaries 'the
Glorious Revolution' Macaulay was to write: 'The revolution,
as far as it can be said to bear the character of any single mind,
assuredly bears the character of the large yet cautious mind of
Halifax.' Macaulay also said of him that: 'Through frequent and
violent revolutions of public feeling, he almost invariably took
that view of the great questions of his time which history has
finally adopted.'

In the most important of his political works, *The Character
of a Trimmer* (which was really a kind of open letter to Charles
II), Halifax not only slyly turns his enemies' taunts back on
themselves by affecting to understand 'trimmer' as a tribute to
his prudent handling of the ship of state, but adopts the term to
characterise his principles of good government and political
stability. In doing so, he expresses some of the most central and
most enduring precepts of Conservatism: respect for the rule of
law ('the laws are jewels' and 'chains of gold' that 'tie up our

unruly passions'), the maintaining of a balance of power between Crown and Parliament to ensure both order and liberty ('our Government is in a just proportion, no tympany, no unnatural swelling either of power or liberty') and government by consent of the governed ('the virtual consent of the whole being included in their representatives' who express 'the united sense of the people' so that 'every act done by such an authority seemeth to be an effect of their choice as well as part of their duty' and spurs them on to 'execute whatsoever is so enjoined *as their own will, better explained by Parliament*, rather than from the terror of incurring the penalty of the law for omitting it'). [my emphasis]

Such is the art of representative government as proffered by the Marquis of Halifax. Leaving out of account the awkward fact that in his times representation through parliamentary elections was a sorry jest in which few could join and averting our eyes from such mercenary considerations as the spoils of office, one passage in his essay (where he contrasts the virtues and vices of 'Monarchy', i.e. absolute monarchy, and 'Commonwealth', i.e. a so-called democratic republic, and rejects both in favour of 'our blessed constitution, in which dominion and liberty are so well reconciled') underlines the essentially oligarchical nature of representative government so conceived:

> 'The Rules of a Commonwealth are too hard for the bulk of mankind to come up to; that form of government requireth such a spirit to carry it on as doth not dwell in great numbers, but is restrained to so very few, especially in this age, that let the methods appear never so reasonable in paper, they must fail in practice, which will ever be more suited to men's nature as it is, than as it should be...'

For all the wit and elegance of his prose, Halifax *examines* nothing. His arguments are but eulogies of the 'this blessed plot of land' variety. ('The Crown has power sufficient to protect our liberties; the People have so much liberty as is necessary to make them useful to the Crown,' runs a typical Halifax clincher). What he does do, however, as I have already observed, is clearly to enunciate the basic constitutional precepts and fine loyal and patriotic sentiments which every Tory holds dear to this day - though just how a latter-day Tory would reconcile his conflicting allegiances should the Crown ever decline to assent to a bill passed by Parliament is the conundrum of conundrums.

Buck's second representative Conservative thinker is Henry St. John, the first Viscount Bolingbroke (1678-1751), a politician much admired by Disraeli. Chief architect of the Treaty of Utrecht which ended Britain's involvement in the War of the Spanish Succession, Bolingbroke shared with Robert Harley, Earl of Oxford, the leadership of the Tory ministry of 1710-1714. Impeached by his enemies after the death of Queen Anne, Bolingbroke lived in exile in France until 1723.

The range of his writings is wider and more philosophical than Halifax's but their political concerns and conclusions are broadly similar, as the three following excerpts (the first from *A Dissertation on Parties*, the second and third from *The Idea of a Patriot King*) show:

'Absolute monarchy is tyranny; but absolute democracy is tyranny and anarchy both. If aristocracy be placed between these two extremes, it is placed on a slippery ridge and must fall into one or the other, according to the natural course of human affairs; if the few who govern are united, into tyranny, perhaps more severe than any other; if they are disunited, into factions and disorders as great as those of the most tumultuous democracy.'

'It is by this mixture of monarchical, aristocratical and democratical power, blended together in one system, and by these three estates balancing one another, that our free constitution of government hath been preserved so long inviolate, or hath been brought back, having suffered violations, to its original principles, and been renewed, and improved too, by frequent and salutary revolutions.'

'To espouse no party, but to govern like the common father of his people, is so essential to the character of a

PATRIOT KING, that he who does otherwise forfeits
the title...The true image of a free people, governed by a
PATRIOT KING, is that of a patriarchal family, where
the head and all the members are united by one common
interest...'

Bolingbroke rejected Hobbes' preposterous notion of an
antediluvian state of 'absolute individuality', considering society
to be natural, and, in accordance with this, presupposing a kind of
original commonwealth. From which it follows that his Patriot King
'can have a right to no more than is trusted to him by the constitution:
and that his people, *who had an original right to the whole by the
law of nature*, can have the sole indefeasible right to that part which
they have reserved to themselves.' [my emphasis]

Such speculations (in which, incidentally, as with most
thinkers of the Age of Enlightenment, a consideration of historical
processes did not seriously figure) might have led to revolutionary
conclusions. But in his thinking they coalesce into the 'one close
system of Benevolence', into a 'gen'ral good...all serv'd, all
serving', each in his allotted place in an 'order' in which 'some
are, and must be greater than the rest' - the 'Heav'n's first law' of
Pope's *Essay on Man*, for which, indeed, Bolingbroke had provided
the philosophy. For democrats, perhaps his most thought-provoking
words are: 'Parliaments have had a good effect on the people, by
keeping them quiet...'

Just as, in the late seventeenth century, under the pressures
of continuing religious conflict and a renewed struggle for
supremacy between King and Parliament, the Marquis of Halifax
moved from moderate Toryism to at least temporary
accommodation with the Whigs so, at the end of the eighteenth
century, under the pressures of the continent-wide upheaval ignited
by the French Revolution, Edmund Burke (1729-1797) began his
political career as a reforming Whig and ended it, to all intents and
purposes, as a Tory. Ironically enough, Burke has indeed been
placed by many Tories at the very pinnacle of the party's pantheon.
(Even more ironically, his spirit is still invoked by parliamentarians
of divers parties as one of the greatest of their brotherhood).

Buck goes so far as to say of him: 'The great contribution to
Conservative political thought in the eighteenth century, and for
succeeding centuries as well, was made by Edmund Burke'; and:

'The most telling statement of the Conservative position is embodied in Burke's *Reflections* and not much is added to these fundamental ideas during the nineteenth and twentieth centuries.' In discussing the contributions of the four politicians he uses to represent Conservative political ideas in the nineteenth century - Peel, Disraeli, Randolph Churchill, and Salisbury - Buck points out that 'they maintained the general framework of political thought which had been stated by Burke.' He usefully summarises this as: 'the respect for the mixed or balanced constitution; the three estates of the realm; the importance of religion; the belief in an aristocracy; the belief in personal rights and property rights; and the recognition of the need for gradual change in institutions as conditions change.' Burke's principles and precepts with regard to the first two of these were, in their essence at least, largely anticipated by Halifax. I shall therefore concentrate on illustrating the last three points as well as Burke's notions of how society began and its organic nature, which have a particularly strong bearing on his views on political stability.

The odd thing is that, notwithstanding the vehemence with which he warns us of the dangers of social engineering because society is to him like a living body, he insists (without offering any evidence and contrary to reasonable assumptions) that society was *not*, and then suddenly, through men's volition, *was*. Thus he accepts the common (and convenient!) idea of his age of the social contract, but utterly rejects Bolingbroke's argument, in his *Origin of Civil Society*, that, since man is by nature a social animal, 'In general we may say, that the foundations of civil or political societies were laid by nature, though they are the creatures of art. Societies were begun by instinct, and improved by experience.' Which is in effect to say that human society has existed for as long as human beings, however long it may have taken to evolve its present forms.

For Burke, the contrary applies - and it is clearly a matter of the greatest concern to him. 'In a state of *rude* Nature there is no such thing as a people,' and he goes on to call this a 'wholly artificial' idea. He maintains (or perhaps one had better say 'supposes') that 'a people' is constituted when 'loose individuals...form themselves into a mass' or 'corporation' by '*common* agreement' [my emphasis], 'covenant' or 'original compact'. Only then do they have 'a true politic personality' which entitles them to be called 'a people'. They may then be said to have a 'general will'. By breaking the covenant between them, they destroy their nationhood - which is what the French had done in overthrowing their monarchy. Such are his arguments in *An Appeal from the New to the Old Whigs* (1791).

Furthermore, the social contract should be looked on with reverence because

> 'It is a partnership in all science, a partnership in all
> art, a partnership in every virtue and in all perfection.
> As the ends of such a partnership cannot be obtained
> in many generations, it becomes a partnership not
> only between those who are living, but between those
> who are living, those who are dead, and those who
> are to be born. Each contract of each particular state
> is but a clause in the great primaeval contract of
> eternal society, linking the lower with the higher
> natures, connecting the visible and invisible world,
> according to a fixed compact sanctioned by the
> inviolable oath which holds all physical and all moral
> natures each in their appointed place.'

Thus, at any rate by the time he came to write his most celebrated work, *Reflections on the Revolution in France* (1790), from which the above passage is taken, Burke's feelings about society partake of the sacerdotal. He is evidently oblivious to how ill such thoughts consort with ideas that, however debatable they may be, are certainly more rational, such as his preceding statement that: 'Government is a contrivance of human wisdom to provide for human *wants*. Men have a right that these wants should be provided for by this wisdom.'

Despite his ardour for reform during his first twenty-three years in Parliament as (to use his own label) a 'Rockingham Whig' and, despite his own protestation, in a speech made early in the year in which he wrote his *Reflections*, that he was 'no enemy to reformation', it is difficult to avoid the conclusion that, consequent to the French Revolution, Burke recognised, not so much the need for change as a regrettable unavoidability which made it imperative that every constitution incorporated the machinery for peaceful change:

'A state without the means of some change is without the means of its conservation...By a constitutional policy working after the pattern of Nature, we receive, we hold, we transmit our government and our privileges, in the same manner in which we enjoy and transmit our property and our lives...Thus, by reserving the method of Nature in the conduct of the state, in what we improve we are never wholly new, in what we retain we are never wholly obsolete.'

Strictly speaking, 'conservation' and hence 'conservatism' are in themselves politically neutral ideas, in the sense that they simply endorse the value of some thing or situation that at present exists or obtains. In a class society, however, they express approval of inequality. Enormous changes in social relationships have occurred, of course, since Burke's day, when even a blind man could see that society was highly hierarchical. Nevertheless - and notwithstanding what may at first sight appear to be an antiquated and wholly superseded attitude to the *demos* - Burke's views on class mirror with astonishing accuracy Conservative views two hundred years later. 'Belief in an aristocracy' was listed above as one of the elements in 'the general framework of political thought' which he handed down to his successors, and like them, he endorses the idea of aristocracy both in the literal or hereditary and in the figurative or natural sense of the term. Of the former he writes in his *Reflections*: 'Some decent regulated pre-eminence, some preference...given to birth, is neither unnatural, nor unjust, nor impolitic...'; while later in the same work, having contemptuously dismissed the case made by Rousseau, Voltaire, and Helvetius (characteristically, without giving them a hearing, but on the conclusive grounds, one gathers, that they are foreigners), he nails his colours firmly to the mast of the *status quo* by roundly declaring: 'We are resolved to keep an established church, an established monarchy, an established aristocracy, and an established democracy, each in the degree it exists, *and in no greater.*' [my emphasis]

With regard to what Burke himself calls 'natural aristocracy', considering his own relatively humble origins, he could hardly but subscribe to what Napoleon, reflecting on his own meteoric career from a distant exile, was to epitomise as *'la carriére ouverte aux talents.'* In his *Reflections*, Burke nominates 'virtue and wisdom...wherever they are actually found' - not 'blood', 'names', and 'titles' - as the sole qualifications for government. However, it should be added that he assumes them to be quite liberally distributed amongst the gentry (since, as he explains in *An Appeal from the New to the Old Whigs*, they have among other advantages 'leisure to read' and are able 'to take a large view...of society') and nowhere declares that the not infrequent absence of such moral qualifications should disqualify the well-bred from office or influence. In his *Appeal*, he defines, or rather describes, 'natural aristocracy' as excellence in a variety of positions of leadership - military, judicial, academic, commercial, simply social, and so forth - and goes on:

> 'Men, qualified in the manner I have just described, form in Nature, as she operates in the common modification of society, the leading, guiding, and governing part. It is the soul to the body, without which the man does not exist. To give, therefore, no more importance, in the social order, to such descriptions of men than that of so many units is a horrible usurpation.'

One could not get much further away than that from the modern idea of democracy as meaning 'one man (or woman), one vote'!

A few lines later, after summoning up a vision of 'great multitudes' acting together 'under the discipline of Nature' and of 'the voice of this grand chorus of national harmony', Burke's rhetoric impersonating reason reaches a crescendo of hatred and hysteria towards the new democratic doctrines:

> 'But when you disturb this harmony, - when you break up this beautiful order, this array of truth and Nature, as well as of habit and *prejudice*, when you separate the common sort of men from the *proper chieftains*, so as to form them into an adverse army, - I no longer know that venerable object called the

people in such a disbanded race of deserters and
vagabonds...Those who attempt by outrage and
violence to deprive men of any advantage which they
hold under the laws, and to destroy the natural order
of life, proclaim war against them.' [my emphases]

Burke's remarkable insight into how the apparently divisive
forces in a capitalist society can, by the harnessing of political
inequality to economic inequality, actually make for political
stability is shown in a passage from his *Reflections* in which
four fundamental tenets of Conservatism - hereditary aristocracy,
meritocracy or natural aristocracy (in a secondary, supportive
role, be it noted, to the fourteen-carat variety), economic
inequality, and political inequality - are seen as acting together
in support of what was summarised above as 'the belief in
personal rights and property rights':

'Nothing is due and adequate representation of a
state, that does not represent its ability, as well as its
property. But as ability is a vigorous and active
principle, and as property is sluggish, inert, and
timid, it never can be safe from the invasions of
ability, unless it be, out of all proportion,
predominant in the representation. It must be
represented too in great masses of accumulation, or it
is not rightly protected. The characteristic essence of
property, formed out of the combined principles of its
acquisition and conservation, is to be *unequal*. The
great masses therefore which excite envy, and tempt
rapacity, must be put out of the possibility of danger.
They then form a natural rampart about the lesser
properties in all their gradations.'

In the context in which we are considering Burke's views
- that of his lasting contribution to Conservative political thought
- it should be remarked that in much of what he has to say he is
speaking for 'men of property' (that is to say, for those who are
markedly better endowed with possessions than the average
person) of *whatever party or none*, and in his or any other time.
In particular, he is a spokesman for the virtues of capitalism.

What he feared above all from the wildfire spread of Jacobinical ideas was that they might eventually lead, via revolution, to State expropriation of property in England. Of the French Assembly he writes:

> 'We entertain an high opinion of the legislative authority; but we have never dreamt that parliaments had any right whatever to violate property...this legislative assembly of a free nation sits, not for security, but for the destruction of property, and not of property only, but of every rule and maxim which can give it stability.'

And a little later he makes his fears absolutely specific:

> 'The great source of my solicitude is, lest it should ever be considered in England as the policy of the state, to seek a resource in confiscations of any kind; or that any one description of citizens should be brought to regard any of the others, as their proper *prey*...Revolutions are favourable to confiscation; and it is impossible to know under what obnoxious names the next confiscations will be authorised. I am sure that the principles predominant in France extend to very many persons and descriptions of persons in all countries who think their *innoxious indolence* their security. This kind of innocence in proprietors may be argued into inutility; and inutility into an unfitness for their estates.' [my emphases]

It is entertaining to recall that within eighteen months of Burke's death Pitt persuaded the Commons, against fierce opposition, to accept a modest proposal for confiscation, namely a tax on incomes of sixty pounds a year and above, 'as an aid for the prosecution of the war' with France, though without any of the dire consequences on the redistribution of property that Burke feared. Income tax was, in any case, repealed at the end of the Napoleonic Wars (on a motion put by one of the leading Whig reformers in the House, Henry Brougham) and it was not reintroduced until the first true Conservative (as distinct from

Tory) administration took office under Sir Robert Peel. Since then - for the first half century mostly at the crippling rate of between 5d and 7d in the pound - it has been a permanent part of 'the social contract'.

In the long view, most of the great parliamentary battles of the century and a half between the Restoration of the Stuart dynasty and that of the Bourbons may be pronounced as 'sound and fury, signifying nothing.' One might consider it fair cause for wry raillery that (despite Philip Buck's confident assertion that from around 1678, when the mutual mudslinging names 'Whig' and 'Tory' came into general use to refer to the two contending bourgeois factions in the English parliament, 'the Tory party shows a fairly continuous development to the present day') before the nineteenth century it is in fact often difficult to distinguish one from the other, except in matters of little moment to most of us today, chiefly concerning loyalty to the Stuart line and, sometimes, though by no means consistently so, adherence to the old faith.

And even then, they might pass back and forth, like actors in a small company playing many parts, or hover in the wings, like the Vicar of Bray, in order to see from which side they might get preferment, since everything ultimately depended on the royal favour. 'The question is,' says Humpty Dumpty in Lewis Carroll's great political satire *Through the Looking-Glass*, 'which is to be the master - that's all.' From our distance in time and outlook, quite contrary to the parliamentary brouhaha and flummery on the occasion of the tercentenary of 'the Glorious Revolution', there seems little sense in awarding marks to one side or the other. As Dryden puts it in his address to the reader prefacing *Absolam and Achitophel* (1681): 'For, Wit and Fool, are consequents of Whig and Tory: And every man is a Knave or an Ass to the contrary side.'

There is a serious point to be made here, though: that the central constitutional precepts and principles characterised above as 'Tory' or 'Conservative' were - and *are still* - more or less common currency among British parliamentarians, so they cannot be used to distinguish between the fundamental aims and values of different parties. In the hunt for these, we might look first at the metamorphoses of Whig and Tory caterpillars into Liberal and Conservative butterflies and see how they hatched in the heat of unrelenting pressure for the extension of the suffrage during the nineteenth and well into the twentieth centuries.

In considering the effects on the nature of the old political parties of their striving, willy-nilly and piecemeal, to accommodate the amorphous masses to the British heritage of constitutional government *without* altering the essential structure of society, it might help to glance first at one other aspect of Burke's attitude to the great 'silent majority' whose interests he (and those of his fellow parliamentarians who ever gave the question any thought) maintained were already properly represented by the three estates whose deliberations determined the 'national interest' and destiny.

Burke acknowledged the truth, laid down by Adam Smith and other economists and by that time generally recognised by thinking people, that labour was the source of all wealth and that, as Burke puts it in *Thoughts and Details on Scarcity*, an essay written in the famine year of 1795 to attract the attention of William Pitt: 'Those who labour...in reality feed both the pensioners called the rich and themselves.' If we knew nothing else about his ideas, such observations, particularly when set alongside such an unequivocal declaration as that in the *Reflections* that 'men have a right to the fruits of their industry,' might lead us to suppose that he was some kind of prototype Socialist.

But as we have already seen, Burke accepted without qualm or question the class and property structure of his society. And as we would expect from such a complete and consummate apologist for capitalism, he was also quite satisfied that what he quaintly called 'commutative justice' generally obtained in eighteenth-century England. In the essay on *Scarcity* he also declaims, with that characteristic way he has of elevating the most mundane and material things into the empyrean: 'The laws of commerce are the laws of nature and therefore the laws of God.' Which flight of fancy was to earn him, from the blistering tongue of Karl Marx, the remark that, 'To the very marrow, he was a commonplace bourgeois.'

Whether or not this son of Ireland felt any compassion for the great ragged army commonly called in his time 'the labouring poor' and whether or not E.P. Thompson is too gentle with him

49

in describing as an 'epochal indiscretion' his most infamous allusion to the masses (in the *Reflections*) as 'the swinish multitude', he certainly seems to have successfully sublimated whatever real concern he might have felt for 'the PEOPLE' in the kind of sublime and vacuous formulae I have cited above. At any rate, the counsel he considered should be given to the labouring poor, in that year of even greater suffering than was their normal lot, was: 'Patience, labour, sobriety, frugality and religion.' In his opinion, 'All the rest is downright fraud.'

CHAPTER 4

The forging of the Conservative Party

> 'Where honest and laborious men can be *compelled to starve quietly*, whether all at once or by inches, with old wheat ricks and fat cattle under their eye, it is mockery to talk of their "*liberty*", of any sort; for the sum total of their state is this, they have "*liberty*" to choose between death by starvation (quick or slow) and death by the halter!'
>
> **William Cobbett, *Rural Rides* (1830)**

Burke's modest origins absolve him of the charge of not living up to the ideal of *noblesse oblige*. Whether or not this has anything to do with his attitude to the masses, these aspects of his mind draw our attention to a missing element in his thinking which was to be of major importance in the development of the Conservative Party - the element of paternalism, or what Disraeli generally referred to as concern for 'the condition of the people'.

Such a charge (of practical, if not of theoretical, neglect of the common people) could not be made against Sir Robert Peel (1788-1850), the politician who, *pace* Buck, has the most genuine claim to be considered the father of the Conservative Party. Not least because, by changing his mind and his policies on major issues on at least three momentous occasions, he split his party - on the first two (concerning Catholic emancipation and parliamentary reform) seriously though temporarily, on the last (the repeal of the corn laws) so fundamentally that it caused a radical realignment of political forces and disabled the Conservatives from serious contention for power for the next twenty years.

Paradoxically, however, in so doing, Peel acted in what has come to be widely seen as the best traditions of his party:

(1) A resolve to put the perceived long-term interests of the country above the interests of the party:

> 'As a minister of the crown I reserve to myself, distinctly and unequivocally, the right of adapting my conduct to the exigency of the moment, and to the wants of the country.' - Peel in 1829.

'When I fall, I shall have the satisfaction of reflecting that I do not fall because I have shown subservience to a party. I shall not fall because I preferred the interests of party to the general interests of the community.' - Peel in 1846, during the debate on the repeal of the corn laws.

(2) The maintenance of political stability through a balanced constitution:

'My object for some years past has been to lay the foundations of a great party, which, existing in the House of Commons, and deriving its strength from the popular will, should diminish the risk and deaden the shock of collisions between the two deliberative branches of the legislature.' - Peel in 1838.

During the debate on the repeal of the corn laws, Peel told the House that, as a Conservative minister, he had done his best 'to ensure the united action of an ancient monarchy, a proud aristocracy, and a reformed constituency.'

(3) The pragmatic adjustment to inevitable change in order to conserve as much as possible of what is cherished. The three most striking illustrations in Peel's career are:

(i) His letter of 11 August 1828 to Wellington arguing that although Catholic emancipation was a great danger, civil strife was a greater one.
(ii) His action to forestall the creation of Whig peers to force through the Reform Bill - a scenario replayed nearly eighty years later in the struggle between the Commons and the Lords over the Lloyd George 'people's budget' of 1909.
(iii) His abandonment of support for the corn laws, defusing a potentially revolutionary situation resulting from the aggregated pressures of labour militancy, the Chartist movement, and agitation against the corn laws.

(4) A real and active concern for 'the condition of the people':

As well as by his conversion to the repeal of the corn laws

and to free trade in general, this was shown in his fiscal reforms (particularly in the introduction of income tax), largely motivated by a desire to cut the cost of living of the working classes by reducing indirect taxation.

All four principles and concerns find expression in his speech of resignation after the irredeemably protectionist Tories, outraged by the repeal of the corn laws, had combined with the Whigs to throw out a government bill on Ireland:

> 'I shall leave a name severely censured, I fear, by many who, on public grounds, deeply regret the severance of party ties - deeply regret that severance not from interested or personal motives, but from the firm conviction that fidelity to party engagements - the existence and maintenance of a great party - constitutes a powerful instrument of government. I shall surrender power severely censured by others who, from no interested motive, adhere to the principle of protection, considering the maintenance of it to be essential to the welfare and interests of the country; I shall leave a name execrated by every monopolist who, from less honourable motives, clamours for protection because it conduces to his own individual benefit; but it may be that I shall leave a name sometimes remembered with expressions of goodwill in the abodes of those whose lot it is to labour and to earn their daily bread with the sweat of their brow, when they shall recruit their exhausted strength with abundant and untaxed food, the sweeter because it is no longer leavened with a sense of injustice.'

As the son and grandson of manufacturers (his father, the first baronet, has his place in history as a forerunner of all the legislation designed to protect factory workers), in his antecedents and in his own career, Peel graphically illustrates the great economic and social changes of his time - the Industrial Revolution, the rise of the middle classes, and (with special relevance to our context) the effect of these changes on the character of the political parties. Considering his origins, it is ironic that his destiny was to lead the party most closely associated with the country gentry and ultimately to be accused by fellow Tories of having 'thrown over the landed interest'.

Of deeper interest is the point that, because of the very fact that his life represents the Tory gentleman at his best, it also demonstrates conclusively the ultimate inadequacy of benevolent paternalism in general and exposes, in particular, the crippling circumscriptions of the Conservative approach to politics. He had the courage to change his mind and his course in the teeth of his most cherished convictions, and that is, especially in a politician, a most admirable quality. Yet not only his career but his most famous testament, the *Tamworth Manifesto* (both in what it does say and in what it fails to say), show that there is no substitute for unfettered thought.

Honourable, scrupulous, conscientious and concerned though he was, lack of foresight led to his inchworm measures for the reform of crying evils, as instanced by years of tinkering with the mechanism of protective restrictions on importing corn until the Irish potato famine forced his hand; lack of imagination dammed up his understanding of the aspirations of the common people; and lack of vision or hard thinking disabled his capacity to search for lasting solutions to the great social problems of his time, as is surely always the case where speculation, theory, and the painstaking construction of ideology are scorned or neglected. Only such deficiencies made it possible for Peel (whom no one could accuse of being a die-hard) to make the extraordinary statement, in the *Manifesto*: 'I consider the Reform Bill a *final* and irrevocable settlement of a great constitutional question - a settlement which no friend to the peace and welfare of this country would attempt to disturb, either by direct or by insidious means.' [my emphasis] Unless it were an appreciation, conscious or unconscious, of self- and class-interest, only a wanton circumscription of his natural powers of intellect could have led him to insist (again in the *Manifesto*) that reason and the righting of wrongs must give way to such Burkean precepts as 'the respect for ancient rights, and the deference to prescriptive authority'. And granting the genuineness of his concern, only one blinkered by the conditioned assumptions and the prejudicial economic doctrines of his time and class (assumptions and doctrines which, it has to be said, served admirably the interests of those who held them) could have got no further in thought and deed than how to ameliorate the harsh conditions of life of 'those whose lot it is to labour'.

If the story of the forging of the Conservative Party out of the old Tories abounds with irony, which it does, it is in large measure a

54

consequence of the internal inconsistencies of Conservative thought. No one illustrates this better than the second of the modern party's founding fathers, Benjamin Disraeli (1804-1881), who played such a prominent part in the sundering of Peel's post-Industrial-Revolution party and subsequently succeeded in re-creating it more nearly in his own image. Political expediency, self-advancement and resentment at Peel's snubbing of his bid for promotion doubtless partly account for the virulence of Disraeli's attack on his leader. However, they do not detract from the sincerity of Disraeli's stance and arguments in declaiming:

> 'Let men stand by the principle by which they rise - right
> or wrong...It is not a legitimate trial of the principles of free
> trade against the principle of protection, if a Parliament, the
> majority of which are elected to support protection, be
> gained over to free trade by the arts of the very individual
> whom they were elected to support in an opposite career. It
> is not fair to the people of England.'

Ironies abound. Disraeli no less than Peel subscribed to a restricted suffrage but was not one of those given, thoughtlessly or disingenuously, to confuse 'the electorate' with 'the people'. Neither had a vested interest in protection for agriculture. Disraeli's concern had more to do with his romantic conception of an English constitution that had always rested on the leading part played by the landed gentry in affairs of state - a political reality until relatively recently not seriously challenged by other social groups (except perhaps in the Civil War) and one which Disraeli sincerely believed to be in the best interests of the whole nation so long as that section of society remained true to its stewardship. Peel, on the other hand, though the son of a manufacturer, was not moved to the major policy change which split his own party through that desire for cheap bread in order to lower the cost of subsistence wages that polluted the motives of so many of the corn law abolitionists. Above all, both of the protagonists had the welfare of the common people at heart.

Despite his severe shortcomings as a thinker - due mainly no doubt to the unremitting pressures of high office in an era of enormous and near-cataclysmic social change - Peel was the greater realist, the one more sensible to the irreversible shift in the balance of social forces that was inexorably making the middle classes, not the landed gentry, the fulcrum of the future. Disraeli combined dazzling parliamentary and political gifts with a profound critique of the present and a powerful vision of the future; he scorned the expedient manoeuvrings of most of his fellow party members, who were concerned at all costs to remain in office or return to power as quickly as possible if ousted. But his vision, fired by a largely mythical past, was of an impossible future, so that despite his great and lasting influence on his party, events carried both it and the country in a quite different direction. Nevertheless, he maintained the four traditions enunciated above with regard to Peel, and (which is our present principal concern) consolidated PROPERTY & PATERNALISM as keystones of Conservatism.

Disraeli's subscription to these central tenets in the Conservative heritage is expressed most cogently (and that this should be so is itself revealing of the cast of his mind) in his novel *Sybil*. But before looking at this it would be as well to glance at two more direct expressions of his political philosophy included in Buck's symposium, since they so well exemplify both the substance and the style of Conservative thinking up to the apotheosis of the Blessed Margaret - its romantic rhetoric, its disinclination to definition, the misty elusiveness (*not* the absence) of its dogma. That a lifetime in politics did not serve to eradicate the protective vagueness of Disraeli's declared views on English 'democracy' is shown by the fact that the first of these two declarations, his *Vindication of the English Constitution in a letter to a noble and learned Lord*, dates from 1835, the year of his fourth unsuccessful attempt to get into Parliament; while the second, a *Speech at the Banquet of the National Union of Conservative and Constitutional Associations* at Crystal Palace, dates from 1872, two years before the start of his second and last ministry.

Nor - despite his attempt to convince the public of his commitment to democracy in his pamphlet *What is He?* (written to explain why, after standing in an 1832 by-election as a Radical, he had thrown in his lot with the Tories); despite his idiosyncratic definition of a democracy (in the *Vindication*) as a 'country where the legislative and even the executive office may be constitutionally obtained by every subject of the land'; and despite the fact that it was under his leadership in the Commons that, in 1867, the second major extension of the suffrage was carried - did he ever become what would be recognised nowadays as a democrat, even of the parliamentary breed.

But this rejection of what he dismissed as the 'democracy of numbers' was, of course, entirely consistent with his paternalism, and indeed its logical concomitant. In his *Vindication* he pointedly distinguishes the 'Commons' - 'an estate of the realm privileged as the other estates...and constituting, even with its late considerable accession of members, only a small section of the nation' - from 'the people'. His point is that the elected members of Parliament, constituting the House of Commons, were not and never had been the representatives of the people (which was an undeniable constitutional fact) although, according to him, Members of Parliament were, together with the Peers, 'the trustees of the nation, not its masters'. And while he abhorred the failure of Parliament properly to protect the interests of the common people (a dereliction of duty dating, he considered, primarily from Parliament's usurpation of the powers of the Crown to act as the nation's umpire - he greatly admired Bolingbroke and particularly his concept of the 'patriot king' - and secondarily from the relinquishment by the Peers of a leading, or at least equal, role in Parliament) he did not, either then or later, disapprove of limitations on the franchise which deprived most of the common people of formal representation in their own governance. In his 1872 *Banquet* speech, alluding to the second Reform Bill which Lord Derby and he had hijacked from Gladstone and his supporters and manoeuvred through Parliament, he declared that 'the great body of the working classes of this country', having 'recently' and 'wisely' obtained 'a great extension of political rights', were now 'in possession of personal privileges - of personal rights and liberties - which are not enjoyed by the aristocracies of other countries'. He described this as 'an adequate concession of political rights' and claimed, revealingly, that such was 'the conviction of the whole country'.

Assumptions of omniscience with regard to the state of public opinion, together with arrogation of the right to speak for others, are, of course, classic symptoms of the sickness of megalomania that so frequently strikes politicians and pressmen. But perhaps the blithe confidence of Disraeli's asseveration is rather to be attributed to the even more dangerous delusion that there is something called 'the country' on the pulse of which it is possible to have one's finger; that such abstractions as 'the mother/fatherland', 'the French nation', 'the German race', 'the English people', and so on, have a reality beyond and above their utility (when used scrupulously and intelligently) as generalisations - and one to which, it goes without saying, these deluded pundits believe themselves to be uniquely attuned. Thus the *Vindication*, without the slightest warrant in the historical record, speaks of 'the English nation' having 'established a popular throne' and having 'invested certain orders of their fellow-subjects with legislative functions', and then proceeds to praise the supposed consequences of a supposed happening that has blessed us with a constitution - 'the matchless creation of our ancestors' - which has 'united equality with freedom' and conferred on us an 'administration of justice...so pure that its exercise has realised the dreams of some Utopian romance...' Who, one might well ask, are the real Utopians - Socialist 'dreamers' or the spinners of conservative myths?

The flowery and fanciful language of the *Vindication* was penned during Disraeli's political immaturity; though, as we have seen, this kind of childishness is not uncommon amongst subscribers to theories of an actual or implicit 'social contract' rooted in the very history of 'the nation'. But if it vitiates his contribution to political thought, his concern for 'the condition of the people' and his championship of 'the rights of labour', however paternalistic their nature, are much to his credit. In his Crystal Palace speech, having enunciated two great objects of his party as 'to maintain the institutions of the country' and 'to uphold the Empire', Disraeli goes on to tell his audience that 'another great object of the Tory party, and one not inferior` to those of which he has been speaking, 'is the elevation of the condition of the people', a prerequisite of which was to 'effect some reduction of their hours of labour and humanise their toil'.

Apart, of course, from the record of relevant reforms during his two administrations (which we shall consider in a moment), there is no surer testimony to the sincerity of his commitment to this cause than the passionate pages of his crusading novel, *Sybil, or The Two Nations*, which projects a remarkably comprehensive picture of the state of England in the early years of Queen Victoria's reign. Disraeli, who had already won a name for himself as a fashionable novelist, was persuaded to write *Sybil* (and the two political novels which flanked it, *Conrad, or The New Generation* and *Tancred, or The New Crusade*) to promote the views of the 'Young England' group of Tory Radicals, who believed that the country's ills were mainly due to the growing predominance of the commercial middle classes (especially since the Reform Act of 1832) and that they could be cured by rallying the working classes under the banner of a benevolent paternalism administered by a rehabilitated monarchy, a regenerated church and a reconstituted aristocracy composed of the more enlightened elements of both the hereditary peers and the captains of industry - an alliance which would have amounted to a kind of semi-feudalistic Welfare State managed through a system of 'guided democracy'.

Sybil (published in 1845) was in part the fruit of a tour through the North of England during which Disraeli and his companions, Lord John Manners and the Hon. George Smythe, saw the factory system at first hand. It tells the story of the awakening of a young nobleman, Charles Egremont, to the condition of the people, largely through his friendship with two Chartist leaders, Stephen Morley and Walter Gerard, and his love for Gerard's daughter Sybil. Thrown into a reflective mood by an outbreak of rick-burning and a disturbing conversation with a tenant farmer on his elder brother's estate, Egremont asks himself:

> 'And the People - the millions of Toil, on whose
> unconscious energies during these changeful centuries
> all rested - what changes had these centuries brought to
> them? Had their advance in the national scale borne a
> due relation to that progress of their rulers, which had
> accumulated in the treasuries of a limited class the
> riches of the world, and made their possessors boast that
> they were the first of nations: the most powerful and the
> most free, the most enlightened, the most moral, and the
> most religious?'

At his first meeting with the two Chartists, Egremont says to Morley: 'Say what you like, our Queen reigns over the greatest nation that ever existed.' But Morley replies (in a passage which focuses on the very heart of the novel and which gives it its second title) that she reigns over not one nation but two, 'THE RICH AND THE POOR', and he stresses how utterly alien each is to the other:

> 'Two nations; between whom there is no intercourse
> and no sympathy; who are as ignorant of each other's
> habits, thoughts, and feelings, as if they were dwellers
> in different zones, or inhabitants of different planets;
> who are formed by a different breeding, are fed by a
> different food, are ordered by different manners, and are
> not governed by the same laws.'

Egremont comes to see that it is so and that the abundant pleasures of life, which he has unthinkingly accepted as his birthright, are rooted in the exploitation of the common people. Philip Warner, a weaver who, despite toiling at his handloom for twelve hours a day for a penny an hour, despairs of being able to keep a roof over the heads of himself and his family much longer, is the very archetype of the dispossessed. 'How did honesty and industry bring us to this?' he muses, and answers himself:

> 'It is that the capitalist has found a slave that has
> supplanted the labour and ingenuity of man. Once he
> was an artisan: at the best, he now only watches
> machines; and even that occupation slips from his grasp,
> to the woman and the child. The capitalist flourishes, he
> amasses immense wealth; we sink, lower and lower;
> lower than the beasts of burthen; for they are fed better
> than we are, cared for more. And it is just, for according
> to the present system they are more precious.'

He bitterly repudiates the fraudulent claim that 'the interests of capital and labour are identical', and declares that:

> 'If a society that has been created by labour suddenly
> becomes independent of it, that society is bound to maintain
> the race whose only property is labour, out of the proceeds of
> that other property, which has not ceased to be productive.'

In scene after vivid scene of high and low life, *Sybil* delivers a withering indictment of a society (whose outlines we can hardly fail to recognise when we look around us today, however changed the detail) in which property comes before people. Then, through the agency of the young parliamentarian Egremont - in the report of a speech that echoes the young Disraeli's speech to the House calling on it to receive the Chartists' National Petition - the author makes a forthright declaration of where he himself stands:

> 'Yes! there was one voice that had sounded in that
> proud Parliament, that, free from the slang of faction,
> had dared to express immortal truths: the voice of a
> noble who, without being a demagogue, had upheld

60

the popular cause; had pronounced his conviction that the rights of labour were as sacred as those of property; that if a difference were to be established, the interests of the living wealth ought to be preferred; who had declared that the social happiness of the millions should be the first object of a statesman, and that, if this were not achieved, thrones and dominions, the pomp and power of courts and empires, were alike worthless.'

Disraeli/Egremont felt his own party was moribund and aspired to lead its regeneration, to restore it to that noble sense of stewardship which he believed had once characterised it:

'Even now it is not dead, but sleepeth; and, in an age of political materialism, of confused purposes and perplexed intelligence, that aspires only to wealth because it has faith in no other accomplishment... Toryism will yet arise from the tomb...to bring back strength to the Crown, liberty to the subject, and to announce that power has only one duty - to secure the social welfare of the PEOPLE.'

The degradation Disraeli describes in *Sybil* mirrors the same inglorious England that Engels portrayed in *The Condition of the Working Class in England*, which was also first published in 1845 - but in Germany, the Victorian reading public being spared this salutary scourge until a translation was issued forty years later. The varied and conflicting attitudes and arguments (not least, for example, over the question of whether poverty is poverty until it is absolute) *Sybil* presents, as well as the range of material conditions - from splendour to squalor - that it portrays, are not so greatly different from those encountered in our own splintered society. That is why Disraeli's expression 'The Two Nations' still strikes home today. And never more so than in differentiating paternalist Tories (or 'One-Nation Tories' as they prefer to call themselves) from 'the New Conservatives'.

Of course, the crusading zeal of the aspiring young politician might have evaporated with the growing triumph of his own career from derided parvenu to honoured elder statesman. How seldom do such youthful ideals survive the surmounting of the slippery slope to success! In Disraeli's case they did, so that his second (and only substantial) ministry, from February 1874 to March 1880, saw the passing of a whole series of laws to improve the lives and labour of the working classes: Factory Acts, an Artisans' Dwelling Act, a Public Health Act, and a Trade Union Act which gave to union funds some protection against claims for damages and granted the right of peaceful picketing.

From this side of the historic watershed of the great Liberal reforming governments of 1906-1914, which laid the foundations of a Welfare State in alliance with a lusty young Labour Party, it is difficult not to think of the Liberals as markedly more sympathetic to the working classes than the Tories. But taken as a whole, the record tells us otherwise. That is no more than we should expect when we consider how the manufacturing and commercial interests were more powerfully represented in the Liberal Party. The miners' leader Alexander Macdonald, who was elected MP for Stafford in the 1874 general election (becoming, in effect, along with another miner who won Morpeth, one of the first two Labour MPs, although officially they sat in the House as Liberals), said of Disraeli's great reforming ministry: 'The Conservative Party have done more for the working classes in five years than the Liberals have in fifty.' Writing about representation of the trade union movement in Parliament after the extension of the franchise to the ever-last-in-the-queue group of workers, the farm labourers, in 1884, Henry Pelling remarks: 'It was not at all clear that the Liberal Party as a whole was more likely to espouse the labour cause than the Conservatives.' He illustrates his point by referring to the 'fair wages' resolution passed by a House of Commons under Tory control in 1891, 'whereby it was agreed that in the awarding of government contracts every effort should be made "to secure the payment of such wages as are generally accepted as current in each trade for competent workmen"'. He describes this as a 'major service for labour.'

In fact - although the 1884 Reform Act was the work of Gladstone's administration, although the 1867 Reform Act of the Derby/Disraeli ministry was the indirect result of the defeat of the Russell/Gladstone Reform Bill of 1866 and although Grey's 1832 Reform Act was only passed when Wellington's forces retreated in face of the King's threat to wipe out the Tory majority in the Lords by creating more Whig peers - the truth is that even when it came to the extension of the franchise, the nineteenth-century Liberals were scarcely less equivocal than the Tories. While Gladstone expressed his belief, as early as 1864, in the right of every man to have the vote, thereby provoking Disraeli's taunt that he had 'revived the doctrine of Tom Paine'; and while unremitting pressure from the radical section of the Liberal Party forced the pace of electoral reform, there was scarcely less opposition to the enfranchisement of the masses among the Liberals than there was in the ranks of the Tories. Robert Lowe (a distinguished frontbencher, subsequently Chancellor of the Exchequer and then Home Secretary), who led the Liberal faction which frustrated the attempt by Lord Russell and Gladstone to widen the franchise in 1866, expressed his aversion, in terms reminiscent of Burke's 'epochal indiscretion', to having his seat dependent on the votes of a class of men he regarded as 'impulsive, unreflecting, and violent' and a prey to 'venality, ignorance, and drunkenness'. Suffice it to say that Hazlitt's sardonic simile likening the Whigs and Tories to rival stagecoaches splashing each other with mud but travelling by the same road to the same destination was almost as pertinent in mid-Victorian Britain as it had been when he made it before the so-called Great Reform Act of 1832.

CHAPTER 5

Radical Liberals and Tory democrats

'The 'Fissical Policy' emanated from the Tory party. That was the reason some of them were strongly in favour of it, and for the same reason others were opposed to it. Some of them were under the delusion that they were Conservatives: similarly, others imagined themselves to be Liberals. As a matter of a fact, most of them were nothing. They knew as much about the public affairs of their own country as they did of the condition of affairs in the planet Jupiter.'

Robert Tressell,
The Ragged Trousered Philanthropists **(1914)**

In short, it is a peculiarly purblind and simplistic kind of historical hindsight that promotes the Liberals as the party of reform in Victorian England, mainly to be accounted for, perhaps, by the hold taken on the popular imagination by Gladstone's crusading zeal. One needs to remember, however, that - with the important exception of the extension of the franchise - this zeal was principally focused on foreign parts, across the Irish Channel or further overseas (reminding one a little of Wilberforce's discrimination in favour of slaves in the West Indies, while the toiling masses at home awakened in his breast no comparable compassion). In *The Common People*, their masterly narrative of two centuries (1746-1946) in the life and struggles of Britain's working classes, G.D.H. Cole and Raymond Postgate declare bluntly that 'Gladstone had never understood or sympathised with the economic claims of the workers.'

Even on the issue of male suffrage, radicals were to be found on both sides of the House; while when it came to questions of social reform to ameliorate 'the condition of the people', neither side could be said to stand unequivocally for progress. What else should one expect from an assembly that, until the election of *two* working-class members in 1874, was wholly composed of representatives of property interests? In other words, in considering the development of democracy and the piecemeal construction of a welfare state, what counts is not the perpetual ritualistic combat between Liberals and Conservatives, but the struggle between social radicals and small-c conservatives of whatever party.

Just as parallel lines (or so we are told by those who understand such abstruse matters) meet in infinity, so do the careers of two political comets - Lord Randolph Churchill and Joseph Chamberlain - apparently travelling in quite separate orbits, converge to illustrate the conflict that was of real historical moment. Son of a leading boot and shoe manufacturer and of the daughter of a London provision merchant, Joseph Chamberlain (1836-1914) sat as a Liberal MP for only ten years and held only two ministerial posts (President of the Board of Trade, 1880-85, and President of the Local Government Board, 1886) in Liberal administrations. Then he broke with Gladstone over the Irish Home Rule issue and crossed the floor of the House, subsequently to serve as Colonial Secretary for Conservative ministries from 1895-1903. Yet his programme of radical reform had a profound influence on both parties and on the social development of the whole country in the second half of the Victorian Age. His most indisputable achievement was, as Mayor of Birmingham from 1873-76, to guide the city into making itself a model for municipal reform, 'parked, paved, assized, marketed, Gas-and-watered, and *improved* - all as the result of three years' active work', as he put it himself. Too modestly, as it happens, since he left out of the account major advances in the provision of educational and cultural facilities and an ongoing commitment to 'the increase of the comfort and happiness of the community'.

In his *Victorian Cities* Asa Briggs draws attention to Chamberlain's doubts that he could do as much, let alone more, for his fellow men as an actor on the national stage as he had done for the citizens of his adopted city. On his election to Parliament in 1876 he remarked to his friend Jesse Collings (a doughty champion of the poor in general and of the agricultural labourer and the smallholder in particular): 'What a fool I am to be willing to go to Parliament and give up the opportunity of influencing the only constructive legislation in the country for the sake of tacking M.P. to my name'; and, while serving as President of the Board of Trade, he commented on the progress of his career to the eminent biographer and statesman John Morley: 'Unless I can secure for the nation results similar to those which have followed the adoption of my policy in

Birmingham, it will have been a very sorry exchange to give up the Town Council for the Cabinet.'

At all events, his commitment to social reform endured (surviving, indeed, his subsequent defection to the Conservatives, with whose views he was more in sympathy when it came to foreign and colonial affairs and also to the question of free trade versus protection) and was forcefully expressed in the general election campaign of autumn 1885, in which Chamberlain's dazzlingly bold 'unauthorised programme', appealing to the have-nots and the have-littles, and especially to the newly enfranchised rural labourers, is generally credited with returning the Liberals to power. Chamberlain argued that, as a consequence of the development of industry, private property had usurped the place of communal ownership; and he counselled the haves to pay 'ransom', that they might continue to enjoy security of property. This they could only do by raising the condition of 'the lower orders' - through the provision of good housing at fair rents; free education; compulsory land purchase to set up a scheme for smallholdings (which was popularised under Jesse Collings' slogan 'three acres and a cow'); security of tenure for farmers; radical revision of the system of taxation; and other measures, including the old Chartist demand for the payment of MPs. 'It went to the extreme limits to which Radicalism could go without becoming Socialism,' say Cole and Postgate in *The Common People*. To which one might add that in one respect of fundamental importance - its challenge to the market basis of landholding and its aspiration to the creation of a protected class of smallholders - it went further than any British government laying claim to Socialist credentials has ever dared to go.

It was such Jacobinical talk that led the moderate Liberal George Joachim Goschen (an ex-merchant banker and director of the Bank of England who, ironically, like Chamberlain broke with Gladstone over Irish Home Rule, became, as a Liberal Unionist, Chancellor of the Exchequer under Salisbury, and, again like Chamberlain, moved all the way into the Conservative Party) to charge his Radical colleague with (says his biographer A. D. Elliot) 'setting class against class; all against property; which he implies but does not actually say is *landed* property.' (Goschen, incidentally, had voted against giving farm labourers the vote). And there is no doubt that the Radicals' efforts to take over the Liberal Party platform, which came so near to success, were mainly responsible for the growing number of defections of businessmen to the

Conservatives. This changing party allegiance of the capitalist classes is clearly capitulated by Harold Perkin in *The Origins of Modern English Society*:

'The threat to passive property mounted by the left wing of the Liberal Party, however innocuous it looks at this distance, was enough to frighten some of them into the arms of the Conservatives. Long before the geological shift in the structure of British politics centred around the Liberal split of 1886 [over Irish Home Rule], which took so many business men as well as landowners into the Tory Party, it is possible, beneath the overwhelming Liberalism of the mid-Victorian business class, to detect anticipatory traces of the drift... The Liberals of course retained a majority of all categories of business MPs except the brewers down to 1885, but the Tory share steadily rose, and when the main break came in 1886 it was the typically corporate interests, finance, railways, shipping and transport, which first gave a majority to the Tories, and the more typically entrepreneurial categories. cotton, coal, metals, engineering, and the merchants, which still remained marginally more loyal to the Liberals. The remoter origins of the modern social structure of politics and particularly the equation of big business and Conservatism, can be traced to the mid-Victorian age.'

On the other hand, it would seem probable that for every disaffected bourgeois it drove away, the populist programme of the Radicals attracted a handful of supporters from the newly enfranchised classes. Thus, had the Liberal Party wholeheartedly embraced a radical agenda in the 1880s, it might have secured the allegiance of 'the lower orders', pre-empted the birth of a workers' party with potential mass support and made itself the natural party of government in a 'fully representative democracy'.

As for Chamberlain's efforts to rally support for the Liberals, far from resting on the appeal of radical manifestos alone, they took the most practical of forms: fostering the recruiting of supporters into local associations and, from 1877, the co-ordination of their activities by the National Liberal Federation, with Francis Schnadhorst, Birmingham-born-and-bred despite his name, as its organising secretary.

Having given working men the vote, not through a process of wise and generous-hearted deliberation but in a succession of political auctions in which the convention-shackled core of each party feared it would be outbid by the other in the contest for popularity, the two illustrious rival parties which together had composed England's competitive oligarchy for so long, were now obliged to set out their stalls to catch - and if they could to hold - the masses on whom their chances of another turn in the seats of political power now principally depended.

Each party emulated the other. In building up a nation-wide grassroots organisation the Liberals were following in the footsteps of the Conservatives, who, with the active encouragement of Disraeli himself, had - to cite only the most salient organisational measure - established the National Union of Conservative and Constitutional Associations ten years earlier, with John Gorst, who had already played a leading part in redesigning the Conservative Party machine, as its honorary secretary. (Gorst was eventually to turn free-trader, break with the Conservatives and, in 1910, to stand unsuccessfully as a Liberal candidate; but during the handful of years during which Lord Randolph Churchill strove to put the imprint of 'Tory Democracy' on the party, Gorst was one of his 'Fourth Party' paladins).

The Tories in turn learned from the tighter organisation of supporters introduced by Chamberlain and his confederates. Lord Randolph Churchill (1849-1895) was among those who had attacked Chamberlain's methods of mustering his forces as 'caucusing'; but he soon came to the conclusion that - as he wrote in a letter to Salisbury - it was 'undeniably the only form of political organisation which can collect, guide, and control for common objects large masses of electors.' Moreover, like Chamberlain, Churchill played the recruiting sergeant, not only by fostering the enlistment of supporters into the party ranks (notably through the setting up of working men's clubs) but through propaganda. And in promoting his own 'unauthorised programme' (the 'Dartford programme', as it came to be called from the place where it was first promulgated) of populist proposals, he followed the example of his illustrious mentor Disraeli by stealing the thunder of reforming Liberals. As we reach this episode in the tedious tale of the jockeying for power between England's two great oligarchical factions, the young Disraeli's derisive charge that Peel had 'caught the Whigs bathing, and walked away with their clothes' echoes mockingly in our ears.

'The dreary negatives of contemporary Toryism,' to quote Philip Guedalla's comment in *Mr Churchill: A Portrait*, were not for the dashing Lord Randolph, and his impatience with them fuelled 'his effort to modernise Lord Salisbury by inoculation with the elastic ideals of Tory Democracy'. Just two months before his political self-immolation, when, as Chancellor of the Exchequer, he had reached the pinnacle of his career, Randolph Churchill, expressing his thoughts in words which, ironically, are reminiscent of Marx's famous comment on philosophy that the point is not to understand the world but to change it, roundly proclaimed: 'Politics is not a science of the past. You must use the past as a lever with which to manufacture the future.' Which is exactly what he tried to do (with the object of furthering his own career as well as his aspirations for his country) in setting out his 'Dartford programme'. Amongst other things, it proposed local government reforms, legislation on land transfer and on tithes, the sale of glebe land and measures to provide agricultural labourers with allotments and smallholdings.

The resemblance of all this to the 'unauthorised programme' which Joseph Chamberlain promoted when he was still a Liberal is striking. And it should be noted that the populist proposals of the 'Dartford programme', emanating from what might be thought of as a distinctly pinkish extreme of the Tory Party, were subsequently adopted as official party policy; just as we need to keep pinching ourselves over the rather astonishing fact that in those palmy days of 'Victorian values' a hundred years ago, the foremost champion of this decidedly radical Conservatism reached the highest elected office within the party, chairman of the council of the National Union of Conservative and Constitutional Associations.

When we turn from particular proposals to seek out the principles underlying Randolph Churchill's 'Tory Democracy', however, we find that, from the point of view of conceptual thinking, they are as insubstantial and as wayward as the 'clouds without water, blown by the wind' to which he scornfully compared his Liberal opponents in a characteristic blast of bombast discharged in a campaign speech at Carlisle in October 1884. At a time of schism in the Liberal ranks over the Irish question and apprehensions concerning democracy and radicalism, he assured his audience and himself that the 'helplessness' of the Liberals 'would compel the English people to turn to the united and historic party, which can alone re-establish your social and imperial interests, and can alone proceed safely, steadily, and surely along the broad path of social progress and reform.'

An address delivered in April of the same year to the Birmingham Conservative Association reveals the thoroughly Disraelian cast of his thinking on the Constitution. Charging 'the Radicals' (and, of course, through insinuated guilt by association, the whole Liberal Party) with 'aversion' to 'the institutions of our country' and with giving 'reasons for their destruction' which - without specifying them, let alone answering them - he characterises as 'multitudinous and specious', he claims that Conservatives defend the Constitution 'on the ground of its *utility to the people*' and on that alone. 'An hereditary throne,' he declares, 'is the surest device which has ever been imagined or invented for the perpetuation of civil order and for that first necessity of civilised society - continuity of government,' while the House of Lords constitutes 'an aggregation of political wisdom and experience such as no other country can produce' and provides '*a powerful check on popular impulses arising from imperfect information.*' Such unexamined arguments are, of course, the staple fare of Tory speechifying. Nor can it be said, however fanciful the dish, that he departs radically from the standard menu in affirming of the Peers that they '*are essentially of the people,*' so that 'every privilege, every franchise, every liberty which is gained by the people, is treasured up and guarded by those who, animated by tradition and custom, by long descent and lofty name, fear neither monarchs, nor ministers, nor men, but only the people, *whose trustees they are...*' [my emphases in the above and following extracts from this speech]

Conservative apologists never have been unduly concerned by problems of consistency in projecting their vision of the good society, so there is no reason to fear that either Lord Randolph or his audience were troubled when he glided on from celebrating 'the glories of our blood and state' as represented by the Crown and the Peers of the Realm to commending the Established Church as 'a centre, a source, a guide of *charitable effort, mitigating* by its mendicant importunity *the violence of human misery,* whether mental or physical, and contributing to the work of alleviation from its own not superfluous resources.' If we feel that talk of charity and the mitigation of human misery (or that part of it at least that is the child of poverty) hardly gets to the root of the problem, at least the injunction that follows - 'And I urge upon you not to throw that source of charity upon *the haphazard almsgiving of a busy and selfish world*' - makes for salutary reading in an age when trickle-down theories of the distribution of wealth are once again in fashion and when private generosity and public parsimony are recommended as the proper palliatives for socially-generated misery. And at least Lord Randolph floated one real remedy on the torrent of his rhetoric: a proposal for 'a large redistribution of the incidence of taxation.'

Despite the disparity in achievement, Lord Randolph Churchill irresistibly recalls Disraeli. Like him, he forced the Elders of the Party to pay attention to him by the sheer brilliance of his attacks on the Opposition - and even more, perhaps, by the derisive darts directed at his own party establishment. Just as the young Disraeli had captained the 'Young England' partisans, so Lord Randolph dashingly deployed his dissident ginger group, which was derisively dubbed the 'Fourth Party' (Parnell's Irish group being the third) but which repaid the mockers in their own coin - and with interest. Both of these Tory young turks were witty and irreverent; neither was over-scrupulous in striking their targets in the House.

As I have demonstrated, they were alike too in their agitprop excursions in the grandiloquent mode, in which sound largely substituted for sense. In fact Lord Randolph Churchill has nothing to contribute to the history of political philosophy but a great deal to contribute to the history of practical politics. At a crucial period in the development of 'representative democracy' he recognised the necessity of roping in the masses and set about it with energy and flair. Since he does not appear to have done this in a spirit of cynical calculation, we may conclude that - as is not infrequently the case in politics - it was his very lack of penetration as a thinker that afforded him the transparency of purpose which made him successful as a tribune of the people. *'No class interests should be allowed to stand in the way of this mighty movement*, [of the people]', he told his Birmingham audience of 'men well acquainted with business, commerce, and trade', who hardly needed his reminder that 'the Tory party of today is no longer identified with that small and narrow class which is connected with the ownership of land', but were doubtless flattered by the recitation. *'Trust the people,'* he enjoined the assembled entrepreneurs, *'and they will trust you* - and they will follow you and join in the defence of that Constitution against any and every foe. *I have no fear of democracy*...To rally the people round the Throne and a patriotic people, that is our policy and that is our faith.'

71

The idioms have changed a little, but such slogans, such rhetoric, have survived as central elements in Tory Party propaganda, and evidently they have lost little of their persuasive power. As for the elusive nature of the philosophy behind the Birmingham speech, I have already remarked that such vagueness, whether studied or involuntary, is, and will remain, a political asset for as long as the great mass of the electorate remains incapable of rational analysis of the society they live in. Which regrettably is still the case, no matter how many contending politicians may unctuously compliment the public on its good sense.

Nevertheless, for all his faults and all his demagoguery, it seems to me, even if I risk the charge of naiveté in saying so, that Randolph Churchill shared with Disraeli a genuine commitment to 'improving the condition of the people'. And what is more important, under his influence the Tory approach to the problem of the common people shifted perceptibly from pure paternalism to a kind of hybrid solution we might describe as 'paternalistic democracy'. Or to put it another way, he contributed greatly to ensuring that Tory paternalism successfully accommodated itself to the demands of a parliamentary democracy accelerating towards universal suffrage. And that was a major political achievement.

CHAPTER 6

Fear the people

> 'There is no period in history - with the exception, perhaps, of the period of insurrections in the twelfth and thirteenth centuries, which led to the birth of the mediaeval Communes - during which a similarly deep change has taken place in the current conceptions of society...a chance combination of accidental circumstances may bring about in Europe a revolution as widespread as that of 1848, and far more important; not in the sense of mere fighting...but in the sense of a profound and rapid social reconstruction...'
>
> **Peter Kropotkin, *Memoirs of a Revolutionist* (1899)**

There is a long-standing and comforting myth that the 'character' of the English people - in blessed contrast to that of more volatile Continental races - has preserved the country from revolution. And considering the monstrous provocations they have repeatedly endured without ever rising 'in unvanquishable NUMBER', there seem to be solid grounds for thinking this. But such serene assurance has by no means always held sway in the minds of the bourgeoisie and may even have been the exception rather than the rule throughout the Victorian Age (not to speak of earlier times) and right up to our 'thirties. On quite a few occasions bourgeois self-confidence must have turned distinctly pale.

'The first and highest duty of a government is to prevent revolution rather than to repress it, to sustain law rather than to revive it, to preserve order rather than to restore it,' Lord Randolph Churchill told a Manchester audience estimated at no less than 12,000 people, in December 1881. The context of his speech was the Irish problem; but nevertheless, when, in his address to the Birmingham Conservative Association referred to above, he commended the exhortation to the House of Commons of their arch opponent, Gladstone, to 'trust the people', surely Lord Randolph's counsel conveyed to the party faithful a subliminal message too - 'or fear them'!

Certainly fear of the people served to remind the combatants in the forever recurring parliamentary mêlée over the question of the suffrage that they had a great deal more in common with their Westminster opponents than they had with the unfathomable working classes whom Disraeli had called through his fictional hero 'inhabitants of a different planet'. And nearly a century after Disraeli raised the spectre of 'the two nations', George Orwell was to comment on 'the idea that there is some mysterious, fundamental difference between rich and poor, as though they were two different races', to which fallacy he ascribed the 'fear of a supposedly dangerous mob that makes nearly all intelligent [i.e. cultivated] people conservative in their opinions.'

To the very considerable extent to which this fear was rooted in sheer ignorance of how the other half lived, felt, and thought, he was right to describe it as 'superstitious'. But that is far from saying it had no rational basis. And if there was still good cause for fear in 1933, when Orwell's *Down and Out in Paris and London* was published, how much more was that true in Victorian England. In fact, despite the clouds of steam produced in all too many instances by panic and prejudice, two eminently reasonable objections (or at least wholly understandable reservations) to proposals to extend the franchise to the working classes stand out starkly enough. Was it wise to admit either the ignorant or the property-less to the body of electors? Since the first of these two deficiencies is the least easily remedied (as we can bear witness to a century later), it is not to be lightly dismissed. For the time being, however, let us simply listen to a few voices objecting to the ill-informed being allowed a say in the government of the country, before tackling the more contentious opinion that the have-nots should not have a vote either.

As we have seen, Gladstone had made it absolutely clear where he stood in principal when, in 1864, he put the burden of proof firmly on the opponents of manhood suffrage. He was far from being either blind or dismissive, however, to the problems that would stem from its introduction. While fully appreciating that the special social disabilities of labouring men were in large measure the cause of their unfitness for much more than a passive role in politics, in an article published in the monthly review *The Nineteenth Century* in July 1878, he expressed concern that in many instances their value as electors would suffer, not only from lack of information and thought, but from 'a degree of subserviency' inseparable from their exceptional dependency on the goodwill of others, in particular employers and landlords. This and other issues he raises in this article remain of central relevance to the question of what 'representative democracy' really amounts to.

Gladstone's mind was made up, then, but it was still full of misgivings. Like him, John Stuart Mill, the foremost liberal philosopher of the mid-Victorian age, certainly wanted to see the extension of the franchise. Indeed, in his *Considerations on Representative Government*, published in 1861, he maintained the equal right of women to have the vote and, in principle, endorsed a fully representative democracy. But he contended that although 'the opinions and wishes of the poorest and rudest class of labourers may be very useful as one influence among others on the minds of the voters, as well as on those of the Legislature...it might be highly mischievous to give them the preponderant influence, by admitting them, in their present state of morals and intelligence, to the full exercise of the suffrage.' This was exactly the point that Lord Randolph Churchill was to make when, in the opening debate on Gladstone's 1884 bill to enfranchise the rural labourers, he inveighed against the swamping of the electorate by the addition of some two millions of poor and grossly ignorant voters; though - doubtless primarily for tactical reasons - he had changed his mind by the time the House voted.

Naturally a host of less sympathetic and not a few wholly hostile politicians and political thinkers employed arguments against the extension of the franchise that were based on the disadvantages which were inseparable from having a great number of voters 'whose minds are unused to thought and undisciplined to study' (to quote Robert Cecil, the future third Marquis of Salisbury). Such arguments, notwithstanding the mixed and not infrequently ulterior motives of their proponents, included many pertinent points concerning the dangers of demagoguery, and collectively they composed a powerful critique of the whole concept of democratic government. For the moment one quite unpartisan comment may suffice to represent these particular fears. In the introduction to the second edition (1872) of *The English Constitution,* Walter Bagehot wrote: 'What I fear is that both our political parties will bid for the support of the working man; that both of them will promise to do as he likes, if he will only tell them what that is; that, as he now holds the casting vote in our affairs, both parties will beg and pray him to give that vote to them.'

After the passing of the Second Reform Act, in the year in which Bagehot's classic study first appeared, the increasingly desperate attempt to stem the tide, flowing, apparently inexorably, towards manhood suffrage, mostly took the form of advocating what Cecil had called, in 1864, a 'graduated suffrage' - a form of progress which, in less specific but also less grudging terms, his party leaders, Lord Derby and Disraeli, had in fact already conceded. Amongst the qualifications nominated as requisite for the privilege of voting were education, intelligence, wisdom, integrity, and virtue (the last unspecified, but doubtless intended to denote subscription, in word if not in deed, to conventional standards of decency in sexual and marital conduct). Let a wry smile suffice, for the time being, as comment, while we turn to look at what surely must have loomed in the minds of the anti-democrats as quite the gravest objection to manhood suffrage: the horrendous prospect it appeared to open up of the radical redistribution of wealth and income.

Again and again we detect - at the very heart of the host of arguments deployed against a wider suffrage - that vindication of inequality in the interests of political stability (that is to say, of the *status quo!*) which Burke made with unexampled effrontery in implicitly equating rapacity with the dispossessed. As with Burke himself, it is by no means always easy to disentangle the gut concern for self from the lofty thoughts of liberty and the like or the pseudo-scientific claptrap concerning 'hidden hands' or 'the characteristic essence of property' into which it is woven. Thus it is quite a relief to read such blunt objections as Robert Lowe's fearful remark that, 'Once give the working man the vote, and the machinery is ready to launch those votes in one compact mass upon the institutions of property in this country.'

A proud distaste for pompous or mealy-mouthed declamation is also one of the attractions of the man who led the Conservatives into the twentieth century, the Marquis of Salisbury (1830-1903). Not that his political testimony is wholly free of humbug. In one of his *Quarterly Review* pieces in particular (published in July 1864), he, whose whole case was based on the defence of property, had the gall to charge his opponents with taking a 'Joint-stock Company' approach to politics. He accused them of leading 'agitation for the extension of the franchise' that is 'purely a struggle for material advantages', while men such as himself (it was implied) were moved by 'emotions far higher than self-interest', by 'self-sacrifice and heroism'. In a passage that might almost have been designed to conjure up the applauding ghost of Coriolanus and reminds one of Lord Valentine's assertion (in *Sybil*) that it was men like his ancestors who had made England what it was - a presumptuous claim which provokes from Stephen Morley such a stinging rebuttal - Salisbury declares:

> 'The sacrifices required of an English politician are heavy enough as matters stand. It is surely enough that he should give his time, his money, and his health to his country, and devote himself to an exhausting labour without reward. To require of him, in addition to all this, that he shall seek the privilege of being permitted to do it by solicitations and compliances which he feels to be degrading, is a heavier trial than the patriotism of the better spirits among the educated classes will bear for any length of time.'

For all that, Salisbury's animadversions against democracy have the great merit of taking us straight to the heart of the matter. 'Revolutions are favourable to confiscation,' Burke had somewhat superfluously proclaimed. His 'solicitude...lest it should ever be considered in England as the policy of the state, to seek a resource in confiscations of any kind...' was now echoed, in the rather less cataclysmic context of parliamentary reform, by Salisbury's warning:

> 'We have now entered upon the descent of the smooth, easy, sloping path of popular finance, on which there is no halting-place to check our career short of *confiscation*. This question of the incidence of taxation is in truth the vital question of modern politics. It is the field on which the contending classes of this generation will do battle...The *proletariat* will not now fight for a *barren share in the business of legislation*, unless it is to bear to each of them a substantial and palpable fruit. The issue between the conflicting forces of society is becoming narrower and more distinct. *The mists of mere political theory* are clearing away, and the true character of the battleground, and the real nature of the prize that is at stake, are standing out more and more distinctly every year...The struggle between the English constitution on the one hand, and *the democratic forces*

that are now labouring to subvert it on the other, is
now, in reality, when reduced to its simplest elements
and stated in its most prosaic form, *a struggle between
those who have, to keep what they have got, and those
who have not, to get it.'* [my emphases in the above and
subsequent quotations from Salisbury's writings]

And just as Burke had drolly dreamed of the rich and powerful
becoming '*prey*' to the destitute, so did Salisbury foresee a 'rising
storm of Democratic *spoliation*' in which taxation would be wielded
'as an instrument of *plunder*.' All this was, of course, nothing more
than an appeal to the healthily possessive instincts of the possessors.
Nor can he be said to have plumbed the philosophical depths when
he did cast around for decent arguments to clothe the naked interests
of his class. For this very reason, the case he makes (in the July
1864 *Quarterly Review* article mentioned above) against 'a wide
extension of the franchise', in fact constitutes as telling an advocacy
of universal suffrage as his most ardent democratic opponents could
have desired:

'To give 'the suffrage' to a poor man is to give him as
large a part in determining *that legislation which is
mainly concerned with property* as the banker whose
name is known on every Exchange in Europe, as the
merchant whose ships are in every sea, as the landowner
who owns the soil of a whole manufacturing town. An
extension of the suffrage to the working classes means
that upon a question of taxation, or expenditure, or upon
a measure vitally affecting commerce, *two day-
labourers shall outvote Rothschild.'*

The gravamen of Salisbury's argument - and one cannot doubt
that if it were a necessary buttress for the continued hegemony of
capitalism its apostles would maintain so still - was that political
power should be proportionate to a man's 'stake in the country',
with 'stake' carrying, of course, the venal and vulgar connotations
not of his life's blood but of his property and his pecuniary holdings
and investments. Such utterly materialistic measurements of a man's
worth - *not* fine considerations of his intellectual, moral, or spiritual
calibre - were foremost in Salisbury's mind in proposing a

'graduated suffrage' and in claiming, with breath-taking confidence, to know and to share the general opinion of mankind on how its affairs should be ordered. '*The common consent of mankind*,' he intoned, 'expressed in the management of their own concerns, has agreed that in the government and administration of *common property*, men should vote in proportion to their shares.'

His most uncompromising dictum on the proper relationship between property ownership and political participation (as manifested, that is, in the periodic privilege of choosing the lawmakers) proclaims: 'Natural right, then, cannot be made to justify an equal suffrage, *so long as there is not equal property to protect.*' But if, without challenging his insolently arbitrary premises, we simply follow where his own logic leads, we see at once that he utterly undermines his own argument (which is of course circular, not to say either simple-minded or disingenuous) by drawing our attention to the possibility, and our thoughts to the desirability, of a drastic redistribution of the nation's 'common wealth'.

The real value of Salisbury's contribution to political thought is that, in his anxiety to defend the *status quo*, he inadvertently illuminates the inescapably fraudulent nature of what purports to be democratic political representation in societies constructed on a system of gross economic inequalities. In short, in complete contradiction to his intentions, he presents us with a formidable critique of 'capitalist democracy'.

How little Salisbury and his class had to fear the supposed rapacity of a predominantly working-class electorate we can testify a century later. As Harold Perkin points out in *The Origins of Modern English Society*, not only Gladstone but also Disraeli took a much more relaxed attitude to the prospect of proletarian voters. As early as 1859, paying tribute to the 'virtue, prudence, intelligence, and frugality' of the artisans who had played such a great part in making Britain pre-eminent among the industrialised nations, Disraeli had recommended that they be permitted 'to enter the privileged pale of the constituent body of the country'. Gladstone went further in speaking of the working classes as 'our fellow-subjects, our fellow-Christians, *our own flesh and blood*, who have been lauded to the skies for their good conduct.' On which words Perkin comments, 'that is, were believed to have accepted so much of the entrepreneurial ideal of a class society based on capital and competition as to be trusted not to use their voting power to undermine it.'

When, with remarkable political agility, Disraeli and Derby 'dished the Whigs' by capturing the credit for the second Reform Bill, the future Lord Salisbury called their coup 'a political betrayal which has no parallel in our annals.' So out of tune with the times did he feel, that he even contemplated abandoning politics. He was to live long enough (besides rising to the highest possible political vantage point) to come to realise that his fears had been childish, to see clearly that the fabric of society remained essentially unaltered by the advance of 'representative democracy'. Indeed, by the time it came to the third major extension of the franchise, the third Reform Bill of 1884, Salisbury, who was blessed with the capacity for philosophical acceptance of the inevitable, had so well readjusted his sense of political balance as to do a deal with Gladstone behind the scenes to ease the passage of the bill through Parliament. His political career, in fact, is quite in consonance with the four political virtues of his party which I enumerated in discussing Peel. It only needs to be added that, as with Disraeli, his opposition to the extension of the franchise, although more unyielding, underlines rather than detracts from his active subscription to the Tory tradition of paternalism.

The centrality of this tradition to whatever can properly be called Conservative philosophy has now been traced from pre-Victorian times into the early years of our century. Since, apart from the partisan opposition to social reform during the Liberal hegemony of 1906-1914, there are no major departures from this paternalist tradition until the Thatcherite hijack of the party, I propose to pick up the thread in the age of consensus that preceded that event and may be said to date from the Second World War, or arguably from the National Government formed in 1931. Before doing so, however, it might be illuminating to glance at one of the most uncompromising of the anti-democrats, one who actually believed that the world had never 'seen a better Constitution than England enjoyed between the Reform Bill of 1832 and the Reform Bill of 1867'. His contribution to the debate, for all its unperceived tendentiousness and its blinkered class bias, stands out, nearly a hundred years after he was writing, as in some ways remarkably prophetic. Let Lecky stand, if you like, for that single strand of

Conservatism of which Cosgrave speaks, for he is, to be sure, the very prototype of a Thatcherite.

William Edward Hartpole Lecky (1838-1903) was, like John Stuart Mill, an intellectual of private means, not a man of affairs. However, in his final years, from 1895 until his resignation through ill-health in 1902, he did sit in the Commons as a Liberal Unionist member of Parliament for his alma mater, Trinity College, Dublin. His most notable works are histories of rationalism and of morals in Europe, a history of England and Ireland in the eighteenth century, and the study with which we are concerned, *Democracy and Liberty* (1896). I shall leave aside his often searching criticisms of the basic concept of democracy in order to concentrate on a few passages which - because they focus more sharply on the trends of the time (in particular on the growing challenge of the trade unions and the evolution of an interventionist and paternalist State) than the writings of most of his conservative contemporaries - are also exceptionally prescient; even though, like Salisbury's animadversions on representative democracy, they grossly exaggerate the threat to the privileges of the bourgeoisie.

> 'In our own day, no fact is more incontestable and conspicuous than the love of democracy for authoritative regulation. The two things that men in middle age have seen most discredited among their contemporaries are probably free contract and free trade. The great majority of the democracies of the world are now frankly protectionist, and even in free trade countries the multiplication of laws regulating, restricting, and interfering with industry in all its departments is one of the most marked characteristics of our time.'

The widespread revulsion against the crying injustices associated with the Industrial Revolution is then alluded to in the most offhand manner imaginable, with the casual remark: 'Nor are these regulations solely due to sanitary or humanitarian motives.' This airy dismissal of a revulsion that in truth provided the driving force which many felt obliged the State to become a guardian of the working classes whose welfare the employing classes had so shamefully neglected, serves for Lecky merely as a preface to a slanderous swipe at the trade union movement - one that is remarkably reminiscent of that guru of the Thatcherites, Friedrich Hayek, not to mention legions of leader writers in the capitalist press.

> 'Among large classes of those who advocate them [regulations] another motive is very perceptible. A school has arisen among popular working-class leaders which no longer desires that superior skill, or industry, or providence should reap extraordinary rewards. Their ideal is to restrict by the strongest trade-union regulations the amount of work and the amount of the produce of work, to introduce the principle of legal compulsion into every branch of industry, to give the trade union an absolute coercive power over its members, to attain a high average, but to permit no superiorities.'

In one of those self-revealing (and *class*-revealing) remarks that presumably explains Lecky's reputation among some commentators for impartiality, he charges the chosen champions of the working classes to whom he has been alluding with having too much power and too little concern for liberty. 'It may be permitted to doubt whether liberty in other forms is likely to be very secure if power is mainly placed in the hands of men who, in their own sphere, value it so little.'

Having summarily disposed of the little matter of the common people and their leaders, Lecky turns again to the issue of the State as an enemy of freedom. The following passage echoes Burke and Salisbury in its fear of democratic depredations on the current distribution of wealth through the deployment of the power of levying taxes, as is stressed by my emphases:

> 'The expansion of the authority and the multiplication of the functions of the State in other fields, and especially in the field of social regulation, is an equally apparent accompaniment of modern democracy. This increase of State power means a multiplication of restrictions imposed upon the various forms of human action. It means an increase of bureaucracy, or, in other

words, of the number and power of State officials. It means also a constant increase of taxation, which is in reality a constant restriction of liberty...*The question of taxation is in the highest degree a question of liberty, and taxation under a democracy is likely to take forms that are peculiarly hostile to liberty...We are steadily advancing to a state in which one class will impose the taxes, while another class will be mainly compelled to pay them.* It is obvious that taxation is more and more employed for objects that are *not common interests of the whole community*, and that there is a growing tendency to look upon it as a possible means of *confiscation*; to make use of it to break down the power, influence, and wealth of particular classes...'

So much for Lecky's foreshadowing of Thatcherism's clarion call to return to *selected* 'Victorian values'. Now for his forewarnings of fascism - ever-impending wherever a would be democratic polity tries to share an estate with the cupidities of capitalism:

'There are other ways in which de*mocracy does not harmonise well with liberty.* To place *the chief power in the most ignorant classes* is to place it in the hands of those who naturally care least for political liberty, and *who are most likely to follow with an absolute devotion some strong leader.* The sentiment of nationality penetrates very deeply into all classes; but in all countries and ages *it is the upper and middle classes who have chiefly valued constitutional liberty*, and those classes it is the work of democracy to dethrone. *At the same time democracy does much to weaken among these also the love of liberty.* The instability and insecurity of democratic politics; the spectacle of *dishonest and predatory adventurers climbing by popular suffrage into positions of great power* in the State; the alarm which attacks on property seldom fail to produce among *those who have something to lose,* may easily scare to the side of despotism large classes who, under other circumstances, would have been steady

83

supporters of liberty. A despotism which secures order,
property, and industry, which leaves the liberty of
religion and of private life unimpaired, and which
enables quiet and industrious men to pass through life
untroubled and unmolested will always appear to many
very preferable to a democratic republic which is
constantly menacing, disturbing, or *plundering* them.'
[my emphases]

It is true that Lecky's apprehensions of democracy leading
to despotism are based on his assessment of the causes that led to
the Second Empire. 'It would be a great mistake,' he writes, 'to
suppose that the French despotic Empire after 1852 rested on
bayonets alone. It rested partly on the genuine consent of those
large agricultural classes who cared greatly for material prosperity
and very little for constitutional liberty, and partly on the panic
produced among the middle classes by the socialist preaching of
1848.' But for all that, it is remarkable how he foreshadows the
rise of fascist states in the 1920s and 30s. One notes, too, his blithe
indifference to the inconsistency of his contentions. On the one
hand, it is the lower orders (for it is, of course, to these he refers
when he speaks of 'the most ignorant classes') who are most
disposed to look to dictatorship for their salvation, while the love
of liberty is an upper- and middle-class virtue; but that, on the other
hand, 'those who have something to lose' will if they can most
likely make sure it is their virtue rather than their property! To
generations affronted by apologia for well-heeled fellow-travellers
of the far right, especially in the years between the two world wars,
it all sounds frighteningly familiar.

We could contrast with Lecky's utterly property-centred
and negative interpretation of freedom, the reflections of a
contemporary of his own class who was also an essentially
conservative thinker, but who did at least make some effort to
understand the situation and attitude of those who had little or
nothing to lose. While personally sharing the concept of freedom
that was natural to Lecky's and his own class, Matthew Arnold
recognised that democracy was opening up for the lower orders
the prospect of another kind of freedom - 'social freedom' or
'equality' - with its own validity. And he refused to accept
that this kind of freedom necessarily implied what its

detractors slanderously call 'the politics of envy'.

Most damaging of all, in fact, to Lecky's whole thesis is the eloquent commentary such passages as I have cited provide on the true significance of what he - *like all persons of his class and time who were either Conservative or Liberal by persuasion or oversight* - called *'constitutional* liberty', which is to say, a kind of liberty that can live very comfortably alongside the harshest deprivation *for others*. Shamefully, nearly a century on, we still cannot claim to have even begun to construct a community in which there is no distinction and no enforced choice - as there should never be - between bread and freedom, liberty and equality.

CHAPTER 7

The age of convergence

'However much it was despised by some in the
seventies and eighties, consensus has usually been
considered one of the marks that distinguish liberal
democracies from less civilized states...Perhaps the
chief difference...Between consensus and conviction
politicians is that the former weigh the consequences of
carrying their convictions into practice or law, while the
latter are determined to implement their
convictions whatever their cost to other people.'

Ian Gilmour, *Dancing with Dogma*

'If you do not give the people social reform, they are going to give
you social revolution,' Quintin Hogg warned his own party during
the debate on the Beveridge Report in the House of Commons in
February 1943. This debate, its circumstances and its outcome,
provides a model lesson in the limitations of parliamentary
democracy. What we are concerned with at present, however, is
what it tells us about the Conservative Party and its capacity to
adapt and survive. As a prominent member of the forty-odd-strong
Tory Reform Group, Hogg was not, of course, a typical Tory
member of the House. But no more, as a general rule, are the official
leaders of any party. For the most part the rank and file take their
cue, willingly or unwillingly, from those who by appointment or
by sheer force of character have won prestige and thus become
opinion-leaders. Perhaps we need to remind ourselves now and
again that in talking about the doctrines and philosophy of a political
party we are, strictly speaking, talking about the views of a minority
of that party. As in society at large, the mass is normally more or
less conformist and politically speaking more or less inert; but that
very fact means that when there is change, it is almost always an
active minority which determines the direction in which the party
moves.

In any case, without falling into the trap of historicism and treating History as a protagonist in its own chronicles, we may fairly say that, as Lecky had clearly foreseen, the concatenation of evolving social and economic forces was pushing all political parties, however disparate their premises, in the same general direction - towards ever-increasing State intervention. It may have taken the common run of men in the property-owning classes a long time to see what was obvious to Socialists from the start: that 'invisible hand' thinking was all very well for eighteenth-century economists but would hardly serve today to save society from disaster in any highly-developed industrialised and capitalist economy; but come to it they had to at the last, though some of them may be kicking and screaming still. Nor should we allow ourselves to be deceived by 'rolling back the State' rhetoric into thinking that the essential reality has been changed by the Thatcherite counter-revolution. However limited its influence on velocity and destination, for the State simply to take its hands off the controls in any modern economy would be to career towards catastrophe.

Values and viewpoints are not confined by party boundaries; but it is still pertinent to recall that 'economic liberty' in anything approaching an absolute sense is historically a Liberal doctrine, while notwithstanding Lecky and his like, their paternalistic traditions made it easier for true Tories to accept the encroachment of the State on economic affairs. In his classic study *Modern British Politics*, Samuel Beer draws attention to this in recounting one of those rare occasions on which fundamental political ideas have been explicitly and directly discussed in Parliament, the 1923 House of Commons debate on Philip Snowden's motion on 'the failure of the capitalist system'. It was the Liberals who led the counterattack, with Sir Alfred Mond, in tabling the only amendment to the motion, admonishing the House that they were faced with 'a clear issue between Individualism and Socialism' and deploying (in Beer's words) 'the old and familiar arguments for free enterprise and free trade that constituted the Liberal orthodoxy.' And Beer points out that while the Conservatives 'attacked Socialism and defended private ownership', that did not mean that they unanimously accepted the Liberal orthodoxy. One distinguished member of the Tory Party, Leopold Amery, not only held forth on the merits of protection (in particular for British farmers) and of Empire development, which were of course old

Tory concerns, but openly advocated State guidance of the economy.

In like manner, Neville Chamberlain, introducing his Import Duties bill of 1932, as Chancellor of the Exchequer in Ramsay MacDonald's second National Cabinet, had no qualms about talking in terms of 'inducing or, if you like, forcing industry to set its house in order'. He was making particular reference to the deplorable state of cotton manufacture and the iron and steel industry, which he considered required 'a thorough reorganisation...if they are even to keep their heads above water in the future.' In fact, as Professor Beer points out in writing about the Conservative Party's 'adaptation' in not only accepting 'the financial burdens of the post-war Welfare State' but in adopting 'the methods and responsibilities of the Managed Economy', its supporters had had time to prepare their minds for further adjustment, since 'interwar Conservatism had taken major steps toward control of the economy.'

Just how far - under the pressure of mass unemployment, declining industries, and increasing balance of trade problems; of the unifying experience of national co-operation in the struggle against Nazi Germany and Japan; and, perhaps above all, of the shock of rejection at the polls in July 1945 - the Conservative Party eventually moved towards Labour's conception of a managed economy, was shown by the *Industrial Charter* drawn up by an Industrial Policy Committee appointed by Churchill. It was composed of five members of the Shadow Cabinet (Butler as chairman, plus Macmillan, Lyttleton, Oliver Stanley, and Maxwell Fyfe) and four back-benchers (David Eccles, Heathcoat Amory, Sir Peter Bennett, and J.R.H. Hutchison). Remarkably, amidst a fusillade of denunciation from the Beaverbrook press and other right-wing quarters for its 'pink socialism' and 'totalitarianism', when this Charter (endorsing the nationalisation of the mines, the railways, and the Bank of England, and proposing new machinery for economic planning and wage-fixing) was put to the 1947 Conservative Party Conference, only three hands were raised against it in an assembly of around 5000 delegates. In the following year, conference accepted an Agricultural Charter which endorsed the principle of guaranteed price supports for farm produce introduced under the Labour Government's 1947 Agriculture Act.

Butler was subsequently to describe the *Industrial Charter* as 'an assurance that, in the interests of full employment and social security, modern Conservatism would maintain strong central guidance over the operation of the economy.' The proponents of the Charter were admittedly on the left of the party; but it would be a mistake to deduce from this either that they in some way misled rather than represented party opinion at the time, or that the Charter was primarily a reactive exercise in self-preservation, designed to strike a note in tune with the spirit of the age - though it was that as well. While it certainly went considerably further than ever before in frankly embracing the policy of State control over the economic health of the nation - and while Churchill certainly spoke for all Conservatives in telling the 1946 party conference that among the party's objectives was: 'To support *as a general rule* free enterprise and initiative against State trading and nationalisation of industries' [my emphasis] - the Charter was equally certainly not at variance with Tory tradition. That was faithfully reflected in Butler's declaration to the House during a debate in March 1947 that 'a good Tory has never been in history afraid of the use of the State.'

And the historical reasons for this readiness to use the State to intervene in the economic life of the nation had more to do with concern, from whatever motives, for improving 'the health and social conditions of the people' (to cite the objective that preceded support for free enterprise in Churchill's statement of aims referred to above) than with questions of economic efficiency or entrepreneurial rights. To put it rather more bluntly than Edward Heath did in his celebrated apology for 'the unacceptable face of capitalism', State intervention had always been necessary to protect the working classes - men, women, and children - from the ruthless exploitation endemic to unregulated free enterprise economic systems. Anthony Eden implicitly admitted as much in commending the *Industrial Charter* to conference:

> 'We are not a party of unbridled, brutal capitalism, and never have been. Although we believe in personal responsibility and personal initiative in business, we are not the political children of the *laissez-faire* school. We opposed them decade after decade. Where did the Tories stand when the greed and squalor of the Industrial Revolution were darkening the land? I am content with Keir Hardie's testimony: "As a matter of hard dry fact, from which there can be no getting away, there is more labour legislation standing to the credit account of the

Conservative Party on the Statute Book than there is to that of their opponents.'"

Such views were by no means confined to Conservatives on the left of the party spectrum, as Leopold Amery, the independent-minded but in general decidedly right-wing thinker cited above, bears witness in a policy pamphlet entitled *The Conservative Future* and published by the Conservative Political Centre in 1945:

'The aim of freedom is the development of human personality. The old *laissez-faire* individualism exalted freedom and personality in principle. But experience has proved that individualism, unchecked and unbalanced, can destroy both freedom and individuality for the majority. In the economic field, indeed, *the old capitalist orthodoxy habitually tended to relegate the majority, under the designation of Labour, to the position of a mere commodity governed by the laws of supply and demand.*' [my emphasis]

As for the question of national economic planning, far from having changed his mind after a lifetime in politics, Amery declares in this policy outline that 'in industry it is for the State to set the course.' And, while clearly sharing the preference for free enterprise expressed in Churchill's conference speech mentioned above, he by no means ruled out public ownership or control, specifically distinguishing the Conservative approach to economic problems from Liberal attitudes on this very point:

'Conservatism has none of the old Liberal objection to the direction and control of industry in the national interest, or even a theoretical objection to nationalisation as such, if the national interest cannot be equally well served without it. But it recognises the greatness of the achievement of individual enterprise in the past and the ordinary Englishman's instinct for doing things his own way, and wishes to give the fullest play to that instinct that the national well-being will allow.'

Amery's pamphlet expresses some weighty reservations concerning nationalisation as a general policy and makes some severe strictures on State Socialism, but at the same time pays tribute to Socialism for having seized the initiative in the field of economics:

'It is on economic policy that Socialism has won its victories, and will continue to win them so long as we confine ourselves to mere negative criticism of nationalisation. We can only win ourselves if we have a better alternative policy for securing both prosperity and stability of employment and are prepared to preach that policy as wholeheartedly and consistently as the Socialists have preached theirs.'

Probably the most startling statement ever made by a Conservative on the relationship between his credo and Socialism is Harold Macmillan's remark, in the course of an interview by *The Star* in June 1936, that 'Toryism has always been a form of paternal Socialism.' This may not quite stand up to serious examination; but if instead of simply dismissing it as mischievous one tries transposing the isms, one sees at once that it is rather more than just provocative. For all his predilection for elfishness, Macmillan had, as usual, a serious intent, which he was to spell out two years later in *The Middle Way*, harbinger of the 'mixed economy' approach to the nation's problems that - amidst all the flowing and ebbing of the tides of nationalisation, denationalisation, renationalisation, and so on and so forth, which caused such turbulence on the surface - underpinned the Age of Consensus which characterised the political scene until the Thatcherite *coup de partie*. With more fidelity to the truth of the matter than his Labour Party opponents, Macmillan called this approach 'planned Capitalism', while freely acknowledging the contribution of Socialist ideas to his own thinking:

'I am led to the conclusion that, for as far ahead as we can see, it is both possible and desirable to find a solution of our economic difficulties in a mixed system which combines State ownership, regulation or control of certain aspects of economic activity with the drive and initiative of private enterprise in those realms of origination and expansion for which it is, by general admission, so admirably suited...The Socialist remedy should on the other hand be accepted in regard to the industries and services...where it is obvious that private enterprise has exhausted its social usefulness, or where the general welfare of the economy requires that *certain basic industries and services need now to be conducted in the light of broader social considerations than the profit motive will supply*.' [my emphasis]

Macmillan's attitude to the questions of State intervention, to planning and social engineering, always had been undoctrinaire. In 1927, in collaboration with Robert Boothby, Oliver Stanley, and John Loder, he had produced a book entitled *Industry and State* which he describes in the first volume of his autobiography, *Winds of Change*, as 'a first essay in devising some coherent system lying in between unadulterated private enterprise and collectivism.' This was at a time when, according to his own testimony, 'the Conservative Party as a whole seemed to have absorbed the old Liberal *laissez-faire* concepts,' and the book was severely handled by the right-wing press, the *Sunday Pictorial* going so far as to call it 'nothing more or less than thinly-veiled Socialism.' Such gibes left him unmoved. Speaking in the 1938 Budget debate, Macmillan told the House:

'Right through the whole national system of industry the State, *whether we call it individualism or Socialism I do not care*, is a partner with the people, and the State today from its own interest has a duty as well as a right to demand effective organisation of commerce and industry in order to produce the results from which the Government may secure its revenue...All modern governments today, *whether of the Right or Left*, must be partners in production and distribution. If we do that, we are going to do far more than by making speeches about democracy which we are so fond of making; about the great advantages it has over dictatorships. We shall be proving that in a Parliamentary and democratic

system we are able to organise the system of
production more effectively than any other system,
that we are able to use the powers of science and
technique to develop wealth unknown before. In this
new world, there is no conflict between government
and industry: it is a partnership between all classes in
the nation to achieve the only means by which we can
carry these staggering burdens and that is to make
them relatively smaller by a continual expansion of the
national economy.' [my emphases]

In the passages cited, the emphasis is on Macmillan's
recognition that free enterprise capitalism unguided by the State
had failed to deliver national prosperity. Bizarre though it may be,
concern for 'the national interest' - and the part played in this by
efficiency in industrial and commercial affairs - by no means
guarantees concern for the welfare of all the nation's citizens, as
Oliver Goldsmith caustically observed a couple of hundred years
ago. But not for nothing was Macmillan the Member of Parliament
for Stockton-on-Tees throughout the years of the Great Depression.
When he writes in *Winds of Change* of 'a world which seemed
now, economically speaking, to have fallen apart', it is clear that
what affected him most deeply was what he calls (in describing the
main theme of *The Middle Way*) 'the twin evils of poverty and
insecurity'. Of the discarded workers of his own constituency he
says, 'I shall never forget those despairing faces, as the men tramped
up and down the High Street in Stockton or gathered round the
Five Lamps in Thornaby'; and of the 'unequalled' relief campaign
he writes, 'But charity, whether of the nation as a whole or from
their neighbours, was not what the men wanted. They wanted work.'
     If there was one question above all others on which, by the
end of the Second World War, all but the most benighted of
politicians had come to agree, it was the utter unacceptability of
mass unemployment, an accord which - along with a general
acceptance of the need for some degree of national planning to
secure economic efficiency - formed the keystone of the Age of
Consensus for the next generation. Professor Beer cites a
memorandum from Sir Anthony Eden to his Chancellor of the
Exchequer, Harold Macmillan (who within nine months was to
replace him as Prime Minister), concerning the inflationary

pressures of excessive demand and of wage claims, but which nonetheless ruled out measures that would lead to dishonouring the Conservatives' commitment to 'full employment'. Eden called such a solution to the country's problems 'politically intolerable'.

One whose ministerial career spanned the great divide between the Age of Consensus and the Thatcherite hegemony (and who may therefore be presumed to have changed his mind and found such a social situation tolerable after all!) is Lord Hailsham, who, as Quintin Hogg, produced one of the most notable statements of consensus-style Conservatism. At any rate, in *The Case for Conservatism*, published in 1947, he quotes without dissent Beveridge's judgement, in *Full Employment in a Free Society* (1944), that few would deny that unemployment, which 'before the first World War appeared as an evil calling for remedy', had come to be considered between the wars 'as the most serious economic problem of its time.' And Hogg concludes his chapters that focus on the problem of ensuring full employment with the hope and conviction that, 'given low rates of interest, high wages, adequate social security (for that is what redistribution means) this terrible scourge can be relegated to the category of minor nuisances.'

As a closely-argued polemic in which conflicting political ideas are presented quite fully, if not quite fairly, *The Case for Conservatism* warrants some scrutiny. In the context of the present polemic, however, I wish simply to record its substantial agreement with the views of other thinking Tories noted above - views which concede a considerable area of common ground between what had become by the 1940s the two principal contenders for power, and at the same time making clear their mutual repudiation of nineteenth-century Liberalism. 'The great heresy of the nineteenth century was self-interest,' writes Hogg, alluding to the long hegemony of Mancunian Liberalism; and in another place, putting the matter in the context of the first two Commandments, he says that Liberalism stands condemned 'because it ignored God and believed that self love was an adequate substitute for our duty towards our neighbour.'

The defection of businessmen from the Liberals which was in the course of time to make the Conservative Party the businessmen's party *par excellence* has already been noted, and in their book on *The English Middle Classes* (1947), Roy Lewis and Angus Maude complain that this had had 'a profound effect on the [Conservative] party, purging it of most of its Tory philosophy and indoctrinating it with that peculiar blend of Whiggery and *laissez-faire* Liberalism which still colours the speeches of some of its leaders.' But Hogg, writing at the same time, had no hesitation in pronouncing *laissez-faire* attitudes as contrary to Conservatism. In a passage referring to Macmillan's book *The Middle Way* and surveying the 'variety of forms of Conservative public ownership as at 1939', he declares: 'It was the Liberals who believed in the essentially unbalanced theory of *laissez faire*,' a principle which (he remarks elsewhere), if 'consistently applied', is 'the mother of economic chaos'. On the other hand, he declares: 'It is completely false to say that Socialism has the monopoly of "planning" in politics.' He points out that neither Churchill nor Eden had a doctrinaire attitude to nationalisation and cites Churchill's wartime statement which emphasises that it would be 'vital to revive at the earliest moment a widespread healthy and vigorous private enterprise' but recognises the increasing role of the State in promoting 'the economic well-being of the nation' and even that 'there is a broadening field for State ownership and enterprise, especially in relation to monopolies of all kinds.'

Just how close the convergence of the contending political philosophies had become Hogg himself makes clear in a chapter on the general election of 1945:

> 'I cannot accept the facile view that the election of 1945 was a choice for or against planning. If it had been, I too, would have found myself among the planners. *Laissez faire* has never been good Conservative doctrine, and though there is much to be said for it in an era of prosperity - in the fierce atmosphere of post-war reconstruction it would have been a fantastic folly to which none but extremists would have subscribed...The key to the nature of the decision in 1945 can be found in a comparison of the two election programmes, contained in the Conservative Manifesto and *Let Us Face the Future*. The most significant fact which emerges from a comparison of these documents is not so much the points of difference, as *the extensive area of agreement.*' [my emphases]

Hogg gives chapter and verse - with regard to foreign affairs and 'Imperial policies', and to the 'reconstruction programme...worked out during the Coalition' for 'full employment' and social security, 'a comprehensive National Health Service', and the provision of decent housing for all - to demonstrate the extent of the consensus. He goes so far as to claim that in 'over 80 per cent of the field of politics the great mass of decent opinion of all parties was agreed as to the best practicable course to take.' And that, if we are to trust his judgement, was a pretty remarkable and utterly unprecedented state of affairs, even allowing for a sizeable deduction from the presumed level of consensus for that prejudicial rider 'decent opinion'. In answer to the questions he began with - 'what was the real choice?' before the electors, and 'what did it amount to?' - he concludes that it was a choice between differences in emphasis rather than in substance:

'There was one further point of identity which tended to be obscured in the flood of ideological controversy. Neither side was committed to the abolition of all controls. Both sides who had manned the Coalition Government were committed to the retention of a fairly full set of wartime controls for a period of years at least from the end of the existing hostilities with Japan. Even after that there was no reasonable authority for claiming that Conservatives were in the least likely to return to a full *laissez faire* economy. The whole trend of our policy for twenty years had been against it. The legislative programme for pensions, housing, the National Health Service, and full employment to which we were fully committed absolutely precluded any such possibility. Wherein, therefore, lay the choice, the vital difference, between the programme of the two parties? It lay in the promise, or threat, of the Labour Party to nationalise the vital industries of the country, and the refusal of the Conservative Party to agree to this course.'

As he remarks in his chapter on Planning, '*Laissez faire* economics were never orthodox Conservative teaching, and Conservatives have only begun to defend them when there appears to be a danger of society swinging too far to the other extreme.' And while the Conservative Party officially accepted the concepts of State guidance over the economy, and even, in certain circumstances, of public ownership, it saw a threat to private enterprise and to individual liberty in the extensive nationalisation programme it feared would ensue from prolonged Labour hegemony.

The *Case for Conservatism* contains some trenchant criticism of the only kind of Socialism that Hogg understands (the State 'Socialism' which is, indeed, the only kind that he shows any signs of knowing anything about). At the same time, it does pay tribute to the humanitarian motivation of much Socialist thinking (though Liberals might protest with some justice that it pays scant regard, if any, to the transformation in this respect of the central values of their creed). It is only right, therefore, to accept at face value the oft-expressed concern for the disadvantaged, with the author recurring again and again to Disraeli's denunciation in *Sybil* of his times' 'triple worship' of acquisition, accumulation, and plunder before 'the altar of Mammon' and his anguish at 'the wail of intolerable serfage' which accompanied it. While one may question how seriously Hogg's book faces up to the problems of achieving social justice (as opposed to what is always the absolute priority for Conservatives: preserving 'the essential fabric of society' - society as it is, of course, based on Property and the grossly unequal shares of Power and Wealth which the capitalist notion of property entails), it is unquestionably a testament in the tradition of Disraelian Conservatism. Such a tradition continued to reign supreme until the bourgeois reaction of our time which thrust into our political vocabulary the appropriately unmelodious term 'Thatcherism', though we might just as aptly describe that harsh philistine creed as 'the neo-Liberal heresy'. To sum up: it is not old-style Tory paternalism but Thatcherite 'libertarianism' that is the foreign body in today's Conservatism.

PART TWO

THE WANING OF THE LABOUR MOVEMENT

'I was at much pains to describe to him the use of *money*, the materials it was made of, and the value of the metals; that when a Yahoo had got a great store of this precious substance, he was able to purchase whatever he had mind to, the finest clothing, the noblest houses, great tracts of land, the most costly meats and drinks, and have his choice of the most beautiful females. Therefore since *money* alone was able to perform all these feats, our Yahoos thought they could never have enough of it to spend or to save, as they found themselves inclined from their natural bent either to profusion or avarice. That the rich man enjoyed the fruit of the poor man's labour, and the latter were a thousand to one in proportion to the former. That the bulk of our people was forced to live miserably, by labouring every day for small wages to make a few live plentifully. I enlarged myself much on these and many other particulars to the same purpose: but his Honour was still to seek: for he went upon a supposition that all animals had a share in the productions of the earth...'

Jonathan Swift, *Gulliver's Travels*
(A Voyage to the Houyhnhnms)

CHAPTER 8

A party in search of an identity

'The fact of the matter is: modern capitalism has not succeeded; it has failed. We are asked in 1959 to believe that if we are only patient, if we only work hard, we will double the standard of living in twenty- five years. That is the same rate of progress as before the war. With all the techniques of modern production...the capitalists of Great Britain can promise us exactly the same rate of progress as before the war.'

Aneurin Bevan at the 1959 Labour Party Conference

'We cannot remove the evils of capitalism without taking its source of power - ownership.'

Neil Kinnock, 1975

In the absolute dog-end days of the Labour Party's supposed endeavour to build a Socialist society through parliamentary power and barely a month before the resurgent forces of Conservatism, largely refashioned in the image of its militant new leader, swept Labour from power, Prime Minister James Callaghan startled the Commons with a challenge that raised the most fundamental issue in political philosophy. 'The question we have to ask ourselves,' he shouted above the uproar of his baying opponents, 'is what kind of society we want in this country. What we have got,' he told them, 'is a totally acquisitive society, and some people are now practising what the Opposition preaches.'

A decade and some down the road to total acquisitiveness, one might ask at whom Callaghan was pointing the finger, and how justly; but the essential truth and the unevadable challenge stand. In that fateful spring of 1979, the people rejected Uncle Jim and bought the glamorous New Conservatism of Maggie Thatcher. It is of continuing importance to consider not only what they got but why they made the choice they did and what they thought they were buying. Accurate answers to these last two questions will uncover the basic values of the nation, while as for what they got, the degree of correspondence between the product progressively unwrapped and the message that sold it is a measure of the maturity of judgement of the British electorate.

Callaghan's impassioned interjection in the debate on an Opposition motion taking the Government to task for its failure to cope with the widespread industrial unrest and the rapidly deteriorating economic situation of that 'winter of discontent' was described by Ian Aitken of *The Guardian* as 'a sudden and highly unexpected flash of old-fashioned Socialist principle.' But the biggest irony is the failure of the Labour Party and of successive Labour governments (since the triumphant post-war days at least) clearly and cogently to project a distinctive vision of the good society. Like the leaders he succeeded, Callaghan had neglected publicly to answer his own question in such a way that any conscientious and reasonably intelligent voter would know what his party stood for. On the contrary, for a not that politically well-educated electorate considering how to cast their votes at the end of a decade or more of manifest national decline, it was not altogether unreasonable to conclude that the Labour Party had little idea where it was going and even less idea of how to get there. It followed that it should therefore give way to a revitalised Conservative Party which at least had the virtue of propagating its notions of how to achieve national prosperity with confidence and enthusiasm - which had, in short, the courage of its convictions. After all, a dynamic approach to problems is attractive and infectious, even if it does tend to distract attention from the need to examine its premises closely.

In rueful contrast, it is a relatively slight and wholly pardonable exaggeration to say that, long before the debacle of May 1979, the Labour Party looked as if it had little left other than a sense of moral superiority to comfort it for its gigantic loss of the faith and fervour of its forebears and its manifest failure to found a Socialist Jerusalem. To persuade a weary electorate to entrust power to it once again, the Party needed to examine itself much more rigorously on what, *in practice*, it had to offer the country which would distinguish its rule from that of its rivals. Whether the voters would then have bought it or not, surely only something that was recognisably *some* brand of Socialism could possibly have fulfilled that requirement.

The story of the uneasy marital relations between the Labour Party and Socialism will be traced in more detail later; but to explain the Party's fateful loss of power in the spring of '79 in terms other than that of the fickleness or the callowness of the electorate, it is necessary to establish Labour's failure to measure up to certain fundamental criteria concerning wealth, work, wages and welfare. A true picture of the state of a nation in these respects, taken together with an accurate analysis of its situation with regard to power and to participation in the polity, will go far to answer the question: what kind of society do its citizens enjoy?

Remarkably, two centuries after the banner of the French Revolution was first raised aloft, the ideals it proclaimed still represent the most quintessential challenge to all societies, whether earlier or later in time. How they rate on the scales of liberty, equality, and fraternity is a question for every ideology and for every polity as it is practised. Spelt out in greater particularity, we are confronted with questions about the relations of State and Government with the people - as citizens, as producers, as consumers, as involuntary supplicants through sickness or other forms of distress, as fledglings and pupils, and as actual or potential dissidents: e.g. as individuals when dissent makes them most individualistic or, most challengingly of all, when they join, form themselves into, or simply constitute through acting as such (as is commonly the case with families) alternative centres of power. (A moment's consideration of this last, family solidarity, aspect of all societies, incidentally, exposes the hollowness of the standard antithesis, which bourgeois liberals are particularly fond of making - as an indictment of Socialism as allegedly inimical to liberty - between individualism and collectivism.) Beyond all this lies the question of the relations of one State with other States and their citizens, and whether these are conducted according to the principles of particularism or universalism.

Another way of approaching the question is through consideration of the distribution of both political and economic power. To take the second kind of power first, all nation-states may be said to imply a commonwealth of sorts, but the vital question is in what sense and in what manner the nation's wealth is held in common. Obviously all nation-states wish to sustain and generally to increase their wealth through commerce and productive labour - but for what and for whom? As for political power, the theoretical scale of its distribution runs all the way from total concentration in the hands of one person, or absolute autocracy, to equal distribution amongst all, or perfect democracy.

From the answers to such general questions we may characterise all political parties, distinguishing in doing so, of course, between precept and practice. In the case of the Labour Party we are obliged to judge its achievements by criteria derived from its origins and history, as well as by its proclaimed principles. At the heart of these, however it is defined and however the definition may shift, lies the idea of equality that is central to all Socialist ideologies. However attenuated this may become in, say, the minds of those who describe themselves as Social Democrats rather than Socialists, it cannot be discarded without changing the character of the party beyond recognition. Nor can it exclude from consideration the more specific idea of economic equality, since it is precisely the importance which the Labour Party attaches to this aspect of equality that most clearly distinguishes it from its principal opponents. Nominal concepts of political equality, equality before the law, social equality and equality of opportunity may suffice for other 'democratic' parties but not for Labour. That party's *raison d'être* may be said to be the conviction that economic equality is the indispensable bedrock of all other aspects of equality.

So we may refine our yardstick to measure Labour's record on more specific issues, especially those concerning social justice, such as the redistribution of wealth and helping the disadvantaged. We may ask such questions as: How does Labour in office treat its own employees - in administration, in the social services, and in the public sector in general? And, in particular, how does it get on with the trade unions? This has to be a touchstone for Labour's success in seeking and holding office, since however many problems the trade unions may cause the Party, they are and always have been a major and integral part of the Labour Movement.

At the same time, just so long as it remains as a whole healthy and vigorous, the trade union movement constitutes a major alternative centre of power to Labour governments, just as it does to governments of any other political hue. So we are brought back from questions of economic power to consideration of the distribution of political power, and we must ask whether, in general, Labour governments try to subordinate other forces that are part of the Labour Movement or seek to co-operate with them as equal partners.

The same question may be asked with regard to other extra-parliamentary forces. Does the Labour record show a commitment to participatory democracy, in respect of both individuals and collectives? All parties in multi-party representative democracies have to pay lip-service at least to civil liberties. The other side of that coin, the more positive concept of people power, is for parties with a stronger emphasis on endorsement of equality. And what of industrial democracy? This is, after all, essentially participatory democracy in the workplace, and so, one might argue, a prerequisite for an equitable distribution of economic power in the widest sense of the term and, more particularly, of wealth, wages, and welfare provision. What part has the Labour Party played in the struggle for industrial democracy?

The following section will give some account of post-World War Labour governments, focusing especially on the Callaghan Government and its demise, with the above questions particularly in mind. At the same time - and unavoidably so - it will highlight the melancholy truth that Labour's story is the story of a party in search of an identity. After the debacle of '79, this became a fact impossible to hide; but the record shows that this uncertainty of purpose, punctuated by explosive discord, stretches right back to the loss of will clearly displayed even before the first majority Labour government had completed a full term in office. And the roots of this identity crisis go back much deeper into the party's past.

CHAPTER 9

How capitalism passed peacefully away

'The truth is that we have had a barrier put to our aspirations, for now the individual is no longer important, whether here or in the East. In Germany, in America, to a lesser extent in Britain, the individual has long been little more than a marketing unit, a gullet that needs feeding, a body that needs clothing, housing, transporting and providing with as much medicinal pap and prepacked pleasure as it can be induced to swallow - all in the interests of higher company profits. In the so-called Socialist states he is an integer of another sort, an underpaid, undertrained, undervalued and completely unindividual unit in the service of a state that as far as one can tell has no function except to exist.'

William Woods, *Poland: Eagle in the East* (1969)

Flashes of 'old Socialist principle' notwithstanding, it was evident enough by the seventies that the Labour leadership had come to terms with the fundamental realities of society as they found it. Reform might still be on the agenda; but anything approaching radical restructuring had long since been ruled out as utopian. It was not simply that a consensus with the other parties on the desirability of a mixed economy was apparently permanently established (for although the balance of the mix remained a matter of significant debate, only the political equivalent of a mad inventor could ever have aimed altogether - or even largely - to eliminate private enterprise), but that the basic features of capitalism had come to be accepted as not so bad as long as society provided a safety-net for the casualties, and, in any case, as probably incapable of transformation except under a dictatorship, as the terrible example of Russia's fate reminded us all.

There was even a tendency to try to talk the facts of life under capitalism out of existence. As early as 1950 Anthony Crosland, who within a few years was to become a leader of opinion in the Party and was to end up as Callaghan's first Foreign Secretary, was proclaiming: 'Britain has *in all essentials* ceased to be a capitalist country.' [my emphasis] And by the time he came to write what has been called 'the revisionists' bible', *The Future of Socialism* (1956), he was even more emphatic, asserting: 'It is manifestly inaccurate to call contemporary Britain a capitalist society.' His more unperceptive comrades had not noticed but capitalism had passed peacefully away.

The nub of his argument was that the intervention of the State in the economic affairs of the nation, employing the tool of Keynesian demand management, had so changed the parameters that it was misleading to use the same term for contemporary Britain as was used to describe the economic organisation of society between the 1830s and the 1930s. And it is undeniable that very substantial changes had taken place in the nature of capitalism, especially (though by no means exclusively) in the crucible of the Second World War and under the planned reconstruction of the Attlee administration that followed. However, a critical intelligence is bound to suspect Crosland's motives in so seismologically shifting the ground of the most elemental ideological contest of the eighteenth and nineteenth centuries as to disarm Socialist thought by the simple expedient of transmuting its infernal old enemy into a quite innocuous old gentleman.

The point I want to stress at the moment though is simply that Crosland's large claim, magnified if anything by his rider 'in all essentials', received a remarkable measure of credence in the higher echelons of the Party (Hugh Gaitskell himself, the Party's leader since Attlee's retirement in December 1955, told a two-day post-mortem conference following Labour's defeat in the 1959 general election: 'In my opinion, capitalism has significantly changed, largely as a result of our own effort') and that this had an enervating influence on its strategy. The implications of this dangerous underestimation of the enemy are most clearly seen by considering the then still surviving Labour objectives of equality in general and of the elimination of poverty in particular.

Contrary to the traditions of the Party, Crosland undervalued (not to mention underestimated the significance of) the very touchstone of Socialism, economic equality, in favour of an ill-defined and sentimental concept of social equality together with a commitment to equality of opportunity viewed most centrally in terms of education. As for Labour as the champion of society's most luckless, in *The Future of Socialism*, Crosland almost seemed to look on poverty as a problem that, through economic growth, would virtually evaporate within a decade or so (note the similarity to the 'trickle-down' talk of apologists for capitalism who are concerned to leave the impression that they *do* give a monkey's about the least advantaged) leaving only so-called secondary poverty, arising from personal disability or misfortune, to be tackled.

Moreover, he gave the impression of looking on class divisions as primarily a subjective phenomenon ('nothing is but thinking makes it so'), writing with some contempt of the curious obsessiveness of 'militant, class-conscious Leftism'. It is true that the best part of two decades later he was admitting, in *Socialism Now* (1974), that extreme class inequalities remained and that poverty was far from eliminated. However, he appeared to attribute the thwarting of his earlier and astonishingly sanguine hopes to rampant inflation and the 'semi-permanent crisis' of the national economy as a whole, rather than to the failure of Labour policies to reflect and of Labour governments effectively to demonstrate that 'exceptional priority' to the elimination of poverty, which he himself had nominated as the defining characteristic of Socialism.

One might remark, in passing, that papal pronouncements have likewise repeatedly avowed a bias towards the poor on the part of the universal church, with similarly disappointing results. But it is more pertinent to highlight a logical flaw of such monstrous proportions in Crosland's thinking that it destroyed his whole case for a laid-back approach to constructing a Socialist society. If no government, Conservative or Labour, appeared to be capable of solving these problems, regardless of whether or not they were to be ascribed to capitalist economics, how was anything that even he might describe as Socialism ever to come about? It was all very well to mock Marxist or other historicist concepts implying some inevitable historical progression towards Socialism, but at least they did offer 'progress'; whereas here, surely, one was left with little more than the politics of historical fatalism?

What all this adds up to, indisputably, is a lowering of the sights of Socialism and, even then, a failure to hit the target. Looking around him in the fifties, Crosland had asked himself: 'Is this still capitalism?' and confidently answered: 'No.' We might more pertinently scrutinise his diagnosis of social ills along with his prescribed remedies and ask ourselves: 'Is this really Socialism?' As a portent of what the Labour Party was to become in the sixties and seventies (not to mention the eighties and nineties) however, *The Future of Socialism* was all too prophetic. From a party promoting Socialist ideas of some sort at least, Labour was reduced to just another Party of social reform, with a mite more, perhaps, of special concern for the poor and, though decreasingly so, for the working class. Nothing more - outside the ranks of its curiously class-conscious Leftists, that is!

CHAPTER 10

Pathfinders for Thatcherism

'For a British government (and nearly every other
government)...[before Mrs Thatcher's] dogmatism was
unusual. In formulating their policies, previous British
governments had traditionally avoided the extremes of a
command economy on the left and of uncontrolled
market forces on the right. Whatever their ideological
banner, Labour governments have never attempted a
fully socialist economy, and indeed have often shown at
least as much respect for market forces as their
opponents.'

Ian Gilmour, *Dancing with Dogma*

Looking back after a decade of Thatcherism at the Labour
governments that preceded it, it is the continuity, not the differences
in financial policy that strikes one most forcibly. An obsessive and
overriding fear of the debilitating effects of inflation dominated
the decisions of the Wilson and Callaghan regimes, sapping their
Socialist will, such as it was. They suffered, in fact, from the
common mental confusion of modern British politicians that
conflates finance with economics and allows the world of finance
to dominate, instead of obliging it to serve, economic purpose. How
ironic that this financial consensus should survive the storm of
Thatcherism; while those elements of social and political consensus
(over such matters as full employment, health and welfare provision,
and even over the rights and due status of trade unions) that -
whatever part concern for maintaining a degree of consensus
may have played in emasculating the Socialist drive - had at
least tempered the ravages of capitalist economics for two
generations, were insidiously eroded or frontally assaulted! Worse
still, under the spell of those peddling the newly fashionable remedy
for inflation, Callaghan and his Chancellor of the Exchequer,
Denis Healey, actually acted as pathfinders for those who were
to supplant them.

With the loss of faith in Keynesian demand management
brought about by the stubborn world-wide recession sparked off in

October 1973 by the Arab nations' use of oil supply and prices as a weapon in the war with Israel and its allies, monetarism, with its seductively simple prescription of curbing inflation through tight controls on money supply, became for many the cure-all. In the words of its arch-priest, Professor Milton Friedman of Chicago University: 'Just as an excessive increase in the quantity of money is the one and only important cause of inflation, so a reduction in the rate of monetary growth is the one and only cure for inflation.' This old doctrine in new guise was enthusiastically embraced by Mrs Thatcher's economic tutors, among them Sir Keith Joseph and Sir Geoffrey Howe, her Shadow Chancellor. The secret subscription to the same doctrine by Callaghan and Healey provoked Labour left-winger Stuart Holland to dub the unholy alliance of supposed political opposites Howleyism, with ironic allusion to the ousted consensus, which had been nicknamed Butskellism after its two leading protagonists, R.A. Butler and Hugh Gaitskell.

'If there has been a Thatcher experiment, it was launched by Denis Healey,' the political editor of *The Financial Times* was to write later. Perhaps the moment when the conversion of Labour's leaders to the new orthodoxy was first clearly exposed was in May 1978. It followed the Chancellor's explanation to the House of his new letter of intent to the International Monetary Fund, concerning the $4.1 billion standby credit it had granted Britain in 1976, in which he reiterated his commitment to maintain monetary control. Under fire from Howe and Kenneth Baker over a six-month growth in the money supply that would mean an annual rate of over 20 per cent, Callaghan declared: 'I am not going to have the great success we have had on inflation dissipated by an increase in the money supply that cannot be contained.' And to Baker's insinuation that the Prime Minister's only way out was to call a general election 'before your chickens come home to roost', Callaghan retorted: 'Your eyes may be fixed on some distant general election, but that is not going to deflect this government from taking any action necessary to keep inflation under control. You can be sure of that.' Five months later, in a Mansion House speech, Healey publicly endorsed monetary policy as the main defence against inflation. (*See Chapter 22*)

It is true that one important difference remained between those determining the Government's financial policies and their shadow opponents. This was over the issue of whether or not fiscal and monetary manipulation were, as ordained by Monetarism's high-priest, the *sole* weapons available to government to curb inflation. By chance, at about the same moment that Denis Healey was spicing his *cordon bleu* Mansion House dinner with a liberal sprinkling of self-gratulation, Ted Heath, the loss-leader of the Tory Party (having travelled his own 'road to Damascus' and renounced his Selsdon Park zealotry) was curdling the blood of a gathering of the faithful in Chelsea with a recitation of the fearful scenario that would face them all should inflation let rip. A new wages' explosion of as little as 10 per cent, he warned them, would double prices in less than eight years, while a return to 20 per cent rises would slash the value of the pound to 50 pence in four years, 25 pence in eight years, and less than 10 pence in thirteen years.

This latest barrage in Ted Heath's dogged campaign to reconvert his party to its old belief in the need for an incomes policy was directed not at the Labour Government, which was still striving to reach an agreement on pay with the trade union movement that would stick, but at the leadership of his own party, at those who had ousted him. In a ringing reaffirmation of the old Tory virtue of pragmatism, he told them: 'We are not having to choose between competing dogmas. We are concerned with the practical questions of running the economy.'

He made his own position absolutely clear in two passages. 'One does not have to agree with all the details of the present policy,' he contended, 'to believe that if that policy fails and wages soar out of control once again we will be taking one giant step back towards the disaster from which we thought we had escaped.' And as for the simplistic fundamentalism of pure monetarism, he demolished it with one hefty swipe of brutal realism: 'I know it is argued that with sound monetary and fiscal policies prevailing, negotiators will come to see the dire consequences of their own actions and learn to behave responsibly. The truth is that, time and again, negotiators, faced with the consequences of inflation and unemployment in the absence of an incomes policy, have made inflationary settlements.'

Ted's target may have been those who had siphoned the Old Liberalism tonic into new bottles labelled New Conservatism, but there were many, both within Labour's ranks and outside them, who were now convinced that the rubicund Denis and even the teetotal, tobacco-shunning, cheery chapel-goer Jim had become hooked on the stuff. It affords wry amusement a Thatcher-Howe-

Lawson-Major-minted 15-per-cent world away to read of the reproachful response of the then director-general of the Confederation of British Industries, Sir John Methven, to the raising of the Minimum Lending Rate to 12½ per cent in November 1978. Speaking for an organisation that was to become quite cravenly reluctant to defend the interests of its own members against the ravages of Thatcherism, Sir John expressed the fear that the Government was relying solely on monetary restraint in its fight against inflation, and that, if this was so, it would gravely damage business investment and the drive to create new jobs in order to cut unemployment and boost economic growth.

The Guardian called the jacking up of the Bank Rate 'a further ominous stride down the monetarist path.' It hoped that the measures were temporary and would jolt the unions into recognising 'the painful alternative of an incomes policy' but could not hide its own fear 'that the squeeze contains an element of overkill which could do long term damage to the British economy.' Three months later, on 8th February 1979, the MLR was raised again to 14 per cent, bestowing on Britain the gift of what were then the highest real interest rates on record.

In a leader entitled 'Between the City and Charybdis', *The Guardian* (10th February 1979) spoke of 'the most savage monetary squeeze in recent memory,' and declared: 'The Government finds itself uncomfortably squeezed between the City, which increasingly controls financial policy (by refusing to buy gilt edge stock to fund the Government's deficit) and the unions, which increasingly control the supply side of the economy.' The paper's principal political commentator, Peter Jenkins, had addressed the threat to national prosperity posed by these two alternative power centres on the previous day, in the course of a trenchant attack on Healey's handling of the economy. Pivoting his commentary on Sir Keith Joseph's sudden and transient conversion to the view that 'monetarism is not enough', Jenkins witheringly declared that, in the depredations of bankruptcy and unemployment it would inflict on the economy, 'Mr Healey's monetarism is the economic equivalent of decimation as a technique of military discipline.' In the event, of course, since Labour was itself wobbling on the brink of decimation at the polls, it was left to Mrs Thatcher's evangelists, from whom Jenkins evidently hoped for national salvation, to decimate British industry as a by-product of its 'economic miracle'.

The Labour left did not take this unholy alliance of its leaders with the City lying down. One of the Government's most persistent critics was Bryan Gould, who at the time of the skirmish in the House of Commons over the money supply referred to above, wrote:

'It is often said that Denis Healey is not really a monetarist but goes through the motions in order to placate the City. The trouble with this, if true, is that he makes such a convincing job of the deception that he simply reinforces monetarist superstitions. Whatever the explanation, the regime over which he has presided in the past year has been even harsher and more damaging than that which would have applied under the Gold Standard itself.'

At the end of the year, as a tidal wave of strikes threatened to engulf Callaghan's struggling administration, Gould castigated the Chancellor for foolishly encouraging 'the myth that the touchstone of success or failure is the monthly figure for growth in M3. Since this figure is entirely at the mercy of the money markets (who can raise it or lower it according to their willingness or otherwise to buy gilts) it is effectively the money markets which now determine the level of deflation required.' In any case, he argued in March 1979, in the Left's last-ditch-before-the-debacle campaign for an expansionary budget which 'would not only improve Labour's election chances and be consistent with Labour's objectives...but would...lay the foundation for desperately needed industrial regeneration,' that deflation was the last thing needed on the brink of a recession:

'The truth is that monetarism is no more than old-fashioned deflation dressed up in a newly fashionable guise. We have a uniquely long and depressing experience of trying to deflate our way out of our problems. It never has worked and it is not working now; manufacturing output is lower now than during the three-day week and is probably falling rather than rising at this very moment.'

With unflagging zeal Gould chastised the Chancellor for so tamely submitting to the City. 'At least in the 1960s and earlier,' he observed, 'deflationary policies were imposed by governments; now it is the money markets which decide policy and the Government has become a helpless bystander.' The present Chancellor 'has handed over control of the economy to the money markets. In two major areas of policy, the exchange rate and domestic money supply, it is the markets rather than the Chancellor who are in control,' he charged. Then he went on to complain that Healey's insistence on 'a stable (and overvalued) exchange rate' for sterling 'means that the foreign exchange markets have a power of veto over anything which might induce them to take a less optimistic view of the pound.'

The strength of Gould's conviction that by bowing down before financial orthodoxy the Government was betraying the whole Labour Movement comes out in rueful reflections on earlier Labour administrations:

> 'The danger for this Government is that the Public
> Sector Borrowing Requirement will become as much an
> albatross around its neck as the balance of payments
> was for the 1964-70 Government and adherence to the
> Gold Standard was for Philip Snowden in 1929-31. In
> conditions of substantial under-utilisation of resources
> of men and money, it is the merest common sense to try
> to put those resources to work.'

And again:

> 'It is...bitterly disappointing to see a Labour
> Government...once again succumbing to the doctrines of
> financial orthodoxy, which are so congenial to Labour's
> opponents both in Parliament and in the City but which
> are so damaging to Labour's aspirations.'

Anyone disposed to dismiss Bryan Gould's scourging of the Callaghan Government for its financial (and hence, in the final analysis, its economic) policies as just the kind of intemperate attacks that were to be expected from an ambitious Labour left-winger could do worse than consider the remarkably similar strictures of that solid, sensible, centrist journalist Peter Jenkins in the article referred to above:

'One aspect of the situation worthy of note is the extent to which what used to be called the 'management of the economy' has passed to the City of London. It is markets which now make policies, not elected governments. For this Mr Healey has himself partly to blame for he has in the past encouraged the financiers in their belief that the Government can be made to dance to the tunes of M3 and the PSBR...Once more a Labour government will have impaled itself upon the financial orthodoxy of the day.'

Despite this intellectual grasp of the half-nelson exercised on 'the financial mind' by a 'money religion' that engendered 'the supposedly sacred nature of certain connections - between the money supply and the level of government borrowing and the external value of the pound,' however, Jenkins had no solutions to offer for overcoming the perils presented by the Scylla of the City. He was far more intent on belabouring Charybdis, i.e. bashing the unions, which, like all respectable citizens, he held to have become a veritable Leviathan.

Where Peter Jenkins and his *Guardian* stable-mate Hamish McRae abruptly parted company with Bryan Gould was in their assumption that, for the present at least, there was nothing for it but to submit to the thumbscrews of the monetarists. McRae was particularly emphatic about this. In a kind of pre-echoing of words that were to become wearisomely familiar, he gave it as his opinion that 'if the general economic policies of a Callaghan/Healey government are broadly similar to those of, say, a Thatcher/ Joseph/Howe one it is because there is no realistic alternative. And the same discipline would act on a Shore/Benn government too.'

Further on in his article on 'Elections and the City' (*Guardian*, 2nd January 1979) he threw in the rhetorical question: 'And is there any evidence that the City could not prove as effective at blocking a *rabid* left-wing Labour government's efforts to control it as the trade unions were in blocking the efforts of both the 1966 Wilson government and its Conservative successor to change the framework of industrial relations?' [my emphasis] No Labour government has ever had the bottle to seriously take on the City in the name of Socialism - nor has the Labour Movement as a whole - and until *that* millennium arrives we cannot know whether McRae is right or not.

Meanwhile, in the later light of the prodigious feats of prestidigitation performed by Nigel Lawson before he discreetly took himself off in a huff as the storm clouds gathered, there is a melancholy pleasure to be had from reading McRae's equally assured judgement that: 'The punishment that the markets can inflict on a spendthrift Government - by driving down the exchange rate and pushing up interest rates - is so great and takes place so rapidly that it has become virtually impossible to imagine a Government being able to set up a short-lived boom by lax fiscal and monetary policies.'

CHAPTER 11

The State as the instrument of Property

'From the moment in which Mr Melmotte had declared his purpose of standing for Westminster in the Conservative interest, an attempt was made to drive him down the throats of the electors by clamorous assertions of his unprecedented commercial greatness. It seemed that there was but one virtue in the world, commercial enterprise - and that Melmotte was its prophet. It seemed, too...that Melmotte treated his great affairs in a spirit very different from that which animates the bosoms of merchants in general. He had risen above any feeling of personal profit...But by carrying on the enormous affairs which he held in his hands, he would be able to open up new worlds, to afford relief to the oppressed nationalities of the over-populated old countries.'

Anthony Trollope, *The Way We Live Now*

It may no longer be *literally* true that in the developed countries of the world the masses have nothing to sell but their labour. But it *is* true that (whatever aberrations may occur, as a consequence, for example, of arbitrary or lawful confiscation) it is and always has been part of the nature of the State - arguably, indeed, its primary role - to protect property. If 'the State' simply stood for the political institutions of a genuinely classless society, one might reply, 'Fair enough!' But, with the arguable exception of a few so-called primitive societies, we have no record of such a society, either past or present. The problem with the concept of a 'property-owning democracy' is that it is a contradiction in terms where property is held unequally, unless, of course, one adopts the absurd or fraudulent position that *real* political equality has nothing to do with democracy.

Inasmuch as property-owners - and in particular larger property-owners - have a preponderant influence on the actions of the State (as two hundred years ago Edmund Burke insisted was right and proper - see Chapter 3 - though he really need not have been so worried about the dangers of this state of affairs being overthrown), regardless of the purposes of any particular government, it is as true now as when the charge was first made that the State is for the most part the instrument of the property-owning classes. Short of revolution, only the most resolute, persistent and sagacious measures of government could significantly shift the balance of control over the machinery of the State away from the large property-owners towards the little people whose principal bargaining power is still their labour. Which is why, of course, any attack on organised labour should arouse the suspicion that it is an attack on the fundamental liberties of the people. The outstanding achievement of the Callaghan regime was that, through its resolution, its tenacity, and its incurable myopia, it gave the Labour Movement as a whole an opportunity to demonstrate its huge potential as a countervailing force.

Despite their submission to the new financial orthodoxy and their consequent catching of a dose of monetarist mania, at least the Labour leaders of those far-off days still believed in the Butskellite concept of 'the management of the economy', a now heretical concept. The New Conservatives, those economic Doctor Panglosses, were already busily deriding this as contradicting Adam Smith's self-evident truth that there is nothing for it but to put one's trust in the 'invisible hand', i.e. in market forces. However, their weakness of will in the presence of the captains of industry rendered the Labour leaders' obdurate adherence to the 'management' tenet of the old faith somewhat nugatory.

Labour's 1974 Manifesto commitment to compulsory planning, which had pledged to strike more than a hundred bargains with key companies, had, by unilateral decision of Harold Wilson and his henchmen, been watered down in the 1975 Industry Act to seeking agreements on medium-term targets and the means of achieving them through a voluntary approach. Tony Benn's fight to uphold the decision of Conference and the Manifesto pledge consequently foisted on the leadership was one of the principal reasons for his transference from the post of Secretary of State for Industry to the less sensitive Department of Energy, an effective demotion that prompted Barbara Castle to commit to her diary the vitriolic but revealing comment: 'We have all suffered from his habit of writing Labour policy by ministerial edict. The Department of Industry enabled him to be all things to the Labour movement with none of the restraints the rest of us face.' With their predominant hold on the Party's National Executive Committee, the Left took up the cudgels again under Callaghan's

117

premiership. But all it could wrest from the leadership was acceptance of the compromise proposed by a joint NEC-Cabinet working party for the passing of back-up legislation empowering the Government to enforce planning agreements where the voluntary approach had failed, should it be thought necessary.

Just how meaningless this watered-down approach had proved to be is made clear by the *Guardian* leader of 22nd August 1978, which asked: 'But why are there so few volunteers?' The writer went on to say: 'The Government lost interest in central planning and the Confederation of British Industry made it clear that compulsory agreements would mean the end of voluntary co-operation elsewhere in the industrial jungle...Agreements became voluntary and there have been few volunteers. Only, to be precise, State-aided Chrysler and State-owned coal.'

Worse still, the Government's one apparent success (outside the public sector) at getting industry to co-operate in planning through friendly persuasion had now turned out to be its deepest humiliation. The disdain of the potentates of capitalism for the views of elected government was impudently demonstrated by the Chrysler management who, having pocketed well over £150 millions in subsidy from the British State since the 1975 rescue operation, proceeded to do a £250-million sell-off deal with the French firm Peugeot-Citroen. It was done behind the backs of the Callaghan Government, who were notified just four days before it was to take effect.

A sharply-etched vignette of the Detroit bosses running rings around the Westminster statesmen is provided by an interchange in the Commons between Labour back-bencher Tom Litterick and the Minister of State for Industry, Alan Williams. 'Why are you in the dark, then?' retorted the back-bencher in response to the Minister's denial that the directors appointed by the Government to the UK subsidiary to keep an eye on British interests as part of the funding agreement had not been consulted. The Minister's somewhat disingenuous explanation was that Chrysler had conducted negotiations with the French motor manufacturers at an international rather than a national level, 'and in this sense...they were less than straightforward.' The comic-cartoon character of the affair is completed by the fact that the Government had neglected to buy an equity stake in Chrysler with its subsidies and was now faced with the probability of having to write off over £50 millions and perhaps more than twice that. For the 23,000 British workers whose jobs were being diced with, however, there was little to smile about. Even when Peugeot-Citroen agreed to take over the UK Chrysler debt, no one assured *them* of a future livelihood.

Another example of this kid-glove approach to employers concerns the notoriously anarchic building industry, which has always operated largely on the basis of casual and temporary labour piped in from pools of unemployed workers. In the interests both of the workers (especially with regard to health and safety and to insurance issues) and, perhaps more significantly, of its own revenue, the Government opened a register of firms in the industry. Unfortunately, however, it decided that registration should be voluntary, with the entirely predictable result (especially as the building bosses became increasingly confident that the Tories would win the next general election and scrap the scheme) that it became yet again a question of 'But where are the volunteers?'

The CBI president, John Greenborough, was technically right, of course, to stress that his organisation was not a party political one, as he did in launching the pamphlet *Britain Means Business*, with its advice to the Government on how to maintain economic growth through tax cuts and the like. But it is a deal more to the point to note the exhortation of Sir John Methven, CBI's director-general, to the bosses attending the 1978 Conference, to stop being apologetic about the way they made their money. For thirty years, he told them (in a side-swipe at those stuck in the mud of consensus politics), employers had not defended the capitalist system properly and it was high time they did.

For Labour's crazy mixed-up-economy kids the times were becoming increasingly difficult. But they knew well enough on which side *their* bread was buttered. As Victor Keegan put it in his *Guardian Notebook* (6th September 1978): 'The CBI's influence tends to be in inverse proportion to the friendliness of the Government in power. It can more easily exploit Labour's desperate need to court industry than it can the natural friendliness of the Tories.' He was even prepared to quantify the arm-twisting powers of this particular capitalists' club as set against the influence of the Left:

> 'Indeed, it could be argued that the Confederation of British Industry has at least 10 times more influence on the Government than Labour's Left. Most of the Left's designs - more nationalisation, more public expenditure and a return to free collective bargaining - have been ignored almost contemptuously by the present Government. Indeed

it is difficult to think of any important concession to the
Left that might not have happened anyway as a result of
the implementation of centrist Labour policies.'

A similar conclusion was reached in Ian Aitken's commentary
(*Guardian*, 7th September 1978) on a book by Michael Hatfield entitled
The House the Left Built (1978). It chronicled the failure of the Left to
make its strength in the Party really tell, despite its success in securing
'the endorsement of a whole catalogue of left-wing policy documents'
as Party policy:

'The fact is that very few of the radical proposals
incorporated in Labour's programme before 1974 have
been even remotely reflected in the subsequent actions of
the Labour Government...The conclusion to be drawn from
all this is that The House the Left Built now looks more
like one of those cardboard cutouts than anything really
substantial in brickwork and mortar.'

Of course, besides the bitter foes outside the Party who were
intent on demonstrating that the milk-and-water Labourism of Uncle
Jim & Co. was actually composed of red blood leeched from
enterprising citizens, there were those in the Party ranks who defended
the Government's record for perfectly honourable reasons, even if
awkward facts obliged them to be a little 'economical with the truth'
(to use a then uncoined but now immortal phrase). Around the middle
of November 1978 *Labour Weekly* published a checklist claiming that
no fewer than 53 out of 68 commitments made in Labour's 1974
Manifesto had been more or less 'carried out'. Then one of the Party's
prospective parliamentary candidates, Timothy Sherwen, delivered a
stinging (and deserved) rebuke to *The Guardian* for its 'cynical attack',
in its first leader of 11th December, on Labour's NEC, together with a
spirited but somewhat less deserved rebuke for the paper's claim that
Labour's promises had received 'pretty short shrift'. Achievements
there undeniably were to the Labour Government's credit; but there
can be no doubt that the verdict of the *Guardian* writers was broadly
speaking correct.

Among those who supported what had come to be called the
Alternative Economic Strategy (which the radical decisions of the 1973
Labour Party Conference substantially embodied) was Stan Orme, by

now Minister for Social Security. In the week before the crucial Party Conference of 1978, he argued strongly for a commitment to use the fast-growing Government revenue from North Sea oil to invest more both in industry and in social welfare provision. 'On the industrial front,' he wrote (*Guardian*, 29th September 1978), 'our support for industry must become conditional on industry accepting a more interventionist policy,' and that the National Enterprise Board should be provided with more funds to back 'winners'. He went on to declare: 'Planning agreements should become a reality in our major firms and a solid start on the road to industrial democracy is needed.' This may sound like pretty radical stuff. But when we set it against the original demands of the supporters of the AES (which, as noted, had received substantial endorsement from Conference); when we consider how negligible - and indeed disdainful - had been the leaders' efforts to carry out the declared wishes of the Party; and when we note Orme's forbearing to point out that Party policy had called for planning agreements that would be enforceable by law; then it becomes difficult to describe it as anything but timid and defeatist. As for the reference to 'a solid start on the road to industrial democracy,' anyone acquainted with the Government's record on this score would be inclined to dismiss it as yet another mocking obeisance to one of the Labour Party's oldest, most hallowed, and most neglected ideals.

Even more eloquent of the dispirited state of the Left, however, was the character of the Minister's plea for more resources for his own allotted province; the more so since he was one of those still ready to speak unabashedly in the romantic terms of 'our egalitarian battle-cry'. Calling on his comrades to defy the Tory clamour for tax cuts based on further reduction in government spending (a monetarist policy which, he argued, would not only cut still deeper into investment in the social and industrial infrastructure, but would by the same token accelerate the recession), Orme declared:

> 'Public spending laid the foundation of the Welfare State. It formed the basis of our caring society *by moderating the insecurity* associated with illness, unemployment, disability, and old age. In doing so it provided, and continues to provide, *an important redistribution of income*. Public spending helps ensure that *nearly everyone has the basic minimum*. This role for public spending must be strengthened. We must recognise that the basic

minimum which was tolerable a decade ago is no longer adequate. The aspirations of our society - *of all families in our society, not just the rich* - move upwards all the time.' [my emphases]

Throughout thirty years of consensus politics such a statement would hardly have been thought controversial coming from the lips of any politician - left, right, or centre - of any party. Indeed, it was a Tory government, Macmillan's, which (in connection with the National Insurance Act of 1959, which in some measure anticipated Wilson's SERPS reform - see Chapter 19 - by introducing into the State's old age pension scheme, with effect from 1961, a system of graduating contributions according to earnings, with subsequent graduated retirement pensions) first proclaimed as a principle that the living standards of the poorest sections of the community should rise at the same rate at which average living standards rose. That Orme's remarks in defending the Welfare State in the speech cited above should have been considered in the least controversial (and, indeed, that he felt they needed to be made at all), is a measure of the vicious swing to both the right and the past which was taking place now that Margaret Thatcher had hijacked the Tory Party. What shocks one, however, is the extreme moderation of those demands for social justice, coming as they do from a Labour left-winger. Was it by such standards that, after three quarters of a century of struggle, the achievements of the Labour Party were to be measured?. Where - or what - was the Socialism? Crosland himself could hardly have demurred at this moderate plea for moderating the ills of capitalism.

After Jim Callaghan had taken the helm, even the most timid hopes of a partial reconversion to Keynesian 'socialism' became childish dreams, as his blunt statement to his first Conference (that of 1976) as leader of the Party and the nation should have made abundantly clear. (See Chapter 21). By the spring of 1979, as Britain began to breathe again after the storm of strikes that has gone down in the history books as the Winter of Discontent, and as the Tories rode ever higher in the opinion polls, it was simply unimaginable that party leaders of the calibre of Callaghan and Healey would go to the country on a Socialist platform.

To their credit, the Left kept up the fight to the bitter end. Early in March, three weeks before the Government was forced by a no-confidence vote in the Commons to declare a general election, the

Labour Co-ordinating Committee, set up at the end of the previous September to mobilise constituency and union support for Benn and other left-wingers on the NEC, launched its own manifesto. It called for an election campaign based on authentically Socialist measures which contrasted with the essentially palliative proposals of the Party leaders. And it spoke up unashamedly for 'labour' as opposed to 'management':

> 'Behind the daily attacks on working people mounted by the newspapers lies a Tory establishment which has no idea what to do next. Industrial management is preoccupied with closure and redundancy, and Britain's plentiful banking and pension funds are flowing abroad or else being invested in pictures, property and other non-productive items at home. Labour has the only answer.'

The unauthorised version of Labour's appeal to the people demanded that the defeat of unemployment be given priority over bringing down inflation, arguing that growing unemployment and under-utilisation of productive capacity were making inflation worse. It called for higher public expenditure, more extensive economic planning and import controls; in short, that the Party should directly challenge the current received wisdom for ensuring national survival in a period of world recession.

The radically democratic thrust of the rebel manifesto is shown by its call for the abolition of the House of Lords, annual election of Labour Cabinets by the Parliamentary Labour Party, meaningful progress towards workers' control, the breaking up of the press monopolies into smaller units to be run by trusts and co-operatives, the abolition of private education, and a Socialist foreign policy that would involve, amongst other objectives, the phasing out of arms exports. Needless to say, none of these near-revolutionary propositions was given the imprimatur of respectability by being officially adopted as part of the Labour Party's appeal to the voters to return it to office.

The Labour Left's failure to make its strength really count is most simply explained by its fear that rocking the boat too violently when the Party was clinging on to power by the skin of its teeth and the courtesy of Liberals, Scottish and Welsh nationalists, and even at times Ulster Unionists, would tip them all into the water. Less superficially, however, it stemmed inexorably from the hierarchical and, in the final analysis, anti-democratic nature of the Labour Party. At the deepest level of all, the failure simply reflected the fundamental flaw in parliamentary democracy and parliamentary Socialism in general and in the Labour Movement in particular, all of which give the last word - and most of the others too! - to Westminster and Whitehall, not to the workers in the street or riding on the proverbial Clapham omnibus.

That I consider the strategy of the Labour Left (even from its own parliamentary-road-to-Socialism point of view) in certain respects misconceived, even to the extent of allowing the Right to pose, with some plausibility, as the true champions of social justice, will become apparent in the course of this essay. But it does not alter the more fundamental fact that the Left was still motivated by a vision of Socialism of sorts, while Centre and Right had effectively abandoned all pretensions to Socialist objectives in favour of 'realism' - i.e. a lowering of sights to seeking the amelioration of the immanent injustices of capitalist society by gaining power through the ballot box. And that is a generous judgement upon the motives of these moderate Labour politicians, taking their expressed concern for the common people at face value.

CHAPTER 12

Juggling with a mixed economy

'...that foul itch of covetousness which is the
explanation of the greater part of the world's activity.'
George Gissing, *The Nether World*, 1889

'If Labour attains an electoral majority and thus dominates the House of Commons, will capitalism meekly abdicate before the onset?' asked the turbulent left-wing professor Harold Laski in the year that Adolph Hitler came to power, *constitutionally*, in Germany. But when, at long last, the Labour Party did, for the first time, capture an absolute majority of seats in the Commons, capitalism was never faced with the awful choice of abdication or the overthrowing of parliamentary democracy by right-wing irreconcilables, since 'the onset' never came. It quickly became clear, even to the most apprehensive of businessmen, that economic enterprise was to remain overwhelmingly in their hands. Indeed, as Ralph Miliband wryly remarks in his study of *Parliamentary Socialism*: 'Private industry enjoyed the co-operation of the Government.'

Since the central tenet of the Labour Party (the notorious Clause IV (4), calling for the workers to receive 'the full fruits of their industry' through 'the common ownership of the means of production, distribution, and exchange') had come to be almost universally interpreted primarily in terms of nationalisation, the extent and degree of success of its nationalisation measures must be a principal touchstone in assessing the seriousness of the efforts of the Attlee administrations to lay the foundations of a Socialist society. At the time he wrote his brilliantly simple exposition of Labour's case, *The Labour Party in Perspective* (1937), Attlee envisaged by far the greater part of industry being taken into public ownership. 'All the major industries will be owned and controlled by the community,' he declared unequivocally, although he did go on to say, 'but there may well exist for a long time many smaller enterprises which are left to be carried on individually.' From other statements in the book, it is clear that it was his absolute conviction that public ownership of the greater part of industry and commerce was indispensable to the building of a Socialist society. 'The root cause' of 'the evils of Capitalism...is the private ownership of the means of life; the remedy is public ownership.' Furthermore, the *primary* purpose of public ownership, as of Socialist planning and economic controls in general, was not to gain efficiency, but to drive towards the goal of equality, with 'the service of the community' displacing 'private profit' as the 'actuating motive' of economic enterprise:

> 'It is the business of the Government to see that the resources of the country, material and human, are utilised so as to produce the greatest amount of well-being for all...I say "for all" because here is the essential difference between Socialist planning and Capitalist planning. There are many advocates of a planned economy who join with Socialists in denouncing the waste and chaos of wealth production. They would seek to substitute for the anarchy of competitive industrialism a planned and organised system, but they still retain their belief in a class society. Socialists believe in a classless society, and the plan which they put forward will envisage a steady progress towards greater equalisation of wealth. In considering what it is desirable to produce in this country they will consider who are to be the consumers. It is no use planning production for a society with its present gross inequalities if your intention is to develop society more and more on lines of equality.'

In other words, State intervention in general and nationalisation in particular were to be recommended not simply to bring greater order and rationality into the nation's economic affairs but to promote social justice.

By the time Labour had the opportunity to put its ideas into practice, the exigencies of war and its aftermath had ensured that the need for a considerable measure of economic planning by the State had become common ground for politicians of all parties, and in some areas even the case for outright nationalisation had been widely conceded. This widespread acceptance of the concept of public ownership, together with subsequent widespread disillusionment, make it all the more important to distinguish between what we might describe as purely economic reasons for support or opposition to such policies and what are at bottom social reasons that might answer in one way or another Callaghan's challenging question, more than thirty years later, 'What kind of society do we want?'

But in those jubilant days of power at last, the Labour Movement was at least united in the belief that a substantial measure of public ownership was desirable. As Kenneth O. Morgan puts it in his study *Labour in Power: 1945-1951*: 'The Labour government in 1945 was bent on implementing socialism as it conceived it, in place of the stagnation and unemployment of the past. Nationalisation was generally agreed to be the vital mechanism in the achievement of this historic objective.' However, the unity was more apparent than real, or perhaps it would be truer to say, more superficial than fundamental, for as Morgan also points out: 'The single most striking difference between the Labour Party's programme in 1945 and that in all subsequent elections down to 1979 [i.e. the latest election at the time he wrote this, for clearly the statement could still stand] is the centrality of nationalization in its overall grand design.' Moreover, as early as the first post-victory Party Conference, that of June 1946 at Bournemouth, with only around one-fifth of industry earmarked for nationalisation, Attlee was telling the comrades: 'The Government has gone as far left as is consistent with sound reason and the national interest.'

Ironically, it would seem that their experience in office in Churchill's wartime coalition government had cooled the ardour of Labour's leaders for outright nationalisation. At any rate, in *The Road to 1945*, Paul Addison cites a letter, dated 12th October 1944, to Richard Acland from Stafford Cripps in which he declares: 'Oh, no, my dear Richard. We have learnt in the war that we *can* control industry.' The same foolish boast was being made, with less excuse, almost thirty-five years later, as Labour slithered towards its most cataclysmic defeat. But in any case, leaving aside the major point that controlling industry in peacetime was a very different matter from controlling it at a time of universally recognised national emergency (and it would be perfectly reasonable to maintain that this extended into the period of post-war reconstruction), just what was the purpose of control? Was it economic efficiency alone, or social transformation too? In Cripps's case a somewhat sombre light

127

will be thrown on this question when we come to consider the thinking of Labour leaders on the status of labour in industry.

In a chapter entitled 'Economic Socialisation' (the term he preferred to 'nationalisation') which he contributed to a three-volume study of *The British Labour Party* published in 1948, Herbert Morrison wrote:

> 'Socialisation should not be regarded as an end in itself. The mere transfer of ownership from private persons or companies to a public authority and management by that public authority is a means to an end - not *the* end. The essential aims are better public service, greater efficiency and economy, and the well-being and dignity of the workers employed in the industry or service. That we should socialise for the sake of socialisation or for the purpose of satisfying a political dogma or slogan would be silly; socialisation for the advantage of the nation is sense.'

As far as it goes, there is not much to quarrel with there. Certainly it is no part of my thesis to insist that nationalisation necessarily equates with Socialism. Perhaps it may in certain circumstances, though there neither is nor has been a single instance of its doing so, which, to say the least, leaves it open to doubt. (And, equally, there are many examples of nationalisation as a key element in the structure of authoritarian States - by which I mean all those that make no bones about banning dissent - and not a few of so-called liberal or social democracies in which it serves as a foundation for private capitalist enterprise and profit.) The issue has been posed in these terms simply because the Labour Party has so posed it by its eternal internecine feud between proponents brandishing it as testimony to their Socialist virility and opponents who may be rationalising their loss of faith in Socialism under the cover of 'realism'. The questions to be put to proponents and opponents alike are:

1) Has nationalisation advanced the cause of Socialism and would more nationalisation advance it further?

2) If it has not, or has only marginally done so, might it produce progress in the desired direction if suitably modified?

3) If it is, by its nature or as a consequence of its misuse, not a vital but a moribund mechanism for implementing Socialism, what other means are there to this end?

4) If some measure of community control over production, distribution and exchange is a prerequisite for Socialist progress, can any of the orthodox mechanisms for such control, or any conceivable modifications of them, serve the advancement of Socialism, without a radical re-ordering of the present system of social relationships and economic ownership?

Uninhibited cynicism might prompt one to ask if this whole argument is anything more than a debate between self-deluding impossibilists on the one hand and open-eyed but button-lipped apostates on the other. However, to jump to that conclusion would not simply painlessly dispose of the questions I have posed, but would beg not a few others in the process. So let us continue to treat them as serious questions and to bear them in mind in further examining Labour's last administration.

The challenge that rings again and again in Labour's interminable debates over nationalisation is Aneurin Bevan's call to hold 'the commanding heights of the economy'. Let us concede at once that such a gain could have been decisive, and that Attlee's pre-war vision of something much nearer to total nationalisation would be superfluous if those 'heights' could be captured without a wholesale State take-over of industry. The verdict of Alan Sked and Chris Cook on how near the first majority Labour ministries came to fulfilling Bevan's more modest ambitions is that: 'The Government, in fact, despite their efforts, had succeeded neither in 'controlling' nor even in capturing the commanding heights...in spite of all the fuss the commanding heights had never really been attacked. The twenty per cent of the economy taken over by the government was to a large extent the unprofitable part, while the profitable sector remained firmly in the hands of private enterprise. Socialist planning of this type was acceptable even to Conservatives.'

Putting aside for the moment the even harsher judgements Sked and Cook make in the same passage of *Post-War Britain: A Political History*, the implications of their verdict clearly go well beyond questions of quantification in nationalising industry and commerce. But, bearing in mind Herbert Morrison's injunctions against a doctrinaire approach to the issue, and focusing on the objectives of nationalisation (to employ Morrison's formula, 'better public service, greater efficiency and economy, and the well-being and dignity of the workers employed in the industry or service'), now that we have been led up the mountain by Bevan's eloquent sermonising, let us descend with him to the plains of practical living. In an NEC debate of 25th November 1947 on a policy document entitled 'Socialism and Private Enterprise', Bevan counselled the comrades: 'What we have to do is to create a framework within which private enterprise can operate efficiently.' As it happens, that is a pretty accurate description of the approach to nationalisation taken by every post-war Labour government, and provided we do not look too closely into the meaning of 'efficient private enterprise', it may even be fairly claimed that to a very large extent nationalisation has achieved that objective. However, whether that means that it has fulfilled the aims set out by Morrison, let alone whether it has assisted in the advance to Socialism, are very different questions.

Of course, once it has been conceded that total or even massively predominant nationalisation of industry and commerce is, under representative government, neither practicable nor desirable, there is nothing to object to, *per se*, in Bevan's formula. But the extraordinary thing is - given the voluminous literature and the interminable talk that had been expended on the subject during the years of preparing for power - that Labour crossed the portals of State power with such a lack of clarity regarding the objectives of nationalisation and the structures best suited to achieving them. (Indeed, until almost the last minute, when, through left-wing pressure in the National Executive Committee, the iron and steel industry was added to the list of coal, gas, electricity, railways, road haulage, Cable and Wireless and the Bank of England, not even the initial targets for take-over had been agreed.)

The consequences of what Kenneth O. Morgan calls the Party's 'extreme and studious vagueness' were seriously disabling, not simply during those pioneering days, but in later Labour administrations and, above all, for the long-term interests of the Labour Party and Movement. In the first place, imprecision, irresolution and poverty of imagination in official thinking led to a complacent falling back on the model of the autonomous public corporation, as advocated by Herbert Morrison. He, as principal architect of the London Passenger Transport Board which had taken over the capital's public transport system in 1933, had the inestimable forensic advantage of having an actual 'socialisation' scalp to his credit. But the trouble with taking the LPTB as a model (or, for that matter, any other existing public corporation - for by 1939 there was a whole string of such bodies, including the Port of London Authority, the Forestry Commission, the British Broadcasting Corporation, the Central Generating Electricity Board, the British Overseas Airways Corporation, the Agricultural Marketing Boards, and a General Post Office which was already evolving in that direction) was that what was needed for each candidate for State take-over was bespoke tailoring to fit its particular needs. And first there had to be agreement as to what those needs were, while those needs in turn could only be rationally articulated in terms of agreed aims.

State regulation was considered desirable to generate 'greater efficiency and economy' (which may be taken as self-evident virtues, even if they do need balancing against other desirables), in the interests of 'better public service', and to provide - in Bevan's formula - 'a framework within which private enterprise can operate efficiently.' Such aims would surely win general assent, as would a proper concern (however that might be defined) for the welfare of those who worked in the public sector enterprises. But even supposing the needs of each particular public enterprise to have been met and its aims fulfilled, unless those separate enterprises worked together to fulfil a general plan, they would be doing little more than aping the beggar-my-neighbour competition of the private sector. For example, in *The Labour Party in Perspective*, Attlee had stressed the need for the co-ordination of transport services:

> 'Road, rail, and sea transport should not be regarded as separate undertakings. They form part of a single whole. At the present time there is nothing to prevent one port being neglected and another developed according to the immediate interests of profit-makers. There is a scramble for business between the various agencies so that goods which ought to go by rail go by road, and vice versa. In a short time the development of air services will bring yet another competitor into the field. The Labour Government will end this chaos.'

Similarly, in discussing Labour's policy for fuel, Attlee treated fuel production as one industry as a matter of course. Yet the need for co-ordination in these two crucially important sections of the nation's economic infrastructure was grossly neglected in those formative post-war years of Labour power. Not until 1965 did any government draw up a long-term development plan for fuel; while no British government has ever got to grips with national transport planning. The chaos of the market still rules! As John Westergaard and Henrietta Resler point out in *Class in a Capitalist Society*, the fact that nationalisation has provided 'a central framework for the long-term development of services and supplies on which the business economy at large depends' itself validates 'the rationale of co-ordination and growth' on businessmen's own terms. This they would all see if they were not blinded by a quite unfounded fear that there is a 'thick socialist end to the thin wedge of *pro-capitalist* public ownership.' [my emphasis] In practice, however, such co-ordination has been rudimentary. What has prevailed instead has been 'the insistence that the nationalized industries should, in normal practice, follow the principles of private commercial enterprise, each pursuing profit maximization for itself', with State-owned industries competing vigorously with one another for business. Only those suffering from the quasi-religious delusions of market mania can seriously believe that such a situation could possibly be in the best interests of a national (let alone an international) community.

The ultimate irony, however, is that notwithstanding this submission of 'Socialist statesmen' to the juju jurisdiction of orthodox economics, market forces have *not* been allowed the same sway in transactions between public and private industry. On the contrary, the prices of products supplied by the nationalised enterprises have not uncommonly been kept so much below what the market would bear that public sector losses have subsidised private sector profit. However deficient Bevan's formula of a publicly-maintained framework for private enterprise to profit from might be felt to be, surely this could not be what he intended? Naturally, this situation of generally low profits - not to mention deficits made good, as well as investment for development provided, through subsidies drawn from the general revenue - has fostered the myth of public sector failure; and that in turn has eroded support for Labour Party policy as a whole. And of course it has been exploited without scruple and frequently without sense by the anti-Socialist parties. Churchill was already wielding this weapon in the general election campaign of 1950:

> 'Socialism, with its vast network of regulations and restrictions and its incompetent planning and purchasing by Whitehall officials, [is] proving itself every day to be a dangerous and costly fallacy. Every major industry which the Socialists have nationalized, without exception, has passed from the profitable or self-supporting side of the balance sheet to the loss-making, debit side.'

But as Morgan points out:

> 'Despite all the hostile propaganda from 'Aims of Industry', the FBI, and Fleet Street, it was significant that there was no general move by the Conservatives after 1951 to reverse the nationalization already achieved, apart from the controversial case of steel, and the separate, limited issue of road haulage. In effect, Churchill and his ministers implicitly admitted the unfairness of many past attacks on industries taken into public ownership in highly adverse financial circumstances, and with, in the case of the railways and the mines, a background of under-capitalization, under-investment, and long-term failure.'

Three decades later, the same kind of propaganda against nationalisation was still being spewed out, not just by party hacks, Grub Street journalists, and businessmen, but by economists of repute. In his *Guardian* 'Notebook' for 4th January 1979, Hamish McRae reflected on an article in *Lloyds Bank Review* by Walter Eltis, a Fellow of Exeter College, Oxford, which appeared to prove conclusively that nationalised industries cost the country more than they produced. McRae's conclusions were somewhat different:

> 'The trouble is (as Mr Eltis partially concedes) the figures do not necessarily prove what they are supposed to. Many nationalised corporations (like coal and the railways) were

not profitable producers of wealth even when they were in
the private sector - and it was partly for that reason that
they fell into public hands. Some, like steel, were
inevitably heading for a deficit as a result of world
pressures. Others, like atomic energy, have such a long
gestation period that it is unfair to compare their sales so
far with their cost to the public purse.'

He went on to draw attention to the standard State industry
situation of uncommercial pricing policies:

'More to the point all of the sales figures for nationalised
corporations ought to be adjusted sharply upwards to make
up for what sales would have been worth if successive
governments had not imposed policies of price restraint -
policies that were ultimately self-defeating.'

Such policies may have been (from any sane and Socialist
viewpoint) profoundly misconceived; but they are certainly not
illustrations of the failure of the public sector to operate efficiently.
They have been deliberately imposed for two purposes. One of these,
the holding down of State industry prices as a counter-inflationary
measure, at least has the merit of not being in itself an *anti*-Socialist
objective, though as we shall see it commonly has dire (and most anti-
Socialist) consequences for the workforce in the public sector. The
second purpose is to provide a good springboard for private enterprise;
and an added irony here is that it is the once-upon-a-time anti-capitalist
party that has been the most assiduous advocate of such a policy. As
Westergaard and Resler so trenchantly put the matter:

'The more complex [the] economy and the more
interdependent its different parts, the greater the need for
some sort of common framework...in the interests of
private industry itself...The case for using public enterprise
- nationalized industry as well as other state agencies and
devices - to provide the preconditions of 'modernization',
economic growth and business prosperity came to be
stressed increasingly during the 1960s, with Labour as the
main spokesman for state stimulation of private
capitalism.'

The thrust of Labour government - if not of Labour Party - policy is most clearly seen in the years in which Harold Wilson convinced himself, and quite a few others, that Labour, not the Tory party, was after all the natural party of government. Wilson, the supreme political pragmatist, rose to power on the hot air of techno-babble, by capitalising on the obvious connection between modernisation and technological progress and playing up the more ludicrous anachronistic aspects of the gentlemen's party. In the age of the sputnik, the shooting-stick had become an inappropriate symbol for the qualities that made men fit to govern others. In the very autumn when Harold Macmillan relinquished the reins of party and national leadership to the Earl of Home (see Chapter 1), the other Harold summoned up the blood of his troops, in a Party Conference debate on an NEC document entitled *Labour and the Scientific Revolution*, with the exhortation: 'We must harness Socialism to science and science to Socialism', to forge a new Britain 'in the white heat of technological revolution.'

At one stroke the Party had wrought the perfect emblem for electoral success. If the nation was to prosper in the modern world, it needed to exploit fully advanced technology in the common cause. Who could argue with that? And here, miraculously, was a party united in the will to see Science harnessed to Socialism, as the 'workers' State' of Soviet Russia was said to have done. As Bartlett puts it (op. cit.), the document 'could be read by the left as denoting new interest in public ownership and initiative, and by the centre and right as a pragmatic bid for modernisation. Crossman applauded this bridging of party differences with science-based socialism to make men masters of technological change. Editorials in *The New Statesman* took the same line, enthusiastically acclaiming scepticism, science and reason as the high road to socialism.'

Unfortunately, however, scepticism was in short supply on all sides. Its absence was exactly what made the document the perfect device for dealing with irreconcilable differences in the Party by promoting an attractively packaged and genuinely unconscious fudge. 'Socialists' of widely varying hues, from pallid parliamentary reformists to revolutionary Marxists, share a susceptibility to the allures of Science. Labour's illusion that it again had a banner to rally round (and as is often the case with illusions, this one did have a striking if transient success) and, moreover, that waving it vigorously might induce swathes of businessmen to sign up as camp-followers, is well illustrated by the reflections which Tony Benn (recently appointed supremo in Wilson's newly-minted Ministry of Technology to replace the left-wing trade union leader Frank Cousins, who, ominously, had resigned in protest at the Government's incomes legislation) imparted to, of all bodies, the American Chamber of Commerce:

> 'Technology challenges governments, whether capitalist, communist, or socialist, and industry whether publicly or privately owned, in such a direct fashion that the common interest uniting them is stronger and more important than the disagreements which divide them. Every society will seek to express this common interest in its own way and in the light of its own history. Here in Britain we start with a mixed economy, and we shall have one as far ahead as I can see. We must therefore make a mixed economy work. Make it successful; make it competitive; look to it to create the wealth we need to do the things we want to do.'

Benn was later to redeem himself from the alternative or combined charges of intent merely to manage capitalism better than the capitalists or of criminal naiveté that such words invited. But for the time being, both for him and for others seeking Socialism along the highway of modernism, such thinking was crippling. It compounded subjection to the partnership myth camouflaging the reality that the State provides the infrastructure (including, let it be noted, that of the Welfare State in general and the social security system in particular) while capitalist tycoons call the shots, with subjection to what Stuart Holland has dubbed the 'mixed economy myth' because of the gross imbalance between public and private sectors, itself reflecting the failure of political will that has allowed multinational firms to capture 'the commanding heights' of Britain's economy.

For however millennial its prospect had already become, those 'heights' remained (doctrinally speaking) the Labour Party's strategic objective right up to the reign of Neil Kinnock. When, following Labour's third successive post-war general election defeat (with the scoreboard showing a loss to Labour since it was last in office of over a million votes), Hugh Gaitskell tried to persuade the Party to ditch Clause IV as user-unfriendly at the hustings, he was heavily rebuffed, but he persisted in his efforts to have it amended so that it should, in his eyes, more accurately reflect the modern Party's aims. He did not succeed in this endeavour; but the 1960 Scarborough Conference (more renowned for the battle over the issue of unilateral nuclear disarmament and for Gaitskell's vow to 'fight and fight and fight again to save the Party we love' from pacifists, fellow-travellers, and - by implication - lunatics) did adopt a statement endorsing both a mixed economy and the 'commanding heights' strategy. The key passage on these issues declares that the Party's:

> '...social and economic objectives can be achieved only through an expansion of common ownership substantial enough to give the community power over the commanding heights of the economy. Common ownership takes varying forms, including state-owned industries and firms, producer and consumer co-operation, municipal ownership and public participation in private concerns. Recognizing that both public and private enterprise have a place in the economy it believes that further extension of common ownership should be decided from time to time in the light of these objectives and according to circumstances, with due regard for the views of the workers and consumers concerned.'

The statement makes clear enough that Labour was not pursuing a policy of wholesale nationalisation and, moreover, that its views on public ownership and control were flexible, not doctrinaire. Before considering whether such an approach could have become a viable route by which to storm the 'commanding heights', let us look more closely at Labour's record in juggling with the mixed economy.

Some of the handicaps that Labour governments have imposed upon themselves in their drive towards the 'commanding heights' (always supposing that this still remained a serious objective after the first flush of enthusiasm for nationalisation had begun to evaporate, as early, according to Morgan, as 1948) have already been noticed. They include the incongruous sack-race stance of price restraint for State-owned industries when dealing with the private sector, on the one hand, and knockabout competition between themselves (as in the case of the power industries) on the other. They also include the related negligent or perverse failure to closely co-ordinate their policy and practice to accord with an overall plan. (That such a plan never really got on to the drawing-board, let alone reaching the assembly lines, seems to argue a lack of conviction in Labour's declared commitment to planning.) Arguably more crippling than these defects was the failure to grasp the nettle of accountability. But before examining that fundamental issue, let us look at the bounds the Labour leadership tacitly set in selecting targets for nationalisation and the circumstances in which they at times transgressed them.

Firstly, just because the issue now seems to have disappeared into a black hole, it should not be overlooked that the national resource which had (along with the railways and minerals) been longest targeted by the Labour Movement was land. The intention of taking land into public ownership - unquestionably the nationalisation proposal with the greatest revolutionary potential of them all - was reaffirmed as Party policy in the 1945 Manifesto, but effectively shunted on to a track terminating (as they tell us parallel lines do) in infinity. At the last Party Conference before the debacle of '79, when a motion calling for farmland to be taken into public ownership, put by the National Union of Agricultural Workers with NEC backing, was once again received with acclamation, Joan Maynard reminded delegates that the Attlee Government had promised in 1946 that the policy would be implemented in the next session. Instead, it had become yet another instance of ritualistic reciting of the creed in place of serious efforts to turn it into reality. It is true that measures had been taken to strengthen the control of representative bodies over land development and that local authorities had been given greater powers to acquire land for public purposes, but the goal of giving the land back to the People was almost as far away as ever.

Secondly, the tacit acceptance that public ownership should be restricted to the infrastructure industries - a growing conviction in the thinking of the core of the Labour leadership that dates back at least to the dispute over steel nationalisation (Hugh Dalton records that despite a clear call from Conference, Herbert Morrison and Arthur Greenwood resisted its inclusion in the '45 Manifesto on the grounds that the City was opposed to the extension of public ownership to manufacturing industry, although the efficient production and supply of steel at reasonable prices was, of course, a basic requirement of almost every other manufacturing enterprise) - deprived Labour (at any rate when conjoined with the policy of public sector price restraint and a predominant motivation of providing a sound framework for private enterprise) of the opportunity of generating profit for the public purse.

Generally speaking, the bounds set by Labour - with a few exceptions justified on such grounds as market domination, as in the abortive and counterproductive attempt to take sugar into public ownership - have been overstepped only to rescue the failures of private capitalism, or perhaps it would be fairer to say, of the capitalist system. (The most famous of these 'failures', Rolls Royce, was saved from bankruptcy by the leaders of the party that had poured so much scorn on the idea of coming to the assistance of 'lame ducks'. This demonstrated that the Tories too were not prepared to see Britain's industrial flagships go down, though some of them would never forgive Ted Heath for the chagrin this caused them.) As Westergaard and Resler point out, the unhappy permutation of piecemeal nationalisation, the taking over of declining industries and 'lame ducks', and uncompetitive pricing policies, has served to discredit 'the goal of full public ownership', since they 'cannot produce commensurate redistribution' of wealth and power. 'In fact, if not by explicit design, it...neatly helps to undermine popular support for the public appropriation of capitalist enterprise at large.'

It is true that, with the confirmation of Wilson & Co. in office in the second (October) general election of 1974, and the subsequent enactment just over a year later of the Industry Bill, Labour appeared to be poised to implement what Phillip Whitehead describes as 'its most radical programme since the war, centred on a National Enterprise Board and a system of compulsory agreements with private industry.' However, the CBI's fear of 'a policy which might shift power fundamentally towards trade unions and away from management' proved to be a 'painted devil'. By subterfuge, stonewalling, and undisguised diktat, Wilson so emasculated the NEB that it could not possibly act as 'the investment primer for the whole economy (let alone take over twenty-five leading companies across the whole spectrum of industry) which Benn and his aides had envisaged.' Instead, it 'was left dealing with the walking wounded of the industrial collapse.' The titanic dimensions of Wilson's autocratic behaviour are graphically illustrated by the fact that the junior minister handling the Bill in committee, Michael Meacher, only discovered that a mere £50 million had been allocated for the Board's use in its first year when a Tory member of the committee challenged him to explain how that figure had been arrived at. Meacher himself considered that 'if it was going to be effective, it probably needed about £1 billion in the first year, and a further billion in each of the next five.'

In the band-aid role it had been reduced to, the NEB did in fact perform a valuable service to the nation - of a kind that any less unintelligently doctrinaire capitalist political party than the Tories had become under the Grantham grocer's daughter would have properly appreciated. Amongst the industries and enterprises Labour's policy of planned investment kept alive, resuscitated, or gave a boost to were coal, oil, steel, shipbuilding, aircraft manufacture, and the motor industry (including BL, of course, as well as the unhappy cases of Chrysler and De Lorean, in which government and nation were ripped off by the beneficiaries). It also gave vital support to sunrise industries (most notably in the micro-chip field) of the kind provided by the State as a matter of course in other capitalist economies, although this public investment was wantonly wasted by the Thatcherites' anorexic approach to the problems of British industry.

The Government's two main objectives were to ensure that the conditions necessary to long-term growth and prosperity were created or consolidated (in which matter they were incomparably more far-sighted than the free-market buccaneers who followed them in office) and to maintain as high a level of employment as possible. Callaghan inherited from Wilson an unemployment burden of well over a million (already the highest figure since the war) which had peaked in September 1977 at over 1.6 million. So it was entirely understandable that bringing it down was a Government priority, since the nation had not yet learned to welcome mass unemployment as a salutary remedy for overindulgence in job-security that would assuredly restore well-being to the body politic. These two objectives (which Labour thought of as mutually reinforcing and the New Conservatives as wholly inconsistent) were very clearly spelt out in a speech made by the Prime Minister in opening a new factory in Birmingham. Defending job-preservation and job-creation measures which were, he said, keeping 300,000 people off the dole, he told his audience:

'We are told that these [job-creation] measures should be
swept away. But I say to you that the simple- minded
recipe of leaving firms to sink or swim unaided in the free
market in a world trading recession, where every country is
scrambling for orders, would mean bankruptcy for many

firms in the Midlands and unemployment for thousands. So we take action to help the firms through this period so that they can emerge healthy and viable at the end of it.'

Under the hammer blows of the worsening world-wide recession, Labour had at least reforged the National Enterprise Board into a more credible shield, even if it was still in essence what Bernard Donoghue, head of the No 10 Policy Unit, described as 'a convenient casualty ward for firms the Government wished to rescue from bankruptcy.' The pitiful £50 million launch budget had been multiplied until its total expenditure and commitments topped £2.5 billion, and on the eve of the Government's demise another Industry Bill was introduced to raise its financial limit to £3 billion, with provision for a further increase to £4.5 billion. An increase in the financial limits of the Welsh and Scottish Development Agencies was also sought. In the Lords debate on the Bill, one crusty Tory peer, Lord Campbell of Croy, with closer approximation to honestly admitting his own hang-ups than to giving an accurate account of the real world, inveighed against the NEB as a bureaucratic institution licensed to 'set forth on pillaging forays in profitable private enterprises', provoking Labour peer Lord Jacques to the even more bizarre observation that if the Opposition resisted all public control they would 'drive people towards communism'!

Official on-the-record Tory policy was more ambivalent but decidedly sour. Speaking as one who would rather die than confess that he was glad that State intervention had saved such prestigious firms as Rolls Royce and Ferranti from the auction rooms if not the scrap-heap, 'Stormin' Norman Lamont, in telling the House that the Opposition would limit the NEB's borrowing power to £3 billion, both complained that the level of return on the Board's investment was well below the average for British industry *and* demanded that it release its holdings in turned-around Ferranti and in the successfully-launched pioneering firm International Computers Ltd. The astounding acumen of the businessmen's party was dazzlingly displayed in both of these instances after it was back in power. Ferranti, flying free of State supervision, was taken to the cleaners by a parasitic entrepreneur, while ICL, Britain's only major computer company, was taken over by a company at the time largely owned by the US multinational ITT, STC, who, in 1990, flogged it off to the giant Japanese electronics firm Fujitsu.

As for the use of public subsidy to sustain livelihoods, to make the right to work a reality, the Tories now making the running were scornful. Thatcherite guru, Sir Keith Joseph, opening a debate on an Opposition censure motion, on the one hand accused the Government of preserving low-paid and unstable jobs at the expense of creating 'new worthwhile jobs', thereby leaving the nation poor and divided, stifling enterprise, and through its 'Socialist' policies paralysing 'adaptation which is the heart of industrial success'; while, on the other hand, he advised the Government not to try to compete with the Japanese and the Americans in the mass-production of what has been called as revolutionary an invention for our age as the wheel once was - the silicon chip. Thus did Sir Keith adapt for a sceptical age the old counsel, 'Let not your right hand know what your left hand doeth.'

To sum up, in judging between the policies of Labour and the Thatcherite Tories, with the long-term prosperity of the nation *and* of industry as the criteria, any mentally sound and moderately detached adjudicator would be bound to award the palm to Labour. The Tories, in fact, have been collectively in the grip of a competition-at-all-costs fever from which few have escaped contamination. From any tolerably sane view of national interests, Labour deserved credit for making some things better than they would otherwise have been and preventing other things from becoming even worse than they did. From the point of view of securing more direct and more enduring benefits to the community from State support for private enterprises, however, the Wilson and Callaghan administrations behaved with selfless generosity in giving away the public's money with scarcely a thought of return. As, for example, in the Chrysler affair referred to in the previous section and in the case of the electronics company Ferranti, a family firm which made huge profits from Britain's *folie de grandeur* 'defence' expenditure. And as for the potential of the NEB and the other State intervention agencies to contribute to progress towards Socialism, the way they were deployed ensured that they supplied still more examples of Labour's almost perverse determination to see (to borrow the title of John Mortimer's novel) 'paradise postponed'.

So does it follow (as the strictures of Westergaard and Resler seem to insist) that having settled for a mixed economy with the cautious option of a 'considering each case on its merits' approach to nationalisation, that the Labour left had unwittingly relinquished all realistic hope of securing sufficient control over the economy to ensure that effective planning would be much more than a paper game? Or had there been all along (as those who framed the Scarborough Conference resolution referred to above apparently believed) an alternative route to the summit that might well have called for more but certainly did not demand wholesale nationalisation? These questions became particularly pertinent in the light of declining public support for nationalisation, which was already down to only around a fifth of the electorate by the mid seventies.

Not only are there good reasons for thinking that the Scarborough resolutionaries were right, but a credible case can be made for maintaining that, even without any further nationalisation, Labour governments could have succeeded in making community interests paramount if they had had the will to do so. The reasons for believing this are in essence very simple and can be summed up by pointing to the enormous clout that, for good or ill, the modern State wields with respect to the economic activities within its ambit. Notwithstanding the powerful and important case made by Stuart Holland in his book *The Socialist Challenge* (1975) to the effect that the multi-nationals dominating what he calls the mesoeconomic sector were escaping from the control of the nation-state - a case which is even stronger now, as the century draws to a close - this point remains true whenever and wherever a representative government makes up its mind that the State it controls will not be held to ransom by private sector interests.

Consider first the historical growth in central and local government employment. Excluding the armed services, this only absorbed some 2 per cent of the workforce in 1891, about 5 per cent in the years leading up to the First World War, about 8 per cent between the wars, over 11 per cent in 1950, and 17 per cent by 1971. With the 7 to 8 per cent of workers in the nationalised industries added, public sector employment had reached about 25 per cent by the early seventies and around 30 per cent by the end of the decade. As for the State's financial muscle (without taking into account its fiscal powers), writing in the mid seventies, Westergaard and Resler calculated that 'the state in one way or another has passing through its hands nearly one-half of the funds generated by economic activity in the country,' and that 'the public sector's contribution to capital investment for the future is on much the same scale.' And this is to leave out of the equation the overwhelming investment of the State in the present and future prosperity of its citizens represented by benefits in kind received through the whole welfare infrastructure - education, health care, and so on.

Of course, for a representative government to wield such clout wantonly would be to invite confrontation and court disaster. But that does not alter the fact that the State carries a most terrific clout which might have been used in alliance with a united Labour Movement to shove society in a Socialist direction. For Labour to have renounced all thought of a 'command economy' was one thing, and wise. For it to have failed to stand up to capitalism on behalf of the community was to reduce the State in which it had put its faith from a paramount power to a supplicant to private privilege. That is what, with a progressive bending of the knee, the Labour governments of the sixties and seventies became.

CHAPTER 13

Labour plays the Great Power game

'Be it thy course to busy giddy minds
With foreign quarrels...'
The King's advice to Prince Harry,
Part Two of *Henry IV*

'The cold war was a marvellous device by means of
which the domestic population could be mobilised in
support of aggressive and interventionist policies under
the threat of the superpower enemy...a highly functional
system by which the superpowers control their own
domains...The question now is whether people can
overcome the attempt to beat the workforce and the poor
into a chauvinist mood so as to tolerate the attack being
launched against them.'
Noam Chomsky (1981)

All political parties, in all countries and at all times, lay claim to
patriotism, to having the best interests of the nation at heart. How
could it be otherwise? (And in a sense the claim is always genuine,
since they sincerely believe it to be so, as, for example, the Petainists
did in Nazi-occupied France). True Socialist parties, however, differ
from other political parties in being at the same time of their very
essence internationalist. (Which is one reason, besides its monstrous
travesty of Socialist ideas and values, why 'National Socialism'
always was a preposterous contradiction in terms, and why
'Socialism in one country' never could be more than a dubious
slogan). This internationalism necessarily arises from the Socialist
analysis of society, which perceives the hierarchical and class-based
character of all capitalist social structures and identifies with the
majority class. However fragmented by the more or less favoured
place of individual members in the hierarchy, that is still in the
final analysis a working class, not an employing class. This in turn
implicates the recognition of common class interests that transcend
national frontiers. (This is just as true of bourgeois parties, of course,
but certain complicating factors inhibit open recognition and

sometimes even awareness on their part.) Socialism, in short, considered as a historical movement reacting to capitalism, always has been a movement placing great value on international contacts and solidarity.

'The Labour Party is the expression in Great Britain of a world-wide movement,' says Attlee in *The Labour Party in Perspective*, and he cites with approbation Bertrand Russell's summary of the essentials of Socialism, with its concluding point that: 'To be fully realised it must be international.' Of course, one is entitled to challenge every value-centred or ideology-centred group or organisation (political, religious, or whatever) on the grounds of whether or not it applies the principles it professes consistently and universally; but this is peculiarly true of Socialist parties when it comes to their handling of foreign affairs, especially when they are in power, for it could be said that their commitment to international working-class solidarity should effectively remove the term 'foreign' from their vocabulary.

It might as well be said at once, that in this respect Labour's record is lamentable. And making every reasonable allowance for the daunting problems of playing a part in restructuring a fractured world order that it faced on coming to power, besides giving it due credit for some positive achievements (making a start, for instance, on the dismantling of empire), the Attlee regime is not simply implicated in this judgement, but it was responsible for laying down the lines (or rather, it would be more correct to say, for faithfully following established custom and practice) by which later Labour governments were generally content to be guided.

The stark contrast between Labour's youthful idealism and its cynical maturity could hardly be highlighted better than by following Tony Cliff and Donny Gluckstein, in *The Labour Party - a Marxist History*, in citing a fire-in-the-belly speech by a constituency delegate at the Labour Party Conference of May 1945:

'The Labour Party should have a clear foreign policy of its own, which is completely distinct from that of the Tory Party. The Socialist revolution had already begun in Europe and was firmly established in many countries in Eastern and Southern Europe. The crucial principle of our foreign policy should be to protect, assist, encourage and aid in every way the Socialist revolution wherever it

appears...The upper class in every country are selfish,
depraved, dissolute and decadent. These upper classes
look to the British Army and the British people to
protect them against the just wrath of the people who
have been fighting underground against them for...four
years. We must see that that does not happen. The
penalty for entertaining any hesitation about the support
for the revolution would be that Labour would wake one
day to find itself "running with the Red Flag in front of
the armoured car of Tory imperialism and counter-
revolution."'

History was to transform that 'bliss was it in that dawn to be alive'
speaker into one of the Party's elder statesmen, deeply implicated
(in particular as Defence Secretary and as Chancellor of the
Exchequer) in its crimes and blunders, for it was none other than
the young Denis Healey, back from playing an honourable part in
the war against fascism.

If expecting the Party to promote revolution was a bit starry-
eyed, its young turks had every right to expect their leaders to strive
to live up to its principles. They had every right to demand that the
Party's triumph at the polls should make a qualitative difference to
history, not just with respect to domestic issues but in the conduct
of foreign and Commonwealth affairs. There is little if any evidence
that it did so. From the start the Attlee Government was ready to
spend - and to do - whatever it took to keep Great Britain in the
Great Powers' League. It was all very well for the golden-tongued
hero of the Labour left, Aneurin Bevan, to proclaim (in July 1948):
'We now have the moral leadership of the world, and before many
years we shall have people coming here as to a modern Mecca...'
The reality was that, whatever good examples it might have been
setting at home, the regime which purported to be the first Socialist
government with a clear mandate from the British electorate was
no moral force abroad; just another tawdry example of the nation-
state rampant. A laundry list of sordid episodes must suffice as
evidence.

With the defeat of Japan in August 1945, the British Empire
and Commonwealth once again embraced a quarter of the world's
population and territory; but over vast tracts of it British rule
was already untenable. In 1947-48 Britain pulled out of India,

Ceylon, and Burma, and abandoned its mandate in Palestine. Forces beyond its control largely absolve the Attlee Government of guilt over the bloody partitioning of India and, perhaps, over the tragic fate of the Palestinian Arabs. However, the catalogue of continuing repression in Britain's other colonies makes sorry reading, with, *inter alia*, the imposition of states of emergency, curfews and the banning of demonstrations; the proscribing of political parties; the banning of newspapers and prosecutions for publishing seditious literature; the shackling of trade unions; the jailing, 'preventive detention', or banishment - not to mention the committing of GBH and lawful murder - of nationalists; and so on (in short, a chronicle of the kind of crimes committed by the British State against its own people a century or so earlier when most of *them* were voteless), in East and West Africa and in colonial territories in the New World.

A charge-sheet of State crimes could include the shooting dead of six African mutineers striking in protest at delays in demobilisation (Kenya, January 1947); an armed police assault on miners taking part in a sit-down strike, in which 21 workers were killed and 51 wounded (Nigeria, November 1949); killings, mass arrests, and savage prison sentences in response to widespread unrest in Buganda (Uganda, 1949-50); a whole series of repressive measures to keep the lid on liberation movements in Nigeria and the Gold Coast; the collective punishment of whole villages during the Malayan emergency (1948-60); and the imprisonment of twelve trade unionists for belonging to an unlawful association (Cyprus, January 1946).

Years later, in 1959, during the Commons debate on the agreement under which Cyprus became independent, with Archbishop Makarios, who had been exiled for a year (1956-57), as its first president, Nye Bevan, now shadow foreign secretary, was to receive a most unwelcome reminder that he had himself been an accomplice in the Attlee regime's repression of freedom fighters. In the midst of a withering attack on the Tories for their folly in suppressing nationalist leaders in the colonies with whom they later had to come to terms, he was 'hoist with his own petard' when he cited the case of Kwame Nkrumah, the first prime minister of the Gold Coast and of Ghana (as the Gold Coast had become on gaining independence in 1957). As the Government benches rocked with mocking laughter, Bevan's mortified colleagues were obliged to break into his cocoon of selective amnesia, though nothing, it seemed, could puncture his impudence. 'All right!' he exclaimed. 'We shoved him in jail. Yes, certainly! If honourable members will restrain their hilarity for a moment, I said this is part of the classic story of these struggles.'

Perhaps only Patrick Gordon-Walker, Secretary of State for Commonwealth Relations in Attlee's second administration, could match such effrontery. Although he was up to his ears in the plot that had enticed Seretse Khama, elected chief of the Bamangwato tribe of Bechuanaland (now Botswana), to England so that he could be banned from the protectorate to placate the South African authorities because he had had the temerity to fall in love with a white woman and marry her, Gordon-Walker denied deceit. He told the House: 'I have done my utmost throughout to preserve honour between man and man in this matter.' Seretse Khama - like Nkrumah and Makarios, and like Jomo Kenyatta in Kenya, among other 'classic' cases - rose in time to the pinnacle of power in his own country through a measure of martyrdom conferred on him by his colonial masters; so perhaps they all had reason to be grateful. Is it not meet then that we outdo Mark Anthony by calling our Statesmen 'Right Honourable'? (Gordon-Walker's frugal habits with respect to open government may be admired again in the context of the sanctions-busting which kept the Rhodesian rebels on the road, recounted in Chapter 30; and further testimony to his dedication to democratic principles surfaced in January 1997 with the 30-years-later rule revelations for 1966, in his words of advice to Harold Wilson on how to handle the embarrassing matter of the war in Vietnam: 'We should search for a policy which, while backing America loyally, allows us a certain more apparent independence of view.')

What we are searching for however, like Diogenes with his lamp in the daylight despondently looking for an honest man, is that 'qualitative difference' alluded to above, and with this in mind it would seem more pertinent to quote the verdict of the authors of *How Labour Governed, 1945-1951*, a seditious if not scurrilous pamphlet that recounts these and other unsavoury stories in some detail:

'To what extent the British Government, as opposed to the colonial governments, was directly responsible for all these colonial crimes is not the main point at issue, although its ultimate responsibility is inescapable. The significant fact is that they could, and did, happen again and again while a Labour Government was in power, no less than they have done under the Tories.'

Perhaps even more shameful was the assistance given to other European powers to regain their right to exploit colonial peoples. British, Indian, and what were described as 'controlled' Japanese troops were used to put down insurrection in the Dutch East Indies and to restore the *status quo ante* until Holland could send troops. As late as 1947 Britain was training and equipping units for a Dutch expeditionary force that grew to over 100,000 strong but none the less failed to prevail over the Indonesian nationalists. Similarly in Indo-China, British along with surrendered Japanese forces operating under their command helped the French to suppress an Annamite rebellion and 'to restore order'.

The current Labour Party Chairman, Harold Laski, spoke for the true Socialists in the Party when he commented on Britain's intervention in Indonesia that it 'makes the British claim to have been engaged in a war for democracy and freedom a hollow mockery all over Southeast Asia'; but there was nothing they could do to control the new masters of State power. This was particularly true in the Middle East. Where Britain's strategic or economic interests were felt to be at stake, the Labour Government made the same assumptions that they must prevail over the rights and interests of other nations as a Tory government would have done. When, on 2nd May 1951, Dr Mossadeq's government asserted Iran's right to her own natural resources by nationalising the Anglo-Iranian Oil Company which controlled the country's oil fields (a measure described by Sked and Cook as 'an act of socialism much bolder than anything ever contemplated by Britain's Labour leaders'), the British Government responded by despatching warships to the Persian Gulf and imposing economic sanctions. Herbert Morrison, who had succeeded Ernest Bevin as Foreign Secretary, was evidently more in sympathy with the kind of British upper-class arrogance displayed by Lord Fraser, the First Sea Lord, when he told a meeting of ministers and the Chiefs of Staff that 'the British public... were tired of being pushed around by Persian pipsqueaks,' than with Labour back-benchers whose consciences were troubling them. At any rate, when Emrys Hughes suggested that Britain's actions smacked of 'nineteenth century imperialism', Morrison coolly replied: 'I think in this case the imperialism is in some respects the other way round.' American diplomacy, combined with cooler consideration of the extent of Britain's military commitments elsewhere, particularly in Korea and Malaya, defused the crisis, and eventually (it was not finalised until 1954) a new deal was worked out. It guaranteed the bulk of Britain's oil supplies, more or less satisfied Iran's honour, and allowed the Americans to get a large finger in the pie. But with such a 'cocky and reactionary pseudo-Pam' (as Hugh Dalton called Morrison, in a mocking comparison with the famous Lord Palmerston of the nation's great-power past) at the Foreign Office helm, Britain had come close to drifting into an imperialistic war.

Quite as bellicose as Morrison was the Minister of Defence, Emmanuel Shinwell (yes, Manny Shinwell, that spunky little Glaswegian Jew who had been one of the leaders of the Red Clydesiders striking for a forty-hour week in 1919), who argued that not standing up to the Persians might embolden nationalists elsewhere and culminate in the nationalisation of the Suez Canal and the collapse of British power throughout the Middle East. Suez was indeed the part of the world where lightning next struck Labour's twilight imperialists. In the middle of the British general election campaign of October 1951, the Egyptian parliament abrogated both the Anglo-Egyptian Treaty of 1936, under which British troops were stationed in the Suez Canal Zone, and the agreement under which the Sudan had been an Anglo-Egyptian condominium since 1899. Again troops, tanks, and warships were promptly deployed against the patriots of another country. 'Morrison's instinctive response,' says Kenneth O. Morgan, 'was again belligerent; echoes of Wolseley and General Gordon were heard in the land,' and the 'bloody little fool' (as Dalton called him on this occasion) had to be overruled by the Prime Minister when he pressed for the escalation of military action. Attlee was at least fortunate in having this crisis taken out of his hands by Labour's defeat at the polls. Five years later, under Sir Anthony Eden, Britain, in collusion with France and Israel, would go to war with Egypt in answer to Nasser's nationalisation of the Suez Canal, much to the official indignation of the Labour opposition; but the truth is that these two incidents in the Middle East in 1951 showed clearly that having a Labour government in power in Britain was no guarantee against gunboat diplomacy.

If Labour's leaders failed to grasp the fact that the Second World War - much more definitively than the First - marked not simply a break in a historical progression, but a total transformation of the international scene; that victory over Germany and Japan did not even offer the option of restoring the *status quo ante*, never mind whether this was to be considered desirable or not; then they are less to be blamed for that (although a greater degree of perspicacity might reasonably have been expected of statesmen who supposedly had a Socialist perspective on the world) than for sharing both the emotional commitment of their political opponents to Britain's 'glorious past' as a great power and their illusion that this role could be sustained in the mid-century world. Socialism in one country may be an unobtainable goal; but had they been wise enough to recognise that Britain was now only cut out to be a bit-part player, had they not been so avid in their desire to strut their hour upon the stage of history, then they might have done far more than they did, both at home and abroad, to further the cause they professed. At least they would not have so tarnished its name by making their country an accomplice in acts wholly inimical to Socialist principles and purposes and, in doing so, come close to reducing Great Britain to the status of a satellite of the United States.

The Labour left saw this danger clearly enough. In November 1946, 58 Labour MPs put their names to an amendment calling on the Government to 'review and recast its conduct of international affairs' in such a way as to 'provide a democratic and constructive alternative to an otherwise inevitable conflict between American capitalism and Soviet Communism, in which all hope of World Government would be destroyed.' In moving the amendment, Richard Crossman accused the Government of drifting away from Labour's election pledges towards an 'exclusive Anglo-American tie-up and of a tie-up between the two front benches.' The bipartisan character of the Government's foreign policy was promptly confirmed by a Tory MP, Captain Crookshank, who declared: 'The Government's foreign policy is, broadly speaking, supported by the Opposition,' and expressed his sympathy for the Foreign Secretary, Ernest Bevin, over the 'stabs in the back' he was suffering 'from his so-called friends.' The conspirators, however, were using rubber daggers: not one of them went into the division lobbies to vote against the Government.

As for the autocrat they had targeted, he was impervious to

their blows and contemptuous of their opinions. On the very day the 1945 general election results were declared, the foreign-secretary-in-waiting had announced: 'British foreign policy will not be altered in any way under the Labour Government.' It is true that the particular policy to which he was referring was that agreed by the wartime Coalition Government of which he had been a member, as he made clear to the House in a mutual backslapping display with the former foreign secretary, Sir Anthony Eden. But despite the important changes in attitude instilled by the chastening experiences of war and the general recognition that Britain's imperial sway could no longer be exercised in the same untrammelled way, that still meant that, in essence, Britain's foreign policy would be Tory foreign policy. Having been let into the club, the Labour statesmen would show they were gentlemen by playing by the rules.

The virtues of a bipartisan foreign policy are commonly taken as self-evident in all countries; but that only highlights the fact that the nation-state is an instrument of tribalism. Parties that profess internationalism yet fail radically to alter their country's foreign policy when they get into power simply illustrate the cynical truth that in politics practice seldom follows precept. But politicians live by the word and, if they dishonour it, deserve to die by it. So whatever allowances may reasonably be made for the practical difficulties of following their principles when in office, it is fitting that the powerless - the ordinary citizens - should constantly rub the politicians' noses in what they have said.

The 'Foreign Policy' chapter in *The Labour Party in Perspective*, for example, opens with the ringing declaration: 'Socialists in all countries are united by a common rejection of the doctrines and ideals of militarism and imperialism,' and goes on to affirm: 'Social justice must be the basis of a peaceful world.' Following a brief but thoughtful survey of the reactions of Labour's supporters to British foreign policy from Victorian times up to the rise of fascism and the civil war in Spain that was still raging when the book was written, Attlee outlines the principal points of the Party's 1934 Conference statement on 'War and Peace', which, he says, 'stands today [1937] as the official policy of the Party...' and 'which it would pursue when given power':

'It based Labour's foreign policy on the collective peace

system through the League of Nations...It regarded the League as a first step towards a co-operative world commonwealth. It rejected the theory of the balance of power and demanded the subordination of national sovereignty to world obligations. It stressed the need for basing the new world order on social justice and demanded far-reaching measures of economic co-operation and world control in economic and financial matters...It declared for an international police force. It stressed the need for world loyalty as against national loyalty. It regarded war resistance as the duty of every citizen, and not merely of organised Labour.'

Attlee makes a special point of declaring that, besides its rejection of Britain's traditional balance of power policy, the Party would not countenance the concept of bipartisan foreign policy:

'It does not agree that there is some policy to be pursued by this country irrespective of what party is in power, a policy which is national and so transcends party differences. There is a deep difference of opinion between the Labour Party and the Capitalist parties on foreign as well as on home policy. *The foreign policy of a Government is the reflection of its internal policy.* Imperialism is the form which Capitalism takes in relation to other nations. A Capitalist Government in Britain...does not consider it [the League of Nations] as a world commonwealth in embryo, because its outlook is nationalist, not internationalist.' [my emphasis]

With respect to these antithetical concepts, in his next chapter, 'The Commonwealth and the Empire', Attlee puts it beyond all possible doubt that his party's principles are to be applied universally, without regard to nation or race. The chapter opens with a frank acknowledgement of Labour's involuntary association with the guilt of imperialism: 'While, on the one hand, it is the protagonist at home of the struggle of the workers against the Capitalists, it is, in relation to the less developed peoples of the world, part of the dominant race which collectively exploits them.' It concludes with a declaration of solidarity with the whole human race:

'One of the vital questions for the future of world peace is the reconciliation of the interests of the white, the black, the brown, and the yellow races. The Labour Party fearlessly applies to this problem the principle of the brotherhood of man. It does not admit that the white race has any right of primogeniture in the world. It holds that the resources of the world must be developed in the interests of all people, and that the standard of life of the inhabitants of Asia and Africa must be raised, and not kept always below those of Europe, America, and Australia.'

Of course, one possible reaction to such elevated declarations is cynicism and sheer disbelief - all too well founded on the observation that politics is a dirty game, and on the suspicion that the only concern of politicians is to persuade others to support them, and that they will say and do anything to secure power. But to take this line, in a society in which we have at least the right openly to debate issues, is to surrender to despair and to become probably more cynical than the worst of those we suspect. Better to take them at their word until we have grounds for disbelieving, and then, piecemeal, to withdraw the credit we have extended them. By treating them as sincere in the first place, we can at least tax them with falling from grace. Besides, like the rest of us, they are more likely to be partly honourable and partly dishonourable than wholly one or the other, and capable of insight as well as subject to self-deception. There is an interesting passage in *The Labour Party in Perspective* in which Attlee takes to task those Labour supporters who, transfixed by the menace of Fascism, were adopting a lesser-of-two-evils attitude to their own government; by so doing they were underestimating the struggle between Socialism and Capitalism, magnifying the differences between Capitalist States and Fascist States, and in their prepossession with national unity encouraging, however unintentionally, 'the subtle introduction of Fascism' at home. The irony and the tragedy is that, ten years later and no longer in opposition but in power, he evidently saw no parallel, but responded to a new menace, that of Soviet Communism, by himself choosing the lesser of two evils, while minimising the distance between his own values and those of American capitalism.

There were, of course, strongly extenuating circumstances to plead in reply to Crossman's charge of an 'exclusive Anglo-American tie-up.' The hot war with the Axis powers had been succeeded, virtually without an interlude of peace, by the Cold War with Soviet power and, to put it mildly, there were already reasons enough for a democratic Socialist State to distrust the intentions of Stalin. Poland, Bulgaria, and Romania were already effectively in the Soviet camp, and within fifteen months the salami tactics of the Communists in Hungary and Czechoslovakia would enmesh those countries too. That is not to say, however, that fear of a Russian attack on the West (inasmuch as it was ever genuinely felt by the Western leaders) was warranted. Sked and Cook bluntly call it 'nonsense' in writing of the panic in Western Europe caused by the invasion of South Korea. Common sense and the evidence concur in concluding that the Russians were as little inclined (if not less!) as their erstwhile allies to plunge themselves into a third world war. The probing and manoeuvring on both sides were part of the age-old balance-of-power game, with neither side now willing to test the other's weakness to destruction, as level-headed peace campaigners well understood long before the amazing Mikhail Gorbachev transformed it into the new received wisdom.

Nor did the rapidly vanishing hopes of reaching an acceptable accommodation with Stalin justify the Attlee Government in coupling Britain to the American chariot. It might even be remarked in passing that the only major demonstration of independence in British foreign policy, the Suez invasion of 1956, which the United States opposed not on ideological or ethical but on pragmatic grounds concerning its own interests in the Middle East, was the act of a Tory government. Although it is only fair to add that their doughty opponents made valiant efforts to rise to the occasion, with Gaitskell comparing Nasser to Mussolini and Hitler because of his take-over of the Canal, and the effervescent Nye regaling the House with such excellent buffoonery as the crack that: 'If the sending of one's police and soldiers into the darkness of the night to seize somebody else's property is nationalisation, then Ali Baba used the wrong terminology.'

The hopes of a better world to come which had helped so many to get through the nightmare years of the war were certainly blighted by the ruthless internal repression and external aggression of the Soviet Union. But they were also blighted by the malign consequences of America's determination to remake the world in its own image. Two days after the opening, on 10th March 1947, of the Moscow Conference of foreign ministers of the wartime allies, at which the future of Germany - still officially envisaged as one country - was the main issue, President Truman, in a speech to a joint session of Congress that was broadcast live nation-wide, assumed on behalf of America the role of global sheriff. The Truman Doctrine, as it came to be called, was full of fine phrases about the choice facing nearly every nation between two ways of life, one 'based upon the will of the majority' and bringing freedom, the other 'based upon the will of a minority' employing 'terror and oppression' to rule the majority. 'I believe that it must be the policy of the United States to support free peoples who are resisting attempted subjugation by armed minorities or by outside pressures,' Truman declared.

The trouble was (leaving aside the megalomaniacal putting-the-world-to-rights presumption involved) that, as Stephen Ambrose says in *Rise to Globalism*: 'The Truman Doctrine came close to shutting the door against any revolution, since the terms 'free peoples' and 'anti-Communist' were thought to be synonymous. All the Greek government, or any dictatorship, had to do to get American aid was to claim that its opponents were Communist.' And so it was to prove, across the continents and for the best part of the next half-century, that the Truman Doctrine became not a torch of freedom to the subject peoples of the world but a terrible threat, reinforcing repression and contributing directly or indirectly to millions of deaths - in Korea, in Indo-China, in Afghanistan, in Angola, and in parts of Latin America, to name just a few of the bloodiest cockpits.

Truth as well as justice was a victim. Ambrose draws attention to the crusading character of the Americans when operating in their idealistic mode, to that Manichaean simple-mindedness that makes them tend to see things in terms of 'a struggle between light and darkness' and equally prone to double-think:

> 'It was difficult for other outsiders, not just Stalin, to understand the American position. Throughout the war Americans had denounced sphere-of-influence and balance-of-power concepts, calling instead for a new era of peace backed by the collective security of the United

Nations, an organization open to all democratic nations. Yet in practice the United States maintained a near hegemony over Central and South America (through the instrument of military dictatorships in most cases). It was true that free elections in East Europe would result in anti-Soviet governments, but it was equally true that free elections in Latin America probably would bring power to anti-American governments.'

To a greater or lesser extent, Britain has been implicated in all of America's post-World-War-II crimes against humanity, since even when its government has not actively collaborated with the United States, it has taken the view that, as a loyal ally, Britain should not oppose them. This is no less true of Labour when in power than of the Tories, who have at least had the excuse that they were not radically departing from their own principles. Indeed, in one crucial case (in addition, that is, to the colonial spats already noted) a Labour government led the way and set the pace for the United States. When the Germans withdrew from Greece in October 1944, Churchill had sent 60,000 British troops to keep the Communist-led resistance movement out of power. As A.J.P. Taylor puts it in *English History, 1914-1945*: 'The British government backed the king of Greece in the name of democracy; though the king's past was far from democratic.' A Commons censure motion protesting at Britain's intervention was backed by 24 Labour MPs, with 23 Labour MPs supporting the Coalition Government and the rest abstaining.

But if that denoted dissent, however feeble, on the Labour benches, the Party's accession to power in July 1945 made not a scrap of difference to the official British position on the issue. In another Commons debate, on 23rd November 1945, Bevin said that the holding of a plebiscite on the controversial issue of the future of the Greek monarchy must await pacification, and with characteristic arrogance told the House that the question was: 'In what reasonable period can I get this country into a tranquil state?' In fact British troops remained in Greece, collaborating with the royalists throughout a bitter civil war that waged from May 1946 to October 1949, the last contingents not being withdrawn until 1950. This shameful episode was instrumental in the proclamation that stood the Monroe Doctrine on its head, since Britain's warning, in February 1947, that it could no longer sustain the burden of military and economic aid to Greece and Turkey led to the United States donning Britain's traditional mantle of paymaster to foreign armies in the balance-of-power game and to the proclamation of the Truman Doctrine as its justification.

In considering the outbreak of the Cold War, the historical record demands recognition of the fact that the Truman Doctrine - like Churchill's earlier 'iron curtain' speech, made in Truman's presence to a university audience at Fulton, Missouri - preceded any clear act of Russian expansionism or aggression, with the arguable exceptions of the Soviet Union's attempts (1) to obtain oil concessions from Iran by postponing the withdrawal of its troops deployed there during the war, and(2) to secure joint control with Turkey over the Dardanelles. The first of these *démarches* was nothing but a mirror image of rights over Middle East oil obtained by Western pressure, while the second reflected the old Tsarist claims to guaranteed passage for Russian ships between the Black Sea and the Mediterranean. In both cases the Russians backed down when their former allies protested. Ambrose comments: 'Stalin was no more ready for war than Truman'; then goes on to record the despatch of America's newest aircraft carrier through the Straits and Truman's remark: 'We might as well find out whether the Russians were bent on world conquest now as in five years or ten years.' In the case of the Iranian oil imbroglio, all the Americans needed to despatch was a stiff note from Secretary of State James Byrnes.

The Truman Doctrine raised the stakes in the poker game with the Russians from an undeclared policy of containment through diplomatic pressures to an open declaration of confrontation. It was America's declaration of Cold War on the Soviet Union. The principal cockpit of this confrontation was Germany, and even if we leave out of account the failure of the United States to take up Stalin's offer of an agreement for a united but neutral Germany (a failure to call his bluff, if bluff is what it was) there are grounds for asserting that America and her principal allies were as responsible as Russia for Germany's forty-five-year division. Perhaps the most telling evidence which supports this view relates to the machinations of General Lucius Clay, the administrator of the American occupation zone. Ambrose - citing Clay's failure to enforce denazification, his inaction with regard to breaking up the industrial cartel system, his ignoring of the Potsdam agreement to limit German industrial production, and his explicit comment that, 'In the event of another war, the Germans probably would be the only Continental peoples upon whom we could rely' - remarks that Clay 'had made the Germans into allies, at a time when most Americans still regarded them as enemies who needed to be punished and re-educated.'

Whatever qualms they still felt about the resurrection of German power and about a permanent rupturing of the wartime alliance with Russia, Bevin and Attlee were in general accord with this pugnacious American stance. 'Both responded to Truman's message [the Truman Doctrine] with enthusiasm,' Morgan says, while Attlee had 'refused to condemn Churchill's ['iron curtain'] speech' when invited to do so in the Commons and Bevin viewed it 'with grim satisfaction.' The House of Commons voted on ratification of the North Atlantic Treaty Organisation on 12th May 1949 (which was, with ironic coincidence, the same day that the Russians lifted their 324-day land blockade of West Berlin). Churchill took the opportunity to taunt the 105 left-wingers who had supported a motion of censure against him for the Fulton speech, in which he had apocalyptically assigned the atomic bomb as God's gift to America so that, in alliance with the other English-speaking nations, it could liberate Eastern Europe and stem the Russian hordes. 'Where are they all now?' he asked. About a hundred simply sat on their hands, with only four voting against ratification.

The influence of Ernest Bevin on the events leading up to the establishment of NATO - and with it the decisive defeat of the American isolationists - was enormous. His advocacy of Western Union in a speech in the Commons in January 1948 led directly to the Brussels Treaty of March 1948 between Britain, France and the three Benelux countries, which alliance became in turn the core of NATO. His prompt response to the proposal of General George Marshall (successor to James Byrnes as US Secretary of State) - in a visionary speech, 'directed not against any country or doctrine but against hunger, poverty, desperation, and chaos,' made at Harvard on 5th June 1947 - 'that the United States should do whatever it is able to do to assist in the return of normal economic health in the world, without which there can be no political stability and no assured peace,' ensured a speedy launch for the Marshall Plan. This was to prove of great importance not only for the rapid recovery of the countries of Western Europe, but also for their continuing co-operation and hence, ultimately, for the European Economic Community and the Organisation for Economic Co-operation and Development.

Historians differ over whether or not Bevin genuinely hoped (as Marshall himself did) that Russia would accept Marshall Aid and encourage the countries of Eastern Europe to do so too, though there is evidence in his favour. Be that as it may, given the intransigence and miscalculation of the Soviet leadership, the consequences of the Marshall Plan were not wholly benign, but divisive too; while with the establishment of NATO, to quote Morgan: 'The polarization of the world between East and West was finally confirmed.'

The consequences of the Cold War for the world as a whole, but especially for the dispossessed masses of the Third World, are incalculable but horrendous. The consequences for Britain are in some respects all too calculable. In collusion with the Great Power delusions of British statesmen, they meant - besides the follies and crimes already chronicled - direct involvement in the devastating war in Korea; complicity in the even more terrible war in Vietnam that spilt over into Laos and tragic Cambodia; complicity in many other acts of slaughter and repression carried out or fostered by the world's preceptor and policeman; the continuation of military conscription for seventeen years after the end of the Second World War; and the imposition of a burden of so-called defence expenditure which was at times greater per head of population than that borne by the United States and which always substantially exceeded that of our other NATO allies. This distorted the economy, constantly diverting precious human, material, and financial resources from being deployed to better the life of the people. It made it more difficult for us to pay our way in the world by trading successfully, let alone to afford much help to less fortunate nations. More directly, our swollen defence budget led to a sickening series of shameful arms deals, in which 'helping our balance of payments' jockeyed with 'sustaining our defence industries and defence jobs' and the age-old shibboleth of 'strategic interests' as justification. (A noisome specimen or two of gun-running deals made by the Callaghan Government on such morally shaky grounds will be examined later.)

The culminating folly of the struggle to retain Great Power status was the development of Britain's own nuclear deterrent, an act mocked, as proliferation gathered pace, in Tom Lehrer's song 'I wanna have a little bomb like you.' With America refusing to share its nuclear power know-how with Britain, despite the substantial contribution British scientists had made to it, Attlee and Bevin (who apparently deployed the cogent argument that it was important for the Union Jack to fly over a British atom bomb), launched this project in secret, without even Cabinet discussion at any stage. It only became public - and indeed parliamentary - knowledge after the Tories had returned to power. After the successful explosion of Britain's prototype atom bomb on the Montebello Islands, off the north-west coast of Australia, in October 1952, Churchill (once again Prime Minister) in a Commons statement, warmly congratulated all those concerned in arming Great Britain with this fiendish weapon, adding: 'I should no doubt pay my compliments to the Leader of the Opposition and the party opposite for initiating it.'

To at least some of those on the Opposition benches this must have been mortifying; but the Labour leaders' love-in with the bomb went on and on. It endured through Nye Bevan's volte-face at Brighton in 1957, when, anticipating his transmutation from shadow to substance following the next general election, he told Conference that to pass the unilateral nuclear disarmament motion they were debating would be to propose sending the next foreign secretary 'naked into the conference chamber...to preach sermons'; through Hugh Gaitskell's contemptuous defiance of Conference when it did vote for unilateralism at Scarborough in 1960; through Wilson's and Callaghan's under-the-counter Polaris submarine nuclear missile development programme code-named Chevaline, pursued with scornful disregard of Labour's 1974 Manifesto pledge not to develop a new generation of nuclear weapons; through Neil Kinnock's neurotic nuclear juggling act ('now you see the bomb, now you don't...') - impelled, like his hesitancy in making anything of the 'peace dividend' which the end of the Cold War offered, by his fear that his political opponents would call him unpatriotic - as he approached, apparently, the threshold of power at the very moment when it was plain for all to see that so far as those in this little island are concerned the unilateralist case had been vindicated by history.

The heart sickens. But what was to be expected from a party whose leaders could have found no answer to the insane logic of Winston Churchill's son Randolph, who, when Britain's strike-force of Vulcan bombers armed with hydrogen bombs became fully operational in 1958, rejoiced because: 'Britain can knock down twelve cities in the region of Stalingrad and Moscow from bases in Britain and another dozen in the Crimea from bases in Cyprus. We did not have that power at the time of Suez. We are a major power again.'? Commenting on Truman's spine-chilling reassurance to General de Gaulle when he expressed his apprehensions of Russian military aggression in Central Europe, that there was nothing to fear, since America would use the atom bomb against any nation that became aggressive, Ambrose writes:

> 'The strategy would later be called massive retaliation. The trouble with it was that even as early as 1945 it bore little relation to reality... Should the Russians realise the West's worst fears and march across the Elbe, the most that bombs could achieve would be retaliation on principal Russian population centers, which would kill tens of thousands but which would not hamstring the Russian war machine. Stalin would match American destruction of Moscow with Soviet occupation of Western Europe. The Red Army was just as effective a deterrent as the atomic bomb.'

All that the nuclear arms race ever did achieve was the ultimate abomination of the doctrine of 'mutual assured destruction', a kind of mutual suicide pact that in the event would willy-nilly take the rest of the world along with the subscribers. Madness there has been aplenty, but as yet no superpower leader mad enough to activate that pact.

Of her own volition - or rather that of her rulers - Britain made as big a contribution to this folly as she was able - punching, indeed, not only above her weight but well above her wit! And by the roll of the historical dice it fell to the first Labour leaders with plenary powers to make the choices that determined Britain's role in the world for the next half-century. Had they chosen differently, and more in accordance with their proclaimed principles, it may well have been too late by the time the Tories returned to office for them to try to reclaim Britain's great power status with any credibility at all. Kenneth O. Morgan rightly says: 'It is easy to go too far in criticizing or debunking the Attlee government.'

Nevertheless, he himself is severe enough in assessing its record on foreign affairs and defence. 'Caught up in cold-war postures' and the defence of 'old imperialist commitments', and responding to a perceived threat from Russia which time 'seemed to show to be increasingly illusory,' he says:

> '...the Attlee government committed Britain to a rearmament programme which was economically damaging and politically naive. The secret decision to commit the country to an independent nuclear weapons programme, which no government minister had the scientific expertise to understand, consorted ill with the proclaimed desire to promote world peace and disarmament.'

He expresses the widespread revulsion against these policies that gathered force in the 'fifties, especially after the launching of the Campaign for Nuclear Disarmament: 'That a British Labour government could involve itself covertly in producing so horrendous an arsenal of destructive weapons seemed at variance with the moral and humanitarian instincts of a party calling itself, in any meaningful sense, socialist.' And he concludes that this 'passionate debate over major aspects of foreign and defence policy...did the party prolonged, perhaps irretrievable, damage.'

As for the long-term consequences for the cause of Socialism in Britain, since the Labour Party, however imperfect, was its main channel, they were baleful indeed. The sad truth is that, far from enabling Britain to claim 'the moral leadership of the world', Labour's adjustment 'to the realities and torments of power' (to quote Morgan again) has meant the sacrifice of more and more of its 'moral capital'. Instead of instilling the courage born of hope and feelings of fraternity, one Labour government after another has collaborated in the conditioning of its subjects - and all citizens of the self-styled 'free world' - to fear and hatred.

CHAPTER 14

Trade wars and tribalism

'Within the tribe the rule of "each for all" is supreme so long as the separate family has not yet broken up the tribal unity. But that rule is not extended to the neighbouring clans, or tribes...Each tribe, or clan, is a separate unity...Therefore, when it comes to a war the most revolting cruelties may be considered as so many claims upon the admiration of the tribe. This double conception of morality passes through the whole evolution of mankind, and maintains itself until now.'

Peter Kropotkin, *Mutual Aid* **(1902)**

If the world at large were like the Bourbons, damned by the verdict that they forgot nothing and learned nothing, we should have cause to despair. But whether or not history signifies anything, the record is not quite as black as that. It suggests, rather, that man learns from the past, but too slowly to keep pace with events, so that the lesson he is learning is perpetually out of date, appropriate for yesterday but not quite applicable today. Like warriors from dragons' teeth, aggressors may spring up anywhere at any time. Conversely, as one of the speakers (though I forget which one - Fenner Brockway, I think, though it might have been Bronowski) so memorably declared at a meeting I went to in my youth to protest at the impending execution of a group of Spanish Anarchists, 'Freedom is indivisible.' It has no frontiers and is nothing essentially to do with national sovereignty. The nation-state is simply the tribe writ large: it partitions mankind on the adventitious grounds of nationality. The struggle for national independence was one of the great epics of the nineteenth century, from the Congress of Vienna to the Treaty of Versailles and, especially for 'colonial peoples', till much more recent times. A historically imperative aspect of the fight for freedom, it was and is none the less far from being coterminous with that struggle, as the early Socialists intuitively understood. It is therefore a matter of particular poignancy to be obliged to look on as statesmen who claim to be Socialists act like any other tribal elders.

Where the 'national interest' more or less coincides with

equity, such primitive viewpoints, though still regrettable, are tolerable. One instance of this state of affairs obtaining during Callaghan's chieftainship was the demand that Britain's burden of contributions to the European Economic Community be lightened on the grounds that it was disproportionate both to the benefits received by Britain and to the country's ability to pay without seriously undermining efforts to improve national prosperity. (One cross-party faction amongst the Brits even appeared to regard the EEC levy as a modern equivalent of Danegeld!) At the time Britain stood third from the bottom of the Community's nine members in terms of gross national product, yet she was easily the main contributor to the EEC budget, with an annual deficit of £1.1 billion (around £20 for every man, woman, and child) between payments levied and payments received, effectively wiping out the whole of the balance of trade in her favour gained from her North Sea oil assets. At the same time her deficit on trade with the other EEC countries was twice the size of her EEC budget payment's deficit, £2.2 billion. Without adding in the folly of the mountainous stocks of surplus food (rising to as much as 5,000,000 tonnes of wheat, 1,500,000 of beet-sugar, 800,000 of milk powder, and 500,000 of butter, some of which was, in November 1978, flogged off to Soviet Russia and Poland at only two-thirds of the price British consumers had to pay for butter in the shops, and at a cost of £25 million to the EEC) and the fact that three-quarters of the EEC's budget was devoted to bolstering farm prices - and hence in EEC domestic terms to overproduction and in global terms to subsidised dumping on the world market - there was reason enough in Britain's extremely unfavourable situation *vis à vis* the Common Market for the tough stance taken by Jim Callaghan and his Minister of Agriculture, John Silkin, against a 2 to 2½ per cent rise in farm support prices demanded by West Germany and France and some cause for congratulations that, with the support of the EEC Commission and Italy, Britain's negotiators secured the promise of a freeze on prices until at least the second half of 1979.

Looking back at what was at the time billed as the mother and father of a row, it is both instructive and wryly amusing to recall the party manoeuvring, factional fisticuffs, and unabashed rationalisations it occasioned. Britain's Minister of Agriculture was charged by his Dutch counterpart with 'pursuing the policies of nineteenth-century capitalism in attacking the small farmers of Europe' for electoral advantage. And while Labour's NEC adopted by the sweeping majority of 19 to 4 a document describing the Common Market as 'an instrument of private profit seeking', the Tories' trade spokesman, John Nott, denounced 'the inherently Socialist manner' in which EEC monies were disbursed and vowed that when they were back in power his party would be 'fighting for the liberal policies of the Rome treaty' against 'the creeping dirigism, the electoral cynicism and the wholly unwarranted destruction of British national interests.' Almost simultaneously, his leaderene, that renowned exemplar of the counsel that the 'soft answer turneth away wrath', rebuffing Callaghan's charge that the Tories' attitude to the Market had been 'acquiescent', sanctimoniously advised the Prime Minister and his colleagues to drop 'their abrasive and critical attitude towards our partners' and to behave 'genuinely as partners'.

In this maelstrom of political manoeuvring, very few could be credited with that 'virtue of small minds', consistency; even fewer with clear-sightedness. Greater truths, such as the long-term development interests of Third World countries and the welfare of peasant farmers - not to mention the landless poor - in far-away places convenient for dumping excess EEC products, got quite drowned out in the din of reciprocal denunciation between members of the exclusive club of EEC politicians.

The ambivalent state of mind of Euro-politicians when called upon to consider the interests of underdeveloped (or as the politicially correct terminology has it, 'developing') countries was thrown into sharp relief in November 1978, during negotiations for a new trade and aid agreement between the EEC and some fifty African, Caribbean, and Pacific nations, to update the Lomé Convention. A proposal to make the new agreement subject to suspension in the event of persistent violation of human rights was strongly opposed not only by the former colonies (whose governments were understandably sensitive to any conditions that appeared to infringe their sovereignty), but by some EEC members too, especially France, while Britain's Foreign Secretary, Dr David Owen, strongly endorsed the proposal. On the other hand, the Callaghan Government was not prepared to accept the argument of the Commons Select Committee on Overseas Development that Britain should actively pursue a policy of industrial adjustment that would foster the importation of manufactured goods from the Third World; while for its part the Select Committee was sceptical of the value of the proposed human rights clause.

The human rights issue had already figured in an attempt by the Labour Government to set a good example to the major non-Communist industrialised nations in their handling of aid to the Third World. In July 1978, following the Group of Seven meeting in Bonn, Judith Hart, Minister for Overseas Development, announced that debts totalling £928 million owed to Britain by seventeen of the world's poorest nations (as defined by the United Nations' poverty yardstick of having an annual per capita income of less than 280 dollars) were to be written off. Five other 'poorest nations' were excluded from this bountifulness because of their serious violations of human rights. The unforgiven were Uganda, Ethiopia, South Yemen, Kampuchea and Vietnam. But amongst those which apparently passed the 'decent society' test were Dr Hastings Banda's squalid little autocracy, Malawi; the military dictatorship of Zia ul-Haq, Pakistan, whose deposed prime minister, Zulfikar Ali Bhutto, was languishing in prison under sentence of death; and a very poor nation-state, Indonesia, whose appalling human rights record may serve to illustrate how tortuous the reasoning, how devious the adjudication must have been in deciding whether to forgive or not to forgive the debtor nations for being too poor to repay the capitalist moneylenders.

In a report published by Amnesty in January 1979 (to mark the thirtieth anniversary of the Universal Declaration of Human Rights) in which at least 110 countries were indicted for abuses, Argentina and Indonesia were singled out for special mention, the former for the disappearance of 15,000 people in the previous two years, the latter for having had no less than 55,000 political prisoners in October 1977. The majority of them had been incarcerated since the abortive Communist uprising of 1965; others were members of different resistance movements, including guerrillas who had fought against Indonesia's illegal annexation of East Timor. At the end of 1978 the Suharto regime announced that it had freed more than 10,000 detainees during that year and that it was now holding 9,700, who it said would be released by the end of 1979.

As a meaningful act of solidarity with the Third World as a whole the Labour Government's debt-forgiveness decision (reached after much debate between ministers over the anticipated loss of 2,400 British jobs over a three-year period) was in any case little more than an encouraging gesture. Responding to a challenge from Robert Rhodes James on the Opposition benches that the House should not have been simply informed of the decision by the

Minister but that parliamentary approval should have been sought for a measure costing the country around £60 million a year, Mrs Hart assured him that the cost would be met from the aid programme already announced and would not entail new expenditure.

Such a rob-Peter-to-pay-Paul approach to figures, such a juggling of monies to counterfeit generosity, always makes it difficult to know just what a government is so virtuously spending, or alternatively and equally virtuously, saving. But judging Labour on its own best self-presentation, as in the challenge of supreme stinginess hurled at the Tories by Labour's spokesperson for Overseas Development and Co-operation, Ann Clwyd, in December 1990, it would appear that Britain came the closest it ever did to hitting the target of 0.7 per cent of GNP set as the UN Second Development Decade (i.e. the 1970s) target for aid from the richer nations to the poorer, in the Wilson/Callaghan years, with 'an all-time high' of 0.51 per cent of GNP. That fell to 0.31 under the tender care of Thatcher & Co. It should be said at once, however, that the top figure claimed for Labour by Ann Clwyd (which is in any case nothing to boast about) is at least a third higher than the generally accepted figures for official British aid during the 1970s, and that Britain's recognised peak performances of over 0.5 per cent occurred in the early sixties under the other Harold, Macmillan. But it is more important to remark how low a priority Third World aid has been to Tory and Labour governments alike, and to note their paramount concerns even when 'in the humour for giving'. Typically, for example, two-thirds of British aid has been directly tied to the purchase of British goods, and arguably has been primarily of benefit to the donor. Truly it is said, 'It is more blessed to give than to receive.'

As in other spheres, the motives of the Labour leadership in the matter of Third World aid were honourable enough. But Socialist objectives were all too often compromised or confounded (as Bentham would surely have judged) through lack of courage to discriminate in their conscientious calculations between the lesser and the greater good. In a number of more extreme cases the consequences of decisions reached after appropriately agonised appraisals were nothing less than baleful.

Above everything else, the Callaghan interregnum was blighted by the swelling spectre of unemployment. As already indicated, Government ministers were right always to take into account the practical effects of their policies and actions on the principle that had, from the 'forties onwards until the noisome eruption of Thatcherism, been accepted by all parties - the right to a job. They were wrong, however, to let it outweigh every other social and moral consideration. One especially heinous instance of this morally debilitating inclination to do a deal with the devil so long as he was offering employment was the Hoffman La Roche affair. This Swiss pharmaceutical leviathan, which was currently selling world-wide some £750 million worth of drugs at an estimated net profit of £150-200 million (and which, incidentally, was heavily implicated in ethically dubious drug-pushing in the Third World), was induced to build a factory in Scotland for the production of vitamin C by a government contribution of nearly one third of the construction costs. The £45 million grant was justified on the grounds that the site of the plant, Dalry in Ayrshire, was in an area of very high unemployment which was on the point of more than doubling to nearly thirty per cent as a result of the British Steel Corporation's decision to end steel-making in the Garnock Valley. However, the price-tag on the 450 permanent jobs to be created was £100,000 apiece.

Moreover, only a few years earlier the beneficiary of this government handout had been caught out in an act of gross exploitation (even by the shameless standards of pharmaceutical multinationals) of the National Health Service, to which it had been selling two commonly prescribed tranquillisers at forty times the rate it charged the Italians. The Wilson Government had accepted an out-of-court settlement under which Hoffman repaid £3.75 million excess profit out of £24 million netted from British sales - and was then allowed substantial price increases! And this was the company that, with the connivance of the Swiss legislative and judicial authorities, had, in 1973-74, played a part worthy of a despot of Mediaeval or Renaissance times, by causing one of its own executives, Stanley Adams, to be tried in camera and imprisoned for industrial espionage. His 'crime' was that he had alerted the EEC Commission to the company's practice of making 'loyalty' payments to retailers to push its products - a practice which breached EEC laws and the trade treaty between the EEC and Switzerland.

But however reprehensible it may have been for a 'Socialist' government to kow-tow in this way to corporate capitalism (even if it was in their judgement 'in the national interest'), at least in the case instanced above the sales products were intended to be life-enhancing, not, as in the most dubious market of all, nicknamed in a notable study by Anthony Sampson 'the arms bazaar', death-dealing. In May 1978 representatives of 149 States - every single member - of the United Nations met in New York to take part in a five-week-long Special Session on Disarmament. Sadly, since its practical achievements were so marginal, the conference could hardly be said to have marked a turning point in world history. But it was the first world-wide attempt to put a brake on the arms race since the 1932 conference held under the auspices of the League of Nations, and it surely served to make many more people realise that, since the invention of weapons of genocidal magnitude, the greatest threat was not that posed by one nation to another, but that posed by the huge hoards of weapons in every corner of the globe to the future of the whole human race. By now, three-quarters of the way through the UN-declared Disarmament Decade, global expenditure on arms was running at around $400 billions a year, a doubling of the spending rate since 1966. The arsenals of Europe alone contained about 11,000 nuclear weapons; and the destructive power of the world's stock of nuclear weapons was reckoned as equivalent to one million Hiroshima-type bombs. Expenditure on military research and development had passed the $30-billion-a-year mark, and represented, according to one estimate, some 40 per cent of all R & D. Estimates of the deployment of manpower on such work ranged from more than half the world's physical and engineering scientists to a quarter of its total scientific manpower.

In a commentary on the UN Special Session, James Cameron pointed out that the world spent more than sixty times as much on equipping each of its soldiers as it did on educating each of its children. As always, it was, of course, the weakest that went to the wall. As Harford Thomas wrote:

'The arms race has been even more damaging to
Third World countries than to the rich. It has
distorted and held back development perhaps more
than any other single factor. It sets up a cycle of
poverty-repression-militarisation. With 95 countries
importing major weapons in 1976, the countries of the
Third World were spending almost three times as
much on arms as they received in development
aid.'

Another baleful consequence, as he pointed out, was the undermining of the economic independence of many countries, 'especially of newly independent countries which become the dependent clients of their arms suppliers.'

To whom are we principally to ascribe this lamentable state of affairs? The blessings of representative democracy are not commonly available in Third World countries. On the contrary, tin-pot dictators and their loathsome henchmen tend to spring up like mushrooms on their soil, and their one unfailing need is to arm themselves against rivals for power and against the people at large. This provides the market for the market-led economies of the democracies. If the demand is there, the capitalist's role is to supply it; ergo, the despots are primarily responsible for the arms trade with the Third World. That at least might be an orthodox economist's analysis.

Viewed from the Cold War perspective, the alternative arch-villains were the Communist countries which threatened stability in so many regions of the world by arming client-states, thus obliging the Western democracies to bolster rival powers. But the problem with apportioning blame according to such Cold War criteria is that the United States on its own, without taking into account its NATO allies, was supplying nearly three-fifths by value of the arms shipped to the Third World, almost three times the arms supplies from the Communist States. One might be tempted to conclude from this that it was from the West that this blight on the Third World principally came, if it were not that the weapons from 'the Free World' were obviously for defence, while the Communists were equally obviously busy arming aggressors. Moreover, from a Manichaean and cataclysmic standpoint it had to be appreciated that if the arms supplied for defence against Communist aggression were sometimes also the means of internal repression, that was at worst an unfortunate side-effect - collateral damage, one might call it. The way Uncle Sam in particular saw it, from the moment he pinned the global sheriff's badge on his own breast, has been pithily put as: 'He may be a son of a bitch, but he's our son of a bitch!' - an attitude which gave us a non-stop picture-show of public enemies from Syngman Rhee to Batista, the Somozas, and Ferdinand Marcos.

Furthermore, if stability and peace really were the principal objectives, it was not always clear that gunrunning was the best way to secure them. Speaking for Singapore to representatives of 87 member-states of the Non-Aligned Movement, at the Belgrade conference of July 1978, Mr S. Radjaratnam stated that since the end of the Second World War 25 million lives had been lost in 133 wars fought in Third World countries. He charged the superpowers with waging war by proxy under the doctrine: 'Let the Third World fight the Third World War.' Undoubtedly strategic considerations did play an important part in the arms trading of the two great rival power blocs; but in the case of the Western democracies at least it has at times seemed simpler and more honest to explain the gun-running as giving in to an insatiable lust to do a deal. For what it is worth, one might even make a plausible case for maintaining that the motives of the Communist gunrunners were generally purer, at least in the sense that they were less swayed by venal considerations.

But in any case, what was it but the Devil's Trade when the two superpowers and their satellites were supplying poor countries with the means of mutual slaughter? A report released by the International Institute for Strategic Studies in September 1978 noted as 'a new development' that a number of countries were placing orders for arms with both Eastern and Western suppliers 'who are clearly in competition.' Four States forged by Western imperialism to fragment the Arab peoples - Syria, Iraq, Kuwait, and Libya - were named as recipients of these presents from the Pandora's Box of the arms manufacturers, and the report noted that the weapons traded were 'technically very well advanced and comparable to systems now being deployed by NATO and the Warsaw Pact.'

In this Devil's Trade, Britain, then as now, did somewhat better than dabble. Writing in *The Observer*, Anthony Sampson pointed out that as the representatives of the 149 member-states of the United Nations were earnestly deliberating in New York on the problem of how to promote disarmament, at Aldershot the Duke of Kent was ceremonially opening the British Army Equipment Exhibition, a bi-annual trade fair designed to promote the export of British weapons, particularly to Third World countries:

'Britain's cross-purposes are well defined. In a carefully written speech at the UN two weeks ago, which was much praised by other delegates, Mr Callaghan spoke of Britain's central role in disarmament, and stressed that the suppliers of arms had a special responsibility to

173

practise restraint. Yet only two weeks later teams of
British salesmen are shouting their wares at an arms
fair, to sell still more guns, tanks and ammunition to
customers abroad. Where exactly does the "special
responsibility" lie?...Among the images of the 1970s
which may look most incomprehensible to our
grandsons could be an arms fair under Royal patronage,
enthusiastically selling weapons to the Third World.'

Weapons were, in fact, amongst Britain's most successful exports,
worth around £1 billion a year to her balance of trade. The
Stockholm Peace Institute computed her share of the global arms
trade in so-called conventional weapons at 9 per cent, ranking her
third equal with France, after the superpowers' slices of 38 per
cent for the USA and 34 per cent for the USSR.

Nor were the Wilson and Callaghan governments of the
'sixties and 'seventies conspicuously more fastidious than the Tories
about the humanitarian credentials of their customers. 'The
beginnings of the British Government's extended role as an arms
salesman were found, oddly enough, under the Labour Government
soon after it came to power in 1964, in the first flush of idealism,'
writes Sampson in a section of *The Arms Bazaar.* Here he chronicles
the way in which a strike-force of Harold Wilson's ministers
demonstrated their marketing skills in a massive three-way arms
deal involving selling to Saudi Arabia British fighters it did not
really want and buying second-choice American fighters with the
proceeds. Every year the Defence Sales Organisation set up by Denis
Healey in 1965 as an agency of the Ministry of Defence organised
a floating bazaar aboard a British warship that sailed half way round
the world to flog weapons to the natives. Ports of call for the three-
month 1978 cruise were in Tunisia, Nigeria, Brazil and Colombia.
This followed the successful 1977 voyage to the Far East which
had secured orders for armoured vehicles from Thailand and the
Philippines and for Hawk training aircraft from Indonesia.

The 'special responsibility' that Jim Callaghan acknowledged
Britain had as a major arms supplier was most conspicuously
displayed in three highly volatile regions of the world - the southern
half of South America, the Persian Gulf, and Indo-China. In South
America two vicious military dictatorships, Chile and Argentina,
had spent 1978 sabre-rattling in a century-old dispute over which

held sovereignty over three small islands at the very tip of the continent, ownership of which also conferred jurisdiction over the adjoining waters and continental shelf. War was averted by a Vatican offer to despatch a special envoy to mediate between the rival powers. But meanwhile both sides indulged in an arms shopping spree, the better to flex their military muscles. France was the market-leader in satisfying these unsavoury customers, but Britain was a keen (not to say crawling) competitor. In July there were disturbing rumours that Argentina was on the point of withdrawing from a very-nearly-clinched £500-million deal to purchase six of Britain's most advanced gas-turbine-powered frigates, each equipped with a helicopter and armed with British Seacat and French Exocet missiles. In high dudgeon after the diplomatic row over its claim to the Falkland Islands, so the story went, Argentina had decided to place the order with the West German firm Blohm and Voss instead. However, ruffled feathers were sufficiently smoothed down again by the end of the year for Whitehall to announce - as Chile's version of 'the Great Dictator', Augusto Pinochet, squared up to Argentina's three-man junta in the Beagle Channel - that one of the triumvirate, the air force commander General Orlando Agosti, was to visit Britain in January as a guest of the Ministry of Defence.

Apart from the obliging policeman who shows Mr Punch how the hangman's noose works by placing it around his own neck, it is difficult to recall a stupidity in the conduct of our affairs of state to match this arming of a hostile, ruthless, and highly unpredictable foreign regime. With one exception. Had it not been for the even greater subsequent lunacy of handing Saddam Hussein the wherewithal to threaten the whole of the Middle East, one might have reasonably assumed that the lesson of this folly would have been branded on the national consciousness for ever, in the months of April, May, and June 1982, by the scorched bodies of British soldiers and sailors on the good ships *Sheffield*, *Sir Galahad*, *Sir Tristram*, and the other British vessels zapped in the South Atlantic conflict by Skyhawks, Mirages, and Exocet-armed Super Etendards sold to the Argies by our American and French allies.

But in any case, such lunacy was outclassed by the callous unconcern over the appalling human rights record of the Argentine regime. In the three years in which the junta had held sway in Argentina by the time Labour lost office in May 1979, its agents rubbed out some 30,000 of their compatriots, men, women and children, about half of whom disappeared without trace. They tortured tens of thousands more and robbed myriads of orphaned children of all knowledge of their parentage. The heart-sickening indifference of the spectator-world to the victims' fate was dramatised by what must surely rank as the supreme triumph of the keep-politics-out-of-sport school of thought, the holding of the World Cup in Buenos Aires in June 1978. As the host-nation's footballing heroes were cheered on to victory in the stadium and the world watched their triumph on its television screens by courtesy of satellite-transmission, other citizens died on the streets and in the cellars in Argentina's 'dirty war'. Such was the progress of civilisation since the days of the Roman circus!

Barely a month later the fans of one of Britain's crack teams, Tottenham Hotspur, could rejoice at the granting of work permits to two Argentinian soccer stars, Osvaldo Ardiles and Ricardo Villa, super-mercenaries bought by their new club for a transfer fee of £750,000. Norman Atkinson, the Labour Party's treasurer and a member of its International Committee, in welcoming the announcement, voiced the widespread concern over the situation of dissidents in Argentina and hoped that political asylum would be facilitated, but added: 'I am convinced, however, that the granting of visas to these two exceptionally gifted footballers will assist that process.'

Experienced political refugees would probably be somewhat puzzled by our Norm's mental processes. Nearer to the mark, surely, were the comments made a few weeks earlier by the Latin America Bureau. It considered that, in dealing with countries in most of which three-fifths of the total income was appropriated by an elite fifth of the population and most of the people were paupers, 'British policy is at sixes and sevens,' and that Labour Party protests about the nature of the regimes, notably in Chile, Brazil and Argentina,' simply could not be squared with Britain's exporting of capital goods, including arms, to a region where 'they not only fail to benefit the vast majority of the population...but actually serve to increase unemployment.' The Bureau characterised the essentially unchanged nature of British policy under Labour with devastating moderation: 'The day-to-day work of the British embassies in Latin America is a difficult and complex one, appearing to stand by civilised values while at the same time doing nothing which would blunt the trade offensiveness of British business.'

CHAPTER 15

The global-stability jigsaw puzzle

'The dead do not know how history is made. They have
fed it with their blood; what comes after, they never
learn...The dead have never spoken...They have
forgotten once and for all the precious uses of the voice.
It is we, then, who must speak in their name. We must
plead the cause in their absence.'

Vasilis Vassilikos, Z

The rationalisations for the even greater lunacy referred to above
were rooted in the 1978-79 revolution that drove Mohammed Reza
Shah Pahlavi from his 'Peacock Throne'. The Pahlavi dynasty owed
its kingdom primarily to the British, who in the aftermath of the
First World War helped Reza Khan (a former officer in the Iranian
Cossack Brigade which was a contingent of the White Russian
forces operating in the southern regions of the Caspian Sea) to seize
power in Persia. The object was to establish a buffer-state against
the threat of Bolshevik expansionism. However, eventually, in 1941,
to counter his friendship with Germany's Nazi regime, the British
joined with Soviet Russia in forcing him to abdicate in favour of
his 21-year-old son. Mohammed Reza reigned as a puppet shah
during the joint occupation of his country by the Red Army and
British forces, from 1941-1946, before securing a spurious and
inherently unstable form of independent power as the ruler of a
key piece of the Truman Doctrine global-stability jigsaw. In 1955,
with Britain and Pakistan, Persia acceded to the Baghdad Pact
initiated by Turkey and Iraq to maintain security and peace in the
Middle East. When Iraq itself withdrew, following the revolution
of July 1958 which overthrew its monarchy, Persia remained a
member of this loose alliance, henceforth called the Central Treaty
Organisation. Within two months of the ousting of the Shah, Iran
(as the country, reverting to its more authentic name, now called
itself) had withdrawn from the pact and CENTO had collapsed.

The Shah had survived by a whisker the threat to his power
posed by the de facto alliance between Mossadeq's National Front
and the Communists of the Tudeh Party, turning the country into a
virtual autocracy after the engineering, in 1953, of a military coup

against his own government. (In one of history's endless ironies, the American colonel who masterminded this coup was the father of the commander-in-chief of the forces launched in the United Nations' authorised Desert Storm campaign against Iraq in January 1991.) With the eager assistance of Western capitalism and NATO gunrunners he had imposed on Persia a high-technology superstructure (with a commensurate standard of living for its elite but only marginal improvements for its impoverished masses) and made it a major Middle Eastern power. Then the sons and grandsons of those 'Persian pipsqueaks' who had so pestered our Herbert in the dying days of his power and glory had struck again, but this time most destructively in the far more virulent form of Shi'ite fundamentalism.

The degree of symbiotic complicity between the 'free world' leaders and the Shah is a measure of their mutual folly and amorality. If the Shah owed his throne to Western imperialism, the leading Western powers became dependent on him for a not insubstantial portion of their prosperity. At the time of the revolution Britain depended on Iran for some 16 per cent of its oil consumption, while Western Europe as a whole received a similar proportion of its needs from the same source. Of America's oil imports, around 10 per cent came from Iran. Israel and South Africa, denied supplies by the Arab states, were highly dependent on Iranian oil, Israel for up to 60 per cent of its consumption, South Africa for no less than 90 per cent. It was a hammer-blow to them when the revolutionary regime joined the Arab boycott against them.

Britain and the United States suffered a serious loss in another respect. Despite Mossadeq's nationalisation of Iran's oil industry, they had retained a strong hold on its products. While the Shah remained on the throne, a consortium led by British Petroleum and including Shell and the five principal American companies continued to market 80 per cent of the country's oil, with the National Iranian Oil Company handling only the remaining fifth. A strike of the country's oil workers, who vowed they would not return to work until the Shah left the country, was not the least of the reasons that persuaded him the game was up. When, after a ten-week break from around Christmas 1978, the taps were turned on again (on the anniversary of Mossadeq's death, a date picked as a symbolic gesture of defiance), it was made clear that the greatly reduced supplies would go to the highest bidders. It was a shaken world market in which, to take an extreme example, Japan, wholly dependent on oil imports for its position as world leader in manufactured exports, was prepared to pay up to 50 per cent more than the official prices set by the Organisation of Petroleum Exporting Countries, while OPEC members were raising their prices by up to 15 per cent. It was anticipated that the total cost to the European Community of oil imports would rise by between 22 and 25 per cent in 1979, and that largely as a consequence of this, EEC growth would be cut by 1 per cent. (In the event, of course, the recession turned out to be much more severe, and for Britain, under the harsh regimen prescribed by the Thatcherites, particularly devastating.) At the beginning of March 1979 the chairman of the International Energy Agency representing most of the world's leading economies issued an alarming warning that the world could not sustain the explosive price rises of recent weeks. Agency members agreed on a 5 per cent reduction in oil consumption, while even in the land of the freedom to guzzle gas President Carter submitted to the Congressional energy committees a standby rationing plan that could limit drivers to little more than a gallon a day if he were to declare an emergency.

For Britain, with its quickening flow from its North Sea assets, the oil crisis would have been the least of its worries had it not been so vulnerable to a downturn in the world economic situation. The almost daily announcements of the cancellation or deferment of lucrative British contracts with Iran had a more direct and immediate impact. *Guardian* economics correspondent Jane McLoughlin described the Shah's downfall as looking like delivering 'a body-blow to British industry.' Around 170,000 jobs in Britain were directly dependent on trade with Iran. Among the Shah's many grandiose schemes was the ambition of making his country the hub of the motor industry in the Middle East, with a production target of a million cars a year by 1985. These were to be built from kits supplied by Western motor manufacturers, including Volkswagen, Renault, the Peugeot-Citroen-owned Chrysler UK, and British Leyland. These schemes, along with export deals involving oil supply facilities, machinery, transport equipment, generating plant, road and building construction, fertiliser production, textiles, and financial services, were all put at hazard by the revolution. And the British taxpayer was seen to be a most audacious gambler, since this vigorous enterprise on the part of British businessmen had been underwritten to the tune of £1 billion by the State-run Export Credits Guarantee Board.

That cool billion, however, was only a fraction of the taxpayer's involuntary stake, only accounting for around a third of Britain's export deals with Iran. The most dubious deals, the government-to-government arms contracts, were outside the ECGB's remit. The Shah was the British armaments industry's most important customer outside the NATO alliance, just as he was America's. Between them, Iran and the second biggest purchaser, Saudi Arabia, accounted for 60 per cent of British arms sales. Orders for billions of pounds worth of military facilities and equipment were on the books when the Shah was driven into exile, including 1325 tanks to the value of £500 million to add to the 900 tanks already delivered, 1000 tank-transporters, anti-aircraft missile batteries with a price-tag of £400 million, four naval vessels totalling £50 million in value, and a whole military-support industrial town to be built near Iran's second biggest city, Isfahan, at a cost of around £1 billion.

These colossal military deals were more dubious than the civil transactions on two accounts. For one thing, they raised more manifest and more exigent ethical questions. It is not possible honestly to consider the arms trade in the way commerce in general is treated, as a morally neutral issue *per se*, simply involving a bargain struck between buyer and seller. But even if such questions are pushed aside, for statesmen if not for merchants, there remains the question of sense. It can be argued that civil contracts are just a matter of business judgement, with which the State need not concern itself (even if that is no longer quite true when the normal risks of business enterprise are reduced or removed by government sponsorship). Military deals, on the other hand, concern in some measure the security and perhaps even the survival of the States that enter into them.

If such reflections seem like resounding statements of the obvious, that only highlights the magnitude of the folly we are considering. The Persia of Mohammed Reza Shah Pahlavi may have appeared admirably suited to the exercise of the talents of the *realpolitik* or tribal school of foreign policy pundits, uniting in one regime, as it seemed to each successive government, of whatever colour, in both Britain and the United States, both their strategic and their economic interests. But *realpolitik* depends for its temporal triumphs on the right reading of reality. Apart from the American-manufactured tragedy of Vietnam, in no other instance, in the whole course of the second half of the twentieth century, have the Western imperialists exhibited such unenlightened self-interest. That is, of course, to leave out of this chronicle of imprudence the monstrous misconception and miscalculation of waging the Cold War that subsumes and is the primal cause of most of their other foreign policy mistakes.

As the blood of insurrectionaries stained the city streets in Iran, the American President, Jimmy Carter, sent (on 11th November 1978) his Secretary of State, Cyrus Vance, National Security Assistant Zbigniew Brzezinski, and Admiral Turner, Director of the Central Intelligence Agency, a note of indignant protest at the poor quality of the intelligence reports he had received on the Iranian situation. A top secret CIA assessment of the situation in mid-August, for instance, came to the almost unbelievably complacent conclusions that 'there is dissatisfaction with the Shah's tight control of the political process, but this does not threaten the Government', that 'Iran is not in a revolutionary or even pre-revolutionary situation', and that 'those who are in opposition, both violent and non-violent, do not have the capability to be more than troublesome.' Apart from the irreconcilable fact that many independent observers, including the more perceptive media correspondents, were far from being so sanguine about the outcome of events (as any diligent newspaper reader could have attested), there was the huge irony that, in a country awash with Western agents listening intently for signs of Soviet aggression, the omnipresent clamour of internal revolutionary upheaval went unheard by imperialism's servants and their masters.

After the fall of the Shah, a wrangle ensued between two Yankee black-belts in the art of *realpolitik*. Dr Henry Kissinger attacked the Carter administration for largely causing, through indecisiveness and a mistimed human rights policy, what he saw as an unmitigated catastrophe. The Shah, he charged, had possessed the means to resist rebellion more strenuously but 'chose not to exercise them' because he had been demoralised by 'doubts about our real intentions'. In response to his interviewer's suggestion that faulty CIA reporting was responsible for America's failure to foresee the crisis in Iran, he showed his mettle as a practitioner of US power politics by skilfully blending pure *realpolitik* cynicism with a tenuous hold on reality. He absolved the CIA of blame and said that its 'emasculation' had weakened America's ability to influence events. Five years ago, he claimed, the Shah's opponents might really have feared CIA covert action. 'Now, realistically, they no longer do.'

Kissinger's salvo provoked a withering reply from George Ball, Under Secretary of State in two Democratic administrations and adviser to President Carter at the height of the crisis, who traced its origins back to 1972, when President Nixon, counselled by Kissinger himself, began to pander to the Shah's 'obsession with elegant weapons'. As a quid pro quo for his guaranteeing oil supplies to the Western powers and policing the Gulf on their behalf, Nixon undertook to provide him with arms to put down the Kurdish rebellion, to send him military advisers and technicians, and to sell him whatever non-nuclear weapons he chose. US arms sales to Iran rocketed from a total of $1.2 billion in the 22 years up to this point, to $19.5 billion during the next 7 years; the financial burden this imposed on Iran led to big cuts in construction and high unemployment. Eventually this economic hardship, coupled with widespread corruption in court circles and the Shah's megalomania, united practically the entire country against him. There was no way America could have kept 'a hated monarch' in power, Ball declared, throwing down the challenge: 'What would Kissinger have done? Sent the Sixth Fleet steaming up the Persian Gulf?'

If unintelligence and complacency characterised America's record in shoring up the Shah, the same is true of Britain's record, as is evident from David Owen's reply to questions in the House from Labour back-benchers expressing disquiet at the Government's failure to foresee the debacle. The most he would admit to was that the cohesiveness of the forces against the Shah might have been underestimated. But he saw this as a matter of judgement and rebutted suggestions that it reflected badly on the effectiveness of our intelligence-gathering services. In short, it could be said of this by no means unique instance, that it showed that the good doctor's conduct of foreign affairs was firmly based on wishful thinking.

There is, however, a lesson of much greater import and much wider relevance to be drawn from the comprehensive disaster that this was. The likelihood of such fatal mistakes is inherent in the restricted terms of reference of the *realpolitik* approach itself. It rules out those considerations of humanity that might alert its exponents to the insufferable nature of certain situations, which may in turn upset all their rigorously pragmatic calculations. When catastrophes ensue for the realpolitikers, it is nothing but poetic justice.

Speculating in *The Guardian* on the destiny of Iran after the Ayatollah Khomeini had replaced the Shah as the man at the helm, and setting his thoughts in the context of a Muslim world struggling like the Third World as a whole for change, Altaf Gauhar wrote: 'In the Third world there is a strong feeling of disappointment with Western Governments who never seem to be able to align themselves with the masses or with their movements.' As expectation such words would be unbearably naive; as a *cri de coeur* in commenting on the conduct of a Western government which purported to subscribe to the ideals and values of democratic socialism, they have irresistible force. Just once - and far too late - David Owen spoke for the Labour Movement as he should have spoken and acted all along, when he told the House: 'These last few months have seen a dramatic change in a country of pivotal importance. We will best maintain our interests and influence by being seen to respect the judgement of peoples of the region and by working with them as they shape their own destiny.' The sorry truth is, however, that in this pivotal period in the history of the Middle East and the Muslim world, the vision of the Labour leaders seldom rose much above those preoccupations that are proper in a nation of shopkeepers.

This 'batting for Britain' style of statesmanship that was to be so brazenly promoted in Thatcher's decade put the Labour leadership on a par with the Grub Street scribblers of the popular press, whose venal and insular perceptions were castigated by Altaf Gauhar:

> 'Unfortunately the whole movement in Iran has been seen by the Western media, mainly, in terms of its effects on the political and commercial interests of Britain and the USA. Not in terms of the human beings involved in the struggle. It was not the tyranny of the regime but the 'British billions at stake' which captured the headlines...To enlist the sympathy of the working classes the media obligingly translated each cancelled contract into number of jobs lost, thus strengthening the impression that Muslim agitators were adding to Britain's economic difficulties.'

With such pressing problems as rising unemployment and the balance of trade on their minds, it was not to be expected that much thought would be spared by Jim Callaghan and his team for the fate of the Persian peasantry and proletariat. But what a comment that is on the criteria for the conduct of foreign policy that represents conventional wisdom in all three of Britain's principal political parties! In Iran, throughout 1978, the blood of militant protest scarcely stopped flowing. 'Tanks won't save the tottering Peacock Throne', warned *The Guardian* in mid-August. The answer to the rioters and to the unacceptable demands for an Islamic theocracy, it said, 'lies in the liberalisation that the Shah says he is trying to pursue, together with a real movement toward the social justice that is supposedly the inspiration of the White Revolution. It does not lie with Chieftain tanks, for when you move an armoured column on one of your own cities you make a confession of abject failure that cannot be disguised.' Three weeks later, on 8th September, Iran's 'bloody Friday', upwards of 3,000 people were massacred by the Shah's soldiers and policemen in Jaleh Square, Tehran.

Relatives claiming their dead from the Behesht Zahra cemetery were charged 'bullet money', up to 3,000 rials (£36) for each bullet found in the bodies of the victims, *Guardian* correspondent Liz Thurgood reported in almost the last of a series of brilliant despatches that earned her the accolade of expulsion from the country. The Labour Government's idea of an appropriate response to 'bloody Friday' was a personal message from James Callaghan expressing sadness 'that the disturbances should have occurred just when Iran was moving steadily towards becoming a leading industrialised society' and hope that 'the violence will not interrupt Iran's progress towards democracy and the Shah's programme of liberalisation.' It assured the Shah that 'Iran's stability and prosperity is of key importance to her friends and allies.' In such wise did the Labour Prime Minister measure up to the highest traditions of responsible statesmanship.

His message was reinforced a couple of weeks later by the messenger himself, when Britain's ambassador in Tehran, Sir Anthony Parsons, made an apparently impromptu and certainly gratuitous speech of commendation at an international trade fair. 'My government,' he told the assembled customers, 'has been heartened by the determination which your government has shown to maintain the stability, security, and progress of Iran along the paths mapped out by the present monarchy. Iran is very important for my country. We wish your government well in these tasks.'

For Britain's Foreign Secretary, the Shah was 'our ally and our friend', and when in an interview on Independent Television's

Weekend World, on 22nd October, Brian Walden pointed out that British-built tanks were being used to suppress opposition on the streets of Iran's cities, Dr Owen, quite unabashed, answered: 'Can you simply take their money, sell them tanks, which you do for a strategic interest, sell them cars, persuade them to hold down the oil price in the interests of the world, generally exert influence with them, and then, when they come under attack, just back off? That is the type of political leadership for which I have total contempt.'

Tribune Group MP Russell Kerr, who with an American sociologist and an Italian Christian Democrat MP had formed an International Commission of Inquiry which spent ten days in Iran at the invitation of the Jurists' Committee of Iran, censured the British Government for 'attempting to shore up a bloody and detested regime' that was facing 'a revolutionary upheaval which we ignore at our peril.' Describing Owen as 'profoundly mistaken in his appraisal of what is going on in Iran,' he rebuked him for his remarks on *Weekend World*: 'It is not enough to say, "We stand by our friends in time of need." This is public schoolboy rubbish which does not enhance the reputation of the Foreign Secretary.'

As the Shah imposed military government on Iran, while simultaneously promising his people to banish 'injustice, corruption, and oppression' from his kingdom, the 'public schoolboy' foreign secretary, accepting the Shah's promissory note, assured the House that we now had a guarantee that in future the government would be based on the constitution and on social justice, divorced from tyranny and oppression. Arms shipments would continue, he told left-wing critics, in the interests of stability in the region, particularly in the light of the recent coup in Afghanistan.

Right up to the very bitter end, Owen remained as cocksure as Kissinger, 'neither repentant, nor even wise after the event', in the words of a *Guardian* article by Patrick Keatley charging the Callaghan administration with playing poodle to the American president. 'We will be perfectly content to be judged by history about whether or not we chose wisely in the national interest,' Owen told the House in a statement made after the shattering of the West's strategic jigsaw in the Middle East. He took this opportunity not only to decline Tribunite Stan Newens' invitation to admit that the policies of Britain and America in supporting autocratic and military government in the Gulf and refusing to recognise the democratic forces in the area had proved a complete failure, but to show no contrition at all for Britain's aggressive marketing of homicidal merchandise.

Such as it is, the rationale behind Dr Owen's stance with regard to Britain's strategic interests (a stance which made him not only staunchly resist strong and constant pressure from the Left to stop arms shipments, but even to reject, until less than a fortnight before the Shah threw in the sponge, the calls for him to advise cancellation of the Queen's projected three-day visit to Iran - a February fixture, with Kuwait and Oman as the other targets, in her upmarket promotion of British goods in the Gulf) was his thinking concerning the forces most likely to succeed to power if the Shah fell. When the Tory right-winger Jonathan Aitken invited him to agree with the Shah's allegation that the recent violence had been stirred up by outside Marxist and Communist troublemakers, the Foreign Secretary dismissed it as a simplification. Yet his own assessment given in the *Weekend World* interview was not so different and exhibited the same brain-numbing addiction to Cold War prejudices. 'I believe it would not be in the interests of this country or the West for the Shah to be toppled,' he told Brian Walden. 'He would be toppled initially by a very Right-wing movement that would soon be disrupted by the Left, and the Left is really Communism and the Soviet Union, and some odd terrorist groupings.'

In part this echoed the 'keep firm hold of nurse' admonitions that emanated from Whitehall to counter criticism of Callaghan's letter of support for the Shah - admonitions that highlighted the reactionary and obscurantist nature of much of the Iranian opposition and pointed out that this put in jeopardy the Shah's whole programme of liberalisation. The truth of this assessment of the rebel forces is not to be denied. However, neither approval of the sound of Iran's *vox populi* nor pretensions to prophecy should have become the mainsprings of British foreign policy. With regard to the latter, even such a wise observer as Altaf Gauhar was disastrously wrong about the course of a revolution in which the warnings of the watchers in Whitehall were fulfilled as ayatollahs came to call all the shots.

And as for approval, in a leader published on the morning after Dr Owen, apologising for the imposition of military government in Iran, faced fusillades from his own back benches and more lethal flattery from the Opposition for his 'robust support' for the Shah, *The Guardian* rightly counselled: 'The stock in trade of British political discourse - moderate, democratic, conservative, reactionary - needs adjustment before it is exported to Iran.' Wisdom (even of the limited, pragmatic sort we call 'enlightened self-interest'), as well as humanity - not to mention fidelity to democratic socialism - would have lain in being guided all along by the principle Owen ultimately enunciated: not, with the *hubris* of imperialism, to seek to determine the fate of a foreign people, but honestly to help them shape their own destiny.

It might be argued that the ultimate futility of the *realpolitik* practised in the Gulf by US, British and Soviet administrations in the seventies was only fully demonstrated a decade later. Then the despotic Ba'athist ruler of Iraq, chosen as a substitute for the Shah in the case of the first two global meddlers and seen as an acceptable surrogate for Soviet-style socialism by the third, to keep revolutionary Islamic forces at bay, turned out to be not a mere monster, but a Frankenstein's monster, out of control of the imperialists of both East and West who had created him. We are still asking: 'When will they ever learn?'

CHAPTER 16

Bulldog in the China market

'Don't help on the big chariot.
You will only make yourself dusty.'
Chinese proverb

'"What did you learn in school today,
Dear little boy of mine?"
"I learned that Washington never told a lie;
I learned that soldiers seldom die;
I learned that everybody's free;
And that's what the teacher said to me.
That's what I learned in school today,
That's what I learned in school."

"What did you learn in school today,
Dear little boy of mine?
"I learned our government must be strong;
It's always right and never wrong.
Our leaders are the finest men
And we elect them again and again.
That's what I learned in school today,
That's what I learned in school."'
**From a song by Tom Paxton,
sung by Pete Seeger in the Carnegie Hall, 1963**

The Callaghan Government's third spectacular in the sorcerer's-apprentice school of statecraft - the feverish bid to sell Harrier jump-jets to China - shows just how muddle-headed, illogical, and threadbare of carefully-considered and consistently-pursued long-term objectives its foreign policy was. The soliciting hit the headlines when Britain's Chief of Defence Staff, Sir Neil Cameron, despatched to Beijing to outbid alluring arms sales propositions from the French, discarded diplomatic discretion and civil service protocol in his eagerness to clinch a deal. 'We both have an enemy at our doors whose capital is Moscow,' he told officers of the 6th Tank Division stationed near Beijing. 'Some of our problems are different, but one thing is absolutely clear to us, and that is the growing strength of the Soviet tank force. We must share, I believe, our common experience so that we are in the best position to take on the Soviet tank force if this should ever be necessary.'

His king-sized gaffe, which he self-importantly described as legitimate discussion of ' defence philosophy', provoked calls for his dismissal from the Labour left on the grounds that it damaged the West's objectives of détente and disarmament pacts with the Soviet Union and that it was an intolerable incursion into the Government's province of policy-making. As *The Guardian* pointed out, in an editorial that was curiously cautious over the issue of whether the Government should dispense with Sir Neil's services, considering that it rightly reproved him for his 'melodramatic and over-simplified way of thinking about the way great power relationships work', President Carter had recently sacked a four-star general for publicly disagreeing with official US policy on South Korea. *Pravda's* comment was more caustic: it cast Sir Neil in the role of the Russian folklore character that symbolises folly, the 'drunken hare'.

The fusillade from the Left provided the Opposition with a field-day to wave the flag and scatter-bomb the mutineers with innuendoes of treason. Disregarding the heterogeneous nature of Sir Neil's critics, who were not confined to the Left, let alone to the few who could fairly be-called 'fellow-travellers', and without admitting that no government could allow itself to be seen as letting its servants determine its policies, shadow defence spokesman Sir Ian Gilmour, speaking on the BBC's *World at One* programme, charged the critics in the Government's ranks with providing capital for Soviet propaganda: 'The pro-Soviet lobby in the Labour Party has got off the mark very quickly - as it always does - and they, of course, are not really on our side.' Labour's top brass moved swiftly, if not adroitly, to defuse the incident, the Prime Minister and the Foreign Secretary both assuring the House that nothing had changed with respect to our relations with either China or the Soviet Union, and that policy was as firmly as ever in the hands of Government ministers. Defence Secretary Fred Mulley blandly declared that, although he would have advised the Defence Chief against using the word 'enemy' if he had had the opportunity to do so: 'There is nothing in the impromptu remarks that Sir Neil made that suggests it should diminish my confidence in him as my chief military adviser.'

The show ran and ran throughout the year, with an ever-growing cast and an ever-thickening plot in which it became more and more difficult to decide who was the seducer and who the seduced. During the last quarter of 1978 mandarins popped up in Whitehall like messages in a Chinese box: in October, Foreign Minister Huang Hua (he who, in one sequence of China's stately courtship dance with the West and its allies, had visited the Shah of Persia on the eve of the Jaleh Square massacre - which was *not* a promising omen!); in November, Wang Chen, Vice-Premier in charge of industrial production; in December, Lu Tung, who, as head of China's Third Ministry of Machine Building, was in effect the country's aviation minister.

In February 1979 Britain's Industry Secretary, Eric Varley, returned the visits, with a retinue of high-powered industrialists representing British Aerospace, Rolls-Royce (which was already giving China a helping hand in its efforts to make 'a great leap forward' by signing a contract for the supply of Spey supersonic engines and licensing their local manufacture), British Shipbuilders, the National Coal Board, and engineering groups Acrow and John Brown. The prize had grown ever more alluring, Varley coming home with a two-way trade agreement with a tantalising £7 billion worth of come-ons. It was the French, the Germans, and the Americans, however, who were actually receiving all the favours. And two weeks before the Callaghan Government fell, it was announced that Dr David Owen himself would go to Beijing in the fond hope of a consummation of Britain's courtship.

What makes following these mah-jong manoeuvres more than a trivial leisure pursuit is their deadly serious context, implicating in the final analysis not just company profits nor even just jobs, but the fate of the whole world. It may have simply been par for the course for a businessman like Sir Kenneth Keith, chairman of Rolls-Royce, to maintain (as recorded by Hugh Hebert in a *Guardian* article tellingly entitled 'Can we enjoy both profits and peace?') that the nation's economic self-interest overrode all moral considerations and to tender as if it were sterling coinage the exceedingly droll Chinese claim that 'Never in our long history have we been aggressive,' to which this real life Undershaft added the clinching argument: 'They've always paid on the nail.' But the intellectual calibre of Sir Kenneth's comments no more measured up to the standards required for the successful handling of the country's foreign affairs than had Sir Neil's. Business acumen untrammelled by too many moral scruples might seem like a sound basis for practical politics, but the intelligent practice of *realpolitik* demands something more, as the careers of not a few migrants from commerce to politics attest.

However much they might have shared Sir Kenneth's viewpoint, though, even the most hard-nosed of ministers could not afford to be so dismissive of the moral issues raised by arms sales to China, since for presentational reasons concern for human rights had to be high on the agenda of the Labour Movement. The tragedy is that, for Labour's party and trade union leaders, bread-and-butter and polling considerations have again and again made it difficult in practice to distinguish between the attitudes of Capital and the attitudes of labour and of Labour. Jobs are inescapably hostage to business profits in the kingdom of capitalism. The welfare of the British working class is in every sense a legitimate and primary concern for Labour; but when it is based on relegating human rights for other peoples to the 'isn't it a pity' category of concern, Socialism is shamed and travestied. When the international committee of the Labour Party's NEC passed a motion calling for a review of policy on arms sales and protesting at the Government's decision to sell Harriers to China (with Tony Benn scourging his Cabinet colleagues for their hypocrisy in rightly condemning offences against civil liberties in the Soviet Union and giving them as a reason for the embargo on selling arms to the Russians, while overlooking China's equally unpalatable record on human rights), the Electrical, Electronic, Telecommunications and Plumbing Union denounced the committee for acting in restraint of trade! 'While Britain is trying to establish trade with China, the National Executive Committee seems intent on disrupting relations as much as possible,' thundered the EETPU, one of whose executive committee members, Eric Hammond (later to win renown in the great miners' strike of 1984 and the Wapping print workers' war of 1986) played the part of tribune of the British workers in the Varley delegation to Beijing.

It was not only with regard to China itself that the embarrassing issue of human rights became entangled with more pressing considerations of commerce and geopolitics. In its handling of diplomatic and trade relations in China's backyard (to adopt a term beloved of American imperialists) the Callaghan Government was also successful in sending a series of conflicting signals about the importance it attached to human rights. The Opposition's attacks on its subsidised shipbuilding for Vietnam (a policy which was also criticised when applied to Poland and India) were brushed aside with the argument that it was vital to save British shipbuilding from devastation during a period of world-wide slump in the industry. Yet when, on Christmas Day 1978, Vietnam, after repeated incursions into its territory by Khmer Rouge forces, launched a full-scale invasion of Cambodia and, a fortnight later, Vietnam-backed Khmer rebels overran the capital, Phnom Penh, Britain's Labour leaders joined in the chorus of indignation conducted by the US Government. On 13th February Judith Hart announced in the Commons that, with the exception of the agreements to supply cargo ships and gas turbines, which would be adhered to 'because of the contractual implications', bilateral aid to Vietnam would cease.

Needless to say, the Vietnamese regime was no paragon in the matter of human rights. However, not only did its record, on the worst estimate, compare favourably with China's, but its trespasses in this field paled into insignificance when set against the horrific crimes perpetrated by the Khmer Rouge against their own countrymen. Whatever the motives of the Vietnamese in invading Cambodia - and obviously they were for the most part rooted in what they conceived their national interest to be - to many Cambodians they came as liberators from torment and slavery. By its callous indifference to the terrible fate that had overtaken the Cambodian people, the Callaghan Government set the tone for the Tory governments that followed. The latter, in contradiction to the normal practice of British governments, refused to recognise the *de facto* government that took over in Phnom Penh and continued to treat the delegates of the infamous Khmer Rouge as the legitimate representatives of Kampuchea (as the country was now designated) at the United Nations. In such a contemptible imposture did the world at large collude for the next decade and more, to the very grave detriment of the Khmer people.

It is true that the full horror of the concentration-camp 'utopia' created by the Khmer Rouge in the fervent belief that they were constructing a society of pure communism was only revealed later by 'maverick' journalists like John Pilger (the Western media's general conspiracy of silence, suppression, and distortion in the face of Khmer Rouge 'heart of darkness' barbarism is itself a story that might well engender despair for mankind). But, belated though it was, enough of it came out in the columns of the more reputable

British papers, as the country was liberated from its silent agony, to deprive the Callaghan Government of the excuse of ignorance for its contemptible policy decisions concerning Kampuchea. Even Prince Norodom Sihanouk, that prince of opportunists (formerly king-pin in Phnom Penh, then held under house arrest by the Pol Pot Government until the day before the capital fell to the Vietnamese-backed rebels), now spoke of that 'Hitlerian and bloodstained regime...under which nearly three and a half million citizens had died from hunger, thirst, sickness, and brutality' and vowed he would not co-operate with the Khmer Rouge - though he subsequently sacrificed his finer feelings in the higher interests of his country and the hope of returning to power again. Moreover, in June 1978 the International Federation of Human Rights had issued a damning report, indicting the Khmer Rouge for mass executions, forced labour, and causing famine and disease.

China countered the Vietnamese invasion of Kampuchea, which rapidly drove the Khmer Rouge forces to the borders of Thailand, by a punitive incursion across the northern frontier of Vietnam. The Soviet Union responded by despatching a missile cruiser and other warships to the Gulf of Haiphong as a warning to China that it would not abandon its ally. As a mocking fate would have it, the Chinese attack (involving according to first reports around 150,000 men) came just three days before Varley's caravan of upmarket commercial travellers was due in Beijing. But while this spot of vexation in the Orient generated some worried expressions in Whitehall and an intensified insistence on the essentially 'defensive' character of the formidable Harrier (which, quite apart from the equivocal nature of all such claims, was authoritatively challenged by Anthony Barnett in a *Guardian* article, pointing out how effective jump-jets could be in enforcing China's claims to the Spratly Group of islands, most of which were held by the Vietnamese and lay in an area of the South China Sea where oil had been discovered), it did not dampen the salesmen's spirits as the £7 billion trade target was agreed. No more than its totally alien attitude to civil liberties and human rights, its accumulation of a nuclear arsenal, and its blunt rejection of notions of détente with the other great 'Communist' empire, did China's act of belligerence deter the Labour Government from seeking to sell it the means to enhance and exercise its power. In this respect the record of the Callaghan Government is hardly to be distinguished from that of any other British government before or since.

Apart from the commercial and national economy incentives for its attitude, there were three other reasons for its morally unwarranted discrimination against Vietnam and in favour of China and its Khmer Rouge protégés over these clashes in Indo-China. The most ostensible reason was the importance of upholding international law in a case involving the violation of a country's national sovereignty and interference in its internal affairs. But to take this explanation seriously one would need to drink oneself witless from a large bottle clearly labelled GULLIBILITY. For one thing, as already pointed out, the customary practice with regard to the recognition of foreign governments (which has nothing to do with approval but a great deal to do with common sense) was contradicted in the case of liberated Kampuchea. And for another, this refusal of recognition was wholly inconsistent with the ready acceptance of the overthrow, by an alliance of rebels and foreign troops (Tanzanian), of another monstrous regime, that of Idi Amin in Uganda - to cite but one recent instance in which outside interference had been gladly tolerated.

Of the other two reasons, one was covert and craven, namely, Britain's acquiescence in America's vindictiveness towards Vietnam. Commenting on this shameful vendetta of the world's most powerful nation against the Third World pygmy that, at a devastating cost to itself, had defeated it, *Guardian* correspondent John Gittings pointed out that the Hanoi regime had been driven into signing the 1978 'Treaty of Friendship' with the Soviet Union by Washington's rejection of every overture Vietnam had made since the end of the war in April 1975. Not even Vietnam's dropping of the demand for reparations for the devastation caused by American military might made Washington relent. On the contrary, in the spring of 1978 the United States vetoed a proposal to channel funds for the reconstruction of Vietnam through the Asian Development Bank. Washington and Beijing were on the point of exchanging ambassadors when China attacked Vietnam, and President Carter promptly reassured the Chinese that the invasion would not affect the normalisation of Sino-American relations, which was 'already an accomplished fact'. According to *The Washington Post*, Beijing was even tipped off in advance that US displeasure would be purely formal, so that its unavoidable public condemnation would neither cause loss of face to the Chinese nor make Washington open to charges of collusion in the attack on Vietnam.

The third non-commercial reason for Britain's less than beguiling behaviour in the Far Eastern farrago was the perfectly open geopolitical objective that had lain at the heart of her foreign policy since the start of the Cold War, and that has had such disastrous consequences, most dramatically in the Middle East: the containment of the Soviet Union and her allies. But even if we accept the bunker mentality of the leading Cold War protagonists in the Western camp in order to judge on their own terms the success of their actual conduct of foreign affairs, the verdict that forces itself on one's mind is ineptitude elevated to the level of folly. The Soviet Union was sufficiently exercised by the prospective sale of jump-jets (which were after all not just high-tech aircraft but unique war machines) to China to make a formal protest, followed by two personal letters from President Brezhnev to Prime Minister Callaghan. British pique at being rebuked and squeals of 'Russian propaganda' in no way detracted from the essential truth of the statement put out by the Soviet news agency, Tass: 'To supply arms to a country whose leadership frantically attacks the idea of détente and preaches the inevitability and even desirability of a new world war means, willy nilly, encouraging the militarism of the Maoists.'

Putting in a strong bid to win the competition for authorship of the most fatuous statement ever made by a British foreign secretary, Dr David Owen told the House that while the sale of Harriers to China could affect our policy of a continuation of détente with Russia, 'What is important is how we ourselves view our foreign policy.' Lest this standing of the truth upon its head should not be deemed a sufficiently dazzling feat, he followed it up with a spot of prestidigitation. No doubt to a generally prejudiced audience his sharp asseveration that 'we must not allow any third country to dictate the scope of our foreign policy' seemed eminently reasonable. But we have only to substitute for the word 'dictate' a word more truthfully reflecting the situation, viz. 'influence', to see that to react to the Russian protest in such an affronted manner was not only simply ridiculous but a negation of rational conduct in the handling of foreign affairs. Still not content with his astonishing performance, Dr Owen tossed into the brew the question-begging non sequitur, 'We want a deeper relationship with China and defence must form part of a balanced development of our relations.' When it was announced, in mid-March of 1979, that he was to go to Beijing in the hopes of clinching a deal, he told the

Indian Journalists Association in London: 'We want to improve Sino-British relations, but not at the expense of our relations with the Soviet Union.' Which was a bit like saying: 'We want to be friends with both God and the Devil', since each of the two pseudo-Marxist leviathans viewed itself as the former and its rival as the latter.

Jim Callaghan showed equally alarming signs of believing he could have his cake and eat it. At a summit meeting of Western leaders in Guadeloupe in January 1979 he joined President Carter, President Giscard d'Estaing, and Chancellor Schmidt in pledging their governments to do everything possible to encourage ratification of the new strategic arms limitation treaty (SALT II) being negotiated between the United States and the Soviet Union. But this unequivocal endorsement of détente had no visible effect on his policy *vis-á-vis* China. 'We must reassure the Soviet Union that we do not have a Chinese card to play,' he told reporters. Yet that was exactly what he had been doing and what he continued to do. Ready enough to accuse the Russians of deeds incompatible with their words, he acted as if he gave no credence at all to Russian fears of Western intentions. In this he showed far less wisdom than some of his own left-wingers and, for example, than such a non-partisan pressure group as the Church and Nation Committee of the Church of Scotland. Its report to the Kirk's General Assembly in May 1978, had pleaded for understanding that the military posture of the Western powers was seen by the Warsaw Pact powers as at least as threatening as their own military capability appeared to the West. Furthermore, the committee pointed out that whereas the Communist world seemed to many in the West a threat to their freedom, many people on the other side of the Iron Curtain saw NATO as an integral part of a basically unjust economic system.

CHAPTER 17

No retreat for Cold War warriors

'The confusion between being 'Left' and being 'East' is over. With the end of this confusion the best defence of contemporary capitalism is broken.'
Royden Harrison, Emeritus Professor of Social History, Warwick University (19th December 1989)

Halfway through the Anglo-Chinese courtship dance, in November l978, Labour's NEC published a discussion document entitled *Cold Peace, Soviet Power and Western Security.* The paper challenged many of the basic assumptions of establishment-thinking in the West about the Cold War, in particular that it was the Soviet Union that had set the pace in the arms race and in the introduction of new weapons systems and that it had overtaken the West in military power. No apology for the Soviet viewpoint, the document conceded that the Soviet build-up had overstepped the legitimate requirements of national security but declared that this was equally true of the West. The authors' primary concern was in fact to show that, as is commonly the case in conflicts between nation-states, the assumptions of those on each side were mirror-images of those on the other, to the serious prejudice of sane thinking. 'There is, of course, the easy assumption in ruling circles in the West that Western purposes are self-evidently peaceful and benign. No doubt the same spirit of self-righteousness informs thinking in the Kremlin.'

In their strictures on what we might call the beam-and-mote syndrome in both camps, the authors were notably restrained. They spoke in the manner of liberal humanitarians and denied themselves the right of those who subscribed (as they did) to a Socialist value-system to denounce the exploitation of Third World countries and peoples by Western capitalism and Western States indulging in economic imperialism, as the following passage on the conflict of Soviet and Western interests in the Third World shows:

'Soviet interference in the Third World is ascribed to a desire to export communism, to incorrigible

expansionism or to the irresistible exploitation of
sensitive situations. Western conduct, in contrast, is
usually described as legitimate efforts to foster their
interests and protect their security and well-being, and
that of the world as a whole. This reasoning is not very
persuasive. It quite conveniently ignores Western,
particularly American, activities in foreign countries
which less partial observers may conclude are at least as
culpable as Soviet ones.'

Even without wholly warranted conviction of the capitalist
'democracies' on the charge of economic gang-rape and robbery
in foreign lands (to leave out of the indictment crimes committed
in their own countries), these arguments are cogent, as the swiftest
of surveys will show. Omitting from the balance sheet the three
regions in which it might be argued US foreign policy has had the
most malign consequences of all, namely, Latin America, the Far
East and the Middle East, let us limit consideration to the two
superpower cockpits of Africa and Afghanistan in which (as Labour
and its dream were wasting away in Britain) the Soviet Union and
its allies were branded by the West as unquestionably the aggressors.
In the explosive Horn of Africa the Americans first intervened on
the side of Ethiopia, in order to counter the arming of Somalia by
the Russians, then on the side of Somalia when it expelled the
Russians, who promptly switched their support to Ethiopia. In short,
unbridled *realpolitik* governed equally the geopolitical manoeuvring
of both superpowers.

In Angola, on the other hand, it was the United States, not
the Soviet powers, which was the first to intervene in an internal
struggle for power that Stephen Ambrose attributes to 'major ethnic
and tribal cleavages' rather than to 'ideological splits over
communism versus capitalism', as the civil war was represented
by establishment-thinking in the West. As a matter of fact, in support
of one or other of the three main contenders for power, no less than
twenty foreign States were happy to trample on the diplomatic
precept of non-interference in another country's internal affairs.
Of the trespassers seven were black African States and one white-
ruled (South Africa), three were NATO members (the USA, France,
and West Germany), and one (Israel) was a US dependant. Of the
eight Communist States that meddled, five (the USSR and its allies)

supported the side that came out on top and three (China, North Korea, and Romania) supported their opponents. That there is precious little cause for self-righteousness and much reason for treating the whole affair as a particularly cynical example of global power politics is underlined in one particular passage of Ambrose's account in *Rise to Globalism*:

> 'American military aid, eventually totalling about $60 million, was sent secretly into Angola by the CIA via Mobuto in Zaire...In addition to [illegally] sending in advisers, the CIA made a de facto alliance with South Africa, which entered the conflict with regular army troops in September 1975. This was the first time South Africa had involved itself in a war in black Africa. It brought about a situation in which Washington, Pretoria, and Peking were fighting side by side, surely a record of some sort for politics making strange bedfellows.'

As for Afghanistan, that thumping headache for the British Raj in earlier times, it provides us with a Spanish-onion-sized opportunity to examine irony after irony as we peel off the concealing skins of moral outrage, clarion calls to defend freedom, and sundry other scraps of puffed-up rhetoric and rationalisation brought to the boil by the Soviet Union's accelerating intervention (so like America's in Vietnam) during 1978-79. But I will restrict myself to mentioning just two of the bigger ironies exposed in this episode. First there was the irony that a resurgent Islam was challenging the economic and strategic interests of both the superpowers, in America's case through revolution in Iran, in Russia's through civil war in Afghanistan. Which, of course, only compounded the irony that Washington, so sensitive to instability in its own so-called 'backyard' of Central America, was either too dumb to appreciate or too dishonest to acknowledge the apprehensions of the Kremlin at the threat posed by Islamic fundamentalism on the march in two big countries with frontiers contiguous to its own mainly Muslim-populated 'Soviet republics'.

The Labour Party discussion document referred to above appeared in a period of heightened Cold War hysteria. There were causes for this on both sides, and as each 'defensive' stratagem was answered by a counter-measure, the rationality of each side's fear was evidently confirmed. Thus misgiving mounted. In the Soviet camp, fear of American hegemony was heightened by the development of the neutron bomb to a stage where it only needed the US President's go-ahead for production to begin. (This bomb was designed in particular to stop tanks in their tracks by wiping out their crews, and thus aimed at counterbalancing the Warsaw Pact's numerical superiority in armour. It was dubbed by some 'the capitalists' bomb' because of its greater respect for property than for people! According to President Brezhnev, the Soviet Union had also invented this weapon, but had renounced its development.) Then the old Bolshevik fear of encirclement was magnified by the rapprochement between the NATO powers and a Communist China stockpiling nuclear weapons, bidding for superpower status, and now hostile to its big brother.

In the West lurid press reports of Soviet Russia's alleged aggressive intentions towards 'the free world' probably did far more to whip up anti-Soviet feelings than did the assiduous (and wholly justified) monitoring of the Soviet States' repression of their own citizens. Surely this must be so, if we are to judge by the fact that public opinion in the 'democracies' did not seem to be excessively exercised by human rights abuses in capitalist dictatorships like Argentina and Chile - except when the victims were European or American citizens. And the captive audience in the West was largely spared the distress it might have been caused had the Western media conscientiously reported the stream of true horror stories about life under Communist China's despotic gerontocracy, Kampuchea's genocidal Pol Pot regime, or the Orwellian Romania of Nicolae Ceausescu. May we never willingly collaborate with those who, like he did, would have us forget and obliterate the past. So let us forever remember that in July 1978 this egomaniacal tyrant was actually accorded by our Queen and her Labour ministers the full honours of a State Visit to Britain.

To cite just three scare stories - circulating during the first quarter of 1978 - as examples of the unflagging campaign to buttress the credibility of Cold War ideology and policies:

1) there were reports (branded by Tass as lies invented to justify the Western military build-up in general and plans to deploy the neutron bomb in particular) that Soviet scientists were

200

developing new strains of killer virus and microbes for military use;

2) unattributable 'intelligence sources' fed the press an imaginative scenario said to be based on NATO insight into Russian plans for a possible thrust into northern Norway by overwhelmingly superior forces deploying rocket-launched chemical weapons;

3) Swedish intelligence agencies warned that at least thirty-six West European cities could be destroyed by six Russian nuclear submarines that had been moved from the Arctic base of Kola to the Baltic port of Libau in Latvia. (To a populace conditioned to believe that a pre-emptive strike sparking off a third world war was to be feared only from 'the other side', the latter report was more likely to impress than President Carter's statement - designed to disarm critics of his arms control policies! - that just one of America's Poseidon submarines, representing less than two per cent of its total nuclear arsenal, could destroy every large and medium-sized city in the Soviet Union.)

In this climate of paranoia concerning Soviet intentions, it was hardly surprising to learn of the launching by 148 members of Congress, in conjunction with numerous illuminati with academic, military, or intelligence 'qualifications', of a bipartisan 'Coalition of Peace through Strength' campaign designed 'to reverse the unilateral disarmament trend which has made the United States militarily inferior to the Soviet Union.' This was notwithstanding the fact that the second of these assertions was not justified by the evidence available and the first was wholly ludicrous. What was even more alarming was the re-emergence of a school of thought maintaining that it was possible to wage and survive a limited nuclear war between the superpowers; that this was precisely what the Russians were preparing for, through the construction of highly-protected command and communication centres which would ensure continuity of government in such an emergency; and that the United States must follow suit.

The thinking - if we are prepared to call it that - behind this call for an urgent reappraisal of America's defence strategy (which incidentally was echoed in Britain by a Tory think-tank calculation that some fifteen million lives might be saved in the event of an unheralded nuclear engagement if civil defence were taken seriously) was that the younger generation of Soviet generals might believe in and successfully advocate a 'war-fighting' doctrine, since they were not old enough to remember the trauma of the Second World War, with its millions of Soviet dead. Both President Carter's National Security Adviser, Dr Zbigniew Brzezinski, and his Defence Secretary, Harold Brown, evidently found it conceivable that the Russians could calmly contemplate a nuclear engagement with the United States. On 25th January 1979, in his annual report on America's military situation, Brown announced a change of strategy from the 'assured destruction' of large Soviet cities to one aiming to include the targeting of every Soviet missile silo. In most pitiable words, he told Congress: 'It is tempting to believe, I realise, that the US threat to destroy a number of cities - along with their population and industry - will serve as an all-purpose deterrent. Unfortunately, however, a strategy based on assured destruction alone is no longer credible.'

Perhaps one should have expected an ambulance to drive up to Capitol Hill, and men in white coats to take the speaker away; but that would be to dream of a normal world in which sanity reigned outside the asylums. For as long as it lasts the human race should never forget that only by unmerited grace or incredible chance did it survive the forty-year stand-off between the two great nuclear-armed camps which we call the Cold War. During this period of purgatory that blighted the lives of a generation and more the avoidance of direct and catastrophic confrontation between the superpowers was perpetually balanced on the knife-edge of that lunatic 'defence' doctrine of 'mutual assured destruction', so appositely giving us the acronym MAD. (Nor should it be forgotten that this period of so-called peace was a lot more like the post-war world of Orwell's nightmare scenario in *Nineteen Eighty-Four* than Cold War warriors would willingly admit.) And during those long death-row years in which mankind seemed to many to be merely enjoying a stay of execution, *no one*, outside the ranks of the *im*moderates - secular or religious peace campaigners, libertarian socialists, and other out-on-a-limb advocates of alternative societies - seriously questioned the sanity of our nuclear statesmen, who are now so ready to congratulate themselves on having saved the world from destruction through their strength of purpose. With such a cornucopia of 'overkill' facilities still at the disposal of our leaders, we dare not say more than that the threat of Armageddon appears to have receded a little. But at least the MAD doctrine is no longer confidently proclaimed as the rock upon which we should build our hopes of salvation from the annihilation of the human race.

If the Cold War is now over, we owe the thaw which brought it to an end above all to Mikhail Gorbachev, whose essential sanity was shown, for example, by these words, spoken to an International Peace Forum in Moscow in February 1978: 'The nuclear powers must step out from the nuclear shadow, and enter a nuclear-free world, *thus ending the alienation of politics from the general norms of ethics.*' [my emphasis] If only they can hang in there long enough, most politicians are the beneficiaries of the extraordinary amnesia of electorates. The world and his wife are not greatly noted for their long memories, so that the many bad and foolish deeds of their political masters are generally soon forgiven through sheer forgetfulness, while the few good and wise ones are seldom indelibly marked up to their credit. Thus it came about that within two years of the revolutions of 1989 and the collapse of the Iron Curtain, Gorbachev had been ditched by the Russian people in favour of another drunken hare, just as President Carter had been, in November 1980, by the citizens of 'God's own country'.

All the same, it is as clear as daylight where the vision was in those critical years of 1978-79 that might have marked a new beginning for the world. Not for Britain alone were the eighties a lost decade; but looking back on Labour's last chance to pursue, if not a Socialist, at least a positively humanitarian foreign policy, it becomes all too evident that its leaders lacked the vision and the courage to let go of their Cold War certainties. (Indeed, the wry truth is that Brezhnev, the procrustean-seeming potentate of the Soviet Union - whom no one would ever accuse of allowing policy decisions to be unduly influenced by humanitarian considerations - had a clearer insight of where a saner future lay. His foreign minister, that great survivor Andrei Gromyko, even showed, in a speech pleading for significant disarmament made to the UN General Assembly in September 1978, that the Russian leaders fully understood the connection between the arms race and world poverty.) Add the fact that, in the proper Labour tradition, the leaders behaved towards the Party in the manner of managers insisting on their right to manage company and workforce, and no movement out of the mental morass was conceivable. Ironically, it was the Party's dissidents whose thinking on détente was genuinely in tune with that of the leader of the Western alliance, Jimmy Carter.

For example, the authors of the NEC document cited above concluded that the commitment of the Soviet Union to détente was 'firm and deep-seated' and their general stance was more supportive of Carter's central foreign policy objective of securing an arms control agreement with the Soviet Union than the lip-service of the Labour leaders as they sought to play their 'China card'. Just how closely in sympathy Carter and the Labour left was is shown by a marvellously candid concession Carter made to 'the other feller's point of view' in a television interview in November 1978, in the course of which he contended that the Soviet Union was no more expansionist than the United States, and went on:

> 'They want peace and security for their own people, and they undoubtedly exaggerate any apparent threats to themselves. They have to be sure that they protect themselves. At the same time, as is the case with us, they would like to expand their influence among other people in the world, believing that their system of government - their philosophy - is the best.'

In short, both Carter and the Labour left were disposed to believe Brezhnev when he said he was seeking 'irreversible détente' and appealed for peaceful coexistence based on trust and confidence between nations to replace the uneasy truce based on the balance of terror provided by the nuclear arsenals of East and West. There was nothing naive in this disposition to believe. It was not wishful thinking. On the contrary, it was rooted in sanity, reason, imagination, the capacity to empathise, and the courage *not* to believe the worst of one's enemies, however at variance their value-systems might seem. For instance, the very fact adduced by the embattled right in the West as an argument for stepping up the arms race - that the Soviet Union was devoting far more of its productive capacity to manufacturing arms than the United States - was susceptible to less paranoiac and more intelligent interpretations. Reporting from Washington on thinking in the US Arms Control and Disarmament Agency, Jonathan Steele wrote, in April 1978:

> 'The view of senior ACDA officials is that the present Soviet leadership is genuinely anxious for strategic arms control. The Russians spend twice as large a proportion of their gross national product on defence as the US.

> The drain is causing increasing consumer problems. Secondly, the present leadership has made a political commitment to the new SALT treaty, and cannot face the alternative of failure. Throughout the 1976 [presidential] election when the Americans were stalling, the Russians continued to push for a treaty. Thirdly - and not necessarily the least important reason - the Russians are afraid that if the arms race goes ahead unchecked, they will lose.'

Even in the case of the USA, 'defence' expenditure, running at 25 per cent of GNP, represented a prodigious waste of the country's resources. For the Soviet Union, trying to keep up was a crippling burden. In Machiavellian minds, indeed, such a calculation may have been considered a conclusive argument for stepping up the arms race, and - mirroring the maxim they pinned on to and professed to despise in their ideological enemies, that 'the end justifies the means' - it may have wholly excused to themselves the lies they told about the military strength of the Warsaw Pact powers.

President Carter's efforts to bring more safety, more sanity, and more humanity into the world have seldom attracted the credit they deserve. That, with the notable exception of the Camp David accord between Israel and Egypt, they were mostly fruitless is arguably more the fault of his 'friends' than of his foes. His sheer perseverance in seeking a new Strategic Arms Limitation Treaty to update SALT I was admirable, even though the bizarre fact must never be overlooked that both SALT I and SALT II (which was signed by Carter and Brezhnev in June 1979 but never ratified by the US Senate!), far from being *dis*armament agreements, were only agreements to limit the multiplication of overkill.

History bears out those who were capable of calmly considering a geopolitical situation in which the 'Communist' powers were if anything even more 'cabin'd, cribb'd, confined' than their 'democratic' enemies. It does not vindicate the more frenzied fears of such Cold War addicts as the astounding Dr Henry Kissinger. In an interview published in *The Economist* in February 1979 Kissinger said that a general nuclear war was unthinkable and would be an 'abdication of moral and political responsibility'. But the main thrust of his argument - that the world 'could be heading into a period of maximum peril' since 'the Soviet Union may perceive a period [of five to seven years]...in which its military power is potentially dominant' and that therefore the United States, instead of increasing its ability to retaliate against a Soviet attack, should strengthen its counter-force capability of destroying military forces targeted against the West - could be taken as supporting the case for a lower nuclear threshold, pre-emptive strikes, and a winnable mini-nuclear war.

Moreover, given his Metternich-like subscription to an often intolerable *status quo* - or, in the modern geopolitical terms he employed, to 'the existing political equilibrium' - and his conviction that the Russians were mainly responsible for upsetting this by their intervention in, for instance, Ethiopia, Angola, Afghanistan, and Cambodia, Kissinger naturally felt that it was a mistake for the Guadeloupe summit to reassure the Soviet Union 'rather than convey the imperative of some acceptable code of conduct.' He believed that behind a facade of unity with President Carter the British, French, and West German leaders shared his view that 'timidity increases our dangers and confuses our policies', and he hoped they would soon speak out. (Kissinger's fear that a new SALT agreement would simply give the West a false sense of security was particularly ironic since he was the chief architect of SALT I, signed in 1972, during Nixon's presidency. His volte-face can be explained, however, by the fact that the two nuclear superpowers were now more nearly equal in military might: Russia had caught up!)

To exude reassurance regardless of the circumstances was the avuncular Jim Callaghan's most conspicuous political talent. Remember his studied air of astonishment, on returning from France's tropical jewel island of Guadeloupe to the bleak winter of a Britain in turmoil, at being greeted by the press gang with demands to know what he thought of the crisis? 'What crisis?' his raised eyebrows, if not his lips, asked. Unhappily, however, heroic imperturbability and soothing sounds proved no substitute for measuring up to reality and taking the appropriate measures, as was soon to be shown at the hustings. While as for his performance on the world stage, how could he expect the Russians to be reassured by mere rhetoric about *not* 'playing the China card' when that was patently his intention.

In his autobiography *Time and Chance*, James Callaghan states that he shared both Carter's conviction that 'both sides possessed far too many nuclear weapons for the purpose of deterrence' and his objective of reaching a SALT II agreement with the Russians. Judging from the way he writes about a memorable meeting in Moscow in 1975 at which President Brezhnev treated Harold Wilson and himself to 'a passionate harangue on the evils of nuclear war', there would also seem to be no doubt at all that he shared Carter's trust in Brezhnev's commitment to 'irreversible détente'. Callaghan says: 'I had no doubt we had listened to the real Brezhnev, and I was convinced of the sincerity of his horror of total war, a sentiment shared by all of us who had experienced the Second World War.' Yet for all the sense and sensibility he shows - such as, for instance, his counsel that 'despite our differences in ideology and philosophy, and notwithstanding the harsh Soviet position on human rights, we should hold a steady course in dealing with the Soviet Union' - he was quite prepared to jeopardise détente with Russia in order to pull off unsavoury deals with China. And for all his expressed conviction that 'it is impossible to believe the security of any one of us was enhanced by the developments of the early 1980s,' the stance taken by him and his lieutenants, most notably David Owen, contributed to the panic over Russia's deployment of SS20s (a temporary advantage which Russia offered to bargain away - an offer which fell on deaf ears) and also helped to lay the groundwork for the West's response with Pershing IIs and cruise missiles, thus heightening not lessening the balance of terror.

In a debate on the defence estimates in March 1979 Labour left-winger Frank Allaun accused Tory MPs and the Tory press of misleading the British people and psychologically preparing them for a war with Russia. There was plenty of substance in the charge when, for example, a Heathite like Peter Walker, who was generally reputed a moderate, could substitute the rhetoric of 'Reds' xenophobia for serious strategic analysis and expect to get away with it, as he had done a year before Allaun's indictment, in a nationally-reported speech to constituency members. In terms reminiscent of the American right, he characterised the West's attitude towards a Russian military build-up which, according to him, would give the Soviet Union the power to 'blackmail' the world within a decade, as 'a perpetual posture of calculated cowardice'. With a fine disregard for historical truth with respect to the age of appeasement, apathy, and general indifference to the fate of foreigners, Jewish or Gentile, not to mention his unrecognisable picture of the current climate of fear and weapon-hoarding, he instructed them:

'Britain's complacency to the Soviet danger is even
more frightening than the disarmament of the 1930s.
Perhaps because Hitler looked nastier and was more
exposed to the media than Mr Brezhnev, perhaps
because his treatment of the Jews and other human
beings was of greater public knowledge, there was at
least some interest in the menace he created.'

(It would have been of greater service to his country - if not to his
party - to repeat the admonition against complacency that the visibly
decaying Brezhnev had made on a visit to West Germany, when he
warned the world: 'It is easy to take peace for granted after thirty
years of it in Europe...' To which he added the poignantly telling
parallel: 'As long as one is not sick, one even becomes complacent
about one's health'.)

Of course, one can consider such onslaughts as Peter
Walker's, along with side-swipes at Labour's Foreign Affairs and
Defence ministers as 'weak and inexperienced', as simply par for
the course in the rough and tumble of British party politics.
Naturally, as the moment for putting to the test that very special
kind of truth that is manifested once every four or five years as the
general will in the polling booths drew close, the Tories played the
patriotic card with ever more shameless abandon. And this despite
the Government's honouring of its pledge to NATO to increase
'defence' spending by three per cent in real terms, in preference to
honouring its 1974 pledge to the British electorate to reduce military
expenditure. But while it might not be quite in order to suggest that
Frank Allaun's charges of conditioning the public for war could
equally have been directed at the leaders of his own party, it is
impossible to avoid the conclusion that, whether for reasons of gross
miscalculation of Russia's intentions or of 'calculated cowardice'
with regard to the verdict of the voters, or both, the Callaghan
Government failed to counteract the long-conditioned fear of a
Soviet attack on the West.

It never was a question of whether there was any reason for
the West to fear the Soviet Union (still less of whether the kind of
society it represented was acceptable) - nor, except in the heads of
absolute pacifists, of massive unilateral *dis*armament - but of calm
consideration of where the greater dangers and disadvantages lay.
Then it should have been a matter of holding (in Jim Callaghan's

own words) 'a steady course' - just so long as it was in a sensible direction and not heading straight for a whirlpool. In fact the Callaghan Government tried to steer in several directions at once, like a pirate ship in the midst of a flotilla of merchantmen unable to make up its mind which was the greatest prize. Did it agree or disagree with Frank Allaun's warning in the March 1978 defence spending debate? 'The threat to humanity is not the possibility of a Russian invasion,' he said. 'It is the arms race itself which is taking us towards a nuclear war.' The fact that we cannot answer this question is a measure of the Government's muddle and its failure.

As has been shown, one of the reasons for this was its determination to treat death-dealing devices as just another kind of commodity to keep the ship of state afloat, an attitude which comes over particularly clearly in Defence Secretary Fred Mulley's remarks during the defence estimates debate of March 1979. He said the Government hoped that sales of British military equipment abroad would amount to £1.1 billion next year, even after allowing for the cancellation of orders from Iran; that these exports were worth 75,000 jobs in Britain; and that they helped to keep down the cost of our own military equipment. And he insisted that the Government would continue to sell such equipment to friendly countries.

Of the difficulty of knowing whether such countries would remain friendly, let alone the question of whether they were the kind of countries we *ought* to be friendly with, he had nothing to say. *The Guardian* did. In a forthright editorial on the fall of the Shah entitled 'Human rights: the best test for the West', it declared:

'Certainly a concern for human rights in Iran, and elsewhere, is a much better starting point for Western policy than the narrowly strategic calculations of Carter's predecessors. A human rights foreign policy encourages people to make free choices. Not only is that good in itself: it promotes Western interests too because the Soviet Union can offer no competition. President Carter should not be deflected by the present uncertainties of Iran from making human rights the foundation of his diplomacy in future.'

Unfortunately, however, *The Guardian* offers a somewhat

less than flawless example of consistency on this score. If anything, it appeared to be even less worried than the Government about either strategic or human rights considerations when it came to flogging jump-jets to China, advising the Prime Minister to 'defend his right to do this deal for what it is: part of the normal pattern of defence transactions with *peaceful* and stable governments, and in no way calculated (these are Harriers, not Tornados to enable or encourage less peaceful behaviour in the future.' [my emphasis] While in two editorials commenting on the Vietnamese invasion of Cambodia, that cockpit of almost incredible inhumanity under the Khmer Rouge, *The Guardian* told its readers: 'The present Cambodian regime can hardly be regarded as desirable by Western liberal standards, though there is no certainty or even probability that any other foreseeable regime would be better'; appeared to give some credence to claims that the Khmer Rouge 'pogroms were over and had in any case been exaggerated'; and went on to make comments of such crassness and such callousness that the guardian spirit of the house must still blush with shame to recall them:

> 'But Vietnam's human rights record, if that is how the countries are to be judged, will not bear much scrutiny either. When one dictatorship invades another, there is only the sterility of international law to fall back on, and here it is the Russians' client which is clearly at fault. But it is a low-grade conflict and does not merit much of the attention which China now wants the United Nations to give it. Only if the Soviet Union and China themselves are foolish enough to allow it to assume big-Power proportions, by alarms on their common frontier, need the West differentiate between one misery-making Asian government and another.'

What is still interesting about this puerile piece of opinionising is that it graphically illustrates how extensively and profoundly the Cold War had corrupted Western thought. Even here, in this contemporary voice of a great liberal paper, straight thinking is driven out by specious double-think in which moral judgement is conditioned by considerations of whether other States are allies or 'friends', or, on the contrary, principal powers or protégés of what President Reagan was to dub 'the evil empire'. In this welter of warped thinking on geopolitical problems in establishment circles, now and again a voice rings out as true as a bell, as in this passage from an address by a Government minister to the Royal Institute of International Affairs at the height of the Far Eastern imbroglio:

> 'The Government's concern for human rights does not stop at the Channel. We must relate our concern for human rights abroad to our own belief in the values we as a society stand for...If we condone or explain away behaviour on the part of others which we know and feel instinctively to be wrong, this will rebound on us and harm our own society. If we do not defend what we know to be right, it will damage our own self-respect as a nation, as well as our standing in the international community...We accept the strategic argument that an unequal world is an unstable world...and we cannot ignore blatant violations of fundamental rights in deciding where and how to help.'

It is a matter for infinite regret that with a Labour government in power one has to pronounce such pure judgements and such unequivocal repudiation of *realpolitik* to be so rare. To add to the poignancy, the minister concerned, Minister of State at the Foreign Office, was Frank Judd, whose subsequent career, after losing his seat in the 1979 general election, as Oxfam's director-general suggests that he was always the most *un*political of politicians in Jim Callaghan's Government. But for the most part, in our fixtures with rival nations, a public-school mentality ruled the behaviour of Labour's statesmen no less than it did that of their parliamentary opponents. The rules dictated a bipartisan attitude to the handling of foreign affairs; and a bipartisan foreign policy might be defined as one in which each party, when in opposition, vigorously assails the government for putting the country at risk, and when in office, behaves as blindly, as unintelligently, and as tribalistically as its predecessor.

CHAPTER 18

Our caring society

'The crowning achievements of the Austrian Republic belonged to the municipality of Vienna. The Austrian workers proudly called it "Red Vienna"...Vienna, which had seemed irretrievably doomed in 1919, was ten years later one of the most remarkable cities of Europe. It had defied death. It had created new life. It had girdled itself with beautiful blocks of flats and garden settlements, with swimming-pools and libraries...Above all it had transformed the Socialist idea of common property, social taxation and social welfare into deeds, and had created among its citizens a new sense of solidarity and social responsibility...it was, above all, a "red city" because it succeeded in realising municipal Socialism in a capitalist country.'

Julius Braunthal, *The Tragedy of Austria* (1948)

For the British people the early forties are the period when, under the pressures of the struggle for the nation's survival, the rhetoric claiming this to be 'the century of the common man' really began to take on some semblance of reality, at least with regard to common standards of living. The people's desire for a decisive break with a past in which suffrage had brought such meagre returns was registered in the general election of July 1945, though not so resoundingly as political mythology would have it, since Labour's victory was founded on a little less than half the total number of votes cast. Nevertheless, history had handsomely recompensed Labour for its long struggle for a parliamentary majority, for the bitter trials and tribulations of its schisms and its long years in the wilderness, by handing it power when it most mattered. It seemed to be a moment of destiny, when opportunity really did knock both for the nation and for the world. 'Now Britain has the chance of leading the democratic revolution,' the Italian revolutionary Socialist Ignazio Silone enthusiastically pronounced.

Just as throughout the nineteenth and early twentieth centuries, from the Congress of Vienna to the outbreak of the First World War, under the pressure of progressive enfranchisement,

Tories and Liberals vied with each other for popular support by proffering the sweetmeats of social reform, so in our time - with the Liberals out of the serious bidding for the contract to run the country - Labour and the Tories have peddled their promises for purchase by vote. Under representative democracy it is necessarily so. Every party, in short, claims to be the party of reform, that is to say, strives to be seen as the party that will most enhance the voters' enjoyment of life. The post-Second World War reforms - reforms for the main part rooted in the wartime coalition's morale-boosting 'land fit for heroes' proposals for a new dawn, and to a large extent resting on consensus - were certainly given a kick-start by Labour's shock victory. That a substantial transformation of what the nineteenth century called 'the condition of the people' took place during the Attlee administrations (which is not, of course, saying was *brought about by* them - a much more debatable opinion) there can be no question. But, in the first place, by the mid eighties - with the Thatcherite counter-revolution fully under way - it should have become obvious to all but the incurably obtuse how narrow the bounds and how fragile the structures of 'the social revolution' of 1945-50 had been. Secondly, social progress in general continued, under Tory as well as Labour governments, in the decades that followed, and more or less in step with the (in twentieth-century terms) fairly rapid and dependable growth of the economy. Thirdly, by the time of the last Wilson/Callaghan governments, the social advance had, on many fronts, stalled.

It may be that a confirmed Labour supporter might reasonably consider a given Labour government - or even each and every known Labour government - preferable to any alternative on offer. But a Socialist must apply stricter criteria, and is obliged to ask not merely: 'Is it better?' but: 'Is it qualitatively different?' And unless he or she can answer: 'Yes', then it does not even begin to measure up to his or her ideals.

In one sense Labour has been the victim of its own success in playing a major role in raising 'the condition of the people' through the development of the Welfare State, and by so doing quietening the clamour for social transformation. In another sense it has been the culprit - by giving way to its fear that its vision of a good society would no longer be attractive to the ordinary voter, cocooned in the new age's material comforts delivered by economic growth and in some measure underpinned by social security provisions, and fearing deprivation through major social change more than through the familiar vicissitudes of the capitalist system. In this manner did Labour, acting under the perceived imperatives of representative democracy, abandon society's 'orphans', the less vocal underclass of the poor and the relatively poor. Whereas they had once formed a majority of the nation (or at any rate a massive minority) they now formed only a negligible fraction of the nation's voters. Lacking solidarity from the general electorate (and such solidarity was never sufficiently fostered by Labour's paternalists), they could be largely neglected without seriously jeopardising - indeed, arguably thereby enhancing - the Labour vote, for to what other party could those disinherited ones turn to look after their interests? Thus have the least privileged been cynically sacrificed to the strategy of consolidating support among the skilled workers and among professionals with tender - but not *that* tender - consciences. (This is roughly the thesis at the core of John Kenneth Galbraith's essay *The Culture of Contentment* (1992), in which he argues that a new development 'in the so-called capitalist countries...is that the controlling contentment and resulting belief is now that of the many, not just of the few...and operates under the compelling power of democracy...[and that] the result is government that is accommodated not to reality or common need, but to the beliefs of the contented, who are now the majority of those who voted'.)

We might measure this massive erosion of Labour's faith and/or its total loss of nerve by contrasting three political pronouncements made by members of the Party's top brass, separated by eighteen years of progressive disillusionment. The first is a clarion call delivered to the Party Conference in 1973, on the eve of Labour's return to power after its fancied drive for a 'white-hot *technological* revolution' [my emphasis] had been so rudely interrupted by Ted Heath's Mark II model Conservatives. The second and third are statements made to *The Guardian* in an interview and a letter by two leading lights of Labour's government-hopefully-in-waiting during the roller-coaster opinion-polling days of the summer of 1991.

In the autumn of 1973, in a belligerent speech in which he promised to wring 'howls of anguish from the 80,000 rich people', Shadow Chancellor Denis Healey won great applause from Conference delegates with these words:

'Our aim is to get power, and we join battle armed with
the most radical and comprehensive programme we
have had since 1945. Its aim is, honestly stated, *to bring
about a fundamental and irreversible shift in the
balance of power and wealth in favour of working
people and their families.*' [my emphasis]

Even allowing for what waggish sceptics might characterise as
providing ample scope for possible 'differentials' of opinion under
the baggy formula 'working people', with its perhaps shrewd
avoidance of any class reference, that still has to be one of the most
ambitiously unambiguous statements of Labour's Socialist
objectives ever made. But let us put the clock forward to 1991.

As a student at Oxford, Denis Healey had joined the
Communist Party, but by the time he made the call to arms cited
above no one could have accused him of being too left-wing.
Margaret Beckett, on the other hand, had moved a long way across
the Labour Party's broad political spectrum (from left to right, as is
almost invariably the case) between 1981, when she supported Tony
Benn in his unsuccessful bid to beat Healey in the contest for the
post of deputy leader, and mid-1991, when Melanie Phillips
interviewed her for *The Guardian* because of her high profile as
shadow Treasury minister. Questioned about her drift rightwards,
Mrs Beckett - inasmuch as she was prepared to admit she had moved
a muscle in that direction - responded in wholly predictable terms
of practicalities and priorities. She spoke of having been made aware
when she was shadowing social security of 'such a great well of
justifiable need that it was really hard to see how you could meet it
all', and went on, in words that perhaps subconsciously echoed
Aneurin Bevan's vacuous dictum that 'Socialism is all about
priorities', earnestly to affirm, 'That's where I think having priorities
is the essence.'

One would be hard put to think up any situation in which one
could quarrel with that; but beyond the commendable fact that she
cares about other people and means to do something about it as a
politician, such musings tell us next to nothing about her political
viewpoint. Compassion does not constitute a political philosophy;
nor is it the same thing as a commitment to social justice. In what
respects, if any, for example, does her way of looking at the problem
of the 'great well of justifiable need' differ from the vision of such

noble exemplars of practical compassion as, say, Mother Teresa or Lord Shaftesbury? Or come to that, from the viewpoints of the more humane and social-minded adherents of political parties she never dreamt of joining?

Applauding the great change she feels 'has taken place in the Labour Party,' Margaret Beckett credits Neil Kinnock with having made the Party 'think about where the country was going and where we were going.' Yet a lengthy and sympathetic interview yields no indication of strategy and no goal except that of amelioration. 'You have to establish a system that's reasonably just and fair, and hopefully start to help people out of the trouble they're in. And if that is not possible, try to give them some feeling of human dignity and respect. Now that is immensely difficult, immensely expensive, and probably will take years of work to get right,' she says mournfully, but adds later: 'At least you can do *something* to alleviate their condition and prevent what would otherwise be a continuing deterioration.'

One is tempted to mock such lucubrations, which suggest nothing so much as a private think-tank from which significant thought has been prudently expelled to produce a controversy-free vacuum. (Are we, for instance, being urged to compare favourably the 'reasonably just and fair system' she posits without prescription with ones that are 'unreasonably unjust and unfair'? Humpty Dumpty may not have been a suitable candidate for tutoring a course in semantics, but at least he was a fine tactician when it came to the manipulation of language). But the words quoted above reveal more than their author (presumably) intends: to wit, that paternalism is still alive and well in the political arm of the Labour Movement, as deeply engrained as it is in old-style religious charity. Moreover, surely the Fabians of yesteryear - if not the modernised variety - would agree that such a dispiriting defence of palliation is hardly hopeful enough to be described even as gradualist reformism.

'I have been on the mountain top and I have seen the promised land,' cried Martin Luther King in a famous peroration. Labour once thought it had seen the promised land, but if it did, it went downhill in quite the wrong direction. At least Bevan was offering his pedestrian aphorism in a context of soaring hopes. Beckett serves it up cold forty years later, after Labour has tinkered with a grossly unjust system through an accumulated term in office of over seventeen years.

The long march of Labour from left to right across the stage of British history was to be dramatised by those who played the leading roles in subsequent events in the Party's leadership contests. When John Smith was elected as successor to Neil Kinnock, following Kinnock's second general election defeat and his resignation as Party Leader, Margaret Beckett became the Deputy Leader; then, on John Smith's sudden death, she was for a short time Acting Leader. Challenging for both the post of Leader and that of Deputy Leader in the leadership elections, she lost out in the first contest to Tony Blair and in the second to John Prescott, who, as Blair's deputy dawg, could turn out to be the last politician of working-class origins to get that high in the Party.

As for Blair, who in the Kinnockio times we are considering held the more modest post of shadow employment spokesman, it is fitting that this man who was to rise right to the top should provide our second contrast to Healey's socialistic war-cry of 1973. The minimalist objectives to which Labour had, by 1991, already descended, from the bringing about of equality to which Attlee's Party once professed to aspire, is crystallised in Blair's advocacy - in response to a symposium of contributions to *The Guardian* on Labour's declared intention of establishing a minimum wage if returned to power - of 'a society where there is a minimum threshold of decency below which no-one should fall.' Winston Churchill proposed something very similar nearly half a century before, and although they might differ as to precisely where that threshold lay, one might well assert that all men of any goodwill whatsoever would say amen to that.(By the end of 1995 Blair had taken Labour so far to the right that the Tory MP for Stratford-on-Avon, Alan Howarth, felt he would be more at home in its ranks than amongst the New Tories, and having crossed the floor, he urged all 'one-nation' Tory MPs to 'join the Labour Party, which is now the torchbearer for their beliefs, and is ready to put them into practice in government')

One might seek to excuse such cautious campaigning by an avowedly reforming and radical party (never mind whether it still claimed to be a Socialist party or not) by ruefully reflecting that to be rejected at the polls three times in succession would be enough to take the heart out of any party that had once held power and continued to remain in serious contention for office. But attention has already been drawn to the essentially defensive, pleading nature of Labour's calls for social justice even before the tempest of

Thatcherite go-getting individualism swept Labour's brick-by-brick experiment in building a better society off the Monopoly board and into 'the dustbin of history'. After all, notwithstanding his advocacy of public spending as providing 'an important redistribution of income' (a claim that will be considered later) Stan Orme's formula for 'a caring society' (see Chapter 11) was not that much more ambitious, proposing little more than 'moderating [financial] insecurity' resulting from personal misfortune. For all that, Orme's unapologetic countering of demands for tax cuts with a call to reduce inequality and deprivation by increasing the 'social wage' marks a significant difference from the embarrassed negativism now prevailing in the Party whenever the issue of the economic equivalent of positive discrimination in education arises.

Labour does have some claim to be considered as, historically speaking, the principal architect of the Welfare State. If, forty years on, it is content for its achievements to be measured against the very modest claim that it is still the most dependable guarantor of the maintenance of 'a caring society', so be it. An attempt to assess scrupulously the relative performances in 'caring' of Labour and Conservative governments between the Tories' return to power in 1951 and the triumph of Mrs Thatcher in 1979 would be tedious and now unrewarding. I shall just glance at the record in the fields of health, homes, and education. Social security will be looked at in the next chapter, in the context of considering more fully the issue of the distribution of wealth and income, upon which, more than on any other, rests the question of social justice.

The National Health Service - launched, as historical chance would have it, by the legendary Nye Bevan - has always been the flagship of Labour's Welfare State campaigns. During the consensus years there was no wide difference of opinion between the parties over the importance of maintaining and developing the NHS, it being generally agreed that around 4 per cent of the national income should be devoted to this purpose. Although the NHS share of GNP fell steeply between 1950 and 1955, from 4.07 to 3.04 per cent, and thereafter rose only slowly to 3.86 per cent in 1964 (the year in which Labour returned to power) and then continued to rise, the superiority of Labour's record in fact falls well short of undeniable. Under the first Wilson governments the NHS share rose to 4.7 per cent, in 1969; but in his essay on 'Inequalities in Health' in *Labour and Inequality* (published in 1972, when the Tories were again in power, under Ted Heath) Nicholas Bosanquet questions the extent to which this surge in health spending should be credited to Labour, since nearly half the increase had its roots in budgeting planned by the previous administration. 'The real Labour years,' he argues, 'the years over which the [Labour] Government had a full measure of discretion, run from 1966 to 1969,' and 'over this period, the additional real current resources available to the Service fell year by year,' from £38 million in 1966 to £7 million in 1969. This hardly amounted to the record of 'enormous expansion' claimed by Richard Crossman in the House of Commons in July 1969, Bosanquet concludes.

Public spending on the Health Service continued to rise (both in real and in share of GNP terms) throughout the seventies *and* the eighties, reaching 5.4 per cent by 1977 but 6 per cent by the time of Margaret Thatcher's third general election victory ten years later. Its persistence as a burning political issue is partly due to the failure of this growth to keep pace with ever-rising demand (resulting both from demographic changes - in particular the greater longevity of the population - and from higher expectations stimulated by the progress of medicine, and especially of medical technology), and partly from the not ill-founded fear that the long-term goal of a powerful faction in the Tory Party is to degrade the National Health Service into a second-class safety-net service for those entirely dependent for the satisfaction of their health needs on the public purse.

However, in considering the question of whether there was a real qualitative difference distinguishing Labour from its opponents during the years of consensus, it is noteworthy not only that significant progress in consolidating the NHS was made under Conservative governments (hospital development, for example, under Macmillan, with Enoch Powell as Minister of Health, or the major reorganisation of the Service piloted by Keith Joseph during Heath's administration), but that the Tories were in some respects more afraid of being open to the charge of undermining the NHS than were their opponents. It was Sir Stafford Cripps who, near the end of Attlee's first administration, first pressed for charges on patients, and Aneurin Bevan only fended off this assault on 'his baby' by agreeing to the forming of a Cabinet committee to monitor and restrain NHS costs. Less than a year later, as 'defence' spending doubled to meet the costs of Britain's entanglement in the Korean War and its other expanding Cold War commitments, with Hugh

Gaitskell now Chancellor, the imposition of half-price charges on spectacles and dentures for adult NHS patients became a principal factor in the resignations from the Government of Harold Wilson, John Freeman, and, of course, Nye Bevan. He described the saving of £13 million out of a budget of £4 billion as 'the arithmetic of Bedlam'. But Bevan had already been pressurised into conceding in principle the possibility of a shilling charge on prescriptions, which Churchill's Government in fact imposed in 1952.

After 'thirteen years of Tory misrule', with Harold Wilson himself now top dog, the voters were treated to yet another dazzling acrobatic display as Wilson's first Chancellor, Jim Callaghan, redeemed Labour's pledge to scrap prescription charges, and his second, Roy Jenkins, slapped them on again in his 1968 crisis budget. So when Heath's Chancellor, Anthony Barber, raised prescription and dental charges three years later, he was only following in Labour's wake. Writing of a later economic crisis over which Harold Wilson presided, with Denis Healey wielding the Chancellor's axe this time, Bernard Donoghue, who acted as Senior Policy Adviser to both Wilson and his successor in No. 10, makes an astringent observation that highlights the fact that, under Labour no less than under the Tories, the social services are the soft underbelly of government expenditure, the first part of the body politic exposed to the knife in any emergency calling for some slimming down. Healey had proposed a 2 per cent cut in the expenditure planned for 1976-77, expecting all the departments of State to be prepared to make sacrifices. But as Donoghue writes: 'Defence, as was often the case, simply refused to accept or even discuss half of its proposed cuts, whereas the cuts in Education, the National Health Service and public industry investment were imposed in full.'

Big differences of opinion over specific issues will occur in any political party that is not strictly regimented; but the Labour Party has never come close (at least when it matters most, i.e. when in power) to agreeing on those 'priorities' which Bevan and Beckett rabbited on about. From any Socialist perspective, Labour governments have made a habit of getting them wrong. Once upon a time - not all that long ago - Britain had a War Office; now that we live in a more civilised age we have a Ministry of Defence. Call a country's expenditure on its armed forces and their weapons of destruction 'defence spending' and most of its citizens will readily agree that it is the number one priority. And, judging by the history of the post-war world, they will not generally be greatly puzzled to hear that the defence of the nation is apparently being undertaken on the other side of the world in a land they have hardly heard of: Korea, say. But in any case, the danger of becoming the victim of military aggression is only one among a host of problems that face a nation, and the degree of risk involved needs to be assessed, as with every other risk.

Straining to be kind to Labour in office, one would still be hard put to pronounce the degree of priority it has repeatedly given to 'defence' as at all judicious. Ministers more exercised by social priorities (*as long, at least, as these have remained their provinces*) have always had a hard time of it, as Donoghue's comment suggests. In the bright new world of post-war Labour-ruled Britain, housing was viewed by every party as one of these priorities. Back in those earlier days of hope and of promises of 'homes fit for heroes' after the First World War, Christopher Addison (a distinguished anatomist who, having turned his attention to the body politic, had become in 1919, under Lloyd George, the country's first Minister of Health, before switching his allegiance from Liberal to Labour in 1923 and concluding his political career as Labour leader in the Lords), had, in A.J.P. Taylor's words, 'more than any other man established the principle that housing was a social service.' Labour considered the right to a decent home to be of such importance that it had promised to set up a separate Ministry of Housing. In the event Housing remained an appendage to Health, as it had been between the wars, so that it became a second major responsibility for Nye Bevan. Notwithstanding his flippant and foolish jest that he devoted only five minutes a week of his time to it, he fought his corner over housing with his customary ardour. Cripps's devaluation package of autumn 1949 not only threatened the principle of a free health service but slowed down progress in the provision of homes. In a letter to Attlee arguing that the need for greater labour mobility meant that 'a reduction in housing cannot be justified on the basis of the existing national emergency,' Bevan complained bitterly that while the 'already gorged and swollen defence estimates' were to be trimmed by no more than £30 million, housing was to suffer cuts of £40-50 million. As Kenneth O. Morgan says: 'The housing programme, now at the peak of its achievement, bore the brunt of the post-devaluation cuts in public expenditure.'

With around one and a half million units (of which two-thirds were new and one-third conversions or restorations) added to the nation's housing stock during the Attlee administrations, Morgan's verdict is that housing 'deserves its honoured role in the saga of Labour's welfare state.' Nevertheless, the 1951 census revealed that the excess of households over houses (at 1.1 million) remained much the same as it had been in the depths of the Depression, twenty years earlier. Bevan had been forced to abandon his goal of 200,000 completions a year, and it was the Tories who first raised the target (at their 1950 Conference) to 300,000, hitting it in October 1953 and surpassing it by over 50,000 the following year. Harold Macmillan, to whom Churchill had given the responsibility of fulfilling the Tory pledge, proudly told the Party Conference in 1954 that he had made housing 'a national crusade', and T.O. Lloyd remarks: 'The housing problem was nearer to being under control than at any time since 1939.'

After its return to power in 1964, Labour published a White Paper calculating that three million families were in need of housing or re-housing in homes of an acceptable standard and setting up a target of half a million houses a year to be reached by 1970, with the objective of solving the problem within ten to fifteen years. Records of over 400,000 completions were achieved in 1967 and 1968, but the figures fell back thereafter, to below 370,000 in 1969, and (with the June 1970 to February 1974 Heath Government in between) down to around 250,000 by 1974. Denis Healey's 1974 budget provided for an expansion of the local authority housing programme, but his 'rough and tough' budget of the following year cut subsidies for housing, as well as food, with the consequence that fewer houses were built or rehabilitated under the Wilson administration of 1974-76 than under Heath's Government.

And so the dreary tale of high hopes repeatedly dashed dragged on into the premiership of Jim Callaghan. By the last full year of Labour rule (1978) public sector housing, at 107,600 including housing association and new town units, had fallen to its lowest level since the first full post-war year of Labour rule (1946), with council house completions down to little over 75,000. Many local authorities were wilfully underspending because of the hostility of the party in control of the council to the whole concept of public housing, with the total amount of Treasury money not taken up amounting to at least £150 million. But in addition, it turned out that the Department of Environment had itself underspent on its housing budget to the tune of £410 million, 8 per cent of the allocation. At the same time, council house sales, running at the rate of 18,000 a year in 1978, were heading for their highest point since the final year under Ted Heath. This led Shelter to censure the Labour Government for its inconsistency in allowing this to happen at the same time as it promoted a charter to improve tenants' conditions and to provide greater mobility for tenants in public housing, all this in an overall situation of crisis in the provision of homes for the people.

In March 1979 Shelter Scotland published a report estimating that 150,000 houses north of the border (8 per cent of the total stock) were below the officially tolerable standard and that half a million people were in urgent housing need. In April nine housing charities, in a joint protest that, for the first time since the war, a general election was being fought without any debate on the supply of housing, claimed that one in five families in England was either homeless or was living in severely substandard or insecure conditions. In such circumstances the publication of Peter Shore's long-awaited Housing Bill, with the tenants' charter as its core proposal, seemed a trifle superfluous. In any case, Labour's rout in the general election swept the bill into oblivion.

Of course, the Socialists in the Party were by no means content with the Government's record in promoting the provision of homes. In a debate at the 1978 Party Conference at Blackpool, Frank Allaun declared: 'Future generations will think us mad when they see that there was a desperate housing shortage on the one hand, and a quarter of a million building workers unemployed on the other.'

Anyone who is at all disposed to take seriously the claim that Labour's objectives (or at any rate its long-term objectives) are - or at least were until comparatively recently - Socialist in character has to reconcile with this assumption the rather remarkable fact that no Labour government has ever introduced a major bill of educational reform. For all its limitations, the Butler Bill introduced by the wartime coalition government in 1944 unquestionably marked a major social advance on a system that had restricted formal education for the mass of the population to the age of fourteen, and in so-called elementary schools. From a Socialist point of view, however, the limitations of the Butler reform were ominous. By providing a clear framework of free secondary education based on three kinds of school (grammar and technical - both of which were already established, though the latter kind was but sparsely distributed - plus 'secondary modern'), the 1944 Act, as A.J.P. Taylor puts it, 'unwittingly created a new class division between those who were clever enough to get into a grammar school at "eleven plus" and those who were not.'

Apart from a certain unease at his use of the word 'clever' (a shorthand expression, perhaps), the only debatable point about Taylor's judgement is whether the 'new class division' was all that 'unwitting'. James Chuter Ede, a former schoolteacher whom Attlee made his Home Secretary, had been Butler's right-hand man in drafting and promoting his Bill, and thus carried no small share of responsibility for its shortcomings. Furthermore, Attlee's first Minister of Education, Ellen Wilkinson (the celebrated 'Red Ellen' of the Jarrow March, who had by now, however, migrated a long way to the right) rejected the Left's argument that the tripartite division of schools, buttressed by the eleven-plus tests, was socially and educationally divisive. 'Her view,' says Kenneth O. Morgan, 'seems to have been endorsed throughout the Cabinet, where such public-school products as Attlee of Haileybury, Cripps of Winchester, and Dalton of Eton lent their voices to the perpetuation of elitism'; while George Tomlinson, who succeeded Ellen Wilkinson on her death as a result of taking an overdose of drugs in February 1947, 'followed a broadly identical policy.'

That policy was to channel into education such increases in resources as the growth of the economy and the competing claims of other Departments of State allowed, but to develop the system on the lines already laid down by the political consensus, on the complacent assumption that this would in due course provide equality of educational opportunity for all. But secondary schooling in particular provides a notable example of areas (and they are not few) in which it has frequently been difficult to talk of Labour policy without first drawing a careful distinction between leaders and led within the Party - a point that calls for closer consideration in the context of the Party as a representative body. Not until July 1951 did the Labour Party officially commit itself to the policy of changing to comprehensive schools, and even then the conversion of its leadership was far from complete. Writing of the first Labour administration after the Party's thirteen years in opposition, C.J. Bartlett says: 'Harold Wilson, with many others in the Labour party, was a grammar school product. These were not readily persuaded that grammar schools had failed as instruments for social mobility.' Wilson, indeed, in the jockeying for a favourable position during the run up to the 1964 general election, swore that the grammar school would be abolished 'only over my dead body.'

The irony is that, spurred on by the growing acceptance of the case for comprehensive schools amongst teachers and educationists, and even more by growing disenchantment amongst parents (and especially middle-class parents!) over the unfairness and inefficiency of the eleven-plus selection system, grammar school products of a different political persuasion gave comprehensive schools their biggest boost. When Ted Heath came into office in June 1970 and appointed none other than Margaret Thatcher as his Minister of Education, less than a third of secondary school pupils were in comprehensives (which were thus normally skimmed of the greater part of the top ability range in their areas); when they left office in February 1974, more than two-thirds were in comprehensives.

Moreover, it was the Heath Government which, in 1973, raised the school-leaving age from fifteen to sixteen, at last implementing an objective that had been declared Labour policy since the school-leaving age was raised from fourteen to fifteen in April 1947 and had long been accepted by all parties as desirable. In tune with Donoghue's dictum on the distortion of priorities, Wilson's first government had, under the pressure of the economic crisis of 1967-68, postponed its intention of raising the school-leaving age for two years, and lost power before it could redeem its pledge.

In his contribution to the 1972 symposium of Fabian essays, *Labour and Inequality*, Howard Glennerster calls this further delay in keeping what amounted to a twenty-year-old promise to the nation's working class (for it was overwhelmingly the children of manual workers who were affected by it), 'scarcely a disaster'. But taken together with the decision made at the beginning of Labour's return to office not to allocate more resources to going comprehensive, it is indicative of a short-termism that throws into doubt the genuineness of its rhetoric regarding the regeneration of Britain - and that is to put the matter simply in terms of conventional patriotism.

As for Labour's proclaimed commitment to move towards greater equality, Glennerster demonstrates that the expansion of educational provision that did occur under Wilson's first administration (of which he was most proud, boasting that for the first time more was being spent on education than on defence) primarily benefited the middle class, with the families of the 28 per cent of the working population who earned their livelihoods by semi-skilled or unskilled labour benefiting from only 19 per cent of the extra spending on education. This was mainly because most of the extra money was targeted on higher education. Wilson is on record as saying that what he would most like to be remembered for was the establishment of the Open University. Indubitably a notable advance in the provision of educational opportunity, this achievement nevertheless illustrates the low priority Labour perpetually gives (in practice if not in intention) to the least privileged. After all, 80 per cent of the Open University's first student intake came from homes with non-manual breadwinners, making it, in Glennerster's words, 'more middle class than the average university.' Furthermore, in September 1978 it was reported that there had actually been a fall between 1973 and 1977 in the number of children of manual workers who had secured places in universities.

Another contributor to *Labour and Inequality*, Dennis Marsden, does not hesitate to castigate Labour's leaders for their 'failures of perception and will', writing:

> 'The leadership was still quite prepared to live with the grammar and the public schools. And there is evidence of a lack of commitment to the ideal of reducing inequality in society. There was a failure to appreciate that economic and structural changes left to themselves will not reduce and may increase inequality. Labour politicians had apparently developed an overpowering coyness about taking any action which would curb or interfere with the existing maldistribution of power or resources.'

He cites as evidence the Wilson Government's failure to tackle the 'ludicrous' legal fiction that Eton and the other public schools are charities and its pusillanimous waging of its declared campaign to make comprehensives the dominant form of secondary schools, during which the Department of Education issued a circular to the local authorities requesting them but not requiring them to submit plans for the reorganisation of secondary education on comprehensive lines. One might well also include its indulgent disregard of the widespread practice of running comprehensives as if they were grammar schools somewhat hampered by the regrettable obligation of accommodating large numbers of 'secondary modern pupils', a brazen subversion of the whole purpose of going comprehensive.

As for failures of perception and of the need for thinking about fundamentals, it can hardly be without significance that all the major reports on the way forward for the nation's education - Crowther, Robbins, and Newsom - were commissioned and published under Tory administrations. But something even more disturbing than complacency was at work. Perhaps more than in any other field, the ingrained elitism of the leaders of the Labour Party was exposed in their handling of education. It raises the issue of what a Socialist vision implies. Must it encompass a striving for real social equality, or might it mean no more than an affirmation of the desirability of unimpeded social mobility? If it *is* no more than the latter, how *can* we distinguish between its fundamental aims and those of the bourgeois parties in liberal democracies, every one of which claims, in the late twentieth century, to be committed to equality of opportunity for all to prove their worth in a meritocratic society?

Ironically, a measure that might at least have proved an earnest of Labour's serious intention of striving for equality of opportunity - Shirley Williams' draft bill that, besides increasing parental choice and broadening representation on the governing bodies of schools, would have funded a pilot scheme to pay grants to sixteen-eighteen year-old pupils, thereby encouraging children from poorer families to stay on at school and perhaps equip themselves for higher education - was on the stocks when Jim Callaghan's Government was forced into the 1979 general election.

Callaghan had seemed to sense the significance of the issue of education, in relation to his 'what kind of society do we want?' challenge to the Tories, when he spoke of 'the great debate'. Yet three weeks before the Government fell, Shirley Williams was telling a conference in London on future trends in education that they were 'a long way short...of the 'mass' higher education system which we used to foresee.' One of the principal speakers at the conference was Dr Richard Hoggart, 'the hymnist of working-class culture', as *Guardian* correspondent John Fairhall called him in reporting him as saying that:

> 'The educational system perpetuated social and economic privilege as much now as it did forty years ago...Hundreds of thousands had been rejected by the education system. No society was civilised if so large a proportion of its population were no more than fillers-in of football coupons and haunters of football terraces. We should not be at ease when the correlation between attendance at certain schools and colleges and many sections of power and influence was as tight, or even tighter, than thirty years ago.'

Despite Hoggart's upbeat conclusion that 'a great opportunity' was in our grasp, Fairhall faithfully captures the predominant tone of his speech in calling it 'a requiem for the hopes that educational developments since the Second World War would make Britain a more democratic society.'

CHAPTER 19

Labour's crusade for social justice

'O, I have ta'en
Too little care of this. Take physic, pomp;
Expose thyself to feel what wretches feel,
That thou mayst shake the superflux to them,
And show the heavens more just.'

King Lear

'He'd come to believe that human pain could not be
cured by attention to individual cases...When he
compared the number of patients he cured with the
number of human beings the world over who could not
buy even the most ordinary medicines, it was enough to
make him shudder. The same with begging. What was
the good of giving money to the poor? The balance of
poverty on the planet remained unaltered. For the world
to change, the system had to change.'

Vasilis Vassilikos, Z

'The dream I have is of a country in which there is...wealth for everyone,
wealth equally distributed (and I don't mean arithmetically distributed)
and in which we do not have two societies,' James Callaghan told
Llew Gardner in the Thames Television programme, *TV Eye*, a week
before Labour lost power. 'As long as there's a hospital patient who
seeks a bed, as long as there are people living in poverty, as long as
there is a single family that hasn't got a home, then there's a great case
for change,' he went on, reciting a litany of hardship and injustice he
had deployed once before as preface to the ringing declaration: 'Our
purpose as a party is to present a bold creative socialist challenge to all
those forces that perpetuate injustice, class division, racial bigotry,
poverty.' And this spirited affirmation in turn recalled the words he
had used on inheriting Harold Wilson's mantle, when he had summoned
up the blood of his followers with the battle-cries: 'Let's root out
injustice; let's pursue equality.'

Such upbeat exhortations have become as foreign tongues to
the Party leadership. It is an almost incalculable distance between

Clement Attlee's quietly confident assertion of 1937: 'No doubt it will be some time before substantial economic equality is achieved, but ultimately it must be...' (which was accompanied by the unequivocal declaration that 'the aim of the socialist State must be equality') and the near-quietist conclusion to a tear-jerking anecdote on chronic poverty from Roy Hattersley's constituency surgery casebook (*Guardian* 4th November 1991): 'If we believe in a more equal society, a more equal society will come.' Equality has been for Labour a quarry forever outdistancing the pursuer. The dream persists but the runner flags, his resolution wilting into mere wish. 'For ever wilt thou love, and she be fair!'

In the opening rally of his first and last general election campaign as Labour's leader, Jim Callaghan, speaking in presciently elegiac tones, told his Glasgow audience: 'We in the Labour Movement may fall short...we make mistakes, but we are still the party of ideals.' Two of the most irreducible of these ideals have to be the first and second of the six characteristics of democratic socialism enumerated by one of his closest Cabinet confidants, Home Secretary Merlyn Rees, in addressing Party members a year earlier, namely the desire to eliminate poverty and the wish to redistribute income and wealth. We are dealing here with men of goodwill, so we ought to be charitable. If their proclaimed goal of equality appeared to be receding into the far future, let us judge Labour's record by the less exacting objectives which most of their political opponents at least purport to share, doing away with poverty and spreading wealth about a bit more.

Taking the second of these aims first, the essential questions are how the distribution of wealth and incomes stood when Rees prescribed redistribution as a principal tenet of democratic socialism, and how distribution had been affected by the fact that Labour had held power for nearly three-quarters of the preceding fourteen years. Rees addressed the subject with admirable candour in pointing out that half the nation's personally-owned wealth was still in the hands of the richest five per cent of its adult population (with the top one per cent of the very wealthy hogging no less than half of that half), and that moreover 'the structure of earnings has remained much the same for ninety years.' As for Labour's influence on this pyramid of economic inequality, his observations were tantamount to an admission that it had been minimal.

Of the contribution of the trade union wing of the Labour

Movement to this close-to-stagnant situation he observed: 'I am bound to say that I doubt the capacity of free collective bargaining to change this structure substantially.' Whether he realised it or not, this effectively sold the pass in the ceaseless conflict within the Movement over calls for wage restraint, in which the Left of the Party as well as numerous trade unionists contended that for the most part the unions were doing little more than struggling to maintain the living standards of their members. Of course, this contention tends to endorse Rees's judgement on the minimal redistributive effects of free collective bargaining. As for the parliamentary wing of the Movement, Rees came perilously close to admitting Labour's complete failure to advance towards its trumpeted objective of a 'fundamental and irreversible shift in the balance of power and wealth' when, in his single concrete proposition, he reasserted 'the Government's commitment to the introduction of a wealth tax.' But we will return to that resurrected weapon later, after looking more closely at the state of the nation with respect to wealth distribution at the time Rees was speaking.

A couple of months earlier, in his Reith Lectures on the changing face of British society, Professor A.H. Halsey had drawn attention to the 'spectacular inequalities' that persisted despite all attempts at redistribution, proffering as one of the most striking illustrations of this socio-economic stagnation a recent estimate that in 1974/75 the richest one per cent of the population got about the same amount in income as the poorest twenty per cent, or, in other words, that they took twenty times as much a head from the common wealth. But focusing on the top and bottom of the ladder is misleading just because the difference is so spectacular and because we are all well-conditioned to the fact that in almost every society there are a few story-book people who are fabulously rich. That they are so exceptional serves as an excuse, and their Olympian state is even portrayed as a kind of blessing in that it lends to the humdrum lives of ordinary people the thrill of watching the wheel of fortune turning, in much the same way that, in his novel *The Power and the Glory* and the travel book, *The Lawless Roads*, which was its source, Graham Greene defends the opulence of the Church in a land of poverty as conferring on the peasantry the gift of forgetting for a while their wretched state. In any case, contend the disingenuous, to share out amongst the many the superfluous wealth of the few would be to attenuate it, *strudel*-like, so much that it would be of no appreciable benefit to the multitude. To see just how specious such arguments are, we need to look at the whole range of income and wealth distribution, not just at the top and the bottom.

As an earnest of Labour's concern about the persistence of gross social and economic inequalities, a Royal Commission on the Distribution of Income and Wealth had been set up in 1975, and in his book based on his Reith Lectures, *Change in British Society*, Halsey used the Commission's findings as a source for tables showing the situation in 1974-75 (the latest year for which figures were available) and for most of the years back to 1959. The 1974-75 figures showed that the income collectively received by the top 10 per cent after the deduction of income tax amounted to just about the same as that collectively received by the bottom 30 per cent; that is to say, on average they got nearly three times more per capita. The top 30 per cent enjoyed more than half (52.2 per cent) the total post-income-tax income, while the share of the bottom 50 per cent was not much above a quarter (27 per cent).

The common contention that the progressive system of income tax had had, over the years, a significant cumulative effect on the distribution of income is quickly dispelled by an examination of the figures. Slight rises (in the order of 0.1 per cent to 0.6 per cent per quantile group) between 1959 and 1974-75 in the share of the total post-income-tax income at the disposal of the lower 60 per cent of income-earners were gained almost entirely at the expense of the top 5 per cent, whose collective share fell from 15.8 per cent to 13.7 per cent, with the top 1 per cent suffering the only dramatic fall, from 5.3 per cent to 4.0 per cent. Despite this, at the end of this period (which covers all but one of Wilson's years in power) the top 1 per cent still had income at their disposal that was nearly a third as much again as the 3.1 per cent of the total available to the bottom 10 per cent. Moreover, the proportionate loss of the top 1 per cent tends to conceal the fact that all the other top quantile groups down to the 40 per cent level actually increased their share of post-income-tax income.

Yet for a number of reasons this still greatly understates the huge disparities in spending power that characterise our society. The single most important reason is that inequalities in the ownership of wealth (and hence in the availability of credit) are even more spectacular than inequalities in personal income. Halsey reproduces from the same Royal Commission report a table showing the percentage shares of estimated personal wealth of given quantile groups between 1960 and 1975. The 1975 figures show that nearly a quarter of the total personal wealth of the UK population was owned by the top 1 per cent, nearly a half by the top 5 per cent, nearly two-thirds by the top 10 per cent, and more than four-fifths by the top 20 per cent, leaving less than one-fifth (18.2 in percentage figures) for the bottom *80* per cent!

It is true that the figures for wealth distribution, in contrast to those for income distribution, appear to show very considerable redistribution from the wealthier sections of the population to the poorer. Between 1960 and 1975 the percentage share of the top 1 per cent fell from 38.2 to 23.2, of the top 5 per cent from 64.3 to 46.5, of the top 10 per cent from 76.7 to 62.4, and of the top 20 per cent from 89.8 to 81.8, while the percentage share of the bottom 80 per cent rose from 10.2 to 18.2. Nevertheless, Halsey finds no convincing evidence to support the contention of 'liberal theorists' that the Welfare State, through its taxation and welfare policies, has substantially reduced 'market inequalities'. On the contrary, he endorses the three principal conclusions of what he calls 'a voluminously and soberly argued empirical account from the Marxist standpoint', *Class in a Capitalist Society* (1975), by John Westergaard and Henrietta Resler: firstly, that the only major shifts in distribution were brought about by the exceptional circumstances of the two world wars; secondly, that such redistribution as has taken place since the Second World War has (in Halsey's words) 'very largely been a spread of wealth to the richest 5 per cent instead of 1 per cent, and much of it reflects arrangements for gifts *inter vivos* - gifts between the living as distinct from those bequeathed at death', whereby 'rich families have passed on their wealth and legally avoided tax'; thirdly, that far from the Welfare State being a 'hugely distributive' force, 'welfare, it would appear, is largely self-financed for the bulk of the population.'

Of the effect of welfare provision, interacting with tax formulae, on the pattern of have-nots, haves and have-lots, the data marshalled by Westergaard and Resler demonstrates that:

'The 'welfare state' does redistribute income. But...this is redistribution between households at different stages of life far more than it is redistribution between households at markedly different levels of income. It is redistribution within classes far more than it is redistribution between classes...The public welfare services are crippled as a means of cutting down class divisions, for two reasons especially. First, because they co-exist with private welfare provisions for the well-off and the wealthy, financed in part from public funds by way of tax concessions. Second, because in general the tax system that feeds them bears down heavily on ordinary wage earners and even the poor.'

The authors show that 'wage earners pay for their 'welfare state' largely out of their own pockets', and that sporadic attempts at 'selectivity' (i.e. targeting through means testing) 'designed to give rather more help to the poorest' have been 'at the expense of the broad masses a little way above them.' And they make a fundamental point about the conspiratorial nature of class power in observing of wage-earners in general: 'They do not have the influence, the proximity to those who make policy and execute it, the sheer self-assurance of privilege, which enable businessmen and high professionals to tap the resources of the state to boost "private" welfare arrangements for themselves and colleagues close to them in the hierarchy.' In fact, as the authors remark elsewhere: 'The public welfare services bear the imprint of [the class] distribution of power' and, like the tax machinery, are geared to 'the needs of a capitalist economy.'

On the wider question of changes in the distribution of income and wealth during the twentieth century, Westergaard and Resler sum up:

'Rising levels of living for every man have gone hand in hand with a marked persistence in economic inequality in relative terms. Exceptional circumstances at times compressed the range of contrasts in income and wealth. Those shifts had lasting effects. But they were confined to the periods around World War II and probably World War I. They formed no part of a continuous trend towards equalization, and they entailed only modest redistribution. Disparities may indeed have widened since the 1950s. They certainly did not narrow significantly, from the early 1950s to the early 1970s, under governments of either political shade.'

There was little difference in the picture by the time Labour lost power in 1979, and it is hardly necessary to add that the following decade brought a distinct darkening of their present and their prospects for the lower ranks of society.

But if the Wilson and Callaghan regimes achieved little in the matter of wealth redistribution, one might be disposed - bearing in mind the severe economic buffeting Britain suffered during the seventies - to plead that, like Rome, Jerusalem could not be built in a day. So let us ask the simpler question: what did Labour do about the more crying needs of the poor, about Margaret Beckett's 'great well of justifiable need'? For is it not reasonable to require of those who speak passionately of social justice that when they are able to act they make the elimination of poverty a high - if not their very top - *priority*?

The first thing to be said about poverty is that it is necessarily a relative concept. It is relative to time, i.e. entailing comparison of the living standards of contemporaries, not of people of different eras stretching back to the Stone Ages. To a large extent it is also relative to place, i.e. primarily a question of comparing the situations of people living within the same or similar societies, like with like, rather than, say, contrasting the living standards of citizens of an advanced technological society with those of Amazonian Indians. This would hardly need saying any more if it were not for the lingering influence of that stony-hearted brood which swarmed through the land while Margaret Thatcher held sway, yapping incessantly that all sections of the population had benefited from rising standards of living generated by the fabulous 'economic miracle' conjured up by 'wealth-creators' such as themselves. Their preferred view appeared to be that poverty referred to some fixed and inerasable line, to be above which was to be properly provided for so long as what was provided was sensibly managed. The attraction of that subsistence-level approach to poverty is that - one way or another! - the problem is eliminated in double-quick time.

Nevertheless when, under the Attlee Government's National Insurance Act of May 1946, Britain's rag-bag of statutory measures and agencies for doling out relief to the financially distressed and destitute was exchanged for a more or less comprehensive social security system, the ultimate yardstick employed was in effect an assessment of subsistence levels. And this assessment was not used to ensure that the non-discretionary entitlements would, on their own, provide subsistence. This was only guaranteed through the discretionary instrument of National Assistance. As the Government acknowledged, in its concern to secure the widest possible consensus both in Parliament and in the country, its Bill was, in the main, Beveridge's proposals in statutory form. In some respects (most notably in its rejection of his recommendation that for actuarial reasons the full implementation of the new pension scheme should be delayed) it improved on Beveridge, but in others it fell well short of his Plan.

As C.J. Bartlett puts it in *A History of Postwar Britain, 1945-74*:

'The choice of flat-rate contributions, determined by what the poorest of those in employment could afford, found few critics at the time. But conjoined with the determination to limit the Exchequer's contribution, the result was basic pensions in 1948 below the exiguous Beveridge subsistence level. This meant the defeat of his hope that in time National Assistance would be confined to exceptional cases as the bulk of the population became entitled to full benefits.'

In other words, notwithstanding the Labour Movement's unshakeable opposition to 'means testing', as an affliction visited by an unjust socio-economic system principally upon the working class, by setting the rates for pension and other non-discretionary entitlements at below subsistence level, the first Labour government that was really in command let the means-testing wolf in through the backdoor.

Its successors, Labour as well as Conservative, accepted this system of the doling out of alms to economic casualties by State bureaucrats - the latter-day equivalents of the Poor Law commissioners - apparently without qualms. It was all very well for John Boyd-Carpenter, Macmillan's Minister of Pensions, to tell the House (in June 1959) that no loss of self-respect was entailed in 'exercising the rights which a Christian and civilised society gives of ensuring that no one should fall below the levels that Parliament has laid down'. It was equally fine for Judith Hart, the other Harold's Minister of Social Security, to appeal (in 1967) to people to take up their *rights*, or for Jim Callaghan's Social Services Secretary David Ennals to rebuke (in 1978) certain members on the Opposition benches for referring to supplementary benefits as 'charity'. The fact remained that many people continued to consider it an indignity to have to apply to the State for assistance when in need, and it is not at all clear that re-christening National Assistance 'supplementary benefits' greatly lessened their distaste at the thought of exposing their sores to the purse-holders of State largesse. Though it is true that the mass unemployment manufactured by the Thatcherite miracle-workers has diminished the stigma by making living on the welfare (an opportunity formerly generally reserved for the working class) a way of life for many middle-class people too - the conferment, indeed, of equal shares of misery!

At all events, in July 1978 the Commission responsible for administering the tarted-up alms scheme reported that every year around 900,000 people failed to claim supplementary benefits to which they were entitled. As Maurice Bruce says in *The Coming of the Welfare State*, whatever else the Welfare State is, 'it is...certainly not Socialism', a truth that anyone pondering the use of the term *Wohlfahrstaat* in Bismarck's Germany would surely readily apprehend. Instead of concerning themselves with devising cosmetic cover-ups to conceal the ugly consequences of the gross inequalities inseparable from free-market capitalism, the Labour tribunes would have done better to exhort the people to fight for their *rights*. That would have been in accordance with the Socialist traditions that demanded that the workers be given 'the full fruits of their industry' and taught that social justice lay in the concept of the commonwealth and the principle of contributing and sharing in consonance with the criteria: 'To each according to his needs; from each according to his ability.'

Most commentators outside the circles of the more extreme free-marketeers seem quite convinced that the Attlee Government was on the right lines in laying down the groundwork for the post-war Welfare State. Thus in *Post-War Britain* Sked and Cook contend:

'In its approach to both these measures [the National Insurance Act and the National Health Service Act] the Government displayed a spirit of true egalitarianism by espousing the principle of "universality". This ensured that their legislation bore a distinctive left-wing stamp;

it also ensured that everyone in future would have equal rights to social welfare.'

Implicitly dismissing without answering the objection that 'it would have made much greater sense to have selected the really poor from the mass of the people and to have given them greater benefits' and that the rejection of this approach meant that 'the needs of the poor were being sacrificed to left-wing ideology', the authors, after stressing Labour's overwhelming desire to consign means-testing welfare systems to 'the bad old days' (which, as I have pointed out, they failed to do), go on to speak of the 'canny realism' in the Government's thinking that 'they would only get the best available...if resources were shared with the rich.'

This was unquestionably a cogent practical reason for adopting the 'universality' principle, as the beneficial effect of middle-class pressure for the maintenance and improvement of standards in the comparable case of State schooling attests. Nevertheless, it remains highly debatable whether this blindfolded impartiality in the matter of basic welfare hand-outs was in the best interests of the least privileged in the long-term. 'Positive discrimination', which was later seen as a powerful weapon in the fight against racial inequality, would surely have served them better. Through its obsession with the 'shame' of applying for National Assistance and its crippled perception of equality, Labour deprived itself of the full potential for using the welfare system as a means of making some small restitution to the workers for the rights robbed from them in the marketplace. But if this looks like yet another indication of Labour's lack of serious commitment to Socialist objectives of redistribution and driving down the road to equality, from a non-partisan but humanitarian point of view there is worse to be said. By its rejection of the case for funding social security entirely out of normal tax revenue, setting a decent inflation-proofed standard of living as the basis for benefits - at a time, too, when openly to oppose such proposals would have been to court widespread unpopularity amongst the voters - Labour lost the chance of outlawing poverty in the pioneering Welfare State.

If we accept that poverty is a relative term, inflation-proofing of benefits fixed at a given moment at a rate ensuring a 'decent' standard of living would not on its own end involuntary poverty, of course, since that decent standard would itself be changing all the time. In an epoch of rising standards such as that enjoyed in the fully industrialised countries since the Second World War, those rises need to be truly reflected at the lowest levels. Apologists for Labour's record in the field of social security might be chastened by the reminder that (as already noted in Chapter 11) it was a Tory government - that of Harold Macmillan - that first officially accepted that the poor should share in the growing prosperity of the nation by laying it down in 1959 that the poverty line that triggered extra help from the State should rise with rises in the general standard of living. (A crystal-clear statement to the same effect, explicitly endorsing the concept of relative poverty, was made twenty years later by Lynda Chalker, when she was Under-Secretary of State in Margaret Thatcher's first administration. In a parliamentary written answer she said: 'It is not sufficient to assess poverty by absolute standards: nowadays, it must be judged on relative criteria by comparison with the standard of living of other groups in the community'.)

Without the will to redistribute wealth in favour of the underprivileged, however, acceptance of what might be called this minimal principle of social justice, in an age when medical and other advances were prolonging life and thus constantly enlarging the proportion of the population that was 'non-productive' (for example, between 1948 - the year that the National Insurance Act, the National Assistance Act, *and* the National Health Service Act all came fully into force on the same day - and 1969, the number of pensioners increased by 75 per cent, 3 million people), meant that the elimination of poverty became an ever more distant social objective. Within five years of the Welfare State train departing from the terminus, its founding father was already lamenting the fact that no less than a quarter of all those receiving retirement or widows' pensions had to apply for National Assistance. By 1969, towards the end of Wilson's first stint in power, nearly 3 out of every 10 pensioners were receiving such assistance in the shiny new packaging of supplementary benefits. By 1973, with Ted Heath in office and the State retirement pension a mite more generous than usual, at about one-third of the average manual wage (for most of the time since 1948 it had hovered around 30 per cent, sometimes falling below that figure), some 1¾ million pensioners needed supplementary benefits. Writing (in *Final Term*) of the situation as it was a couple of years later, before the introduction of SERPS, Harold Wilson says that 2 million of our 7 million retirement pensioners and no less than half of the nation's elderly widows were dependent on supplementary benefits. Between 1948 and 1962 the total number of people having recourse to National Assistance nearly doubled to top 2 million. By the following year more than 2½ million people were wholly or partly dependent on National Assistance, with a further million who either did not realise they were entitled to it or shunned the role of supplicant. In *Change in British Society* (1978) Professor Halsey states:

> 'Four and three-quarter million Britons receive money from the Supplementary Benefits Commission. In other words, four and three-quarter million are living at the government's own estimate of the poverty line. And there are more below it who do not claim their due.'

A report published by the Department of Health and Social Security in July 1978 stated that around £2 billion a year was being paid out as supplementary benefits to about one-tenth of the population, that is, to more than 5 million people. The product of a two-year review of the supplementary benefits system, the report was greeted with both bouquets and brickbats - bouquets for the precedent in open government set by the comprehensive publication of the working papers upon which it was based; brickbats for its assumption that no more money would be made available to operate the system and that more rigorous restrictions would have to be imposed on discretionary payments and on the right of appeal against the refusal of assistance, proposals for policy changes which indeed foreshadowed the even harsher tightening up that took place when, in 1988, the Thatcher regime introduced its euphemistically-named Social Fund. The failure of the Attlee Government to measure up to Beveridge's requirements for comprehensive social security in the first place - and of every succeeding government to face up to the problem - was now coming home to roost, as the swelling ranks of poor pensioners and of those thrown out of work began to put an intolerable strain on the supplementary benefits system. In the words of the DHSS report: 'On any realistic assessment, the scheme will have to deal with large numbers of claimants for a long time to come; it is a safety net into which many more people will fall than it was originally intended for.'

This chronic situation drew even gloomier comments from the chairman of the Supplementary Benefits Commission, Professor

David Donnison, when he addressed the annual conference of the British Association of Social Workers a couple of months later. That fewer than half of the unemployed were still able to draw unemployment insurance benefit meant that the insurance scheme designed to keep up the income of those who lost their jobs had collapsed, he told the delegates. Like many one-parent families and families in which the breadwinner was poorly paid, most of the unemployed were now at least partially dependent on supplementary benefit, and in some parts of the country the service was breaking down under the pressure of the demands on it. In an ominous foreshadowing of the evaporation of caring ('compassion fatigue' was the ironic expression later popularised by the media in the analogous case of fading response to calls from charities for donations to help them fight famine in the Third World) that was to characterise the Thatcher help-yourself decade, Donnison observed:

'As the British people have lost confidence in progress, no longer feeling that society can afford to help the poor without holding back the steady advance of everyone else to greater affluence, they have become less tolerant of those who live on incomes provided by the taxpayer. That includes civil servants and social workers along with social security claimants.'

We are unlikely to doubt where Donnison's sympathies lie. All the same, his scrupulously non-partisan, unreproving way of putting an attitude that cannot quite escape the charge of callousness might lead us almost unconsciously to swallow the highly questionable assumption that the nation's economic troubles and the consequential deceleration in growth had deprived it of the resources to cope with poverty or, at the very least, that to find adequate resources would be to demand too great sacrifices of the general population. Paradoxically, the other big danger is that by focusing our attention on the problem of the provision of social security we may lose sight of the sheer dimensions of the poverty we are concerned with - and hence of the kind of society in which we live. For although it is true that in the late twentieth century the severely deprived have come to constitute only a minority of the population of the more advanced nations, they remain so substantial and persistent an element in such countries as ours that we can no longer talk in Crosland's optimistic terms of a merely residual or 'secondary poverty'. On the contrary, it is all too evident that the two-thousand-year-old saying, 'The poor are always with you,' is as true of our times as it was of Jesus Christ's.

In 1975, for example, Help the Aged estimated that around one million of the elderly were living *below* the poverty line, a figure consistent with Age Concern's calculation in October 1978 that poverty persisted for as many as 2½ million out of the 9 million people in retirement. If we raise our definition of deprivation by just twenty per cent, we find that more than half the nation's 'senior citizens' were poor. Such was the second-class citizenship awarded to a large fraction of the people of the Welfare State when their working lives were over. Large numbers of those who had not yet started working for wages but were the nation's future, its children, commonly suffered from the low pay of their parents - to such an extent that by the end of the Thatcher decade it was reckoned that a quarter of British children were growing up in poverty - a dispossessed fraction which by 1995 had been revised upwards to one third. As for the total numbers of the poor, in 1976, at about the mid point of Labour's last inglorious period in office, it was calculated that nearly 10½ million people - around a fifth of the nation - were living on, below, or no more than twenty per cent above the poverty line.

The big change we ('we', that is, in the advanced Western-style societies) have experienced in the last half century is that for the first time poverty has unquestionably become the affliction of a minority. And to that extent capitalism (when harnessed with representative democracy and the Welfare State, neither of which is exactly a natural stable-mate for it) *has*, at long last, delivered the goods. Comparing the purchasing power of male manual workers earning the median income of just over £1 a week in 1905, with that enjoyed by male manual workers with median earnings of just over £60 a week in 1976, Professor Halsey reckons that 'we can safely say that they also represent at least a tripling of real income.' He goes on to remark: 'Nor can there be any doubt that the ordinary manual worker and his wife are very much less the slaves of toil than they were in Edwardian England.' As he says: 'Their market freedoms, whether as earners or spenders, have been transformed.' When, not long after taking over the reins of power from the stricken Sir Anthony Eden, Harold Macmillan told the country, 'Most of our people have never had it so good,' (words which, when recycled by the Grub Street hucksters as 'you've never had it so good', sounded like a Tory taunt to the have-nots or a vulgar come-on to the punters), he was doing no more than telling the truth. That was within a dozen years of the end of the most exhausting and near-mortal combat the country had ever engaged in; and the exponential growth of the advanced economies, whether they had been victors, vanquished, or neutral in the titanic conflict of 1939-45, was to continue more or less unabated into the early seventies, raising general living standards more rapidly than ever before or (so far at least) since.

In February 1978 the Central Statistical Office recorded in its annual supplement on 'Economic Trends' that real incomes had doubled between 1953, when the consumption boom began, and the summer of 1976, when it hit its peak, not long after the great pragmatist Harold Wilson, with that juggler's sense of timing for which he was celebrated, had handed over the golden balls of the State to Sunny Jim. During 1977 living standards fell: only by about one per cent, but the sense of standing on an escalator that would in time carry everyone to prosperity gave way to that gloomier mood to which Donnison alludes - and to a what-we-have-we-hold family-laager frame of mind that left little room for concern for the underclass who never had enjoyed a secure place on the escalator.

A high proportion of this 'submerged fifth' (to adopt a term from history) was naturally composed of some of those who, in a modern civilised society, were considered either too young or too old to be expected to work for wages. They were, in short, dependants by reason and by right of their age. Writing about the problem of the provision of social security at the end of the sixties, Bartlett notes that the ratio of children and pensioners to the working population had risen from 488 to 1000 in 1941, to 655 to 1000 in 1969. Commenting on the fact that 'Britain's overall performance in social welfare ranked below that generally achieved within the EEC', he alludes to the extenuating circumstances of Britain's recurrent economic crises and slow growth, and points out that much of the rise in welfare expenditure during the Wilson ministries was simply absorbed by rising numbers of dependants. 'In these circumstances,' he observes, 'the plight of the poor could only have been relieved by a radical redistribution of wealth.'

But that is precisely what Labour's top brass had set their minds against. As early as April 1949, Attlee's second Chancellor of the Exchequer, Sir Stafford Cripps, laid down the principles which - with the full approval, of course, of their generalissimos - all succeeding Labour chancellors were to follow:

> 'There is not much further immediate possibility of the redistribution of national income by way of taxation in this country; for the future, we must rely rather upon the creation of more distributable wealth than upon...redistribution...Total taxation, local and national, is now more than 40 per cent of the national income, and at that level the redistribution of income entailed in the payment of Social Services already falls, to a considerable extent, upon those who are the recipients of these services. We must, therefore, moderate the speed of our advance in the extended application of the existing Social Services to our progressive ability to pay for them by an increase in our national income. Otherwise, we shall not be able to avoid entrenching, to an intolerable extent, upon the liberty of spending by the private individual for his own purposes.'

That *ex cathedra* pronouncement, made in the context of a budget founded on a TUC-endorsed wage-freeze, is of immeasurably greater significance than all the Healey-style rhetoric of the irreversible-shift-of-power and squeezing-the-rich-till-the-pips-squeak varieties, since it spells out the rules that Labour imposed upon itself in the struggle for social justice. It was as if Samson had bound himself. What scope was left for the pursuit of equality, or even for the abolition of poverty and the guaranteeing of adequate social welfare for all? As for pulling down the pillars of the temples of capitalism, Heavens forbid!

Cripps was voicing his overriding concern for the private individual's 'liberty of spending' (assenting, in effect, to the common proposition that everybody has the right to do what he pleases with 'his own property') as Labour's purported social revolution was still supposedly in full swing. Yet, like any other reputable politician, he put his emphasis not on the problems of sharing fairly wealth produced by common effort, but on the need to increase the size of the cake. 'Let the people eat cake crumbs' - to revamp a celebrated piece of apocrypha. The world created by capitalism was not, at least in its essentials, to be disturbed. Social progress - including whatever creeping steps towards greater equality, if any, were envisaged - was to depend on economic growth steadily increasing the national income. Ruling politicians would play no more than a subsidiary role to capitalism's celebrated 'trickle-down' benevolence by doling out to the most disadvantaged 'the superflux' in the State's coffers.

This always was a fraudulent prospectus for bringing about equality, of course. Even given increasing prosperity for all classes, since when have the more affluent been content to see their differentials diminishing? And no way would they accept that they ought to receive a *smaller* share of the new wealth created than the less affluent! Indeed, to their way of thinking, they were entitled to a share of the new wealth fully proportionate to the hoard they already had! But however devoid of Socialist content such an attitude might have been, it did at least hold out some hope of improvement in the lives of the grossly underprivileged as long as growth kept coming. Throughout the fifties and sixties, notwithstanding the recurrent economic crises and a worrying decline in her trading position in an increasingly competitive world, Britain enjoyed her longest period of sustained growth this century. By the time Wilson lost power in the summer of 1970, however, the prospects already looked gloomier, with Anthony Crosland confessing that he had been too complacent in pinning all his hopes for a more equal society on growth when he wrote *The Future of Socialism*. Six months before the debacle of May 1979, one of the then doughtiest champions of the poor challenged Labour to confirm or deny its presumed identity as a party of radical reform. In an article in *The Guardian*, the director-general of the Child Poverty Action Group and of the Low Pay Unit, Frank Field, who was himself to become a Labour MP by winning Birkenhead in the forthcoming election, wrote:

'If, in the foreseeable future, the economy fails to grow
at a greater rate, Labour will be forced to choose
between ditching its role as the reforming party or
breaking the post-war political consensus...The agent for
lowering the political temperature, while at the same
time removing the stains left by society's grosser forms

of poverty, is a steadily rising national income. The
promise to the "haves" was that injustice could be
painlessly removed; they would not be required to make
real, only accept relative cuts in their living standards.
Economic growth would guarantee that the real income
of the "haves" rose while only part of the largesse was
transferred to the "have nots".'

From Crosland's insistence that 'in a democracy low or zero growth
wholly excludes the possibility' of the substantial transference of
resources to the poorer sections of society, Field drew the conclusion
that in the situation then obtaining - one of low growth with
ever-rising numbers of people becoming dependent on State
welfare as a consequence of demographic changes and increasing
unemployment - 'Labour will not only have to abandon its
commitments to creating a more equal society but stand idly by
as the poor suffer real cuts in their standards of living.' The
gravamen of his case was that Labour's only alternative was to
abandon consensus politics in favour of 'a determined policy of
redistributing existing resources.'

When the sixth report of the Royal Commission on the
Distribution of Income and Wealth was published in the summer of
1978, it had carried an addendum by three of its members who argued
that income distribution could be improved by political will. But where
was that will to be found? Certainly not among the top Labour
leadership, who were wholly engrossed in the struggle against inflation
and the concomitant campaign to break-in the trade unions by saddling
them with another incomes policy. The project amounted to a straitjacket
for working-class aspirations. Not even the most exploited groups of
workers got a fair crack of the whip from the Callaghan Government.
The poverty lobby, which had bitterly pronounced that the plight of the
poor had grown worse under Labour in the sixties, was now only willing
to reduce the charge slightly by adding a question mark. On the eve of
the 1979 general election Ruth Lister, Frank Field's successor at the
Child Poverty Action Group, asked: whatever happened to James
Callaghan's pledge of a crusade against poverty? There was nothing
for the poor in any of the party manifestos, she protested. Yet again,
the cry of the poor was falling on deaf ears. And the callousness was
compounded by the fact that 'the people's party' was in power and had
ruled for the past five years.

CHAPTER 20

A marriage on the rocks

'The trade unionists...having had their minds so fully occupied with the idea that Parliament is the all-important institution, and never having even hoped to see all workers organised industrially, have failed to realise what enormous power lies in industrial solidarity.'

Tom Mann, *Memoirs* **(1923)**

Moving the address of thanks for the King's Speech in the Commons on 16th August 1945, just after the victory of the Allies over Japan, Major John Freeman told the House that this was 'D-Day in the battle of the new Britain.' In those 'bliss-was-it-to-be-alive' days no one in the triumphant ranks of the 'we-are-the-masters-now' party could have dreamt of the bitterness of the battles that were to come - not those they fully expected to have with their acknowledged political opponents (the 'class enemy', or even the 'vermin', as some Labour members thought of them), but those that were to take place within the ranks of the Labour Movement itself. A third of a century later fratricidal strife threatened to shatter the Movement, as the dominant forces in its parliamentary wing clashed with the trade union battalions that more directly represented the Party's 'working-class' constituency.

Abetted by a press almost wholly hostile to Labour and near-to-universally antipathetic to trade unions, the Tories have been so successful at selling their twopence-coloured broadsheet portrayal of the so-called Winter of Discontent to the electorate at large that it has become - even for many habitual Labour voters - the authorised version of that social upheaval, to be recited by right-wing cheerleaders at election after election as conclusive evidence of Labour's unfitness to govern. The message it punches home is of the gross irresponsibility, greed and intolerable anarchy that prevail whenever law and government fail to keep union power firmly in check. 'What kind of society is this that breeds such selfish callousness?' Margaret Thatcher, with that breath-taking effrontery that comes so easily to her, demanded, lusting after her 'glorious summer'.

The photomontage of rubbish piled high in the streets, the dead denied burial, the sick forsaken by nursing orderlies, and the like, that became imprinted on the mind's-eye of the public, testifies to the easily-won supremacy of image over information and of emotional orgasm over intellectual appraisal. What does on first consideration astonish, though, is that this tabloid travesty of the true story of the Winter of Discontent has gone largely unchallenged by Labour. On first consideration, that is - until one reflects how much more unpalatable for Labour the conclusions of any more carefully-considered analysis must be. For the Winter of Discontent came close to dispelling for ever the illusion that a Labour government has one great and undeniable advantage not enjoyed by its opponents when they are in power - a hotline to the unions that can ensure at least a tolerable measure of industrial peace. The truth is that for many years after the war Labour's leaders were able to make this claim with some credibility. Then, like the lover in Dylan's song, they threw it all away.

The term Labour Movement is, of course, much more than a piece of rhetoric expressing a general sympathy between the purposes of the Party and those of the trade unions. Affiliation to the Party theoretically conferred on the unions enormous - indeed, predominant - power in the formulation of its policy and the election of its leadership. As David Coates says in *Labour in Power?*: 'It is facts like these that give credence to the repeated Conservative claim that the Labour Party in office is the creature of trade union control.' In certain respects the integration of party and affiliated unions is so intimate (Kenneth O. Morgan calls it 'intimate symbiosis') that to talk of the separate wings of one movement and of the dialogue between them may be said to be a tool of analysis rather than a description of reality. Yet by their nature they remain - and cannot but remain - distinct and alternative centres of power; and that natural tension between them which makes of them one structure (a tension inherent in the Party's origins at the beginning of the century as the Labour Representation Committee) may shift so far out of balance as to threaten disintegration. Indeed, considering the potential for conflict between them and the many actual clashes that have occurred (particularly during periods when the Labour Party has been in office), it is a matter for some wonder that - contrary to the view assiduously propagated in the press - the unions have generally behaved with such remarkable restraint that the couple has managed to rub along together for so long.

Time and again (to speak, as is customary, in terms of leaders and elites, not of the common ruck) loyalty to the Party - or to put it more precisely, concern for its prospects at the polls - has overridden trade union interests. This loyalty was, understandably, at its height during the days of hope of Attlee's first administration, when at least it could be claimed that 'the social wage' was being pushed up substantially. A White Paper published in February 1948 in effect called for the freezing of personal incomes except where rises were justified by increased productivity. Despite the fact that there had been no prior consultation with the TUC - let alone union rank and file, this policy was agreed to at a special conference of trade union executive delegates by a majority of 5,421,000 to 2,032,000. It was endorsed by the following TUC Conference, and was not overturned until the autumn 1950 Conference. Then, under the pressures of a rapidly rising cost of living caused principally by the devaluation of sterling in September 1949 and the outbreak of the Korean War in June 1950, wage restraint was voted down by the small majority of 222,000.

Even before a pay pause had become official TUC policy, considerable restraint had been exercised by the unions, as is shown by the fact that the general level of wages was in real terms lower in 1948 than in 1947. Sked and Cook note that: 'From 1948 till August 1950 wage rates rose by only 5 per cent while retail prices rose by 8 per cent. Indeed between 1945 and 1951 average weekly wages rose in real terms by only 6 per cent.' In other words, they say, quoting another's analyst's caustic comment: 'Under six years of socialism the workers had to work a great deal of overtime to improve their standard of living by a tiny 1 per cent a year.'

In his *Years of Recovery: British Economic Policy 1945-51*, Sir Alec Cairncross draws attention to another fact which makes this restraint even more remarkable. In a capitalist economy the price of labour, like that of other commodities, is of course largely determined by supply and demand. Thus periods of labour surplus have always tended to mean hard times for the workers and their families, whilst periods of labour shortages are times of opportunity for increasing their prosperity by militant action or the threat of it. Yet, as Cairncross points out:

'That money wages rose so little when real wages were stationary or falling and unemployment was down to

300,000 is striking testimony to the influence of the trade-union leaders. Hourly wage rates after March 1948 rose no faster than in the mid-1930s, between 1934 and 1938, when unemployment was around two million.'

It is neither coincidence nor perversity which makes periods in opposition, normally speaking, those in which the Labour Movement is most united. In saying this I am not simply making the obvious point which applies to any party defeated at the polls, that, notwithstanding the painfulness of post-mortems and of abrasive debate about how best to adjust their programme and tactics, the will to win next time will tend to draw them together. I am making a point more specific to Labour: that when the Party is out of office it is natural for those in all the echelons of the Labour Movement to feel like comrades in adversity, but when the Party is in power, constitutionally-speaking it represents 'the national interest', while the unions, separately considered and even considered collectively, merely represent sectional interests. (That too might seem blindingly obvious, but far too little account is taken of this fundamental fracture in the Movement in serious analysis, as distinct from partisan squibbery.) So, notwithstanding the fierce debates that took place within the Movement over such momentous issues as 'the bomb' and whether Clause IV should be considered as anything more than an example of junkable antiquarianism, as Hugh Gaitskell hopefully positioned himself for a victory at the polls that never came, Labour's matrimonial difficulties during the 'thirteen wasted years' were as nothing to the turbulent times it experienced after it returned to power under Harold Wilson's leadership.

Wage restraint may not have been an article of faith for Labour governments (as it is, with respect to 'ordinary workers', for what one used to be able to distinguish as 'the bourgeois parties'); but in running a capitalist economy in a situation of slow growth, of a problematic balance of trade, and of recurrent sterling crises, it was no less a practical imperative for them than it was for the Tories. Above all, it was seen by every Chancellor of the Exchequer, of whatever party, as the main means to bind the serpent of inflation. The efforts of Wilson and his Chancellors, James Callaghan and Roy Jenkins, to stem the tide of the trade unions' drive, sometimes to improve but often simply to maintain or recover the position of their members in the pecking order, span Labour's whole period in office between 1964 and 1970.

The details of the four formal stages of wage restraint decreed during those years are of little interest now. What remains significant is the retrogression from the attempt at voluntary co-operation - exemplified by the Joint Statement of Intent on Productivity, Prices and Incomes signed by representatives of the Government, the TUC, and employers' organisations in December 1964, and also by the Prices and Incomes Board set up in April 1965, which had only monitoring and advisory powers - to the Government's mobilisation of powers of compulsory restraint under the 1966 Prices and Incomes Act. Twenty-three Labour back-benchers defied the Government whip when the Bill was pushed through the Commons on the ominous date of August 4th. Nor was this downhill path to division in the Movement taken without protest from trade union leaders as well as the rank and file. Yet it is still significant that it was not until the autumn of 1968 that the Government's wages policy was repudiated by the Movement's two principal annual conferences. Both rejections were by crushing majorities, nearly five to one at the Party Conference and nearly eight to one at the TUC's. And even then, at their conference, the workers' delegates agreed to the TUC's own policy of voluntary restraint, though admittedly only by the tiny margin of 34,000 votes.

The climax of this collision between the two wings of the Labour Movement came a few months later, with the publication in January 1969 of *In Place of Strife*. This White Paper, intended as the basis of legislation designed to pacify industrial relations, had its origin in the disappointment of Wilson and some of his colleagues with the Donovan Report. In February 1965 the Labour Government had announced the appointment, under the chairmanship of Lord Donovan, of a Royal Commission on Trade Unions and Employers' Associations, though as Joe England and Brian Weekes acidly remark in their essay *Trade Unions and the State: A Review of the Crisis* (1981): 'No one doubted that trade unions were intended to be the main target for investigation.' The Commission as a whole, however, was certainly well-disposed towards the trade unions (one of its members, indeed, was the TUC's general secretary, George Woodcock), and its report, published in June 1968, came down decisively against legal coercion as a solution to Britain's industrial relations problems. In taking this view, it showed far more wisdom than Wilson and his Secretary of State for Employment and Productivity, Barbara Castle (the minister principally responsible for the Government's White Paper), who perhaps shared Nye Bevan's incomprehension that workers could strike against 'a workers' government' and were certainly fearful of the electoral consequences of failing to bring the unions to heel.

In *Place of Strife* made twenty-seven specific proposals, including the establishment of a permanent Industrial Relations Commission, a Register of Trade Unions and Employers' Associations, and new kinds of industrial arbitration - ideas to which the Donovan Report had already given currency without arousing much controversy. In his autobiography, James Callaghan cites his own contemporaneous note recording his feeling that '90 per cent of the White Paper is not only acceptable but welcome', and certainly most offence was given by those three proposals (out of the total of twenty-seven) that contained coercive and penal clauses. These chiefly concerned provisions for compulsory arbitration in intractable inter-union disputes, for compulsory ballots before strikes deemed to constitute a serious threat to the public interest, and (mimicking a hamstringing clause in America's notorious anti-labour Taft-Hartley Act), for the imposition of a 28-day cooling-off and conciliation period before a strike could take place. The main thrust of these proposed sanctions was directed against strikes in 'essential services' and unofficial strikes, the latter constituting, according to the Donovan Commission's calculations, no less than 95 per cent of the total number of strikes.

Further testimony to the embarrassing gap between establishment notions of labour discipline and the insubordinate reality was provided by the Prime Minister himself, who appealed for sympathy to an audience of City worthies in a speech at the Guildhall (in so doing, implicitly identifying himself with them and his troubles with theirs, of course), by telling them: 'We face the problem of an assertion of the power of the factory floor.' As Bartlett wryly remarks, with reference to the ascendant influence of shop stewards: 'The government's dismay over the rise of shop floor wage bargaining was a little ironic given its own encouragement of productivity deals, which of course required that type of approach.' He also notes that: 'Incomes policy had been circumvented in other ways, so that the Prices and Incomes Board concluded that its effect between 1965 and 1968 had been to reduce incomes by no more than one per cent a year...'

In any event, in an atmosphere of growing militancy the national leaders of the unions were obliged either to get out in front or be seen as irrelevant by the rank and file. The number of strikes rose from an annual average of 1,181 in the four years before Labour regained power to nearly 1,500 in both 1964 and 1965, and to nearly 2,000 in 1966. It continued to climb steadily through 1967 and 1968, then steeply to well over 3,000 in 1969 and to not far short of 4,000 in 1970, the year in which, in June, the Tories were returned to power under Ted Heath. As for the man-hours lost through strike action, these rose at the rate of around two million strike-days a year between 1967 and 1969, when they reached about 6,800,000 strike-days. It is not easy to calculate the effects of industrial action on the counter-inflation policies of the governments trying to impose them; but despite the common assumption that the effects of such action are devastating, it is a fact that the increase in retail prices was held to an average of below 6 per cent between 1968 and 1970, but rose to 8.6 per cent under Heath.

When Wilson insinuated to his receptive Guildhall audience that the Government had been right in contending that the State needed more statutory powers to control the unions, he had already lost the battle. What is astonishing is that Harold and Barbara ever thought that they could win it (without destroying the Labour Movement in the process, that is). Despite all warnings - including a mutiny in the Commons when the White Paper was debated on 3rd March 1969 in which 55 Labour members voted against it and about as many again abstained, the NEC's decisive rejection by 16 votes to 5 on 26th March, and the strong opposition of the TUC which had been forthrightly expressed from the beginning and never showed signs of wavering - they pressed on with their shackling proposals from January to June, when at last, given pause by a crushing rebuff inflicted by a special TUC conference held at Croydon, they began a face-saving withdrawal. On 17th June, Robert Mellish, the Government's Chief Whip, reported to the Cabinet that more than half the Parliamentary Labour Party was opposed to the penal proposals and that there was no chance of their being pushed through the Commons. The next day the Labour Movement gave birth to the celebrated illusionist Solomon Binding.

Harold Wilson in his memoirs and Barbara Castle by report both claimed that with the threat of penal legislation hanging over them the unions had moved forward farther in a matter of weeks than they had in forty years. (Why 'forty' one can only speculate, but it can hardly be coincidental that that would have taken the scenario back to the despondent aftermath of the near-revolutionary clash between the State and the unions in 1926, in which the leaders of both wings of the Movement had, with few exceptions, played such a pusillanimous part). But the fact was that Labour's would-be statespersons had had their bluff called and had capitulated. Apart from the undertaking given in the trade unions' own counter-proposals (the so-called *Programme for Action* drawn up by the TUC and endorsed by the Croydon conference, which Barbara Castle contemptuously dismissed as a 'pious hope') that they would submit to the rulings of the TUC General Council in inter-union disputes or face suspension, virtually only one additional concession was wrung from them. It was a 'solemn and binding' but not legally enforceable pledge from the General Council that affiliated unions would observe the TUC's own guidelines on the containment of unofficial strikes.

As James Callaghan says: 'This whole episode was a venture bound to end in tears.' Certainly he was a great deal more canny than the Prime Minister and his fiery redhead, whom Callaghan characterises as galloping ahead 'with all the reckless gallantry of the Light Brigade at Balaclava.' In a note he wrote at the time which makes her sound much more like that ultimate conviction (i.e. 'I am always right') politician, Mrs Thatcher, than he perhaps intended, he also distinguishes between those whose unqualified support for the White Paper he considered implicated them in 'the shabby and squalid intellectual dishonesty which pretends that these clauses are going to solve unofficial strikes and, therefore, are vital for our balance of payments problems' and the passionately sincere (but presumably dumb) redhead: 'Barbara is a different case; she believes passionately in any job she is doing at the time...and she is absolutely convinced, but there is no reason why the rest of us should be.'

Callaghan thought the White Paper 'contained excellent ideas' but had a flaw which he clearly considered fatal:

> 'But the paper was flawed by ineffective proposals for legal sanctions as a solution to the problem of unofficial strikes. Both industrial strikers and unions would be liable to fines, *but it would not be the employers who*

*would take the strikers to court. The Government itself
would make an order having legal effect, thereby
bringing the state directly into conflict with the men
concerned.'* [my emphasis]

Whether or not this dispassionate analysis implies that he saw no objections in principle to such proposals, but only objections, regrettably, on pragmatic grounds, it is undeniably shrewd. Such a conflict between workers and State might be welcome to politicians of other hues (though even then such pugnacity might be deemed rash); but to politically literate Labour politicians it could only spell FOLLY.

Callaghan is equally Olympian in his casual allusion to the fact that, far from being privy to the drafting of the White Paper, as a known opponent of its more draconian measures, he was deliberately kept in the dark. He was, after all, in addition to being Home Secretary, particularly closely associated with the trade unions as Party Treasurer, and was a member of the Cabinet committee on industrial relations, which was vouchsafed no sight of the White Paper prior to its coming before full Cabinet. Yet all we get in his autobiography touching on this 'oversight' (to put the impropriety in diplomatic terms) is the oblique observation that 'the issue had not been considered in the usual manner by Cabinet committee so there were many rough edges and unanswered questions.' A somewhat nicer concern for the workings of inner party democracy and constitutional government might prod a person into voicing some more astringent comment. For example, that this devious and deliberate bypassing of the Cabinet committee most pertinent to the issue under consideration provided just a foretaste of the monstrous-regiment-of-Woman government that was to come in a decade or so.

But however complex and disingenuous or, as he would have us believe, transparent and straightforward Callaghan's motives might have been, his stance served him very well in the long term, winning him widespread union support in the contest for the leadership that took place after Wilson sprung his resignation on the Party in the spring of '76. Indeed, moves were afoot during the crisis provoked by the schismatic proposals of *In Place of Strife* to persuade Jim to challenge Harold for the leadership, and if Harold had not backed down, it seems certain he would have faced a shoot-out. In his contemporaneous note cited above, Callaghan takes pains to refute the allegations being 'put around' that his opposition to the penal proposals in the White Paper was to be explained as a prelude to a bid for the top job. But such a reading of his conduct is not necessarily incompatible with his insistence that his opposition reflected his judgement as to what was prudent and in the best interests of the Party. At any rate, Denis Healey makes no bones about his rival's ambitions in his autobiography: 'Callaghan campaigned publicly against them ["Barbara's proposals"] in the hope of winning enough trade union support to force Wilson out and take his place.'

What may be regarded as of much greater moment than these questions of, on the one hand, conspiracy and vaunting ambition, or on the other, opposition directed solely by disinterested judgement and sense of duty, are the consequences to the Party and to the whole Labour Movement of the internecine strife unleashed by *In Place of Strife*. And here Healey's verdict on what he calls 'six months of civil war throughout the Labour movement', severe though it is, seems fully justified:

> 'The Government had wasted six months on a hopeless fight, *which had caused permanent damage to our relations with the trade unions, without making them any less necessary to our survival. In Place of Strife* did for Wilson what the hopeless attempt to delete Clause Four from the Party Constitution had done for Hugh Gaitskell.'
> [my emphasis]

It seems improbable that I can be the first person to observe that periodically the Labour Party seems to exhibit a death-wish. To say this is not to associate oneself with those don't-rock-the-boat chants to which - whether from simplicity or deviousness - many Labour supporters are addicted. Such pleas are nothing more than a sort of obscurantist electoralism. Politics that fail to transcend the pursuit of power and pork barrels are simply squalid and (except for the winners) meaningless. But while meaningful politics necessarily entail the clash of differing viewpoints within every party with any pretensions to being democratic, not simply between the parties, this does not adequately explain why the Labour Party repeatedly tears itself apart in full view of the public eye. Certainly in the case of *In Place of Strife* conflict plunged from a properly combative passion into an abyss of unreason and self-mutilation. One can hardly doubt that, far more than the industrial unrest that engendered the thought of such desperate remedies in the minds of the White Paper's most ardent supporters, the public spectacle of this strife played some part in the defeat of the Party in the general election of June 1970. Certainly the distrust the episode sowed between the two wings of the Movement was still reverberating menacingly in the Winter of Discontent.

Moreover, whenever Labour politicians talk regretfully of the abandonment of the post-war consensus in British politics, they should be brusquely reminded that it was not the Tories but Labour that first reached for the legal truncheon to subdue the unions. It was his adversary's example that Ted Heath emulated in introducing his industrial relations legislation. Indeed, the first thing to be said about the Industrial Relations Bill, which was enacted on 6th August 1971, after no less than 450 hours of debate spread over 60 days (in fact it absorbed one-third of the Government's legislative time during that session of Parliament), is that the Tories were right in maintaining that it was, to use Lord Wedderburn's phrase, 'in line of descent' not only from their own *Fair Deal at Work* but from *In Place of Strife*, and that both were offspring of the Donovan Report. (They might well have gone further than they did in rubbing in the point that their 1968 proposals could reasonably be assumed to have played no small part in prodding Labour into matching their bid for public favour by abandoning the party's traditional dependence on voluntary co-operation between government and unions to maintain acceptable industrial relations 'in the national interest'.)

For despite important differences of emphasis, particularly concerning situations in which individual rights sometimes came into conflict with collective rights, there was more in common than at variance between the Heath-Carr prescriptions and the nostrums so reluctantly withdrawn by Wilson and Castle. Each scheme involved the State registration of trade unions, which was supposed to confer on them the protection of the law, balanced, of course, by legal obligations. In each scheme industrial courts had an important role. Each of them had provisions for secret ballots before industrial action was taken and compulsory cooling-off periods. Each of them, in short, constituted a step down the road to the Corporate State. Additions to the State's coercive armoury under the Industrial Relations Act included powers for the Government to apply to the newly-minted National Industrial

Relations Court for restraining orders under 'national emergency' injunctions, and for Government intervention in cases concerning the disciplining and expulsion of members by the unions to which they belonged. The pretext for assuming this particular power and for the outlawing of the closed shop, which would likewise serve to weaken the solidarity of workers in dispute with their bosses, was the Tories' celebrated concern for 'the right to work' so long as you could find it and could stomach the terms that the 'free contract' of employment imposed upon you.

From the point of view of a party representing the employing classes and prone to thinking of the trade unions as, at best, a bit of a nuisance and, at worst, a threat to 'the spheres in their courses', doubtless this all seemed eminently reasonable. Even supposing that to be the case, however, there remains the problem of tactical consistency. Considering that those who conceived the Industrial Relations Act were not academicians from Lagado but experienced players of the power game, it is a little surprising that they seemed to be gripped by a strange kind of schizophrenia. The muscle-flexing that formed the substance of their strategy in squaring up to the unions could have made some kind of sense if they had had the will to follow far enough in Mussolini's footsteps (although at some hazard even to *parliamentary* democracy). But it was accompanied by the make-believe thinking that it could be seamlessly joined to a let's-all-be-reasonable approach that is best exemplified by two provisions in the Act: one, for the registration of trade unions; two, for collective agreements to be made legally binding if both parties assented. Not only was this agreement-into-contract offer shunned by the unions, but like the outlawing of the closed shop it was not even generally favoured by affected employers. As for union registration, this was not made obligatory, but only those unions that did register were, in effect, to be considered to be unions. But, regrettably, declining to call a lion legally a lion does not make it a lamb. Despite the loss of legal privileges which cost the unions £10 million in taxes and in pension funds, the TUC instructed its affiliates not to register. Only twenty-one unions chose legitimisation by the State in preference to strength through solidarity with the rest of the organised labour movement. One of these cancelled its affiliation to the TUC and the other twenty were expelled.

Like its Labour predecessor, Heath's Government turned from efforts to combat inflation through voluntary co-operation between

257

the Government, the CBI, and the TUC, to statutory control, starting in November 1972 with a 90-day standstill on prices, pay, dividends, and rents, and moving on through two more stages designed to impose strict limits on rises in prices and incomes. The attempt to keep the lid on demands for a better standard of living was challenged again and again by many groups of workers, including gas-workers, power engineers, local authority manual workers, civil servants in their first ever strike, dockers, railwaymen, and above all by the miners, who showed twice that the Government's edicts did not run in the face of workers' militancy.

What the Industrial Relations Act did achieve was a spectacular rise in the number of days lost through strike action. From an average of hardly more than 2 million in the first post-war decade and of well under 4 million between 1955 and 1969, the figure shot up to nearly 11 million in 1970, to over 13½ million in 1971, and to almost 24 million in 1972, the highest total since 1926. The Act designed to put the unions on a leash in fact provoked the rebirth of the political strike in Britain. According to one estimate twice as many workers took part in official and unofficial strikes against the Industrial Relations Act in 1970-71 as were involved in the entire year's more strictly industrial disputes. In keeping with its anti-revolutionary traditions, the TUC refused to call for industrial action against the Act, but for all that, Joe England and Brian Weekes are broadly right in their judgement that: 'Rank-and-file activists joined with the trade union leaders in opposition to the Act, thus bringing about *one of those rare occasions when all levels of union power were operating in the same direction at the same time.*' [my emphasis]

The Tory Government had acted as its own agent-provocateur without ensuring that it could cope with the situation it had provoked (as was most dramatically illustrated by the case of the Pentonville Five, in which a one-day general strike in protest at the imprisonment of five dockers for breaking the industrial relations law was only forestalled by the Law Lords cooking up a pretext for their release from jail). It is true that the same might be said of the authors of *In Place of Strife*, but since the unions were at least nominally their allies, Harold and Barbara, unlike Ted, did at least have some grounds for flattering

258

themselves that they might seduce them into lying down on the procrustean bed of State-regulated industrial action. Since the Tories could hardly share such delusions, theirs must have been engendered by faith in the intimidatory power of the State *per se*. But ''tis the eye of childhood that fears a painted devil.'

Their folly did a singular service to their adversaries, throwing them into each others arms again after the bitter squabbles occasioned by the imprudent attempt of one of the partners to restrict the liberties of the other. The question asked by Ted Heath, however, after the miners' militancy had put industry on a three-day working week and virtually forced him to go to the country - 'Who governs Britain?' - remained unanswered.

CHAPTER 21

A contract dishonoured

'You will eat, bye and bye,
In that glorious land above the sky;
Work and pray, live on hay,
You'll get pie in the sky when you die.'

Chorus from a song by Joe Hill,
The Preacher and the Slave

Following the humiliation of the Tories by the miners, the Labour
Movement (to speak mythically) returned to power on 1st March
1974 apparently more purposefully united than at any time since
the first Attlee Government. Denis Healey's fighting-talk reference
to 'the most radical and comprehensive programme...since 1945'
was no exaggeration. Had it 'honestly stated' what the Party's
leaders were resolved to do, their goal might even have been
described as social revolution. According to the manifesto Labour
put before the electorate, its aims were:

(a) To bring about a fundamental and irreversible shift in the balance
of power and wealth in favour of working people and their
families;
(b) To eliminate poverty wherever it exists in Britain and commit
ourselves to a substantial contribution to fight poverty abroad;
(c) To make power in industry genuinely accountable to the workers
and the community at large;
(d) To achieve far greater economic equality - in income, wealth
and living standards;
(e) To increase social equality by giving greater importance to full
employment, housing, education and social benefits;
(f) To improve the environment in which our people live and work
and spend their leisure.

More specifically, the parliamentary wing of the Movement
was committed to what amounted to a 'social contract' with the
trade union wing of the Movement, pledging what David Coates
justly describes, in *Labour in Power?*, as 'radical and innovatory

260

policy in the fields of industrial relations, housing, prices, social benefits, investment and industrial democracy.' These undertakings stemmed from the *Statement on Economic Policy and the Cost of Living* drawn up by the TUC-Labour Party Liaison Committee and published in February 1973, which embraced (in Coates' summary):

(a) what it termed 'a wide ranging and permanent system of price controls', particularly on food;
(b) a new approach to housing and rent, to include the repeal of the 1972 Housing Finance Act, the long-run municipalisation of private rented property, the public ownership of required building land, and the building of at least 400,000 houses a year;
(c) the strengthening of public transport, and experiments with free public transport in major conurbations;
(d) a large-scale redistribution of income and wealth, by wealth taxes, gift taxes, and steeply progressive direct taxation;
(e) the end of prescription charges, and an immediate rise in pensions, with pensions thereafter to be annually updated in line with average earnings;
(f) the expansion of investment and the control of capital by further public ownership, by the extension of state supervision of private investment, and by new measures of control to prevent excessive investment overseas;
(g) the extension of industrial democracy, by bringing investment policy and closure policy into the scope of collective bargaining.

As Coates comments, the 'contract' was 'significantly quiet on the question of incomes policy'. In joint pursuit of the return to power of a Labour government, neither party to the 'contract' wished to fan the embers of the bitter recriminations provoked by the clash over *In Place of Strife*. None the less, there was undoubtedly an understanding that the union leaders would do their best to moderate wage demands as a quid pro quo for what could fairly be claimed, if the promises were delivered, as a major advance in the social wage.

The second (or should it be called the umpteenth?) honeymoon between the two partners composing the Labour Movement lasted scarcely longer than the seven months between the February and October general elections of 1974, in the second of which Wilson obtained a working majority. Nevertheless, in the opening period of his tenure it really looked as if the Government meant to keep its side of the bargain. In her diary Barbara Castle called Harold Wilson 'custodian of the Manifesto' and spoke of his 'playing it straight down the line of party policy.' Ted Heath's obnoxious Industrial Relations Act was repealed, to be replaced by the much less threatening Trade Union and Labour Relations Act, which was followed up by the positively worker-friendly Employment Protection Act of 1975. Agencies with powers to intervene in the labour market were set up: the Advisory Conciliation and Arbitration Service, the Health and Safety Commission, and the Manpower Services Commission held out real promise of more protection and security for working people. Progress both in the workplace and in wider social fields was made by other legislation, including the Sex Discrimination Act of 1975 and the Race Relations Act of 1976, and by the Government's redeeming of its pledge to repeal Heath's 1972 Housing Finance Act - an act which is a notable example of the tireless ingenuity of the capitalist State in shifting the burden of subsidising the poor from the backs of the well-to-do to those of the hard up. (It was this act that led to the surcharging and disqualification of the twenty-one Clay Cross Labour councillors who refused to implement Government-imposed increases in council housing rents.)

The return of Labour brought an expansion of local authority housing programmes and measures to discourage the sale of council housing. A rent freeze was imposed and the Price Code and Price Commission were retained, with stricter controls applied to price increases, while the Pay Board was abolished and, in July 1974, the compulsory wage restraint imposed by Heath was ended. Pensions and child allowances were raised and there was a substantial increase in the subsidy of basic foods. Thus, despite increases in income tax and in excise duties on cigarettes and alcohol, plus an extension (most notably to petrol) of goods liable to Value Added Tax, the cost of living was broadly contained, with a little redistribution of income to the less advantaged.

But in regaining power when it did, as the global recession really began to gnaw at the economy, Labour had accepted a poisoned chalice. There is no question that it had a harder task to cope with than any previous post-war government in guiding the country to carve out a living in harshly competitive international trading conditions. Engrossed for the first decade and a half since the end of the Second World War in the chimerical project of retaining her great-power status; obsessed with her 'special relationship' with America and her vanishing role as mother country of the Commonwealth; and induced by these illusions of grandeur - reinforced by entrapment in her nightmare of the Soviet threat - to divert far too much of her capital and human resources to the development, production, and deployment of arms, Britain had lost her chance of exercising a decisive influence on the rebuilding of Europe. Meanwhile the six founding members of the European Economic Community (including, of course, another nation, France, which still had many grand illusions to shed) were more prudently laying the foundations for a common prosperity. The Treaty of Rome between the original 'six' was signed in March 1957. Britain's first bid for EEC membership, made during Macmillan's second ministry, was vetoed by De Gaulle in January 1963; and her second bid, under Wilson, was again vetoed by De Gaulle, in November 1967. Not until January 1972 was Britain's application accepted, with Ted Heath, now Prime Minister, succeeding at his second attempt, having led the British negotiating team in the first bid.

Leaving aside the crucial loss of the opportunity to play a major part in determining the structure and thrust of the Community, by this time Britain's chronic under-investment in many of the most rewarding areas for international trade had left her at a grave disadvantage compared with her principal competitors. Britain's relative decline from around the mid-fifties can be roughly measured by a few facts and figures. The growth of her economy was both slower and more unsteady than that of her main competitors. During the fifties Britain's gross national product had risen in real terms by about 30 per cent, compared with an average rise of 80 per cent for EEC members. In 1950 Britain's GNP, at $47 billion, had been worth not far short of two-thirds of the combined GNPs ($75 billion) of the six states which were to forge the EEC; but by 1970 her GNP only equalled a quarter of the EEC's aggregated GNP, $121 billion as against $485 billion. In 1961 Britain ranked 9th out of 25 in the International Growth League of the Organisation of Economic Co-operation and Development, one behind West Germany and one ahead of France. By 1966, a few months before Wilson's bid for EEC membership, Britain's ranking was down to 13th, with France in 7th place and West Germany in 10th. By 1971, with Britain on the point of being allowed to join the club, the relative rankings were Britain 15th, France 9th, and West Germany 5th. By 1976, the year in which (in April) Callaghan took over the reins from Wilson, Britain had fallen to 18th place, while West Germany ranked 7th and France 11th. In per capita terms there was in 1961 near equality between the three countries, at a figure a little more than half that for the then top-ranking country, the United States. By 1976 France and West Germany had narrowed the gap with the US (itself now overtaken by Sweden, Switzerland, and Canada) and both far outstripped Britain. Although her per capita product had doubled in the 1966-76 period, it now stood at less than three-fifths of France's and not much over a half of West Germany's.

Weathering the storm of the recession the world had entered into in the autumn of 1973 was made more difficult by the ill-advised push for growth that had been launched by the Heath Government with Anthony Barber's candy-floss budget of March 1972, along with its massive tax cut of £1.38 billion. The most conspicuous consequences of 'the Barber boom' (in many ways a foreshadowing of the lunatic Lawson boom of 1986-89) were a spectacular increase in investment in property speculation and the sucking in of a spate of imports for consumption. Added to the unavoidable extra imports burden caused by rocketing world commodity prices, the consumer-imports' boom resulted in a record balance of payments deficit of £1.12 billion in 1973. In the following year the deficit shot up to £3.32 billion.

The balance of payments crisis was a major factor in precipitating a sterling crisis, with a flight from the pound in June 1972 and a persistent decline in its exchange rate. In March 1976 it fell below the $2 level for the first time ever, reaching its lowest point of under $1.16 the following October, and not rising to $2 again until the second half of 1978. These crises induced the Wilson Government to take advantage of Britain's Special Drawing Rights with the International Monetary Fund at the end of 1975, and subsequently, in September 1976, to apply for the maximum permitted standby credit of $3.9 billion. During the following two years the pound stabilised, Britain's balance of payments improved, and inflation fell. But naturally the economic crisis was overcome by cutting public spending, and equally naturally, the cuts were largely at the expense of the social wage, affecting the health service, education, housing, land acquisition by local authorities, food subsidies, public transport and roads. And these cuts began with

Denis Healey's first budget after the Wilson Government's tenure had been confirmed in the October 1974 general election.

The interim budget of November 1974, says Coates, 'foreshadowed much that was to come', beginning a retreat from the subsidies and price controls promised in the social contract, and from the tight discipline over private firms anticipated in the debates when Labour was in opposition. Citing the Chancellor's admission to the House that in his view the ever-swelling public sector borrowing requirement had reached 'a disturbingly large figure which one would never accept under normal circumstances', Coates comments: 'The Government was well aware that an immediate and drastic reduction in public sector expenditure could only bring a large fall in output and employment in its wake. But Ministers had at least succumbed to the view that public sector spending had to be curbed, no matter what the Labour Party in opposition had believed, and the November 1974 budget made a series of small beginnings.'

This overriding objective became explicit in the budget of April 1975, which Healey himself called 'rough and tough'. By a combination of higher levies on personal incomes and consumption (income tax was raised 2p to 35p in the pound, VAT on most luxury goods was increased to 25 per cent, duty on tobacco and alcohol went up and duty on private cars was raised from £25 to £40; while corporation tax remained unchanged and capital gains tax was reduced for farmers and small businesses) and planned cuts of £900 million for the fiscal year 1976-77 in subsidies for food and housing and in 'defence' spending, the public deficit was to be brought down to 8 per cent of national output in 1975-76 and to 6 per cent in 1976-77.

As the biggest constituent in public expenditure in a 'welfare state', what can collectively be considered as the 'social wage' is invariably a victim of cuts. Moreover, these cuts were made in the context of rising unemployment (excluding Northern Ireland, more than 450,000 people lost their livelihood during 1975, nearly 150,000 more during 1976, and over 200,000 more during the first nine months of 1977, when the unemployment total peaked at 1,380,000; by the end of Labour's last period in power there were more than twice as many people out of work than when they took office in March 1974) and unremitting government pressure to hold down the wages of ordinary workers. Coates remarks that to a 'shift from control to exhortation in the Labour Government's relationship with the private sector, and to the erosion of the social wage by limits on government spending, the November 1974 budget added a third and later much more significant development in policy: *the beginning of the respecification of the social contract as an agreement pre-eminently concerned with controlling the rate of increase of earnings.'* [my emphasis]

The Government's strategy for countering inflation and coping with the economic crisis was made brutally clear by Healey's 'rough and tough' budget and the drumhead recruitment of trade union leaders to discipline their own troops into accepting a 'voluntary' limit of £6 as a maximum weekly wage rise during the twelve months commencing in August 1975 - the formal Stage One of the Wilson/Callaghan Governments' everlasting incomes policy. The consequence of this keeping-capitalism-on-the-rails strategy was that even for workers who managed to hold on to their jobs, in most cases wage rises barely kept pace with the rising cost of living. Far from stepping confidently along a road that could lead to that promised goal of a 'fundamental and irreversible shift in the balance of power and wealth in favour of working people and their families', the workers, like Alice and the Red Queen, found themselves running hard to stay in the same place.

'Within fifteen months of taking office,' says Coates, 'the Labour Government was back to explicitly cutting the living standards of its electorate by at least 2.5 per cent over the year, on the Government's own figures.' Dennis Kavanagh, in *Thatcherism and British Politics: The End of Consensus?* (1987), notes an 'actual decline in the average citizen's standard of living in 1976 and 1977.' Not until its last year in power, in fact, did those who formed Labour's natural constituents begin to recover from the body blows they had been dealt. The rise in 1978 of 6.3 per cent in real personal disposable incomes reported on the eve of the general election by the Central Statistical Office was the sharpest rise since the 8.6 per cent rise of 1971-72; but it did little more than restore the buying power of the average citizen to that which he had enjoyed when Wilson outmanoeuvred Heath during the election campaigns of 1974.

So much for the Labour leaders' favourite alibi of irresponsible wage demands as a principal cause of the shattering of their last hopes of building Jerusalem. As for the more specific charges against the trade union wing of the Movement, levelled not only by Labour's opponents but by Party members too, before dealing with the final showdown between the Labour Government and the unions, it is necessary to blow away the miasma of misrepresentation spread by a media motivated more by its repressed fear of the potential power of organised labour and an instinctive antipathy to collective action by workers than by concern for keeping the public properly informed. For the record shows that almost without exception the union leaders made extraordinary and exhaustive efforts to accommodate the demands of their political allies. It also shows that, far from being a pre-eminent cause of inflation, as bourgeois propaganda and popular misconception would have it, wage claims during this period were as a rule fuelled by the remorseless rise in the cost of living. Indeed, social history almost invariably shows that widespread popular unrest is a reaction to worsening conditions.

Following the near-terminal marital breakdown during Wilson's previous premiership, the trade union leaders had apparently set their faces firmly against wage restraint policies. The furthest the TUC chiefs would go was to support (in *Collective Bargaining and the Social Contract*, June 1974) sober guidelines for the maintenance of real incomes. Yet within less than fifteen months of Labour's regaining power wage restraint was on the agenda again, with the most influential trade unionist of all as its leading advocate. In May 1975 Jack Jones, general secretary of the Transport and General Workers Union (and according to Barbara Castle's diary, perceived by her officials when she was Employment and Productivity supremo as 'the archetypal trade union villain), proposed to the TUC/Labour Party Liaison Committee of which he was chairman that to safeguard the Social Contract the movement should be asked to agree on a modest flat-rate rise for the next pay round. The figure settled on was £6, representing around ten per cent of average earnings. The policy was endorsed by the General Council of the TUC and Congress accepted it by an overwhelming majority in September.

The policy purported to be voluntary, but Sked and Cook describe it as 'effectively compulsory', since, under the Price Code, sanctions were threatened against any firm which breached the limit in a pay settlement and tried to recoup its higher labour costs by raising prices. Furthermore, Martin Holmes, in *The Labour Government, 1974-79*, implicitly contends that it meant the end of the Social Contract, writing that although the TUC document supporting the £6 policy was entitled *The Development of the Social Contract*, 'the language of the Social Contract had been made redundant, and could not disguise the fact that this was incomes policy on the traditional lines of restricting wages to reduce inflation.'

Moreover, it even failed to fulfil the minimalist objectives of the trade union movement: the maintenance of real incomes. In praising the trade union movement for its 'voluntary agreement', Healey himself admitted that the majority of trade union members would suffer 'some reduction in real take-home pay.' Yet for the most part the agreement stuck, and the Chancellor was able to report to the House in April 1976 that, 'with only a few months of the current wage round left to run, we know of no instance where wages are being paid in breach of the £6 pay limit.'

Stage Two of the pay policy, running from August 1976 to July 1977 inclusive, brought a similar measure of success for official policy. An agreement between the Government and the TUC for a maximum rise of 4.5 per cent was ratified overwhelmingly by a special congress in June 1976, and even though for most workers this meant a rise in money terms of less than half that received in the previous pay round, it was implemented without a single official trade union challenge.

Of the first two stages of the Wilson/Callaghan Government's pay policy David Coates writes:

'These two years of successful pay restraint stand as clear evidence of the loyalty of trade union leaders to this Labour Government, and their willingness to subordinate their wider policy aspirations to Government pressure. They stand too as evidence of the trade union leaders' hold on the loyalty of their own membership and of the weakness of any rank-and-file movement of protest against pay restraint and trade union incorporation. Not even the left-wing union leaders most hostile to what they saw as TUC capitulation to bankrupt Treasury orthodoxy could galvanise mass support against policies which explicitly cut living standards, failed to prevent price rises, and allowed unemployment to grow. By August 1977 the Labour Government could legitimately claim that it had achieved a degree of working class co-operation over a long period that no Conservative Government could match, and had in the process cut back significantly the pressure of wages on industrial costs.'

It is hardly surprising that falling living standards and growing disenchantment at the Cheshire Cat nature of the Social Contract promises led to the withdrawal of co-operation by the unions with the Government's policy of pay restraint. Even so, the withdrawal was itself gradual and, for another year, quite remarkably restrained. Far from kicking over the traces, the TUC continued to accept the policy in principle, while striving to hold on to its mantle of authority by promulgating an 'orderly' return to free collective bargaining. The purchasing power of the pound in the pocket might dwindle day by day, but the customary gap of twelve months between settlements should continue to be observed, it preached, and settlements due before 31st July should not be deferred in order to evade the limits laid down for that stage of the pay policy.

It might be felt that in giving an explanation for its supine attitude that 'the Government is not likely to be deflected from its present course of action', the General Council was abrogating its responsibility to give active leadership to the trade union movement in defence of working-class interests. But while there may be grounds for arguing that counsels of restraint were in the longer-term interests of the Labour Movement as a whole, is the same to be said of the TUC decision that the already trumpeted campaign to increase the target for low-paid workers from a £30 minimum to £50 should be deferred until times were better? Likewise, what is to be said of a government formed by a party purporting to champion the interests of working people that discriminates against its own employees by imposing a ten per cent limit on public sector rises, regardless of wage and price movements in the economy as a whole - especially bearing in mind the high proportion of low-paid workers in the public sector? In undermining Labour's strongholds, such questions were to become as Joshua's trumpets.

The Government made it clear that it would hold the line against breaches of the twelve-month rule, rebuff all attempts to recoup loss of real earnings since 1975, reject spurious (i.e. non-self-financing) productivity agreements, and impose sanctions against private firms agreeing to settlements that exceeded its stipulated maximum of 10 per cent. Even the TUC's guidelines - never mind the Government's stipulations - fell somewhat short of what trade unionists in general, along with their capitalist masters, are pleased to call 'free collective bargaining'. Yet the General Council's decisions were ratified by sizeable majorities (no less than 7.1 million to 4 million in the case of the twelve-month rule) at the September Congress.

Only one union, the firemen's, openly defied the edicts of the Labour establishment by calling an official strike in pursuit of its claim for a 30 per cent rise. The Government's response was to mobilise the Green Goddesses (the antiquated fire-engines used by the army) - neither the first nor the last time a Labour government has deployed soldiers as strike-breakers. After eight weeks out, from mid-November 1977 into the New Year, the firemen were strong-armed into accepting the 10 per cent on offer, on the understanding that they would not be held to the 'norm' fixed for subsequent stages of Labour's pay policy.

Just over half way through Stage Three, in the middle of February 1978, the Department of Employment was able to claim that over 96 per cent of the wage settlements reached in the current pay round had been within the Government's guidelines. Without resorting to more draconian measures to enforce its will, such a high degree of success was not sustainable, but surprisingly, considering the many claims that exceeded 10 per cent and the strength of the rank-and-file pressure for more money that built up, it turned out that even by the end of Stage Three the Government had succeeded in holding the annual rate of increase in earnings to 14.2 per cent. (This figure meant that there had been some *restoration of lost living standards* for some employees, since it was 6.4 per cent above the rate of growth of prices.)

There is no question that the continued collaboration (however reluctant) of the TUC in Stage Three was crucial to the Government's relative success in holding down the incomes of rank-and-file workers, just as it had been the decisive factor in the previous stages of the pay policy. When the firemen called for support in the name of the principle of free collective bargaining which the TUC had just reaffirmed, the General Council rebuffed them, resolving by 20-17 to uphold the policy of wage restraint during Stage Three, and even the Government's strike-breaking measures provoked little more in the way of solidarity from other unions than sighs of regret. The most stunning victory of all for the political overlords was the taming of the miners. Ably abetted by the miners' president, Joe Gormley, the Government persuaded the 232,000-strong National Union of Mineworkers, vanguard of the British working class, to drop its claim for a 90 per cent rise and accept around

10 per cent. Their loyalty to the Labour Government was hailed by the Prime Minister publicly thanking them in the House.

What needs explaining most is not the popular myth of union power (for the persistence of which one would have to anatomise in particular the baleful influence of the media - *and not only the popular media* - in promoting ignorance and prejudice), but the essential subservience of the trade union establishment to the political leaders of the Labour Movement. This perception of a predisposition to acquiesce (to put it at its lowest) lies at the heart of Coates' penetrating analysis of the twilight of Labourism. As he points out, the power of the union leaders was almost wholly negative. When they disagreed with Labour's political leaders, they could argue, haggle, and temporise, but in the end, if the terms fixed upon still remained too unpalatable, they could do little more than decline to co-operate. That at least is how they seemed to see it. And given the nature of the British trade union movement, perhaps that is how it really was. In any case, those union generals who were most powerful on paper lacked the will to shape events. As the Social Contract, which - together with its indispensable underpinning of a heterodox economic strategy - they had played such a large part in forging, disintegrated before their eyes, they looked on as helplessly as small children robbed of their candy by bigger boys. Coates describes the situation lucidly:

> 'Trade union leaders could resist particular details, could block and negotiate, and (where their members' direct co-operation was required) could exercise some kind of veto on particular policy options. But they could not define the agenda of proposals that the Government put before them, nor the context within which policy had to be formulated; and so in the end they proved unable to prevent the transformation of the social contract from its initial character (of a set of concrete and immediate legislative proposals that favoured the working class), into its later form (as a vehicle of wage restraint, buttressed by general statements of aspiration and vague long-term commitments to social change). The drift to incomes policy, the rise in unemployment, and the Government's resistance to the TUC's expansionist policy stand as major pieces of evidence against the thesis of excessive trade union power, and make clear that the visibility of trade union leaders was

less an index of their power than of their subordination. The
story of the relationship between this Labour Government
and the trade union movement after 1974 is one of the
transformation of the national trade union leadership into
vital junior allies of the Cabinet in the implementation of
incomes control - policemen in their own arena of action,
visibly pursuing policies with which they were uneasy
within limits set only by the sporadic degree of rank and file
protest to which they were subject.'

The Wilson/Callaghan Government of 1974-79 presented the
Labour Movement with its most unmistakable moment of truth. Even
if the British Labour Party had been a very different animal (closer in
nature, perhaps, to the dreams of its left-wingers), we would still have
been witnessing, while it lasted, an interlude of collaboration, a passing
period of symbiosis, between two very different creatures, possessing
not the complementary powers of Labour theory, but antithetical kinds
of power: on the one hand, State power - the power to command and
coerce (an arrogated power in essence, notwithstanding all the
paraphernalia of elections and mandates); on the other hand, people
power - the negating power of inertia, withdrawal, resistance, and
outright defiance, whenever the positive power of freely-willed co-
operation was withheld.
It is highly questionable what the workers had really gained by
their reasonableness and restraint. Sympathy perhaps, from a few 'men
of goodwill', but nothing remotely resembling any form of Socialism;
neither with regard to the serious pursuit of social justice, nor even (to
whittle down Socialism to little more than common-sense
Keynesianism) to a credible attempt to manage the economy so as
markedly to mitigate the ravages of capitalism during one of its manic
downswings. In short, it became clear for all with eyes to see that the
so-called Social Contract was what its most far-sighted critics had
always called it, the 'social con-trick'.
It is particularly ironic, in view of the absolutely central position
assumed by the State in Labour (as in Marxist) thinking (before the
'modernisers' had done their work that is), that the two men of power
who dominated the fateful period after Harold Wilson had slipped away
with an '*après moi la deluge*' twinkle in his eye, Callaghan and Healey,
are commonly represented as strong and decisive leaders. And yet both
of them had apparently lost all confidence in the countervailing powers

of the State in its relations with capitalism. With more than a tinge of a fatalism that would have been fitting enough for a faithful free marketeer, one of their Cabinet colleagues, Shirley Williams, confessed to the 'Youth Charter Towards 2000' conference in February 1977: 'We are seeing the increase in unemployment throughout the industrial world, and it is a problem for which we have no real answer.' In fact, by their allegiance to essentially monetarist policies and their refusal to adopt 'New Deal' type strategies, they contributed to unemployment rather than countering it. When, in 1991, Norman Lamont told the Commons that higher unemployment was a price well worth paying to bring down inflation, he was assailed by a storm of protests from the Labour benches. Yet when Healey had been Chancellor, he had cut public spending and sacrificed jobs to counter inflation, in contrast, as Dennis Kavanagh points out, to the Heath Government's reflating of the economy when faced with rising unemployment.

Kavanagh clearly considers Healey's spring 1975 budget a watershed in post-war politics: 'In March 1975 Denis Healey's budget abandoned the commitment to plan for full employment, choosing to cut instead of increase the deficit, a historic breach with one of the main planks of the post-war consensus.' It has been too little remarked that the rejection of Keynesian strategies for dealing with recession began not with the Thatcherite fundamentalists but with the responsible Labour statesmen who preceded them. Absolute confirmation of the new orthodoxy in Labour's economic thinking came in James Callaghan's speech to his first party conference as leader and Prime Minister in 1976:

> 'We used to think that you could spend your way out of
> recession and increase employment by cutting taxes and
> boosting Government spending. I tell you in all candour
> that that option no longer exists, and that insofar as it ever
> did exist, it only worked on each occasion since the war by
> injecting a bigger dose of inflation into the economy,
> followed by a higher level of unemployment as the next
> step.'

An obsession with curbing inflation at any cost and a conviction that it was wage pressure above all that induced that inflation - all part of an essentially monetarist and anti-Keynesian (not to say anti-Socialist) credo that foreshadowed rampant Thatcherism - led Labour's leaders to behave like the legendary Dutch boy who stuck his heroic finger in the hole in the dyke. This not being a tale of derring-do, however, but a gathering storm in real life, Labour's last-chance ministry was, by the time the country shuffled discontentedly into Stage Four of the prices and incomes policy in August 1978, near the point of being swept away by a deluge of demands that it deliver some semblance of what working people had been promised in the Social Contract between the political and the industrial wings of the Labour Movement.

CHAPTER 22

Who does govern Britain?

'Old-fashioned patriotism has become the almost
exclusive property of the working class, whose tribal
loyalties are kept alive every Saturday on the football
terraces. History is ordaining not that the workers of the
world unite, but that the executives, bankers, and
entrepreneurs erase national differences to advance their
own interest.'

Alan Clark (1978)

The problem facing the last Labour government was not simply
that faced by all governments, of reconciling - or if not
reconciling, then at least of successfully balancing (within the
confines imposed by economic exigencies) - demands from the
competing vested interests that made up its own constituency,
while dishing out minimal portions of appeasement to the
electorally most threatening sections of its antagonists. It went
far deeper than that, for it was a problem posed by the manifest
failure of Labour's political wing to deliver its promise of a
new society in which the rules of the game would not be heavily
weighted against the interests of 'the common people' - a
promise that lay at the very heart of its appeal.

No one had laid down the premises of the Social Contract
between government and people more plainly than Harold
Wilson did, when he told the 1972 Labour Party Conference:
'There can be no road to national agreement, national
unity...except on a basis of social justice.' That at least made it
sound as if he had learned the lesson of the bitter strife that had
come close to tearing the Labour Movement apart under his
administrations in the sixties; and whether through cunning
prescience or the devil's own luck, he was to relinquish the
burden of office before the times grew tumultuous again. The
ironic paradox is that his successor, who had shown much more
prudence than Wilson had during Labour's civil war over *In
Place of Strife*, now that he held the reins of sovereign power
and found himself faced by a restless multitude, displayed

arrogant inflexibility, poverty of imagination, and a grossly inadequate concern for the demands of social justice. Hubris had struck again!

Of course, not all the preconditions of a workable accommodation between the Government and the unions were transparently questions of social justice. For example, in the annual round of wage settlements which was propelled in large part by inflation, the issue of differentials posed one of the thorniest problems of all. As commonly represented, as a demand for maintaining the status quo (or for restoring some real or supposed status quo ante) of inequalities, this had at best an oblique and equivocal relationship to the concept of social justice. But for the very reason that Labour was holding office at a critical time in the life of the nation, when the concept of the Welfare State had come to seem to many to be at odds with the demands of national economic prosperity in a fiercely competitive world, the Callaghan Government had a rare opportunity. They could have seized the moral high ground by proclaiming unequivocally that in any pay policy the first call on 'spare' resources must be the claims of the least privileged sections of society. That could only have meant that once the essentials of the economic infrastructure had been provided for, the social wage and more generous remuneration for the low-paid must take priority, and that as far as it lay in the Government's power, there should be no discrimination in this respect between its own employees and workers in the private sector. Then - and only then - would it have had the right to expect the country to heed its exhortations for restraint 'in the national interest'. But instead of acting in accordance with the principles of social justice, the people's government squandered its moral authority by its Janus-faced policies of appeasement towards the strong and intransigence towards the weak. It is true that the official guidelines did allow for more favourable treatment of low-paid workers, but as we shall see, this subtle genuflection in the direction of equity was more honoured in the breach than in the observance.

At all events, at this fateful moment for the British people a sort of stubborn steadfastness masquerading as 'strong government' held sway, revealing yet again that deeply unattractive paternalistic streak that is so characteristic of Labour's tribunes. Notwithstanding ritual obeisances to the doctrine of full consultation, the mind-set of the Labour leaders was more suited to autocracy than to representative government, with Cabinet (or even just *inner* Cabinet) deliberations issuing in what amounted to rule by ukase. Such procedure is anything but foreign to the traditions of British Cabinet government; but it is totally at odds with the proclaimed tenets of the Labour Movement.

In the face of overwhelming opposition, clearly and repeatedly voiced in the democratic forums of the Movement, all the way up to the theoretically sovereign Party Conference, those who held the purse strings decreed a 5 per cent norm for an imposed Stage Four and stuck to it, effectively declining to bargain with their own followers not only over pay but over any other aspect of the Government's economic policy. Yet at the same time, in a White Paper issued in July 1978, the Government called for the reaching of tripartite agreements - between Government, unions and employers - to counter wage-induced inflation. Its contention was that in the absence of such agreements its duty was to fix norms for pay rises. Yet in doing so it took little or no account of considerations of equity, thinking it sufficient to promulgate a percentage-increase figure that in its opinion the economy could afford. Ironically, it did eventually reach some measure of agreement again with the General Council of the TUC (a 'concordat' as it was called by leaders who, it seems, were insensible to the unfortunate Corporate State associations of that term), but only after the storm had broken over the Government's head. It was in any case no more than a fig-leaf donned in the desperate hope of persuading the public that Labour was still the party best able to handle the unions, since in the context of such widespread discontent the union leaders were quite unable to deliver the assent of their rank and file.

Compared with the year in which Callaghan took over from Wilson, 1977 had seen a threefold increase in the number of working days lost through strikes, with the total figure reaching only a little short of ten million. Relatively speaking, 1978 provided a lull. What was ominous, however, was that whereas unofficial stoppages in the motor and engineering industries, together with a considerable contribution from the official firemen's strike at the end of the year, had accounted for a large proportion of the work-time lost in 1977, now that the unions were reasserting their commitment to free collective bargaining, the groups of workers ready to take action to defend their interests or to support their claims practically covered the waterfront of organised employees. Among workers who resorted to some kind of industrial action to supplement the purely verbal persuasive powers of their negotiators were, in the public sector: porters and other ancillary staff in hospitals, including telephonists and laundry workers, ambulance crews, social workers, social security staff, teachers, caretakers in schools and colleges, firemen, refuse workers, traffic wardens, civilian police workers, prison warders, customs officers, industrial civil servants, ministers' drivers, dockyard and other defence industry workers, post office engineers, shipyard workers, dockers, tugmen, pilot ships' officers, airport workers, rail and tube workers, bus crews, steelmen, and miners; and in the private sector: North Sea oilmen, petrol tanker drivers, Channel ferry seamen, construction workers, motor industry workers, lorry drivers, bakers, bottle factory workers, draymen, print-workers, journalists, television broadcasting technicians, stagehands, and bank staff.

That by no means exhausts the list of those who were prepared to use 'industrial muscle' to get their way, and those not listed not only embraced such traditional musclemen as the power workers, but extended to university dons and to such unimpeachably respectable professions as medicine. In April the British Medical Association warned the Government that there would be a mass exodus of medical practitioners from the National Health Service if they failed to negotiate appropriate recompense for their services. Polite society and such pillars of the establishment as the capitalist Press might in such cases refrain from their customary cant of 'blackmail' by strikers, taking refuge, if challenged on the similarity of behaviour between common workers downing tools and doctors and surgeons downing stethoscopes and scalpels, in the contractual relationship of such professional people to public services; but what was it in truth but pressure on the community's most tender spot? And some idea of what the BMA considered to be appropriate rewards for those whose 'vested interests' it represented may be gathered from the claim put in on behalf of consultants for an 80 per cent increase!

Harold Wilson's admonition concerning the conditions for national unity referred to above omits in my citation one crucial phrase: '...on a policy adequate for dealing with inflation and unemployment...' And there was the rub. One fine day in the autumn of 1978, Labour's dauntless double-act, Jim and Denis, yoked together in their three-legged dash for stable sterling undefiled by devaluation, vowed, each in his own way, to stand fast against the inflationary clamour of the multitude. At the annual Mansion House junketing for Chancellor, bankers, and merchants, Denis came right out of the closet by openly admitting his predilection for monetarism, adding with characteristic swagger that the government in which he served was the first for very many years 'which has given monetary policy the importance it deserves.' He made it crystal clear that it would be his main weapon in the struggle to hold down inflation.

Meanwhile, at the Anglo-German summit meeting in Bonn (on the eve of negotiations for a European Monetary System which Britain did not, in the event, join until Margaret Thatcher was badgered into doing so by her Cabinet colleagues more than ten years later), Prime Minister Callaghan told Chancellor Schmidt of his government's determination to meet one of the central preconditions of a durable EMS, no return to high rates of inflation. Making one of the major unintended understatements of the century, he warned: 'There may, as a result of our policies, be some industrial disturbances this winter. But I hope our European friends will not think that the UK has gone down the plug-hole as a result.'

For a fistful of reasons it was the eruption at the Ford Motor Company a month earlier that really breached the dyke, although the full flood did not come for several more months. Among these reasons was, of course, the chance factor of the point at which union agreements at Ford ran out, which happened to be after the transition from Stage Three of Labour's pay policy - for which there had been at least a semblance of voluntary agreement between government and unions - to the diktat of Stage Four, during which sullen acquiescence gave way to defiance. The paramount factor, however, was the Ford workers' undoubted right (speaking in conventional capitalist 'free labour market' terms) as employees of by far the most profitable motor manufacturing firm in Britain (which incidentally turned out the second largest number of vehicles of all Ford's foreign-based factories) to a far higher rise than the 5 per cent limit the Government sought to impose. Thus, as Callaghan puts it in his memoirs, 'the Ford pay claim [became] the bellwether of the flock.'

The 15 unions organising the 57,000 manual workers at Ford (and the involvement of so many unions - itself a consequence of Britain's antiquated craft-based organisation of labour - naturally acted as a green light to great swathes of their members employed elsewhere) had in fact agreed on a rather egalitarian claim of £20 all round, which was equivalent when averaged out to around 25 per cent. (It is worth noting in passing, because of its bearing on the whole question of the responsibility and restraint, or otherwise, of trade unionists under the Wilson/Callaghan regime, that in their previous settlement the Ford workers had agreed to an increase lower than the average Stage Three increase, rejecting the advice of their leaders to push for more.) The Ford strike began on 22nd September, in response to the management's insistence on sticking to the official pay limit, and within three days the whole workforce was out.

The fragility of government when it will not or dare not fall back on brute force to ensure that its edicts are observed was laid bare by a 9-week strike that ended with the acceptance of an offer of 17 per cent, over three times more than the limit, thus exposing the so-called Labour Movement for what it is: an expedient alliance of two separate centres of power with only occasionally coinciding interests - an alliance perpetually threatened by schism. In this withdrawal of co-operation which heralded a wholesale workers' revolt, the social illusions and shibboleths by which we normally live (and on the altars of which, it is true, we sometimes even immolate ourselves) - national identity and national unity, party allegiance, group loyalty, duty to employers or to others in authority over us, and the like, along with such assorted cosy assumptions as that we are all equal before the law; that universal suffrage confers political equality; that, consequentially, a distinction can and should be made between the withdrawal of co-operation for economic reasons (potentially justifiable) and 'political strikes' (*per se* unjustifiable); and that organisations established to promote the interests of particular groups of workers in a market economy should be expected to subordinate their members' economic interests to higher considerations, even to some hypothetical 'national interest' - all were revealed by a lightning flash as the stinking ordurous heap of sanctimonious humbuggery they are.

The right of the trade union wing of the Labour Movement to part company with a Labour government and go its own way was bluntly asserted by Ron Todd, chairman of the union team on Ford's national joint negotiating committee, who was later to become general secretary of the Transport and General Workers' Union:

'We have undergone a great deal of self-sacrifice to help the country overcome inflation. Now we believe is the right time to reintroduce free collective bargaining. This is all we want. *The response of Ford reflects Government policy, and we are reflecting trade union policy. It is getting to the stage when to mention free collective bargaining is to sound revolutionary.*' [my emphasis]

Todd accused Ford of using the Government's pay guidelines as a pretext for refusing to bargain. But while no one could doubt that, like just about every other employer, it would use whatever arguments came to mind to deprive its workers of most of the fruits of their labour, it was certainly not in its interests to provoke a mass walkout by making what *it* must have felt, hardly less than Todd & Brothers, to be 'a derisory offer'. Both sides knew perfectly well that the unions' biggest quarrel was with the Government they had helped to put into power, as Ford's chairman, Sir Terence Beckett, indirectly told them when, in a speech at a conference in London on international planning a couple of days after the walkout, he called it 'a strike against the Government' and added that 'the situation we are in depends on something wider than the Ford Motor Company.' He inadvertently underlined the speciousness of most attempts to distinguish between legitimate industrial action and 'political strikes' by subsequently remarking that the dispute had been 'made into a political rather than an industrial issue.'

In fact a kaleidoscopic rearrangement of forces at once took shape, implying - without, of course, formally bringing into being - new alliances expedient to new circumstances. These were alliances (grotesque, even unholy, if you like) between the two sides we are not to suppose exist in industry and commerce, namely, capital and labour, and more ominously in the long run, between large numbers of ordinary working people who had up till then always instinctively backed Labour and the standard-bearers of so-called 'free enterprise'. The TGWU general secretary, Moss Evans, who, as Ford erupted, had warned the Government that it should expect a similar explosion from more than a million public sector manual workers when their claims were turned down, began to talk of joint union-employer protests if sanctions were imposed on firms to repress free collective bargaining.

A captain of industry and a labour leader did just that at a conference in London organised by the British Institute of Management. They spoke as if with one voice against the inflexibility of a policy that had already imposed crude pay norms for three years and that left little scope for negotiating over problems of differentials and anomalies. Calling for a national body to adjudicate on such matters, the chairman of BIM's economic committee, Sir Fred Catherwood, warned the Government: 'You can do these things for one year and two years and with sanctions and a miracle even three years. But when you go into the fourth year, especially when people didn't expect a fourth year and expected an election, then you are in dead trouble.' While guest speaker Ray Buckton, general secretary of the Associated Society of Locomotive Engineers and Firemen, argued that freedom to bargain over the rate for the job was a prerequisite of efficient and competitive industry. No firebrand, the studied moderation of his position was made very clear by his statement that: 'I hope the 5 per cent policy does not disintegrate, but I hope the rigidity does.'

If the Government would not listen to its friends, in the belief that they were betraying Labour's cause, did it have to be deaf to those who were nominally its foes but who in this case at least shared with it the common purpose of paying as little to the workers as possible? To be deaf even when those 'foes' spoke with the prescience of the London Chamber of Commerce and Industry was to be daft too. Its October report, published a fortnight after the Ford walkout, drew attention to the dilemma faced by companies which 'are able - and willing - to pay more than the norm' and fear a protracted strike more than Government sanctions:

> 'The attitude of the unions suggests that, unlike the first three phases of pay policy, the opposition will be both vociferous and sustained. Faced with an intransigent trade union movement and with no legal powers to bind the unions to wage agreements and only ineffectual sanctions to reinforce it, the pay policy depends for its survival on the goodwill of companies. And the Ford experience has severely taxed what goodwill is left.'

The Chamber predicted that sanctions (for which it had earlier in the year actually expressed approval, provided machinery was established for the right of appeal) would be destroyed as a weapon with which to enforce the Government's pay policy by a settlement at Ford that would inevitably exceed the norm, and that this would signal the demise of Stage Four. The only thing wrong with the Chamber's prophecies was that it could not believe that Ford would hold out for as long as it had in 1971, merely to save a pay policy it regarded as totally unrealistic.

As for warnings of the probable dire *political* consequences of the Government simply standing its ground, these came thick and fast from the ranks of those whose allegiance it had to retain in order to survive, and we are at liberty to draw our own conclusions as to whether ignoring them demonstrates strength or stupidity. One day after the stoppage became total, Ford stewards delivered a letter to No. 10 which warned the Prime Minister that the 5 per cent pay limit was seriously jeopardising the chances of the Government winning the forthcoming general election and that 'proposals that we should work for the return of Labour MPs are being openly derided' on the shopfloor. Down at Dagenham, *Guardian* reporter John Andrews sampled some of this derision for himself. 'I don't mind if Mrs Thatcher comes in,' he was told by one young worker who saw himself as 'a slave putting nuts and bolts into engines'. A fellow worker who had been with the company for thirty years and felt he had been reduced from a position of prosperity to the status of a peasant, said the Government should appreciate that they had gone along with it to get the country on its feet, and expressed the view - to which it is hard to take exception without excoriating the kind of society that generated it - that: 'If you work for a firm and they're making money, you're entitled to more.'

The sharply diverging purposes of the two wings of the Labour Movement were summed up by a convenor of shop stewards picketing Ford's tractor plant at Basildon when he pointed out to the man from *The Guardian* that they were acting in accordance with the trade unions' agreed return to free collective bargaining and told him: 'The majority feeling is that we won't keep a Labour Government at any price, and our first job as union officials is to do our best for our members - not to keep the Labour Government in office.'

A more fundamental criticism of this still professedly Socialist government that had rejected as impractical the propositions of the 'alternative economy' strategists for overcoming Britain's economic malaise and was wholly and desperately engrossed in making the late-twentieth-century model of capitalism that it had inherited work, came from the local Labour Party in Southampton, where more than 4,000 Ford workers were on strike. In an emergency resolution tabled for the following week's Party Conference at Blackpool, it declared: 'We reject the idea that trade unionists should be loyal to the Government over their 5 per cent policy because this will only hold down wages to prop up the capitalist system.'

Far from being restricted to rank-and-file dreamers in the constituencies, however, critics of the Government's pay policy within the Party itself included its treasurer, Norman Atkinson, MP for Tottenham, who declared unequivocally on ITV's *News at One* that the Labour Movement could not and would not endorse, nor drift into, statutory wages control. His warning that the Government was 'in grave danger' of being deserted by its traditional supporters was echoed in the motion from Wavertree constituency party on which the debate on pay policy took place at Blackpool on 3rd October. That motion made it clear that wage planning would only be acceptable in the context of a planned economy embracing planned prices, profits, and investment as well.

Since the TUC, at its Congress at Brighton a month earlier, had overwhelmingly rejected (indeed, it might be said, contemptuously dismissed, as a show of hands was all that was needed to put the matter quite beyond doubt) Government policy on pay, with all but four of the forty-one members of the General Council coming out openly against it, and since at the Party Conference the trade union delegates comprised over half the total number of delegates and wielded in aggregate more than 6 million votes out of the total of 6¾ million, the outcome of the battle at Blackpool was never seriously in doubt. The five-per-cent flagship was blown clean out of the water in a two-to-one defeat for the Government, while a motion approving its general economic strategy went down by 3,626,000 to 2,806,000.

The Party's political leaders put the best face they could fashion on the humiliation they had suffered at the hands of the trade union wing of the Movement. That old trouper Sunny Jim turned in a vintage performance. Simulating irrepressible

284

optimism and unshakeable strength, he delivered with comradely bluffness the steely message that the Government's policy would not change come hell or high water, and that if its plea for pay restraint went unheeded, it would be duty bound to resort to further monetary measures to hold down inflation. Redoubled assurances of moderation, trustworthiness and loyalty to Labour came from union leaders, and in response to pow-wow noises from Big Chief Callaghan, David Basnett, general secretary of the General and Municipal Workers' Union, gave tongue on behalf of the TUC to their ever-readiness to take part in further talks on pay and other economic matters. But when Basnett assured Conference: 'Our alliance remains firm', he was papering over a chasm. There was in reality little left for the Party's leaders but the slender hope that the nation's resurgent workforce would refrain from demanding rises greatly in excess of 5 per cent.

The workers at Ford were already fighting for six times as much. With little sense of realism, sundry politicians and political commentators continued to talk of the possibility of a settlement at Ford of as little as 7 or 8 per cent, or at the worst of one just staying within single figures. But within three weeks of the Labour Party Conference Ford's resistance had buckled and it was suing for peace with an offer two and a half times the dictated 'norm'. This was swiftly followed by a 'final offer' of 16½ per cent, which, when it in turn was spurned, was eventually raised to 17 per cent, with some loosening of the work-discipline strings that had been attached to the 'final offer'. It was all very well for the Prime Minister to tell the Commons that the Ford workers would be no better off with a 17 per cent rise after a nine-week stoppage than they would have been if they had accepted 5 per cent in the first place. The dispute had cost Ford £450 million, and, what was for Callaghan more to the point, had comprehensively called his bluff, diminishing the Labour Government's authority not only in the eyes of the trade unions and the employers, but of the general public as well.

The Government could only choose between the unthinkable option of openly conceding defeat, the semi-suicidal option of maximum retaliation against Ford to which being true to its vows would impel it, or the face-saving option of taking whatever measures might serve to veil the fact that it had been utterly routed. Needless to say, it chose the third, or dissembling option. Accordingly, the Ford Motor Company was inscribed on the blacklist of recalcitrant firms which, for whatever reasons, had exceeded the 'norm' laid down for collective agreements.

During Stage Three of its prices and incomes policy the Government had assumed powers, under the Price Code it had conveniently inherited from the Heath Government, to penalise blacklisted employers. It was able to deny them contracts and business with public authorities, discretionary grants and aid, including selective employment subsidies, and export credits. Given the size and purchasing power of a public sector which at that time itself directly employed nearly a third of the nation's workforce, these powers of persuasion were potentially formidable, and conceivably had already served to keep in line many more firms than were ever named. Officially the blacklist was 'confidential', a guilty commercial secret between Government and culprit unless the latter chose to disclose it; but it appears that when Ford's name was added to it, it numbered around sixty firms. (At its peak there were believed to be about 170 names on the blacklist.)

As a major multinational, however, Ford was in a different league from the other blacklisted culprits, and when it came to the crunch the sanctions with which the Government had armed itself proved to be rubber teeth. Healey huffed and puffed in the Commons about how the Government would continue to do its duty to the nation as a whole honestly and courageously; but the 'tim'rous beastie' of substance hiding behind Healey's ballooning sound-bites was his sober observation that, in using their discretionary powers, ministers would take into account such factors as unemployment. On the same day Industry Secretary Eric Varley notified Ford that sanctions would be imposed, and that these would include *recommending* a number of nationalised industries to switch to Leyland when replacing vehicles. In addition, certain investment grants would be withheld, but these would not include the £150 million loan agreed on for the company to develop the new car plant due to open in 1980 at Bridgend in South Wales. The British Government had secured this commitment from Ford in the face of fierce competition from at least two other EEC countries, West Germany and Ireland.

The truth was that it was not Ford but the Government that was over a barrel. The nation's need for economic development and more jobs was too great to really punish Ford. But even if the Government had been hell-bent on imposing sanctions of metal-bashing proportions, the damage it could inflict was very limited. For example, a total public-sector ban on buying from Ford would have cost the company upwards of £80 million; but as we have seen, this was a flea-bite compared with what the strike had cost it. In the event, the penalties imposed were nearer to £8 million than to £80 million. In a passage in his autobiography, Callaghan himself comes near to frankly acknowledging that the whole sanctions policy was based on bluff:

> 'In one respect sanctions resembled the nuclear deterrent, in that they were most effective when they were not used. In another respect they were totally different, for when used would hardly have caused Ford a scratch. They were a gesture of disapproval and as such no one in the Cabinet was enthusiastic about employing them.'

If the Government had been playing a game of bluff because ministers believed that holding down incomes was the key to controlling inflation, the opposition parties and the more sophisticated members of the employing class in general had been perpetrating a double bluff on the workers. On the one hand they volubly protested on grounds of principle against what they considered to be the Government's arrogated, arbitrarily exercised, and unjustified powers of intervening in pay bargaining in the private sector (somehow they did not feel the same indignation about the attack on 'free collective bargaining' when it came to Government interference with statutory pay boards and other nominally autonomous bodies in the public sector). On the other hand they secretly welcomed the weapon Government policy gave them in resisting pay claims. In February the Opposition had divided the House over the practice of blacklisting; but with support from the Liberals the Government had fended off the challenge, despite the abstention of eight Labour left-wingers. When the Tories finally made up their minds to throw down the gauntlet again over the whole issue of sanctions, and it became all-important to rally round their banner all the forces they could drum up, the director general of the Confederation of British Industries, Sir John Methven, in a speech to the Parliamentary Press Gallery, succeeded in reconciling these contradictory feelings and in giving the appearance of speaking up for all those who dissented from the Government's pay policy, irrespective of their particular point of view. The Government was pursuing a legitimate end by unconstitutional means, he argued, while slyly adding, as if it were a consideration that carried weight with him, that the pay policy had no support from the TUC. On the other hand some employers came in for a rebuke for their complaisance over the Government's interference with 'the rights of management', in taking the short-sighted and unprincipled view that the interference helped them in their own pay negotiations. The policy was rigid, he said (making a bid for near-universal approval), yet at the same time pay bargaining in the UK was a 'shambles' that should be replaced by a system (unspecified) in which wages were determined by 'the competitive pressures of the market place', with the private sector setting the pace. Meanwhile the general public should be led to a better understanding of economic cause and effect. Thus spake this quintessential market-place philosopher, fully equipped with state of the art flexible thought-processes.

The most profound lesson to be learned from the Callaghan Government's humiliation at the hands of the Ford Motor Company - that in the global jungle of international capitalism the governments of sovereign states are puny when they come up against the economic power of major transnational corporations - was little remarked on at the time. This was largely because the Government was paradoxically let off the hook by its defeat in the Commons on an Opposition motion condemning sanctions, which allowed ministers to maintain that the other parties were responsible for undermining its ability to control private sector pay. The Government regained its footing on the following day, ten days before Christmas, by calling a confidence vote which it knew would swing the Scottish Nationalists back behind it since they would not wish to jeopardise the holding of the referendum on devolution by bringing about the dissolution of Parliament. But even so the Government only won the vote after the Prime Minister had told the House that sanctions would be abandoned. The curtain was brought down on the final scene of the pantomime after the inherently comical spectacle of a deputation from the CBI visiting Number 10 to thank a Labour government for dropping the threat of sanctions against its members.

Ted Heath's rhetorical question 'Who governs Britain?', to which the general election of February 1974 had appeared to give - from a constitutional point of view - the wrong answer, was being posed again. This time it was in terms of the trade union wing of the Labour Movement challenging a Labour government. But at a deeper, more tectonic level could be detected the rumbling of an even more crucial challenge, that of global capitalism to 'the right to self-determination' of the nation-state.

CHAPTER 23

The winter of discontent

'The curse of the British working class is their willingness to settle for so little. They are disciples not of the politics of envy but the politics of complacency. That is why they are so regularly ignored when the demands of the middle classes (who suffer from no such inhibition) increasingly dominate the policy agenda of both major parties.'

Roy Hattersley (1996)

As the Ford workers bolted themselves onto the assembly line again for their extra seven or eight quid a week take-home pay, the leaders of the National Union of Miners, bent on restoring differentials internally as well as regaining their overall front-runner position, banged in a claim for between 20 per cent (for the lowest-paid surface worker) and 40 per cent (for coal-face workers) for 232,000 pitmen, plus a four-day working week, with the additional sting of a demand for an eight-month agreement so that settlements should revert from March (the current date for contract changes) to the previous settlement month of November, a strategically much more favourable month for putting pressure on the Coal Board. Rubbing salt into the wound, the Government's Stage Three 'philanthropist', NUM president Joe Gormley, emphasised that his union was bargaining 'in a free collective bargaining situation, not fettered by outside considerations,' and that he expected the Board to do likewise. Perched on his butt in his editorial office, meditating on the happy lot of a coal-face worker already enjoying on average a 'healthy' 20 per cent productivity bonus under the miners' Stage Three settlement, the *Guardian* leader writer had no problem in pronouncing the proposition of paying a pit person a basic wage of £110 a week to be 'blatantly ridiculous'.

The horizon looked distinctly menacing as 1978 - itself dubbed by shadow chancellor Geoffrey Howe, in a catalogue of industrial confrontation, 'the year of the bloody-minded' - drew to a close. As the miners' claim was lodged, half a million civil servants were about to be incited to go for four times the Government's prescribed norm by the Pay Research Unit, the independent body responsible for monitoring their pay. Since the administrator of the Unit was a prime ministerial appointment, this was a major embarrassment for the Government, although it had given no guarantee that it would fully implement the Unit's recommendations. A 40 per cent claim for more than a million local government workers was already on the table, alongside similar claims for over 300,000 health service workers. The gas-workers' Christmas card for the Government was a 20 per cent demand, with the water-works delivering a copycat card. A six-week strike of provincial journalists over a claim for a £20-a-week rise started on 4th December. Threats to Christmas cheer came from television technicians, bottling factory workers, and draymen, though in the event they did not add up to much gloom or excessive abstemiousness. A strike of social workers which had begun in Newcastle and two London boroughs in late August escalated at the end of the year, with some 1,300 (from about a tenth of NALGO's social work branches) out and more set to join them. A five-and-a-half-week strike of bakers responsible for the production of seventy per cent of the nation's daily bread ground to an end twelve days before Christmas in bitter division, with the union settling for little more than half its original claim.

All this, however, was little more than a blustery prelude to the storm that was gathering. The public service unions announced 22nd January as their big Day of Action, and despite the Government's parliamentary reprieve, the political barometer fell in consonance with the weather. The old year slipped away with temperatures diving towards zero and widespread sleet and snow showers. Then 1979 - 'this year of decision and advance', as Prime Minister Callaghan called it, with deaf-and-blind but regrettably not dumb optimism, in his New Year Message - made its entrance as if nature were intent on providing the most apposite possible metaphor for the state of the nation, with Britain (in the *Guardian's* description) 'littered with abandoned cars as thousands of motorists ended their holiday weekend journeys trapped in snowdrifts or trapped behind other vehicles on icy roads.' The exceptionally cold weather continued to grip the country (with brief let-ups) throughout January and for the best part of February, compounding the problems imposed by wilful disruption.

The threat of a strike of petrol tanker drivers had been hanging over the nation's head since the end of November, when they set 3rd January as the deadline for agreement on their claim. As the year ended, troops were put on standby to be ready to take over deliveries to essential services. The deadline was put back a week to give the drivers time to consider eve-of-crisis offers from most of the oil companies, and a nation-wide strike was narrowly averted by a settlement raising the basic wage to £78 without strings, with fringe benefits bringing the total value of the rise for most drivers to between 13 and 15 per cent. Even so, unofficial action hit some parts of Britain, in particular Greater Manchester, where bus services were cut and some schools had to be closed because they ran out of heating oil. In Northern Ireland direct action by tanker drivers rapidly stoked up a crisis, and for seventy-five hours the country was under a state of emergency, with several hundred additional troops despatched from the mainland to drive and escort supplies of oil for vital services. Secretary of State Roy Mason was accused of extending his colonial attitudes into the field of industrial relations by Seamus Mallon of Ulster's Social Democratic and Labour Party, who reminded him that in 1974 a Labour government had stood by as a political strike of right-wing Loyalists toppled the Northern Ireland administration.

The biggest disruption to the life of the nation was caused by the tanker drivers' counterparts in general haulage. A week before Christmas delegates representing 40,000 lorry drivers had also fixed on 3rd January as the date for an all-out strike if their claim for a £65 a week basic (an increase of around 20 per cent) had not been conceded. It was not, and within twenty-four hours they had a stranglehold on the country. 'Lorry strikers cut country's supply lines', cried the front-page headline of *The Guardian* on 5th January. This was above a report that the icy weather, colluding with the strikers, was turning common-or-garden vegetables into luxuries in many parts of Britain, and that anticipated not only that pig and poultry farmers might have to slaughter their stock 'within the next few days as animal feedstuffs supplies fail', but the even direr forewarning that the non-delivery of newsprint might bring the presses to a halt.

When James Callaghan returned from his mini-summit meeting with the leaders of the three other major NATO powers in semi-tropical Guadeloupe (where the Prime Minister had been captured on film strolling across the sands with Audrey) to a bleak Britain, he ran straight into heavy flak. On this occasion his celebrated sangfroid simply provided more ammunition for an overwhelmingly hostile press and opposition politicians. Doubtless there was the malicious intention of misrepresenting him as callous and complacent behind the apocryphal quote 'Crisis? What crisis?' But it was not in fact such an outrageous travesty of what he actually said, in playing that grubby old card brought out by ruling politicians of whatever party when charged with responsibility for the deplorable state of the nation - the one that calls the critics unpatriotic. 'Please don't run down your country by talking about mounting chaos,' admonished Uncle Jim. 'If you look at it from outside, you can see that you are taking a rather parochial view. I do not feel there is mounting chaos.'

But whoever's fault it was, mounting chaos and something awfully like a crisis there manifestly was, even though it was obviously in the interests of capitalists in general and Tories in particular to exaggerate it. On the day of Callaghan's return, John Harvey-Jones, one of the three deputy chairmen of Britain's fourth biggest company, Imperial Chemical Industries, reported that 19,000 of its 90,000 employees were already involuntarily idle, and warned that the company would be forced to close by the end of the following week if the lorry drivers' strike was not called off. 'If we are not careful the whole pack of cards will collapse,' he said. Which is what the CBI began to envisage the next weekend, in predicting that a tenfold multiplication of the current total of 175,000 lay-offs would be caused by the combined effects of the ongoing road haulage dispute and the one-day rail strikes called by the locomen's union for the coming Tuesday and Thursday.

These dire and doubtless disingenuous predictions (which, in the event, were not fulfilled) were eagerly exploited by the leaderene of the Opposition - doubtless motivated by a burning desire to repay in kind the shame the miners had inflicted on a Tory prime minister five years before - in calling for the proclamation of a State of Emergency. From Callaghan's ministers the predictions provoked indignant cries of deliberate exaggeration. Perhaps that well-known mental characteristic of politicians, selective memory syndrome, meant they really had forgotten the even more fearful foreboding of their own Chancellor, voiced three days before the CBI warning, that two million people could have been made idle by the following week if the current and planned industrial action was not called off.

After the road transport disputes were over it was reported that they had caused at the peak point 235,000 lay-offs. The biggest single casualty of the road haulage strike was the massive Sheffield complex of the British Steel Corporation, which was shut down, with the laying-off of its 14,000 workers, through a blockade imposed by picketing lorry drivers. When the official figures were published in March, it transpired that the overall loss of production in January caused by the collusion of strikers and weather amounted to 8.2 per cent, which actually brought January 1979's total production figure to 8 per cent below that achieved during the three-day-working-week period under the unhappy Heath, so perhaps the dishonours were after all about even. The ICI estimated it had lost about £100 million from the road haulage strike, which ended in most areas on the last day of the month, with the general acceptance by the drivers of £64 for a 40-hour week, just £1 short of their original claim.

Of much greater moment than this economic sabotage so far as the formation of the folk memory of the Winter of Discontent is concerned - and thus for its long-term political repercussions - was the revolt of rank-and-file workers in local government services and the NHS. The most obvious reason for the lasting impression of this revolt is that - apart from industrial action in water or fuel supply or in public transport - the services provided by these workers impinged most directly on the lives of ordinary people. The Day of Action and its aftermath might have provided a salutary reminder of just how much was owed by society to the day-after-day dedication of the mostly ill-paid manual workers in these social services. Instead of which, this kicking over of the traces by the menials who customarily kept the machines of civilised living running so unobtrusively, seems to have provoked, more commonly, incomprehension and resentment. That this was the general reaction among ordinary folk may be reasonably inferred from the consideration that, had it not been so, 'superior people' able to command a public hearing could hardly have got away with such outrageous slanders against the public service workers as they did.

To this crucial war of words I will turn presently, after a brief account of the direct action to which the manual workers in local government and the NHS resorted in pursuit of their claims, pausing here only to draw attention to the brinkmanship repeatedly practised by the powers that be in their attempts to buy off trouble at the minimum possible cost. It was public knowledge a week before Christmas that 22nd January was to be a Day of Action involving up to one and a half million members of the four principal unions organising workers in the public services, 'the most co-ordinated industrial action since the General Strike of 1926', as a *Guardian* reporter put it. Alan Fisher, general secretary of the union with the greatest number of public service members, the National Union of Public Employees, had warned at the time: 'The stage is now set for a major confrontation in the public sector unless the Government is prepared to move quickly and decisively to end the low pay of the nation's underpaid workers.'

Yet it was not until four weeks later, just six days before what the Government - if one is to judge from its inertia - hoped would be little more than a jumbo-sized demo, that Callaghan gave another inch on its inflexible five-per-cent formula, by accepting full-time weekly earnings of less than £60, instead of less than £44.50, as providing a case for special treatment under the low-pay criterion. In consequence of this late concession, with its promise of Government funding, two days later, on the Thursday night before the Monday D-Day, the local government employers upped their offer to between 8 and 9 per cent, while at the same time the water authorities raised their offer to 33,000 manual workers to 11.5 per cent. On the same day British Gas and unions representing 40,000 manual workers agreed to set up a working party to examine a 20 per cent claim. The water and sewage workers won themselves a 16 per cent package early in February without having to lace up their bovver boots, with the power and gas workers doing even better by the time their settlement was due. The dispute with the local authority workers was allowed to drag on into March, when they finally settled for 9 per cent plus £1 on account while comparability studies were carried out. (The actual basic rates for a 35-hour working week, under what Environment Secretary Peter Shore imaginatively described as a 'fair - even generous - settlement', were raised by 50 pence a living day to £45.90 for the lowest-paid group and to £51.75 for the highest, as against the £60 target the workers had been aiming at.) It is true that 6.9 per cent of the water workers' package was for a projected increase in productivity, but then productivity was more measurable in the water industry, as in gas and power supply. More to the point, one naturally suspects, is that industrial action in such essential industries has such an immediate, brutal, and comprehensive impact on economic and social life.

But if the Government hoped that the Day of Action would be no more than a passing show, Fisher and his companion commanders leading the host of public sector workers into battle never expected the walls of the five-per-cent citadel to come tumbling down on 22nd January. The Day of Action was intended as an impressive display of solidarity and resolve (which it was), to be followed by such skirmishes and acts of attrition - selective strikes, go-slows, and the like - as turned out to be necessary to ram home the point that they would not be fobbed off with 5 per cent or little more. In some areas council workers moved at once into unofficial strikes of indefinite duration. In others the action was more of a hit-and-run nature. Much depended on local initiative, as in a guerrilla campaign. This was similarly so with ancillary hospital workers, and even in some instances with nurses. Here and there, graves remained undug, icebound roads ungritted, soiled bed linen unwashed.

In a number of areas, schools were closed down from the Day of Action onwards by striking caretakers, and by early February well over a thousand schools in England and Wales were shut. The 37,000 schoolchildren in the Labour-controlled London Borough of Haringey were among those who enjoyed an unexpected holiday, as the council was one of those which had decided not to try to keep its schools open without having caretakers on duty. One Haringey school, Creighton Comprehensive, provided a perfect microcosm of a nation at odds, since its head teacher, Molly Hattersley, was the sister of the Secretary of State for Prices, Roy Hattersley, shortly to be lumbered with the thankless task of smoothing the way to a truce with the public sector workers. Those parents protesting against the closure of the school were confronted by counter-demonstrators composed not only of caretakers, but of teachers (with their own demands in the pipeline), pupils, and other parents who took a more sympathetic view of the caretakers' strike.

In the midst of all this agitation of workers in local government, the civil servants prepared to go into action, fixing 23rd February as the date for a one-day all-out strike, to be followed by selective strikes. These small-scale manoeuvres had quite spectacular results, gumming up the Government's data-processing operations and even stopping its cheques. The unions' campaign was ably abetted by the Government itself. By suspending civil servants taking part in selective strikes, it escalated the action. In Scotland the Government actually succeeded in paralysing itself by suspending thirty-nine civil servants who refused to do work normally undertaken by colleagues. The suspension of thirty-nine people for declining the role of scab labour provoked a walk-out by 30,000.

With indomitable disregard for prudence and the findings of the Pay Research Unit, the Government produced towards the end of March the incendiary offer of 7 per cent, thereby enflaming the normally very moderate Inland Revenue Staff Federation to instruct its members to black all work on the Budget, and the civil service unions jointly to call an all-out strike for the following Monday, 2nd April. Just minutes before the Government was defeated in a vote of confidence in the Commons, on Wednesday 28th March, the First Division Association, representing some 10,000 top civil servants, announced that its members would support the strike. This was surely the very apogee of the Government's achievements. It had succeeded by almost unsurpassable ineptitude in uniting against itself its 600,000 own white-collar employees, divided by their membership of nine different unions, and ranging in rank from office cleaners and all the others constituting the more than fifty per cent who earned less than £65 a week, to senior civil servants with five-figure salaries and the power to bend the ears of ministers. On the last Friday in March the Government tried to retrieve some semblance of being in control of the problem by raising its offer to 9 per cent, with a promise of further rises, based on the recommendations of the Pay Research Unit, to be paid on 1st August and on 31st March 1980. However, its divide-and-rule ploy, masterminded by special agent Roy Hattersley, of seeking to reach a separate accommodation with the smaller unions, failed to avert the unprecedented situation of a government going into a general election campaign while under siege by its own civil servants, with the pitched battle of 2nd April being followed up by ongoing guerrilla warfare.

And yet other bread-and-butter struggles (involving such diverse groups of disaffected workers as tool-men, engineers, printers, stagehands, and Post Office workers) accompanied the Tweedledum-versus-Tweedledee battle of the polls - and in some cases, notably that of teachers in England and Wales (though their Scottish colleagues had already won a famous victory) rumbled on long after the last bit of election litter had been swept up.

One of the longest-running guerrilla campaigns during the Winter of Discontent - and the one that caused the most bitter recriminations - was that of the ambulance crews. So incensed were London's 2,500 ambulancemen by being offered, a week before the public sector workers' Day of Action, an extra 5 per cent (it represented an increase of between 85 pence and £2.50 for drivers and crewmen whose highest wage was £47) that their shop stewards declared, in defiance of union instructions, that no emergency services would be provided during the 24-hour strike due to run from seven a.m. on the 22nd January. The threat was dropped on the night before the strike, but in Birmingham, Coventry, Solihull, Cardiff, Glasgow, Inverness, Fife, and Strathclyde 999 calls went unanswered. By the end of the month emergency-only ambulance services were the general rule, although in some areas cover had to be provided at times by troops or police till towards the end of March.

Hospitals were hard-hit from the beginning. By early in February, as the result of industrial action by ancillary staff, more than half and perhaps as many as two-thirds of the country's 2,300 hospitals were restricting admissions and only providing full treatment to urgent cases. In a few instances some of the nursing staff took part in short strikes, even on one occasion at Great Ormond Street children's hospital.

Fisher's NUPE (with 124,000 members making up nearly half the total of ancillary hospital workers, 12,000 members forming more than two-thirds of the ambulance crews, and over 80,000 nursing members out of the total of some 350,000 nurses and midwives) was in the vanguard of the fight for more generous rewards for health workers, and was the last union to agree to the final offer of 9 per cent plus £1 on account pending comparability agreements, only settling at the end of March after being outvoted by the other unions represented on the national pay bodies. The main still-outstanding grievance of the ambulancemen, many of whom were fully-trained paramedics, was that while, like the local authority manual workers, they had won the principle of comparability, they had not succeeded in securing a guarantee that they would be treated as emergency service workers on a par with firemen and the police.

Alan Fisher himself, who had played such a prominent part in championing the cause of the low-paid, was portrayed by press and politicians as if he were the Grand Demon in a Pandemonium of trade union villains bent on orchestrating what the Prime Minister described at one point - as the disruption of hospitals rose to a crescendo - as 'free collective vandalism'. But before lending an ear to the mouth-to-mouth fighting that resounded from one end of the kingdom to the other in those bitter days, and especially before trying to divine what creeds the clamour really expressed, it might be as well to lay down a few markers by which to measure how exorbitant, or not, were the demands for a larger share of the nation's cake that came thick and fast from just about every quarter.

Figures for the situation in April 1978, released by the Department of Employment at the end of October, recorded the average earnings of men over twenty-one as £86.90, of adult male white-collar workers as just over £100, and of women over eighteen as £55.40. On the Sunday after the public sector workers' Day of Action, league tables based on the latest statistics available from the Department of Employment were published by *The Observer*. They compared the gross average weekly earnings of forty different groups of workers in April 1975 and April 1978, breaking them up into four divisions that helped to show how successful each group had been in playing the snakes-and-ladders wage-bargaining game while their betters got on with their game of Monopoly. With a few exceptions (water workers, gas workers, firemen, miners working on the surface, secondary school teachers, and senior civil servants, for example, had slipped downwards, while draughtsmen, car workers, toolmen, and electricity power engineers had scrambled upwards) their relative positions were much the same in 1978 as they had been in 1975. It is important to bear in mind, of course, that the tables tell us nothing else about the relative rewards of working in different occupations, not even how long it was necessary to work to get the gross earnings indicated.

In the top division, with over £100 a week gross in 1978, were top managers (£149.60) [a somewhat vague category, this: a couple of months earlier the Opinion Research Centre had defined 'top managers' as 'those earning over £12,000 a year, i.e. more than £230 a week], electricity power engineers (£136.10), marketing/sales managers and executives (£131.40), teachers in higher education (£121.30), office managers (£116.10), senior civil servants (£113.70), production and works managers (£110.50), miners working at the coalface (£109.20), accountants (£107.40), and secondary school teachers (£102.70); in the second division, with £84 to £100 gross, were primary school teachers (£99.90), electricians in industry (£95.10), draughtsmen (£92.00), steel workers (£91.70), miners working on the surface (£91.20), policemen (£91.00), car workers (£90.70), toolmakers (£89.80), train drivers (£86.00), plumbers (£85.30), clerical/executives in the Post Office (£84.80), and heavy goods lorry drivers (£84.20); in the third division, with £70 to £84 gross, were gas workers (£81.50), printers outside London (£81.10), food-processing workers (£80.50), firemen (£79.90), bricklayers (£79.20), railway workers (£78.80), electricity supply workers (£78.00), water workers (£74.60), painters and decorators (£73.90), and dustmen (£70.40); and in the bottom division, with less than £70 a week gross, were general clerks (£68.40), nurses (£68.20), clerical officers in the civil service (£62.90), female bank workers (£62.00), caretakers (£61.50), farm workers (£57.70), catering workers (£57.00), bespoke tailors (£43.00), and female retail food workers in England and Wales (£42.20).

Commenting on these pay league tables, and noting among other points that between 1975 and 1978 'the gap between many white-collar, high-income people in the private sector and people in manual labour had widened', Robert Taylor made about as sensible remarks as anyone on the free-for-all situation which had lead to the insurrection of the Winter of Discontent. He called the tables 'the expression of a leap-froggers' system in which workers strive, through fragmented and localised bargaining, to hold their position relative to workers in other work-places and other industries. The most that workers tend to seek...is to climb a rung or two above those whose pay they traditionally compare with their own.' Is not this exactly what we would expect from people conditioned from birth to struggling for a decent livelihood earned in a secure job in a competitive capitalist society? Taylor, who starts his commentary by implicitly rejecting notions - from either left or right - that there was anything revolutionary behind the mass industrial action of the British workers, with the dismissive remark that 'envy of the super rich, or a revival of class warfare, is not the inspiration behind [their] anger and frustration', goes on to make the shrewd observation that 'from some points of view, it may be just as well that most workers do not relate what they earn to incomes throughout the national labour force.'

Whether it is 'just as well' that in general they are not at all well-informed (which is partly what the blessing amounts to!), and that they do not concern themselves overmuch with questions of how society works and whether it gives everybody a fair deal or not, is a matter of opinion, responses to which will vary according to whether the idea of democracy is taken seriously or is just thought of as a useful buzzword. Had 'most workers' made a practice (with the help of the trade union bureaucracies, say) of casting their eyes much higher up the pyramid than where they stood, at the incomes of those who would probably not, except jocularly, regard themselves as members of 'the national labour force', they would have found such fascinating figures as these to compare with the earnings of ordinary workers listed above. The takings of Michael Edwardes, the South African miracle-worker appointed to turn round struggling BL, were estimated at £100,000 per annum (approaching £2,000 a week) and those of dream-child Lord Grade of Associated Television at £150,000 (nearly £3,000 a week). The Chairman of the British National Oil Corporation garnered £50,000 (over £960 a week) and the Chairman of the National Enterprise Board £36,265 (just short of £700 a week). The Prime Minister's salary at that time was £20,000 per annum (£386+ a week) and Cabinet ministers salaries £13,000 (£250 a week). Up till June '78 MPs were paid £6,270 (£120+ a week) and thereafter £6,897 (£132+ a week). The salary of TUC general secretary Len Murray worked out at about £175 a week.

Among the ironies to savour if we include really superior people in our survey of rewards for contributing to the common weal are these. The man with the dazzling name who had been appointed to chair the Royal Commission on the Distribution of Income and Wealth, Lord Diamond, was paid £9,225 per annum for a 2½-day working week, i.e. at a weekly rate equivalent to about £355 - a 'rate for the job' which was to be matched by the salary of the chairman of the Pay Comparability Commission when it was set up in March 1979 (see Chapter 24). A more direct bit of comparability was thrust under the noses of Ford's assembly-line workers, who, as they contemplated an offer of £3.40 pay rise to bring them a sumptuous wage of £72.40 for a forty-hour week, heard that their boss, Sir Terence Beckett, was to get a whacking £459 a week rise, bringing his salary to £54,000 per annum, or around £1,038 a week.

As the clamour from ordinary workers for more money was translated into action, the sympathies of even the fairer sections of the press tended to wane. For instance, Robert Taylor, the 'sensible' observer cited above, began to call the leading campaigning union NUPE 'a four-letter word', while the high-decibel expression 'greedy' was liberally deployed in the media against wage demands. In considering - at least with regard to the lower-paid sections of 'the national workforce' - whether union demands were reasonable or 'irresponsible', one marker is indispensable, namely, the figure alighted on by the Government as the borderline below which earnings would be officially accepted as 'low pay'. This figure was £44.50, and the incomes policy White Paper laid it down that pay increases could be above five per cent if the resulting wage did not exceed that sum. The Government claimed that this was a proper updating of the figure of £30 set by the TUC as a minimum pay target in 1974.

Official acceptance of such pitiful pay (a gross wage of less than one tenth of Sir Terence's *rise*) as adequate invites bitter comment - and direct action! It hardly deserves the reasoned response it got from NUPE's Alan Fisher, who criticised the Government's figure on two scores. In a letter to the Chancellor of the Exchequer of August 1978, he pointed out that, to get as much as he could get on supplementary benefit, a man with two children would have to earn £46.28 gross, and that with three children he would have to earn £53.62. Furthermore, Fisher said, the TUC's unrevised target had been for a minimum basic rate, not for minimum earnings. He maintained that the TUC figure had been calculated as two-thirds of average earnings, and that updating it on this basis would give a minimum basic figure of £60. It is this figure that NUPE and the other unions organising the manual workers in local government and the health service had agreed on as their target.

CHAPTER 24

The battle for Britain

'Never before in the history of human conflict have so
few owed so much to so many.'

Apocryphal

If history is a consideration of why things happened rather than
being merely a chronicle of events (just 'one damned thing after
another,' as Saki memorably put it), if 'the sound and the fury' do
in fact signify something, then we should listen to the voices of *all*
those on its stage, the less as well as the more vocal, the less as
well as the more articulate - and listen even harder to hear the
thoughts that remain unspoken. At times of social upheaval, the
masses break their bonds and, becoming more than the instruments
of others and more than merely a chorus, mock by their actions
Carlyle's dictum that 'the history of the world is but the biography
of great men.' It will not do to talk of the Winter of Discontent as a
kind of collective insanity (though certainly it was a mass getting-
out-of-hand with a vengeance). Nor will it do to treat it primarily
in institutional terms, ending up with the kind of conclusion such
treatises covertly begin with, such as, in this case, that events
demonstrate conclusively that the trade unions had grown too
powerful and/or had failed to adapt so that they could effectively
represent the interests of their members in a changed world.
(Although the latter point is undoubtedly true in ways that little
concern the apologists for capitalism and its warped social
relationships who customarily produce such treatises.) To get to
grips with the Winter of Discontent it is necessary to realise or
recall how ubiquitous and pervasive was the deliberate disruption
of the everyday life of the country.

But beyond that, the point of the account given above of the
course of the Winter of Discontent is simply to serve as a backcloth
to the really significant action: the mental and moral agitation
seething beneath superficially material (and indeed materialistic)
objectives - agitation that challenged the very basis of society. As
had happened to France in 1968, the integrity of British society
was called into question in 1979. And it is a reflection on the
inadequacy of Britain's left-wing intelligentsia in the late seventies

that they failed to rise to the occasion, failed coherently to articulate, cogently to crystallise the common cry of 'it's not fair'. They left the field clear for the self-serving apologists for a society which, however fluid it might appear to have become, remained ineradicably hierarchical in character, to croak loathesomely 'the politics of envy, the politics of envy'.

What did the young Major Freeman intend by his challenge to the elected representatives of the people, during those first elated days of peace after the long struggle against fascism, that this was 'D-Day in the battle of the new Britain'? Surely he meant that, progressively at least, the old social divisions would be demolished, the old injustices done away with, the old inequalities banished from the land by a Labour Movement which had at last won power for the people at a time that gave it a fighting chance of victory in a campaign to construct a good society? The charge against Labour's leaders - and more especially against those who themselves came from a working-class background - is that they allowed themselves to be seduced by 'the sweets of office' into defecting to the ranks of the elite. For however rosy the prospects for Socialism may have appeared in those heady post-war days, by the time of the third round of Labour rule in the mid-seventies, at the latest, the fraudulent nature of the Party's prospectus for transforming society by parliamentary means must have been patently obvious to those who had themselves been transported by the magic boxes of the polling booths to the high seats of power and privilege that representative democracies provide for their really successful politicians.

As the manual workers in hospitals, schools, and local government services took to the streets to support their Day of Action, the Prime Minister was starring in a very different arena, as guest of honour at Granada Television's lunch for 'What the Papers Say' press awards. In addressing the representatives of an 'estate' not greatly distinguished for its record of speaking fair of organised labour, James Callaghan (theoretically chief tribune of the workers) felt impelled by the crisis he did not recognise to acknowledge that 'events in recent days' had been 'a setback, not just for the Government but for the nation as a whole.' He said that what was happening was 'a social, indeed a moral question, much more than a matter of law', hoped 'that these events will make us ask what kind of people and what kind of society we want to be', and concluded with an affirmation of faith that 'the good sense of our people' would prevail. Perhaps the optimistic conclusion was no more than an obligatory obeisance from a politician displaying his democratic credentials and bidding for re-election. Yet once again he could not be faulted for recognising that profound questions were raised by the current social scene. Whether his vision held any answers is another matter. If some of the superficiality in his contemporaneous presentation of the problems posed by the Winter of Discontent can be attributed to the astute manoeuvrings of an active politician at the very centre of the web of so-called 'democratic' politics, the same excuse cannot be made for his retrospective comments. But perhaps one should not expect the passion for self-justification to diminish with loss of power. At all events the judgements he makes in *Time and Chance* on two of his most prominent opponents during the Winter of Discontent, Moss Evans and Alan Fisher, are grossly unjust because his portrayal of the situations in which they found themselves is wholly superficial, either from a natural inability to perceive or from a studied intent to deceive.

Not that penetrating, nor even honest, commentary and analysis was readily to be found amongst the communicators of the time. With rare exceptions, the common purpose of politicians, journalists, and priests alike was rather to clothe the unaccustomed starkness of social division with homily and platitude, however the message might vary according to where the spokesman located the mystic heart of 'the nation'. The trade union tribunes spoke bluntly enough, as was their wont, but were little disposed to dig beneath the surface and expose the treacherous foundations upon which their whole *raison d'être* rested. Inasmuch as a national debate took place, the central issue was (to reduce it to manageable if oversimplified terms) whether it was better for the incomes of employees to be determined by 'free collective bargaining' or through negotiating machinery established by the State, based on national economic targets laid down annually (with the approval of Parliament) by the government of the day. A long-standing exponent of such a policy, Transport Secretary William Rodgers spelt it out a bit at the beginning of 1978:

'I believe that the time has now come to stop thinking of incomes policy as a temporary expedient and to begin to accept it as a necessary - and obvious - component of economic management and social planning...An orderly search for a settled incomes policy would be widely

welcomed. It would be a voluntary policy, reached by
agreement between all those involved, Government,
trade unions, employers, and resting on the broad
approval of public opinion. TUC backing would be
essential.'

Although events could hardly have proved him more wrong
in judging the moment to be propitious for promoting such a policy,
in pointing to the fear of inflation as the spur for those who
advocated it, he could not have been more right. Almost without
exception this was what mainly, if not entirely, motivated them,
and lack of concern for wider and deeper questions raised by the
great wages race condemned their advocacy from the start. On the
same day that Rodgers flew his kite, the Chief Secretary to the
Treasury, Joel Barnett - backing up his bosses, the Chancellor and
the Prime Minister, who were already floating 5 per cent (or little
more) as a suitable figure for the next stage of a pay policy from
which the unions had already made up their minds to withdraw
their co-operation - made it all too clear who was to bear the brunt
of the policy for incomes which he rightly declared the Government
must have:

'In the national interest, and not least in the interest of
maintaining and improving public services, it must be
understood that if public sector wages take a bigger
share of the national cake then - if we are not simply to
finance inflation by printing money, as our predecessors
did - the consequences are clear. And surely, as night
follows day, so excessive public sector wage settlements
must be followed by cuts in public services. The
alternative of financing higher public sector wages from
higher taxation is not an option open to us.'

Barnett's warning contains everything that characterises the
Callaghan Government's surrender of Socialist purposes to the
forces that rule capitalist society. The actual employees of a
supposedly Socialist government - its natural allies - are to be
penalised for contributing their working lives to exemplifying the
proposition that there is another, fairer and more rational, way of
organising society. Not only are public sector workers to be

306

discriminated against in comparison with workers employed to enable individual capitalists to pile up profits (perhaps for the cogent reason that the government has far greater leverage against its own employees than it has against workers in the private sector, though Barnett's intimation that to further increase the proportion of the nation's wealth tied directly to the public sector would be inimical to 'the national interest' powerfully suggests his subjection to orthodox capitalist thinking with regard to the production of wealth). But inasmuch as they succeed in wringing from their State bosses higher rewards for their labour than those superior servants of the State are willing to concede, they are also to be held responsible for whatever cuts the Government decides as a consequence it must impose on public services. That public services must be sacrificed in such circumstances is taken as read.

So much for the Social Contract, the admirable aims of which had to be subordinated to a 'national interest' which, in some mystical, almost Hegelian, sense is thought of as subsuming all personal and sectional interests. Such evasions of the pain of scrupulous thinking are firmly founded on the shallow supposition that there is some measure of justice in the way that that notorious 'national cake' is shared out between the individuals who collectively constitute the nation. Alternatively, the only principle operating is the cynical conviction that the only cause for concern is the relative strengths of those competing for a bigger slice of the cake. What a mouldy state of affairs!

If, on the contrary, it is accepted that justice should come into the equation, a paramount point that Barnett conveniently leaves out is the heavy concentration of low-paid workers in State employment - a concentration persisting through administrations of different political persuasions that tells us much about the 'natural' relationship between leaders and led, bosses and bossed, which overrides all ostensible ideologies. But Barnett was far from being alone amongst ministers in the Callaghan Government in warning public sector workers that unless they accepted the Government's pay policy they would be jeopardising not only the amorphous 'national interest' in general but, in particular, public services and even their own jobs. Besides repeated doses of homily pills from Prime Minister and Chancellor, a series of more specific threats - alternating with or even accompanying nauseous wheedlings - issued from the throats of sundry leaders of 'the people's party'.

For instance, a couple of days after the Ford workers settled for their 17 per cent, the Environment Secretary, Peter Shore, announced that the Treasury's rate support grants for 1979/80 would be maintained at 61 per cent of approved expenditure and that rate increases should not exceed 10 per cent. This ceiling on rate increases, he said, would cause local authorities no problems provided they made wage settlements within the Government's 5 per cent guidelines. Geoffrey Drain, general secretary of the National and Local Government Officers' Association, promptly attacked the Government for failing to provide enough funds to pay their workforces adequately, although in truth it was nothing but normal practice for whatever government happened to be in power to subsidise the Welfare State and the general social wage by, in effect, a levy on the pay packets of public sector workers rather than raising sufficient revenue through general taxation. This is but part of a general principle that, contrary to the common misconception that Welfare States are in the main funded by redistributing wealth from richer citizens to the less affluent, makes the middling sort and even the poor for the most part pay for their own State benefits. Although it was to be further perfected by the Thatcherite counter-revolutionaries, such a principle was, as we have seen, clearly enunciated by Labour's own economic guru, Sir Stafford Cripps, in the early days of the building of Britain's post-war Jerusalem. (See Chapter 19)

In a debate in the Commons while the battle with the local government and health service workers raged in the streets outside, Education Secretary Shirley Williams (later to become one of 'the Gang of Four' who broke away from the Labour Party to set up the Social Democratic Party) told the House that to concede what the local authority employees were still holding out for, 15 per cent, would mean either a rate increase of 20 per cent or the loss of 30,000 teaching and 20,000 other jobs in the education service in England and Wales. Bill Rodgers (who like Williams was to become a founder member of the SDP, along with Roy Jenkins and David Owen) did not scruple to plead with the poorly-paid workers in public transport to moderate their demands for a decent living in favour of the elderly and disabled, warning the busmen that if the settlement they succeeded in exacting was considered to be inflationary the Government would have to abandon its plan to legislate for a national half-fare scheme for those groups.

Time and again the Government lent credence to the Tory capitalistic view that workers in the public sector were featherbedded and that it would be better for the country if many of them were shaken out into the dole queues. A Treasury paper submitted by the Chancellor for Cabinet discussion - just as the leaders of the manual workers in the NHS and local government began to sell to their members the 9-per-cent-plus-£1-on-account settlement of their dispute - asserted that breaching the 5 per cent barrier would have to mean renewed stringency in Government expenditure. Mixing menace with mendacity, it intimated that workers in central and local government had not yet experienced any of the rigours of market forces. Four leaders of white-collar public service workers jointly denounced the absurdity of Government policy which allowed the Treasury to disseminate its view that public sector jobs should be shed at the same time as a special programme to create 50,000 extra jobs was announced. 'It is high time the Treasury were told to adjust the cash limits to provide fair pay settlements in the public sector,' they declared.

Perhaps the most glaring example of a philosophy in which it was thought unexceptionable for ordinary workers and their families to be called on to make disproportionate sacrifices to support a Welfare State that, when everything is taken into account, has always provided bigger benefits for the well-to-do, is to be found in the Government's handling of the problem of funding the nationalised railways. (Though 'handling' is not quite the way to put it, considering its studied determination to keep the problem at arm's length. It has been insufficiently remarked that for Labour governments no less than for Tory administrations the pseudo-constitutional separation of government from the managements appointed to run nationalised industries has been a great blessing to the politicians, especially whenever there was 'trouble at t' mill'.) Higher productivity from a reduced workforce was called for in a report from the Commons Select Committee on Nationalised Industries published at the end of August 1978. The report welcomed the substantial progress made by British Rail during the previous two years towards reaching its target of cutting its deficit by 55 per cent by 1981. However, it noted that this was mainly attributable to a staff reduction of about 6 per cent and a fall in earnings per member of staff of about 4 per cent. In a stunningly perspicacious comment, if they were speaking for the workforce in making it, the Committee doubted that 'a further fall in real average earnings would be considered desirable.'

From the start of municipal and State ownership, public transport in Britain, on both road and rail, has been an industry notorious for maintaining a perpetually precarious fiscal balancing act between expenditure, revenue, and subsidy through the extensive practice of overtime working, operating as an irresistible lure to workers paid at low basic rates. (For example, the bus drivers Rodgers appealed to only hoisted themselves out of the poverty pay basic rate of £34.49 for a 40-hour week by working on average 12 hours a week overtime, frequently including Saturdays and Sundays.) Paradoxically, technological advances, which with the slashing of the country's once-unsurpassed network of services had reduced British Rail's labour force from 446,000 in 1950 to 178,000 by the beginning of 1979, tended to reinforce reliance on overtime (with little concern for the health and safety factors this raised). Yet the financial costs of investment in new technology continued to increase the pressure to cut down on manpower. The railway unions claimed that staff shortages exceeded 12,000, and that if British Rail conceded their claim for a reduction in the basic working week to 35 hours, this would provide 28,000 more jobs. Yet, with exemplary timing, just as last-minute efforts were being made to persuade the locomen's union not to go ahead with its planned series of one-day strikes in support of a bonus claim, BR management released plans for a manpower cut of 20,000. This was raised a month later to between 30,000 and 40,000, the redundancy figures BR said would be necessary if it were to grant an industry-wide bonus scheme.

To make matters worse, there were clear signs that ASLEF's leaders were quite prepared to see a rundown in BR's manpower, provided it was achieved through voluntary 'wastage', in order to get a bonus for the locomen, a stance that was completely unacceptable to NUR general secretary Sid Weighell. He declared that, on the contrary: 'The unions should jointly oppose attempts by management to drastically reduce manning levels.' At the same time, Weighell threatened an overtime ban if BR refused to cut the basic working week and to offer 'realistic' pay rises. In the wake of the 9-per-cent-plus-£1 deal just won by the local authority workers, BR management's notion of realism was, apparently, to offer the railwaymen 6.38 per cent, an offer which only exceeded the 5 per cent 'norm' because the Government had agreed that full-time wages that were still below £70 after a 5 per cent rise could be topped up by up to £3.50. The three rail unions were told that one likely consequence of a settlement that exceeded BR's cash limits would be the raising of fares for the second time that year.

Yet again the State's own employees were being told that they should accept low wages so that the public would not have to pay higher prices, with a Labour government mimicking its political opponents in rejecting the option of raising the living standards of public sector workers by providing more money for public services through general taxation. The dead man's handle operated by Sir Stafford Cripps (that 'superb Christian planner', as one of his biographers dubs him), in ruling out more radical 'redistribution of national income by way of taxation', still stopped the workers in their tracks as they strove for a better standard of living. Yet no consideration of facts which manifestly added up to a serious deterioration in the situation of many people employed in the public sector, precluded Prime Minister Callaghan from pouncing triumphantly on the Leader of the Opposition when, during the first week of that fateful election campaign of spring 1979, she added to her constantly reiterated charge of overmanning in the public sector the warning that if the recommendations of the recently established Pay Comparability Commission exceeded the labour costs allowed for in public sector budgets, it would almost inevitably lead to cuts in services, job losses, or both. 'This is the kind of blunder that can upset industrial peace, which has been so hardly won,' crowed Callaghan, as if he and his ministers were entirely innocent of ever issuing such GBH-type threats.

It was a nice irony that, aside from the few trade union leaders who seriously took up the cudgels on their behalf, the most vigorous defence of the interests of the public sector workers came from the dethroned King of the Tories, Ted Heath, during the course of his personal campaign in support of the principle of an incomes policy - a principle which the Thatcherites were busy denouncing as a heresy from the true path of capitalism. Interviewed on television in a programme which incorporated a film showing him having the poignant experience of being feted in a Lancashire miners' club, he made it crystal clear that he considered it neither fair nor sensible to treat workers in public services or nationalised industries less favourably than those employed in the private sector:

'Let us say that a government tries to hold down the public sector, while on the other hand the private sector gives much higher increases in wages. Those people in the public sector don't accept that. We've learnt that from experience. They say, "Why, because we're in a nationalised industry, because we're public servants in hospitals or elsewhere, because we are nurses or firemen, why should we have worse treatment than those who are working in the private sector?"'

Callaghan may have recognised that there were moral issues underlying the revolt of the public sector workers; but, as with his grudging concession on low pay on the eve of their Day of Action, so it was with his concurrent implicit admission that they never would accept the status of second-class citizens in wage bargaining: only when browbeating had patently failed to intimidate them would he grant the irrefutable justice of their case. He announced that machinery would be established for the continuous review of public sector pay on the basis of comparability with private industry, i.e. of 'the rate for the job'. Seven weeks later, three weeks before the Government fell, Hugh Clegg, Professor of Industrial Relations at Warwick University, was appointed (at what, the Prime Minister made clear, in answer to the doubts expressed by Labour back-bencher Arthur Lewis whether such several-fingers-in-the-pie people were the right sort to consider the pay of the lower-paid, *was* 'the rate for the job' for such posts, i.e. £18,510 for a full year's work) to chair the Standing Commission on Pay Comparability. Its first reports, he told the House, on the pay of local authority manual workers, NHS ancillary workers, ambulancemen, and university workers, would be made on August 1st. The Commission remained standing until it was knocked on the head by Mrs Thatcher in 1980. The VIPs' equivalent of the tribunal set up to see fair play for the PBI of the public sector, the Top Salaries Review Board chaired by Lord Boyle of Handsworth, PC, not only preceded the Clegg Commission by eight years but effortlessly survived its decease.

Like the wages councils (the origins of which lie in the trade boards set up by a bill of 1909 which was introduced, under a Liberal administration, by the man who was to become the century's most considerable Tory statesman, and the final smothering of which was to be engineered in 1993 by the ministry of its least considerable

Tory statesman), the Clegg Commission was, of course, a deviation from the creed of free collective bargaining to which both sides of industry and all parliamentary parties in theory subscribed - or at least had subscribed until relatively recently. In both 1900 and 1979 there were good reasons for this deviation, and strangely one of the most telling reasons was central to both cases, though they sprang from radically different causes. A biblical lifespan before Clegg's collectivist butterfly was broken on the wheel of the first of the Thatcherite kickback anti-combination laws, Winston Churchill had succinctly identified this central reason for the need for State intervention as the absence of 'parity of bargaining' between management and labour to secure 'a decent provision for industrial workers'. Churchill's target was 'the sweated trades' in which workers could be exploited without the restraint of union organisation. The target for Clegg and his colleagues was the biggest boss of all, the government, so that in a sense the State was being enjoined to intervene against itself - or at least against those who, *pro tempore*, held the stewardship of the State and all the powers that went with it.

The trouble with the incomes policy concept which by the seventies had lodged in the minds of more than a few people of varying party allegiances or none at all was that there were two entirely distinct, and indeed antithetical, reasons for the growing disenchantment with the doctrine and practice of free collective bargaining. On the one hand, there was the *weakness* of the workers, in such situations as Churchill had inveighed against or in such cases as public sector workers in the caring services; on the other hand, there was the *strength* of the workers - that is, of those groups of workers who were in a position (to use the smear phrase so liberally applied by the anti-union media) to 'hold the country to ransom'.

Unsurprisingly, the beginning of the wider dispersal of the pay policy proposition coincided with the renascent power of the trade union movement in the post-war years and gathered strength as economic growth weakened. Equally unsurprisingly, many trade unionists and most of the Labour left became totally wedded to a practice that was really a true expression in the labour market of the doctrine of *laissez-faire* capitalism. Thus came the wry consequence that in the great crisis faced by the Labour Movement in the winter of 1978/79 its most ostensibly radical members were in one key respect - that of wage-bargaining - closest in their thinking on industrial relations to the most reactionary of the Tories, who were harking back to the heydays of unfettered capitalism in the nineteenth century. Of course, Labour supporters in the Jim-'ll-fix-it-if-you-let-him-pay-policy bed were equally incompatible. They were all deeply - and rightly - concerned about the effects of inflation on living standards. But while some of them were there primarily to consummate State control over the workers, others had climbed in with the hope of securing fair play for groups of workers who had not done so well out of a free-for-all. However, as we shall see, others just as concerned about workers who failed to get a square deal out of free collective bargaining took a death-before-dishonour stance towards the Government's Stage Four propositioning and to the whole thrust of the Labour leadership's project for a permanent incomes policy.

'Union is strength' and 'united we stand, divided we fall' are the commonest slogans strung across the banners of British trade unions, and the truth of these precepts is in theory well understood by trade unionists and by the Labour Movement as a whole. But every party and every movement, despite the common purposes which bind the members together, has in-built centrifugal forces stemming from the fact that it is actually composed of an alliance of more or less disparate elements. Indeed, to talk of a 'movement' at all may be an indispensable generalisation but is nevertheless a dangerous one, since it tends to obscure or to iron out significant differences and disagreements. The breakdown of Britain's consensus politics under the pressure of faltering economic growth brought increased dissension to the Tory Party as well as to Labour. But the Tory centre held, carrying the Butskellites with it (though perhaps with some heartache and maybe even a twinge of conscience or two - and in the longer term with potentially suicidal consequences for the Party) as it moved markedly to the right. Labour's tragedy is that at this most critical moment it was a movement deeply divided, and no one should be surprised at its rout by the New Tories, whose message seemed more in tune with the spirit of the age. 'Dispirit of the age', perhaps one should say, since its principal characteristics were the loss of optimism in general progress through steady economic growth along with a concomitant switch to an every-man-his-own-enterprise approach to life.

Just how divided the industrial wing of the Labour Movement

had become may be gauged by listening to the bitterly discordant voices of some of the trade union leaders. The Brighton Congress of September 1978 may have given the impression of organised labour united against the concept of a national pay policy by its overwhelming backing for a return to free collective bargaining. However, by his very defence of this hallowed principle, in putting the motion composited from all the separate trade union resolutions rejecting the Government's plea for a Stage Four, the miners' general secretary, Laurence Daly, exposed free collective bargaining as a force that fragmented the trade union movement. He insisted that he was not advocating a system in which, in pressing their claims, workers ignored the interests of other workers, or of the community as a whole. Commending it to Congress as an apposite metaphor (evidently he was much pleased with it, since he was recycling it from an address he had made to a Durham miners' gala), Daly likened free collective bargaining to 'free collective motoring, all right unless it turned into free collective suicide, with everyone choosing his own side of the road.' One might take the charitable view that it mattered little what he said, since everyone knew that the motion he was speaking in favour of would be carried overwhelmingly; but to draw attention with such unconscious clarity to the way free collective bargaining worked and to why it never could serve the interests of the community as a whole did seem a little unfortunate.

More pertinent and perceptive comment on the British trade union movement came from the chair, in the opening address by David Basnett, general secretary of the General and Municipal Workers' Union. Mindful of the high probability of a general election being called within a month or so (how was he to guess that three days later Callaghan - in a delirium of hope that, given a little more time, a majority of the electorate would come to see it his way and conclude that his government was after all best fitted 'to carry on with the task of consolidating the present improvement in the country's position' - would announce his Russian roulette decision to soldier on into a fifth session of Parliament?), Basnett was understandably at pains to be conciliatory. (This, indeed, seems to have been a characteristic of his in his dealings with other union leaders and with Government ministers, and for which pains he is dismissed by Denis Healey in his autobiography as 'weak and vacillating in our years of travail'.) So he took care to avoid providing the common enemy with ammunition to fire at the Labour Movement, and urged his fellow trade unionists to work and vote for Labour in the sensibly measured terms of calling it the best of the parties on offer to deal with discrimination and poverty.

To the unions' dispute with the Government over the pay policy issue he only alluded obliquely (and in a way which indicated that he was by no means wholly unsympathetic to the case for a pay policy), in criticising some sections of the Labour Movement for being too often prepared to trade off the social wage for an increase in the pay packet. And gently probing closer to the heart of the problem of worker solidarity in a capitalist society, he reproved the unions for forgetting about the inequalities which still existed in income, housing, and education. Of course, his allusion to making 'the final assault on discrimination, inequality, and poverty' was ludicrously hyperbolic talk from a member of a mountaineering expedition which had hardly trekked as far as the foothills of social injustice. Still, at least his speech suggested that for trade unionists with any vision of a better society there was a great deal more to be thought about than the next pay claim.

Basnett's unreadiness to put his trust in paternalistic politicians was already on record. He clearly saw that government intervention in wage bargaining only further loaded the scales against workers in the public services. Early in May 1978, as Government ministers hoisted their England-expects-every-man-to-tighten-his-belt-again flags, Basnett repeated his call for the TUC to set up a special committee to provide 'better co-ordination and mutual support' for unions in dealing with the Government's 'unilateral policies' of pay control in the public sector. And nearly a year before the Clegg Commission was set up, Basnett called for pay research reviews to draw comparisons between public and private sector earnings. He also suggested that the pay of nurses and the police should be index-linked to that of workers in manufacturing, as had already been conceded to the staff of another emergency service, the fire brigades.

Index-linking, so long as it was honoured, would have the great advantage of guaranteeing that without having to take industrial action themselves, the public service workers to whom it was granted would benefit from the strength and fighting spirit of the private sector workers with whose labour rewards it had been agreed theirs should correspond. By contrast State-sponsored pay review bodies, although conceived (like commissions entrusted with reviewing social security benefits, or more wide-ranging commissions like Diamond's) as independent, were nothing more than advisory bodies - as was made brutally clear by the Callaghan Government's cavalier treatment of the unwelcome findings of both the Burnham Committee on salary scales for teachers in State schools and the Pay Research Unit on Civil Service pay. Furthermore, they were constantly subject to external pressures as well as to internal prejudices. State-sponsored pay review bodies are at best but frail props in the struggle for a fair deal for workers, particularly under such a constitution as Britain's, which not only grossly distorts the representation of the people but, in the absence of any constitutional checks and balances, effectively permits an elective dictatorship to ride roughshod over opposition to its will. The Tory hegemony which followed the rout of Labour in 1979 was all too amply to demonstrate this by - to cite just three examples germane to the present discussion - its severing of index-linking for firemen and its abolition not only of the Burnham Committee but also of the wages councils that had formerly afforded a shabbily minimal protection to the weakest of society's wage-slaves. Nevertheless, such official bodies had proved their value to those sections of workers whose jobs were covered by their reviews, simply by providing the ammunition with which they could fight their own battles. Whatever their philosophical implications, in practice these bodies tended to bolster rather than to undermine free collective bargaining. Propositions for a national pay policy were quite another matter, with disturbing echoes of the Corporate State.

Despite the paucity of its theoretical underpinnings, the British trade union movement has always had a healthy distrust of government, which its experience of operating under Labour rule has, to say the least, done nothing to remove. But no such qualms - nor even the consideration that if a party of a different colour gained power, its leaders would have few scruples in making the most of any convenient precedent set by Labour - sounded in the voices of those who spoke at Brighton in favour of the motion from the National Association of Local Government Officers calling for recognition of the need for government intervention in wage bargaining, particularly in view of the inescapable fact that it would always have a more or less direct influence on the determination of pay in the public sector.

In putting the motion, Glyn Phillips made the cogent criticism of 'free collective bargaining' that in twenty years as a union negotiator he had never seen it operating freely in the public sector. Deploying metaphor more deftly than Daly, he made the caustic comment that he was 'tired of putting empty buckets down the well of free collective bargaining and pulling empty buckets back.' And reason was also on his side when he argued that it was illogical to tell the government to keep out of wage bargaining when concern for every other major aspect of the country's economic life was accepted by the trade unions as part of its remit. Of course he was right to call this opposition to government intervention 'self-interest'. But on what else was the whole competitive economic system in which the Labour Movement had schooled itself to acquiesce, and on which the trade unions had modelled themselves, based but the perpetual clash of conflicting interests?

The two most persistent and most voluble trade union champions of the Government's case were the general secretaries of the National Union of Railwaymen and of the Union of Post Office Workers. In supporting the NALGO motion at Brighton, Sidney Weighell of the NUR focused on the futility of winning big wage settlements only to see them eaten away by higher inflation, while the postal workers' leader, Tom Jackson, arguing that a consensus between government and unions on the amount of money available for wage rises was imperative, made the incontrovertible assertion that free collective bargaining never produced fairness in the distribution of wages. But he spoke as if he knew nothing of those irreducible factors in the equation of wealth distribution that are inseparable from societies operating in accordance with the imperatives of private capitalism.

Tom Jackson succeeded David Basnett as TUC president, so he was in the chair when the General Council rejected by a tied vote the attempt to cobble together a semblance of accord between government and unions ten weeks after the raspberry Congress had blown in Brighton. The pair of linked statements which the General Council was asked to endorse had been drawn up in five weeks of beggars' horse-trading between the Chancellor and the TUC's economic committee. The exasperated Healey calls the statements 'helpful...guidance on pay', and it is true that they were anodyne enough, with neither side giving away anything of substance, unless the sympathetic nod towards low-paid workers in the public sector can be so described. Basnett found their rejection 'incomprehensible', and perhaps he was right, inasmuch as their acceptance would have made little practical difference to union negotiators, while their rejection was bound to highlight the disunity of the Labour Movement. But for anyone with reasons for doubting the Government's good faith, the thrust of the proposed agreement - with its paramount stress on controlling inflation (together, of course, with its implied acceptance of government oversight in wage bargaining) - was bound to have seemed objectionable.

At all events, it was so diplomatically non-committal in its details that it threw the Council into a welter of confusion, so that its members hardly knew why they were voting for it or against it, or at least were doing one or the other from mutually contradictory convictions as to what it meant or did not mean. Jackson, who knew by his very whiskers what he felt, was put in the unhappy position of being obliged by custom to use his casting vote against the proposed accord. This may help to explain why, in attending a House of Commons luncheon for assorted members of the political cognoscenti the following day, he was quite unable to contain himself, laying about him and roundly abusing handfuls of his General Council colleagues by name - which hardly helped matters. His sentiments did him credit, certainly. 'When did the movement march towards Socialism behind the banner of free collective bargaining - a banner saying, "As much as you can get, and to hell with the unemployed?"' he asked belligerently, and presumably with purely rhetorical intent. But unhappily, in asserting that 'what we are going through is an aberration', he only exposed the tenuousness of his hold on reality, as became all too evident a few weeks later, when a delegate conference of his own union agreed to slap in a pay claim of 24.4 per cent.

To cries of derision from those he had abused, he could only retort: 'If there is to be a rat-race, if there is to be a free-for-all, we must be part of the all.' Exactly! That is the standard premise of bargaining - collective or individual, wage or whatever - in capitalist society. Every union in the land was formed, organised, and henceforth operated on that basis, to look after its own members. To use Jackson's scornful words, they were guerrilla groups, each group pursuing its own interests, and inasmuch as his highly emotive talk of 'the rapacious pursuit of self-interest' had validity, it did not represent the *end* of trade unionism (as he would have it), but its whole history, with only intermittent examples of wider solidarity. And little had ever been done either by the trade union movement collectively or the Labour Movement as a whole to amend this situation of working people divided and ruled by capitalists. Certainly the attempts of successive Labour governments to control the proportion of the national wealth that was paid out in wages had nothing whatsoever to do with the fair and judicious distribution of the incomes of working people, whether in or out of trade unions, let alone with the gross inequalities of living standards across the population as a whole.

A particular target of Jackson's animus was the NUPE leader Alan Fisher, who was unable to share Jackson's confidence that the rejected agreement would have ensured at last a square deal for public sector workers. If Fisher believed that Messrs Callaghan, Healey & Co. were only interested in conjuring up a nostrum with which they could convince the country that Labour was the party that could secure national unity through concord with the unions, events were surely about to prove him right, since it took a mass revolt of workers to shift the Government from its 5 per cent formula even for the low-paid. Although it was too late to save the country from vandalisation by the Thatcherites, Denis Healey at least had the grace eventually to admit to the folly of the Government's five-per-cent-fixation. James Callaghan, on the contrary, seems to have regarded standing firm for 5 per cent as an act of faith. In his account in *Time and Chance* of the abortive meeting between himself, the Chancellor, and the Secretaries for Employment and Industry, on the one side, and the General Council of the TUC, on the other, which took place shortly before the September Congress that torpedoed Stage Four, he takes Fisher (the only opponent he names) to task for arguing that 'the whole policy had been unfair. Coming from him,' asserts Callaghan coolly, 'this was singularly wrong-headed for his members, who were among the lowest paid, had benefited more than most other groups as the policy had been deliberately tilted in their favour.'

This particular canard was also given wing, just as the fateful general election campaign got under way, by someone who should perhaps have stuck to duck-shooting. Sports Minister David Howell used a presidential address to his own union, the Association of Professional, Executive, Clerical and Computer Staff (APEX), as a vehicle for a scathing attack on the 'madness' of free collective bargaining. He singled out (though not by name) for the harshest criticism the ingrate public sector trade union leaders whose members, he claimed, had gained most from the Social Contract but had led the revolt against it. Callaghan may have been referring simply to the pay policy in rebuking Fisher, in which case he was just plain wrong, since, during Stage Three at least, pay rises in the public sector had lagged behind those in the private sector. In extending the case for a reprimand to the wider issue of the Social Contract, Howell was guilty of self-deception, if not of the greater crime of conspiring to deceive others - and others who were comrades marching with Tom Jackson, Sid Weighell, and Uncle Tom Cobleigh along what they fondly imagined to be the road to Socialism.

There were plenty of people who, while they were not prepared to accept a Labour government controlling workers' wages simply in order to control inflation, could nevertheless see the point of a trade-off between pay rises and a bigger 'social wage' to jack up the general standard of living. Some of the most telling criticism of the Callaghan Government at the Brighton Congress concerned its failure to deliver its side of the bargain called the Social Contract and its unwillingness to treat organised labour as a partner whose views should at least be given serious consideration. As it happens, it was Fisher who put the composite motion calling on the Government to adopt the economic strategy favoured by the unions (including more public ownership, increased State investment in manufacturing industry and public supervision of investment, more house-building, the use of North Sea oil revenues to boost public service employment, a rapid increase in the overall level of economic growth, and the redistribution of wealth to reduce the massive inequalities in society). And it was another of the Labour leaders' *bêtes noires*, the general secretary of the Association of Scientific, Technical and Managerial Staffs, Clive Jenkins (Healey gratuitously characterises him in *The Time of My Life* as 'the maverick left-wing leader of a professional union whose members mostly voted Tory'), who led the attack on the Government's monetarist policy, moving the composite motion demanding the restoration of cuts in public expenditure and the ending of cash limits which were preventing local authorities from implementing legislation and therefore of fulfilling their mandates. 'The United Kingdom today is a bucket of cash, a reservoir of capitalism,' he piped belligerently. 'Let us use this money to irrigate the public sector.'

A third black bellwether, Moss Evans of the TGWU, led the demand that the Government should make the reduction of unemployment its top priority, the main key to which, most unions had long believed, was a cut in the basic working week, the elimination of 'excessive and systematic levels of overtime', earlier retirement, and more holidays. He said that trade union research indicated that full acceptance of a 35-hour week could create 750,000 new jobs, of which 200,000 could be in the public sector. If the expectation that all this could be achieved 'without loss of pay and without being impeded by any 5 per cent policy' sounded a little hopeful to some, the gravamen of his complaint - that while social security benefits had taken some of the sting out of unemployment 'there is just no adequate compensation for being without a job' and 'we are still as far away from full employment as before the war' and with predictions of far worse times to come - was fully justified.

These three principal opponents of pay policy are not open to the charge of being only concerned with putting more money into the pockets of their members (or to put it in the Chancellor's abusive terms, pandering to 'greedy people'), and the most often vilified of the three, Fisher, made an unanswerable response to Healey's gibes about 'confetti money'. Asked by Peter Jay in a radio interview if it would not be better to have 5 per cent settlements all round, he replied that 'in an ideal situation' that was so. 'But of course the problem that our people have got is that if everybody else this year settles at a higher level, and it looks very much as if that is going to be the case, if they in order to help the Government were to settle at a much lower figure, it would only mean that an already low-paid group would find themselves in an almost desperate situation.' And talking about ideal situations, one might note that Moss Evans went on record as being willing to contemplate an incomes policy, but only in the context of a Socialist society.

The point is, of course, that instead of making a frontal assault on free collective bargaining in the tradition of the World War I donkeys in charge of our lads on the Western Front, Labour should have spent those three years of grace that the trade union movement gave it by its restraint, in conceiving and promoting a fairer system of rewards for work. Seeking to excuse the Party leaders for neglecting to do so, one might surmise that they thought such a project impossibly utopian, to which the reply has to be that it is always for utopia that one must strive. More probably, it never even occurred to them that it was a matter meriting some of their precious time.

Few Labour politicians at that time seem to have succeeded in getting it on record that they were that much bothered even about the plight of the low-paid, never mind the immensely complex issue of fair pay in general and the tangled web of conflicting interests, jostling differentials, and shameful status-squabbling into which capitalist competition has driven all of us workers. But since I take the elimination of poverty-pay as a *sine qua non* for taking a first step along that road to Socialism, let us give one Labour MP who did speak out loudly and clearly the last word here. On the night of the public sector workers' Day of Action, the Tories launched an attack on the Government's handling of the industrial crisis. A 'somnolent Commons debate' was 'lit up' by Jeff Rooker 'with a passionate appeal to the Government to try to see things through the eyes of the low-paid', according to *The Guardian*, who promptly invited him to contribute to its series on 'The Pay Race'. Among the points he made in his speech and his article were the following.

He said that the seeds of the present troubles had been sown over the past three years of an incomes policy that was not directed in substance to the low-paid, and that in fact the Government's own figures showed that they had lost ground in relation to average earnings. They could not be blamed for getting extremely angry and bitter at being forced to take industrial action in order to have their case heard. One reason for the build up to the present troubles was the lack of a co-ordinated government policy for dealing with the public sector. The Prime Minister should appoint Ministers specifically to look after wages and conditions of service in the public sector, and to see that no group, whether it had or had not the muscle to take industrial action, should be allowed to fall behind 'to such an extent that its members have bitterness and anger in their hearts and are prepared to take action which they know damages themselves and their families.'

Rooker made it clear that he had never advocated a free-for-all, 'but I have never yet supported the rigid incomes policies imposed on the workers of this country, in the main by senior civil servants who have never done a real day's work in their lives, aided and abetted by a Cabinet that is so wretchedly lacking in people who have worked in industry.' He ended his article with some words of wisdom for his leaders: 'So long as "incomes policy" operates as "pay restraint" we shall deserve our present difficulties. Preaching by Ministers will not bring about even the minimum changes. A little real leadership might just do it.'

CHAPTER 25

In the national interest

'I am more interested in the Gross National Happiness
of my people than the Gross National Product.'
Jigme Singye Wangechuk, King of Bhutan (1988)

'Where Plenty smiles - alas! she smiles for few -
And those who taste not, yet behold her store,
Are as the slaves who dig the golden ore -
The wealth around them makes them doubly poor.'
George Crabbe, *The Village* (1783)

One of the many early warnings of the wrath to come should the
Government refuse to change course had come from the praetorian
guard of the Labour Movement in the first week of July 1978 - before
the TUC Congress, before the Labour Party Conference, before the
Ford strike, and nearly half a year before the onset of the Winter of
Discontent. At their conference in Torquay the miners' delegates
had carried unanimously a motion demanding the termination of
the Social Contract, which (with either conscious or unconscious
irony) they equated with government intervention in pay bargaining
and stringent controls on public spending. What was needed, they
considered, was an alternative economic strategy designed to reduce
unemployment and raise living standards through stimulation of
the economy. Emlyn Williams from South Wales had a message
for the political leaders of the Movement which they would have
been wise to heed. After chiding his own executive for not always
abiding by conference decisions in the past, he promised that the
miners would negotiate responsibly, 'but not with a government
that is prepared to take cognisance of the dictates of the IMF and
forget its dedication to Socialism.' The miners had remained loyal
to Labour even after their industry had been 'almost completely
massacred' under Wilson's first governments, he pointed out; but,
he admonished the Callaghan Government: 'If we are talking about
loyalty, loyalty must be two-sided. *They* must be loyal to those
who elect them.'

However it might be in feudal contexts, such reciprocal loyalty
is unquestionably indispensable to every functionally efficient

society with any pretensions to being democratic. But precisely therein perhaps - at least in their own conceit - lay the Labour leaders' get-out. Representative government provided them with the constitutional fiction that as ministers of State they represented the interests of every citizen, which in theory at least liberated them from the views of those who had actually voted them into power. In particular, so long as the prime minister can command the support of his own parliamentary party (and for that he possesses formidable powers of patronage, besides almost literally holding in his hand the immediate political fate of the MPs forming it), and provided that party retains a working majority in the House, he is the final arbiter of 'the national interest'. Thus one fiction reinforces the other and vice-versa. All that needs to be added is the arrogance of power - and that comes naturally when others defer to us.

That interests differ, sometimes so greatly as to be irreconcilable even through compromise, makes 'the national interest' a riddle it is impossible to solve. It can only make sense if either the words are construed as meaning 'the greatest good of the greatest number', or 'the nation' is assumed to have a reality independent of the individuals who compose it, thereby making it possible to maintain that 'the national interest' surmounts the interests of any number of particular individuals and the common interests of groups. Holding such a belief would in no way help to determine wherein that greater interest lay. It would remain a matter open to dispute, unless we were prepared to make the further assumption that a particular person or group of persons was peculiarly equipped to perceive that greater interest. Eschewing such metaphysical unrealities and such philosopher-king concepts, we are left with Bentham's formula. Wherein lies the greatest good of the greatest number is still of course subject to argument, but at least it gives us something tangible to argue about. Besides, it is unquestionably the prevailing assumption in representative democracies that this is the proper criterion for decision-making, and furthermore, that it should be at least substantially determined in terms of the material welfare of the general populace. That is why it *should* be reasonable to assume that those parties which have the greatest stake in a hierarchical form of society would have the greatest difficulty in convincing the voters that they were the best fitted to look after 'the national interest'.

The paradox is that despite their obvious preponderant concern for the better-favoured sections of society, who by definition constitute only a minority, the Conservatives (except, arguably, in 1945) have never had much of a problem on this score. Cocooned in their unshakeable conviction that theirs is the patriotic party and that their leaders are thus the natural leaders of the nation (even though they can hardly be said any longer to have patently been born to rule), they generally have little difficulty in persuading themselves - and hardly more in persuading others far beyond their natural constituency - that whatever they do is 'in the national interest'.

Labour's leaders, on the other hand, notwithstanding the great betrayal of 1931 and despite the fact that their natural constituency should provide them with permanent majority support in the country, have remained susceptible to the charge that theirs is a class movement. As one illustration of this hypersensitivity one might cite their near-paranoiac nervousness when faced with criticism of the wing of their movement that - despite the growth of professional unions and the tendency of trade union members to distance themselves from their class origins as they become more affluent - remains firmly rooted in working-class history and culture. It is nothing less than ludicrous that privileged people with easy access to the nation's political commentary box get away with dinning into the heads of the general public the false perception that what the trade unions peculiarly stand for is the promotion of sectional interests (or 'vested interests', to use the more or less meaningless slur most commonly used as a vehicle for this hostile propaganda) inimical to the common good. Instead of deriding such charges as the bogeyman balderdash they are and making a serious effort to enlighten the public regarding the power structures that so affect their lives, the political instinct of the leaders of the Labour Party has almost invariably been to be defensive and apologetic. Such a stance, of course, far from placating the class enemies of the trade union movement, has only served to feed their ineradicable animus and simultaneously to supply them with further 'proof' of its justification. At the same time it has widened the natural fault-line in the Labour Movement and nudged the Party establishment into the arms of the bourgeoisie. At no time did these latent schismatic predispositions become so manifest as during the Winter of Discontent.

Of course, holding a substantial portion of the middle ground is an imperative in the politics of representative democracy. With its natural appeal to present and potential stake-holders and steak-eaters, the Conservative Party has - at least during periods of fair economic growth - done this almost effortlessly. For Labour the problem has been greater, as John Cole (later to become the doyen of the BBC's political commentators) noted in a challenging and perceptive article published in *The Guardian* after the miners had thrown down their challenge to Ted Heath:

> 'The reason for Labour's perpetual pussyfooting over income tax, which goes back at least to Hugh Gaitskell's pledge in the 1959 election, is clear. The classic nightmare of many Labour MPs is of finding themselves standing on the doorstep of a prosperous industrial worker and Labour voter, being rebuked for raising income tax to pay for higher family allowances and better schooling for the inordinately large families of the less well-paid, who, to add political colour and venom, are probably Irish, West Indian, or just feckless. If Britain's main party of the Left, created to foster a social revolution, is not able or willing to carry out the campaign of public education that such attitudes demand, there seems little hope of any turning-point.'

Cole's prescient reflections, five years before the deluge drowned the Labour dream, on the prerequisites for inducing the nation to accept an incomes policy as a normal part of its life are worth returning to. For the moment I shall simply add, for its bearing on Labour's problem with its own identity, Cole's one direct allusion to class, made in the context of comments on the deeply ingrained assumptions about the proper 'pecking order' that prevail in British society. 'Because Marxists talk too much about class others talk too little about it,' he writes. 'Class remàins a potent fact in our political attitudes.'

Yet in Denis Healey's memoirs one may read with astonishment his view, expressed in an obituary on Ernest Bevin written for the Norwegian paper *Arbeiderbladet* more than twenty-two years earlier, that 'a policy based on class war cannot have a wide appeal when the difference between classes is so small as Labour has made it.' What can one say, except that this must surely rank among the supreme triumphs of the art of wish-fulfilment?

And, perhaps, that it must have greatly eased the burden of his lucubrations when it came to tinkering with the taxes to know that the class problem had to all intents and purposes already been solved.

Cole is right, of course, in saying that Marxists make too much of class, though a great deal of their over-insistence might be excused as a necessary corrective to the popular and complacent pretence that it has ceased to be of any real significance, culminating in the absurd Foster-Son-of-Thatcher pronouncements that the classless society is now being ushered in. As for many of Labour's leading lights, while they may be anxious to distance themselves from Marxist doctrine, it is difficult to shake off the suspicion that their main problem is that they find the whole subject of class deeply embarrassing. A decreasing minority of them come from working-class backgrounds anyway. Or, like many others in our times, they may feel they have pulled themselves up by their own boot laces, and beyond a residue of sentimentality, this may have left little but a strong belief in equality of opportunity. If they still recognise the realities of social advantage and disadvantage, that might still be enough to make them fight on behalf of what remains their main constituency; but as they themselves get nearer the top, the lure of *national* leadership, with all its illusions of conciliation and unity, becomes too strong to allow them to use their heaviest weapon, that core constituency itself, to batter down the doors of privilege. That can only be done through conflict amounting ideologically speaking (and in some degree if necessary *actually*) to civil war, and real social conflict is what they have come to dread.

On the plane of ideas one can readily accept Healey's statement that 'Socialism emphasises...consensus rather than confrontation'; but where consensus is not attainable and crying injustices persist, the choice becomes one between confrontation and capitulation. This soft reluctance of Labour's leaders to engage the enemy (even to admit there is an enemy, apart, that is, from the mutinous elements in the ranks behind them, and *they* are quite another matter and are not infrequently subjected to drumhead justice by their field commanders) comes out strongly in an illuminating passage in Callaghan's memoirs:

'Society is in a permanent state of flux and I had learned that it is not enough to enforce changes in the fulfilment

328

of ideals. These require changes also in human attitudes and relationships which will only be both permanent and of benefit if they are attained through education, persuasion and understanding, not through coercion. There will be conflicts among such groups and between them and Government. I was not content that these should be resolved by the exercise of muscle alone. We should use rational means to reconcile differences between groups, to persuade them that they are all part of the common weal which determines the quality of our society as a whole.'

This is desperately jejune stuff, and there are few other pauses for thought in the course of the author's pedestrian chronicling of events from which to piece together such semblance of a philosophy as underlay his political career. The paragraph quoted is part of a passage in which he recalls reflecting - on finding himself 'at the head of our national business' (and his citing of Bagehot's description of the prime minister's position is perhaps significant) - on the question 'What did I want my Administration to stand for?' and strongly reaffirming the place of moral judgements in politics and the central purpose of Labour governments to eliminate social wrongs and promote social well-being. Clothing these unexceptionable bare bones with an ounce or two of flesh, he says that 'the class system had grown less rigid during my lifetime but it was still a millstone that hampered progress, as was gross inequality'; and tells us that 'men and women are not born equal in the sense of being equally endowed, but equal opportunity is a basic principle of social justice' and that much working-class talent and creative ability still go to waste. Napoleon Bonaparte might have said as much. Indeed he did, in his famous promotion of the concept of 'la carrière ouverte aux talents.'

So far, then, there is nothing distinctively Socialist about Callaghan's political 'philosophy'; indeed, nothing at which one-nation Tories like Rab Butler, Harold Macmillan, or Ted Heath - nor even the more militant breed of 'new Conservatives' who displaced them - might demur. 'Socialism,' Callaghan continues, 'should concern itself with the weak and underprivileged whoever they are - the poor, ill-educated, disabled, or coloured.' There can be few members of other modern political parties who would not contest the implied claim that Labour

329

has something of a monopoly of such concern; none at all, perhaps, if we remove the word 'coloured' from the list of the disadvantaged.

What is more revealing - especially when considered in the context of Callaghan's constant preoccupation with the power of the trade unions - is the somewhat equivocal observation which follows: 'We were always painfully conscious that the idealism of the Labour Movement could come into conflict with its materialistic aspect - but we claimed it was the aim of socialism to reconcile the two.' It is hard to see why any kind of Socialist whose creed is rooted in egalitarian principles (and however shallowly, Callaghan's kind seems to be so rooted) should be troubled by a supposed antithesis between idealism and materialism, since a concern for the rational stewardship of the means of life is fundamental to every form of Socialism, and equity in sharing supplies the rest. In a very real sense, indeed, surely it is largely in concern for the equitable provision of material 'goods' that the 'idealism' of which he speaks lies.

If there *is* a problem of reconciliation between these supposed opposites for the Labour Movement, it is only because it has in the main continued to accept the mores and the *modus operandi* of individualistic capitalism - a socio-economic system in which idealism (or at any rate idealism of the socialistic sort) and materialism are indeed irreconcilable. As a practising politician leading an uncommonly busy life, it may well be that Callaghan found all too little time for thinking about the theoretical basis of his actions. But this is no rarefied academic point, since it has a crucial bearing on the nature of the Labour Party and on its relations with the Labour Movement as a whole, and in particular on labour organisations condemned to operate in the context of capitalist society. In the final analysis, the options the trade unions were faced with, from their formation, were to adapt to the capitalist realities - by making themselves, in effect, just another kind of interest group in a highly competitive world - or to react by forging themselves into revolutionary forces. It is hardly to be wondered at that in the history of the world's labour movements, organisations that took the latter course (like America's Industrial Workers of the World and the CNT in Spain) are very much the exception. Even where political awareness has reached a level high enough for the recognition that Socialist ideals are simply irreconcilable with capitalism, trade unionists have usually felt forced to adapt their weapons to the imperatives of the capitalist world in order to survive. By definition, Labour's political wing - and especially its parliamentary echelons - have been relatively free from the exigencies confronting the defence corps of the workers, and the politicians of a movement that gradually abandoned even a gradualistic approach to social revolution have long since forfeited their right to tender a Socialist critique of the unions.

Callaghan's attitude to the unions was highly ambivalent, while being easily understandable and completely rational in terms of the power struggle. Trade union strength was to be welcomed as a subordinate ally of the political leadership of the Labour Movement; as an alternative centre of power, it was intolerable. 'Jim Callaghan belonged to the generation of Labour leaders which had come to depend on the trade union block vote for protection against extremism in the constituencies; moreover, the trade unions had provided his main political base in the previous decade,' writes Denis Healey. 'That base was now crumbling.' Exactly! Though no one not afflicted by Carlyle-like great-men-of-history delusions could have gone on to attribute the crumbling of this base (as Callaghan also does by implication - see *Time and Chance*, Chapter 14) to trade union titans being succeeded by incompetent and untrustworthy dwarfs (who by a remarkable coincidence were generally also markedly more left wing).

What Callaghan is really getting at in his nebulous allusion to the potential for conflict between idealism and materialism in the Labour Movement becomes clear in his next paragraph, in which, following a reference to the nationalisation of the coal mines and the drawing of a hazy and equivocal distinction between ownership and function in the exercise of power, he writes: 'We had limited but by no means removed the power of wealth to exploit [he can say that again!], but whilst we were engaged in doing this, new sources of power had grown up.' Evidently he did not include the trade unions in his 'we', since in the sentence that follows he lists, alongside such overtly capitalist forces as the multinational corporations, 'the post-war strength of the trade unions' as among 'other great sources of power that could and sometimes did exercise their veto against the national interest.' The point is not whether trade union power could be or ever has been used against 'the common weal' (to adopt the less objectionable expression Callaghan himself employs in the paragraph that follows, which I quoted above). Of course it could be and has been. The point is that the generalissimo of the Labour Movement could look upon the workers' organisations which had given birth to it, as enemies to Labour's purposes.

This distrust (to put it at its lowest) comes out more explicitly in his first speech to Labour Conference as Prime Minister and Party leader, the core of which was about the danger of - to use Callaghan's hugely question-begging expression - 'paying ourselves more than the value of what we produce' and pricing ourselves out of our jobs. He went on, in a passage that sounded uncannily reminiscent of the sanctimonious cant about widows' savings and the like commonly to be heard at Tory Party conferences, to say that 'the twin evils of unemployment and inflation have hit hardest those least able to stand them. Not those with the strongest bargaining power, no, it has not hit those. It has hit the poor, the old and the sick.' Pinning onto the organisations formed to defend workers' interests the principal responsibility for the plight of those unfortunates, he continued, in a comment which implied that the principal enemy of Labour's socialistic and humanitarian purposes was not competitive capitalism but militant trade unionism: 'We have struggled, as a Party, to try to maintain their standards, and indeed to improve them, against the strength of the free collective bargaining power that we have seen exerted as some people have tried to maintain their standards against this economic policy.'

Leaving aside the hard facts that the trade union movement did not accept as the way forward the economic strategy adopted by the Government but despite that was for years remarkably co-operative in trying to implement it, the point here is not to do with the dubious merits of so-called 'free collective bargaining', but that the unions had never been offered a fair alternative to fighting their corner. The central theme of John Cole's *Guardian* article cited above was 'our growing awareness of and unease about the inequitable distribution of income, wealth, and privilege...' which raised 'problems which dip deep into our relative valuation of human beings and their contributions to society.' As Heath's Government struggled to make *its* incomes policy stick, Cole pronounced: 'The failure to tackle such issues, the failure often to acknowledge their relevance, makes the search for permanent counter-inflationary policies fruitless.'

However, Cole addressed himself particularly to Labour, since that was the party it was most natural to assume would be concerned about such issues, but with no optimism at all that it would summon up the will to emulate the Swedish social democrats in 'educating its supporters about the relationship between social justice and incomes policy...The Labour movement's leaders - the Shadow Cabinet, National Executive, and TUC General Council - have neither the unanimity nor stomach for any such campaign.'

How right he was! But the principal reason for Labour's failure to grapple with this fundamental but explosive issue (which was to blow the Party into the wilderness five years later) was, for a supposedly Socialist movement, a more discreditable one than natural nervousness about the discord that would arise from stirring the great cauldron of differentials in pay and status. Can one doubt that for many of those who made up Labour's establishment (and who by the same token had done quite nicely, thank you, out of an unjust social system) it was a matter of little concern? 'Socialism is about equality or it is about nothing,' Attlee had once said. Well, equality had long since been laughed out of court in Labour establishment circles as a utopian, and in any case undesirable, objective. 'Social justice', as a far more flexible term, was still acceptable language. However, even among Labour's grassroots' activists, the issues it raised tended to take second place to pushing for policies through which they convinced themselves they were demonstrating their unchallengeable Socialist credentials, as Cole acidly commented:

> 'The Labour Party currently purports to be in a
> radical mood, measured principally by the length of
> its public ownership commitment. Personally I prefer
> to measure its radicalism by the apparent depth of
> commitment to redistribution of wealth and income.'

This failure to grasp the very prickly nettle of differentials between the rates of remuneration - not simply of workers with differing skills and tasks (a problem of which the political leaders as well as the trade union leaders were all too conscious), but between what amounted, economically speaking, to different classes of citizens: 'professionals' and tradesmen; non-manual and manual workers; 'skilled, semi-skilled, and non-skilled' workers; administrators, executives, clerks and typists; managers and operatives; and so on and so forth; not to mention the great divide between shareholders and units of the labour force - vitiated almost all the calls for sanity from commentators, politicians, and alarmed trade unionists alike. A good example of this fatal flaw in the arguments of the do-let's-be-sensible brigade was provided by Harford Thomas in the 'Alternatives' column of *The Guardian*, precisely because his thinking was profound and prescient yet still lacked the indispensable element of a consideration of distributive justice.

In an article quaintly entitled 'No chance for the meek in today's rip-off society', written as the 1978 season of party conferences moved towards its end with the Tories opening their talking-shop in Brighton, Thomas forcefully propounded the case for a fundamental rethink 'of our political and economic structures' because 'the old order of things is manifestly unsustainable (not only in the UK but throughout the developed world)...we are in a period of transition, possibly to what will later come to be seen as the post-industrial era...' Endorsing the general thrust of thinking in the Ecology Party, and drawing on David Steel's address to the Liberal Assembly in which he declared that 'economic debate was still based on the assumption that standards of living could be doubled every twenty-five or thirty years' and that this assumption was false and profoundly dangerous, Thomas lumped together 'the parties of big business and big unions' as more or less equally culpable 'for the defence of the old order.' While that showed a fine disregard for questions of relative advantage, there was more than a grain of truth in his exceedingly uncomfortable assertion that 'the two big parties are totally committed to the status quo, in the sense that they have no ideas beyond the manipulation of the consumer rat-race to their own particular vested interests.' He claimed that 'in essence they share the same philosophy', that this could be summed up as 'I want what I want and I want it now', and that another way of saying this was 'free collective bargaining'.

If this was putting his whole fist in the scales of judgement, and if it was a mite disingenuous to talk, as he did, of 'a quite *new* [my emphasis] kind of class division between the haves and the have-nots *within the labour movement* [his emphasis], between the strong and the weak, between the ruthless and the well-behaved' (not to mention the use of the word 'today's' in the title of his article), the gaping hole in his thesis - as is so often the case with the prophets calling for a new and sustainable economic system - was the studied avoidance of the issue of the prevailing distribution of wealth. 'Make more, sell more, earn more' ran a *Guardian* leader on the dispute at Ford, taking the orthodox capitalist line on 'wealth creation' and wages. To which, taking that other matter commonly called 'the national interest' into account, one might add 'export more'. But as Thomas' article shows, even those 'green' enough to see the flaws in such prescriptions (which reduce people to economic units and society to a national labour force) tend to be negligent of natural demands for a fair share of what is going. If 'the national interest' means anything, even its purely material aspects can certainly not be adequately defined simply in terms of *general* economic prosperity. It demands facing up to the problems of fair distribution, as Oliver Goldsmith showed an awareness of more than two hundred years ago, advising his readers 'to judge, how wide the limits stand/ Between a splendid and a happy land' and declaring: 'Ill fares the land, to hastening ills a prey,/ Where wealth accumulates, and men decay.'

'Not everyone is convinced by the morals and practices of the market place,' wrote Thomas, citing as dissenting voices the Labour leaders, Callaghan, Healey, and Michael Foot. Which was wry, since in most matters apart from the pay policy (the purpose of which had nothing to do with social justice and almost everything to do with controlling the wages of organised labour in order to restrain inflation) they submitted to market forces rather than grappling with them. Also absolved from his grand remonstrance against the Labour Movement was Sid Weighell, the trade union leader who, in his rage at those in the movement who could not agree that it was in the best interests of the workers to continue to go along with the Government's pay policy, provided everyone who loathed the unions with a singularly damning quotation to bolster their prejudices. 'If you want the call to go out that the new philosophy of the Labour Party is the philosophy of the pig trough and those with the biggest snout get the biggest share, I reject it. My union rejects it,' he told the 1978 Party Conference.

'I am convinced that many of the inequalities and injustices we experience today across the whole of British industry are largely due to so called free collective bargaining,' Weighell had written the previous February, in a *Guardian* article entitled 'Time to halt the mad pay scramble'. He argued that an incomes policy 'is the only way to ensure that some measure of social justice can be inserted into pay bargaining,' declaring it incomprehensible that those 'who want socialist planning to deal with the rest of our resources,' could 'want a free-for-all market system about pay.' And after the Movement had booted out the Government's policy he warned, in another *Guardian* article, of 'a very real danger of social breakdown worse than that which led to the rise of fascism and Nazism.'

Unfortunately, neither jeremiads nor impassioned pleas for 'rational behaviour on all sides' to avoid 'open warfare' were any substitute for the failure of the Movement, through all those years since the Attlee Government had launched British Socialism on its first sea-trials, to work out and agree on a credible strategy for, at the least, a steady advance towards social justice - least of all in the matter of the distribution of wealth and incomes. I reject the pig-trough philosophy and my union rejects it, Weighell had declared. But when the time came for the NUR to put in its next pay claim, in April 1979, it was obliged to submit to the inexorable pressures of capitalism, in order that its members should be able to keep their heads above the swirling waters. It asked for a rise of between 12 and 13 per cent, in line with the miners. A few days later official figures revealed the annual rise in earnings between February 1978 and February 1979 to be 14.9 per cent.

With all these plugged-in communicators putting in their penn'orths on the deplorable state of the nation, it was not to be supposed that the most elect of communicants (whose job, after all, was preaching) would abstain from getting in on the act. In mid-January the Archbishop of Canterbury, Dr Donald Coggan, delivered the first of a series of thunderclap sermons on 'irresponsible strikes' which was to lead to a clash with the NUPE leader Alan Fisher. The debate between them would lead right to the heart of the matter. Stressing everyone's 'duty and responsibility to the community at large,' Coggan declared: 'We need to be more concerned with what is right and less concerned with our rights.' Eleven days later he told his fellow peers of the realm that the right to strike was being used 'far too soon and far too readily and far too irresponsibly', that the strikers had made their point and that he believed 'the average Britisher has the right to say "enough is enough" and look for a return to normal procedures for settling disputes.'

He spoke of 'the sheer pitilessness of much of what is going on,' a charge he reiterated in Folkestone on 11th February. In the course of a sermon in which he acknowledged that there were 'some areas where employees are still badly paid' and that 'some salaries and some salary rises...are out of all proportion to the work done or to the good achieved for the community by those who receive them,' he said that Keir Hardie, who had emphasised the need for brotherhood in the trade union movement, would have had some caustic comments to make on these features of society 'if he were in Britain today'. He went on to suggest that 'he'd have something even more caustic to say about the sheer pitilessness...which injures the old and the very young who can't retaliate even if they wanted to; which leaves the dead unburied and the sick and dying uncared for.'

Coggan might have had a special insight into the cure of souls, but Fisher's 'flock' had wide experience in the care of bodies, and he was not to be deterred from defending his members by the archbishop's accusations that some of them were prey to the 'forces of selfishness' and had abandoned 'pity...mercy...and that sense of brotherhood in the nation'. Inviting the primate to come and meet striking hospital and other public employees to hear at first hand about the problems of the low-paid, Fisher declared: 'Our members are not pitiless. They are caring people. That is why they work in the public sector. That is why up to now they have been prepared to work for such pitiful financial reward. That is why they have been so concerned about the recent spending cuts which, more than they [i.e. his members] are doing now, have closed hospitals and put the sick on to longer waiting lists.'

Into this cockpit in which the archbishop and the trade union leader were engaged in hot disputation about morals and conduct in public life, the Church Commissioners tossed a most embarrassing bundle of propositions, like a bishop's illegitimate baby left at the church door. The Commissioners were already on record as not considering that the Government's incomes policy applied to the clergy. In November 1978 the General Synod had been told by the First Church Estate's Commissioner, Sir Ronald Harris, that the policy was not statutory and did not apply to the self-employed (which technically the clergy were), and that since the greater part of any increases in stipends would come from voluntary donations and would not lead to increases in prices or charges, they would not be inflationary. However dubious this argument was (and dubious it did indeed appear to be, especially when four months later it was learned that the Church had imposed

337

rent increases of 40 to 45 per cent on its 6,000 tenants in Paddington), there was certainly a good case for a substantial rise for the parish clergy. Most vicars and rectors were only being paid between £2,900 and £3,250 a year (although incremental payments in kind were by no means inconsiderable), and the proposed rises, averaging around 13.8 per cent, would in most cases only bring them up to weekly incomes of between £63 and £73, at the bottom end not that much above the £60 minimum demanded by the public sector workers.

The really serious damage to the credibility of the Church's claim to moral leadership of the nation came when, a fortnight after Coggan's most stinging rebuke to the trade union movement, the news broke that the Commissioners had awarded an 18 per cent rise to the bishops and no less than 28 per cent to residentiary canons. The pay of most of the forty-three diocesan bishops was to go up from £5,615 to £6,660, the Archbishop of York's salary from £9,245 to £10,960, and the Primate of All England's salary from £10,590 to £12,555. Opposition led by the Bishop of Liverpool, David Sheppard, who urged that, in view of the national crisis and in solidarity with low-paid workers in the public sector, rises for the clergy should be limited to 8 or 9 per cent, failed to deflect the Commissioners from their munificence. Firm in their faith in the divine right of material differentials for spiritual beings, they argued that whereas average earnings elsewhere had risen by more than 200 per cent between 1970 and 1979, even with the current award, bishops' pay would only have gone up by 79 per cent. Nevertheless, one was talking about *rises* not far short (in the case of the bishops) of half a year's pay for many public sector workers, and as Fisher had remarked in a caustic comment on that perverse but near-universal devotion to percentages in pay bargaining: 'Percentages give least to those who need most, and most to those who need least. At the end of the day, ten per cent of nothing is bugger all.'

Notwithstanding his commendation of Keir Hardie and his reference to Christianity as having inspired the trade union movement, it is difficult not to conclude that there was an element of class-conditioned prejudice behind Coggan's attack on the striking workers. At the very least there was poverty of understanding of their predicament behind his sanctimonious injunctions to trust in 'normal procedures' and Christian prayer to put things right. And without question the picture of 'pitilessness' he painted was too lurid by far - however satisfying it may have been to his taste for histrionic homily. What authenticated cases were there of the old, the young, the sick and the dying callously left to their own devices?

It may be that in his eyes the most heinous sinners were the striking gravediggers. It is almost certainly true that the refusal in certain places to bury the dead and the picketing of graveyards and crematoria caused widespread offence, even though a substantial proportion of the outrage expressed in Parliament and the press may well be accounted for by awareness, on all sides, of the irresistible propaganda opportunity afforded to Labour's opponents by such industrial action. When Environment Secretary Peter Shore made an emergency statement in the Commons in response to a call from his opposite number in the shadow cabinet, Michael Heseltine, only one member of the House stood up for the gravediggers. Accusing his fellow MPs, with few exceptions, of 'indulging in a bout of utter hypocrisy', Dennis Skinner declared: 'There is no one, but no one, in this House who would do the job these people are doing for a take-home pay of £40 a week.' But in urging his comrade to consider what his 'sense of priorities and values' were, Shore's indignant retort was more finely attuned to the popular predisposition to pay greater respect to the dead than to the living. For all that, his appeal to the striking gravediggers for 'some sense of common fellowship and decency between members of the same community' might have been better addressed to all those untroubled by the thought that the relative comfort of their lives rested on the backs of ill-paid fellow citizens.

The question is, what was meant by all these fine words? In real life there may commonly be chasms between the powers and privileges of one brother and another; but we hardly take that as a mark of 'brotherhood'. 'Fellowship', 'common weal' (to go back to the passage in Callaghan's memoirs cited above), and 'community' (except in a purely geographical sense) all carry connotations of common interests. Even 'the nation' commonly does. But apart from tribal-minded confrontations with other more or less artificially circumscribed 'nations', wherein lie the common interests when the stakes held differ so inordinately in size and the individual and sectional interests are commonly so much in conflict?

Skinner's impatient outburst at what he felt to be the intolerable humbuggery of most of his fellow MPs over the gravediggers' strike was a graphic example of a general charge he had made before against the leaders of his party. In the course of a joint meeting of Labour's Home Policy and International Committees held in November 1978 to discuss the economy with the Chancellor, he accused both Healey and Callaghan of not caring about the working classes, declaring that there was all the difference in the world between what *they* called 'the national interest' and the real interests of working people.

We need not get side-tracked into fruitless discussions about who 'the working classes' are, or whether they really exist any more. All we need to do is to remember that it remains essentially true that the great majority of people still have little to sell other than their labour power: they are workers, not capitalists, even if they have been inveigled into buying a fistful of shares in some privatised 'public utility' or other. If we consider how very few people exercise any considerable influence on the political and economic decisions that determine the life of the nation; if we further consider with what shameless cozenry the nation's wealth, to which all contribute, is shared out between a grossly affluent few and the general populace (a broadly unchanging truth encapsulated in the name adopted by the radical theatre company '7:84' to highlight the holding of 84 per cent of the country's wealth by 7 per cent of the population) - and all in the name of 'the national interest' - how can we not conclude that, to realise their trumpery dreams of national leadership, to strut a while upon the stage of history and then to be elevated to the Olympian status of elder statesmen, the leaders of a party which had proclaimed its paramount purpose to be 'to bring about a fundamental and irreversible shift in the balance of power and wealth in favour of working people and their families', had sold out the people?

CHAPTER 26

No love lost for Labour

"'Luk what's happened wi' all his talk. National
Gover'ment, an Labour nowhere. 'Tain't no use talkin'
socialism to folk. 'Twon't come in our time though Ah
allus votes Labour an' allus will."

"Vote for none on 'em, say I. All same once they get i'
Parli'ment. It's poor as 'elps poor aaaall world over.'"
                              Mrs Bull and Mrs Dorbell in
                 Walter Greenwood's *Love on the Dole* (1933)

'In 1979, come to that in 1976, everyone was fed up
with the political grandeur of trade unions. Power in few
and uncomprehending and above all, sectional hands
meant abuse and distortion, high unit costs, a declining
currency creating a competitive edge to be wasted in the
next round-dance of wage claims. Arthur Scargill with
his "bag of crisps" dismissal of a 16.5 per cent increase,
was the outward and visible sign of lost grace, of a
received idea leeched for blood. The unions were too
strong, the workers too strong: policies of full
employment had meant anti-economic overmanning. To
say that all this had to change was sudden truth.'

Thus *Guardian* opinionator Edward Pearce, in a pendulum-has-
swung-too-far-in-the-other-direction polemic, discharged nearly a
decade and a half after the Winter of Discontent. As a crystallisation
of a fallacy with momentous consequences - embellished with a
little *de rigueur* twopence-coloured demonising in the Thomas
Carlyle tradition - it could hardly better express the popular
perception of the State of the Nation in the final months of Labour's
last government. And - notwithstanding its breathtaking political
naiveté (or is it disingenuousness?), most fundamentally in its
strictures on the concentration of power 'in few...and above all
sectional hands', as if, in any hierarchical society, things could
possibly be otherwise, its blatant bourgeois prejudice, and its

341

barefaced misrepresentation of the realities of power and privilege in Uncle Jim's Great Britain - by the very act of reflecting popular opinion in a 'representative democracy' it does, of course, go a long way towards explaining the calamity of Labour's loss of power in the only watershed general election since that of 1945.

But besides the desperately ignorant and shallow nature of Pearce's denunciation of the unions, there are two specific objections to the picture he in part sketches and in part insinuates, one concerning the relationship of unions to their members, the other concerning the place of politics in the lives of workers and the related issue of their attitude to the Labour Party. In his zeal for chastising both unions in general and that even bigger body of culprits he calls 'the workers', in particular, Pearce takes no pains to distinguish between the organisations, their officers, and their rank-and-file members. That officials and payers of subs were not infrequently at cross-purposes apparently makes no difference. All were too strong for his cultivated nostrils.

Yet as the rift grew between the trade unions and the Labour Party during 1978, more perceptive observers also noted the general decline in the deference of rank-and-file trade unionists to the views of their own official leaders. Some commentators even went as far as to talk of a new syndicalism. A few days before the end of the harsh month of January 1979, for instance, Peter Jenkins wrote in *The Guardian*: 'In the last few weeks we have seen the coming of age of syndicalism.' This was going a deal too far, since in most cases the insubordination had little intellectual basis or grasp of power structures. However, it does serve to underline the spontaneity and elemental force of the revolt against the establishments (trade union just as much as governmental) of workers with their feet firmly on the shopfloor. Their own official leaders had the option of going along with the revolt - and so in some sense continuing to lead - or being swept aside.

But syndicalism is not just a theory concerning the effective organisation of workers to promote their own interests *vis-à-vis* those of their employers (although it certainly is that). It recognises that those conflicting interests have their roots in a socio-economic structure that extends far beyond the factory gate and is shored up by a legislative political system that arrogates to itself the right to take decisions which profoundly affect the lives of working people, both inside and outside the workplace. At its core is a belief in the primacy of industrial action over political action in furthering the interests of the workers. In their distrust of and disgust with party politicians, whole swathes of workers were in the winter of 1978-79 emotionally poised to accept the syndicalist case; but the means for widely propagating it did not exist. Beyond the passing moment, with its strictly limited issues and possibilities, the people, ideologically purblind, were unable to seize their destiny. From such a state of mental turmoil and disillusionment, with no intellectual creed to foster sustained constructive struggle, the natural outcome is political cynicism, whether its mood be angry or apathetic. In these circumstances it is no cause for wonder that large numbers of workers broke their voting habits and switched to 'the class enemy' or simply abstained. Although they did themselves no service by their polling-booth revolution, what they did do is to teach the Labour Party (or rather those few in it capable of learning) that the Party exists to serve the Labour Movement, not the other way round.

To the consequences of this widespread political disgust I shall return presently, after considering one particular factor in the industrial revolt that gave rise (and lent a little validity) to the notion of the resurgence of syndicalism. But first I am impelled to make a more general reflection on the standard of the debate provoked by the revolt, for its bearing on the fidelity, or otherwise, of prevailing perceptions not only of the 'national crisis' of '78-'79 but, more fundamentally, of the nature of the society which shapes, or at least delimits, our lives.

Perusing contemporary accounts of and comments on the Winter of Discontent, one is struck at least as forcibly by the prevalence of intellectual confusion (at times even of a world-turned-upside-down bewilderment) as by the chaos on the streets. Of course, one has the advantage of hindsight; but the value of contemporary observations (beyond those intrinsic in the faithful recording and graphic portrayal of events) lies in their far-sightedness, and this is gravely impaired whenever - for whatever reason - coherence of viewpoint is lacking. Disingenuousness was only to be expected from those striving for advantage in the cockpit of party politics, and few rose above it. And in greater

343

or lesser measure the same may doubtless be said of many other protagonists in the great debate. But to ascribe to the generality of those contending for public approval some kind of clear-eyed Machiavellianism is at once too cynical and too flattering. What is in question is clarity of vision, not simply of representation. In politics conspiracy is ever present, but purposed deception will not suffice as an explanation of the welter of inconsistent arguments and incompatible postures commonly adopted, on the same or different occasions, by one and the same person in sounding off about this great challenge to the world as he or she knew it. What answering the challenge all too often revealed - making all due allowance for the complexity of the issues raised - was a grievous deficiency of moral and intellectual integrity (i.e. wholeness), a reliance on reach-me-down responses to profoundly unsettling events that could be no substitute for a coherent *Weltanschauung*.

What was hard for any observer to overlook was that 'shopfloor' ferment I alluded to above, with the associated factor of the key role of shop stewards, that gave rise to thoughts (not to say fears) of syndicalism. Implicitly or explicitly, the issue of leaders and led was raised repeatedly (though seldom with reason and honesty reigning over rage) by columnist and politician alike - and better than any other issue it serves as a touchstone for assaying their fundamental social attitudes. What almost all of them shared was a consuming preoccupation with the problems of control of the industrial workforce. Which is not to be wondered at. One may, if one chooses, put this all down to a perfectly natural concern about the serious disruption of the rhythms of the nation's life, with the hardships that caused to many 'innocent' people. That *was* conspicuous or latent in just about every comment made on the crisis. What was near-to-universally *absent* amongst the authorised communicators was any sense that they recognised that they occupied a quite different circle in the matrix of society from those inhabited by the workers on whose conduct they were pronouncing. This gave them (the opinionators who were claiming to speak for the *public* interest) a *vested* interest in stability - which is actually only an undoubted good when everything is at least approximately all right. Irrespective of the particular postures they adopted on the issues of the day, with rare exceptions they acted in essence as 'pillars of the community'. Purporting to speak for it, they had not the honesty to see, the candour to admit, their own thoroughly *un*representative nature - a disability for their spokesman's office they could only counter by a leap of imagination and empathy. Most of them were incapable of making such a leap, since whatever doubts they might have felt about the soundness of the prevailing order were, in the final analysis, really quite superficial.

This comforting - and perhaps partially self-inflicted - blindness is well illustrated by the commentaries of Peter Jenkins. Acclaimed by his peers as 'Journalist of the Year', he certainly exhibited an outstanding propensity for contaminating shrewd and perceptive comment with prejudice and exaggeration. In an article written on the eve of the Prime Minister's visit to the 1978 moment-of-truth TUC congress in Brighton, counselling Callaghan 'to resist too fond an embrace from his union allies' lest a love-in with organised labour should turn off the voters, Jenkins described both the national and the local leaders of the trade union movement as 'finally, and fully, paid-up members of what is in effect the ruling class'. He postulated a bleak scenario of 'diminishing prosperity' in which they served '- as in these last few years - as a sturdy prop to a crumbling establishment'. And he made these extravagant aspersions without giving the slightest indication that he saw himself as anything other than a disinterested social observer. This characteristic missing of his presumed aim of producing really penetrating analysis is, ironically, underlined by his acknowledgement that 'the rank and file haven't done so well' in a period of Labour rule in which (according to him) 'trade unions as institutions have never had it so good.' But then the great constant in his commentary is his liberal bourgeois animus against organised labour and Socialism.

For all that, it is worth citing his testimony on what (from an essentially establishment point of view) had gone wrong, as quite representative of the more sophisticated kind of press comment on the unions. Although his critique is never in danger of seriously challenging his own fundamentally orthodox view of what kind of amendments might bring about a stable and viable socio-economic structure, at least it eschews simplistic or downright dishonest conspiracy theories. He recognises 'the non-revolutionary, even downright conservative character of the British trade union movement' and considers that 'the ultimate threat to the political system in Britain does not stem from the ambitions of trade unions to wield political power...[but] from continuing economic failure,' largely stemming (in his view) from the formidable 'immobilising force of the unions' and the 'inflationary and disorderly travesty' that collective bargaining had become under the halfway 'corporatist' system of the Labour Government's 'trade union connection'. Nor will Jenkins have any truck with the simple-minded or artfully-fashioned fallacy that subversion within the unions is the root of the problem. 'The role of Trotskyists or other troublemakers is real but exaggerated.' On the contrary, Jenkins frankly acknowledges that what was shaking society was 'the militant pursuit of higher wages by *a broad section of the community*' - a pursuit which the national trade union leaders had largely lost control of. 'I have never known them to be more alarmed,' he reveals. 'If the country becomes ungovernable *it is not because of the power of the unions*, it is rather because of their powerlessness to govern their own members.' [my emphases] And in a passage in an earlier article that well illustrates his own proneness to mixing perceptiveness with perversion of realities, he writes:

> 'In office Labour will confer further privileges upon trade unions and, at least to some extent, manage the economy according to their interests or desires, only to discover once more - as now - that a rank-and-file revolt prevents the union leaders from delivering on their side of the bargain for more than a year or two at a stretch.'

Jenkins obviously saw that it posed something of a riddle to expect 'institutions of collective bargaining...which live by the law of competition' (which, with more honesty than many commentators, he admitted to be the trade unions' situation) to exercise 'corporate responsibility'; but he never grappled with it, perhaps because his deepest underlying wish was to see, not reconciliation between the two principal partners in the Labour Movement, but rather divorce. He was clear-eyed about 'the underlying conflict of interest between the industrial and political wings of the Labour movement', sardonically characterising the sentiment and vows that kept them hitched together 'the doctrine of ultimate compatibility', and openly recommended them to call the whole thing off after the government house they intermittently cohabited had been repossessed by the Tories, as he correctly assumed was about to come to pass.

The limits of Jenkins' understanding of radical unionism is highlighted by a passage (in the article from which the quotations in the preceding paragraph are taken) that carries interesting echoes of Denis Healey's strictures on Moss Evans' lack of commitment to the Labour Party. Managing to be both acute and obtuse at one and the same time, Jenkins writes of Moss Evans:

> 'He is an exponent of a trade unionism more akin to aggressive American-style business unionism than to the governmental approach of the British trade union "establishment". His philosophy is of the market place. His job is to do that which is within his power to bargain on behalf of his members...he thinks in terms of firms, not the nation.'

While in one respect the comparison with 'American-style business unionism' may be illuminating, it is profoundly misleading in others, including its intimations of an accommodation with capitalism, which Jenkins reinforces with a subsequent remark that Evans 'in this respect at least [i.e. his market-place approach to his job] is nearer to Mrs Thatcher than to Mr Callaghan.' As Jenkins has himself observed just before the paragraph quoted above, 'upbraided by his General Council colleagues' for 'laying out a welcome carpet for Mrs Thatcher,' Evans responds with 'an attack upon those who would make themselves the slaves of a corporate state.' Having supplied himself with all the pieces necessary to complete the jigsaw, Jenkins fails to see that Moss Evans' position lies not to the right, but decisively to the left of most of his colleagues and of the Labour Party leaders.

In broad terms the same kinds of virtues and the same ultimately crippling limitations are to be found in editorial comment in *The Guardian*, for which at that time Peter Jenkins served as principal political columnist. Like him and in common with the media at large, the paper's overriding concern was with the control of labour and the containment of its economic costs. It did try to peddle the line that the trouble was mainly due to the 'harebrained militancy of stewards', conveniently interpreting the responses to a poorly-designed opinion poll as meaning that 'the silent majority's' claim that they were not properly represented by their union leaders referred not to the national leaders but to local ringleaders. But this was before it became patently obvious that the country was faced with a general (to use Jenkins' phrase) 'peasant revolt in the trade union movement'.

In the longest of all its many hand-wringing leaders on the Winter of Discontent, published two days after the peasants' 'Day of Action', *The Guardian* spoke openly of 'disorganised labour responding to no one's leadership'. Almost sounding as if he was biting back the word 'rabble', the leader writer made it clear that in his view the striking workers had forfeited through their indiscipline the unions' claim to a 'place at the top table'. This was far the most wide-ranging and searching of the paper's leaders on these troubles. Besides dealing in the staple platitudes of union power, law and order, and the overriding rights of the community at large, it raised the issues of 'social justice' and 'national cohesion', the 'hierarchy of needs' which society should recognise, and the 'sense of grievance and...desperation' which had driven (by implication, moderate) trade unionists to join 'the militants' in 'the great pay panic', disregarding the effects of their actions on 'a public against which they have no grievance'. In the final analysis, however, it added up to the standard frugal fare of paternalistic preaching and piety. The promise pregnant in the leader's title, 'How we are and how we might be', never was going to be delivered by a writer who could not understand that the vicarious satisfaction of seeing their tribunes 'at the top table' was no longer enough for plebs who felt they were entitled to a more generous slice of the cake.

To get some sense of the climate of opinion, it can be more rewarding to examine journalistic comment than that of the protagonists. Practising politicians, particularly those at or near the top of the greasy pole, naturally tend to be more inhibited in speaking their minds, for fear of offending one or other section of the voters. One can even see this in the contrast between interventions (at the height of the 'peasant revolt') by the former prime minister - now, blissfully unencumbered, free to vent a Coriolanus-like disdain for the multitude - and the more guarded comments of the incumbent PM. In his new column in the *Financial Weekly* magazine, Sir Harold Wilson maintained, like Peter Jenkins, that the problem was not that the unions were too powerful, but that their leaders were not powerful enough to keep their own members in order. 'My experience suggests,' he wrote, 'that only strong union leadership - not unenforceable legislation - is the way to control the situation.' That was all very well, from an establishment point of view, but strongly suggested *schadenfreude*, especially as it contained no prescription for the reimposition of that order and sense of discipline in the ranks for which his successor in the top job (not to mention many a trade union general) yearned just as much as - and a deal more urgently than - he now did.

Interviewed on Thames Television a week before Wilson's weighty words were exchanged for a more serviceable currency, the beleaguered James Callaghan assumed a tone of judicial detachment, appropriate to the unruffled leader of the nation, towards the heated debate over the behaviour of the unions. 'I am trying to repair relations with the trades unions. We must not treat them as enemies, even though they are not the whole of the community,' he told Llew Gardiner. Instead he directed his 'friendly fire' at the softer target of (to use a favourite expression of his Chancellor's) the 'silly billies' within the unions, chiding the public-service strikers for trying to 'get more out of the bank than there is in it', and reprimanding shop stewards for misleading the rank and file. If there is cause for wry reflection in observing Labour's predominantly union-elected commander-in-chief pleading - in his 'Little Father of the Nation' role - with his fellow countrymen not to judge too harshly the movement which had forged his own party and remained its core power base, his superciliousness towards the authentic functional leaders of the workers is breathtaking. It was only to be expected that one so exalted by fate should endorse the 'officers' mess' view that a major cause of the trouble for which the unions were held to be primarily responsible was the formal devolution of power that they had generally adopted (although a better understanding of the findings of the Donovan Commission would have been enough on its own to scotch such a silly explanation). To go on to assert that the problem lay with shop stewards who did not properly understand the basic tenets of trades unionism was gratuitous insult as well as arrant (and arrogant) nonsense.

But it is only one example of a more general proneness of those busy carving out political careers for themselves not only to scapegoat but to patronise the 'trench-comrade' leaders of mutinous workers. Instance comments made by two purportedly left-wing

349

Labour MPs to Martin Holmes when he was researching for his study of those dismal days. Talking about the salient part played by NUPE in the public sector dispute, Joe Ashton remarked: 'Fisher had taken over a tame union up to 1968 then came great recruitment but the recruits, tea ladies, cleaners and the like, weren't union officials. The officials were got from Ruskin and were militant and wanted to [prove it]. Suddenly ambulance men and hospital porters on strike found they were headline news and were on TV - like the miners.' The second comment is even more intriguing, in view of the subsequent elevation of the man who made it. 'The graduate officials in NUPE thought about the working class as if they had stepped from the pages of a history book. They fitted the working class into economic models which were political science fiction.' It may be true that many a good activist has ended up in some sort of wonderland by becoming too heavily addicted to Marxist (or perhaps pseudo-Marxist) theory, which one assumes to be the target of Neil Kinnock's sarcasm. But the people he is satirising *were* taking part, vigorously, in a struggle that was all too real. It seems inherently improbable that they could out-fantasise any politician (if such there was) who still seriously believed that Labour was on the way to emancipation of the working class (or whatever substitute for that old-fashioned concept they favoured) as long as they could get enough people to vote for them.

In any case, however the balance lay between shrewdness and sneers in these acid comments on extra-parliamentary militants, they tend to conceal one truth of enormous - and perhaps fatal - consequence for the Labour Party and the Labour Movement. Fully-paid-up supporters of Labour probably have more reason to know - and certainly more reason to regret - that the great mass of electors are essentially *a*political. To put it another way, their approach to the political menu on offer, with dishes concocted by the competing parties, is essentially - and perhaps sensibly - *à la carte*. Between meals their appetite for politics is very limited. They prefer to be left alone to get on with their own personal lives, leaving it to others to play political games. If politics were marginal to our lives, there would be nothing to be said against that; but in complex societies it may affect them profoundly. Lack of interest can only mean lack of insight, and in politics no less than in commerce, the ill-informed have no freedom of choice. For a party like Labour, which, if we are to take it seriously, is offering an ongoing prospectus of reform leading to a qualitatively different kind of society (and a party, moreover, which functions, in theory at least, through democratic decision-making processes), such a situation is disastrous.

On the eve of Labour's downfall, Ralph Miliband wrote:

'Regrettably, the idea that the Labour Party is set on the socialist transformation of Britain is dishonest nonsense. A fair number of its members do want such a transformation; but most of its leaders do not and are indeed actively opposed to it. They are also in secure control of the party. Their purpose today is the same as it has always been: to manage Britain's capitalist society somewhat differently than the Tories.'

But paradoxically the case is not greatly altered if we decline to take Labour's 'road to Socialism' (or wherever else the promised land is now to be found) project seriously. It may have been mere rhetoric to Labour's leaders all along; but to supplant the Tories as 'the natural party of government' (as Wilson perhaps once sincerely believed was well within Labour's grasp), it was *necessary* rhetoric, for the Party had to offer more than sound government and low taxes to outbid the parties whose attractions were more obvious to businessmen, professionals, rentiers, and the middle classes in general, along with all those who aspired to the pneumatic lifestyle of such superior people. The Party may never have come within a thousand miles of bringing about that 'fundamental and irreversible shift...' that the real Socialists in its ranks aspired to, but to enthuse the party-workers and to hold the allegiance of an electorally-decisive number of citizens, it had to convince them that the ground gained in their favour could be held and extended. It had to persuade them that this could only be done by continuing to (at the least) nibble away at the powers and privileges of the better-favoured sections of society and by doling these out among the generality of the people. Yet as another Marxist pundit, Eric Hobsbawm, was once again ruefully pointing out, in a plea for a common front against Thatcherism made two years after Mrs Thatcher's second and greater rout of Labour: 'Even at the peak of its forward march (1951) they [British socialists] had failed to convert one third of the British workers, and since then Labour's working class support has plummeted.' With the structural changes in kinds of remunerated employment (in particular the shift from manual to non-manual labour and the shift from production requiring many hands to more automated forms of mass production), even before the decimation of Britain's manufacturing industry by Thatcherite economic policies, occurring alongside the increasing affluence of many workers, Labour always was in danger of suffering a serious haemorrhaging of dependable support.

It is conveniently overlooked by most of those who rightly inveigh against the country's plight (in being in the second decade of the Thatcherites' permafrost grip, contrary to the four-times-expressed choice of a very clear majority of the participating electorate) that since the Second World War neither of the two major contenders for power ever has won majority support in a general election. Moreover, since the resurrection of the Liberals as a serious spoiler of the Box-and-Cox system of taking turns at enjoying the fruits of office, no winning party has secured the endorsement of as much as 44 per cent of those electors who have bothered to cast their votes. As for the government that Callaghan inherited, its mandate rested on a 39.2 per cent share of the votes cast in October 1974 - a lower share than that won by any of its Tory successors. Since Wilson led Labour into its last two general election victories, in February and October 1974, when it took respectively 37.1 per cent (0.8 per cent less than the ousted Tories!) and 39.2 per cent, Labour's percentage share of the vote has been 36.9 per cent (1979), 27.6 per cent (1983), 30.8 per cent (1987), and 34.2 per cent (1992).

In the concluding passage of the section of *Time and Chance* covering his premiership, Callaghan claims that: 'Contrary to the myths which have sprung up since 1979, Labour did not lose support in the general election - our national vote was in fact slightly higher than it had been nearly five years earlier in October 1974, when we had won more seats than the Tories.' He goes on to say: 'It demonstrated how much steady understanding and support existed for what we had tried to do.' There are more ways of deceiving than peddling trays of pork pies. It is quite true that, *in a larger turnout*, Labour did pick up another 50,000-odd votes in 1979. But Callaghan's rosy representation of a deeply gloomy reality is more than economical with the truth: it is positively parsimonious. In his next sentence Callaghan implies that Labour's defeat was mainly due to Tory abstainers returning to the colours. But well over a million voters withdrew their support from the Liberals in 1979, and precious few of them can have redeployed their vote to demonstrate assent to Callaghan's contention that: 'The Labour Government of 1974 to 1979 had no reason to feel ashamed, and much to be proud of.'

Besides which, thirty-four years since Labour had been given its first real chance to show what it could do for the people, with four further chances along the way, it could only rally about the same numerical support it had attracted in 1974, i.e. around 11½ million, while the Tories, back in form again, were pulling in the punters in the old numbers of well above 13½ million. And although it is true (and important to bear in mind) that the country was delivered into the hands of the Thatcherites by only one third of its enfranchised inhabitants, Labour could only manage to retain the allegiance of 28 per cent of the British electorate. If that was not a stinging rebuff for a people's party, what would be?

But there are other figures which in some respects cast an even more sombre light on Labour's decline. Any party whose intentions were really radical should have been deeply disturbed by the evidence that an ever-growing proportion of the electorate did not see a great deal of difference between the parties competing for their support. In polls taken during the general elections, Gallup found that those who felt the parties were 'much of a muchness' rose, in percentage terms, from 20, 20, and 29 in the fifties, to 32 and 37 in the sixties, and up to 41 (as against 54 who were still persuaded there were 'important differences') in 1970, when Heath led the Tories back into power. The last two figures - 41:54 (with 5 per cent 'don't knows') - are what the needle on the gauge of election-year perceptions pointed to throughout the seventies, except for a slight widening (to 38:57) in February 1974. Gallup took a reading about halfway between general elections in 1977 and came up with a figure indicating that hardly more than a third (34 per cent) of the voters saw 'important differences' between the parties, with no less than 60 per cent considering them 'much of a muchness'.

Of course, it may be that the social democrat tendency in the Labour Party would view such a narrowing of perceived differences between the parties as a cause for self-congratulation rather than alarm, as showing that the voters feel at ease with Labour, as a 'moderate' and 'responsible' party. And it is undeniable that in a representative democracy a party intent on taking power must try to occupy the middle ground. But if there was any sense of satisfaction within the Labour Party at this situation (as the striving for respectability since 1983 suggests must have been the case), it was thoroughly misplaced. It could only mean that the Party was contending for supremacy on ground on which its opponents generally had the advantage, for the very tangible reasons already indicated. The forces of inertia, of small-c conservatism, are formidable in every society, and it is these customary modes of perception of the people at large, much more than its avowed opponents, that any radically reformist party must overcome. An intelligent strategy - even for not especially radical leaders of what had to remain (however unfortunate the term might be felt to be) in some sense a 'workers' party' - would have aimed at moving the middle ground decisively (though not too far and not too abruptly, now that the groundwork had been done by the Labour administration of 1945-50) to the left, by implanting the notion that Labour's policies were practicable, reasonable, and really rather moderate. It could have been mooted that the parties which opposed them were essentially elitist and never could properly represent the interests of the ordinary voter. Since this latter charge would have been so demonstrably true (at least in the case of the Tories), it should not have been beyond the bounds of sensible aspiration and steady striving to get the people to see it.

What was needed, in fact, was a sustained campaign (such as Sweden's social democrats had undertaken) to secure a permanent bias in Labour's favour - a campaign incorporating the building up of a mass membership of the Party (not simply of the unions), aiming at genuine and not merely passive or menial participation, and with an ongoing programme of political education conceived (as education always should be) as an all-ways dialogue, not a from-the-top-downwards process. In suchwise it should have been possible to form a critical mass of citizens who identified with Labour, not just at election time and not just from sentiment, but from awareness and comprehension of social structures and social dynamics. Despite certain formidable handicaps (particularly those concerning media control and bias), the Labour Movement did in fact have the means to carry out such a programme through an organic network of working-class institutions which gave it a potentially decisive advantage over its opponents.

Foremost amongst these institutions were, of course, the trade unions themselves. Before it started to decline under the frontal assault of anti-union legislation - and even more through the attrition resulting from the half wanton half wilful regeneration of mass unemployment - union membership had reached a peak of over 13 million, 54 per cent of the national workforce. (Indeed, in March 1979 two researchers, James Curran and John Stanworth, estimated that around 60 per cent of eligible recruits - i.e. remunerated employees excluding top management and the self-employed, as well as the unemployed - had joined up.) Of course, even though the correlation between union membership and voting Labour was once high, there never was any question of the Party being able to take for granted the support of trade unionists in the polling booth, and the spectacular growth of the white-collar unions made the reckoning less and less certain. But that does not alter the fact that, potentially, the trade unions constituted an effective channel to counteract the overwhelmingly anti-Labour bias of the commercial media, and that for the most part that potential was only exploited in a sporadic, tactical, narrow, and thoroughly unimaginative way. As for the course in political economy that could have been a standard part of the package deal of union membership - well, for the vast majority 'could have been' is what it was.

CHAPTER 27

Tory blandishments and
Labour hubris

'The antics of Presidents and Senators had been
amusing - so amusing that she had nearly been
persuaded to take part in them. She had saved herself in
time. She had got to the bottom of this business of
democratic government, and found out that it was
nothing more than government of any other kind. She
might have known it by her own common sense, but
now that experience had proved it, she was glad to quit
the masquerade; to return to the true democracy of life,
her paupers and her prisons, her schools and her
hospitals.'

Henry Adams, *Democracy* (1880)

For anyone who still puts his or her faith in the Labour Movement
for the eventual emancipation of the British people, the reasons
that come to mind for Labour's long neglect of what was once so
important to it - political evangelism - are profoundly dispiriting.
Paternalism, vanguardism, leaderism, leave-it-to-me-ism: these are
ways of denoting the same psychic inhibition, a political vice of
minds conditioned by the mores of a hierarchical society which
many no longer even recognise as such - a vice no less anti-
democratic in a tribune of the people than in patrician or priest.
Add to the prevalence of such frames of mind amongst Labour
leaders the structural schizophrenia produced by the yoking together
of institutions - those of organised labour and those of The Party -
whose purposes are much more often at odds than in harmony, and
the wonder is rather that so many people of a Socialist persuasion,
through generation after generation, ever could have imagined that
Labour was a vehicle adapted to travelling towards the destinations
they desired to reach.

Testimony tainted by its source it may seem - and testimony
given with an ulterior motive it most certainly was - but when,
shortly after what he described as the 'sustained rally in support of

Labour' at the 1978 TUC Congress, the shadow chancellor, Sir Geoffrey Howe, addressing Kirklees Chamber of Commerce on problems of industrial relations, spoke of 'the myth of a movement whose assumed solidarity on all issues no longer exists', he rather understated the truth. And however tendentious his thesis, there was much substance in his comment on the loss of trust between trade union leaders on the one hand and shop stewards and rank-and-file strikers on the other: 'This steady erosion of traditional union solidarity seems to follow from the increasing politicisation of the union movement, which changes the trade unions themselves from being the servants of their members into their would-be masters.'

Sir Geoffrey's touching concern for the plight of 'ordinary' trade unionists was part of the strategy (by no means new, of course) of weaning enough of them away from Labour to piece together a Tory majority at the polls. The Tory benches are never short of barking dogs when an opportunity arises for verbally savaging the trade unions, but the more ill-trained beasts were now, for the most part, held on a short leash. In view of the almost certainly crucial part played in Labour's defeat in May 1979 by defectors who were union members (and, of course, in view of the decimation that the future held in store for the trade union movement), it is worth underlining the fact that, when still in opposition, the Tories did not indulge their instincts to launch a general offensive against the trade unions. It is true that in the heat of parliamentary battle, when enthusing the troops behind them, even front-benchers did now and then get over-excited. During a Commons debate after the public service workers had followed the lorry drivers into action, John Nott (soon to find himself C-in-C Trade) charged that the nation's economy had been subcontracted to the trade unions and responsibility for law and order to the TGWU, winding himself up to a positive paroxysm of rage with talk of 'workers' soviets', while he who would be Maggie's Chancellor hereafter spluttered on about 'trade union tyranny' and 'collective mugging'. But they were after all speaking in a heady atmosphere of competitive soundbiting in which the Prime Minister himself lashed mutinying unionists with talk of 'collective vandalism'.

Sometimes the Tory Thespians put on a double-act. In response to the assumed majesty of Callaghan's New Year message to the country, with its appeal for a sense of responsibility in wage bargaining, the histrionic Heseltine (soon to be overlord of the Environment) projected fire and lava onto the unfortunate Prime Minister's head. Denouncing him as personally responsible for pulling 'the rug from under his own leader' when Wilson had tried to rein in the unions, he thundered: 'The monster that he unleashed has now turned on him.' Meanwhile, more emolliently in Guildford, the emerging Energy supremo, David Howell, counselled his constituency party to remember the noble history of the British trade union movement, speaking more in sorrow than in anger of its present fall from grace and chiding Callaghan for setting back 'the course of responsible unionism disastrously' by his 'five per cent speeches' and 'strong arm methods'.

For the most part blandishment was the name of the game. Not only did a velvet-gloved fistful of Tory generals (in addition to Howe and Howell, Maggie's faithful Willie Whitelaw, shadow home Secretary; Sir Keith Joseph, shadow industry Secretary; Jim Prior, shadow employment secretary; and the generalissimo herself) very nearly fall to quarrelling amongst themselves for supremacy with regard to the absolute purity of their intentions towards the trade unions (Sir Geoffrey went as far as telling the staff at Smith Square - *on* the record, of course - that if the unions had not existed it would have been necessary to invent them: 'How else to represent the individual and the group interests of those who earn their living in a complex industrial society?' he intoned). Several of them even made proposals, for all the world as if they were a serious part of the Tories' agenda which they had every intention of implementing if they were returned to favour, which amounted to advocating taking a step or two towards industrial democracy - a hallowed Socialist ideal oft hymned in the Labour Movement and shied away from whenever it was in a position to do something practical about it. Sir Geoffrey, for instance, propositioned the unions to accept some reform of industrial relations in return for a pledge of a bigger say for employees through works' councils and/or employee-share schemes. Peter Walker (who had been Secretary of State for Trade and Industry during the miners' assault that knocked out the Heath Government in 1974 and who, as Energy Secretary, was to find himself in a key position for the 1984 replay), scoring a bull's-eye against his opponents with his comment that Labour's 'social contract failed because it was irrelevant to ordinary workers', who 'saw it as a one-sided arrangement allowing TUC barons to strut the corridors of power but reaching down to the shopfloor in the form of nothing but wage controls,' spoke of 'the need for a new social contract to contain wide-ranging proposals for workers' participation and profit-sharing'. He was also shrewd enough in his wooing of the lower orders to observe: 'When, as Mrs Thatcher says, we are trying to get the votes of doubting Labour supporters, we must recognise that individual freedoms are not just the freedoms of the market place.'

Doubtless this lovey-dovey talk sounded like yet more pie-in-the-sky to most workers; but the promise at the heart of the Tory wean-'em-from-Labour campaign, that a Tory government would get off their backs, was appealing enough, and coming from the free-market party, not entirely implausible. As another of Ted Heath's former lieutenants, Jim Prior, put it in a sophisticated party political broadcast 'aimed' (as Ian Aitken reported) 'directly at Labour's traditional supporters in the trade unions' and transmitted as the brothers' talked their way through what was to prove an essentially redundant conference agenda at Blackpool: 'We aim to break out of this damaging cycle [of national incomes' policies] and restore a system of responsible and realistic pay bargaining, free from government interference.'

Early in the first week of the New Year, Margaret Thatcher outlined on London Weekend Television's *Weekend World* what James Prior was to dub 'the Moderates' Charter' to replace 'Labour's Militants' Charter'. Her proposals did not sound so threatening, except perhaps for the call to outlaw strikes in public utilities, and this was quickly remodelled as a proposal to give pay guarantees in exchange for acceptance of a no-strike rule in vital public services. In fact the general thrust of the Tory criticism of the trade unions, with its principal emphasis upon problems connected with picketing, the closed shop, and keeping essential services running, doubtless sounded reasonable enough even to most trade unionists.

By their ceaseless assaults on militant (i.e. forceful) unionism, the Labour leaders manufactured bullets for their political opponents to fire at the trade union wing of their own movement, making it possible, for instance, for Jim Prior provocatively to welcome the Government's recognition of problems over the closed shop, balloting before strikes, picketing, and breach of agreement. As for the Tories' frankly avowed objective of breaking the link between the unions and the Labour Party (an objective, incidentally, which was fully endorsed by the Liberals, on whose indulgence the Government had principally depended for survival from the time they saved it from defeat in March 1977 until they abrogated the Lib-Lab pact in June 1978), what was that to the average apolitical trade union member? Most of them would not have seen the fraudulence of the argument (which erupted most cholerically when a Trade Union Committee for a Labour Victory was set up to second union officials to help Labour candidates in the Party's key 100 marginal constituencies) that trade union power should not be deployed in politics, nor even have felt affronted by Mrs Thatcher's arrogant assertion that 'politics belongs to Parliament'.

Besides which, the Tory critics of trade union affairs (no less than critics from other parts of what, when it comes down to it, is the almost seamless fabric of the establishment-minded) were normally careful to distinguish between the decency of the ordinary union member - matching that of the ordinary British voter - and the subversive activities of 'extremists', or 'industrial terrorists', as Sir Geoffrey dubbed them in an intemperate outburst to his constituency party. The grandees of the quintessential British establishment party might not have cared to put it this way, but they clearly recognised that, at least while Labour was in power, top people in the trade union movement were, however regrettably, part of that establishment. Thus Whitelaw graciously offered organised labour's own establishment a helping hand by promising that a Tory government would legislate to strengthen 'the moderates', telling an audience at Lancaster University: 'We will confront the militant wherever he seeks to undermine traditional standards and the rule of law - and in doing so we will defend the position of respectable workers and trade union leaders.'

On the same day Sir Ian Gilmour, shadow defence secretary, speaking in Liverpool, claimed that a government which acted in accordance with Margaret Thatcher's proposals for trade union reform would have the backing of the vast majority of trade union members, who 'are deeply ashamed of the tiny minority of wreckers.' As the lorry drivers' strike reached its climax, the lady herself used very much the same terms. Amidst the 'mounting chaos' which had been created, according to her, by the 'ruthless determination' of 'a few men', she urged employers to call on the forces of the law to defeat the 'flagrantly unlawful action' of men who 'are wreckers in our midst, not the mass of trade unionists.'

As already indicated, part of the strength of Tory propaganda concerning what had become, as the Winter of Discontent stormed on, a burning issue around every fireside, was its generally temperate and reasoned presentation. Another stemmed from the genuine moderation of the man charged with the principal responsibility for dealing with policy on industrial relations on behalf of the party that was soon to take power. (And it should be marked how central this issue was to the Tories, not just because of their repeated humiliation by union power during Heath's administration - though that supplied highly combustible emotive fuel to their thinking - but because the trade unions were the greatest single obstacle to their project of setting finance free.)

One illustration of Jim Prior's essential fair-mindedness and will to see the point of view of others is provided by the debate on the closed shop, a practice against which both Tories and Liberals were forever fulminating. A particularly emotive issue for those hostile to collectivism, it is not always easy to judge to what extent opposition to this practice stems from genuine scruples of conscience, as distinct from being motivated by a desire - natural enough at least to members of the employing classes - to deprive the workers of their full strength to wrest a good return for their labour. (Similar considerations, incidentally, apply to picketing, not to mention strikes, especially secondary and sympathy strikes.) It may not always be easy to judge, but it is always silly not to be suspicious. Instance the side-swipe delivered by Ian Gow when the Commons agreed to let him introduce a Private Member's Bill on picketing (the second bill on this subject to be allowed to proceed in the space of twenty-four hours, incidentally). Purporting to champion the individual against 'coercion' and the risk of losing his livelihood should his union card be taken away from him by disciplinary action (a risk largely removed in 1988, by the way, by the Thatcher Government's third Employment Act), Gow felt no compunction in invoking 'the founding fathers of the trade union movement, and indeed the founding fathers of the Labour Party,' who 'would be appalled to know that nowadays workers are being conscripted into the unions as a precondition of employment instead of joining it willingly.' In contrast Prior - who would not be suspected by many of conspiring to grant all power to the workers - went out of his way, when commending 'the Moderates' Charter' (see above) to the country, to promise that any amendments a Tory government made to the law affecting the closed shop would meet 'the objections of many trade unionists to so-called free-riders.'

More remarkably, this old-style 'one-nation' Tory made it clear to the 1978 Party Conference at Brighton that he fully accepted what might be described as the post-war settlement of capital with labour:

> 'It is my passionate belief that the Conservative Party
> will never be able to govern effectively, and the country
> will never be able to prosper, until we have learned to
> understand, learned to work with, and learned to
> become part of trade union activity. Trade unions are a
> powerful body now present in our institutions and in our
> everyday life, and we have to learn to understand this,
> and try to come to terms with them.'

That must have stuck in the craw of his lady leader, who in 1981 was to reward Prior for his considerable contribution to her general election victory by shunting him into the politicians' equivalent of the elephants' graveyard, Northern Ireland. Margaret Thatcher's personality was an unpredictable factor in the Tories' campaigning. It is probably largely forgotten now by those who then collectively constituted public opinion that the Tory leader trailed Uncle Jim in terms of personal popularity all the way to the polls, acting as a drag on her party's progress rather than a fillip to it. And this is by no means adequately accounted for by the presumed male chauvinist prejudice against her, which in any case was in the event at least partly counterbalanced by an equally unreasoning female chauvinist prejudice in her favour, as I can personally bear witness.

It may seem like a contradiction in terms to say of one who was to display such sorcery in the acquisition and wielding of political power to call Margaret Thatcher a fantasist, but that is what she was. In the first place, she patently had less understanding of her country - its social structure, its place in the world, and above all its past (her perception of English - and I do mean *English*, other British folk being almost entirely beyond her ken - history had hardly progressed beyond that 'our island's story' stage which an indulgent teacher in her schooldays might have judged adequate in a junior school pupil) - than any other British prime minister, in this century at least. In the second place, her mind had an incurable tendency to run to excess. Talking to Brian Walden, in the *Weekend World* programme referred to above, about the industrial strife, she declared that 'anyone who does not use power responsibly must expect his position to be reconsidered by Parliament', but had preceded this sweetly reasonable remark with the ludicrously inflated assertion that 'unions have been given enormous powers by Parliament', which 'has placed them above the law.' On another occasion she told a fellowship of financiers that the Labour Government had 'left no stone unturned to extend the powers and privileges of the trade unions.'

But perhaps her finest flight of fancy on this subject came in her reply to the Queen's Speech in the final session of Parliament before the downfall of Labour, when she denounced the Prime Minister for buying off the unions in the first three stages of the Government's pay policy by huge increases in public spending, coupled with giant strides towards socialism, brought about by increased nationalisation. Of course, as Oscar Wilde pointed out before Dr Goebbels could copyright the saying: 'Nothing succeeds like excess.' What principally distinguishes Margaret Thatcher from Adolph's Arch-Liar, one may presume, is that she had no idea her mind was bolting. Complexities were really beyond her, qualifications (which disable certainties and are akin to doubts, which are in turn close to treason) foreign to her nature. Her world was black and white, like a B-movie starring one of the few foreign statesmen she did not abhor. This, of course, was the secret of her success as a populist politician. However astonishing it may sometimes seem, she really believed what she was saying.

For one of her impassioned, utterly self-persuaded, wholly adamant nature, it must have taken superhuman effort to rein herself in during those endless months of waiting before the bugle sounded for the last great charge that won the war, but she did just about manage it, though now and again she bared her teeth. When Walden suggested her approach was rather confrontational, she protested: 'Eleven millions - do you think I'm going to be in confrontation with eleven millions?' But a few weeks later, in the more congenial arena of the *Jimmy Young Show*, she momentarily showed her true self, a tomboy spoiling for a fight, declaiming that if the trade unions confronted our essential liberty, 'by God, I will confront them.'

Margaret Thatcher took power in May 1979 as the leader of a team that was still predominantly pre-Thatcherite and paternalist in outlook. Irrespective of the extent to which this was imposed upon her by the realities of the balance of power at that time within the Tory Party (in which, at least so far as people with experience in central government is concerned, 'one-nation' modes of thought still held sway) - as opposed to the part played by political cunning in fielding a team composed principally of moderates - it had certainly worked to her advantage in the campaign to subvert the allegiance of trade unionists to Labour. The half hidden agenda which her mind was busy concocting to deal with the 'collective bullying' of the trade unions (as she once called the process of collective bargaining) is more clearly reflected by a confidential report leaked to the press, almost twelve months before the watershed general election, than in most of her own relatively guarded pronouncements. Drafted by one of the most constant of her political beaus, Nicholas Ridley (who incidentally had been sacked by Heath as Minister of Trade for opposing Heath's U-turn back to consensus politics), and apparently commissioned by the man who came closest to being her guru, Sir Keith Joseph, this report (which, significantly, was never submitted to full shadow cabinet discussion), listed the industries and services in which it was considered a Tory government would be most vulnerable to defeat in the case of a head-on clash with the unions. It made proposals (including certain denationalisation measures, the building up of stocks to lessen the impact of strikes, mobilising special squads of police and non-union drivers, and cutting off State benefits to strikers) for counteracting union power, and frankly recommended paying up when striking unions 'have the nation by the jugular vein.'

The significance of the Ridley report is multiplied by the fact that its leak followed hard on the heels of another leak, of a report in which a senior Tory, Lord Carrington, warned his leader that a future Tory government would be unable to defeat certain powerful unions and recommended that a higher priority be given to emergency planning. Sir Geoffrey Howe might reassure the public, in an authorised press release early in February 1979, that: 'We have no class war to wage.' But who can doubt that the swelling Thatcherite faction was all along planning for the day when it would seem opportune to open hostilities against the unions. When Prior pledged in his 'Moderates' Charter' speech: 'We shall proceed by consent as far as possible,' it carried no sinister overtones of 'and by the rack if necessary'. Doubtless he was doing no more than expressing his belief in trying to reach agreement through negotiation, while registering the Tories right, if returned to power, to legislate as they saw fit after due consultation. His leader's temper was utterly different, as was to be revealed halfway through the 1979 election campaign.

It is seldom easy to gauge the impact on the general public of even widely-disseminated political speeches, and epithets like 'keynote', let alone 'historic', inevitably get overworked. But in one sense at least Margaret Thatcher's remarkable speech of 16th March 1979 (delivered in, of all places, Jim Callaghan's constituency city, Cardiff) is truly historic, since, with the lady poised for a take-over, it marks the end of one era - that of the wartime and post-war consensus - and the beginning of another: the hegemony of the New Conservativism. That she yearned for an end to consensus politics she made clear with characteristic directness, combined with a flattering tribute to the evangelising traditions of Wales, which had taught her that 'if you've got a message, preach it,' she told her audience, before going on to declare:

> 'I am a conviction politician. The Old Testament
> prophets didn't say: "Brothers, I want a consensus."
> They said: "This is my faith. This is what I passionately
> believe. If you believe it too, then come with me."'

The main burden of her message was that 'the bulging Socialist State', falling back on unworkable 'collective alternatives' for free enterprise and stifling 'the natural energy of the people' and 'the elemental human instinct' which drives 'the individual to do the best for himself and his family', was responsible for Britain's economic decline, in which we were caught up in a 'spiral of low productivity and low wages.' Stripped of pejoratives and rhetoric, her wide-ranging speech was a call for a return to capitalist individualism and a minimalist State levying low taxes.

Time was to prove it what a less gullible public would have seen it at once to be - with its easy assurance of national regeneration and prosperity for all willing to work for it - a fraudulent prospectus.

(One quite specific fraud concerns the lady's exploitation of the subject of North Sea oil. 'The windfall of the century' which 'should have been husbanded and deployed in long-term investment' instead of being 'treated like a win on the pools and an invitation to spend, spend, spend,' she admonished, with a side-swipe attributing profligacy particularly to the Labour Left, who as it happens had argued strongly but unavailingly for Britain's increasing revenue from its oil to be used as a nest-egg for exactly that, national investment. (A more canny electorate would promptly have mentally reclassified the lady's withering indictment as a Freudian revelation of what would be most likely to happen to this waxing but transient source of wealth if she got her hands on it, rather than as a fair description of Labour's record on the matter.)

But this is not a speech in which to look for genuine insight or to treat seriously as honest argument; but rather, one to admire for its masterly timing in chiming in with the prevailing mood of a thoroughly disgruntled electorate, and for the sheer impudence of the speaker's claim that her own party in fact represented all that was best in the Labour Movement, without the degeneracy of the conduct (such as 'flying pickets', 'kangaroo courts', 'the merciless use of closed shop power', and sundry other pernicious practices which had turned 'worker against worker, society against itself') into which some of its sections had fallen - epitomised as 'the officious, jargon-filled, intolerant Socialism practised by Labour these last few years.' In the most audacious thrust of all - all the more wounding for its substantial truth - she mocked her enemies for 'the bizarre transformation of the Labour Party which always used to be so proud of its radicalism', charging it in effect with abandoning its ideals:

> 'Labour, the self-proclaimed party of compassion, has
> betrayed those for whom it promised to care. There used
> to be, in this country, a Socialist movement which
> valued people, had dignity and warmth. What a world
> away from the officious, jargon-filled, intolerant
> Socialism...' etc., etc.

For a politician whose essential credo hosannas the inestimable blessings which spring naturally from competitive individualism under a 'free enterprise' capitalist system, and who harbours an inveterate hatred of Socialism (a few years later she was to proclaim from her pinnacle of power that Socialism was totally alien to the character of the British people, and to boast that she had vanquished it both at home and abroad), this was the most infernal humbuggery. But for all that, it may be that her refusal to be reined back any longer by the caution of her counsellors, plus the sheer audacity of her assault on Labour, were decisive in the seizure of the citadel by the caterpillars of New Conservatism.

When, at the first Congress after the rout of Labour, the TUC General Secretary, Len Murray, spoke of trade unionists who had voted Tory, and who subsequently, in the light of the new government's policies, were regretting it, *The Guardian* took issue with his assumption that the Callaghan Government's hard line on pay was the principal reason for the switching of votes. 'It is, to say the least, just as reasonable to argue that his [a hypothetical worker's] defection contained a massive protest vote against union behaviour during the last winter of discontent,' the paper declared. Well, it is certainly true that in looking for the motives which determine where the voter puts his cross in the privacy of the polling booth, it is no use taking it for granted that reason, or at least enlightened self-interest, will prevail over emotion, nor even that the mark will represent some consistency of feeling and conduct on the voter's part. So it seems very likely that disgust over the Winter of Discontent, or at least over some of its manifestations, played some part in Labour's defeat, and that this 'disgusted vote' was swollen by the choices of not a few of those who had themselves behaved militantly enough in the battle with the Labour Government. But it seems even more likely that the decisive factors were disillusionment with apparently unending pay restraint under Labour and the converse conviction in the punters' minds that they would be 'better off' under the Tories, ever ready with the ever seductive message of 'more of the money you've earned left in your pocket to spend as you please'.

Tory propaganda against the level of public expenditure that the Callaghan Government and Labour-controlled councils considered necessary or appropriate, and against the commensurate rates of taxation they levied, and for higher incentives for skill and enterprise, was designed to appeal almost as much to skilled workers as to the entrepreneurial, rentier and professional classes. *In The Conservative Party from Peel to Thatcher*, Robert Blake makes the point that: 'It was, perhaps surprisingly, not true that the highest taxpayers were the only category to favour lower taxation. Those whose incomes were rising from whatever base felt even more strongly about the matter. It was clear too that a large section would be happy to opt out of parts of the Welfare State.'

It should not be forgotten that the labour revolt against the pay policy actually began not with an offensive by the great army of the very low-paid but amongst engineering craftsmen protesting about the shrinking of differentials and mutinying against their own generals. Commenting on the 1983 general election (in which there was admittedly a major complicating factor in the alliance between the Liberals and the breakaway Social Democratic Party), Blake writes of the skilled working class deserting Labour 'in droves'. In fact in 1983 Labour only secured 39 per cent of the trade unionists' vote, with the Tories taking 31 per cent and the Alliance 29 per cent. The Tory share of support from this category of voters was actually down from 40 per cent in 1979, but the defection from Labour was even more massive.

In 1979 Labour gathered in half the organised-labour vote, but the swing to the Tories from this section of the voters was higher, at 7 per cent, than the overall swing of 5.2 per cent. Moreover, Denis Healey points out in his memoirs that it was manual workers in particular who deserted Labour, with the Party's support actually rising by 5 per cent among white-collar workers and by 8 per cent among the professional middle class. In *The Times Guide to the House of Commons, May 1979* Ivor Crewe notes the 'exceptionally high swings [to the Tories] in two types of affluent working class areas', with Labour losing two seats (Birmingham Northfield and Hornchurch) in which car workers formed a significant proportion of the electorate, and suffering big swings against them in two others (Dagenham and Barking) and in New Towns such as Harlow, Basildon, and Hertford and Stevenage. The swings in these constituencies varied from 8.2 to 13.9 per cent. Not till the third general election battle against the Iron Lady, in 1987, did Labour begin to recoup these grievous losses in its natural core constituency, with its share of the organised-labour vote rising to 42 per cent. Even by 1992, with the Tory host led into battle by the incomparably uncharismatic John Major, Labour could not carry with it half the trade union voters, 31 per cent of whom gave their votes to the Tories and 19 per cent to the Liberal Democrats, compared with Labour's share of 46 per cent of the total poll.

In the course of a lengthy conversation with Kenneth Harris covering the whole of his political career, published in *The Observer* in November-December 1978, James Callaghan acknowledged that one factor in the ousting of the Wilson Government in the general election of 1970 was the abstention of trade unionists, who 'did not turn up to vote because of what they thought was the attitude of the Labour Government to them.' As already remarked, he was not prepared to be as candid when it came to their verdict on his own record as a prime minister. But besides the hard facts, we have the testimony of his own Chancellor, whose recognition of the indispensability of the trade unions to Labour has already been noted in the context of Wilson's abortive attempt to shackle them. But before calling Callaghan's principal co-conspirator to give evidence, let us listen to some other witnesses from the Labour camp to supplement those Cassandras from sundry quarters whose voices we have already heard.

First one might cite the general warning of the man who had been the Labour Government's most powerful ally in the launching of its pay policy, and who had 'loyally' (as the follow-my-leader gang - what we might call the O'Grady Says Tendency - like to put it) continued to back the Government through two further stages of pay restraint. On retiring as general secretary of the TGWU, Jack Jones warned the Government that any attempt to introduce a fourth stage, in the teeth of the general opposition of the trade union movement, would be 'counter-productive and bad for unity'. That was in March 1978. In May the general secretary of the Electrical, Electronic, Telecommunication and Plumbing Union, Frank Chapple (who might well have been considered an uncertain friend by some Labour supporters, but who was at any rate admired by the erratically-judging Labour Chancellor) made it crystal clear that the imposition of a Stage Four could do irreparable damage to a labour movement which people had joined to improve their living standards. Four days later, at his union's annual conference at Margate, Alan Fisher threw down his dramatic challenge to the Callaghan Government: 'If they will fight with us on low pay, we will fight with them in a general election.' In July, after it had become as clear as daylight that the Government and the unions were on a collision course, Labour back-bencher Martin Flannery told a Chancellor who was still exuding confidence about the prospects for the economy and for continued co-operation from the trade unions, that the five-per-cent pay limit 'played right into the hands of the Tories electorally and in many other ways.' How right he was!

For a man so little given to admitting his multitudinous mistakes, Denis Healey's subsequent candour concerning the five-per-cent straitjacket is remarkable. Former Labour MP Phillip Whitehead, researching for the Channel 4 television series and book *The Writing on the Wall*, records two of Healey's *mea culpas*. On the general point of the Government's insistence on pushing on with a Stage Four, he says: 'I remember very well in my own area, one of the wisest and most moderate of all trade union leaders, the regional organiser of the Transport and General, Ernie Hayhurst, saying to me, "Denis, it will not work another time; you'll have to find some other way." But we didn't listen to this advice; we were carried away by the degree of success we'd already had.' (Healey harks back to this particular warning in his own memoirs: 'I was warned during a visit to Leeds by his [Moss Evans'] union's regional officer, one of the wisest and most upright men I have known, that it would be simply impossible to operate a national incomes policy for another year.')

And on the ill-chosen five-per-cent figure which, as Harold Wilson was to comment, 'Ministers bravely, but somewhat unrealistically, nailed...to the masthead', Whitehead quotes Healey as saying: 'I'm convinced now that if we had said we want settlements in single figures, we'd have come out with probably something like 12 per cent overall and retained the support of the unions, avoided the Winter of Discontent, and won the election. But hubris tends to affect all governments after a period of success, and by golly it hit us.' 'Hubris' is what he called it too in *The Time of My Life*: 'Our hubris in fixing a pay norm of five per cent without any support from the TUC met its nemesis, as inevitably as in a Greek tragedy...If we had been content with a formula like "single figures", we would have had lower settlements, have avoided the winter of discontent, and probably have won the election too.'

Men (and women!) who have successfully grappled their way up the heights of power (and the summit only just eluded Denis Healey) are not much given to humility, even in retrospect, so there is much merit in Healey's 'hubris' admissions. Regrettably though (for all his many talents, his wide sympathies, and his breadth of mind), he does not appear to have been able to apply the virtue of humility to producing a more searching scrutiny of his own record in office, nor in particular of its sorry conclusion. He writes as he talks, with wit, charm, vivacity, and vividness, but too often like one who cannot spare the time to examine his own convictions and his own judgements, and who therefore frequently fails to carry conviction when criticising others. He seems to think, for example, that the argument of the Labour Left 'that the Callaghan Government had sacrificed the workers for the sake of middle-class votes, and that we could recover our position only by moving left' (an argument which is certainly not immune to serious objections) can be dismissed by a couple of sentences on the manifest disillusionment of working people with Labour, garnished with a sardonic citation of Brecht's incisive poem on the East Berlin workers' rising of 1953 that only serves to illustrate Healey's own aptitude for getting hold of the wrong end of the stick. As ever, he wades into the fight, especially when it is against 'the Left', with enormous zest, but it is all too apt to make little more sense than a John Wayne movie punch-up.

With regard to the particular point at issue - whose fault was the 1979 knockout blow to Labour? - he writes: 'The Winter of Discontent was not caused by the frustration of ordinary workers after a long period of wage restraint. It was caused by institutional pressures from local trade union activists who had found their roles severely limited by three years of incomes policies agreed by their national leaders; they felt, like Othello when he had to give up soldiering, that their occupation was gone.' The unsettling effects of having 'activists' in any institution (from the government downwards) should certainly not be underestimated; but leaving aside the not negligible point that, at least so far as trade union officials - from shop stewards upwards - are concerned, to be active on ordinary members' behalf is precisely what they have been elected or appointed for, Healey's own evidence (as given above) hardly bears out his verdict. He might not like it, but much more in accordance with the realities recorded in these pages is the judgement of NUPE research officer, Reg Race, as transmitted to Phillip Whitehead:

> 'The Labour Government of Harold Wilson and James Callaghan was destroyed by its own actions. It was destroyed by its action in increasing unemployment. It was destroyed by its actions in attacking public expenditure. It was destroyed by its relationship with the Labour Movement, which deteriorated very markedly...To blame

trade unionists is therefore looking at the symptoms rather than the causes...for what subsequently happened.'

Juxtaposing two more comments on the conflict between the two wings of the Labour Movement, as recorded by Whitehead, makes the ultimate collision seem as inevitable as Thomas Hardy's re-creation of the encounter between the *Titanic* and the iceberg in *The Convergence of the Twain*. The first is again by Reg Race, explaining why his union was prepared to go right up to, but not over, the brink:

'We reasoned that it was a good time to do it, first of all because the economy was relatively buoyant at that time...second because we knew that the Government was coming up to a general election and we said to ourselves, "Well, the Government will not risk the possibility of a confrontation with the trade unions over an issue of this kind"...And we therefore went deliberately out of our way to publish in advance documents which described the justice of the claims of the workers concerned.'

The second comment illustrates what has already been detailed, the brinkmanship of James Callaghan. Talking to his aide Tom McNally, the indomitable PM argued:

'We'll not get any agreement out of them after a general election. But with a general election imminent we might get them to go along with it...The gun was there, the gun was loaded, and in those circumstances the trade unions surely wouldn't pull the trigger and let in a Tory government.'

An impartial observer might feel that was trying to put all the blame on the other side, i.e. on the rival wing of the Labour Movement, as well as being a teeny weeny bit unbalanced as a statement of the balance of power between the two parties to the quarrel. But as a description of the state of conflict between them, of the confrontation between incompatibles who were nevertheless indispensable to each other in playing the game of 'representative democracy', it is fair enough. If either side can be said to have backed down in the end, it was too late. Labour met its nemesis.

CHAPTER 28

Raising the status of labour

'When you get to No 10, you've climbed there on a little ladder called "the status quo". And when you're there, the status quo looks very good.'

Tony Benn (1995)

'The identity of all classes of labour is one thing on which capitalist and communist doctrine wholly agree. The president of the corporation is pleased to think that his handsomely appointed office is the scene of the same kind of toil as the assembly line and that only the greater demands in talent and intensity justify his wage differential. The communist office-holder cannot afford to have it supposed that his labour differs in any significant respect from that of the comrade at the lathe or on the collective farm with whom he is ideologically one. In both societies it serves the democratic conscience of the more favoured groups to identify themselves with those who do hard physical labour. A lurking sense of guilt over a more pleasant, agreeable, and remunerative life can often be assuaged by the observation "I am a worker too" or, more audaciously, by the statement that "mental labour is far more taxing than physical labour"...'

J.K. Galbraith, *The Affluent Society* (1958)

Labour's defeat in May 1979 could, at the time, be plausibly construed as no more than a setback caused, primarily, by temporary disunity within the Movement. In fact it was a debacle.

Of course, for both Labour politicians and Labour trade unionists the shared experience of finding themselves out in the cold was enough for the semblance of a common movement to be patched together again. But beneath the high-decibel defiance of the Tory triumph, progressive demoralisation set in, not principally because of the succession of general election defeats suffered by

373

Labour or the body-blows delivered to the trade unions by the Thatcher Governments' anti-combination laws, but, more fundamentally, from the Movement's crisis of identity. It was not the shop-around voters alone who became increasingly unsure about what Labour really stood for (beyond the punters' unwavering conviction that it would always want to take more money out of their pockets than would the other parties). Labour members themselves, constantly bombarded by exhortations from the Party illuminati to rethink and modernise, could hardly be expected to know in what direction they were supposed to march, nor why - though they could hardly have failed to get a strong impression of their leaders' impulsion to proceed down whatever path seemed most likely to take them back into power.

'To thine own self be true' and so forth. But how can one be true to oneself if one is not sure who one is? An unmistakable sign of Labour's loss of belief in itself was that the words 'socialism' and 'socialist' accelerated, as it were, out of circulation. The Party establishment, and all those who looked to such blethering bellwethers to lead them out of the mire, had substantially accepted the pejorative connotations so liberally smeared onto Socialism's back by its implacable foes.

Back in the dream-time when Clement Attlee offered his common-sense testament to the common people, he carefully distinguished the character of the Labour Party from that of other national parties promoting social reform. 'They see a form of society in existence which they think to be right although it may require some alterations. Socialists see a society which is wrong and must be replaced by another.' He stressed that 'a Socialist Government must have always very clearly before it its ultimate aims and ideals. It must work throughout with the object of attaining them. It must not rest content with minor successes. It must, even when dealing with immediate problems, keep in mind always the goal to which it is tending.' In those aspiring days Attlee felt pretty clear about whither Labour should be tending. 'Socialism is about equality or it is about nothing,' he declared; and as we have seen in the chapter on 'Labour's crusade for social justice', he did not mean by 'equality' something satisfactorily nebulous like 'in the sight of God', conveniently negotiable like 'before the Law', or pragmatically pointless, as in the American colonies' Declaration of Independence.

A significant feature of Labour's last premiership was Callaghan's cavalier attitude to the concepts of Socialism and equality, which he emphatically endorsed when it suited his purpose and shrugged off when it did not. Instances of his deploying the rhetoric of Socialism at salient campaigning moments have been cited in earlier chapters. At other junctures - as has also been noted - he was at pains to distance himself from such 'extreme' views in order to highlight his claim to being not simply a party leader but the leader of the nation. Some particularly illuminating demonstrations of this chameleon facility were provided by his extended conversation with Kenneth Harris of *The Observer* referred to above.

Towards the end of the interview Harris invited him to comment on the fact that 'some Labour Party members - some people who aren't Labour Party members - say "The Labour Party is no longer Socialist."' Harris asked him: 'What do you think they mean by that?' The gist of Callaghan's 300-word reply, which meandered past signposts to the 'Broad Church' of Labour, scattering along the way reminders that Labour was not a *class* but a *national* political party, containing wholly unexplicated references to 'the principles of democratic socialism', and injunctions to Socialists in the Party to remember that many other members 'are concerned about ethical problems, or about environmental problems, or social problems,' but 'are *not* so interested in a form of society as such' (as though the question of 'the organisation of society' were an esoteric and ritualistic preoccupation) - the gist of his reply was, 'Ask them rather than me.'

So, a third of a century down the road from '1945 and all that', the man who was now Labour's leader seemed to have little idea to where, after all that winding and twisting, it was leading. But then that did not appear greatly to trouble him. And to Harris's related follow-up question - 'You don't think, in fact, that some people have lost faith in the Labour Party because prominent supporters of the Labour Party, not just politicians, seem to have done very well for themselves and have "crossed over to capitalism"?' - Callaghan responded even more dismissively. 'Everybody's standards have gone up,' he said, remarking (in words pre-echoing Kinnock's Conference taunt to his Militant opponents a few years later about miners with holiday homes in Marbella) that pensioners from his constituency city of Cardiff who would once have got no farther than Barry Island for a brief annual break might now take their holidays in Spain. 'That kind of criticism leaves me totally unmoved,' he told Harris.

Not much sign of dedication to the ideal of equality there! Except for a kind of sickly afterglow, even more pallid than Crosland's, amounting to little more than a commitment to social mobility, along with, of course, a decent little life dealt out to all and sundry. A revealing interchange earlier on in *The Observer* interview seems to bear this out. Harris had alluded to talk in inner political circles a few years back that Ted Heath's Chancellor of the Exchequer, Anthony Barber, had thought of putting Callaghan's name forward as the next Managing Director of the International Monetary Fund (now *there* was a commendation for an erstwhile Labour chancellor!) and Callaghan admitted to having seriously considered leaving politics should such an opening arise. 'But you don't regret not having gone?' asked Harris. 'I should say not!' replied Sunny Jim. 'Look how lucky I've been. My life has been very good to me. It ought to be a lesson to everybody who thinks at some time in his life that the door has closed on him,' he added, with log-cabin-to-White-House-style logic. Well now opportunity had knocked for Callaghan's Downing Street gardener, Len Hobbs, too, in the probably unanticipated form of being able to treasure a portrait of himself, nervously fingering his tie, alongside the Labour Prime Minister in a national newspaper publishing the story of 'Callaghan: My Way to the Top'.

Such verbal commerce with journalists is admittedly but small change when weighed in the balance with a politician's actions and inactions. Midway through the April '79 election campaign, on the day after Margaret Thatcher's belligerent anti-consensus speech, with its audacious claim to occupy the territory of radicalism and idealism (even of the old, true Socialism!), Callaghan counterclaimed that 'the centre ground' as well as 'the Left and radical ground' was now held by Labour, who represented co-operation between employers, employees, trade unions, and government, in contrast to the 'reactionary' divisiveness generated by the New Tories. At a press conference in London he attacked 'man and master' class distinctions as damaging for output, living standards, and jobs. 'It is time we ended this status business and had a single status and stopped separation between white-collar workers and blue-collar workers,' he averred, in a ringing Humpty-

Dumpty kind of declaration with which the apostle of a classless Britain who was so miraculously elevated to *primus inter pares* eleven years later would have had no quarrel. (John Major told a gathering of businessmen in St Ives, Cambridgeshire, in February 1994: 'Those artificial distinctions between blue- and white-collar workers are outdated, absurd, damaging, and they should be put in the dustbin immediately and never taken out again.')

It is true that the boy from Brixton would not have wholeheartedly endorsed Callaghan's pledge that the next Labour government would press for voluntary agreements between management and shopfloor - with the deployment of statutory back-up powers if necessary - for the establishment of representative committees to enable companies to discuss with their employees plans for investment, closures, expansion, and other matters affecting them. But leaving aside the question of what such 'consultation' would really amount to, considering that the Labour Government had just dropped a sadly emasculated Bullock, how much faith were authentic advocates of industrial democracy (even those who would settle for colonial-government-style consultative councils) expected to invest in such a pledge anyway?

The truth of the matter is that with all of the parties canvassing for the workers' votes, and even the Tories (Dr Strangelove clones always excepted) fearful that worker-power could derail their agenda if they got back into office, and accordingly operating in their notion of appeasement mode, industrial democracy was the flavour of the moment. Worker co-operatives were not only being promoted by the Liberals, in particular by Jo Grimond and John Pardoe (admittedly the Liberals' advocacy was in some measure motivated by their awareness of the Trojan-horse potential of worker co-ops *vis-à-vis* the power of the Labour Party/trade union bloc; but it was genuine in its way, even enlightened in its conception - not that distant from the vision of some within the Labour Movement itself - of worker co-ops as a more human and more individual-friendly alternative to giant nationalised corporations and socialistic paternalism), but even condescendingly subscribed to by thinking Tories. When the Government bill to set up a Co-operative Development Agency came before the Commons in April 1978, Kenneth Clarke told the House that his party welcomed the kind of co-operative which engaged in commercially-sound exercises and did not rely on subsidies or preferential treatment, and the bill was given an unopposed second reading. And with whatever degree of sincerity or insincerity it might have carried in each case, general endorsement of the concept of industrial democracy was given by a whole string of Tory illuminati, including Prior, Nott, Howe and Walker.

(A sure indicator of just how transformed the scene had become fifteen years later, through the vigorous exercise of Tory mastery, was provided by an easily-overlooked news report of comments made by Employment Secretary David Hunt on the social standing of the battered and depleted trade union movement of the nasty nineties. Speaking after an address to the Industrial Society in which he had gone out of his way to make it gratuitously clear that the trade unions could not expect to be given 'preferential status' - and, as it happens, not long after friendly overtures to the Government from the new TUC general secretary, John Monk, and the first formal invitation since the Tories had returned to power for a government minister to address a TUC conference - he admonished the unions to purge themselves of 'class-war delusions' and to 'recognise their own limitations.' The man with the top job in industrial relations, Cabinet minister in a government which had abolished the National Economic Development Council - the body set up by Macmillan's Government to promote dialogue between the national government and the two sides of industry - bluntly told the unions that they could have no direct role in determining policy. 'The corporate state is wholly discredited. It will not be restored'.)

The trouble was that the bodies representing the employers' interests - the Confederation of British Industries, the Institute of Directors, and, of course, the Tory Party - were naturally implacably opposed to giving the workers a statutory right to representation on company boards. The more reasonable Tories were ready to underwrite - with good grace if not with enthusiasm - a code of practice to foster industrial democracy (or, more accurately, to foster the impression that they were in favour of industrial democracy). Their most substantial shadows on employment and industry, James Prior and John Nott, made this clear to the Party's trade unionists' advisory committee in a letter (written in mid-May 1978, just before, as was known, the Government's subterranean writhings on the issue were about to break surface) which offered workers perhaps the most worthless promise ever made, even if it were to be honoured by the next Tory government: *that company law should be amended to make it incumbent on directors to have as much regard for the interest of employees as for those of shareholders.*

Equally predictably, the Tories were unshakeable in their conviction that workers who were not union members should be at no disadvantage when it came to representation on company boards. This point was also put most forcibly by the director-general of the CBI, Sir John Methven, who in an intervention accusing the Government of 'biased ideology' and obsession with extending trade union power, charged that its proposals would make millions of employees who were not trade unionists 'second-class citizens' - unlike their brother workers enrolled in unions, who were, presumably, 'first-class citizens', just like their capital-wielding bosses and the rentier masses. (It is worth noting, in passing, that in contrast to this display of humbug put on by the boss class there were a few authentic democrats - Eric Heffer for one - who were critical of the unions' insistence that they should be the sole channel of representation for workers on company boards in any scheme that should be set up.)

The great irony is that the unbiased non-ideological mental marsh-ground from which Sir John's explosive gas arose was not so different in character from what lay beneath the Prime Minister's decisive words about Labour's future intentions and his equally decisive present inactivity. While for obvious and inescapable tactical reasons Callaghan could not repudiate the union claim to a dominant role in the worker-representation element of the proposed consultative boards, in fact what real interest he had in the promotion of industrial democracy mirrored that of the bosses. The allegation that he sought an extension of trade union power was frankly risible (indeed, the exact opposite of the truth) and he concurred with his ostensible opponents on the two principal arguments which made some capitalists look not wholly unfavourably on the concept of industrial democracy. The most fundamental of these is succinctly put by Callaghan's Senior Policy Adviser, Bernard Donoghue: 'High hopes were also briefly entertained that British industry might be regenerated by the introduction of greater industrial democracy. The argument was that if British employees became more involved in the decisions affecting their working lives they would work harder and show more commitment to the success of their firms.'

The other, subsidiary, argument for industrial democracy which was naturally shared by all who were complacent about the capitalist system is alluded to in Keith Harper's *Guardian* report on the letter from Prior and Nott to that society for the protection of the curious hybrid species of Tory trade unionists referred to above. 'Mr Callaghan has long been using the carrot of industrial democracy, however far removed from the Bullock principle, as a method of continuing to win union co-operation on further pay restraint.' As a matter of a fact, with his big stick still concealed down his trouser-leg, he had just had the temerity to dangle this chimerical carrot before the noses of the presumed donkeys of APEX (the Association of Professional, Executive, Clerical and Computer Staff) assembled on May Day for their annual delegate conference.

(On the broader field of capitalist societies as a whole, the same considerations are powerful arguments for promoting not only shareholding by a company's own workforce, but the widespread ownership of shares in general, the 'popular capitalism' of Tory - and sometimes of Liberal - rhetoric. The millennium would be reached by this route in the unlikely event of shares ever being spread sufficiently widely and sufficiently evenly to equalise economic power. Perhaps some such dream had possessed the minds of the members of the Labour Party's Home Affairs Committee who in June 1973 endorsed a plan for a take-over of capitalism in Britain through the introduction of legislation obliging employers to issue equity shares to their workers, who would thus be enabled to build up a potentially controlling capital fund. 'A significant move towards workers' control,' according to Ian Aitken in a forty-inch front-page *Guardian* report which incidentally congratulated Left-wing MPs on the committee for their near-unanimity in recognising, like the more sensible comrades to their right, the 'foolishness' of the NEC's attempt to commit the Party to the nationalisation of twenty-five leading companies. No one explained why, if the implacable opposition of the property-owning classes to the latter strategy was certain, they could be expected to accept revolution - or what they would call 'robbery' - by stealth: a flaw transmuting a theoretically brilliant strategy into a 'vain fantasy...as thin of substance as the air.')

These arguments, which seemed cogent to both Callaghan and his official opponents, are not disreputable. Indeed, in an abstract way they are sensible enough for ordinary workers to understand and agree with. However, they are not exactly at the heart of what 'industrial democracy' has to mean if 'democracy' means what Abe Lincoln said it does: 'Government of the people, by the people, for the people.' And of course we all believe in that, don't we?

The Committee of Inquiry on Industrial Democracy appointed in late 1975, with the distinguished historian Alan Bullock as chairman and Jack Jones as its most prominent trade union member, reported to the nation on 26th January 1977, after which, according to Denis Healey: 'The Government spent an inordinate amount of time on this issue.' Whether that is true with respect to its importance is a matter for individual judgement. (Donoghue - hardly an egregiously radical witness - writes that the Bullock Report, for all its shortcomings, might have led to 'a major social advance and contributed to the greater efficiency of British industry'.) What is certainly the case is that, whether or not they were thinking through their bottoms the while, the ministers sat on the report for an inordinate amount of time, not publicly responding until almost the end of May 1978. The main reason for the delay, according to Trade Secretary Edmund Dell (of whom more in a moment), was the problem of how to deal with firms which simply refused to discuss employee-participation on their boards with their staff or with the unions.

Just as the publication of Bullock had been preceded by pre-emptive strikes from the forces whose covert conviction was that the truest expression of industrial democracy - maybe even of democracy itself - was 'one share, one vote' (Nicholas Goodison, chairman of the Stock Exchange, had chimed in on cue with a perfect exposition of Burkeian democracy: that control was inseparable from the rights of property and that it should continue to lie with shareholders who put up risk capital - to which Colin Fowler of Eastleigh Labour Party tellingly retorted that workers often committed to one firm 'the risk capital of their working lives'), so it was when it came to the Government's response to Bullock. The day before the Government White Paper was published, the Institute of Directors went ballistic, its Director General, Jan Hildreth, shooting off missives to the nation's top businessmen urging them to warn their workers that 'their jobs, standards of living and indeed all their happiness, are all in jeopardy.' If the Government were allowed to carry out its presumed intention of imposing trade unionists on boards of directors: 'The board would cease to be an executive *devoted to serving the customer* and would become a committee designed to bicker over the distribution of wealth between shareholders and employees.' [my emphasis] Even codes of practice, according to this high priest of Mammonism, 'will only facilitate destructive meddling', when 'the end we should all be seeking is prosperity.'

The Institute's 30,000 directors, along with all the other worthy wealth-creators, need not have got their knickers in a twist. When the

Government at last lobbed its delayed-inaction device to deal with this explosive issue into the public domain, its proposals turned out to be, in the words of Victor Keegan of *The Guardian*, 'a pale reflection of the original Bullock proposals,' and a *Guardian* leader commented approvingly: 'Short of abandoning worker participation altogether...*Mr Callaghan could have done little more to appease the (righteous) wrath of the CBI.*' [my emphasis]

The central recommendation of Bullock was that there should be parity on company boards between representatives of the shareholders and representatives of the workforce, with a third smaller group of independent directors co-opted by joint agreement of the other two groups - the so-called $2X + Y$ formula. It was argued that: 'It is unreasonable to expect employee representatives to accept equal responsibility unless...they are able to have equal influence on the decision-making process.' After the report's publication, some critics from the Left pointed out that what Bullock was offering was the appearance, not the actuality, of parity. Amongst these critics was a 33-year-old firebrand named Neil Kinnock, who, writing in *The New Statesman*, called the $2X + Y$ formula 'incredible' and said that in practice it would give worker directors 'responsibility without power'. Kinnock, seething with revolutionary indignation, concluded: 'Far from being an assault on either ownership power or on corporatism, Bullock's recommendations provide a democratic face for capitalist hierarchy.'

But since the report was now in the safe hands of a Cabinet committee chaired by Shirley Williams, and with the Prime Minister himself taking a close oversight, it did not matter a whole lot whether or not Bullock was deadly from a capitalist point of view or hopelessly defective from a revolutionary point of view. It was certain to be defused until it was harmless enough for toddlers to handle. The principle of parity, which the majority on the Bullock committee had at least been at pains to underline as a theoretical objective, was simply ignored in the White Paper, which substituted the proposal that the aim should be to give workers in companies employing more than 2,000 people (the same figure as in Bullock) the right to appoint one third of the directors.

Whatever its faults, the Bullock Report argued its case closely and produced a detailed scheme for implementing its proposals, for which it was condemned as 'ill-thought-out, rigid and legalistic' by *The Guardian*, in a leader which proceeded to justify its antipathy by pointing out that: 'Participation, statutory participation, and a lot tougher and more rigid than anything this Government is contemplating, has long been the order of the day in Germany, Scandinavia and the rest of Western Europe. It may not have caused their relative industrial peace and plenty. But it has certainly not subverted it.' Notwithstanding the repeated broadsides *The Guardian* was in the habit of firing at the antediluvian attitudes and practices of both sides of British industry, and the paper's professed attachment to the concept of industrial democracy as a potentially regenerative force, when Change actually knocked at the door, it turned its coat inside out as adroitly as a quick-change artist and became in a twinkling a champion of near-geological evolution. Bullock had tried to rush things, it claimed, attempting 'in one jump to impose in this country a system which had evolved over decades on the Continent.' Much more to its taste was a White Paper which substituted fudge for forceful argument and an almost endless chain of buckets of conciliation for resolution.

The Bullock Committee majority had been anxious to dispel fears that their proposals could lead to worker representatives gaining control of company boards: 'It is no part of our intention to make recommendations which could possibly produce such a result,' their report says reassuringly in one passage. Just how unthreatening to capitalist control the Callaghan Government's White Paper was may be judged by its almost somnolent reception in the Commons from a Leader of the Opposition noted for her stridently combative responses. 'We welcome proposals that will lead to greater involvement by the whole workforce,' the lady purred, going on to comment with a more characteristic caterwaul: 'These proposals seem to be very different from the Bullock version - and rightly so.' Indeed *The Guardian* noted with satisfaction that the plans sketched in by the White Paper 'bear a striking similarity to "minority Bullock" - the counter-proposals produced by the three industrial members of the committee of inquiry.' The paper chided the CBI for its continuing hostility to reform despite the fact that this sober minority composed of three of its leading members appeared to have had the biggest influence on the Government's thinking!

Presumably without intentional irony in its allusion to the most savage of all satires in the English language, *The Guardian* described the White Paper as 'a modest, heartening proposal'. 'Modest' for sure! Not only had it 'discreetly ditched the essential feature of Bullock' now that *enfant terrible* champion of the Bullock approach, Jack Jones, was safely retired. The Government had also made it quite clear that it was its intention to proceed towards its simulation of industrial democracy by voluntary agreements between companies and their employees reached through negotiations so patient that, as *The Guardian's* leader-writer noted, to reach the point of exhaustion when 'the fall-back formula' of arbitration to break absolute deadlocks would come into play 'presupposes two consecutive Labour victories at general elections before a single (compulsory) worker director took office...hardly a recipe for instant revolution.'

If further reassurance was needed that thoughts of the tocsin and of barricades in the boardrooms were out of place in steady heads, it could have been found in the character of the man in charge of the ministry principally responsible for issues concerning company law. Edmund Dell was the very model of a minister specially designed for the use of social democratic governments worried that they might inadvertently make the bourgeoisie bolt. Despite having been one of Denis Healey's CP comrades at Oxford, 'the ultra-cautious Edmund Dell' (as Joel Barnett - not exactly an impetuous soul himself - describes him in *Inside the Treasury*) had developed the perspective of a businessman rather than a politician. By the time he had become 'the ultra-moderate Minister of Trade' (as a *Guardian* leader called him), his attitude was, in the words of the paper's political correspondent Simon Hoggart, 'almost apolitical...scarcely interested in party politics' but 'keen to do a good administrative job.' Just the chap to defuse such a politically-charged issue as industrial democracy, one might feel.

Hoggart was reporting - nearly six months after the publication of the White Paper and shortly after the CBI had bluntly reaffirmed its decision (as Hoggart puts it) 'to have no truck even with a watered-down version of industrial democracy', and with Cabinet ministers still not in accord over the question of whether worker-directors should be directly elected from the shopfloor or only through union channels - on the resignation of Dell, who had decided not to stand for Parliament again in the next general election, but to return to his old firm, the Guinness Peat group, which he was eventually to chair. Dell's replacement as Trade Secretary, and billed as a much tougher proposition for the CBI to tackle, was a forty-year-old newcomer to the Cabinet destined to have to soldier on through four Labour general election defeats before becoming a household name. Who can say whether, granted more than a few meagre months of office, John Smith would have won his spurs in battle with the intransigent CBI over the issue of industrial democracy? As it was, to use the metaphor deployed by both Healey and Donoghue, the whole business 'ran into the sand'.

The extent of Jim Callaghan's disappointment at this trickling away of hopes for some measure of shopfloor suffrage may be gauged from the fact that he has nothing at all to say about the fate of Bullock in his autobiography. The report is simply referred to as a document he was waiting for in the hope that it 'would help create a framework of joint responsibility' in industry. Nowhere else in a detailed chronicle of his political life does industrial democracy get a mention.

Not that he was short of excuses for his government's failure to make any significant progress on this long-standing Labour commitment. for one thing, quite apart from the general hostility of the employers, with no overall majority in the Commons, legislation could not be pushed through without winning some support from MPs in other parties. For another, according to the opinion polls the issue aroused little interest amongst rank-and-file trade unionists in general. And more importantly in terms of getting the Prime Minister off the hook, there was much division of opinion in and some strong opposition from the higher echelons in many trade unions. While the TUC general secretary, Len Murray, went on record as thinking that the debate about industrial democracy was 'of pivotal importance for the 1980s' and that the Bullock Report was 'a signpost for the future', *The Guardian* was not far out in calling Jack Jones 'the one union leader wedded to Bullock'. Among the big unions whose leaders were opposed to the worker-director proposals or who had strong reservations about them were those of the miners (NUM), the electricians (EETPU), the engineers (AUEW) and the construction workers (UCATT), plus the second biggest general union (NUGMW).

Some progress was made in areas of the public sector, where - provided the major unions organising labour were not, like the NUM, hostile - the Government had more elbow for persuading managements to go along with the introduction of some measure of industrial democracy. However, experience in these public sector areas, which included steel-making, the railways, and the Post Office, tended to highlight the incompatibilities between labour organisations in Britain and the concept of industrial democracy. On the railways, for example, it was reported to the annual conference of the NUR just three weeks before the deadline given to British Rail to come up with a full plan for worker participation on the Board, that while the NUR and the white-collar rail union TSSA were in accord, ASLEF was declining to co-operate.

Because of the long association of their union with the campaign for workers' control, the experience of the Post Office workers was particularly poignant. The unions representing Post Office staff had reached agreement with the Board, broadly on the lines of the Bullock recommendations, within a week of the publication of the report. A combination of ironing out residual difficulties and Government stalling delayed the launching of the two-year experimental participation period agreed on until 1st January 1978. Two days after the publication of the Government's White Paper response to Bullock, the annual delegate meeting of the Union of Post Office Workers received the first report-back of their representatives on the PO Board. As the written report they tabled underlined, what they were taking part in was 'certainly not the workers' control envisaged by our forebears when they established the UPW nearly 60 years ago.' Furthermore, it became clear during discussion that the worker-directors felt inhibited from playing a full part on the board through their fear of undermining the bargaining tactics of the union's general secretary and its official negotiators. It turned out that the seven people who were on the board specifically as representatives of the unions and the workforce did not even meet as a group to co-ordinate their interventions to the board's proceedings.

This is but an indication of the genuine and serious problems that worker-participation on company boards posed for the unions. The deepest apprehension of all - that worker-directors could lose the trust of their work-mates by becoming too closely identified with management policy - was deployed with Jesuitical cunning by Tories and others who had no real sympathy with the idea of industrial democracy. Nevertheless, it is hard to avoid the conclusion that opposition in the unions to moves towards greater industrial democracy - moves which long pre-dated Bullock - was generally rooted not in any commitment to the collective power of the workers and the fear of undermining it, but in the awareness of union establishments that it would undercut their own power. After all, shifts in the power of determining the unions' actions from their general staffs to shopstewards in the front-line met with similar sustained hostility in many parts of the trade union movement, not to mention, as we have already seen, in the political wing of the heroic Labour Movement. However, only by looking back from the shadow boxing over Bullock to earlier debates in the Movement can we see how profoundly equivocal has been the attitude of many Labour politicians to the idea of industrial democracy. That is what we shall now do.

CHAPTER 29

Ambiguities of workers' control

> 'I am not a labor leader. I don't want you to follow me
> or anyone else. If you are looking for a Moses to lead
> you out of the capitalist wilderness you will stay right
> where you are. I would not lead you into this promised
> land if I could, because if I could lead you in, someone
> else would lead you out.'
>
> **Eugene Debs, quoted by John Dos Passos,**
> ***U.S.A.* (1938)**

In their compilation of documents published in 1968 as *Industrial Democracy in Great Britain* and republished in paperback form in 1970 as *Workers' Control*, Ken Coates and Tony Topham in effect treat the shopsteward movement and the campaign for industrial democracy as one movement. Despite the dangers of misunderstanding arising from the fact that some of those associated with the shopsteward movement have been too closely identified with movements pursuing political power (most notably the Communist Party, but in the final analysis the Labour Party too) with agendas which are ultimately inimical to workers' control, there are good reasons for doing so. Both the shopsteward movement and the industrial democracy movement strike (writing in the 1990s one feels more inclined to say 'struck') at the dominant twin traditions of political and industrial Labourism: centralism and paternalism. The never-ending struggle in the Labour Movement between democrats and autocrats - the struggle, to spell it out, over who is to be sovereign, the union leaders or the rank-and-file, the Party or the people - is so central to the question 'what does Labour really stand for?' that it calls for far more attention than I can afford it. Besides what has already come out in the course of this narrative and argument, I must content myself with pointing to a few significant contributions to the industrial democracy debate prior to Bullock (basing my references mainly on Coates and Topham), before, in the next chapter, glancing at the issue of democracy within the Labour Party.

Coates and Topham, the publication of whose book fortuitously coincided with the widespread ferment of 1968, intended to do more than make a contribution to the study of labour history. They also aimed, as they say in their preface, 'to provide a practical textbook for *active* students of trade unionism, industrial relations and working-class politics.' [my emphasis] It may be assumed that this was one important factor in their decision to limit the scope of their book to this century. As part of their documentation of what might be called the heroic age of the workers' control movement in Britain - i.e. the years preceding and immediately following the First World War - they include an extract from the autobiography of Tom Bell, the once-upon-a-time Clydesider Wobbly, in which, having remarked that in those 'pioneering days' (to borrow the title of his memoirs) both Fabian guildsmen and syndicalists 'were a source of confusion and distraction for the militant workers; the syndicalists by exorcising all parliamentary action, the Fabians by dragging in their fetish of the State,' he goes on to declare, with wholly unconscious irony: 'With the Russian Revolution most of the problems disturbing both syndicalists and guildsmen were clarified and the best elements from both camps found themselves by 1920 in the Communist Party of Great Britain.'

Whether or not some are born to lead, it often seems that many are born to be misled. It may well be that the common acceptance of the myth that worker-power had triumphed in Soviet Russia was the decisive factor in the outcome of the debate over industrial democracy in Britain in the crucial years between the wars and while Labour was for the first time really in power, from 1945-51. Certainly the 'Workers' State' had, in this as in so many other matters, a most baleful influence on the British Labour Movement. The early extinguishing of the movement for industrial democracy in Soviet Russia itself exposed the 'Workers' State' as fairy-tale rhetoric hiding an ugly reality. (Scarcely a month after the Bolsheviks gained power, they set up a Supreme Economic Council, *Vesenka*, to which all existing economic authorities, including the All-Russian Council of Workers' Control, were subordinated, while the trade unions became mere agents of the so-called Soviet Socialist State. Of the factory committees and other institutions of workers' control which had flourished after the February Revolution, and which had indeed played a major role in the Bolsheviks' ascendancy, Richard Pipes says in *The Russian Revolution, 1899-1919*, 'By 1919, they were only a memory.') But outside the small Anarchist and Anarcho-Syndicalist movement, this was little understood among Socialists or progressive intellectuals in Britain, or indeed in other bourgeois democracies. As Richard Crossman writes in his introduction to *The God that Failed*: 'A very few men can claim to have seen round this particular corner in history correctly...most of those who are now so wise and contemptuous after the event, were either blind, as Edmund Burke in his day was blind, to the meaning of the Russian Revolution, or have merely oscillated with the pendulum - reviling, praising, and then reviling again, according to the dictates of public policy.'

But there is a world of difference between the visions of a good society that led the six intellectuals (Arthur Koestler, Ignazio Silone, André Gide, Louis Fischer, and Stephen Spender) whose self-analyses make up this book first to embrace and then to repudiate the travesty of Communism that was shackled onto the people of Russia and its empire, and later onto Soviet Russia's East European satellites - and between the truly liberating aims of many other people in the decadent bourgeois democracies of the twenties and thirties who, to a greater or lesser extent and for a greater or lesser period of time, became dupes of Soviet Communism - and those like the Webbs for whom the great attraction of the 'new civilisation' was its paternalistic order.

In that appalling apologia for Stalin's nightmare State, *Soviet Communism: A New Civilisation* (first published in November 1935), the Webbs refer to what they call Stalin's 'epoch-making address' of June 1931 to a conference of leaders of industry, in which that titanic thinker made it clear that he had fully absorbed the lessons of that (in the Webbs' words) 'episode of "workers' control"', with its 'leaderless chaos and widespread inefficiency' which had 'led Lenin, in June 1918, to supersede "workers' control" in the direction of industry by one-man management, under the orders either of the State and the municipality...or of the consumers' co-operative movement.' The Webbs explain that 'the extrusion of the profit-making entrepreneur' had led to 'one of the characteristic diseases of non-profit-making enterprises' which 'the Bolsheviks termed "depersonalisation"'. For the benefit of his industrial general staff, Stalin defined this in his speech as 'complete absence of responsibility for the work performed, absence of responsibility for machinery, lathes and tools.'

In the section on the establishment of the Supreme Economic Council, the Webbs write: 'The idea of the "self-governing

389

workshop"; the dream of the anarchist and the syndicalist, which had misled whole generations of socialists, had to be abandoned. Workers' control, though not eliminated for other functions [?!], was definitely deposed from management.' Thus do the Webbs, acting in their capacity as Socialist historians and theoreticians, dispose of the revolutionary force of the factory committees, as their Bolshevik heroes had done in real life.

Elsewhere in their mighty paean to the 'new civilisation', with that patrician disdain which came so naturally to these self-appointed tribunes of the people, they curtly explain what might not have occurred to a more common breed of democrats. 'In any highly evolved industrial society, whatever its economic or political constitution, the citizen as a producer, whether by hand or by brain, in his hours of work, must do what he is, in one or other form, *told* to do...' [*authors'* emphasis] However, anxiety that the interests of the ordinary worker might not, after all, have been properly represented in the Workers' State is quite misplaced. As the Webbs tell us, union 'membership was, by mere majority vote in each factory, made compulsory for all those at work,' with 'trade union dues [being] stopped from wages, and any trade union deficit [being] met by one or other of the forms of government subsidy.' As in any other kind of Corporate State (though the Webbs refrain from drawing attention to such unhappy analogues), this was simply a rational arrangement, because 'the unions became, in substance if not in form, government organs.' The liquidation of that foolish Utopian dream of workers' control was not to be regretted, however, since, the Webbs reassure us, 'the workmen's most effective control over industry was afforded by the fact that the government's boards or commissions had, in their membership, a large proportion of the leaders of the trade unions.' No one reading such words could be in the least surprised to learn that the authors had no time, any more than Joe Stalin himself had, for those 'leftist blockheads' (Stalin's description) who think that Socialism has something to do with equality. But to pursue that point would be to stray too far from our present concern.

The Webbs' approbation for such a totalitarian society, complete with a snugly-fitting straitjacket for the workers, cannot be passed off as an unfortunate consequence of an understandable sense of jubilation that in one great country at least 'capitalism had been overthrown and communism was being constructed in its place,' as the Webbs might have put it. Their problem was that they had a most *un*peculiar, a most unregenerately respectable conception of what representative democracy is. Which is to say, they swallowed - hook, line, and sinker because it all tasted so good to such self-confident candidates for prominent roles as leaders of enlightened opinion - the constitutional myth that representative democracy is, well, some sort of democracy. In *A Constitution for the Socialist Commonwealth of Great Britain*, a verbal panacea offered to an undeserving public in 1920, they labour mightily to distinguish between democracy 'as an "organ of revolt"', deployed 'when people were "subjects" and not themselves the sovereign power', and democracy once that revolt has succeeded, i.e. democracy 'as an "organ of government"', patiently explaining that 'in the completely democratised community' government is carried out by those whom the electors have designated to be 'not their governors, but their agents or servants, chosen for the purpose of carrying out the people's will.'

Applied to the idea of democracy in the workplace, this ripe cerebral wisdom (combined with what the Webbs claim to be - without troubling to substantiate it - the universally unfavourable experience gained from 'innumerable experiments in almost all industries and services, in all civilised countries, during the past hundred years, in every form of "self-governing workshop"') leads inexorably to the irrefutable conclusion that collective criticism by subordinates of those designated to manage is as out of order as is individual criticism. 'The relationship set up between a manager who has to give orders all day to his staff, and the members of that staff who, sitting as a committee of management, criticise his action in the evening, with the power of dismissing him if he fails to conform to their wishes, has been found by experience to be an impossible one.' And no arguing!

Beatrice Webb's detestation of the concept of workers' control was positively virulent. In an entry in her diary for 4th May 1926, forecasting with jubilant confidence the imminent collapse of the General Strike, she predicts: 'Future historians will, I think, regard it as the death gasp of that pernicious doctrine of "workers' control" of public affairs through the trade unions, and by the method of direct action. This absurd doctrine...introduced into British working-class life by Tom Mann and the guild Socialists,' was, in Russia, 'quickly repudiated by Lenin and the Soviets [a politically necessary misrepresentation, the latter reference, since the revolutionary Soviets of workers, peasants and soldiers were an icon to the Socialist movement everywhere], and the trade unions were reduced to complete subordination to the creed-autocracy of the Communist Party.' (What an ally she would have been for Wilson and Callaghan in their struggles to bridle the unions!) Her following remarks - on the Italian fascists (who would not have seized power, she implies, had not the champions of workers' control incited the workers into seizing the factories), make it transparently obvious that she had no objection to subordination (of others, of course) as such, only to the subordination of the workers to private capitalists, against whom they should, presumably, democratically revolt, before, having triumphed at long last, democratically submitting to the 'managers' of their very own State.

Again and again the combination of the sheer glamour that the 'Socialist State' held for the British Labour Movement with the immense ignorance of those in its ranks of what life was actually like under the Bolsheviks (an ignorance that was arguably even greater amongst those who had had the 'benefit' of a guided tour in Soviet Russia - and that applies quite as much to the fellow-travelling intellectuals as to trade unionists), muddied the debates in Britain over workers' control. It may be that the standpoints of the principal protagonists in these debates were essentially determined by their own mind-sets, by where they stood on the real left-to-right political spectrum which reflects degrees of libertarianism shading into higher and higher degrees of authoritarianism. But these were people who had made up their minds. On audiences of workers' delegates composed largely of those with (as the equivocal expression goes) 'open minds' on the issue, arguments deploying - whether disingenuously or not - 'the Russian experience' must have carried great weight.

In his influential book *Socialisation and Transport* (1933) Herbert Morrison, with whatever-suits-my-argument logic, taunted his 'critics in the Labour Party...who so often wrongly persuade themselves that they are on the Left,' and 'find it difficult to believe that the Russian Communist Government can do any wrong,' with yet being (unlike himself) quite out of step with the Soviet Government over workers' control. 'The Russian Soviet mind,' he told them, had evolved 'from the doctrine of workers' control in its crudest form [we have already seen what it became in its most refined form!]...to a position which broadly...corresponds to the general outlook of the Labour Party's Policy Reports on Transport and Electricity.' So there!

Herbert Morrison played a decisive role in shaping the form that public ownership was to take in Britain, since the National Government (formed under the leadership of Ramsay MacDonald after his Labour administration had been shattered, in August 1931, by bitter discord over the budget cuts demanded by Snowden, with the Prime Minister's backing, to cope with the world economic crisis, the last straw being the proposal to slash unemployment benefit, which was rejected by ten of the twenty-one ministers in the Cabinet) substantially adhered to the scheme for a unified London transport system which Morrison, as Minister of Transport in the minority Labour Government, had drawn up after negotiations with the existing undertakings and had been almost ready to implement when the Government fell.

The London Passenger Transport Board, launched in 1933, bore most of the features which were to characterise the public corporations established to implement later nationalisation measures. These features included a very high degree of autonomy and of financial independence, with a management predominantly drawn from business circles and only marginally subject to government or parliamentary interference, a minimum of consumer-interests' input, and the whole issue of employee-participation in management sidelined. Actually, in the case of the LPTB, the green light given by the Labour establishment to capitalists comfortable with a monopoly set-up so long as they were controlling it (and it should not be forgotten that far from distinguishing 'State Socialism' from 'free' capitalism, monopoly - albeit ideally achieved through wheeling, dealing, fixing, and so successfully competing as to wipe out one's competitors, rather than through legislation - is the natural goal of 'free market' capitalists) could not have been clearer. In this case the board was appointed by a body of trustees: not even the chairman was appointed by the Government. And who was the first chairman of the LPTB? Why, the man who was already the biggest cheese in the business of making money out of Londoners' needs for a public transport system, Lord Ashfield. As for a voice for the workers who actually ran the buses, trams, and tube trains, one officer of the TGWU was made a part-time member of the board - after (and this was a point of principle on which the Labour

Movement establishment was thereafter to insist whenever a worker was appointed to the board of a public corporation) relinquishing his trade union duties and responsibilities.

At the Labour Party Conference in 1932, moving an NEC resolution calling for the establishment of a publicly-owned transport industry managed by a National Transport Board, Morrison assaulted the advocates of workers' control with a great windbag of a speech from which banalities and vulgarities tumbled in equal measure. (The quality of Morrison's mind can be gauged by his buffoonish thrust against 'the syndicalist demand of "the mines for the miners"' in *Socialisation and Transport*: 'and presumably,' he chortles, '"the dust for the dustmen"'). Boiled down to its pauper's-fare ingredients, Morrison's message was that people should be appointed, by the appropriate minister, to sit on public boards for their 'individual capacity', not 'to do anybody a good turn', nor because they represent any interest. This was especially so in the case of transport, since everyone, including 'the former shareholders', had an interest in it, and, should the principle of the representation of interests be granted validity, each would be clamouring for a seat on the board.

And to clinch the argument, this model of 'paternalistic Socialism' warned delegates that 'within a year' of being appointed to the board, a workers' representative 'will be regarded by the rank and file as a man who has gone over to the boss class and cannot be trusted any more. You all know that is true. He will become more and more impressed with the work of the Board and the case of the Board. It would be better, if you want a trade union fighting policy, that your officials should not see too much of the other side, but should have a free hand to bargain...' Such was Herbert Morrison's faith in the integrity of his brothers!

Not that his point about the danger of defection to the boss class was not pertinent enough, as anyone who has seen for himself the common effect of granting employees marginal representation on management boards and governing bodies (not to mention anyone with adequate knowledge of the history of the Labour Movement!) can testify. But then the advocates of workers' control were not cap-in-hand supplicants for a seat or two on the boards of industries and utilities which were taken into public ownership. They were calling for the workers to have a statutory right 'to an effective share in the control and direction of the industries which their labour sustains', by which they generally meant that at least '50 per cent of the representation on Managerial Committees shall be accorded to workers' nominees.' (Besides which, for the most part they held firmly to the good old trade union principle of mandating delegates - not 'representatives' - with those who elected them retaining the right of recall if they were not satisfied with their delegates' performance.)

The half-share-in-control claim referred to above is part of a resolution from the General and Municipal Workers' Union put to the Trades Union Congress in 1933, and the resolution ended with the bold Socialistic demand: 'This ultimately requires that the control of industry be taken out of the hands of profit-seeking proprietors, and that "Proprietor control" be replaced by "workers' control" in which the trade unions shall be the recognised nucleus of representation for the whole of the workers - manual, clerical, technical and supervisory.' Not the least interesting thing about this resolution is that - this ultimate, revolutionary aim apart - it broadly foreshadows the central recommendations of the Bullock Committee forty-four years later.

At the Labour Party Conference of 1933, Charles Dukes, who had moved the workers' control resolution at the TUC conference, put on behalf of the GMWU a similar resolution, which, although it was (presumably for tactical reasons) markedly moderated and less specific, still called for a statutory right 'to an effective share in control...' etc. In speaking to it, Dukes tackled head on what he called 'the bogy' of 'interests', roundly declaring that 'a more absurd argument could not be put before a conference of Socialists' than that, for instance, on nationalisation of the mines, the miners were to be denied 'a statutory right to run an industry to which they had given their lives.' He pointed out that 'we have all got our interests,' advising delegates to face up to that fact and secure an adequate share of control over their own industries. 'If I understand the meaning of a socialised industry, it is that it is not merely to be a change of ownership; it is to mean more than the mere creation of a rentier class and leaving the control of industry very largely in their hands.'

At the 1932 Party Conference, in the course of speaking to a TGWU amendment to the NEC resolution on nationalising transport, Harold Clay chided Morrison for talking as if they were already living in a Socialist society. 'This is a class society, whether we like to admit it or not; and whether we say that interests will be represented or not, interests will be there. Every interest except that of the people who are actually doing the job.' While rejecting the syndicalist label ('I went through that movement like many others'), Clay declared: 'I believe in political democracy, but I do not believe that can become complete until you have industrial democracy.' And he commented caustically on the NEC report on this issue: 'One of my difficulties in reading this report is that *it appears to assume the permanency of the commodity status of labour*. That, I think, is a fundamental objection. It assumes that the Board will be a kind, benevolent sort of thing that will give to labour an opportunity to learn more about the job. Good heavens! We can teach them more about the job than they ever knew.' [my emphasis]

At the 1932 TUC conference, John Cliff of the TGWU attacked the General Council's report on the management of socialised industry for offering the workers nothing more than Whitleyism [see below]: discussion but not determination, consultation but not executive powers. While G. M. Hann of the Shop Assistants' Union, demanding 'representative industrial authority on which the workers are in a permanent majority by the simple right that they are the biggest factors in industry,' charged that 'public utility control is not workers' control, and it is bordering on perfidy to put that forward as a substitute for workers' control.'

In this struggle for the hearts and minds of the members of the Labour Movement on this crucial issue, the champions of workers' control had the better of the argument but could not win it against the power of the trade union and Party establishments. Coates and Topham sum up the outcome of the battle, with reference to the anodyne formula agreed between the TUC and the Party and reported to Conference in 1935: 'Much debate, and many votes which appeared to favour the principle of workers' control, were...reduced to the most minimal guarantee of a "statutory right" for trade unions to be represented on the board of socialised industries.'

Just how far the Labour Establishment had moved towards grooming itself for full acceptance in the club of the bourgeois democrats is indicated by a commentator unsympathetic to such democratic extremism as workers' control. In *Nationalization in British Industry* (1966, revised edition 1973), Leonard Tivey writes:

'In the outcome of these arguments it became accepted
that workers' participation would mean that some trade
unionists would be appointed to management boards,
and that the trade unions might suggest who these
should be. But they would nevertheless be chosen by the
Government and would retain no ties with their unions.
They would not act as spokesmen for union policy.
Instead, trade union views would be pressed through
compulsory advisory and consultative machinery.'

Having succinctly summed up a power structure in which the
essentially adversarial and supplicatory relationship of labour to
capital and to management remained unchanged, Tivey goes on to
comment:

'The settlement of this issue after 1935 meant that the
main lines of nationalization methods were decided. In
principle, the Labour movement had accepted the
public-corporation model recommended by the Liberals
and initiated by Conservative Governments. There were
some modifications in practice - such as the rights of
trade unions to consultation, and more explicit powers
of control by the Government - but the main structure of
the new institutions was clear and widely accepted by
all parties. A current of opinion in favour of more direct
representation of workers in management has continued,
but so far it has had little effect.'

Contrast this sidelining of the once vigorous campaign for
workers' control with the enthusiastic response to the call to arms from
the Tailors' and Garment-Workers' Union at the Trades Union
Congress in 1925. The brave little tailors moved:

'This Congress declares that the trade union movement
must organise to prepare the trade unions in conjunction
with the party of the workers to struggle for the overthrow
of capitalism. At the same time Congress warns the
workers against all attempts to introduce capitalist schemes
of co-partnership which in the past have failed to give the
workers any positive rights, but instead have usually served

as fetters retarding the forward movements. Congress further considers that strong well-organised shop committees are indispensable weapons in the struggle to force the capitalists to relinquish their grip on industry, and therefore pledges itself to do all in its power to develop and strengthen workshop organisation.'

Patently a call for the workers to rely on their own direct-action power at the point of production ('in conjunction with the party of the workers' is no more than an aside), this resolution in the spirit of revolutionary syndicalism (its mover, a Mr E. Joseph, made no bones about its 'more or less revolutionary character') was carried on a card vote of 2,456,000 to 1,218,000.

What happened to freeze this revolutionary ardour? Within nine months of this clarion call the TUC leaders had made Britain safe again for bourgeois parliamentary democracy by scuttling the General Strike. In such a fundamentally undemocratic, class-riven power structure, fanciful ideas of workers' control (or anything remotely resembling it) could not be countenanced. Predominant opinion among trade union leaders was at one with that of the Labour Party establishment, and remained so during the critical period of post-war Labour power when the infrastructure industries (coal, civil aviation, public transport, electricity, gas, iron and steel) and the overseer of public finance, the Bank of England, were nationalised.

In her Fabian Tract of January 1951, *Workers' Control?*, the Labour MP Eirene White describes a situation in which the once-strong current running for workers' control has been successfully dammed and diverted by the powers that be:

'At Bridlington in 1949, the TUC General Council restated its attitude in the light of its initial experience of nationalised industries. Substantially this statement reaffirmed the 1944 position [defined in *An Interim Report on Post-War Reconstruction*, a document generated from the liaising of the Economic Committee of the TUC and the Labour Party's NEC, and endorsed almost without debate at the 1944 Trades Union Congress], giving pride of place to the public board, with full consultation, but leaving executive responsibility firmly in the hands of management.

"Consultation does not imply diffusion of authority,"
said the Council, "nor is direct workers' representation
in management acceptable." On the contrary, the
General Council underlined the need for a trade unionist
taking a full-time appointment on a Board to sever his
formal connection with his union. Where part-time trade
unionists serve, they must come from unions not
directly connected with the industry.'

The TUC has generally been blessed with a talent for seeing
all sides of the question and accordingly never coming down so
decisively on one side or another as to make it difficult to change
its position and still appear to be leading from the front. A 1953
report dismissed advocates of workers' control as a minority (an
objection applicable to anyone who puts forward an idea before, as
the saying goes, its time has come) unsettling the ranks by
propagating 'out-of-date ideas about industrial relations' and
'traditional ideas of what constitutes industrial democracy' which
'*lead to criticism of the existing structure of nationalisation*', [my
emphasis] when the instilling of a proper understanding of the
purposes of 'joint consultative machinery' would have avoided
'disappointment and frustration' amongst those who had wrongly
assumed that it conferred some 'executive power to workers'
representatives'. A 1963 report, after preambling upliftingly around
the theme that 'one of the purposes of trade unionism is to protect
and enlarge the freedom and dignity of the individual worker,' and
then proceeding downhill to the difficulties of doing this in the
context of 'a complex industrial society' in which decisions are
largely 'made by business organisations and by Governments,' has
the cheek and duplicity to conclude that the workers and their unions
are themselves largely to blame for this unpromising situation
because they did not press harder for industrial democracy: 'Past
efforts in the direction of securing for working people a greater
degree of participation in the decisions which affect them have
largely been ineffective, partly because of the low priority that
unions have accorded to these activities...'
At bottom, of course, lay Humpty Dumpty's ever-present
challenge: 'Who's to be the master?' For those for whom it is
unarguable that the wealth of nations is most successfully generated
by private capitalism, it can only be the businessmen who so

benevolently provide jobs for others and 'create wealth' for all. For State Socialists - politicians and trade unionists alike - the answer, though different, is just as clear: for State Socialists of the purest and simplest sort the answer is equally pure and simple - the State; for those with mixed feelings, i.e. the mixed-economy merchants, the answer is either the State or one of those benevolent private bosses, according to what is on offer. For all these paternalistic people workers' control simply does not figure in the equation, except in the inside-out form of how to control the workers. The overriding problem, in fact, for both free-marketeers and State Socialists (plus all shades of paternalists in between) is how to provide capital with the labour it needs to fulfil its divine purpose, to go forth and multiply.

Certainly the concept of industrial democracy did not much exercise the mind of that ex-worker-firebrand Emmanuel Shinwell when it came to piloting through the Commons that nationalisation measure which more than any other seemed to some at the time to mark the emancipation of the workers. The National Coal Board, appointed by Shinwell, as Minister of Fuel and Power, and composed of 'persons appearing to him to be qualified as having had experience of, and having shown capacity in, industrial, commercial or financial matters, applied science, administration, *or the organisation of workers*' [my emphasis], had the duty of establishing machinery to consult with the trade unions on 'questions relating to the safety, health, or welfare' of employees and 'other [unspecified] matters of mutual interest'; but not only were there to be no worker representatives on the Board, but statutory provision for consultation with the workers actually employed in the industry (as distinct from their union officers) was pronounced by Shinwell to be 'superfluous' to 'the existing conciliation machinery', until the astonishment of MPs *on the opposition benches* prompted him to change his mind.

In more radical times, Labour's policy on taking over the mines (always to the forefront of its programme) had been one of confiscation without compensation ('restitution', its champions might with some justice have called it); but since then hearts - and brains - had softened, at least in leadership circles. In a revealing passage in his autobiography *Conflict without Malice* (1955), Shinwell writes that one of his biggest problems was how to reach agreement with the owners on compensation for pits that in most instances were so run down that without massive investment they would yield little or no profit, and indeed might involve losses to the owners. Not everybody concerned in the matter saw things in quite the same way. 'The miners themselves,' says Shinwell (in a great leap of empathy with the 'caryatids of civilisation', to use Orwell's memorable words), 'did, of course, include many whose bitter experiences precluded any feeling of sympathy for the owners.'

Of course, workers in the industry had rather less reason than their ministerial comrade to be complaisant about the way the nation at last took over the pits; but there were others, too, who did not share the Minister's magnanimity. Putting to the 1948 Labour Party Conference a resolution calling for the immediate nationalisation of the iron and steel industry, without compensation and instituting 'a complete scheme of control by the workers engaged in the industry' (a 'principle...to be applied to all industries nationalised, past and present'), Mr H. Ratner of Salford North District Labour Party commented caustically:

> 'When the workers voted for the Labour Government in
> 1945 they did so in the belief that the nationalisation of
> the basic industries would take the burden of rent,
> interest and profit off the back of the industry, but in the
> nationalisation of the coal industry, the Bank of
> England...and the other industries...the principle adopted
> is that the ex-owners of the industries are guaranteed
> more or less the same amount of money in the form of
> compensation as they were getting before in the form of
> dividends. All that has happened is that the State has
> taken over the running of the industry for the benefit of
> the ex-owners...'

He intemperately demanded that 'the first charge must be not compensation to the ex-owners, but the interests of the working class and the freedom of the country as a whole: the giving to the workers in the industry of a decent standard of living...'

At the behest of the NEC the Conference rejected this motion in favour of an amendment from the Association of Engineering and Shipbuilding Draughtsmen that effectively gutted it of all its radical elements. Truth, however, was on the side of the comrades of Salford North DLP. Who could feel surprised that, despite expeditiously redeeming the relevant pledges in Labour's 1945 manifesto, the Attlee Government's 'nationalisation measures were not accorded great respect by British socialists,' as Sked and Cook put it, with some moderation, in their *Post-War Britain*? And they explain why:

> 'As time went on the defects of the programme became ever more apparent. To start with, it seemed that many of the previous owners had been compensated over-generously; £164,600,000 was paid out, for example, to the mine owners, leaving miners to think that the fruit of their labour was destined even yet - and for some time to come - to find its way into familiar pockets. Moreover, since these former owners were now able to invest this money in much more profitable enterprises, *it seemed as if the Government had really rewarded capital instead of labour*. Thus nationalisation signified no new beginning for labour. No transformation of its relationship with capital occurred. In practice all that happened was that the state bought out the former owners and allowed the former management to remain. Labour was accorded no greater say in industrial decision-making, and since it shared in no profits it gained no economic benefit either.' [my emphasis]

So, in the first place, while nationalisation may have given a wee fillip to the 'dignity' of labour for those who were freed from their former masters to be marshalled instead by the State, without any significant move in the direction of industrial or economic democracy it did nothing to change the essential status of the worker from what pioneer Socialists had had no hesitation in calling him, namely, a 'wage-slave'.

Secondly, Sked and Cook strip away the pretensions of Labour's nationalisation measure to amount to anything more than what might be called techno-socialism:

> 'Finally, there was the criticism of Labour's policy (from the socialist point of view) that in spite of all the fuss the commanding heights had never really been attacked. The 20 per cent of the economy taken over by the government was to a large extent the unprofitable part, while the

profitable sector remained firmly in the hands of private enterprise. *Socialist planning of this type was acceptable even to Conservatives.*' [my emphasis]

Sked and Cook could have added, ' - all the more so since the breaking-even-rather-than-profit-making target generally set by government for nationalised industries meant, in effect, that, whether they were subsidised or not, the way they were run amounted to a concealed subsidy to private industry and commerce.'

Truth, too, came out of the mouths of Tories and Liberals (however ulterior their motives might have been) when the Coal Nationalisation Bill was debated in the Commons. The miners had a proud campaigning tradition not just for nationalisation, but for workers' control. Probably the most celebrated of all the calls for workers' control is that of the Reform Committee of the South Wales Miners, whose pamphlet of 1912, *The Miners' Next Step*, actually warned the workers that State nationalisation would simply benefit society's landlords and capitalists, and calling for industrial democracy, declared: 'Any other form of democracy is a delusion and a snare.' And when the mines came close to being nationalised after the First World War (following the temporary wartime nationalisation) the Miners' Federation of Great Britain was telling the Sankey Commission it wanted fifty per cent representation in management. All such aspirations had melted away by 1945, and for the most part it was not Labour MPs who drew attention to this when at last the pits became public property. Describing the reception of Shinwell's bill in the House in *Labour's First Year*, J.E.D. Hall focuses in particular on three members of the opposition parties:

'It was a Bill, said Anthony Eden, to set up a State monopoly for the production of coal and nothing else. Would the evils disappear once it came under the aegis of the State? Was this the nationalisation the miners wanted - or thought they wanted? The old cry "the mines for the miners" had no place in this Bill. The same men would be managing the mines as before, observed others. Where else could the Minister get them? The miner would go to the same pit and get the same lamp from the same man, said Major Lloyd-

George. He would go into the same cage, be lowered by the same man - and would see the same expression on the face of the pony! Would it make all the difference if the boss was different? One of the complaints under private enterprise was that the boss was so remote. But this one would be even more remote. The boss would be a board composed of nine men - "nine bright shiners" Harold Macmillan called them. They would not be elected by the mining community. The miner would have only one source of employment and he could not change his employer. Surely from the miner's point of view this could not be called a "good swap."'

One Labour back-bencher who, to his credit, did have something to say about the question of bosses, old and new, was the MP for Belper, George Brown, who argued that in the coal mines in particular, 'a very wide measure of industrial democracy is essential.' In the midst of the euphoria of the Labour victors around him, he sounded a decidedly wistful note: 'When I am in my division I frequently stay with mining friends. The last time I was there I was sitting by the fire with two old stalwarts; one of them, who was gently chiding me and pulling my leg, turned to his friends and said, "You know, it will be the same thing under another name."' That is the kind of native wisdom to which George Eliot pays tribute in Middlemarch, where an old rural labourer, told that the coming of the railway's 'a good thing', replies, 'Aw! good for the big folks to make money out on,' and says of all the changes he has seen, 'an' it's been all aloike to the poor mon.'

In *Labour in Power*, Kenneth O. Morgan writes of the State take-over of the pits: 'No single measure in the earlier phase of the Attlee government aroused more genuine or spontaneous enthusiasm than did the nationalisation of the coal-mines. On Vesting Day, 1 January 1947, there were mass demonstrations of rejoicing in mining communities from South Wales to Nottingham, Yorkshire, Durham, and Fife, as the flag of the NCB replaced the ensign of the old, discredited private coal-owners.' Had the miners had a better understanding of what they had been fobbed off with, one might have strained one's ears to catch the faintest sound of cheering. But then how many of those Labour politicians who were convinced they were representing the best interests of the vanguard of the Labour Movement understood the point of Macmillan's remark: 'This is not nationalisation; it is State capitalism'?

The kindest comment - still commensurate with the truth - one can make on the tragic failure of the Labour leaders (political and industrial) to proceed towards the genuine 'socialisation' (ironically, that was the term that Herbert Morrison preferred to 'nationalisation', though with democratisation excluded, what he gave the Movement was 'bureaucratisation') of industry when they had the chance is Sked and Cook's: that the question was approached with 'timidity and naiveté' and 'with no imagination whatsoever'. In all too many cases, however, it would probably get nearer the heart of the matter to point the finger at their fundamentally anti-democratic mind-sets and at that ingrained paternalism which hoards power like others accumulate wealth - though perhaps the two kinds of covetousness are simply opposite sides of the same coin. Most of these authoritarians were too fly to oppose the idea of workers' control with quite the aristocratic scorn and candour of Sir Stafford Cripps, whose pronouncement of the present impossibility of 'worker-controlled industry, even if it were on the whole desirable' raised a storm in Conference. (Among those he provoked was the Salford North delegate referred to above, who scathingly remarked that he was 'once a Socialist' but now 'we wonder whether he knows in which party he is'.) But, as the saying goes, there is more than one way to skin a cat, and in the light of the perfidy and pusillanimity that (in those years chronicled by Coates and Topham) repeatedly thwarted comrades struggling to gain for the workers a real voice where it mattered most, in their working lives, the sly slaughtering of Bullock - the last (?final) act in the long campaign for workers' control - was all too predictable.

CHAPTER 30

Labour's leviathan

'Open government is a contradiction in terms. You can
be open, or you can have government.'
                    Sir Humphrey Appleby in BBC Television's
                                              Yes, Minister

'When he asked me if I was hungry, he really forgot for
a second or two that he was nothing but a servant of the
state. Then he became quite human and showed that he
still had some soul left. Nothing strange about that. To
be hungry is human. To have papers or not to have
papers is inhuman. It is against nature's laws. That's the
point. There is a good reason for being the way he is.
The state cannot make use of human beings. It would
cease to exist. Human beings only make trouble. Men
cut out of cardboard do not make trouble. Yessir.
Excuse me, I mean: yes, sir.'
                    Ben Traven, *The Death Ship* (1926)

In opposition Labour can generally be relied on to champion liberty,
at home and abroad. [STOP PRESS. This sentence was written
before shadow home secretary Jack Straw showed his determination
not to be outflanked to the right by the most reactionary Home
Secretary since the war on the issue of law and order, by
substantially endorsing increased powers for the police and security
services to bug and burgle 'in the public interest' contained in
Michael Howard's 1997 Police Bill.] In office what it does is quite
another matter. This is only partially explicable in ideological terms.
Managerialism is only one strand in Labour's ideology. Besides
which, though it might be considered an onerous brief to have to
defend Labour against the charge that it is the dominant strand, on
the other hand Labour rightly argues, in contradiction to the specious
claims of Tory 'self-styled libertarians', that in capitalist societies
(no less than in feudal ones) the authority of the State can be - and
not infrequently has been, both in pre-democratic and in
'democratic' ages - protective of the relatively powerless rather

than oppressive. Labour, in short, rightly refutes the charge that it is *more* authoritarian than its Tory opponents, whether these be of either the paternalistic or the self-styled libertarian variety. As a more or less sincere exponent of what we have come to call, with a minimal measure of analysis, 'democratic socialism', it is, all in all, *less* so.

Labour rightly underlines the negative and atomising nature of the traditional 'liberal democratic' attitude to liberty, which largely ignores the dearth of freedom implicit in the gross inequality in the power to choose which is immanent in capitalist society - an in-built situation memorably captured in Anatole France's observation that the millionaire and the tramp are equally at liberty to sleep under bridges. The Socialist realisation that liberty and equality are not rivals but inseparable partners should be Labour's greatest strength. However, as with a number of other fundamental issues, Labour has always been afraid to take the offensive on this score - an irony to which we will return.

Less tainted by moral nannyism so far as social (and particularly sexual) behaviour goes, it is not to be denied that Labour's 'good shepherd' tendencies show that it has more in common with Tory paternalism than it can comfortably admit. What out of office is nothing more than another set of contending opinions is transmuted by the assumption of 'democratic' authority into a prescriptive mandate: exhortation becomes command. This follows ineluctably from the nature of the State and of government as an instrument to implement reforms, especially when these add up to a potentially substantial restructuring of society foreshadowing an attempt to 'remould it nearer to the heart's desire'.

No degree of commitment to the ideal of freedom is proof against the corruption of power, as that quintessential Whig historian Lord Acton, mentor and intimate friend of Gladstone, warned a hundred years ago. 'Power tends to corrupt,' he wrote, 'and absolute power corrupts absolutely. Great men are nearly always bad men.' Nine years after Acton's death the last government formed by that party which believes itself to be peculiarly touched by the grace of truly cherishing civil liberties, laid down the very corner-stone of the institutional dominion wielded by the executive (or to speak more precisely, by the prime minister and a handful of his chosen fellow hierarchs) under the British system of government. On Friday 18th August 1911 an Official Secrets Bill that had been introduced in the Lords and accepted without amendment was presented to the Commons. Within thirty minutes it had been pushed through all its stages, and four days later, having received the Royal Assent, it was law. To those few Members who had still been in the House during that outstandingly inglorious half-hour in the annals of British parliamentary government, the Bill had been represented by the ministerial mountebanks charged with ensuring its passage as an uncontroversial measure designed solely to strengthen the powers of the State to tackle the menace of foreign spies. In fact, nominally at least, it gave (*and gives*) the government in power total control over the dissemination of official information, and with it, draconian sanctions against civil servants, journalists, and the citizenry in general who handle or pass on that information without being authorised to do so.

Labour may not assume that special grace alluded to above, but it does make particular claims to upholding the democratic rights of the people. So it is instructive to contrast the critical assaults launched by Labour on the erosion of liberty and democracy since the State became a tool of the New Tories with the record of Labour in power - particularly during the Wilson/Callaghan period, since that provides the closest parallels in concern and response, while at the same time quite accurately reflecting Labour's whole in-office record. The aspects of governance we shall focus on are those concerning State secrets and government confidentiality, along with the operations of the security services, the police, and the judiciary to safeguard them against the prying eyes of its citizens. The issue which looms over all these matters is the inherent conflict between executive power on the one hand and democratic accountability on the other. Such accountability - to the representatives of the people in Parliament and ultimately to what may be called (in theoretical discussion of representative democracy, at least, though the term is hardly strictly in accord with British constitutional realities) 'the sovereign people' - is dependent on the right to know, together with the actual possibility of finding out. The final years of the Wilson/Callaghan regimes threw up two spectacular examples of the absence of the right to know under Britain's system of parliamentary government, besides numerous lesser ones. One of these two spectaculars, which we shall look at later, concerned the Government's failure to enforce the sanctions it had itself imposed on the rebel regime in Rhodesia. The other pitched the executive into open conflict both with the more independent-minded members of the legislature and with the Fourth Estate (and equally pitched the Labour leadership into conflict with both wings of the Labour Movement) through a secrets trial which surpassed in absurdity the Whitehall 'spycatcher' farce with which, when its turn came, the Thatcher regime was so brilliantly to entertain us.

The ABC trial (as it came to be known from the surnames of the men in the dock) had its source, like so many other noxious emanations of those times, in the Cold War alliance and the supposed 'special relationship' between Britain and the United States. In February 1977 the Home Secretary, Merlyn Rees, told the Commons - to supportive remarks from his shadow, Willie Whitelaw, and from other members of the official Opposition, and outraged cries from the unofficial opposition behind him that he was behaving like the Czech authorities did towards the signatories of Charter 77 - that he was sticking to his decision to deport two American citizens in the interests of national security. One of them, Philip Agee, was a former officer of America's Central Intelligence Agency who had undoubtedly angered his erstwhile masters by his revelations about the CIA, though Rees naturally denied that CIA pressure had anything to do with his decision. The other, Mark Hosenball, was a less street-wise idealist whose dad, Neil, was actually a senior legal adviser to the US space-flight agency, NASA, the National Aeronautics and Space Administration. Mark Hosenball was employed by the London *Evening News*, and according to his editor, Simon Jenkins, he was being victimised by a Labour Home Secretary for being 'a Left-wing investigative journalist'.

Since Rees' original decision, in November 1976, that the presence in Britain of these two men whom he clearly looked on as Cold War subversives was 'not conducive to the public good', both of them had submitted themselves to what Jenkins described as the 'charade' of appealing to the tribunal of 'three wise men' instituted by Heath's Government in 1971 to consider - *in camera* and with no independent powers to detail either charges or evidence, or even to name, let alone to summon for cross-examination, witnesses, and no authority to do more than make *sub rosa* recommendations to the Home Secretary - appeals against such deportation orders. Following Rees's confirmation of his decision, Hosenball applied for and was granted the right to a judicial appeal. This, however, served only to underline the absolutist nature of the Home Secretary's powers. The Lord Chief Justice, Lord Widgery, speaking for all three judges at the hearing in the Queen's Bench Divisional Court, made it clear that under the law the imperatives of natural justice were overruled by those of public security as perceived by the Home Secretary. 'Where matters of public security are in issue and where a minister has certified that certain matters should not be disclosed, they will not be disclosed.' The court did not know what the offence was, but it was only concerned with whether the minister had acted in good faith, which of course was not in question, and whether he had committed any procedural error, which he had not. Accordingly, it refused to quash the deportation order.

In due course the deportations were carried out. But the rumpus the deportation orders had aroused, far from dying down and becoming as stirring as *yesterday's* shock-horror news, was greatly amplified, even before the orders were implemented, by the news that three supporters of the Agee-Hosenball Defence Committee had been arrested by Special Branch officers and charged, after forty-four hours in police custody, under Section Two of the Official Secrets Act. The three accused were John Berry, who had served for four years in the Royal Signals Corps as a Signals Intelligence specialist, Crispin Aubrey, a reporter on *Time Out*, and Duncan Campbell, a freelance journalist and regular contributor to *Time Out*, *Undercurrents*, and *New Scientist*. What had brought these three together, making them, in the eyes of the Special Branch, co-conspirators, was an article in *Time Out* entitled 'The Eavesdroppers', co-authored by Mark Hosenball and Duncan Campbell, on whose researches it was largely based. It was reading this article and relating it to his army service that had prompted Berry to go to the offices of the National Council for Civil Liberties and talk to members of the Agee-Hosenball Defence Committee. Berry told them that he had followed the affair with particular interest because of his SIGINT experience, commenting:

'Both the extent of intelligence activities of this nature and the resources which the British Government deploys in this area are largely unknown to the public. The fact that they remain unknown is due in no small measure to the considerable pressure placed on people who have or have had access to the facts. It appears to me that secrecy is one of the most important keys to power and the existence of an organisation spending vast sums of money in the total absence of public control should do much to dispel any illusions about the democratic nature of our Government.'

The Home Secretary had already demonstrated how to spatter egg all over his own face in this unsavoury imbroglio. Now it was the turn of the Attorney-General, Sam Silkin, to show that he was not to be outdone when it came to clowning. Just as the decision to deport Agee and Hosenball was solely the Home Secretary's, so the decision to apply to the High Court for permission to prosecute the ABC trio, on the basis of the meagre evidence of serious conspiracy unearthed by Detective Superintendent Harry Nicholls and his team of subversion-busters, was the Attorney-General's alone. Labour was committed by its 1974 manifesto to progressing towards more open government, and in particular to reforming the Official Secrets Act. Even more specifically, Merlyn Rees had - only that last November before Sam Silkin had to make up his mind how best to deal with the troublesome trio - announced the Government's decision (in line with the recommendations of the Franks Committee set up by Heath's Government) to replace Section Two of the Official Secrets Act with a less catch-all formula, adding: 'Although the operation of the Act is a matter for the Attorney-General, it will no doubt be open to the Attorney-General to take into account the Government's intention to introduce legislation on the lines I have indicated in considering whether to bring prosecutions under Section 2.' Rees made it clear that the Government accepted that 'mere receipt of official information should no longer be an offence.' Yet as the NCCL predicted at the time of the ABC arrests, when it was still possible for sanity to prevail over a policy of mutton-headed repression of Britain's dissidents: 'In contrast with the Labour Party's manifesto, which promises more open government, Mr Callaghan and Mr Rees have in the last four months made it clear that the Labour Government will harass and intimidate any journalist who attempts to investigate matters which the Government wants hidden.' The Government had already wielded the State cudgel against two American truth-revealers. Now it was about to blunder into a hornet's nest by an assault on British journalists and the freedom of the press, and even, as we shall see shortly, on the hallowed privileges of Parliament.

The ABC affair dragged on damagingly, while the Right Honourable Samuel Silkin chewed his nails and agonised and Harry Nicholls and his team took a crash-course in the anti-democratic nature of British government by rummaging through the thousands of damning documents seized from Duncan Campbell's Brighton flat. Doubtless because of the embarrassment of bringing prosecutions solely dependent on a part of the Official Secrets Act that the Government itself had admitted was untenable, in May further charges were heaped on the heads of the terrible trio. These were brought under Section One of the Act, which was commonly understood to apply only to espionage on behalf of a foreign power. The fishing operations and scissors-and-paste labours of the Special Branch sleuths brought the calendar round to November before committal proceedings could be held. The opening of the trial itself was still nearly a year away, but a cloudburst of protest was about to precipitate copious quantities of indignation, derision, and defiance on the Government's head.

The prosecution's principal witness in persuading the magistrates that those charged had a case to answer was to have been a man who was not even prepared to accept the magistrates' direction that his name should be given to the defence in confidence. So the utterly mysterious Lieutenant-Colonel A (as he was denominated) was replaced by the somewhat less mysterious Colonel B, whose name was revealed in writing to the accuseds' counsels, though not, of course, to the accused themselves. It was, however, no masterly feat of espionage to work out his identity, since he obligingly gave his army number in open court and referred to a specific issue of his own regimental journal, *The Wire*, in which his name and post had been published. Colonel B, who testified in the magistrates' court that his own testimony was damaging to the national interest since 'there should not be any public discussion of Britain's SIGINT activities at all', before making the positively Kafkaesque observation that 'the regulations governing the secret handling of this intelligence are themselves secret', was unmasked by *Peace News* and *The Leveller* as a Colonel Hugh Johnstone - a revelation of great moment, no doubt, to Soviet intelligence!

One could say the colonel then became a household name, since his name was subsequently broadcast on radio and television, batted about in the House of Commons by unruly MPs, launched on red balloons released by dissidents from London's GPO Tower, and even carved in ten-foot-high letters on the beach at Whitley Bay, Northumberland - all of which, according to the prosecuting authorities, made him damaged goods from an intelligence point of view. For prosecutions were now brought against the two campaigning journals and against the National Union of Journalists, whose own publication, *The Journalist*, had given further unwanted publicity to the by now utterly unmysterious colonel in the course of citing motions submitted by branches for debate at the annual delegate meeting of the NUJ, to be held at, yes, Whitley Bay.

In May the three journals were fined for contempt (£200 in the case of *The Journalist*, £500 each for the campaigning journals which had first exposed the unhappy colonel) by the Queen's Bench Divisional Court, again presided over by Lord Widgery. The Court of Appeal upheld the High Court judgement, but on 1st February 1979 the five Law Lords unanimously overturned the ruling and awarded costs against the Crown. (The fines had, in any case, failed to deter *Peace News* from further acts of subversive defiance. To demonstrate 'its opposition to official secrecy, not only in theory but in practice', it published another account of Signals Intelligence work - this time by a former Royal Navy conscript - and revealed the identity of the recently-appointed head of MI6, the first time a British intelligence chief had been publicly named while still in office. And, with maximum provocation in the timing, it committed these criminal acts a week and a half before the ABC trial was to open. Yet they went unpunished.)

Meanwhile the right-to-know row had moved from Whitley Bay to Westminster, the very centre of the constitutional web. The fabled blessings of the British constitution spring from the separation of powers invested in the State between the executive, the legislature, and the judiciary; but the country was about to witness a series of unseemly brawls between the rival arms of the State. When Jo Richardson, followed by three other Labour MPs, provocatively named the once incognito colonel during question time in the House, the Director of Public Prosecutions - at the urging of the Attorney-General, Sam Silkin - promptly warned the Press, through a memorandum to the Press Association, that publishing Colonel B's real name could constitute a contempt of court. This was notwithstanding the fact that it had already reached the ears of millions of people half an hour earlier, through broadcast reports of proceedings in the House.

413

But there was a much bigger 'notwithstanding' than that, for MPs may say what they please in the House so long as it is within the Rules of Order, and Parliament has an unfettered right to publish its proceedings. The DPP certainly had no powers to gag Hansard. To the credit of the Fourth Estate, not a single newspaper allowed itself to be intimidated by the DPP's warning; but the question remained, 'Did Parliament's right to full publication extend to the Press?' All members of the House are jealous of its privileges, and it was a Tory MP, Graham Page, who described the DPP's action as 'a contempt of Parliament', submitting to the Speaker that it was a prima facie breach of parliamentary privilege, while the most forthright intervention in a subsequent debate on the issue came from the redoubtable right-winger Enoch Powell, who declared: 'I cannot imagine a more direct assault upon the essential privilege of this House.' Unsurprisingly, when this hot potato was passed to the Commons Committee of Privileges, composed of senior members of the House *and including the Attorney-General*, it was far more cautious - not to say mealy-mouthed - in its pronouncements, exonerating the DPP on the grounds that his warning had only been guidance, and failing to grapple with the vital issue of whether the privilege of free speech in Parliament extended to the reporting of it by the media.

Concern for the rights of the Fourth Estate (at least in so far as it constitutes a just-about-indispensable publicity machine for elected politicians!) was not the only cause of conflict between 'the High Court of Parliament' and the judicial arm of the State. Members pressing for a debate in the House on the freedom-of-speech issues arising from the ABC affair unexpectedly won assent from Michael Foot as Leader of the House, only to find themselves gagged by the Speaker's ruling that the matter was now *sub judice*. Then in November the threat of a punch-up between the legislative and judicial arms of the State, following an MP's complaint that the secrets trial judge, Mr Justice Mars-Jones, had shown disrespect for Parliament by neglecting to observe the convention that permission must be sought before referring to ministerial statements published in Hansard, was again only averted by shunting the issue into that misty marshalling yard for mislaying matters which embarrass the establishment, the Commons Committee of Privileges.

All this time the machinery of State justice was grinding on inexorably to crush the menace of the ABC conspirators. Aubrey's alleged offences were the least serious; but when the trial proper at last got under way on 5th September, both Berry and Campbell still faced a charge under Section One of the Official Secrets Act that carried a maximum penalty of fourteen years in prison, since they had turned down plea-bargaining offers from the prosecution. The case had only be running for ten days when the first trial judge, Mr Justice Willis, ordered a retrial because some other pestilential journalist had referred in a broadcast to the presence on the jury of a former member of the Special Air Service (he had, in fact, been chosen by his fellow jurors as their foreman) and of two other jurors who had signed pledges to observe the Official Secrets Act.

Defence counsel had already raised the awkward question of just how impartial the jury could be said to be by protesting that, contrary to accepted practice, the jury panel for the ABC trial had been vetted by the security services. Leading counsel for the Crown, John Leonard QC, admitted the vetting, elucidating the issue with the observation: 'Anyone who is known to have been disloyal would obviously be disqualified.' Which in turn prompted the NCCL to challenge the Attorney-General to make it clear who decided if a person was loyal or not for the purpose of jury selection and on what criteria the decision was made. The clash over jury-vetting in the ABC case led to the official (but secret!) guidelines drawn up in 1975 *for the benefit of prosecuting counsel* being made public, and to the revelation that there had been twenty-five previous occasions during that period when the Crown had weeded out 'unreliable' jurors. Suspected vulnerability to intimidation and/or bribery accounted for about half of these and assumed partisan sympathies in 'terrorist' cases in Northern Ireland to the bulk of the others; but the guidelines made it clear that suspicions of 'disloyalty' could be invoked in cases brought under the Official Secrets Act.

When the stalled trial was restarted, on 3rd October, it was under Mr Justice Mars-Jones, since Mr Justice Willis had had the good fortune to fall sick with tummy trouble. The flimsy nature of the case pieced together against the ABC trio was at once made obvious to the thickest plank on the jurors' bench by the prosecution's announcement that it would be offering no evidence on the most serious charge against Duncan Campbell: that he had collected information about defence communications which was prejudicial to the safety and interests of the State. Mr Leonard (over whom, as Lord Hutchinson QC was to remark in his closing speech as counsel for Campbell, 'an amazing change' had come 'since those early weeks when you first heard him make his original address to you') implicitly admitted that he had been much impressed by the quantity of the material submitted by the defence to prove that the material found in Mr Campbell's possession was already in the public domain. (Not the least droll revelation during this exceedingly droll affair was that this journalist with what Mr Leonard considered an unusual interest in Signals - though Leonard himself described Campbell as 'a qualified and brilliant scientist' - was the co-author of an Open University book on the subject which was about to be published, and that a copy of this book containing much allegedly classified information had been found in his briefcase when he was arrested.)

Mr Leonard's admission showed how badly briefed the distinguished barrister was; but his pretext for the charge having been brought in the first place was truly risible. 'When I opened the case originally, I told the jury that much of the information was no doubt culled from published sources. It was the Crown's contention, nevertheless, that Campbell had committed an offence because much of the information was added to and interpreted with his observations as a skilled scientist, and was built up so as to be likely to be of value to an enemy.'

The real offence, it was thus made clear, was the application of *unauthorised* intelligence to the scrutiny of the State's security operations as published strictly for the attention of its own designated servants; plus the communicating of this information in an accessible form to 'the common people'. Campbell had acted, in fact, as a kind of civic spy, in the spirit of Crispin Aubrey's affirmation to his fellow journalists at their Whitley Bay conference that it was their duty to inform the public about matters they could not find out for themselves, 'not to support those people in positions of power who simply wish to avoid embarrassment.'

Having begun to unravel, the case against the conspirators unwound itself into a virtual nullity at a quite giddy rate considering its constitutional gravitas. After a day and a half of legalistic argy-bargy in its absence, the jury was instructed on 24th October to ignore all four remaining charges under the 'spies'' section of the Official Secrets Act, which left only four Section Two charges, carrying a maximum penalty of two years' imprisonment, to be dealt with. On 6th November the jury was directed to return a 'not guilty' verdict on one Section Two charge against Crispin Aubrey. Now, instead of the formidable nine-count indictment the State had levelled at them in the first place, the three defendants faced only one charge each under the less serious Section Two. On 10th November, motivated perhaps by concern that the prosecution might be utterly discredited and the law appear 'a ass' if all the defendants got off scot-free and he was left with no one to pass sentence on, the judge directed the jury to convict the most vulnerable of them, the ex-corporal John Berry, on the one remaining charge against him. For this direction Mr Justice Mars-Jones earned himself a rebuke from a former Lord of Appeal, Lord Devlin, who pronounced it 'contrary to modern authority' to deprive a jury of the right to acquit.

In the event a vengeful State secured convictions against the upstart journalists as well as against the disloyal ex-soldier, after the jury had agonised over its verdicts for nearly sixty-eight hours and spent three nights in a hotel. And Mars-Jones proved himself a judicious chap after all by the leniency of the sentences he dished out on 17th November: six months suspended for two years for Berry, conditional discharges for three years for Aubrey and Campbell.

But there was no hiding the truth that it had been a State-sledgehammer-to-crack-three-subversive-nuts' affair which had cost the taxpayer a quarter of a million pounds and the Labour Government a great deal more in wasted credit. The very fact that the trial judge had felt constrained to warn both the media and demonstrators showing their solidarity with the defendants that it was 'improper' to try 'to influence the jury's verdict' and dangerous to 'ignore the sub-judice principle and to comment on criminal proceedings during their currency', and then in his summing-up, after flattering the jury by calling it 'the last bastion of freedom', to tell its members they must put out of their heads the campaign to secure the acquittal of the three men, showed how futile it was to try to silence those not prepared to accept that a State describing itself as democratic had the right to keep secret from its citizens whatever it chose.

As this tangled tale of contumacious citizens challenging the authority of the State (Rex v. John Citizen, one might call it) unfolded, the Labour establishment had become increasingly jittery, its rank and file increasingly restless. On the day the ABC trial opened in the Old Bailey, GMWU general secretary David Basnett, chairing the TUC conference at Brighton, postponed debate on an NUJ resolution calling for the prosecutions to be dropped and for the introduction of a Freedom of Information Act. Since pressure from Basnett, TUC general secretary Len Murray, and other members of the General Council failed to persuade the NUJ delegation to remit its motion to the General Council for a quiet interment, it was ruled out of order on the grounds that the matter was now *sub judice*, provoking NUJ president Dennis MacShane to walk out of the conference. Before the decision to impose a gag on the parliament of labour had been confirmed, MacShane acidly remarked: 'We find it highly ironic that a motion about freedom of information should have its debate suppressed by the TUC General Council. He went on to assert that the real problem with his union's motion to the TUC conference was not legal but political. 'A general election is looming and it is clear that the TUC wants no debate which will involve major criticisms of the Government. The Government's track record on official secrets is a shiny black spot in its general record.'

In the ranks of the Labour Party itself, inside as well as outside the PLP, rebelliousness over the Official Secrets brouhaha and the issues of freedom of information and freedom of expression flourished. The attempt by the DPP to gag the press when the ABC affair was aired in Parliament had provoked more than fifty Labour MPs to sign a motion condemning his interference. A similar number of awkward squaddies called for a PLP meeting to discuss the ABC prosecutions. A few Labour MPs publicly - and doubtless many more privately - had urged the Attorney-General to drop the charges against the ABC trio. Now that the trial was over, one of those who had gone public on the matter, Robin Cook, called the 'token' sentences a moral victory for the defendants, suggested the Attorney-General should resign, and declared: 'The Home Secretary must introduce, as a matter of urgency, the long-overdue reform of the Official Secrets Act.'

And in this most ticklish business the Government was quite bereft of that excuse which so often served to extenuate its inaction or backsliding. For nominally at least there was almost universal agreement in the House on the need to reform the Official Secrets Act, and there were enough genuine champions of more open government on the Tory benches to have made it devilishly difficult for the Opposition leaders openly to resist a vigorous push for reform had one been forthcoming. One Tory MP with a particular personal reason for interest in the ABC affair was Jonathan Aitken, who in 1971 had himself been acquitted on a Section Two charge arising from his despatches to *The Sunday Telegraph* on the war in the Nigerian province of Biafra. When the ABC trial was over he commented that the Attorney-General had been 'badly advised by the security services' and had 'made an expensive error of judgement in preferring the Section One charges.'

Outside the party cockpit, striking endorsements of the call for reform came from two pillars of the State whose lives had been spent in the defence of law and order. With the ABC 'conspirators' still in the dock, the former Metropolitan Police Commissioner, Sir Robert Mark, published his memoirs, in which he said he would like to see Section Two of the Official Secrets Act repealed, but that if it remained in the Statute Book he would still hope to see it increasingly ignored. And at almost the same moment a Law Lord, Lord Justice Scarman, addressing the Royal Institute of Public Administration, made a sweeping attack on government obsession with secrecy. He called for a Freedom of Information Act on the lines of those enjoyed - and shown to be workable - in Sweden and the USA, but correctly predicted that the Government would 'totally fail to formulate any general principle governing the right of access to official information.'

Despite its promises the Government showed little inclination seriously to reform this discredited Act and still less to honour Labour's 1974 manifesto commitment to introduce a Freedom of Information Bill. On the contrary, its White Paper on these issues was rightly described at the Blackpool Conference of 1978 as 'a mouse', and when the Liberal MP Clement Freud succeeded in getting a private member's Freedom of Information Bill on to the floor of the House, Government ministers in effect colluded with the Opposition front-bench to water it down and wreck it. Their unholy alliance was superfluous, however, as the Government fell nine days before the bill was due to come up for full debate, and it was thus consigned to the wastepaper bin.

'A story of unrelieved folly on the part of the Crown,' pronounced *The Guardian* on the day the ABC trial ended so humiliatingly for the prosecution. There's nothing uncommon about folly in the history of government, whatever the political colour of the rulers. What was outstanding about this particular specimen of folly was the extent to which the government in question damaged its reputation in the eyes of its own supporters and made itself stink in the nostrils of those not inconsiderable sections of the electorate whose libertarian leanings left them with little or no meaningful choice but to vote for Labour or stay at home. For MacShane was not overstating things all that much in saying after walking out of the Brighton congress to show his disgust at being gagged that the Callaghan Government had 'the worst record of any this century in trying to limit the freedom of expression.'

On the other hand, it was Callaghan's misfortune that it was during his premiership that the noisome evidence of one of the most shameful episodes in the post-war history of the British Commonwealth bubbled to the surface, since it was his predecessor who was chiefly to blame. But as one speaker in the 1978 Labour Conference debate on open government exclaimed, if Labour had legislated earlier for the public's right to know, the country might not have had to wait ten years to hear the truth about the oil sanctions scandal. He was alluding to the fact that when the white-settler government led by Ian Smith resolved on UDI (unilateral declaration of independence), the Wilson Government, having persuaded the United Nations to impose mandatory sanctions on Rhodesia, gave every appearance of actively and wholeheartedly participating in the blockade (even to deploying British warships to patrol the seas off the port of Beira, in the Portuguese colony of Mozambique, over a period of nine years), while secretly conniving at the flouting of the law and the subterfuges by which Western companies (including Shell and British Petroleum, a company in which the British government held a controlling share) conspired to keep the oil flowing which kept the rebel government's war-machine running which prolonged the war which piled the corpses high.

This murky business began to come to light in June 1976, with the publication in the USA by the United Church of Christ of *The Oil Conspiracy*, a report based largely on information leaked to a shadowy anti-apartheid organisation called Okhela, led by the Afrikaans poet Breyten Breytenbach. At about the same time 'Tiny' Rowland, head of Lonrho, a company with major interests in southern Africa, made allegations to the British Government about sanctions-busting operations. The publication in Britain, in March

1978, by the Anti-Apartheid Movement and the Haslemere Group, of another report, concentrating on sanctions-busting by Shell and BP, followed by questions in the House, made it imperative for the Government to act. Thomas Bingham, QC, an obscure London barrister who was destined to become the highest justice in the land, was commissioned to investigate the allegations, and he presented his report to the Foreign Secretary, Dr David Owen, on 22nd August 1978.

Four weeks passed before the report was released, but by then *The Guardian* had published a leaked draft; and although it was at once clear that Bingham had stuck strictly to his brief to investigate the conduct of the British oil companies - as distinct from the conduct of government ministers and civil servants - vaporous intimations of an accusatory finger hovered menacingly over many a venerable head. Rarely outside Lilliput has such nimble footwork, such deft passing of the buck, been seen amongst such eminent men of affairs. Within days of Bingham's findings being delivered to Dr Owen, a pre-emptive strike was launched by the verdantly-styled Lord Greenhill of Harrow, permanent secretary at the Foreign Office between 1969 and 1973, who, as one of the two government-appointed directors on BP's board since leaving the Civil Service, was still in a somewhat sensitive position with regard to this affair.

The principal subterfuge employed by Shell and BP to comply with British law without getting on the wrong side of the white-man's-burden regimes ruling South Africa, Mozambique and Southern Rhodesia was to fix up an oil-swapping arrangement with Total - a French company quite unhampered by scruples about propping up another white-paternalist regime by sanctions-busting - under which it would supply Ian Smith's rebel government with oil and have its own stock replenished by the British companies. (So cynical did this deal eventually become that the swapping degenerated into deliveries from the same Shell Mocambique depot as had been used to supply Rhodesia before the rebellion, with the ownership of the oil being first recorded in the books as transferred to Total.) Greenhill (who curiously enough turned out not to have been interviewed by Bingham) frankly admitted to having known about this swapping scam while he was still at the Foreign Office; then promptly shifted the burden of responsibility to the Commonwealth Relations Office by pointing out that it was the

Commonwealth and Colonial Secretary, George Thomson, who had held the oil-embargo talks with Shell and BP.

Thomson is an interesting figure partly *because* his is not a name which reverberates widely outside the diminishing ranks of Labour's elder statesmen, yet he was just the sort of sound back-up man needed to cement firmly into place the well-earned reputation for responsible politics of the Labour establishment. An old and faithful friend of both James Callaghan and Denis Healey, Thomson began his career appropriately as editor of the comics *Dandy* and *Beano*; rose under Wilson's command to Cabinet rank, becoming Minister without Portfolio and Chancellor of the Duchy of Lancaster, with special responsibility for negotiating with the EEC the terms for Britain's entry (after Labour had been turned out of office by the 1970 general election, along with Labour's new Deputy Leader, Roy Jenkins, and Harold Lever, he resigned from what was now the Shadow Cabinet over Wilson's acceptance of Tony Benn's proposal for a referendum on British membership of the Common Market); accepted the offer of appointment as one of Britain's two EEC Commissioners after Ted Heath had secured British entry; and, to purloin Healey's witticism, 'some would say, completed the circle by ending it as a [life] peer and Chairman of the Independent Broadcasting Authority.'

It was this very model of the great and the good who in each generation shore up our venerable institutions who was now in the telescopic sights. He did the only thing he could: he grassed on his co-conspirators by confessing that he was a mere conduit for communications between the sanctions-busting buccaneers and his own skipper. Less than a week after the putting about of a disclaimer that the Wilson Cabinet had ever been informed of the nose-thumbing smuggling ops, Thomson released a six-page dossier bluntly stating that Cabinet papers 'confirm that I conveyed in writing to the Prime Minister and other Ministers most directly concerned a full account of all that passed at my meetings on behalf of the Government with the oil companies.'

He went on to assert that following UDI 'the most vigorous national and international efforts to bring down the illegal Rhodesian regime by sanctions' had been initiated by the Labour Government, but that they had been 'forced painfully and reluctantly to face the fact that so long as South Africa and Portugal refused to operate the sanctions there was no chance of ending the rebellion' swiftly, since open confrontation with those countries, as well as military intervention in Rhodesia, had been ruled out as unwise and/or quite impracticable. Prosecution of the British oil companies for breaking the sanctions would only have given comfort to the rebels, so we did the best we could, Thomson claimed, which was 'to prevent any further British oil reaching Rhodesia...Of course, the arrangements which began in 1968 were a second best. They did not prevent Rhodesia getting her oil since that was outside our power. But they did mean that the Government was ensuring that British companies under their jurisdiction were observing British law and that was of capital importance in maintaining the pressure on Smith for a negotiated settlement.'

Whether or not it is possible for anybody who has not wholly surrendered to cynicism to consider this apologia as anything better than a tale of pusillanimity and deception, Thomson's account was largely borne out by a vigorous defence of the oil companies' conduct by Shell's chairman, Sir Frank McFadzean, which appeared in *The Times* on the day before Thomson spilled the beans. Sir Frank claimed that the British oil companies had made it clear that oil could only be prevented from reaching Rhodesia by imposing a blockade on South Africa, which the British Government was never prepared to do. 'Once the Government appreciated that the substance of its sanctions' policy was beyond its grasp, all efforts were devoted to trying to keep the companies and their staff within the letter rather than the spirit of the Order.' Hence the oil-swap deal with Total, about which, McFadzean said, there had been several discussions with the Government.

The inescapable implication of George Thomson's statement as to who was in the know was that Roy Jenkins (who was Chancellor of the Exchequer at the time), Michael Stewart (Foreign Secretary 1965-66 and 1968-70), Denis Healey (Defence Secretary 1964-70), probably James Callaghan (who moved in 1967 from the post of Chancellor to that of Home Secretary), and of course Harold Wilson himself, were perfectly well aware of what was going on. While Sir Charles le Quesne, who as head of the Foreign Office's West and Central African Department at the time said that he had been told by the oil companies that they could not prevent their South African subsidiaries from delivering oil to Rhodesia, threw in for good measure the name of the wayward George Brown, who was Foreign Secretary from August 1966 to March 1968, and remained Deputy Leader of the Labour Party (to which post he had been elected in 1960) until he became a life peer in 1970.

To Lord George-Brown, as he whimsically became, we shall return after taking an unsightly squint at the reactions of the others in the frame. Roy Jenkins took refuge behind the self-denying principle of not commenting on matters pertaining to his time in office in Britain since becoming President of the EEC (a post he had conveniently taken up in 1976 and held until January 1981, when he became free to join the 'Gang of Three' and become figurehead of the Social Democratic Party); Messrs Callaghan and Healey kept uncharacteristically quiet and Michael Stewart said as little as possible; while the creature at the centre of the web sent up a circumlocutory smoke-screen which revealed neither qualms of conscience nor any disposition to accept personal responsibility for the total failure of the oil embargo. For such uncomfortable feelings was substituted an exemplary candour in naming others (James Callaghan, Fred Lee, Arthur Bottomley, Michael Stewart) whose almost constant attendance at meetings of the Cabinet or Cabinet committees during the period concerned almost certainly made them privy to whatever his Government could have been said to know. Unfortunately, however, according to him, nobody could remember anything about the reports to the Cabinet to which George Thomson was referring.

As for the parvenu peer who was (like Roy Jenkins) a failed contender for Labour's top job, and in 1976 resigned from the Party, Lord George-Brown washed his hands of the matter, without directly answering the allegations against him, by saying that he was not personally or departmentally involved in the sanctions' supervision; described the debate about who did what and who knew what as 'distasteful and unseemly' and Wilson's call for the publication of all the relevant Cabinet papers 'an insidious, sinister, and malicious attempt which made Cabinet government as we have known it impossible in this country'; attacked David Owen for failing to invite Ian Smith to come to Britain for talks; denounced what had been his own party and the Liberals for feting 'a leader of thugs and murderers' (*viz.* Joshua Nkomo) when 'he came openly to this country'; and announced that he would vote against a renewal of sanctions.

To go back to Bingham, after all the finger-pointing, dodging and weaving which had preceded publication - plus, of course, the leaks about what the worthy man of law was going to say - when the authorised and carefully circumscribed report of this squalid affair was officially released on 20th September, it was naturally a bit of a damp squib as far as new revelations go, though it did add a little to the record and confirmed in a generally no-names-no-pack-drill kind of way the collusion between the British oil companies and both Wilson's and Heath's administrations. One passage in the report referred to a Government note of a meeting, on 21st February 1968, between George Thomson and top executives of Shell and BP, which left no doubt that the Government knew about the massive leaking of British oil to the rebel regime and that the Government's main concern had been to devise a verbal construction which could be deployed in reporting to Parliament on the implementation of sanctions without making any demonstrably false statement or arousing suspicion, while at the same time cloaking the truth, which was that so far as oil supplies went the British blockade was a masquerade. The solution was simple. 'No British company is supplying POL [petrol, oil or lubricants] to Rhodesia' should and did satisfy most supporters of sanctions, since British companies had been responsible for 85 per cent of the country's needs. And the statement diverted attention from the profoundly disturbing fact that while Rhodesia's oil consumption had fallen after UDI, it quite soon returned to its former level and then rose to a figure double the 1965 rate.

This aide-memoire of 21st February 1968 was on its own all but conclusive in answering the question of whether Harold Wilson himself was party to what really amounted to a conspiracy to deceive Parliament and the British electorate, not to mention the international community, since a copy was sent to No 10 Downing Street for the attention of the Prime Minister's private secretary, Michael Palliser (who by the time this came to light in Bingham's report was Sir Michael Palliser, head of the Foreign Office), and no one could believe he would not have drawn his master's attention to such an important matter. In the teeth of ever-inflating implausibility, Wilson persisted in his well-I-didn't-know tactics, even going so far as to scapegoat his civil servants, Palliser and Burke Trend, who was secretary to the Cabinet at the time. It could have been an oversight on Palliser's part, due to pressure of work, was Wilson's line, while Burke Trend was fingered for not bringing the matter before the Cabinet, as he should have done. Among the hosts of people who evidently had difficulty in summoning up sufficient credence in Sir Harold's version of events was his party's International Committee, which declined to nominate him for re-election as Vice President of the Socialist International because of his embroilment in the oil sanctions scandal.

Of course, it was not Labour ministers alone who (to understate the matter) were under suspicion, since the charade of oil-swapping carried on after the Tories took office in 1970 and continued until the reversion to direct sanctions-busting in 1972, and this blatant flouting of British law and UN sanctions went on at least until 1976. 'Nobody knew and everybody knew, because we were collectively determined not to know,' Enoch Powell told his fellow MPs, unfairly, doubtless, to the Labour left and a few but not many others. But the situation was different for the Tories. In the first place they had what was - in terms of the party political cockpit at any rate - the near-perfect excuse that when they came to power they simply (in the words of their foreign affairs spokesman John Davies) 'carried on the policy established by the Labour Party'. And in the second place they did not have the same degree of proclaimed moral commitment as Labour to the defeat of a white-settler oligarchy (indeed, most Tory MPs had a great deal of sympathy for the rebel 'colons' and a sizeable section of their parliamentary party, not to mention the party in the country, was wholly opposed to sanctions), and, by the same token, they were much less susceptible than Labour to political damage from charges of dirty dealings arising from sanctions-busting revelations. The canniest Tories could see clearly enough that their best course was to sit back and enjoy the barney on the Government benches.

The biggest damage to Labour - since, sadly, it would be vain to pretend that this dishonourable affair was of great moment to the great body of the electorate - occurred within its own ranks, with further grave erosion of the faith of many active supporters in their leaders. Two weeks after the Bingham Report was published, an emergency resolution calling for a full public investigation and for prosecution of those implicated in breaking sanctions was passed by Party Conference. Further investigation into the extent to which ministers were in the know was also called for. 'Our reputation and our credibility as a party, as a government, and as a nation, is firmly on the line,' said Ernie Ross of AUEW-TASS in moving the resolution. The 89-year-old anti-colonialist and civil liberties campaigner Lord Fenner Brockway told Conference that, acting on information from Dr Kenneth Kaunda, he had warned the Wilson Government eleven years before that sanctions were being broken and was told that the Zambian President had been duped by a 'fabrication' planted on him. 'I'm not suggesting,' he said, 'that most of the members of our Labour Government at that time, or even of the Tory Government, were aware of what was happening. But some must have been, and even at the cost of some exposure, the integrity of our party demands that a full investigation - with all the Cabinet papers available - be made for our honour.'

West Aberdeenshire delegate Mrs Mary Panko said that it was only to be expected that the Tories, under Heath, were involved in the affair, 'But I'm damned if I will take it from a Labour government.' But like the rest of us, take it she had done, did, and would. When, at the beginning of November, Sir Harold offered to let Parliament see all the Cabinet papers relating to the breaking of the sanctions against Rhodesia, provided the other Prime Ministers concerned (i.e. Ted and Jim) agreed, was it at all Pygmalion likely that he was being serious, man? Or was he laughing up his sleeve, secure in the certainty that his fellow statesmen would see to it that an open and rigorous inquiry would never be up and running? It is true that, from an initial 'nyet' response from both Heath and Callaghan, they did make the political calculation that it would be more prudent to agree that Cabinet papers could be made available to a Special Commission of inquiry composed of members appointed from both Houses; but even that apparent major concession was hedged around with the proviso that the papers should first be scrutinised by the commission chairman, who would then decide whether or not they would be put before the commission!

(Moreover, the inquiry was to be held in private, in order - to quote the Lord Chancellor's subsequent assurance to his fellow peers - 'to limit the risk of public pillorying and limit the damage that might arise from the publication of Cabinet papers and documents.' Perhaps the fellow went in fear of the pillory himself, since his name was Lord Elwyn-Jones, and, as Sir Elwyn Jones, he had been the Attorney-General who, on 17th July 1968 - i.e. four months after the crucial meeting between Thomson and the British oil companies mentioned above - asking for adoption of the full mandatory sanctions ordered by the Security Council, told the

Commons: 'The move to comprehensive sanctions will make it much more difficult for sanctions breakers to carry out illicit deals under the cover of legitimate transactions.' Perhaps it is an earnest of Labour's resolve to stamp out sanctions-busting that, according to Elwyn Jones's successor as Attorney-General, our old friend Sam Silkin, in an answer in the Commons in the first week of November 1978, while the biggest fine for this crime had been £50,000, the smallest - was it for smuggling in chewing gum, or what? - had been a swingeing £10. And since the imposition of sanctions, there had been just 34 prosecutions, which suggests either that the general blockade was remarkably effective, or that it leaked like a sieve, perhaps because the responsible authorities had been turning a blind eye to other criminals besides the executives of the oil companies.)

Besides which, there was the longstop of the Lords, and there was every reason for confidence that the Tory peers would never wear it! (Someone really ought to make a study of how helpful the House of Lords has been to the Labour leadership!) When the proposal was put before the Lords, a week after going through the Commons, Lord Hailsham declared that 'Bingham was enough, perhaps too much', and that the Commons should not ask the House of Lords to 'compromise our own honour, our own integrity, and our fundamental constitutional principles.' His central objection was that full disclosure of what had gone on would break two vital constitutional principles: the confidentiality of advice given to ministers by civil servants and the confidentiality of Cabinet documents and discussions.

A ringing endorsement of his argument came from a former Minister of State at the Home Office. As an official adviser to Michael Stewart and Roy Jenkins in the early years of the oil scam, and at one time secretary to Hugh Gaitskell, Lord Harris of Greenwich (as the homespun John Harris had become in 1974) naturally spoke with strong fellow-feeling. 'I am certain many of my former colleagues must have approached the appointment of this body with a great deal of repugnance, breaking, as it does, virtually all the conventions that attach to the confidentiality of Cabinet and Ministerial discussions.' Lord Harris was one of four Labour peers (the others were Lord Paget of Northampton, the Reginald Paget who had represented that city from 1945 until his elevation in 1974; Lord Gordon-Walker, who as Patrick Gordon-Walker had once held the posts of both Commonwealth Secretary and Foreign Secretary; and Lord Glenamara, who before his transmogrification had been plain Ted Short, Deputy Leader of the Labour Party and Leader of the House of Commons) who joined the Tory peers in kicking out the Special Commission proposal by 102 votes to 58.

When the Commons had debated the matter, on 1st February 1979, it was the shadow leader of the House, Norman St John-Stevas, who made the most revealing remarks. 'We are embarking on a dangerous course - dangerous first of all to the reputation of this country,' he said, adding that the inquiry would be an 'inquisition into the whole process of government, and parliamentary government as we have known it, and into the assumptions on which it is based.' He was absolutely right: telling the people the truth could seriously damage the health of those running the body politic shop. All those who cherished our proud heritage of parliamentary government could breathe a deep sigh of relief at the common sense and steadiness of the Lords, and perhaps at the fact that, as St John-Stevas pointed out, they were at that moment in the midst of one of the gravest crises the country had faced since the war. Who had time, he might have added, to worry about Rhodesia's thirteen-year-old civil war (or what and who had fuelled it) while Britain was in the throes of its own civil war - the Winter of Discontent?

Two months almost to the day after Ian Smith's government plumped (on 11th November 1965) for UDI, Harold Wilson had told the Commonwealth Prime Ministers' meeting in Lagos: 'The cumulative effects of the economic and financial sanctions might well bring the rebellion to an end within a matter of weeks rather than months.' According to Lord Walston (who was Under Secretary of State at the Foreign Office from 1964-67; was identified by Bingham as the Government minister to whom BP and Shell first reported, in April 1966, the massive leakage of oil through the sanctions barrier around Rhodesia; who held informal talks with both the Portuguese foreign minister and the South African Prime Minister, Dr Vorster, to try to bring more pressure on Ian Smith to return to legality; and who claimed to have been a 'hawk' in favour of military intervention to break the rebellion), Wilson's astonishingly optimistic forecast was 'greeted by most of us [presumably behind Harold's back] with derision at the time. It was clearly not according to the facts of the case as known by virtually everyone.'

We have all heard of the man who thought his wife was a hat, so it is perhaps conceivable that Wilson believed his own upbeat rhetoric in Lagos; and it is just about possible that when he met Ian Smith on HMS *Tiger* in December 1966 for talks about terms for a return to legality, Wilson was unaware of the extent to which British oil companies were involved in sanctions-busting. But to ask history to believe that he was still as blissfully ignorant of this scandalous conduct by the time of his second fruitless meeting with Smith, on HMS *Fearless* in October 1968, is to stretch credulity thinner than the dough in *apfelstrudel*. Yet he went on acting out his talking-from-strength charade on the world's stage. Moreover, Britain had signalled, for all the world to see, that the principle from which she would not shift was NIBMAR ('no independence before majority rule'), yet if we are to take the word of Ian Smith's predecessor as Prime Minister of Rhodesia, Sir Edgar Whitehead, if the concessions offered by Wilson in the *Tiger* talks had been accepted by the rebels it would almost certainly have postponed the introduction of colour-blind majority rule 'beyond the end of the century'.

To top up the cup of gall proffered by Labour seigneurs for popular consumption, on the day that Ian Smith was granted a visa to visit the USA to seek support for his plans for progress towards majority rule, and that the Labour Party Conference debated the sanctions-busting scandal, the Deputy Leader of the Party and the Government, Michael Foot, told a Tribune rally, in the course of defending Jim Callaghan's decision to put off going to the country, that one of the reasons this was a good decision was that there had been a real danger that the Rhodesian crisis would have reached its climax during a general election in Britain, or at a time when there was either a Tory government or perhaps no effective government at all. The crowning irony in this tale of perfidy is that it was the Tories under Maggie Thatcher, with Lord Carrington leading the British Government's negotiating team, who, after fourteen years during which Britain (for most of the time under Labour) had, in effect, stood on the sidelines washing its hands in crocodile tears, at last brought the rebellion and civil war to an end, with the Lancaster House Agreement of December 1979, thereby making it possible for the fully-independent nation of Zimbabwe to come into being under majority rule in May 1980.

Like every other historical period, the Wilson-Callaghan years yielded a cornucopia of crimes of State power. Among the subjects which would have to appear in anything like a comprehensive survey, and regarding which the State would have a serious case to answer, would be: legal justice in Northern Ireland, the unaccountability of the security services, phone-tapping, police files, the 'sus' laws, the prison services, immigration law and administration, political asylum, secret treaties, secret 'defence' projects, suppression of the historical record and the related 30-year-rule delaying the release of documents. Instead of attempting such a survey, which in any case could only be tackled here in summary terms, I have chosen to recount two unsavoury stories at some length. Not just because they *are* spectaculars, but because, as the saying goes, the devil is in the detail, and only by looking at the details does one become aware, not simply of the general historical record, but *of the way we are governed.*

Everybody knows that absolute rulers commit crimes against their subjects; but the pretence in constitutional theory is that democratic States do not really have rulers and subjects: they have elected and accountable governments and citizens entitled to hold them to account. The reality is rather different. Lord George-Brown was absolutely right: all government, whatever steps may be taken to make it more open, is founded on secrecy, on keeping the governed in the dark, at least until it is too late for the governed to take over the governing. Only so can it work. Which (as St John-Stevas did not quite say) makes even representative government the enemy of democracy.

CHAPTER 31

Hope deferred

'We've found out in this war how we're all neighbours and we haven't got to forget it...We've been doing some hard thinking lately, and we haven't got-a stop when this job's finished. I mind you saying to me after the last war, this must never happen again. But it has happened. We stopped thinking ourselves and left it to other people...We've made a fine big war effort, and when it's all over we got to see we make a fine big peace effort. We can't go back now we've made a start. There's no two ways about it. Look at that Dunkirk. There wasn't no unemployed there. Every man had a job to do and he done it. And a job's what we got to see they have in peacetime. There mustn't be no more chaps hanging around for work what don't come. There mustn't be no more slums neither; no more dirty filthy backstreets, and no more half-starved kids with no room to play in. We can't go back to the old way of living. Leastways not all of it. That's gone for ever, and the sooner we make up our minds about that the better...We got-a all pull together. That's how I look at it anyway.'

So runs the dialogue between two elderly Home Guards, played by Percy Walsh and Bernard Miles, in *The Dawn Patrol*, a British wartime propaganda film produced by the Ministry of Information. What seems remarkable about it from the perspective of the very different ethos of half a century later is the confidence it exudes that it is expressing not some sectional viewpoint but a national consensus. Healthy scepticism might suggest that showing such a film in the nation's cinemas was just another cynical move in the never-ending game of getting the people to do the bidding of the powers that be, and some acquaintance with State propaganda when the British had their backs to the wall a generation earlier (the promises of making 'a land fit for heroes' and all that jazz) only lends credence to such a sour interpretation. Yet without getting starry-eyed about the Dunkirk spirit or whatever, there are good reasons for thinking that, for the first time ever, the British had indeed reached something like a national consensus.

In its homely way, *The Dawn Patrol* was calling for the slaying of the 'five giants' - Want, Disease, Ignorance, Squalor, and Idleness - named by Beveridge as barring the way 'on the road to reconstruction'. And the whole country was behind him. (This is one of those very rare instances in which such an assertion is almost literally true: The British Institute of Public Opinion reported an astonishing 86 per cent backing for the Beveridge Report, with support from employers and the upper middle classes almost as strong as from manual workers. For once the people had told the politicians in no uncertain manner what was 'in the national interest'.) If the same was less assuredly true of the party which had held sway for so long (and one must avoid the fallacy of giving all the credit to Labour for the establishment of a modern Welfare State in Britain: the Beveridge Committee, after all, was set up under the wartime coalition government; the Education Act of 1944 was primarily down to Rab Butler; the policy of establishing a National Health Service on an every-citizen's-right basis was endorsed by Churchill in March 1944 in a speech which made it clear that the purpose was 'to ensure that everyone in the country, irrespective of means, age, sex, or occupation, shall have equal opportunities to benefit from the best and most up-to-date medical services available'; and perhaps most importantly of all, in a White Paper of May 1944 the Government had pledged itself to maintain 'a high and stable level of employment after the war'), there were 'One-Nation' men in its ranks to remind their ultra-conservative colleagues of the likely consequences of opposing speedy and substantial reform.

'If you do not give the people social reform, they are going to give you social revolution,' Quintin Hogg, echoing Disraeli, had warned, as was noted in the last chapter of the section on the development of the Tory Party. When, to the astonishment of the Tories, an ungrateful country rejected the appeals of its great war-leader and returned Labour to power in July 1945, it looked to many people like the first step in a bloodless 'social revolution' which would at least deliver a markedly more democratic and egalitarian society. What was not easy to see in the euphoria and effulgence of that marvellous summer was that the foundations Attlee's Government was laying down were certainly not those for a classless society. There may have been no more suitable firm available, but Labour was simply the wrong builder for the construction of a Socialist democracy. What the people got from Labour was not so much a new contract - for a contract implies, however misleadingly, at least some measure of equality between the contracting parties) as a new - and admittedly kindlier - dispensation. There was a contract (an implicit one: a kind of 'gentlemen's agreement', in fact!), but it was between the new ringmasters of the political circus and an establishment whose power was not subject to the vicissitudes of electoral politics - the economic ruling class - and it precluded any serious pursuit of social transformation.

The unspoken deal was for Welfare Capitalism (with parliamentary democracy thrown in as a 'free gift', of course): a rockbed of security for the individual citizen, administered by the State, to deliver a basically contented and co-operative workforce to employers, with a dirigiste element not so much greater in scope than had already been seen in America under Roosevelt's New Deal. And ironically, the handling of the issue that had given some of them nightmares, nationalisation, could only reassure the men of property that they had little to fear from the New Order.

Firstly, the old rhetoric of general nationalisation had been dropped from Labour's official pronouncements, so that only basic industries, national transport and communications, and utilities - collectively constituting the nation's material infrastructure - were targeted. Secondly, there never was any question of confiscation, such as had been proposed by some of the more Socialist-minded members of the Party (R.H. Tawney, in his 1921 book *The Acquisitive Society*, for example) in the past. On the contrary, such generous compensation was paid to the dispossessed capitalists that they were frequently better off than they had ever been, considering the commonly rundown state of their former assets, while the 'pensions' they drew from the now State-owned enterprises remained a serious drain on national resources for many years afterwards. Thirdly, those appointed to head these State enterprises, as well as those placed in influential executive and consultative positions, were drawn largely from the ranks of the capitalists themselves.

Most comforting of all was the fact that it was obvious from the start that the new regime accepted that in the 'mixed economy' the private-enterprise sector would massively predominate, and indeed that the Labour junta preferred it that way. Second in importance only to this in putting to rest the fears of the rentier class, was the adoption of the Morrisonian conception of nationalisation (or as Morrison himself preferred to call it, presumably without intending irony, 'socialisation'): giant State corporations aping in most respects their private-sector counterparts. Organised from the top downwards, they displayed no more than a genuflection towards the principles of participatory democracy (with regard either to producers or to consumers) and showed scarcely more concern for accountability to the people through their representatives in Parliament. (With respect to the workforce in the public sector, attention has already been drawn to the large share of blame for acceptance of this undemocratic situation which attaches to the leaders of organised labour. Their failure to demand a bigger say for the workers in State enterprises - especially at the crucial moment of their establishment - may be ascribed in part to timidity or to a naive trust in their political counterparts, the Party leaders, but surely is primarily to be accounted for by the paternalistic and power-seeking attitudes they shared with them.)

Moreover, the State corporations were run primarily as a springboard for successful private enterprise, particularly with regard to international trade. This functional subservience, combined with the need to counter inflationary pressures, made it imperative to hold down wage rates in the public sector to as low a level as possible, and certainly below the 'rate for the job' in the private sector. Thus, as with State education and State provisions for looking after the health and general welfare of the working populace, far from undermining capitalism, nationalisation (as conceived and operated in Britain) shored it up by effectively subsidising the cost of labour.

Almost as baleful in its consequences as the conduct of this Caliban itself was the obsession it induced in the minds of Labourites with the ever-stale-to-putrid but never-quite-dead controversy over the whole issue of nationalisation. Should there be more of it? Should there be less of it? Should 'we' just hold on to what 'we' have? Tory acceptance of some measure of government control of the economy, including a degree of nationalisation, was a *sine qua non* of consensus, since it figured so largely in the minds of their principal adversaries. None the less, Tory instinct (which was not without cogent arguments to back it up) was, of course, to stem the dirigiste tide, and if possible to turn it back. Until the Thatcherite horde swept across the landscape, the Tory counter-offensives to claw back State-acquired enterprises were limited to a few industries like steel, sugar, and shipbuilding. But the battles over nationalisation, denationalisation, and renationalisation diverted attention (and proletarian vigour) from more significant issues, especially ones concerning social justice, to which the whole phoney war was quite irrelevant.

Labour's 'fine frenzy' of reform scarcely outlasted its first post-war period in office. It became obvious soon after it was returned to power in February 1950 that it had run out of steam, and that it was undecided or at odds as to its destination. Within little more than eighteen months Attlee, acting in the spirit of autocracy conferred upon him by Britain's glorious constitution, took an effectively unilateral decision to go to the country. Despite achieving its highest support ever, beating the Tories in its share of the poll by 48.8 to 48 per cent, Labour came out of the general election of October 1951 with 26 fewer seats than the Tories (whose overall majority was 15), largely because of the collapse of the Liberal vote - a lesson in the flaws of first-past-the-post voting systems which it failed to learn then, and perhaps never will learn. It had to wait fully thirteen years for its next chance to show what it could do.

Never mind! As noted at the beginning of this lamentable tale of Labour's downhill 'progress' since World War II, the leader of the Party (since December 1955), Hugh Gaitskell, and the PLP's super-egghead, Anthony Crosland, were satisfied that, while much remained to be done, the decisive battle had already been fought and won in 'this blessed isle': capitalism had been tamed and transformed. If not into a handy tool for fashioning 'the future of socialism' by each new Labour government as it took its turn in office, then at least (it was assumed) 'the people's governments' would have enough leverage to persuade the capitalists to co-operate with them.

At every stage in its life Labour has been excoriated, by assorted pundits basically antipathetic to socialistic and egalitarian objectives, for its reluctance to relinquish 'outmoded traditions' and to change with the times. But Crosland's widely-acclaimed achievement in rethinking Socialism was actually to downsize the dreams - *and the undertakings* - of the Labour Movement almost to vanishing point. Mind you, in one respect his thinking was, *pro tempore*, sound (although naturally this was not a point he was keen to draw attention to). As long as the consensus lasted (and in those days few in establishment circles foresaw its demise), it did not make a great deal of difference which of the contenders was, for the time being, in power: the capitalist tiger would be contained within 'tolerable bounds' by Keynesian economic adjustments and its ravages would be redressed by Welfare State provisions. And so we dreamt and drifted through those 'thirteen wasted years' ('wasted', in particular, for the PLP's ambitious understudies waiting in the wings for their turn to 'strut their stuff'), during which, however much it lagged behind the more royal progress of other nations, Britain's GNP grew steadily and almost everyone's standard of living rose, so that it was simply a matter of fact and a cause for mutual gratification when Harold Macmillan pointed out that: 'Most of our people have never had it so good.'

To the extent that they felt this to be true, most people were naturally little concerned about which party was in power or whether the government and its policies could be described as more or less 'socialistic': if the kind of capitalism that was on offer seemed to be working for them, they were 'not bothered'. That was obvious from the general election results (Macmillan's 1959 victory - the third in a row for his party - was unprecedented, and raised the Tory catch to its highest point ever, 13,749,830 votes); but it was spelt out more explicitly by the public opinion pollsters, who reported a diminishing number of 'loyal voters' as the years went by. In 1951 only about a fifth of those questioned said it made little difference which party was in power; by 1964, assuming the opinion polls accurately reflected the views of the nation, nearly a third of the electorate thought it hardly mattered who won the elections.

That was the year in which Labour's new leader - elected to succeed Gaitskell after his death in January 1963 - just managed to wrest the reins of government from Supermac's successor, Alec Douglas-Home. Harold Wilson was the first Labour leader since the war who had a left-wing reputation. But what he offered the country was not a Socialist but a 'scientific' revolution, a moderate commonsensical Englishman's version of the 'scientific socialism' which had supposedly prevailed in Russia since the Revolution. Just as 'electricity' was a talisman for the Bolsheviks, so 'advanced technology' was to be Labour's Excalibur. The recipe for a regenerated 'land of hope and glory' included a smidgen of the Stalinists' equation of Socialism with State planning and industrialisation and a generous dollop of their obsessive concern with productivity.

Of course, for both geophysical and ideological reasons, a command economy like that of the Soviet Union was (blessedly!) not in the frame in Harold's swinging Britain, though his party continued to invest a deal of faith (though not much else) in a pallid version of State capitalism. However, the reality beneath a rhetoric which lent the appearance of a deep divide between Labour and its opponents was the confirmation of Labour's capitulation to capitalism. The strategy, such as it was, of 'harnessing science to socialism' (see Chapter 12) depended for its success on a formula acceptable to all the parliamentary parties because it threatened none of them: producing more and selling more in a highly competitive global marketplace where the conditions of trade were set by free-enterprise capitalism; and so to creep and crawl towards the millennium of an ubiquitous prosperity (within the bounds of our own 'promised land', that is) which the Party might plausibly represent as the 'virtual reality' of Socialism.

Such at least appeared to be the situation so long as those Party people whose opinions really counted (those who were of Labour's own upper class) were not prepared to grasp the nettle of redistribution. And the premise of the Age of Consensus - of the maintenance of an equilibrium that might, according to personal and party apperceptions of a well-adjusted polity, swing gyroscopically gently out of balance of a focal point subliminally-projected but mutually-apprehended by the chattering classes, without upsetting the basic stability (i.e. without fundamentally disrupting the status quo!) - was that capitalism would deliver ever higher standards of living to everyone. This would happen, whatever the starting points on the magic moving staircase, thereby reducing controversial questions concerning the redistribution of wealth and income to no more than subsidiary, if not quite marginal, problems.

While its acceptance by the Party establishment and its 'loyalist' henchmen betrayed their minimal concern for social justice, the premise did retain a certain air of plausibility throughout the fifties and sixties, despite the somewhat sluggish and erratic performance of the British economy and the sterling crises which partially crippled Wilson's 'scientific revolution'. But the first major oil crisis, of 1973 (see Chapter 21), trashed the illusion that capitalism could be depended on to deliver ever greater national prosperity, and that, with a minimum of fiscal tinkering, 'social justice' would trickle down to everybody. It took another fistful of years for the crunch to come; but the consensus between the parties, which previously only Labour's 'outside left' had seriously challenged, came increasingly to be recognised as no longer viable. No one put the situation more bluntly than anti-poverty campaigner Frank Field: 'The promise to the "haves" was that injustice could be painlessly removed...Economic growth would guarantee that the real income of the "haves" rose while only part of the largesse was transferred to the "have nots"'. And he warned that Labour would be forced to choose between abandoning reform and breaking the consensus. (See Chapter 19)

But the Party leaders - unlike the advance guard of the rampant New Toryism - lacked either the conviction or the courage (or perhaps both) to make a clear choice. Their dilemma was already an old one when Field challenged them. It could be traced through every deflationary and regressive Labour budget measure since 1964. But the embracing of the monetarist doctrines of their supposed political enemies by Healey and Callaghan in 1975/76 (see Chapter 21) should have made it clear to all but the incurably myopic (who would have to await the Winter of Discontent for the scales to be torn from their eyes) that a choice had been made, and that it was a choice in favour of the interests of capital, not of labour - not of working people, and still less of the poor!

Having almost completely abandoned the idea of extending public ownership as a route towards Socialism; having been proved deceived in their faith that capitalism with a light Keynesian touch on the tiller would deliver the goods, so that redistribution to bring about their 'minimum standard of decency' conception of social justice (see Chapter 18) could happen almost unnoticed, without pain and above all without confiscation; and finding themselves economically becalmed, or worse, in choppy seas; in order to sustain their new status as national statesmen, Labour's leaders turned on their own followers, substituting control of the masses for their emancipation. Except in the most extreme circumstances, an amorphous population is little to be feared by its governors; workers organised under their own leaders are quite another matter. So of course controlling the masses took the form, above all, of deploying the machinery of the State to rein in the unions - a task in which they were perfidiously abetted by not a few captains of the workers' battalions. (With due allowance for the constrictions imposed on authority by an established system of parliamentary democracy, it was not so different really from the terrible story of the aftermath of the Russian Revolution, in which the proletariat was enslaved by its 'liberators' partly through the instrument of its own organisations. Different at least principally in degree rather than in principle; and, in the final analysis, in spirit hardly different at all from the Thatcherites' brimstone-and-treacle prescriptions for industrial peace.)

Hence the slanderous attacks by Labour leaders on militant unionism (the Party was hardly back in office after those 'thirteen wasted years' than its reputedly left-wing leader was denouncing, with sublime even-handedness, 'luddites' whether in the boardrooms or the trade unions; while little more than a month after consolidating his power in the spring election of 1966, he was diligently denigrating 'England's' ever-exploited seamen by dubbing them dupes of Communist conspirators who had inveigled them into striking 'against the State, against [note the cunning conflation of quite separate species] the community') which accompanied the never-relinquished claims for Corporate-State-like control of wages and regulation of the unions; hence the abortive attempt to override the disappointingly cautious counsel of the Donovan Commission by imposing the gospel according to Saint Barbara; and hence the ever-rising strife in Callaghan's kingdom which finally drowned Labour's dreams in the Winter of Discontent.

Hence, too, in the decades of disillusionment and desertion which followed the debacle, the substantive endorsement by Her Majesty's Loyal Opposition, of the reforms by which the New Tories hamstrung the organisations which constitute the only effective countervailing force (short of revolution) against capitalism's unrelenting drive for a cheap and pliable workforce to man its machines. Their record in office shows that this accommodation to the agenda of their political opponents was no painful one for most of the Labour Party leaders, nor for a solid core of 'loyal' or simply careerist Labour back-benchers. (Yesteryear's 'beer and sandwiches at No. 10' - the jibe the Press has never grown tired of - only went to show that usually a deal could be done with the union bosses to keep the lads in order, as it had been most momentously in 1926.) But the morale-sapping years of rejection at the polls, with a shocking rout in '83 succeeded by a deeply disappointing defeat in '87 and an absolutely 'gobsmacking' one in '92, induced more shameful accommodations: dishonest concessions to the specious claims of the caterpillar classes that universal welfare - even, perhaps, universal health care, and in the end universal education - has come to cost more than the country can afford and will have to be cut back to a more basic (or if you would rather put it that way, minimally 'decent') level, with everyone having the 'choice' of topping things up for themselves and their families with 'their own money'. In short, that for the satisfaction of desires beyond this basic State-guaranteed level, it has to be left to 'the market' to supply the wherewithal to match what is called in the ludicrous cant of capitalist economics 'demand'. For Labour's leaders, it was anything, anything at all, to exorcise the spectre still crying out for redistributive justice! Until things had reached such a pass that in many matters concerning 'the condition of the people', including the will to wield taxation in such a way as to 'shake the superflux' from the grasp of 'the stinking rich', Labour had ended up markedly to the right of the heirs of the Liberal Party.

This soft-shoe shuffle rightwards provoked, in the dying days of Labour rule and in the early years of the Thatcherite hegemony before Labour morale collapsed, a campaign within the Party and the Movement to reduce the huge deficit between democratic principle and oligarchic (not to say autocratic) practice in Labour's decision-making processes - a campaign which reached its climax in a pyrrhic victory for 'the democrats' at the Special Conference at Wembley in 1981. It had actually taken an eternity for this perennial burning issue to come to the boil. Time and again throughout the whole life of the Labour Party the issue had flared into open conflict. But, to restrict the tale to the post-war years and to put the matter in a most summary fashion, the indictment was that while party activists had indefatigably puffed out their dream signals (about 'capturing the commanding heights of the economy', 'effecting an irreversible shift in the balance of power and wealth in favour of working people', etc., etc., etc.) and diligently drafted resolutions and prospectuses for putting them into practice (an 'Alternative Economic Strategy', a 'Social Contract', a 'Wealth

Tax', and so on and so on, *ad astra*) - *and* succeeded in persuading Conference to support them - the Labour leaders had responded patronisingly by lecturing them on political realities, or simply shrugged their shoulders without bothering to waste their breath, and got on (as one children's story puts the facts of political life) with their 'ruling and fighting'.

The crux of the matter was (and is) the contradiction between the constitutional *fiction* of the sovereignty of Conference (together with the subsidiary fiction of the supreme authority of the NEC between one Conference and the next) and the insurmountable *fact* of the actual autonomy of the PLP. It is insurmountable (except, of course, by insurrection) because it is rooted in the higher authority of the State constitution, which confers on Members of Parliament - as representatives not of political parties but of geographical conglomerates of electors - the right to decide what is best for the national polity. Thus the reality behind the theory of representative government (in which 'the sovereign people' are represented by a 'sovereign parliament' which they have elected, but effective power is in most circumstances in the hands of a caucus called the Cabinet, headed by a Prime Minister with quasi-autocratic powers) is in effect imposed on the political parties competing for parliamentary seats, regardless of what their own constitutions lay down.

The Labour Party's assimilation of and by what must be - of all the national constitutions with any claim at all to being 'democratic' - the most centralised and the most hierarchical of all (so much so that with respect to a party in power the situation approximates to 'democratic centralism'!) has practically guaranteed its inutility as a tool for social transformation. Perhaps no commentator has made this point more forcefully than Gregory Elliott does in his remarkable synoptical history and critique of the Labour Party, *Labourism and the English Genius* (1993). And it is a point which is so fundamental to the issue of radical reform in quest of a more equal society that it reduces (relatively speaking) to little more than academic interest the complex question of the degree of democracy which the Labour Party theoretically offers its members and the long and involved tale of conflict between leaders and led in the Party and the Movement, a story which has often been told in part but, to my knowledge, has never been given the full treatment it merits as a study in the myths and realities of institutional democracy.

One possible objection to the case I have been making is that Labour never has been a Socialist party. It is a point that is made, with varying shades of sincerity, from diametrically-opposed standpoints, by radical left-wing critics (commonly of Marxist or semi-Marxist persuasion) and by 'moderate' apologists intent on fending off left-wing criticism. From the left, Gregory Elliott makes the point with characteristic incisiveness:

> 'Labour is not now - and never has been - a socialist party. Throughout its history it has comprised a coalition of *social reformers* and *reformist socialists*, the latter in a permanent minority, whether among parliamentarians, trade unionists or individual members. As its very name suggests, Labour was founded to advance the interests of the labouring class within capitalism, via reforms, not to create a qualitatively different form of society; to *ameliorate*, not *abolish*, capitalism. At the same time however, the accretions of the 1919 Constitution - in pride of place, Clause 4 section (4) on the 'common ownership of the means of production' - have bred the illusion, stretching far beyond Labour's own ranks, that Labour has been committed to the goal of socialism, its members differing not over the destination, but only as to tactics and timing; or, when this became unsustainable, that a socialist rank and file was pitted against a treacherous leadership from whom the party could be rescued. As recent events have demonstrated, the leadership/ ordinary members dichotomy is a myth, though a beguiling one, inspiring the everlasting project of restoring the Labour Party to a socialist vocation it has never possessed.' [author's emphases]

All of this is true (as well as, incidentally, being uncontaminated by any desire to excuse, or at least to extenuate, Labour's gross historical failure), and it is a most important truth; but paradoxically it is to an extent misleading. Yes, committed Socialists have always been in the minority in the Party, and one might go further and say that they have had a wholly disproportionate influence, at least on its propaganda nexus with the public. But then activists, by definition, always do have a disproportionate influence on whatever group within which they are operating, and in politics activists tend to be more *ideologically* committed than others; or, to put it the other way round, their ideological commitment tends to make them activists. In a sense, they tend to be 'extremists', accentuating the differences between their party and other parties. So it is only to be expected that in the Labour Party commitment has more often than not meant advocating 'more socialism'.

As with the Party proper, so with the larger Movement. So that it is by no means as clear as Elliott's statement suggests that in the political *life* of the Party and the Movement and their constituent parts (i.e. in the expression of their 'democratic will') Socialists have always, or even usually, been in the minority. Without in any way implying the existence of a similar measure of support for each side of the perpetual left-right argument, Labour's story might be better described as a ceaseless contest between activist 'mods' ('moderates' or 'modernisers', it makes little difference) and activist 'rockers' (radicals who, by taking Labour's and their own rhetoric seriously, rock the boat) for the ear and the support of those in the wider Movement and the world outside it, i.e. of the electorate.

(Incidentally, it is pointless, if not disingenuous, to complain that the disproportionate influence of activist minorities usurps the rights of 'silent majorities', since - without getting bogged down in the intractable problem of distinguishing between actual 'public opinion' and its often tendentiously *assumed* varieties - 'mass democracy' only works, inasmuch as it may be considered to work at all, through the agency of those prepared *actively* to participate in its processes. It is the self-evident truth that democracy cannot be *passive* which makes what we call 'representative democracy' a contradiction in terms. All of which highlights the fact that activists who are 'moderates' - i.e. whose attitudes are more or less conservative with a small c - are no less part of the minority who are active than are 'extremist' activists.)

There are also problems - despite their reasonableness and their usefulness as descriptive terms - with Elliott's antithesis between *social reformers* and *reformist socialists*. It is not that the distinction itself is not clear, but that those so distinguished have frequently failed to see that there is such a distinction and that, if they had seen it, they would probably have been even less clear as to which category they belonged. They might even quite reasonably have claimed to belong to both! This is, of course, one of those irresolvable problems in analysis, especially when applied to a subject such as human thought and behaviour, in which inconsistencies are endemic.

One can illustrate the difficulty by pointing out that as late as the mid-nineties, by which time a sober-sided and utterly dependable Party had begun openly courting the middle class, on the pretext that it had been vilely abused by its long-cohabiting Tory partner, the personable New Labour leader would still now and again speak of 'democratic socialism'. Flatulent rhetoric, no doubt, largely attributable to concern for keeping on board the Party's 'other ranks', or at least the old soldiers amongst them. Not altogether, though. In some instances the use of such obsolescent language by Labour politicians and supporters is surely to be ascribed to lack of understanding of what they are saying (as is shown by the growing practice, approved at the highest level, of treating 'democratic socialism' and 'social democracy' as if they were interchangeable terms) - and even of who they are: a cognitive and identity problem compounded and confounded.

Indeed, the emphatic and utterly unequivocal nature of Elliott's analysis raises the problem of just how seriously we are to take the socialistic-sounding pronouncements made on occasion by every Labour leader over the years. For instance, to go back more than half a century, but only two-thirds of the way back through the Party's lifetime on which he comments so confidently, what are we to make of Attlee's unambiguous endorsement of Socialist doctrines and values in *The Labour Party in Perspective*, samples of which have been displayed earlier? Are we to take him at his word - or at least his word in 1937 - or not? It may be that Elliott would be prepared to make such a charge, but what more damning indictment could there be than the assertion that all such pronouncements by Labour leaders never were more than hot air to stoke up the fire in the bellies of their followers?

Indeed, the emphatic and utterly unequivocal nature of Elliott's analysis raises the problem of just how seriously we are to take the socialistic-sounding pronouncements made on occasion by every Labour leader over the years. For instance, to go back more than half a century, but only two-thirds of the way back through the Party's lifetime on which he comments so confidently, what are we to make of Attlee's unambiguous endorsement of Socialist doctrines and values in The Labour Party in Perspective, samples of which have been displayed earlier? Are we to take him at his word - or at least his word in 1937 - or not? It may be that Elliott would be prepared to make such a charge, but what more damning indictment could there be than the assertion that all such pronouncements by Labour leaders never were more than hot air to stoke up the fire in the bellies of their followers?

One of the paradoxes of political thought in Labour circles is that, despite the Party's affiliation to an international movement which coalesces around a body of ideas we recognise as kindred enough to be grouped under the common ideological term Socialism, many Labour politicians are as wary of the very concept of ideology as are most of their Tory opponents. Which does not, of course, mean that there *is* no ideology behind their political projects (indeed, that the truth is quite the reverse has already been demonstrated with respect to Tory thinking in Part One of this essay). It is only that those who do not recognise its presence disable themselves of the possibility of scrutinising it, and thus of explaining it to others, as well as - and even more importantly - of justifying it to themselves or of amending it because they cannot justify it. For Tories this *un*perceiving is in some ways a strength, since it bolsters their self-assurance by hiding from themselves their own prejudices. (Besides, in any context with any claim at all to being democratic, what they really stand for will not stand the light of day for a full five minutes.) For Labourites it is a grave weakness, unless they subconsciously subscribe to pretty much the same tenets as their political rivals.

Distrust of ideological thinking is so prevalent among British and American politicians that it has been identified as an Anglo-Saxon characteristic; but it would be more rational to ascribe it to the more evolutionary development of society and politics in Anglo-Saxon lands than to postulate a predilection for pragmatism peculiar to the progeny of their native soil. At all events, Labour politicians tend to pride themselves on their pragmatic approach to issues, as if to think too deeply about them is to disable oneself when it comes to making practical decisions. (The same is true of union leaders in Britain - as well as in America - and while this may have little effect on their day-to-day activities, since their immediate concerns are of a more practical nature than those of the politicians, the long-term effects of this limitation in modes of thinking are surely of vast if incalculable significance.) For the most part they reject Marxism (or rather, the ersatz condensed concoctions they take to be the bones of the matter) without coming anywhere near to understanding it, and they are temperamentally hostile towards anti-Statist forms of Socialism like Anarchism and Anarcho-Syndicalism, their conceptions of which are even more rudimentary and distorted.

But the point is not that they accept or reject any particular ideology ('ethical socialism' might serve if those who subscribe to it had taken the trouble to work out exactly what it meant to them, so that they could offer us a clear and honest prospectus, instead of fecklessly using the expression as an easy way of distancing themselves from more managerial forms of socialism, including what they benightedly call 'communism'). It is that, by neglecting rigorously to examine the bases of their own thinking and to analyse the structure of society and identify the forces within it which they might harness to haul it towards clearly denoted destinations, they disarm themselves against imposture - inflicted against themselves as well as against others! They suffer from the failing reprehended by J.S. Mill as 'the inability of the unanalytic mind to recognise its own handiwork' - and more to the point, we suffer from the botched handiwork of their inept operations on society! Such food as they offer the intellect on the subject of Socialism and its prescriptions for curing social ills is about as nourishing as the diet in a World War II POW camp run by the Japanese army. For the most part it is insipid, sloppy stuff about 'the brotherhood of man' and the like, samples of which we have already tasted. (See Chapter 25). The prize for the ultimate pronouncement in the 'pragmatic socialism' genre has got to go to Herbert Morrison's definition of Socialism as 'what Labour governments do', but scarcely more illuminating is Nye Bevan's blinding revelation that 'Socialism is about priorities'. All this shows an indifference to, if not a contempt for, serious thinking about Socialist principles - perhaps even of serious thinking about principles, full stop. No wonder the 'socialist' faith of Old Labour could not make a stand against the evangelising fervour of the New Tories!

It is no accident that the only unmistakably socialistic doctrine in the Labour Party's constitution (which is almost entirely concerned with organisational matters) should again and again have

447

become a bone of contention between the Party's leaders and the Movement's rank and file - or at least enough of them to produce some pretty ferocious dogfights. I refer, of course, to the clause introduced into the constitution in 1918 (see the extract above from Gregory Elliott's book) as one of the (ultimately seven) 'Party objects'. As amended, this famous - or as some would have it, infamous - clause reads as follows:

> 'To secure for the workers by hand or by brain the full fruits of their industry and the most equitable distribution thereof that may be possible upon the basis of the common ownership of the means of production, distribution, and exchange, and the best obtainable system of popular administration and control of each industry or service.'

The clause is more famous than familiar. which is to say, more read than understood and more talked about than read, otherwise it could not have given rise to so much accidental (as distinct from deliberate) misrepresentation. Three or four observations are indispensable. Its first *and* primary point echoes the historic demand that workers should enjoy the fruits of their labour and calls for the equitable distribution of the wealth they produce. Outrageous demands indeed! It nowhere mentions nationalisation, which make its references to 'common ownership' etc. and to 'the best obtainable system of popular administration and control' etc. open to wide interpretation - even among the intellectually honest. It is followed by a fifth objective ('generally to promote the political, social and economic emancipation of the people, and more particularly of those who depend directly upon their own exertions by hand or by brain for the means of life') framed in much more general - and thus vaguer - terms, which nevertheless gains strength from the specifics of Clause IV (4). (Incidentally, in his entry on this offensive clause in his *Brewer's Politics*, Nicholas Comfort points to an intriguing parallel in the subversive thinking of the American president who also gave us that dangerous definition of democracy as 'government of the people, by the people, for the people'. Abraham Lincoln concluded his contribution to a discussion of tariff law which took place in 1847 with the remark that to secure 'for each laborer the whole product of his labor, or nearly as possible, is a most worthy object of any good government'.)

Such was Labour's covenant with those dependent 'upon their own exertions...for the means of life' which - within a few years of the Party's brief chapter of glory in leading a nation reforged in fire - faint-hearts had concluded was inimical to the re-election of Labour to power. For timorousness or treachery had set in long before Tony Blair made his successful bid (in 1994-95) for the extinguishing of the clause which 'the lost leader', Neil Kinnock, had contemptuously dismissed as 'tunes of glory'. At the post-mortem conference following Labour's third successive general election defeat in 1959, Hugh Gaitskell, wilfully misrepresenting the offending clause as calling for '100 per cent state ownership' and as implying that that was 'the only precise object we have', called for its deletion from the constitution. He was rebuffed, but (as Comfort puts it) the 'modernisers' continued to see it 'as an albatross' around the Party's neck.

The Labour left saw it quite otherwise. It helped them cling to their hope that the Party might yet prove to be an agency for social transformation. The myths and realities behind the tenacious defence of Clause IV are well expressed by Tony Cliff and Donny Gluckstein in *The Labour Party - A Marxist History* (1988):

> 'In a body where symbolism frequently outweighs reality, this is the holy of holies. It is the most pious of Labour's many pious resolutions, yet its words are important. They mark *the conversion of the Labour Party into a 'socialist' organisation, or, to be more exact, a mass reformist party* distinct from the two openly capitalist parties...it was drafted by [Sidney] Webb...*as a conscious means of staving off revolution.* It was the fear of mass action which forced them to take this step...There is an important difference between Clause Four in 1918 and Clause Four today. Seventy years ago it registered the high water mark of workers' pressure on the Labour Party. Since then the imminence of revolution has never been so great. But Clause Four remains in the party constitution - a relic of days gone by. In this sense it must now be defended as a sign of Labour's commitment to a minimal anti-capitalist

position which some leaders would like to forget.'
[authors' emphases]

Gregory Elliott, in the paragraph following the passage from *Labourism and the English Genius* quoted above, declares firmly: 'Although the revisionist enterprise of amending the 1918 Constitution faltered, Labour did in fact make the transition from Clause 4 "socialism" to social democracy *in the late 1950s and early 1960s.*' [author's emphasis] At the time few of those on the left can have recognised that - despite their rout of the revisionists - the decisive transition of which Elliott writes had occurred. Paradoxically, perhaps this was just as well, since there was no alternative *parliamentary* channel for propagating Socialist solutions to society's problems (nor will there be as long as Britain's absurd first-past-the-post system of electoral gambling prevails). As for the contentious clause itself, it remained of totemic importance to the Left, and as late as 1983 was overwhelmingly reaffirmed as 'the central aim of the Labour Party', with Conference explicitly demanding 'repossession of all parts of the public sector privatised by the Tories.'

It may be that the Left's staunch attachment to Clause IV was largely to be accounted for by continuing support within the Party for nationalisation. By 1987, however, under the hammer blows of the Thatcherite 'counter-revolution', this particular enthusiasm had waned to such an extent that the NUM resolution to Conference calling for all industries privatised by the Tories to be renationalised was heavily defeated. Doubtless what persuaded delegates to give up their addiction was the pusillanimous argument that to renationalise the industries concerned would entail paying the new private 'owners' something in the region of £15 billion. And given the unfortunate focusing of Labour minds on the secondary issue of public ownership called for in the second part of section (4) of Clause IV, this 'how can we possibly afford to buy back our own property?' defeatism may well explain why the Party's single explicitly Socialist aspiration was eventually consigned to 'the dustbin of history' with relative ease.

For others, however, the question of public or private ownership of 'the means of production, distribution, and exchange' is not, *in itself*, of paramount importance (though the impact which different forms of ownership may have on the kind of society we live in is quite another matter). For such Socialists it is the issue of social justice which is at the heart of the matter. Shortly after Tony Blair's slyly oblique targeting of Clause IV at his first Conference as Party leader, a history research student at Sussex University, Jacqueline Tratt, in a piece written for the 'Face to Faith' column of *The Guardian*, lamented 'the death of Labour's Clause Four' as 'final acknowledgement of the triumph of competition and the market'. She put down the moral impasse we are in to the fact that: 'In the post-Thatcher era, there are not enough votes any more in social justice. The Labour Party has learned the lesson and is adapting its policies and constituency accordingly...'

'And after fifteen years out of office,' she goes on, 'who can blame them?' But that is being altogether too charitable. My own critique is grounded in the conviction that while it may be possible for Labour to abandon all commitment to Socialism without serious damage to its reputation (its moral reputation, that is; its cerebral reputation is another matter), it cannot without dishonour desert the cause of social justice. One can see the logic of the case for ditching the old Clause IV - even if one cannot agree with it and cannot respect the dissembling fashion in which it was foisted on the Party. But healthy scepticism could not but question whether (as was claimed) honesty, with itself and with others (honestly admitting, that is, that bringing about 'the common ownership of the means of production, distribution, and exchange' was not now, if it ever had been, the Party's aim), was the real reason for the determination of the 'modernisers' to amend Labour's constitution. Was it not, rather, the almost antithetical concern for flexibility, for room to manoeuvre, to avoid being pinned down by the mercenaries of a hostile media?

After all, the best safeguard against being charged with failing to deliver on promises is not to make any. But since that is hardly a practicable strategy for winning over the voters, politicians usually fall back on the second-best safeguard, which is to make promises which are so general in character (such as, 'to improve the country's economic performance and raise standards of living', or even, 'to strengthen the position and prestige of the nation in the world') that it is often difficult to disprove their claims to have fulfilled them. Vagueness is the politician's friend, which is why an abstract principle like 'social justice', which needs a lot of defining to mean much at all, is much to be preferred as a declared objective to the old 'full fruits of their industry' promise, while 'fairness' is even better, since it is so flexible as to mean whatever its advocate chooses it to mean. (Nothing illustrates this better than what that pre-eminent precursor of the Blairite 'modernisers', Anthony Crosland, did to the word 'equality' by liberating it from the sordid shackles of being thought of as having some connection at least with considerations of material wealth.)

In Clause IV as refashioned for the dawn of the new millennium (the old millennium of the mind, having signally failed to live up to its promise, could pass away unmourned except by eccentrics) one ancient relic remained, in the astonishingly bold declaration that Labour was 'a democratic socialist party'. But the main engine for its stated aspirations was clearly to be private capitalism, surfing the seas of the 'free market' somehow (unlike the merchants in the Temple) on a wing and a prayer, *in the public interest*. And Labour's new Clause IV passes the acid test for flexibility with flying colours. Although it is true that those parties contending with Labour for 'the trust of the people to govern' (as the final words of the glossy rewrite puts it) would have placed the emphasis on different aspects of the goodies on display, apart from that haunting echo of the bold challenges of a more heroic age just mentioned, there is nothing to which *any* of them could take exception. Or not openly at any rate!

Not that there is anything wrong with what New Labour says it 'believes', it 'is committed to', and it 'will work for'. All, all, are honourable aspirations - if they are more than pious hopes. Which is to say, *if* - despite the unpromising withdrawal from socialistic solutions and the present invisibility of convincing alternative solutions - the words express an underlying and invincible will *for something like a transformation of society*. For nothing short of such a transformation can turn those aspirations into realities.

And the trouble is we have been waiting (and not *just* waiting, either, but working. too) for such promises to be fulfilled for half a century or more, those of us whose lives span the years from the war to stop the tidal wave of conquest unleashed by the great dictators, and perhaps go back to (in J.B. Priestley's words in his trenchant *Letter to a Returning Serviceman*) 'the sickening muddle, darkening to tragedy, of the Twenties and Thirties'. And as it says in *Proverbs*: 'Hope deferred maketh the heart sick.'

In an article written for *The Guardian* four months before

the shock re-endorsement of the Tory hegemony in April 1992, Dennis Kavanagh spoke of the irony that 'Mrs Thatcher changed Labour more than she changed her own party. As her own party discreetly tries to distance itself from her, so Labour has come to terms with much of her work.' Entitled 'The phoney wars', the article makes two further salutary observations for the consideration of those disposed to put their faith, or at least to invest too much hope, in returning Labour to power. The point is not spelt out, but the first and more fundamental observation implicitly warns against expecting too much of changes of government in our kind of society. 'Apart from political careers and party fortunes, do general elections actually make much difference?...The only post-war elections that can be said to have made a difference...were those of 1945 and 1979, and historians may well conclude that even then the new governments confirmed change that was already under way.' The second observation relates to those incredibly enduring illusions about the Labour Party. 'Mrs Thatcher said that she wanted to kill off socialism in Britain, and it is often said that she did so. This is wrong; it died long ago. Under Wilson and Callaghan Labour was concerned above all with gaining and retaining office. Party politics was a battle between the ins and the outs.'

Of course, one can only choose between choices which actually exist (or in exceptional circumstances such as revolutions can perhaps be made to exist), and for anyone with any sense of the fundamentally equal worth of all human beings there is simply no contest between New Labour and the New Tories. Launching a UNICEF report in 1993, the fund's (since deceased) American executive director, Jim Grant, expressed his faith that:

> 'The day will come when the progress of nations will be judged not by their military or economic strength, nor by the splendour of their capital cities and public buildings, but by the well-being of their peoples: by their levels of health, nutrition, and education: by their opportunities to earn a fair reward for their labours: by their ability to participate in the decisions that affect their lives: by the respect that is shown for their civil and political liberties: by the provision that is made for those who are vulnerable and disadvantaged: and by the protection that is afforded to the growing minds and bodies of their children.'

Now that would be worth voting for; and a Labour Party with a real commitment to social justice would be a social reform party worth supporting and working for, even if its new aspirations fell sadly short of its old ones.

But what assurance can we reasonably feel (even if we are sanguine enough to believe that private capitalists in general can somehow be cajoled, cudgelled, or otherwise manoeuvred into a position few of them or their predecessors have ever taken before - a position, that is, of making 'the public interest' their paramount concern) that New Labour will deliver on its (admittedly far more modest) promises where Old Labour for the most part failed? Just over a century ago, in the course of a lecture on the American economist Henry George, whose *Progress and Poverty* was creating such a stir on both sides of the Atlantic, the social philosopher and philanthropist Arnold Toynbee apologised to his working-class audience for the indifference and callousness which had generally characterised the attitude of 'the middle classes...not merely the very rich' towards their hard and not infrequently dire situation. 'Instead of justice we have offered you charity,' he said.

It is difficult (perhaps impossible) for people of a paternalistic turn of mind to recognise the difference. But to my way of thinking Charity was what Labour offered the ordinary people - the real wealth-creators - of post-war Britain. And after it had been chipped away as Britain's relative ranking in the league of nations' wealth listings declined, in order not to jeopardise the privileged life-styles of the seriously rich and those hanging on to their coat-tails, it turned out to be meagre charity at that. Social Justice never was seriously on the agenda.

That is the truth, and we should not hide it from ourselves. Old Labour never came anywhere near to being as good as its word. Maybe, by some miracle of self-transformation, New Labour will shape up to its more modest proposal of ushering in an age of kinder capitalism supervised by 'democratically-elected' paternalists - a proposal not so different really from Plato's ideal of rule by philosopher-kings!

PostScript

Not long after writing this I re-read Michael Young's far-sighted look into the future, *The Rise of the Meritocracy: 1870-2033*, which was first published in 1958. It occurred to me that nothing could provide a more fitting postscript (or should one rather say 'post-mortem'?) for the sorry tale of the Labour Party than the following passage from that scintillating satire:

> 'The Labour Party made the inevitable compromise with the new society it had done so much to create: it ceased to exist. Fewer and fewer electors, however brawny, responded instinctively to the appeal of "labour". Drawn upwards by their aspirations for their children...[they] conceived of themselves as a cut above the labourer at the bottom of the heap. The canny leaders of the...Party...recognised full well the need for change. They scrapped the appeal to working-class solidarity and concentrated on the middle class, partly to capture new sections of the electorate, more to keep pace with their own supporters who had, in their outlook, moved upwards from their point of origin. One of the symptoms of rampant ambition was the upgrading by name alone of occupations which could not be upgraded in any other way...rat-catchers were called "rodent officers", sanitary inspectors "public health inspectors", and lavatory cleaners "amenities attendants". Employers conformed to the changing *mores* by dismissing their "workers" and hiring none but technicians, clothed in white coats instead of dungarees. The Labour Party finally made the same adjustment. "Labour" was a millstone; "worker" was taboo; but "technician", what magic was there! And so the modern Technicians Party was born, catering in the broadest possible manner for technicians by hand and by brain.'

UTOPIA AND REALITY

'A map of the world that does not include Utopia is
not a map that I want to look at.'

Oscar Wilde

Alternative societies

As the dominant personality of British politics in the 1980s, and
acclaimed leader of a capitalist counter-revolution against welfare-
state 'socialism' which reverberated around the world, Margaret
Thatcher attracted a positive cornucopia of colourful nicknames,
adulatory or derisory, and sometimes both at the same time.
Amongst them were 'the Iron Lady', 'Attila the Hen', 'the Great
She-Elephant', 'the Blessed St. Margaret', 'Laura Norder', and
'She-who-must-be-obeyed'. None, however, was more revealing
of the woman's mind-set (nor of the Narnia-like hold it exercised
over the country she ruled for nearly twelve years) than that
deceptively unalarming girl's name, 'Tina'. An acronym of her
relentlessly reiterated assertion, 'There is no alternative', it
epitomises a style of political debate (or rather of the stifling of
such debate) - engendered by tunnel-minded vision and rooted in
dogmatic certitude - which she did not, of course, invent (the great
dictators of her youthful days were consummate practitioners of
the art of what she liked to call 'conviction politics'), but which
she did bring to an exquisite height of perfection in the context of
quasi-democratic politics.

Thatcher and her acolytes never 'won the argument' - as they
were accustomed to boasting they had done - since (with rare
exceptions), togaed in the dignity of first principles and self-evident
truths, they did not deign to treat opposing points of view seriously.
But in a manner quite remarkable for a still nominally pluralistic
society, they did - aided and abetted by a largely like-minded media
and with only a wavering opposition in Parliament - to an
extraordinary extent drown out contrary voices and circumscribe
the agenda for 'sensible' political debate. But perhaps it was not so
remarkable after all. With so many 'socialist' redoubts (including
those engineered by the Liberal economist John Maynard Keynes

to counter unemployment and recession, and which were for a third of a century seen as indispensable to the strategy of Labour governments, and assent to which was, indeed, part of the consensus with their opponents) already surrendered by Labour's establishment even before the Tory triumph of 1979 - and with that triumph soon followed by abject admissions by both Denis Healey and by that once-upon-a-time fiery Welsh radical Neil Kinnock, after his elevation to the Labour leadership following Michael Foot's rout in the 1983 general election, that henceforth market forces would be accepted by Labour as the principal agency of prosperity - it might be felt that the New Tories' hegemony in the field of political thought had not been so hard won.

After all, leading Labour luminary Anthony Crosland had sold the pass as early as 1956 with his absurd contention that capitalism had already passed away; and although it would take another three decades for the concept of 'socialism' to be effectively expunged from Labour's 'authorised version' of the New Jerusalem, no Party leader subsequent to Attlee ever seriously purported to aspire to more than managing capitalism (or non-capitalism, as Crosland would have it) better than its naked but unashamed advocates. Heath's celebrated censure of 'the unpleasant and unacceptable face of capitalism' exhibited by the sleazy Lonrho affair of 1973 provoked no withering retort from Labour regarding the manifest social evils emanating from the grip of private capitalism on the nation's economy, which had once been a general conviction in its ranks. By the 1990s capitalism's shining virtues had become so apparent to the Labour establishment that its leader, whizz-kid Tony Blair, could recycle Ted Heath's disingenuously selective strictures with a silly sally about 'the unacceptable face of privatisation'.

Yet the no-alternative-to-capitalism assumption common to the politicians of all parliamentary parties in Britain (and in every other representative democracy in the world) has given us, in the last two decades of 'the Century of the Common Man', 2-4 million-odd unemployed (with a doleful tally from the European Union countries collectively of upwards of 20 million jobless) and ever-increasing inequality - arguably, indeed, mass poverty. (And that is to say nothing of less blessed realms sustaining - if that is not too mocking a way of putting it - four-fifths of the world's population.) The competitive caterpillars of capitalism have gnawed away at the pillars of the Welfare-State structures built in the aftermath of the great war against fascism, and now threaten to bring the temple down round our ears 'because we cannot afford its upkeep' and to replace it with a more modest, well, poorhouse really. It is truly astonishing that such reactionary and downright dishonest arguments have the remotest chance of prevailing in the counsels of supposedly democratic societies in the late twentieth century! But the truth is that, half a century on from William Beveridge's brave Bunyanesque call to slay the 'Five Giants on the Road to Recovery: Want, Ignorance, Disease, Squalor, and Idleness', they are all alive and kicking back, even if their victims are no longer the majority of our compatriots but only a quarter or so, with the rest of us in the main subject less to hard times than to fear of them.

This is where the practical, down-to-earth, realistic politicians (many of them pleased to call themselves 'radicals') have brought us, with 'revolutionary' redefined in New Labour's *Dictionary for Modernisers* as 'referring to an organisational structure enabling the Party leader to take the decisions necessary for winning power, unhampered by the time-wasting restraints involved in processing them through the Party's democratic machinery' - or something to that effect. (See the leaked report - deliciously entitled 'The Unfinished Revolution' - produced by consultant Philip Gould for Tony Blair and published in *The Guardian*, 12th September 1995.)

As we all know, utopias are, by definition, impossible of realisation, so nothing more needs to be said to shoot down an alternative vision than to call it 'utopian'. Denis Healey's approach to the eradication of social evils, like that of all the Labour leaders he served under, is that of the Fabian inch-worm. He is an admirer of the dissident Polish philosopher Leszek Kolakowski, and in *The Time of My Life* he cites with approval (as 'not an ignoble vision' which 'will do far more to help real people living in the real world today and tomorrow than all the cloudy rhetoric of systematic ideologies') Kolakowski's comment that while it 'does not sell any of the exciting ideological commodities which various totalitarian movements - Communist, Fascist, or Leftist - offer dream-hungry youth', and while 'it has no prescription for the total salvation of mankind', democratic socialism requires, besides 'commitment to a number of basic values, hard knowledge and rational calculation' and also 'an obstinate will to erode by inches the conditions which produce avoidable suffering, oppression, hunger, wars, racial and national hatred, insatiable greed and vindictive envy.'

Silenced in his own country for his unacceptable independence of mind, Kolakowski had ample reason to distrust all-embracing ideologies. But in deploying his words as a kind of apologia for his own record as a politician, Healey was perhaps unaware of Kolakowski's earlier ringing affirmation of the value of utopias. In an essay entitled *The Concept of the Left*, written in the turbulent period following Khrushchev's devastating speech on Stalin's dictatorship to the Twentieth Congress of the Soviet Communist Party, Kolakowski declares that 'the Left cannot do without a utopia', a word he uses ('deliberately and not in the derogatory sense that expresses the absurd notion that all social changes are pipe-dreams') to speak of 'a state of social consciousness, a mental counterpart to the social movement striving for radical change in the world.' His argument is that 'as a conservative force', the Right needs not utopia but 'fraud', since it 'strives to idealise actual conditions, not to change them', unless it be to revert to a former state it considers more desirable; but 'the Left cannot give up utopia because it is a real force even when it is merely a utopia.' To the 'pipe-dreams' jibe he opposes the weight of history:

> 'Much historical experience...tells us that goals unattainable now will never be reached unless they are articulated when they are still unattainable. It may well be that the impossible at a given moment can become possible only by being stated at a time when it is impossible...*The existence of a utopia as a utopia is the necessary prerequisite for its eventually ceasing to be a utopia.*'

And again he writes:

> '*The striving for revolution cannot be born only when the situation is ripe, because among the conditions for this ripeness are the revolutionary demands made of an unripe reality.*' [author's emphases]

It may or may not be that the Kolakowski who wrote the words cited by Healey would stand by his more youthful thoughts on revolution and utopias; but however great may seem the descent in hopes and aspirations from Kolakowski's revolutionary Marxist days to his state of mind when he wrote that tribute to the stoical virtues of democratic socialist politics, the views expressed are not in fact incompatible. However much talk of 'an obstinate will to erode by inches the conditions which produce avoidable suffering' may denote a more pessimistic perception of the obstacles to be overcome and of the time-scale over which they may be surmounted, the need for radical change - as distinct from mere amelioration - remains an imperative for the reformed Kolakowski. And if he now feels that the cost of swift revolution is too great or makes its consolidation too unlikely (though these are not issues he discusses in the passages cited), he can hardly be recommending as a positive good any slower progress towards radical change than it is possible to make by non-violent means.

Revolution through a process of cumulative reform would be another way for stating this attitude. Such is (or at least was) the prescription of Fabian Socialism. Yes, it is 'not an ignoble vision'. But it does demand an apprehended destination and some idea of how to reach it. Furthermore, if more revolutionary routes are rejected, some sense of progress towards that destination must be felt by those who buy tickets in the hope that at least their children or their grandchildren might reach it - a sense which, to say the least, it has been hard to feel after the sidelining of semi-socialist programmes under the Wilson and Callaghan Governments, not to mention the major reversals suffered under the New Tory regimes.

As the twentieth century draws to a close, must we just be grateful that it looks like ending, in Eliot's words, 'not with a bang but a whimper'? What seems most eroded is not those 'conditions which produce avoidable suffering' but the will to change them. Across the length and breadth of Europe and beyond, the 'democratic socialist' parties (or at least their leaders) appear to have no alternative vision to offer the people than the 'free market capitalism' of their ostensible opponents, or at best a customised version of this glorious free-for-all (all with the dosh, that is) alluringly packaged as 'the social market' - an elusive concept pioneered by that once potentially revolutionary force the German Social Democratic Party and eagerly taken up by David Owen in the days when he believed that his SDP was going to 'break the mould' of British politics.

The best part of a century earlier (when abject poverty was

indeed far more widespread even in the industrialised nations) vision was not so wanting among those who called themselves Socialists - and even Labour Party leaders were proud of that label then! Shortly before World War I, writing - in *Socialism and Syndicalism* (1913) - from an avowedly Fabian-gradualist and emphatically anti-syndicalist standpoint, Philip Snowden, observing that 'every political party in the United Kingdom claims to be a party of Social Reform' (to which he could have added that such a claim was indispensable in a representative democracy), proclaimed an essential distinction between 'Social Reformers' and 'Socialists', and that it lay in the Socialists' rejection of the assumption 'that it is possible to abolish social evils...without changing the basis of the economic structure of society.' He maintained that 'there cannot be extremes of wealth without all the moral and social evils which inevitably spring therefrom', and declared: 'No so-called reform touches the problem unless it lessens the power of capitalism to appropriate socially-created wealth.'

And he went on to make an observation which might have served as a warning to all his successors as Chancellors of the Exchequer in Labour administrations, each one of whom half-seriously thought to bring Socialist equality a little nearer through the redistribution of income and wealth, and to effect this with the instrument of taxation. Citing facts and figures for those opening years of 'the Century of the Common Man', Snowden demonstrated that the accumulation of wealth by the wealthy was proceeding far more rapidly than the levying of revenue from that wealth, and that if this were not so, the cry would go up that the taxes were tantamount to confiscation. And as for welfare reforms and rises in the workers' standard of living, although these were obviously to be welcomed, the principal beneficiaries of such advances were (as they always must be under capitalism) those who gained as employers from the workers' higher productivity or as landlords or traders from their greater spending power.

Snowden never was the sort of man one would call a dreamer or a visionary, let alone a revolutionary, yet in those days of hope (eleven years, that is, before he became Labour's first Chancellor of the Exchequer in 1924 and eighteen before he accepted that high office for the third time, when Ramsay MacDonald formed his so-called 'National Government' in 1931, following a general election campaign during which Snowden described the programme of his erstwhile Labour comrades as 'Bolshevism gone mad' - Labour has never been short of turncoats) he looked forward sanguinely to 'the gradual acquisition of political power by the democracy and the gradual transformation of the capitalist system into a co-operative commonwealth'. Eight decades later, New Labour's leaders must surely find such a belief about as utopian as you can get!

Only the present is real: the past is a story and the future a vision. Yet the truth is that there are always *many* alternatives to the tyranny of the present moment - alternatives waiting to be conceived and bounding far beyond the narrow confines of withered imaginations. '*The Left* doesn't accept the reproach of striving for a utopia,' Kolakowski boldly declares in the essay cited. [author's emphasis] And around the turn of the century, when the continuing poverty of the masses in even the wealthiest nations gave ample cause for despair, there was not the present dearth of people bold enough to imagine a just society and to proffer their 'utopias' to others. Such utopias were of two principal kinds, emblematic or analytic. By emblematic I mean presenting a picture of a more desirable society, as Bellamy did in *Looking Backward* (1888) and William Morris did in *News from Nowhere* (1890). By analytical I mean attempting to demonstrate that it is actually possible to change things radically enough to call it creating a new kind of society. These attempts were, in effect, assaults on the 'there-is-no-alternative' mentality in general (a mentality which tends to be prevalent at all times in most places) and, in particular, on the hegemony over the human mind of the capitalist concept, with all its malign offspring: from its Malthuses and Social Darwinists of yesteryear, to its Thatcherites, emasculated Socialists, and obscurantist 'Social Marketeers' of our times. And if we find the case those earlier Socialists made - *something like a hundred years ago* - at all convincing, we must conclude that 'the common man' has been led by the nose through the trials and tribulations of 'his own century'.

The economic system we know as capitalism - a system which, with the fall of The Wall and the effectual capitulation to its sworn ideological enemies of 'Communist' China, more or less holds sway from one end of the earth to the other - depends for its success on the accumulation of wealth to produce yet more wealth. Accumulation is, as it were, the seed corn which must be saved to provide the wherewithal of future consumption. That much is unarguable. How it is saved (whether by individuals or, in some form or other, by the community) is another matter, as is how it is used for the generation of more wealth. And a separate question altogether is how that part of the wealth produced which is not set aside as seed corn but consumed should be distributed. And from the point of view of the people of a country as a whole, however wealthy or otherwise their 'nation' may be, how else should the success of capitalism be judged than by whether it delivers the goods to each and every one of them, or fails to do so?

'Nowhere is the old cliché "Poverty in the midst of Plenty" more easily applicable than in the later years of the nineteenth century in the United States,' writes Peter d'A. Jones in *An Economic History of the United States since 1783.* 'Recurrent economic crises, maldistribution and unintelligent exploitation and wastage of natural resources gave rise to a rich literature of protest and to governmental intervention in economic life - to social criticism and social reform.' Foremost among the critics was the self-taught economist Henry George, whose central idea for remedying the ills of capitalist society, a single tax on that commodity which he believed to be the inalienable right of every human being to use, namely land, winged its way around the world (not only to other English-speaking countries but to realms as far-flung and disparate as China and Denmark), and its force is not yet spent.

This idea was given its fullest development in a book published in March 1879, almost exactly a hundred years before that addle-pated archangel of resurgent capitalism seized that Box-and-Cox State of complacent consensus which its more tradition-minded citizens still most like to call Great Britain. *Progress and Poverty* - dedicated 'To those who seeing the vice and misery that spring from the unequal distribution of wealth and privilege feel the possibility of a higher social state and would strive for its attainment' - is subtitled '*An inquiry into the cause of industrial depressions and of increase of want with increase of wealth*', and its author devoted the greater part of his fairly short life (1839-1897) to propagating his single-tax remedy for this deplorable state of affairs. Although both his diagnosis and his cure may be highly simplistic, Henry George's one big idea - that the expropriation and exploitation by the few of the land which rightly belonged to the many and which properly constituted the very basis of the *common*wealth was the primary cause of society's ills, and that these ills could be remedied by an appropriate system of taxation - remains a great idea which has been sorely neglected by the Left. That it is a great idea should be obvious from the simple fact that it is patently totally unacceptable to the Right!

More germane to the present polemic, however, is Henry George's passionate indictment of an economic system erected on the expendable lives of the many without whom its triumphs could never have been won, and his equally passionate affirmation that this blighting of lives is not a sacrifice which is necessary for the creation of wealth. Remember, the book which asserts this was written more than a hundred years ago! Yet despite the great elevation in the general standard of living in the most developed countries of the world since then, and despite the welfare safety-nets their societies have strung up to catch those so stricken by ill-fortune of one kind or another that they cannot adequately help themselves, the judgements delivered in *Progress and Poverty* - however dated their forms of expression may make them appear - are in their fundamentals no less just and true today. Consider, for example - in the sombre light of the current condition of the disjointed 'Western' societies, intermittently roughly in step then stumblingly at odds, as they straggle along towards the millennium - the following passages:

'The wrong that produces inequality; the wrong that in the midst of abundance tortures men with want or harries them with the fear of want; that stunts them physically, degrades them intellectually, and distorts them morally, is what alone prevents harmonious social development.'

'In the very centres of our civilisation today are want and suffering enough to make sick at heart whoever does not close his eyes and steel his nerves.'

'Between democratic ideas and the aristocratic adjustments of society there is an irreconcilable conflict. Here in the United States, as there in Europe, it may be seen arising. We cannot go on permitting men to vote and forcing them to tramp. We cannot go on educating boys and girls in our public [i.e. State] schools and then refusing them the right to earn an honest living. We cannot go on prating of the inalienable rights of man and then denying the inalienable right to the bounty of the Creator. Even now, in old bottles the new wine begins to ferment, and elemental forces gather for the strife!'

As the above passage indicates and the extracts given below make explicit, Henry George is no simpleton, to believe that universal suffrage ushered in 'government of the people, by the people, for the people.' Or to put it another way, he well understood that political democracy is but a bauble without economic democracy.

'All the dull, deadening pain, all the keen, maddening anguish, that to great masses of men are involved in the words "hard times", afflict the world today. This state of things, common to communities differing so widely in situation, in political institutions, in fiscal and financial systems, in density of population and in social organisation, can hardly be accounted for by local causes. There is distress where large standing armies are maintained, but there is also distress where the standing armies are nominal; there is distress where protective tariffs stupidly and wastefully hamper trade, but there is also distress where trade is nearly free; there is distress where autocratic government yet prevails, *but there is also distress where political power is wholly in the hands of the people.*' [my emphasis]

'To educate men who must be condemned to poverty, is but to make them restive; to base on a state of most glaring social inequality political institutions under which men are theoretically equal, is to stand a pyramid on its apex.'

The riddle Henry George set himself to solve was why accelerating economic progress should bring, to so many, not security but poverty. 'The great enigma of our times,' he called it. The book opens with a positively rhapsodic evocation of progress:

'The present century has been marked by a prodigious increase in wealth-producing power. The utilisation of steam and electricity, the introduction of improved processes and labour-saving machinery, the greater sub-division and grander scale of production, the wonderful facilitation of exchanges, have multiplied enormously the effectiveness of labour. At the beginning of this marvellous era it was natural to expect, and it was expected, that labour-saving inventions would lighten the toil and improve the condition of the labourer; that the enormous increase in the power of producing wealth would make real poverty a thing of the past. Could a man of the last century - a Franklin or a Priestley - have seen, in a vision of the future, the steamship taking the place of the sailing vessel, the railroad train of the waggon, the reaping machine of the scythe, the threshing machine of the flail; could he have heard the throb of the engines that in obedience to human will...[and so on, and so on]...could he have conceived of the hundred thousand improvements which these only suggest, what would he have inferred as to the social condition of mankind?...Plainly, in the sight of the imagination, he would have beheld these new forces elevating society from its very foundations, lifting the very poorest above the possibility of want, exempting the very lowest from anxiety for the material needs of life...And out of these bounteous material conditions he would have seen arising, as necessary sequences, moral conditions realising the golden age of which mankind have always dreamed... Foul things fled, fierce things tame; discord turned to harmony! For how could there be greed where all had enough? How could the vice, the crime, the ignorance, the brutality, that spring from poverty and the fear of poverty, exist where poverty had vanished? Who should crouch where all were freemen? Who oppress where all are peers?'

To men and women of goodwill 'at the beginning of this marvellous era' who had such reasonable visions, 'progress' brought bitter disillusionment:

'The march of invention has clothed mankind with
powers of which a century ago the boldest imagination
could not have dreamed. But in factories where labour-
saving machinery has reached its most wonderful
development, little children are at work...large classes
are maintained by charity or live on the verge of
recourse to it; amid the greatest accumulations of
wealth, men die of starvation, and puny infants suckle
dry breasts; while everywhere the greed of gain, the
worship of wealth, shows the force of the fear of want.'

Of course the picture is too stark to portray accurately the advanced
democracies of our times. Yet without casting our eyes any further
afield, into Third World territory, when he goes on, 'The promised
land flies before us like the mirage', we can see clearly enough that
our condition is not so different from the one he is writing about.
And in one passage in particular he speaks of a state which is
common to most of our 'superior' societies today, the tolerating of
the existence of a section of sub-citizens left out of normal
participation in their society ('socially excluded', as the current
cant has it) through that very fact - poverty:

'It is true that wealth has been greatly increased, and
that the average of comfort, leisure, and refinement has
been raised; but these gains are not general. In them the
lowest class do not share. I do not mean that the
condition of the lowest class has nowhere nor in
anything been improved; but that there is nowhere any
improvement which can be credited to increased
productive power. I mean that the tendency of what we
call material progress is in nowise to improve the
condition of the lowest class in the essentials of healthy,
happy human life. Nay, more, that it is to depress still
further the condition of the lowest class. The new
forces, elevating in their nature though they be, do not
act upon the social fabric from underneath, as was for a
long time hoped and believed, but strike it at a point
intermediate between top and bottom. It is as though an
immense wedge were being forced, not underneath
society, but through society. Those who are above the

point of separation are elevated, but those who are below are crushed down.'

Henry George lived and laboured - as seaman, hired hand, printer, journalist, editor, and newspaper proprietor - in the fastest-growing capitalist economy in the world. From Philadelphia and New York in the east to San Francisco in the west, he saw for himself both the marvels and the miseries of that era of exponential increase in the nation's wealth, which is why he could write about them so vividly. From inconspicuous beginnings, he became a man of renown, so that one of his biographers noted that his death 'was followed by one of the greatest demonstrations of popular feeling and respect that ever attended the funeral of any private citizen in American history.'

With regard to lineage, one could not be much farther removed from this American witness against the social system bequeathed to the world by capitalism than was Prince Peter Kropotkin, who was born only three years after Henry George, but lived long enough to see the Bolsheviks seize power in the one country which the prescient French historian Alexis de Tocqueville foretold in 1835 (in his brilliant study *Democracy in America*) might one day come to compete for global supremacy with the lustily-growing young republic in the New World. Paradoxically, however, the mature Kropotkin was in his way no less a self-made man than Henry George. Only so could he have made that almost unimaginable mental journey from his origins as scion of one of Tsarist Russia's most distinguished aristocratic families to a maturity in which his life was dedicated to the realisation of Anarchist-Communism. A member of the Corps of Pages, the most select military academy in Russia, at the age of fifteen; Siberian explorer at the age of twenty-two; acknowledged, when he was barely into his thirties, as an eminent geographer who had transformed understanding of the physical formation of the continent of Asia; he threw away his privileges and his honours to join the International Working Men's Association (the First International) and work for the liberation of labour from enslavement to capital. His activities as a revolutionary propagandist earned him imprisonment both in Russia and in France. From the former he escaped after more than two years in detention; from the latter he was released by the authorities, after more than three years in French prisons, following a sustained campaign involving men and women from the worlds of scholarship and the arts in many countries, united in their indignation that a man of such distinction should be so persecuted for the non-violent propagation of his anti-Statist views.

He took refuge in England, where most of his more substantial works were written. Besides further contributions to geography, these included a book on Russian and French prisons, a history of Russian literature, a history of the French Revolution, and many works more directly promoting his Anarchist philosophy, notably his most famous book, *Mutual Aid* (1902), the subtitle of which was '*A Factor of Evolution*'. Title and subtitle taken together clearly indicate Kropotkin's purpose, which was, by showing the importance of co-operation both in animal societies and in human societies (and even in relationships between different species), to counter the common overemphasis on competition as the driving force of evolution, which in turn served to justify the fiercely competitive nature of contemporary capitalism. In his Anarchist writings as a corpus, Kropotkin shows himself to be in some respects the most fundamental and uncompromising of all the critics of capitalism. Two of his books, *The Conquest of Bread* (1892) and *Fields, Factories and Workshops* (1898), are most pertinent to the present argument: that it would have been perfectly possible to bring economies to the same stage of development as capitalism has done without committing the crimes and incurring the heartaches which every advanced society has suffered in becoming 'advanced', and from which they still suffer today. It is from the first of these two books that most of the following extracts will be taken, but as a preface to crystallise Kropotkin's attitude to the capitalist order and to questions concerning the wealth of nations and the distribution thereof, perhaps one can not do better than quote from the statement of principles which he drew up for himself and his two co-accused for their trial for sedition in Lyons in January 1883.

Contrary to the common assumption of political economists that freedom and equality are naturally at war with each other, the Anarchist-Communist credo of this statement treats them as mutually dependent. Having set out their demand for freedom for every human being and their consequential rejection of 'the governmental idea', the contumacious 'scoundrels' in the dock audaciously brandished a concept which in the context of capitalism is most commonly cant - the concept of 'free contract' - to contrapose to 'the principle of authority' in human relationships. Then they affirmed their adherence to the age-old idea of the commonwealth:

> 'We believe that capital, the common patrimony of humanity, since it is the fruit of the collaboration of past and present generations, should be at the disposal of all, so that none should be excluded from it...We desire equality, actual equality, as a corollary or rather as a primordial condition of freedom. From each according to his abilities, to each according to his needs...Scoundrels that we are, we demand bread for all; for all equally independence and justice.'

The core argument of *The Conquest of Bread* (like that of *Progress and Poverty*) is that, whatever may have been the case in earlier ages, the productive capacity of modern industry and agriculture had rendered deprivation superfluous for *any* section of society, so that were the distribution of wealth equitable, poverty would be but a page in history:

> 'And if in manufactures as in agriculture, and as indeed through our whole social system, the labour, the discoveries, and the inventions of our ancestors profit chiefly the few, it is none the less certain that mankind in general, aided by the creatures of steel and iron which it already possesses, could already procure an existence of wealth and ease for every one of its members. Truly, we are rich - far richer than we think; rich in what we already possess, richer still in the possibilities of production of our actual mechanical outfit; richest of all in what we might win from our soil, from our manufactures, from our science, from our technical knowledge, were they but applied to bringing about the well-being of all. In our civilised societies we are rich. Why then are the many poor? Why this painful drudgery for the masses? Why, even to the best paid workman, this uncertainty for the morrow, in the midst of all the wealth inherited from the past, and in spite of the powerful means of production, which could ensure comfort to all, in return for a few hours of daily toil?'

Kropotkin represented one strand in the rich weave of Socialist ideas contending for the public ear in those days. But he could confidently speak on behalf of all Socialists (revolutionary and gradualist; Marxist, Anarchist, and Social Democratic) concerning their fundamental critique of capitalism. One could not possibly do that today, even on behalf of most of those parties still prepared to admit to a nodding acquaintance with and some sympathy for Socialist ideas, since they have no such critique and little self-knowledge with regard to what they really stand for besides getting into power as quickly as possible. Yet, *mutatis mutandis*, the indictment of capitalism with which Kropotkin answers his own questions is as true of the capitalist dispensation today as it was when he made it. And that is so even of the great liberal democracies. For the masses in what used to be called the Third World (while the illusion lingered that the command economies of the so-called Soviet states offered another way), it is true just about word for word:

'It is because all that is necessary for production - the land, the mines, the highways, machinery, food, shelter, education, knowledge - all have been seized by the few in that long story of robbery, enforced migration and wars, of ignorance and oppression, which has been the life of the human race before it had learned to subdue the forces of Nature. It is because, taking advantage of alleged rights acquired in the past, these few appropriate today two-thirds of the products of human labour, and then squander them in the most stupid and shameful way. It is because, having reduced the masses to a point at which they have not the means of subsistence for a month, or even for a week in advance, the few can allow the many to work, only on the condition of themselves receiving the lion's share. It is because these few prevent the remainder of men from producing the things they need, and force them to produce, not the necessaries of life for all, but whatever offers the greatest profits to the monopolists. In this is the substance of all Socialism.'

Moreover, proclaims Kropotkin, human progress is a collective achievement, and everyone has the right to enjoy its fruits:

'Millions of human beings have laboured to create this civilisation on which we pride ourselves today. Other millions, scattered throughout the globe, labour to maintain it. Without them nothing would be left in fifty years but ruins...Science and industry, knowledge and application, discovery and practical realisation leading to new discoveries, cunning of brain and of hand, toil of mind and muscle - all work together. Each discovery, each advance, each increase in the sum of human riches, owes its being to the physical and mental travail of the past and the present...All things for all. Here is an immense stock of tools and implements; here are all those iron slaves which we call machines, which saw and plane, spin and weave for us, unmaking and remaking, working up raw matter to produce the marvels of our time. But nobody has the right to seize a single one of these machines and say: "This is mine; if you want to use it you must pay me a tax on each of your products", any more than the feudal lord of mediaeval times had the right to say to the peasant: "This hill, this meadow belong to me, and you must pay me a tax on every sheaf of corn you reap, on every rick you build". All is for all! If the man and the woman bear their fair share of work, they have a right to their fair share of all that is produced by all, and that share is enough to secure them well-being. No more of such vague formulas as "The right to work", or "To each the whole result of his labour". What we proclaim is THE RIGHT TO WELL-BEING: WELL-BEING FOR ALL!'

And in a passage a little further on in the book - following a bitter commentary on the fate of French workers whose insistent clamour for jobs *after* the 'success' of the 1848 revolution was answered by the new masters of the republic with the threat of being shot down by the forces of the State - he emphasises the fundamental difference between reformist calls for full employment and revolutionary demands for social justice:

'The "right to well-being" means the possibility of living like human beings, and of bringing up children to

472

be members of a society better than ours, whilst the "right to work" only means the right to be always a wage-slave, a drudge, ruled over and exploited by the middle class of the future. The right to well-being is the Social Revolution, the right to work means nothing but the Treadmill of Commercialism. It is high time for the worker to assert his right to the common inheritance, and to enter into possession of it.'

The fraudulent character of 'free market' capitalism is laid bare in such withering words as these:

'In virtue of this monstrous system, the son of the worker, on entering life, finds no field which he may till, no machine which he may tend, no mine in which he may dig, without accepting to leave a great part of what he will produce to a master. He must sell his labour for a scant and uncertain wage. His father and his grandfather have toiled to drain this field, to build this mill, to perfect this machine. They gave to the work the full measure of their strength, and what more could they give? But their heir comes into the world poorer than the lowest savage...We cry shame on the feudal baron who forbade the peasant to turn a clod of earth unless he surrendered to his lord a fourth of his crop. We call those the barbarous times. But if the forms have changed, the relations have remained the same, and the worker is forced, under the name of free contract, to accept feudal obligations. For, turn where he will, he can find no better conditions. Everything has become private property, and he must accept, or die of hunger.'

But while he would never have apologised for giving first place to ethical considerations in his arguments, Kropotkin was not simply moralising. He well understood that it was contrary to the whole character of private-enterprise capitalism to put the community first - a hard fact which seems to have eluded the subtle cerebrations of such as Anthony Crosland:

'It is absolutely impossible that mercantile production should be carried on in the interest of all. To desire it

473

would be to expect the capitalist to go beyond his province and to fulfil duties that he *cannot* fulfil without ceasing to be what he is - a private manufacturer seeking his own enrichment. Capitalist organisation, based on the personal interest of each individual employer of labour, has given to society all that could be expected of it: it has increased the productive force of Labour. The capitalist, profiting by the revolution effected in industry by steam, by the sudden development of chemistry and machinery, and by other inventions of our century, has worked in his own interest to increase the yield of human labour, and in a great measure he has succeeded so far. But to attribute other duties to him would be unreasonable. For example, to expect that he should use this superior yield of labour in the interest of society as a whole, would be to ask philanthropy and charity of him, and a capitalist enterprise cannot be based on charity.'

Of course, the State can oblige capitalists operating within its jurisdiction to pay some tribute; but it is natural to their motivation and *modus operandi* to do so grudgingly and in as mean a measure as possible. And now that the capitalist system is really global (though before our century began Kropotkin wrote, in *Fields, Factories and Workshops*, that 'capital knows no fatherland', observing that it migrated to wherever profits were highest), with international finance and transnational corporations setting the pace, the opportunities to evade, defy - or even to exploit for yet higher profits - the demands of the crumbling Sovereign State are legion, so that even the national bourgeoisies sometimes have cause to regret the boundless powers of capital.

The Conquest of Bread began life as a series of articles for the French-language papers *Le Revolté* and its successor, launched after its suppression, *La Revolte*. *Fields, Factories and Workshops* develops many of the themes of *The Conquest of Bread* - among them the need for the integration of industry and agriculture, of town and country, of schooling and work, of manual and intellectual tasks; and the desirability of counteracting capitalism's tendencies to centralisation, to the division of labour, and to the restless hunt for markets, by fostering a high degree of regional self-sufficiency.

It illustrates them with a wealth of detail and statistical evidence drawn both from study and from direct research during the author's travels in Europe and America. The central theme is again the perfect possibility of supplying all the necessities to all the people of the advanced nations. A more complex and scholarly work than *The Conquest of Bread* (though Kropotkin's ingrained scholarship - his scrupulous concern for evidence, accuracy, and reasoned argument - is ever present in his writings), a sociological treatise rather than a polemic, *Fields, Factories and Workshops* does not lend itself in the same way to excerpting, although it powerfully reinforces the argument of the earlier book. Furthermore, its innate concern for such subjects as (to use modern terminology) 'the conservation of resources', 'sustainable development', and care for 'the global commons' makes its message as resonant today as ever. I shall simply cite from the concluding chapter Kropotkin's heartfelt cry - 'What floods of useless sufferings deluge every so-called civilised land in the world!' - and his appeal to 'the unprejudiced mind':

> 'For centuries science and so-called practical wisdom
> have said to man: "It is good to be rich, to be able to
> satisfy, at least, your material needs; but the only means
> to be rich is to train your mind and capacities as to be
> able to compel other men - slaves, serfs or wage-earners
> - to make these riches for you. You have no choice.
> Either you must stand in the ranks of the peasants and
> the artisans who, whatsoever economists and moralists
> may promise them in the future, are now periodically
> doomed to starve after each bad crop or during their
> strikes, and to be shot down by their own sons the
> moment they lose patience. Or you must train your
> faculties so as to be a military commander of the
> masses, or to be accepted as one of the wheels of the
> governing machinery of the State, or to become a
> manager of men in commerce or industry." For many
> centuries there was no other choice, and men
> followed that advice, without finding in it happiness,
> either for themselves and their own children, or for
> those whom they pretended to preserve from worse
> misfortunes.'

But the promised future, insisted Kropotkin one hundred years ago, has arrived:

> 'Modern knowledge...tells thinking men that in order to be rich they need not take the bread from the mouths of others; but that the more rational outcome would be a society in which men, with the work of their own hands and intelligence, and by the aid of the machinery already invented and to be invented, should themselves create all imaginable riches.'

Kropotkin was right. Man had reached a plateau from which he might have struck off towards the promised land - had he had a better sense of direction. The productive capacity of industrially developed societies was such that it could have delivered well-being to all; ceaseless struggle for civic rights had won a general if grudging acknowledgement that the common people had some right to a say in their own governance; and the masses upon whose constant toil, as Kropotkin said, everything depended, had created and were creating self-help and mutual-aid organisations which they could have used to wrest their rightful heritage from their masters, as more and more of the disinherited joined their ranks.

On the plane of intellectual debate Socialist ideas were gaining ground rapidly; but the prospects for seriously challenging the hegemony of capitalism depended on solidarity, and although the Socialists were in essentials at one in their repudiation of capitalism and their reasons for doing so, they were much at odds in their strategies for replacing it and in their blueprints for post-capitalist society. These divisions lay behind the break up of the First International, although the immediate causes had more to do with bad relations between Karl Marx and the foremost champion of Anarchism, Michael Bakunin, the details of which are not pertinent to this discussion.

However, co-operation in the common struggle and many friendships continued across this divide, and it was the outbreak of war which brought about a more decisive rupture in the Socialist movement. Despite the repeated calls from Socialist international congresses for non-collaboration with the State in the event of war, which was firmly pronounced another evil endemic to capitalism, when the nation-states called them to the colours, relatively few

476

Socialists became war-resisters. International working-class solidarity was easily swept aside by the old nationalistic passions and prejudices that masquerade as patriotism. Ironically, spurred on by his intense hostility for everything that the Kaiser's Germany stood for, Kropotkin himself, whose whole life had been dedicated to the emancipation of humanity, supported the war, even signing, along with fourteen other well-known Anarchists, a manifesto declaring as much. Despite their illustrious names, the signatories, together with the few scores of others who subsequently endorsed the manifesto, were a small minority in the Anarchist movement, whose delegates to the Amsterdam international congress of 1907 had called for war to be met by insurrection, and most of whose leading figures (now that Socialists in one army's trenches were slaughtering Socialists in 'the enemy's' trenches) staunchly continued to urge maximum possible resistance and preparation for revolt. But such unmistakable expressions of the unrelenting opposition of most Anarchists to the war did not inhibit Lenin from exploiting Kropotkin's manifesto to slag off Anarchists in general as 'social-chauvinists'.

Although he had nothing to gain from it, Kropotkin's support for the war was inevitably seen by erstwhile comrades as a terrible betrayal. Of himself as well as of their common cause, since in the final analysis it is impossible to reconcile it with his own life and teachings. Be that as it may, over two other issues pregnant with misfortune for the future of Socialism, he was prescient indeed. These issues concerning possible forms of government in societies considering themselves Socialist, the issues of collectivism and parliamentarianism, are usually associated with two different kinds of Socialism - the former with 'State Socialism' (as in the 'Soviet' system), the latter with 'Social Democracy' - which are thought of as antithetical rather than akin. For Kropotkin, however, they have the same species of worm in the bud, and while they may not be equally undesirable in their effects, are nevertheless simply different methods for an elite to exercise authority over the people. His fears for the future of Socialism were that such authoritarian forms would prevail over the Anarchist-Communist form for which he stood. Unhappily, he lived to see one of these fears fulfilled in his own country, while we have lived to see the other fulfilled in ours.

Since the authoritarian nature of the so-called Marxist States is hardly a matter of debate amongst those who consider themselves democrats, we will take the uncontroversial issue of collectivism first, again using *The Conquest of Bread* to present Kropotkin's opinions. As we have seen, for Kropotkin freedom and equality were interdependent: neither could exist without the other. In the following passage, which incidentally relates to his rejection of the theory of 'surplus value' ('all wages' theories have been invented after the event to justify injustices at present existing,' he says acidly elsewhere) he makes it clear that a collectivist revolution would leave the common people in a position of servitude:

'Collectivism, as we know, does not abolish the wage system...It only substitutes the State, that is to say some form of Representative Government...for the individual employer of labour. Under Collectivism it is the representatives of the nation, or of the Commune, and their deputies and officials who are to have the control of industry. It is they who reserve to themselves the right of employing the surplus of production - in the interests of all. Moreover, Collectivism draws a very subtle but very far-reaching distinction between the work of the labourer and of the man who has learned a craft. Unskilled labour in the eyes of the collectivist is *simple* labour, while the work of the craftsman, the mechanic, the engineer, the man of science, etc., is what Marx calls *complex* labour, and is entitled to a higher wage. But labourers and craftsmen, weavers and men of science, are all wage-servants of the State - 'all officials', as was said lately, to gild the pill. Well, then, the coming Revolution could render no greater service to humanity than by making the wage system, in all its forms, an impossibility, and by rendering Communism, which is the negation of wage-slavery, the only possible system.'

He went on to warn that after the revolution the people would be patient no longer and that if food were not forthcoming they would plunder the bakeries. It would end up with the people being shot down and the capitalists lending their support to the so-called revolutionists as 'the champions of *order*'. Thus 'the Revolution itself will become hateful in the eyes of the masses.' One month

478

less one day after Kropotkin's death on 8th February 1921, a devastating realisation of this prophetic warning came to pass when Red Army troops were launched against the naval base of Kronstadt, whose sailors, many of whom had strong Anarchist leanings, had mutinied in defence of the gains made by the revolution. Kropotkin also warned against trying to coerce the peasants to provide food to the cities instead of treating and trading with them fairly, illustrating the folly of coercion from the events of the French Revolution. But the Bolsheviks were deaf to all such warnings, as the terrible story of what almost amounts to the reintroduction of serfdom in Russia shows.

At the beginning of a chapter on possible objections to his kind of Communism, Kropotkin writes:

'It is not for us to answer the objections raised by [i.e. 'against'] authoritarian Communism - we ourselves hold with them. Civilised nations have suffered too much in the long, hard struggle for the emancipation of the individual, to disown their past work and to tolerate a Government that would make itself felt in the smallest details of a citizen's life, even if that Government had no other aim than the good of the community. Should an authoritarian Socialist society ever succeed in establishing itself, it could not last; general discontent would soon force it to break up, or to reorganise itself on principles of liberty.'

Well, such societies did establish themselves, of course, and in the author's native land one such society lasted about as long as a man's allotted span, which may be thought to prove his words far too optimistic, especially as the causes of its demise were a deal more complex than 'general discontent'. For all that, Kropotkin had signposted one of the worst possible deformations of the noble idea of Socialism, a deformation which has so discredited that name that one doubts it ever will fully recover its former good reputation.

As with a woman, there is more than one way of abusing a good idea, and it may be done without ill-intent. Some passages in the chapter on 'The Collectivist Wages System' may be cited as exposing the kinship between the ostensibly mutually antagonistic social systems of collectivism and what would more accurately be called capitalist parliamentarianism. The chapter opens challengingly:

'In their plans for the reconstruction of society the collectivists commit, in our opinion, a two-fold error. While speaking of abolishing capitalist rule, they intend nevertheless to retain two institutions which are the very basis of this rule - Representative Government and the Wages' System.'

The Anarchist principle of the proper distribution of responsibilities and rewards in the community are clearly enunciated in the declaration of Kropotkin and his comrades to their judges in the Lyons trial: 'From each according to his abilities, to each according to his needs.' *In The Conquest of Bread* Kropotkin argues that the collectivists may think they will put right injustices by acting on their principle of remuneration, but in fact they will only perpetuate the evils of capitalist calculation:

'The collectivists say, "To each according to his deeds"; or, in other terms, according to his share of services rendered to society. They think it expedient to put this principle into practice, as soon as the Social Revolution will have made all the instruments of production common property...Of course, in a society like ours, in which the more a man works the less he is remunerated, this principle, at first sight, may appear to be a yearning for justice. But in reality it is only the perpetuation of injustice. It was by proclaiming this principle that wagedom began, to end in the glaring inequalities and all the abominations of present society; because, from the moment work done began to be appraised in currency, or in any other form of wage, the day it was agreed upon that man would only receive the wage he should be able to secure for himself, the whole history of a State-aided Capitalist Society was as good as written; it was contained in germ in this principle.'

But Kropotkin does not denounce the wages' system only because of the gross injustices of its consequences. At the heart of his condemnation is his repudiation of the idea that it is possible to weigh and measure a person's worth to the community:

> 'Human society would not exist for more than two
> consecutive generations if everyone did not give
> infinitely more than that for which he is paid in coin, in
> "cheques", or in civic rewards. The race would soon
> become extinct if mothers did not sacrifice their lives to
> take care of their children, if men did not give
> continually, without demanding an equivalent reward, if
> men did not give most precisely when they expect no
> reward.'

The only way out of the 'blind alley' into which 'middle-class' (i.e. capitalist) society has led us, he says, is to demolish its institutions:

> 'We have given too much to counting...We have let
> ourselves be influenced into *giving* only to *receive*...We
> have aimed at turning society into a commercial
> company based on *debit* and *credit*.'

If all this sounds like 'primitive Christianity', the comparison would not have embarrassed Kropotkin, although he was not a believer, and not just a preacher either, but a revolutionary. After the revolution, he writes:

> 'We will set to work to demolish the last vestiges of
> middle-class rule: its morality drawn from account-
> books, its "debit and credit" philosophy, its "mine and
> yours" institutions.'

As for the other issue in respect of which Kropotkin draws a parallel between collectivism and capitalist democracy, that of 'parliamentarianism', it might be felt that he is grossly unfair to proponents of the latter. After all, it is true that the degree of fraud in what we call representative democracy is commensurate to the degree in which citizens may be said to have a say in choosing their representatives. And it is also true that the quantitative differences between one-party totalitarian States and multi-party States with substantial civic rights - free elections, equality before the law (in theory, at any rate), freedom of the press, and so forth; things we rightly value - may be so great as almost to amount to a qualitative difference. But even taking into account the advances in capitalist democracy (notably votes for women and the development of social welfare systems) since the time he was writing, Kropotkin's radical criticism of 'parliamentary democracy' is still valid. One hundred years ago, he maintained that representative government had already proved its impotence 'to discharge all the functions we have sought to assign to it.' Which was not in the least surprising to him, since he was conscious of 'the absurdity of naming a few men and saying to them, "Make laws regulating all our spheres of activity, although not one of you knows anything about them!"'

Capitalism and parliamentarianism, he considered, enjoy a mutually beneficent symbiosis, and both systems operate in the interests of the middle classes. (Of his time, of course: it is anything but clear what we mean by that term nowadays.) One cannot fault his succinct description of the historical development of representative government; but it is more important to see that in essence the same reality still obtains:

> 'Built up by the middle classes to hold their own
> against royalty, sanctioning, and, at the same time
> strengthening, their sway over the workers,
> parliamentary rule is pre-eminently a middle-class
> rule.'

Similarly, he writes:

> 'A society founded on serfdom is in keeping with
> absolute monarchy; a society based on the wage
> system and the exploitation of the masses by the
> capitalists finds its political expression in
> parliamentarianism.'

Such rhetoric has gone quite out of fashion, of course, particularly in what used to be thought of as the workers' party; but it is none the less true for that. Kropotkin goes on to speak of forms of administration appropriate to the kind of society for which he was campaigning:

'But a free society, regaining possession of the common inheritance, must seek, in free groups and free federations of groups, a new organisation, in harmony with the new economic phase of history.'

Kropotkin's fears that the anti-revolutionary Socialists' project of gaining power through the ballot box would result in the bourgeoisification of the political leaders of the workers have been amply borne out by history. Look where you will, the record shows that whatever the proclaimed intentions of parliament-centred Socialist parties when in opposition, in office they ineluctably act primarily as the agents of the capitalists.

Moreover, 'taking power' in what is, constitutionally speaking, the nation's sovereign institution, invariably induces in the victors the assumption that they have won the right to take the final decisions on behalf of the nation, despite the fact that the capitalist system ensures that, inasmuch as the measures pushed through parliament are anti-pathetic to capitalists, those decision-making powers are largely illusory. Even when in opposition (and perhaps as far from power as Labour was when led by Michael Foot), with respect to their own movement, the leaders of the parliamentary party mentally arrogate all political power to themselves. This has been demonstrated innumerable times in the history of the Labour Party, but never more explicitly than by the spat during Foot's leadership over Peter Tatchell's talk of the need for extra-parliamentary action to defeat Thatcherism. And this ridiculous assumption that a *Socialist* movement can differentiate between *political* power (to be accepted by every supporter as the province of the party politicians) and *industrial labour* power (in which it is conceded that the workers' union leaders have primary - though not ultimate - rights of decision-making) lies behind almost every significant rupture in the solidarity of the Labour Movement. It also means that both wings of the movement have usually been fighting with one hand tied behind their backs. Truly, the case against parliamentarianism from a Socialist (and indeed from a plain democratic) point of view is infinitely more damning than that presented in his 1961 book, *Parliamentary Socialism*, by Ralph Miliband, who naturally failed to see that such radical strictures as those made by Kropotkin applied equally to 'true Marxist' parties.

If Kropotkin's vision was of a more utterly transformed

society than most 'utopias', he was only one of hundreds of nineteenth-century Socialist intelligentsia who dared to dream, who - unlike normal well-to-do people of his time, who (like Julian West's contemporaries in Bellamy's fictional utopia) were capable of going about their business with eyes averted from that nether world which underpinned and indeed made possible their own - were inwardly compelled to contemplate the life of the masses and yearned to make it better. And far from being impractical dreamers, these men and women were, certainly from a sociological point of view, the best-informed people in their society. The 'Tina' sneers of 'utopianism' are turned back on the mockers when Kropotkin writes in *The Conquest of Bread*:

> 'It has always been the middle-class idea to harangue about "great principles" - great lies rather! The idea of the people will be to provide bread for all. And while middle-class citizens, and workmen infested with middle-class ideas admire their own rhetoric in the "Talking Shops", and "practical people" are engaged in endless discussions on forms of government, we, the "Utopian dreamers" - we shall have to consider the question of daily bread...and...with this watchword of *Bread for All* the Revolution will triumph.'

His words carry a mental health warning for constitution-mongers, even those of the more altruistic variety, like Charter 88ists, who look to constitutional formulas for the salvation of society.

And remember those words of Kolakowski's: '*The existence of a utopia as a utopia is the necessary prerequisite for its eventually ceasing to be a utopia.*' All progress starts inside people's heads. And yes, 'bread for all', 'homes for all', 'worthwhile jobs for all' - even such modest demands are 'utopian' whenever and wherever they are not statements of an established social situation, and whenever and wherever it is not universally held to be absolutely unthinkable that it should be otherwise. Or that such things are any more than what we owe to one another - these things and everything else implied by the idea of living together and accepting one another as equals.

Having such utopias in our heads - and being resolved to do whatever we can to manifest them - is not a denial of realities. Of course, it is no good taking the attitude of the proverbial hayseed who upon being asked the way by a stranger replied, 'Well I wouldn't start from here if I were you.' But facing up to reality is not the same thing as surrendering to it. Those who are serious advocates of Socialism cannot do other than work through whatever seem to them the least unsatisfactory organisations or institutions already in being, while exerting what pressure they can to push them in the desired directions and to change them in the desired ways when the opportunity arises, until the time seems ripe to replace them with something better.

Which is why, while organisational forms more serviceable to the furtherance of Socialist objectives are gestating, British Socialists who have not opted out have to use the Labour Movement (both its political and its industrial wings) and the established institutions of so-called 'representative democracy' - but without illusions (which amongst other things means tactical voting to try to keep out the worst candidates up for election, not childish ideas of party loyalty) and without giving up their dreams. Heirs to the noble aspirations of nineteenth-century forerunners, Socialists living in the twilight of the twentieth century bear the burden of having been witness to the repeated rape of Socialist ideals, rape committed most traumatically of all not by strangers or sworn enemies but by family members claiming to subscribe to those ideals.

The twilight Socialists have a choice between three options:

(1) acquiescing in programmes promulgated by party leaders who, at the best, may be genuinely persuaded that all they are doing is sensibly modifying Socialist tenets to match modern times, or, at the worst, may be cynically refashioning their beliefs to maximise electoral support, but who in any case are certainly not propagating Socialism as distinct from social reform;

(2) quiescing, i.e. turning their backs on the struggle;

(3) fighting on to reignite, regenerate, re-propagate those brave ideals dreamed up by the utopian heralds of a new society.

SOURCES AND SELECT BIBLIOGRAPHY

(An asterisk indicates that a work has been cited in the text and that the author's name is to be found in the Index. Newspapers and periodicals cited also appear in the Index. Other works listed here have either been consulted during the writing of this essay or have contributed to it by being in my mind.)

FACT OR FACTION?

Paul Addison, *Churchill on the Home Front 1900-1955* (Cape 1992)
Paul Addison, **The Road to 1945: British Politics and the Second World War* (Cape 1975)
Stephen E. Ambrose, **Rise to Globalism: American Foreign Policy, 1938-1980* (Penguin 1980)
Leopold Amery, **The Conservative Future: An Outline of Policy (Conservative Political Centre* ?1945 - in Buck, q.v.)
Evelyn Anderson, *Hammer of Anvil: The Story of the German Working-Class Movement* (Gollancz 1945)
Anonymous, **How Labour Governed, 1945-1951* (Syndicalist Workers' Federation n.d. ?1957)
Paul Avrich, *Kronstadt 1921* (Princeton 1970)
Paul Avrich, *The Russian Anarchists* (Princeton 1971)
C.R. Attlee, *As It Happened* (Heinemann 1954)
C.R. Attlee, **The Labour Party in Perspective* (Gollancz 1937)
Walter Bagehot, **The English Constitution* (1867, 2nd edn. 1872)
Joel Barnett, **Inside the Treasury* (Deutsch 1982)
C.J. Bartlett, **A History of Postwar Britain, 1945-74* (Longman 1977)
Samuel H. Beer, **Modern British Politics: A Study of Parties and Pressure Groups* (Faber 1965)
Thomas Bell, **Pioneering Days* (Lawrence & Wishart 1941 - extract from Coates and Topham, q.v.)
Tony Benn, *Arguments for Democracy* (Cape 1981)
Tony Benn, *Arguments for Socialism* (Cape 1979)
Tony Benn, five volumes of diaries, 1963-1990
William Beveridge, **Full Employment in a Free Society* (1944)
William Beveridge, **Social Insurance and Allied Services* (1942)
Robert Blake, **The Conservative Party from Peel to Thatcher* (Fontana 1985)
Viscount Bolingbroke, **A Dissertation on Parties* (1773-4 - extracts from this and the next two titles in Buck, q.v.)

Viscount Bolingbroke, *The Idea of a Patriot King* (1747-8)
Viscount Bolingbroke, *Origin of Civil Society* (1754)
Nicholas Bosanquet, *'Inequalities in Health' (in Townsend and Bosanquet, q.v.)
Julius Braunthal, *In Search of the Millennium* (Gollancz 1945)
Julius Braunthal, *The Tragedy of Austria* (Gollancz 1948)
Gerald Brenan, *The Spanish Labyrinth: An Account of the Social and Political Background of the Civil War* (Cambridge 1943)
Asa Briggs, *Victorian Cities* (Odhams 1963, Penguin ed. 1968)
Asa Briggs, *Victorian People* (Odhams 1954)
J.A.C. Brown, *Techniques of Persuasion: From Propaganda to Brainwashing* (Penguin 1963)
Maurice Bruce, *The Coming of the Welfare State* (Batsford 1961)
Philip W. Buck, *How Conservatives Think* (Penguin 1975)
Tony Bunyan, *The History and Practice of the Political Police in Britain* (Friedmann 1976, Quartet 1977)
Edmund Burke, *An Appeal from the New to the Old Whigs* (1791)
Edmund Burke, *Reflections on the Revolution in France* (1790)
Edmund Burke, *Thoughts and Details on Scarcity* (1795)
James Burnham, *The Managerial Revolution* (Penguin 1945)
Sir Alec Cairncross, *Years of Recovery: British Economic Policy 1945-51* (Methuen 1985)
James Callaghan, *Time and Chance* (Collins 1987)
John Campbell, *Nye Bevan: A Biography* (Hodder & Stoughton 1987)
Barbara Castle, *The Castle Diaries, 1964-1976* (Macmillan 1990)
Randolph Churchill, *'Speech to the Organization of the Conservative Party, at Birmingham, 16 April 1884' (from extract in Buck, q.v.)
Tony Cliff and Donny Gluckstein, *The Labour Party: A Marxist History* (Bookmarks 1988)
David Coates, *Labour in Power?: A Study of the Labour Government, 1974-9* (Longmans 1980)
Ken Coates and Tony Topham, ed., *Workers' Control* (Panther 1970)
William Cobbett, *Rural Rides* (1830)
Gabriel and Daniel Cohn-Bendit, *Obsolete Communism: The Left-Wing Alternative* (Deutsch 1968)
G.D.H. Cole, *Self-Government in Industry* (Bell 1917)
G.D.H. Cole and Raymond Postgate, *The Common People, 1746-1946* (Methuen 1938-56)
Lord Coleraine, *For Conservatives Only (1970 - from extract in Buck, q.v.)
Nicholas Comfort, *Brewer's Politics* (Cassell 1993)
Patrick Cosgrave, *Thatcher: The First Term* (Bodley Head 1985)
Ivor Crewe, *The Times Guide to the House of Commons, May 1979* (Times Books 1979)
Anthony Crosland, *The Future of Socialism* (Macmillan 1956)

Anthony Crosland, *Socialism Now* (Macmillan 1974)

Richard Crossman, *The Diaries of a Cabinet Minister, 1964-1970* (Hamish Hamilton and Jonathan Cape 1975-77)

Richard Crossman, ed., *The God that Failed* (Harper & Row 1950)

Benjamin Disraeli, *'Speech at the Banquet of the National Union of Conservative and Constitutional Associations at Crystal Palace, 24 June 1872' (from extract in Buck, q.v.)

Benjamin Disraeli, *'Vindication of the English Constitution in a letter to a noble and learned Lord' (1835 - extract from Buck, q.v.)

Milovan Djilas, *The New Class: An Analysis of the Communist System* (first pub. in English 1957, Allen & Unwin 1966)

Bernard Donoghue, *Prime Minister: The Conduct of Policy under Harold Wilson and James Callaghan* (Cape 1987)

A.D. Elliot, *Life of Lord Goschen, 1831-1907* (1911)

Gregory Elliott, *Labourism and the English Genius: The Strange Death of Labour England?* (Verso 1993)

Cecil S. Emden, *The People and the Constitution* (Oxford 1933)

Joe England and Brian Weekes, *'Trade Unions and the State: A Review of the Crisis' (Industrial Relations Journal, 1981 - in McCarthy, q.v.)

R.C.K. Ensor, *England 1870-1914* (Oxford 1936)

Eric Estorick, *Stafford Cripps* (Heinemann 1949)

Alan Freeman, *The Benn Heresy* (Pluto 1982)

Milton Friedman and Rose Friedman, *Free to Choose: A Personal Statement* (Secker & Warburg 1980)

Paul Frolich, *Rosa Luxemburg* (Gollancz 1940)

John Kenneth Galbraith, *The Affluent Society* (Hamish Hamilton 1958)

John Kenneth Galbraith, *American Capitalism: The Concept of Countervailing Power* (Hamish Hamilton 1957)

John Kenneth Galbraith, *The Culture of Contentment* (Sinclair-Stevenson 1992)

Henry George, *Progress and Poverty* (1879)

Ian Gilmour, *Dancing with Dogma: Britain under Thatcherism* (Simon & Schuster 1992)

William Ewart Gladstone, *'Is the Popular Judgement in Politics more just than that of the Higher Orders? - 2' (in Goodwin, q.v.)

Howard Glennerster, *'Education and Inequality' (in Townsend and Bosanquet, q.v.)

Michael Goodwin, ed., *Nineteenth-Century Opinion: An Anthology of extracts from the first fifty volumes of The Nineteenth Century, 1877-1901* (Penguin 1951)

Philip Guedalla, *Mr Churchill: A Portrait* (Hodder & Stoughton 1941)

Marquis of Halifax, *The Character of a Trimmer* (1699 - extract from Buck, q.v.)

J.E.D. Hall, *Labour's First Year* (Penguin 1947)

A.H. Halsey, *Change in British Society* (Oxford 1978)

Michael Harrington, *The Other America: Poverty in the United States* (Macmillan, New York, 1962; Penguin 1963)

Michael Hatfield, **The House the Left Built* (1978)

F.A. Hayek, *The Road to Serfdom* (Routledge 1944)

Denis Healey, **The Time of My Life* (Michael Joseph 1989)

Paddy Hillyard and Janie Percy-Smith, *The Coercive State: The Decline of Democracy in Britain* (Fontana 1988)

Quintin Hogg, **The Case for Conservatism* (Penguin 1947)

Stuart Holland, **The Socialist Challenge* (Quartet 1975)

Martin Holmes, **The Labour Government, 1974-79: Political Aims and Economic Reality* (Macmillan 1985)

Eric Hopkins, *The Rise and Decline of the English Working Classes 1918-1990: A Social History* (Weidenfeld & Nicolson 1991)

Peter d'A. Jones, *The Consumer Society: A History of American Capitalism* (Penguin 1965)

Peter d'A. Jones, **An Economic History of the United States since 1783* (Routledge & Kegan Paul 1956)

James Avery Joyce, *The War Machine* (Quartet 1980, Hamlyn 1981)

Dennis Kavanagh, **Thatcherism and British Politics: The End of Consensus?* (Oxford 1987, 2nd ed. 1990)

J.C. Kincaid, *Poverty and Equality in Britain: A Study of Social Security and Taxation* (Penguin 1973)

Leszek Kolakowski, **Marxism and Beyond: On Historical Understanding and Individual Responsibility* (Pall Mall 1969)

Peter Kropotkin, **The Conquest of Bread* (1892)

Peter Kropotkin, **Fields, Factories and Workshops* (1898)

Peter Kropotkin, *The Great French Revolution* (1909)

Peter Kropotkin, **Memoirs of a Revolutionist* (1899)

Peter Kropotkin, **Mutual Aid: A Factor of Evolution* (1902)

Nigel Lawson, **The New Conservatism* (Centre for Policy Studies 1980)

William Edward Hartpole Lecky, **Democracy and Liberty* (1896 - extract from Buck, q.v.)

Bernard Levin, **The Pendulum Years: Britain and the Sixties* (Cape 1970)

T.O. Lloyd, **Empire to Welfare State: English History 1906-1976* (Oxford 1979)

Anatoly Marchenko, *My Testimony* (Pall Mall 1969; Penguin 1971)

Roy Lewis and Angus Maude, **The English Middle Classes* (Penguin 1953)

W.E.J. McCarthy, ed., **Trade Unions* (Penguin 1972, 2nd ed. 1985)

Harold Macmillan, **The Middle Way* (1938 - extract from Buck, q.v.)

Harold Macmillan, **Winds of Change, 1914-1939* (Macmillan 1966)

Tom Mann, **Memoirs* (1923, Macgibbon & Kee 1967)

Herbert Marcuse, *Soviet Marxism: A Critical Analysis* (Routledge & Kegan Paul 1958)

Herbert Marcuse, *One-Dimensional Man* (Routledge & Kegan Paul 1964)

Dennis Marsden, *'Politicians, Equality and Comprehensives' (in Townsend and Bosanquet, q.v.)

Ralph Miliband, *Parliamentary Socialism: A Study in the Politics of Labour* (Allen & Unwin 1961)

Ralph Miliband, *The State in Capitalist Society* (Weidenfeld & Nicolson 1969)

John Stuart Mill, *Considerations on Representative Government* (1861)

C. Wright Mills, *The Marxists* (Dell, U.S.A., 1962; Penguin 1963)

Kenneth O. Morgan, *Labour in Power* (Oxford 1984)

Kenneth O. Morgan, *Rebirth of a Nation: Wales 1880-1980* (Oxford & University of Wales 1982)

Herbert Morrison, *'Economic Socialisation' (in Tracey, q.v.)

Herbert Morrison, *Socialisation and Transport* (Constable 1933)

Peter Nettl, *Rosa Luxemburg* (Oxford 1966)

A.R. Orage, ed., *National Guilds: An Inquiry into the Wage System and the Way Out* (Bell 1914)

George Orwell, *Down and Out in Paris and London* (Gollancz 1933)

George Orwell, *Homage to Catalonia* (Secker and Warburg 1938)

George Orwell, *The Road to Wigan Pier* (Gollancz 1937)

Thomas Paine, *The Rights of Man* (1791-92)

Jenny Pearce, *Under the Eagle: U.S. Intervention in Central America and the Caribbean* (Latin America Bureau 1981)

Sir Robert Peel, *'Address to the Electors of the Borough of Tamworth' (1834 - extract from Buck, q.v.)

Henry Pelling, *A History of British Trade Unionism* (Penguin (1963)

Henry Pelling, *Origins of the Labour Party, 1880-1900* (Oxford (1965)

Harold Perkin, *The Origins of Modern English Society, 1780-1880* (Routledge & Kegan Paul 1969)

Richard Pipes, *The Russian Revolution, 1899-1919* (Fontana 1992)

K.R. Popper, *The Open Society and Its Enemies* (Routledge & Kegan Paul 1945, revised fifth edition 1966)

J.B. Priestley, *Letter to a Returning Serviceman* (Home & Van Thal 1945)

Joseph G. Rayback, *A History of American Labor* (The Free Press, New York, 1966)

Patrick Renshaw, *The Wobblies: The Story of Syndicalism in the United States* (Eyre & Spottiswoode 1967)

W.G. Runciman, *Relative Deprivation and Social Justice: A Study of Attitudes to Social Inequality in Twentieth-Century England* (Routledge & Kegan Paul 1966; Penguin 1972)

Marquis of Salisbury, *articles from the *Quarterly Review*, 1860-1865 (from extracts in Buck, q.v.)

Anthony Sampson, *The Arms Bazaar* (Hodder & Stoughton 1978)

Victor Serge, *Destiny of a Revolution* (French edition ?1937, English translation published by Hutchinson n.d.)

Victor Serge, *Memoirs of a Revolutionary* 1901-1941 (translated from the French by Peter Sedgwick, Oxford 1963)

Victor Serge, *Year One of the Russian Revolution* (first published in France; Peter Sedgwick translation, Allen Lane 1972)

Emmanuel Shinwell, **Conflict without Malice* (Odhams 1955)

Alan Sked and Chris Cook, **Post-War Britain: A Political History* (Penguin 1979)

Philip Snowden, **Socialism and Syndicalism* (Collins 1913)

I.N. Steinberg, *In the Workshop of the Revolution* (Gollancz 1955)

John Stevenson and Chris Cook, *The Slump: Society and Politics During the Depression* (Cape 1978)

Julian Symons, *The General Strike* (Cresset 1957)

R.H. Tawney, **The Acquisitive Society* (Bell 1921)

R.H. Tawney, *Equality* (Allen & Unwin 1931)

A.J.P. Taylor, **English History, 1914-1945* (Oxford 1965)

E.P. Thompson, **The Making of the English Working Class* (Gollancz 1963, Penguin revised ed. 1968)

Leonard Tivey, **Nationalization in British Industry* (Cape 1966, revised ed. 1973)

Alexis de Tocqueville, **Democracy in America* (1835)

Peter Townsend and Nicholas Bosanquet, ed., **Labour and Inequality* (Fabian Society 1972)

Herbert Tracey, ed., **The British Labour Party* (Caxton 1948)

Beatrice Webb, **Diaries* (ed. M.I. Cole, Longman 1952 and 1956)

Sidney and Beatrice Webb, **A Constitution for the Socialist Commonwealth of Great Britain* (Longman 1920)

Sidney and Beatrice Webb, **Soviet Communism: A New Civilisation* (Longmans 1935, 3rd ed. 1944)

K.W. Wedderburn, **'The New Politics of Labour Law'* (University of Durham Industrial Relations Group, 1983 - in McCarthy, q.v.)

John Westergaard and Henrietta Resler, **Class in a Capitalist Society: A Study of Contemporary Britain* (Heinemann 1975, Penguin 1976)

Eirene White, **Workers' Control?* (Fabian Society Tract 1951 - extract from Coates and Topham, q.v.)

R.J. White, **The Conservative Tradition* (Adam & Charles Black 1950 - from extract in Buck, q.v.)

Phillip Whitehead, **The Writing on the Wall: Britain in the Seventies* (Michael Joseph and Channel 4, 1985)

Harold Wilson, **Final Term: The Labour Government, 1974-6* (Weidenfeld & Nicolson and Michael Joseph 1979)

George Woodcock and Ivan Avakumovic, *The Anarchist Prince: A Biographical Study of Peter Kropotkin* (Boardman 1950)

William Woods, **Poland: Eagle in the East* (Deutsch 1969)

E.L. Woodward, *The Age of Reform 1815-1870* (Oxford 1938)

FICTION?

Henry Adams, *Democracy* (1880)
Lewis Carroll, *Alice's Adventures in Wonderland* (1865)
Lewis Carroll, *Through the Looking-Glass and What Alice Found There* (1871)
Benjamin Disraeli, *Coningsby, or The New Generation* (1844)
Benjamin Disraeli, *Sybil, or The Two Nations* (1845)
Benjamin Disraeli, *Tancred, or The New Crusade* (1847)
John Dos Passos, *U.S.A.* (Constable 1938, Penguin 1966)
George Gissing, *The Nether World* (1889)
Walter Greenwood, *Love on the Dole* (Cape 1933)
John Mortimer, *Paradise Postponed* (Viking 1985)
Ben Traven, *The Death Ship* (1926)
Robert Tressell, *The Ragged Trousered Philanthropists* (abridged edition Grant Richards 1914, first full edition Lawrence & Wishart 1955, Panther 1965)
Anthony Trollope, *The Way We Live Now* (1875)
Vasilis Vassilikos, *Z* (Macdonald 1969, Sphere 1970)

UTOPIAS

Robert Ardrey, *World's Beginning* (Hamish Hamilton 1945)
Edward Bellamy, *Looking Backward, 2000-1887* (1888)
Jack London, *The Iron Heel* (1907)
William Morris, *The Dream of John Ball* (1888)
William Morris, *News from Nowhere* (1891)

DYSTOPIAS

Aldous Huxley, *Brave New World* (Chatto & Windus 1932)
George Orwell, *Animal Farm: A Fairy Story* (Secker & Warburg 1945)
George Orwell, *Nineteen Eighty-Four* (Secker & Warburg 1949)
Michael Young, *The Rise of the Meritocracy: An Essay on Education and Equality* (Thames & Hudson 1958)
Yevgeny Zamyatin, *We* (first English language edition 1924; Cape, in translation by Bernard Guilbert Guerney, 1970)

Thanks for the material substance of this lamentation are due to the many people - scholars, social campaigners, journalists, or whatever - who have mined it, and to those Socialists who have striven to keep the faith and to propagate it. Thanks are also due to the politicians who have laboured so hard and so profitably to prove my case. To those who rightly conclude that 'we woz robbed', everything else is due.

INDEX

[Post-World-War-II governments are indexed under the names of their prime ministers, with the page references to matters primarily to do with their administrations following the other references.]

Attlee, Clement, 125-6, 131-2, 146-51,
153-5, 217, 221, 224, 229, 333,
374, 436, 445-6, 457; 88, 103, 105,
138, 156 *ff*., 213, 219, 234-6, 239,
243, 248, 260, 336, 402, 404, 433-4
Aubrey, Crispin, 410-17
Austria, 212
Bagehot, Walter, 75, 329
Baghdad Pact, 177
Baker, Kenneth, 109
bakers' strike, 291
Bakunin, Michael, 476
balance of payments and of trade, 113,
161, 166, 173-4, 183, 243-4, 249,
253, 263-4
Ball, George, 182
Banda, Hastings, 168
Bangladesh, 12
Barber, Anthony, 220, 264, 376
Barnardo, Thomas, 14
Barnett, Anthony, 193
Barnett, Joel, 306-7, 384
Bartlett, C.J., 23, 224, 235, 242
Basnett, David, 285, 315-16, 318, 418
Batista, Fulgencio, 172
Beaverbrook, Lord, 88
Bechuanaland. *See* Botswana
Becket, Margaret, 215-16, 220, 234.
Becket, Sir Terence, 281, 302
Beer, Samuel H., 87-8, 93
Bell, Tom, 388
Bellamy, Edward, 1 *ff*., 6-8, 18, 462, 484
Bellamy, Paul, 6-7
Bellos, Alex, 10
benefits, supplementary, 236, 239-40,
302
Benn, Anthony Wedgwood, 23, 114,
117, 123, 135-6, 139, 191, 215,
373, 422
Bennett, Sir Peter, 88
Bentham, Jeremy, 325
Berry, John, 410-17
Bevan, Aneurin, 99, 129-32, 147-8,
156, 162, 215-21, 251, 447
Beveridge, William, 86, 94, 234-5,
239, 433, 458
Bevin, Ernest, 150, 152, 158, 160-1, 327

Bruce, Maurice, 236
Brzezinski, Zbigniew, 181, 202
Buck, Philip, 33, 38, 40-2, 48, 51, 56
Buckingham, Lisa, 16
Buckton, Ray, 282
building industry, 119
Bulgaria, 156
Bullock Report, 377 *ff*., 387, 395, 405
Burke, Edmund, 31, 41-51, 54, 63, 76-8,
82, 116, 381, 389
Burma, 148
Burt, Thomas, 62
Burnham Committee, 317
Butler, R.A., 22, 88-9, 223-4, 329, 433
Butskellism, 24, 109, 117, 314
Byrnes, James, 159-60
Cairncross, Alec, 248
Callaghan, James, 99-100, 108 *ff*., 117-22,
127, 162, 174, 183 *ff*. 188 *ff*., 206 *ff*.,
220, 227, 228-9, 245, 249, 251,
253-5, 271 *ff*., 284-5, 291-3, 295,
298, 301, 304-9, 311-12, 314-17,
320-21, 323, 328-32, 335, 339,
345, 347, 349-53, 357-8, 362, 365,
369, 371-2, 374-7, 379 *ff*., 392, 408,
411, 420, 422-4, 427, 430, 440, 453,
460; 25, 103, 104, 140-2, 166-7, 169,
213, 222-3, 234-5, 242, 259, 264,
266, 275-80, 287 *ff*., 324, 342, 367
Cambodia, 161, 168, 192-4, 200, 206, 210
Cameron, James, 171
Cameron, Sir Neil, 188-9
Campaign for Nuclear Disarmament,
131-2, 162
Campbell, Duncan, 410-17
Campbell of Croy, Lord, 141
Canada, 264
Canterbury, Archbishop of, 336-38
Carlyle, Thomas, 303, 331, 341
Carr, Robert, 256
Carrington, Lord, 364, 430
Carroll, Lewis, 35, 48, 216
Carter, James Earl (Jimmy), 179-82,
185, 189, 194, 201-2, 204, 209
Castañeda, Jorge, 11
Castle, Barbara, 117, 251-3, 256-8,
262, 267, 440

Resler, Henrietta. *See* Westergaard, John and Resler, Henrietta
revolutions of 1848, 73, 84, 472
Rhodesia, 408, 420 *ff.*
Richardson, Jo, 413
Ridley, Nicholas, 364
Rifkin, Jeremy, 16
Rippon, Geoffrey, 27
road haulage strike, 292-4, 357, 360
roads, 131, 264
Rodgers, William, 305-6, 308
Rolls-Royce, 140-1, 190
Romania, 156, 199-200
Rooker, Jeff, 323
Roosevelt, Franklin Delano, 434
Ross, Ernie, 426
Rousseau, Jean Jacques, 44
Rowland, 'Tiny', 420
Royal Society of Health, 17
rural labourers, 62, 65-6, 69, 75, 138, 300
Ruskin College, 350
Russell, Bertrand, 146
Russell, Lord John, 62-3
Russia (Tsarist and post-Soviet), 12, 104, 389, 468-9, 476-7
Russian Revolution, 30, 388, 440, 468
St John-Stevas, Norman, 429, 431
Salisbury, Robert Gascoyne-Cecil, 3rd Marquess of, 42, 66, 68-9, 75-82
Sampson, Anthony, 171, 173-4
Saudi Arabia, 174, 180
Save the Children, 13, 15
Scargill, Arthur, 341
Scarman, Lord, 419
Schmidt, Helmut, 196, 279
Schnadhorst, Francis, 67
seamen's strike (1966), 440
Seeger, Pete, 188
Shakespeare, William, 76, 145, 149, 380
share-owning democracy, 379-81
Shelter, 222-3
Sheppard, David, 338
Sherwen, Timothy, 120
Shinwell, Emmanuel, 151, 400-1, 403
shipbuilding, 190-2
shop stewards, 251, 344, 347-50, 357, 371, 386-7, 398

Shore, Peter, 114, 223, 295, 308, 339
Short, Ted, 429
Sihanouk, Norodom, 193
Silkin, John, 166
Silkin, Sam, 411-14, 418, 428
Silone, Ignazio, 212, 389
Singapore, 173
Singleton, Roger, 14
Sked, Alan and Cook, Chris, 26, 129, 150, 156, 236-7, 248, 267, 402-3, 405
Skinner, Dennis, 339-40
Smith, Adam, 49
Smith, Ian, 420, 423-4, 429-30
Smith, John, 217, 384
Smythe, George, 59
Snowden, Philip, 87, 113, 393, 461-2
social contract, 16, 41-3, 48, 58, 260-1, 265 *ff.*, 275, 307, 321, 324, 359, 441
Social Democratic Party, 308, 368, 424
social democrats (German) 460, (Swedish) 332-3, 354
Social Fund, 239
social security. *See* benefits, supplementary; Beveridge; means testing; National Assistance; National Insurance; pensions; welfare state
social wage, 121, 217-18, 248, 261, 264, 276, 308, 316, 321
Somalia, 198
Somoza, Anastasio, and family, 172
Soros, George, 10-11
South Africa, 149, 178, 199, 420-3, 429
South Yemen, 168
soviet communism, 9, 11, 152, 155-6, 186, 373, 388-92, 437-8, 459, 462, 471, 477-80
Soviet Union, 152, 155 *ff.*, 166, 174, 177, 187, 188 *ff.*, 197 *ff.*, 263, 388-92, 437-8, 459, 479
Spain, Spanish Civil War, 153, 165, 330
Spender, Stephen, 389
Stalin, Joseph, 156-7, 163, 389-90, 459
standards of living, 32, 34, 121-2, 212-18, 228-30, 233 *ff.*, 258, 260-1, 266-70, 311, 314, 319-22, 324, 375-6, 381,